Spelling:
Basic Skills for Effective Communication

Spelling:
Basic Skills for Effective Communication

edited by
Walter B. Barbe
Azalia S. Francis
Lois A. Braun

Zaner-Bloser, Inc.
Columbus, Ohio

© 1982, Zaner-Bloser, Inc., 2500 West Fifth Avenue, Columbus, Ohio

All rights reserved. No part of this book may be reproduced or transmitted in any form or by any means, electronic or mechanical, including photocopying, recording, or by any information storage and retrieval system, without permission in writing from the Publisher.

Designed by Thomas M. Wasylyk.

ISBN No. 0-88309-118-6
Reorder No. 320199

Contents

Overview 1

SECTION ONE

Perspectives 15
   Introduction 15
   JERRY ZUTELL, Children's Spelling Strategies and Their
      Cognitive Development 16
   DONALD H. GRAVES, Spelling Texts and Structural
      Analysis Methods 29
   EDMUND H. HENDERSON, Correct Spelling—an Inquiry 34
   HOWARD E. BLAKE AND ROBERT EMANS
      Some Spelling Facts 37
   PATRICK GROFF, Speaking and Spelling 45
   WALTER T. PETTY, Handwriting and Spelling:
      Their Current Status in the Language Arts Curriculum 53
   ROBERT J. FITZSIMMONS AND BRADLEY M. LOOMER,
      Excerpts from Spelling: Learning and Instruction—
      Research and Practice 61

SECTION TWO

Issues 81
   Introduction 81
   ROBERT L. HILLERICH, Let's Teach Spelling—
      Not Phonetic Misspelling 82
   BRUCE CRONNELL AND ANN HUMES, Elementary
      Spelling: What's Really Taught 89
   PATRICIA McCUNE IRVINE, If You're Not a Spelling
      Genius, Beware of Friday 94

DONALD C. McFEELY, Syllabication Generalizations:
  Help or Hindrance to Communication 98
ALBERT J. MAZURKIEWICZ, What Do Teachers Know
  About Phonics 104
ALBERT J. MAZURKIEWICZ, What the Professor Doesn't
  Know About Phonics Can Hurt! 114
LAWRENCE M. KASDON, Phonics? Phonetics? Phonemics?
  A Reply to Mazurkiewicz 129
RUSSELL TABBERT, Dialect Difference and the Teaching of
  Reading and Spelling 132
DONNA SCHWAB KLIGMAN, BRUCE A. CRONNELL,
  AND GARY B. VERNA, Black English Pronunciation and
  Spelling Performance 135
ALBERT J. MAZURKIEWICZ, Toward a Spelling Reform 142

SECTION THREE

Foundations of Instruction 149
  Introduction 149
  PAUL R. HANNA, RICHARD E. HODGES, AND JEAN S.
    HANNA, The Alphabetic Base of Spelling 150
  EDGAR DALE, JOSEPH O'ROURKE, AND HENRY A.
    BAMMAN, Pronunciation and Spelling 164
  JAMES WHEELOCK BEERS AND CAROL STRICKLAND
    BEERS, Vowel Spelling Strategies among First and Second
    Graders: A Growing Awareness of Written Words 192
  MARILOU R. SORENSEN AND KRISTEN JEFFERS
    KERSTETTER, Phonetic Spelling: A Case Study 198
  JAMES W. BEERS, Developmental Strategies of Spelling
    Competence in Primary School Children 203
  SHANE TEMPLETON, Spelling, Phonology, and the
    Older Student 210
  TOM NICHOLSON AND SUMNER SCHACHTER,
    Spelling Skill and Teaching Practice—Putting Them Back
    Together Again 217

ALBERT J. MAZURKIEWICZ AND JANE GOULD,
   Spelling Preferences and Instructional Considerations 222
EMMETT ALBERT BETTS, Spelling and Phonics 231

SECTION FOUR

Classroom Practices 247
   Introduction 247
   THOMAS D. HORN, Test, Then Study in Spelling 248
   RONALD L. CRAMER, Diagnosing Skills by Analyzing
      Children's Writing 249
   EMMETT ALBERT BETTS, Perceptual Learning:
      Phonics Countdown 252
   DUANE R. TOVEY, "Sound-It-Out": A Reasonable Approach
      to Spelling? 262
   KENNETH CADENHEAD, BARBARA ASHWANDER, AND
      MARVIN USSERY, Helping Children with Spelling 272
   CAROL J. FISHER, ROBERT RUBINSTEIN, VALERIE
      SELLERS, SHIRLEY T. SHRATTER, AND SALLY E.
      TODD, How to Take the YUK Out of Spelling 274
   ANN SOFGE, Teacher-Made Tapes Provide Auditory Aids 280
   PATRICIA CAMPANILE-HAPP, In Spelling We Try Harder .. 284
   TIMOTHY R. BLAIR, Spelling, Word Attack Skills 287

SECTION FIVE

Students with Special Needs 291
   Introduction 291
   WENDY M. GOLLADAY, The Teaching of Spelling to Low
      Ability Students 292
   STEVE GRAHAM AND LAMOINE MILLER,
      Spelling Research and Practice: A Unified Approach 297
   MARYANN FEOLA CASTELUCCI, Can We Assume our
      Remedial Reading Students Know How to Use the
      Dictionary? 319
   KENNETH W. HOWELL, JOSEPH S. KAPLAN, AND
      TERESA SERAPIGLIA, Spelling: Diagnosing Basic Skills ... 322

SECTION SIX

Word Lists 339
    Introduction 339
    W.S. GUILER, Primary-Grade Words Frequently Misspelled
        by Higher-Grade Pupils 341
    LESLIE W. JOHNSON, One Hundred Words Most Often
        Misspelled by Children in the Elementary Grades 347
    DALE D. JOHNSON, The Dolch List Reexamined 348
    CHARLES MONROE WALKER, High Frequency Word List
        for Grades 3 through 9 356
    EDWARD FRY, The New Instant Word List 365
    ELIZABETH SAKIEY, EDWARD FRY, ALBERT GOSS,
        AND BARRY LOIGMAN, A Syllable Frequency Count 371

Index 383

Overview

Children in schools today can usually read better than they can spell, chiefly because reading instruction is conducted more efficiently than is spelling instruction. Training programs stress reading while placing relatively little emphasis on spelling, and so teachers are less confident in their ability to teach spelling than reading. Moreover, teachers are not usually familiar with the literature devoted to spelling, and base their instruction more on tradition than on the results of spelling research.

The purpose of this book is to provide teachers with a resource that comprises diverse opinions on learning to spell, as well as an overview of the research on spelling. The selections in the book have been drawn from many sources, and were written by some of the most prominent names in language arts. A single text such as this is not intended to replace intensive pre-service and in-service training, but does attempt to give teachers the information they need to develop an appropriate spelling curriculum.

In this first chapter, we shall preview the remainder of this book by answering some of the questions teachers frequently ask about spelling. Our answers will be relatively brief, because a more complete response can be found in the articles that follow in later chapters. For those teachers who wish to pursue a question even further, we suggest consulting the references that follow the selections in the book.

What is the most effective way to teach spelling?

No single way of teaching spelling is correct for all students or teachers; on this the experts agree. There are some practices that are strongly supported by research, and others that the research suggests are of questionable value. The best advice we can give a teacher is to consider the information summarized by Fitzsimmons and Loomer in the next chapter and make a decision based on the studies they present.

It is important to remember that what works for one student may not work for another. Students vary with respect to their perceptual or modality strengths, and also other dimensions of learning style. For example, some students can easily visualize words in their correct form. These students would profit more from repeated exposure to whole words rather than practice in phonetic analysis. Other students, however, may have poorer visual memories, so providing them with many opportunities to see words will not bring about spelling improvement. These non-visual students should be taught to spell using their stronger auditory or kinesthetic modalities.

Remember also that teachers favor those spelling methods that they find most helpful to themselves. Often, these methods reflect the teacher's modality strength. There is nothing inherently wrong with this tendency, so long as the teacher makes provisions for those students who have different modality strengths.

Be flexible and experiment when teaching spelling. Do not hesitate to try something new or to abandon a practice that is not working. And, most important, keep in mind that the purpose of spelling is to communicate clearly through writing, so give your students many opportunities to write and encourage the use of the words they have learned during the spelling lesson.

Is a basal spelling book really necessary?

The answer, of course, is no. Textbooks are not "really necessary" in any subject. They are a convenience to both teachers and students, in much the same way that dimensional lumber is a convenience to a cabinetmaker. Any good woodworker can fell a tree, cut the lumber to size, dry it, and plane it smooth; the process adds tremendously to the project being undertaken, but it can be done. The same is true about textbooks. Any good teacher can start from scratch and develop the materials necessary for spelling, reading, or other school subjects. But is the effort involved worth the benefit that results? In a few cases, yes, but in most cases, the answer is no.

Spelling texts, for all their shortcomings, perform several useful functions. They provide teachers with a basic word list, activities that feature the words, and a structure within which spelling can be taught. Children find many of the games and activities in spelling books motivating, and spelling books often provide a link between spelling and other subject areas.

The major problem with spelling series is that teachers rely too heavily on them. Spelling books are only tools. They do not teach spelling— teachers do. Some publishers promise that their text is a complete spelling program, but it never is and never can be. A spelling text, or any other textbook for that matter, is in the same category as the chalkboard, overhead projector, pencils, and paper: they are all classroom aids. Teachers have no trouble deciding when and how to use these classroom aids, and if they approach a spelling series with the same attitude, they will have no trouble using it appropriately.

Does it make sense to teach spelling "rules"?

The answer is a qualified yes. It does make sense to teach spelling "rules," but students should not be expected to memorize them or use them exclusively in spelling words with which they are unfamiliar or about which they are unsure.

English is a surprisingly regular language; the /b/ sound, for example, is almost always spelled with the letter *b*. Because of this regularity, there are some general rules that describe the relationship between written and spoken words. On the other hand, there are so many exceptions to the rules that the correspondence between language sounds and their written counterparts is imperfect. In a classic study of spelling conducted at Stanford University, a computer was programmed to spell using "rules." To test the efficiency of the rules, the computer was then asked to spell 17,000 of the most frequently used words. It was able to spell only 50 percent of the words correctly, but spelled an additional 37 percent of the words with only one error.

Hanna, Hodges, and Hanna, whose contribution is found in a later chapter, summarize the results of the Stanford study by asserting that:

> But what this finding does point to is the generalization that nearly half the words in ordinary usage can be correctly spelled solely on the basis of a functional understanding of the relationships between spoken sound and written symbol.

Spelling rules, then, do have some value, but students should not be expected to memorize all of them or rely on them exclusively when attempting to spell words. Making students aware of the "*i* before *e*" rule and the "two vowels go walking" rule, as well as the other regular patterns, will certainly have a positive effect on students' ability to spell as well as their knowledge of our language. These rules alone, however, will not make children good spellers, and in some cases, if they are overstressed, will cause more problems than they will solve.

What is "invented spelling"?

Invented spelling is an offshoot of the current interest in the writing process. Composition is being stressed in more and more of our nation's elementary schools, and even children in kindergarten and first grade are being encouraged to "write" their thoughts, feelings, and experiences. Because these children have not yet developed the ability to spell words correctly, they invent spellings for the words they use.

Rather than being a problem, invented spelling is now accepted as a stage through which children progress as they become mature spellers. Zutell, Beers, and several other of our contributors describe the manner in which children's spelling strategies change as they become older.

One of the most problematic aspects of invented spelling is the name itself. Many teachers and parents object to the concept—not because of what it is, but because of what the name implies. *Invented spelling,* they believe, is just a euphemism for *incorrect spelling,* and should not be permitted. One way to avoid this problem is to substitute the term "developmental spelling" for *invented spelling,* and explain that a child's first efforts at spelling or composing will seem as primitive as initial attempts at speaking. Parents and teachers will then see that encouragement, modeling, and reinforcement, the factors that influence children's speech, can also contribute to the development of correct spelling.

Is there a relationship between handwriting and spelling?

Logic suggests handwriting and spelling are related, but the evidence supporting the relationship is not overwhelming. In a doctoral dissertation published in 1973, Strickling compared the oral and written spelling performance of 136 fifth-graders. She found that their mean oral spelling score on the Morrison-McCall Spelling Scale was 27.6 words correct out of a possible 40, while the mean written score was 23.3. The correlation between written spelling errors and two measures of writing legibility were .60 and .56. Strickling concluded that:

> The lower mean score on the written spelling test was due mainly to handwriting errors because: a) Words missed on the written spelling test because of handwriting errors were spelled correctly on the oral test. b) The number of words missed on the written spelling test because of handwriting errors was positively correlated with the errors made on the handwriting tests. c) When the words missed on the written spelling test because of handwriting errors were added to the written spelling score the total was essentially the same as the score on the oral spelling test.

A similar finding was reported by Milone, Wilhide, and Wasylyk at a meeting of the National Council of Teachers of English. They examined the handwriting and spelling of 750 sixth-grade students in public schools in South Carolina. Spelling was assessed using twenty words that were frequently misspelled by elementary school children, and handwriting was evaluated using a 1-to-5 scale, with 5 being the most legible.

Of the students whose handwriting was rated as either 4 or 5, almost 95 percent had 4 errors or fewer. Students with the least legible handwriting had very low spelling scores, with 80 percent having 7 errors or more and 50 percent having 10 errors or more.

The evidence reported by these researchers suggests that there is a strong relationship between handwriting and spelling. Children with legible handwriting spell better than children with illegible handwriting, perhaps because legible handwriting permits the correction of errors. Good handwriting does not cause good spelling, but poor handwriting does seem to prevent children from becoming competent spellers.

Should spelling words be grouped and taught according to common characteristics?

In some spelling series and in many teacher-developed materials, words are grouped according to common characteristics, such as the /f/ sound spelled *ph*. The chief advantage to this practice is that the students may come to associate the words on the list with one another, and by remembering how to spell one, they can recall the correct spelling of the other words.

Grouping words according to common characteristics allows spelling progress to be assessed in an interesting way. In scoring the weekly spelling test, it is possible to determine not only how many words the student has spelled correctly, but how many times the letters that were the basis of the lesson were correct. For example, in a twenty-word test on *ph* words, a student might get only 14 of the 20 words totally correct, but may have spelled the *ph* letter combination correctly in each word.

Should I test then teach, or vice versa?

The evidence supporting the test-first approach is very strong, as several of the articles in later chapters point out. Correcting a pre-test contributes as much to spelling progress as any other practice that has yet been investigated.

Should a teacher decide to use the test-first method, there are two other issues that must be resolved. One is whether or not to let students prepare for the pre-test. We recommend letting students take the test "cold," because this gives a better estimate of their pre-instruction level of ability. Part of the benefit of the pre-test is gained through correcting errors, and if the number of errors is spuriously low because of preparation, then the effectiveness of the pre-test will be diminished.

Another issue is whether or not to encourage students to complete activities featuring words they already know how to spell. The extra practice these activities give will strengthen spelling skills, but students may become bored by having to study words they already know. On the other hand, a student may have guessed at a word on the pre-test and spelled it correctly, but really should be studying the word further. Teacher judgment is the only way to resolve this issue. If a teacher believes that a student truly knows the words and needs no additional practice in them, then there is no reason to study them. This student should be allowed to move on to other words. If a teacher thinks a student's performance on the pre-test is an overestimation of the student's abilities, then more studying should be encouraged.

Is there a logical sequence to spelling skills?

Spelling skills seem to follow a sequential order that resembles the sequence of reading skills. Knowledge of single consonant sounds precedes recognizing blends, and spelling one-syllable words comes before spelling multi-syllabic words with inflectional endings. What is unclear is which consonants or vowels should be taught first, or which digraphs are the most difficult.

Spelling textbooks offered by major publishers differ somewhat from one another in their presentation of skills. The references that follow the Cronnell and Humes article appearing in Chapter 3 include several studies of the content of popular basal spelling series. These references can be obtained from the Southwest Regional Laboratory at 4665 Lampson Avenue, Los Alamitos, California 90720.

A typical scope and sequence chart of a basal spelling series is presented on the following pages. This particular chart summarizes the skills taught in the Zaner-Bloser spelling series. The offerings of other publishers are similar.

What is spelling reform?

The correspondence between written and spoken English is strong, but it is not perfect. We have only 26 letters in our alphabet, and use more than 40 speech sounds. Moreover, many non-English words have been introduced into our language. As a result, spelling our language can be quite a challenge.

In an effort to reform our orthography and make spelling a more logical proposition, some educators and a few public figures have suggested that changes be made in our written language. George Bernard Shaw was perhaps the most well-known advocate of orthographic reform, while among our contributors, Betts and Mazurkiewicz are staunch supporters of this concept.

The recommendations made by different proponents of reform vary greatly. Extremists argue that the source of the problem should be attacked directly by developing a new alphabet in which each sound of the language has a single written symbol. Such a radical reform is virtually impossible to undertake, and would probably not accomplish the purpose for which it was intended, because our spoken language is constantly undergoing change through usage. The word *enough* might logically be spelled "inuf" for the next several decades, but what happens if its pronunciation changes to /enuf/, as it may well do?

A more moderate type of reform is to accept "popular" spellings of some words, for example, "tho" for *though*. Such simplified spelling would make life easier for most schoolchildren, but would certainly meet with resistance from their elders.

Finally, the least objectionable type of reform is to teach acceptable alternate spellings. In the next chapter, Mazurkiewicz presents an argument that is most appealing, even to those of us who are rooted in traditional orthography. As Mazurkiewicz indicates, when teachers become aware of acceptable alternate spellings, they seem quite willing to teach them. It is reasonable to assume that the teaching of acceptable alternative spellings will be the first type of spelling reform that enjoys widespread support in American schools.

Is the weekly cycle of spelling instruction a good idea?

The pattern of spelling instruction used by most teachers and recommended by most publishers involves one lesson per week, with a review offered every four or five weeks. On Monday, students have either a pre-test or are introduced to the words for the week through a reading selection. Using the week's words takes up Tuesday's lesson, a mid-week test or further usage is featured on Wednesday, and on Thursday students learn the important characteristics of the words. The weekly post-test occurs on Friday.

There is nothing magical about this weekly pattern, and in fact, many teachers criticize its inflexibility and marginal effectiveness. There is good cause to question this pattern, but abandoning it entirely may be a case of throwing out the baby with the bath water. A certain amount of structure is necessary in teaching any subject, and spelling is no exception.

Rather than rejecting a weekly pattern entirely, some teachers have modified the pattern to suit their needs. For example, instead of beginning the cycle on Monday, start on Tuesday, and have the post-test on the following Monday. This practice permits two days of non-related activity to precede the final test, giving a better indication of how well the students have learned the words. Another possibility is to use the Monday-to-Friday cycle, but only use the textbook for three days. Substitute teacher-developed activities or materials for the two days of textbook activities that have been dropped, or use the two days to

SCOPE AND SEQUENCE

Grade 1	Grade 2	Grade 3	Grade 4
1. matching letters, shapes, and symbols	1. short *a*	1. short *a, e*	1. short *a, e*
2. rhyming sounds	2. short *e*	2. short *o, i, u*	2. short *i, o, u*
3. initial sounds	3. short *i*	3. short vowels	3. short vowels
4. initial sounds	4. short *o*	4. short *e* spelled *ea*	4. vowel sound in *book*
5. final sounds	5. short *u*	5. vowel sounds in *book, cup*	5. schwa
6. initial *l, t*	6. review and practice	6. review and practice	6. review and practice
7. initial *d, c*	7. long *a*	7. long *a, i, o*	7. long *a*
8. initial *f, g*	8. long *e*	8. long *a* spelled *ai, ay*	8. long *e*
9. initial *j, s*	9. long *i*	9. long *o* spelled *o, oa*	9. long *i*
10. initial *b, h*	10. long *o*	10. long *e* spelled *ea, ee*	10. long *o, u*
11. initial *p, r*	11. phonograms *ow, old*	11. long *i* spelled *igh, ie, y*	11. long vowels
12. initial *n, m*	12. review and practice	12. review and practice	12. review and practice
13. initial *y, v*	13. phonograms *ow, ew*	13. *r*-controlled *o*	13. /är/, /âr/
14. initial *w, k*	14. phonograms *ay, ake*	14. *r*-controlled *o, e, ea*	14. /ir/, /ur/
15. initial *z*, review	15. phonograms *ing, ill*	15. *r*-controlled *i, u*	15. /ôr/
16. short *a*	16. phonograms *ent, and*	16. *r*-controlled long *a*	16. /ėr/
17. phonograms *an, at*	17. phonograms *ell, all*	17. *w*-controlled *a*	17. /ər/

Lesson

Grade 5	Grade 6	Grade 7	Grade 8
1. long *a*	1. long *a*	1. short vowels	1. long vowels
2. long *e*	2. long *e*	2. long vowels	2. long vowels *a, e, i, o, u*
3. long *i*	3. long *i*	3. long vowels/variant spelling *o, i,* and *u*	3. vowel review
4. long *o*	4. long *o*	4. *r*-controlled vowels	4. vowel spelling patterns
5. vowel sound in *blue*	5. /ū/, /ü/	5. *r*-controlled vowels	5. *r*-controlled vowels
6. review and practice	6. review and practice	6. review and practice	6. review and practice
7. /ar/, /ār/	7. short vowels *a, e, i, o, u*	7. hard, soft *c*	7. *ei, ie*
8. /er/	8. short vowels *a, e, i, o, u*	8. hard, soft *g*	8. vowel spelling patterns
9. /or/	9. spelling of short *i* in accented and unaccented syllables	9. spelling /f/, /k/, /s/, /z/, /zh/, /gz/	9. schwa
10. /ô/	10. schwa	10. variant spellings of *s*	10. schwa
11. /ə/, /ər/	11. /əl/, /ər/	11. variant spellings of *nk, ng*	11. vowel groups
12. review and practice	12. review and practice	12. review and practice	12. review and practice
13. /k/, /j/	13. /är/	13. variant spelling of *z*	13. hard, soft *c* /k/, /s/
14. /z/, /zh/	14. /èr/	14. consonant letter *v*	14. soft sound of *g*
15. /sh/, /ch/	15. /îr/, /âr/, /īr/	15. consonant clusters	15. silent consonants
16. schwa	16. /ôr/	16. doubled consonants	16. double consonants
17. vowels /u/, /ū/, /ü/	17. *oy, oi*	17. silent letters	17. /sh/, /ch/

(Continued)

Grade 1	Grade 2	Grade 3	Grade 4
18. short *e*	18. review and practice	18. review and practice	18. review and practice
19. phonograms *et, en*	19. initial consonant clusters *sl, pl*	19. soft *c, g*	19. initial *kn, wr, gu*
20. short *i*	20. initial consonant clusters *br, tr*	20. consonant digraphs *wh, ch, tch*	20. silent letters
21. phonograms *in, ick*	21. initial consonant clusters *gr, fr*	21. initial consonant clusters *dr, pr*	21. initial *squ, qu*
22. short *o*	22. consonant digraph *sh*	22. initial consonant clusters *gl, bl, cl*	22. initial *str, scr*
23. phonograms *ot, og*	23. consonant digraph *th*	23. final *mp, nd, st, ck*	23. final *ld, nd, nk*
24. short *u*	24. review and practice	24. review and practice	24. review and practice
25. phonograms *ug, ump*	25. suffix *ing*	25. possessive singular	25. irregular plurals
26. long *a*	26. noun plurals adding *s*	26. suffixes *er, est*	26. *-s, -es* added to words ending in *y*
27. phonograms *ave, ail*	27. verb ending *-s*	27. *-ing, -ed* doubling last consonant	27. *-ing, -ed* after *y*
28. long *e*	28. suffix *ed* no base change	28. *-es* added to words ending in *ss, ch, sh, x, tch*	28. *-ing, -ed* after final *e*
29. phonograms *eat, eet*	29. contractions	29. suffix *ly*	29. *-er, -est* added to bases that double consonants or drop final *e*
30. long *i*	30. review and practice	30. review and practice	30. review and practice
31. phonograms *ide, ike*	31. vowel sound in *boot*	31. vowel sound in *cow* spelled *ou, ow*	31. contractions
32. long *o*	32. *r*-controlled vowels	32. vowel sound in *boot*	32. homophones
33. phonograms *old, ose*	33. consonant digraphs *sh* and *th*	33. compounds	33. compounds
34. long *u*	34. homophones	34. homophones	34. gardening words
35. initial *fl, cl, bl, pl, sl*	35. compounds	35. contractions	35. school words
36. initial *br, gr, dr, cr, tr*	36. review and practice	36. review and practice	36. review and practice

Grade 5	Grade 6	Grade 7	Grade 8
18. review and practice	18. review and practice	18. review and practice	18. review and practice
19. prefixes: *dis, mis*	19. /sk/ *sc, sk, sch*	19. suffix *ion*	19. prefixes: *co (m, n), pre, post, sub*
20. *-er, -est* added to words ending in *y*	20. /f/ *ph, gh*	20. suffixes	20. prefixes: *un, mis*
21. suffixes: *ment, ous*	21. suffixes *ary, ery, ory*	21. Latin word parts	21. prefixes
22. suffixes: *ness, able, en*	22. suffixes: *ant, ent, ance, ence*	22. Latin roots	22. suffixes
23. suffixes: *er, or*	23. prefixes: *in, im, pre*	23. Greek roots	23. suffixes: *ist, ery, ary, ory*
24. review and practice	24. review and practice	24. review and practice	24. review and practice
25. synonyms	25. plurals	25. antonyms	25. synonyms
26. antonyms	26. words beginning with *ex*	26. synonyms	26. compounds
27. homophones	27. compounds	27. homophones	27. compounds
28. abbreviations	28. compounds	28. contractions	28. coined words
29. singular and plural possessives	29. open compounds	29. compound words	29. commonly misspelled words
30. review and practice	30. review and practice	30. review and practice	30. review and practice
31. compounds	31. commonly misspelled words	31. commonly misspelled words	31. Latin roots: *spect, aud, vid, vis*
32. commonly misspelled words	32. commonly misspelled words	32. words from other languages	32. Latin roots: *port, ject, duct, tract*
33. commonly misspelled words	33. emotion words	33. coined words	33. Latin roots: *ped, capit, tain, ten, tin*
34. household words	34. weather words	34. math words	34. automotive words
35. animal words	35. sports words	35. geography words	35. career titles
36. review and practice	36. review and practice	36. review and practice	36. review and practice

work on vocabulary development or editing written materials. The latter two activities are excellent ways of helping students generalize spelling skills to other areas of the curriculum.

What can I do about students who score well on the weekly test but spell miserably at other times?

Spelling is not the only subject in which students have difficulty generalizing what they have learned, but for some reason, the problem is more noticeable in spelling. What seems to exacerbate the situation is that students misspell relatively simple words that they use regularly, such as *there* and *their, to* and *too, beautiful, except,* and *separate.*

The reason that students fail to generalize their spelling skills is that a week's instruction on a word list produces only minimal competence, not mastery. For students to master a list of words, they need ample practice, meaningful application, and reinforcement. These aspects of instruction must be provided by a teacher who is genuinely interested in spelling, and will require an extended period of time.

To encourage generalization of spelling skills, make writing an important part of the curriculum, particularly the editing aspect of the writing process. Students who have many opportunities to write and rewrite their thoughts are continually exercising their spelling skills in ways that go beyond the weekly test.

Another way is to involve all the educationally relevant learning modalities (vision, audition, and kinesthesia) in spelling instruction. All too often, spelling texts favor a single modality; students with other perceptual strengths are forced to rely on their weaknesses when learning to spell. Moreover, even students with a modality strength the same as that favored in the spelling text will suffer, for they may not be able to transfer what they have learned in their strongest modality to other modalities. For example, auditory students who use a text that is phonics-based may never learn to proofread their work in order to catch misspellings.

Third, devote time to vocabulary development. In a later chapter, Dale and O'Rourke state that:

> The lack of a solid relationship between spelling and vocabulary skills is apparent when students spell *bare* as *bear, there* as *their, fete* as *fate.* The significance of choosing the correct letter in spelling is easily seen in words such as *homily* and *homely, blackhead* and *blockhead, mallet* and *mullet, winch* and *wench, cook* and *kook.*

Students who have strong vocabulary skills rarely confuse homonyms and are familiar with root words and inflectional endings. Invariably, these students are better spellers than their peers who have underdeveloped vocabulary skills, and their spelling ability persists beyond the weekly test.

Should I develop my own word list?

Because of their dissatisfaction with basal spelling texts, teachers sometimes prefer to develop their own word lists and conduct their spelling instruction as part of reading, composition, or other subjects. They base their decision on two factors, the first of which is that the word list contained in the basal series does not feature all the words students use in their everyday reading and writing. The second factor is that basal series do not usually contain enough of the words that are used in the individual subject areas of social studies, arithmetic, and science.

We are reluctant to suggest to teachers that they develop their own word lists for spelling instruction. It is a good idea to build a supplemental word list that contains words used frequently by students in a given class, school, or region, and to include in the supplemental list specialized words from different content areas. Compiling a word list from scratch, however, will require a great deal of effort and your list will probably include many of the same words you would find in any spelling series.

In the final chapter of this text, we have included a number of popular word lists, some of which were based on research conducted over fifty years ago. The remarkable thing about these lists is the degree of overlap among them. There are certainly exceptions, for example, the word *television,* which was unknown fifty years ago but is among the most frequently used words today. But by and large, any list that purports to contain the words most often used by children will look very much like other similar lists. Teachers are better advised to spend their time augmenting an existing list rather than developing one from scratch.

Concluding Comments

As can be seen from the content of this first chapter, we believe that there are no simple answers to questions that are raised about spelling. Our language, although it is comparatively regular, is not highly predictable in its written form. Moreover, students vary with respect to the characteristics that influence spelling ability. Given these two sources of variability, it makes sense to adopt an eclectic approach to spelling instruction, one that embraces pedagogically sound practices yet permits enough flexibility to meet the needs of individual students. Teachers should have no reservations about using a well-designed textbook as the basis of their spelling instruction. They should also feel free to supplement the contents of the book with materials offered by other publishers or developed by themselves. The more variety that teachers can bring to the spelling curriculum, the more likely it is that students will become good spellers.

There is one aspect of spelling that we have not yet discussed: spelling conscience. Several of our contributors touch on this subject, for it is a critical element in spelling success. No matter how effective instruction is, students will not become good spellers unless they develop a spelling conscience. They must *want* to spell right before they will do so with any consistency.

A spelling conscience, pedagogically sound materials, and a varied curriculum all contribute to spelling success. There is an additional ingredient, however, that is more important than any of these—the teacher. It is the teacher who selects materials, designs the curriculum, and instills in students a spelling conscience. If a teacher is concerned about correct spelling, then it is likely that the students in her or his class will be competent spellers.

REFERENCES

Milone, M., Wilhide, J., and Wasylyk, T. "Spelling and Handwriting: Is There a Relationship?" Paper presented at the National Council of Teachers of English, Spring Convention, 1982.

Strickling, C. "The Effect of Handwriting and Related Skills upon the Spelling Score of Above Average and Below Average Readers in the Fifth Grade." *Dissertation Abstracts,* 1974, 34(7), 3717-A.

SECTION ONE

Perspectives

- Children also need opportunities to compare and contrast words on a variety of levels (sound, structure, syntax, semantics) so that they might systematically discover and utilize both intraword and interword patterns of organization.

   Jerry Zutell

- Children spell better when they are using language with a purpose; when they are using the response meaning and word study exercises.

   Donald Graves

- . . . a compromise must be made between learning enough rules to give a system for spelling, but not so many that the learning of such rules becomes a burdensome task.

   Howard Blake
   Robert Emans

INTRODUCTION

There are probably as many different perspectives on spelling as there are authors willing to express their beliefs. We can not present all the major perspectives that have appeared in the literature in recent years, but we can make the reader aware of several that have immediate application in the classroom.

In the lead article in this section, Zutell points out that children's progress in spelling is both quantitative and qualitative. That is, as children mature, not only can they spell more words, they use more sophisticated strategies to do so. Graves follows with a review and update of Cohen's classic study of the content of spelling texts, and Henderson discusses in a personal way ". . . why children do not and cannot learn to spell."

It is always comforting to know that there are "facts" to guide our educational efforts; Blake and Emans summarize the "facts" that are known about spelling and clarify the sometimes murky waters of terminology. Groff introduces the issue of speaking and spelling, one that appears again in the next chapter, and Petty discusses the change in status that both spelling and handwriting have undergone in the years since Sputnik. Fitzsimmons and Loomer close the chapter with a highly useful summary of what works and what doesn't work in spelling.

Children's Spelling Strategies and Their Cognitive Development

JERRY ZUTELL

A growing research literature [particularly Read (21), Beers and Henderson (3), Beers, Chapter Three and Henderson, Chapter Twelve of *Developmental and Cognitive Aspects of Learning to Spell*], has pointed to sensible and developmental patterns in young children's spellings. The present study has attempted to elaborate and extend this line of research in three ways: by examining the responses of a broader range of children—those in grades one through four—by examining their attempts at spelling more complex word patterns (see below), and by investigating the relationship between the developmental nature of children's spelling strategies and their overall intellectual maturation in terms of Piaget's model of cognitive stages. Thus, four specific hypotheses were tested through data collection and analysis:

1. The quality of children's spelling would improve as their grade level increased;
2. as the word categories became more complex, children's spelling strategies would be less sophisticated;
3. there would be an interaction between grade level and word complexity; and
4. there would be a significant correlation between children's spelling strategies and their cognitive functioning.

In order to make the procedures and results of this study clearer for the reader and to elaborate on the rationale behind the study, it will be necessary to provide some specific background information regarding the three variables of word complexity, quality of spelling response, and Piaget's stages of cognitive development. Thus, each of these will be examined in more detail, especially as they apply to the plan and content of this study.

Pages 52–73 of *Developmental and Cognitive Aspects of Learning to Spell*. © 1980 by the International Reading Association. Reprinted by permission.

Word Complexity: The Nature of the Writing System

The English spelling system has long been condemned by scholars and educators as highly irregular and, thus, difficult to master. Appeals for reform (15) and attempts to teach reading using a simpler system (i.t.a.) have dotted the reading-spelling literature. Yet recent computerized and linguistic analyses (11, 24, 6) have progressively discovered more regular patterns below the surface of phoneme-grapheme (sound-letter) correspondences. Chomsky and Halle, in fact, argue that English orthography (the spelling system) appears to be a near optimal way of representing underlying meanings.

In order to understand such reasoning, a brief historical perspective may be helpful. At an early point in its history, English seems to have had a closer, simpler match between phonemes and graphemes. Since that time, the orthography or spelling system has become relatively stable, especially since the invention and widespread use of the printing press—the use of which made consistent spelling highly desirable. Contrary to popular understanding, it is the phonology or overall pronunciation system which has undergone and continues to undergo more radical changes, naturally affecting sound-letter relationships. However, since phonological changes are not random, but do follow some basic principles (26), the relationship between the phonology and the orthography, the pronunciation and writing systems, is *systematic* if not simple and direct. Furthermore, since changes in pronunciation are much less "visible" and "controllable" than changes in spelling, a stable writing system that preserves relationships in meaning at some expense to sound-letter correspondences has the advantage of allowing speakers of differing dialects and historical periods to recognize the same meanings, although their pronunciation may vary.

On the one hand, such an analysis based on generative phonology has a great deal of explanatory power. It especially makes sense in terms of the mature reader who can quickly and efficiently recognize many written words, get their meanings directly, and *then* produce the appropriate pronunciations in oral reading. On the other hand, such an explanation fails to account for the difficulties of beginners who have neither much experience with print nor a knowledge of the history of English phonology. This is particularly true for the beginning speller who must generate the printed form of a word having its pronunciation available to him. Thus, a slightly different, complementary perspective—one more akin to Venezky's analysis (24)—is necessary if we are to understand the relationship between word patterns and children's spellings.

From this point of view, the writing system can be analyzed in terms of a series of patterns which provide a high degree of regularity, if not simplicity. These patterns fall into four broad categories:

1. *Letter-Name Sound Correspondences.* The alphabetic principle is, of course, an essential component of the English spelling system. However, it is important to recognize that sound-letter correspondences are not always as straightforward as they seem. Letter names and letter sounds are not always simply related. In fact, short vowel spelling patterns typically violate young children's letter-name-sound expectations! Thus, only a very few words (e.g., *me*, but not *met* or *meet*) can be spelled correctly using simplistic sounding strategies (see Beers' chapter for a comprehensive review).
2. *Structural Patterns* exist in words in which the presence of one or more letters affects the pronunciation of others. Silent letters are typically structural markers. "Silent e" and consonant doubling patterns are common examples of structural markers. Contrast, for example, the spellings and pronunciations of *hop* vs. *hope* and *hopping* vs. *hoping*.
3. *Inflectional Patterns.* In English spelling, changes in tense, number, and part of speech are often indicated by word endings (*-ed*, for past tense, *-s* or *-es* for plural). These meaning-bearing elements are typically spelled the same even when they are

pronounced differently because of different phonological environments. Contrast the different pronunciations of -ed marking past tense in *kissed* vs. *planned* vs. *lifted*.
4. *Derivational Patterns*. Words that are derived from the same root often retain the same spelling for the root element, although in the context of the overall word, pronunciations may change. Contrast the different pronunciations of *a* in *nation* vs. *national* or of *i* in *combine* vs. *combination* or of *c* in *medicine* vs. *medical*.

Given the hypothesis that the complexity of the pattern to be spelled would affect children's spelling strategies, the above analysis contributed to the selection of what types of word patterns children might be asked to spell. Five specific kinds of words were used: Short Vowel, Long Vowel, Past Tense, Consonant Doubling, and Derivational Pairs of Words. (For more information, see Appendix.)

Rating Children's Spellings

Since an expanding body of literature has indicated that children's misspellings are quite sensible and that there is a systematic developmental change in how children misspell words [see Read (*21*) and the chapters by Henderson and Beers in *Developmental and Cognitive Aspects of Learning to Spell*], it was evident that right-wrong tabulations of children's spellings would hide the key element of qualitative change. Instead, a scale was developed which rated errors according to their quality and sophistication. The criteria for scoring incorporated those used by Beers (*2*), but this system was also modified and extended to include analysis of examples of the five different word patterns being used in the study.

More specifically, all spellings were rated on a six point scale (0–5). A 0 rating indicated an uninterpretable response, 1 a letter-name response and, at the other end, 5 indicated a correct spelling. Ratings of 2, 3, and 4 indicated different stages of awareness of the particular pattern being examined. (A full diagram of the rating system by word pattern category is available in the Appendix.)

Cognitive Stages: Piaget's Perspective

For Piaget, the critical question in developmental psychology has always been an epistemological one: How is knowledge acquired? And his model of the process of acquisition is basically biological: Learning is an adaptive function mirroring the more inclusive biological paradigm of the adjustment of the organism to its environment. Thus, the underlying invariant process remains: 1) assimilation of the new to the old, 2) accommodation of the old to the new, and 3) the achievement of a balance or equilibrium between the internal demands of the system and the constraints of external reality.

Therefore, growth is neither simply a matter of maturation nor one of absorption. It depends upon the interactions of several factors: internal maturation, the action of objects, social transmission, and equilibrium. The first three are, of themselves, insufficient to account for learning since "A whole play of regulation and of compensation is required to result in a coherence" (*19*). For Piaget a flexible internal regulation, "progressive equilibration," coordinates all other factors into an organized system.

Learning depends not only on the stimulus, but on the structure or system the learner has available to process it. The qualitative differences in these available structures, and in the way in which the organism is capable of dealing with physical experience, delineate the stages of cognitive development. Piaget (*18*) enumerates four major cognitive stages: sensorimotor, preoperational, concrete operational, and formal operational. Since in the present study we are most concerned with children's spelling strategies when many of them are making the transition from preoperational to concrete operational thinking, we will examine some of the differences in thinking that distinguish these two stages.

Preoperational children are bound by, or "center" on, the perceptual states of objects. Though they are aware that these objects may be changed from state to state, they are unable to compare them across states without centering on perceptual cues of limited value. An analysis of one of the typical tasks Piaget presents to school age children will clarify and elaborate this stage of centration-decentration. The problem chosen is the classic conservation of continuous quantity (20).

The child is presented with two glasses of equal size, equally filled with water. The water from one glass is then poured into a thinner, longer container. The preoperational child now typically judges that the thinner container has more water, since the level is higher. He "centers" on the perceptual state of the water and considers only one aspect of the problem. He "centers" on the height. If an extremely thin, elongated container is introduced, he may even successively vary the relevant dimension. He may now decide that thickness is more important and judge that the shorter, thicker glass contains more water. But he is unable to consider both aspects—higher but thinner vs. shorter but wider—simultaneously in seeking a solution. In Piaget's terms, he lacks compensation.

The operational child, on the other hand, may approach the problem from one of two different but equivalent points of view. Having the ability to combine classes (like height and width), he may judge the quantity of the water to be the same by compensating for one dimension in terms of the other. He may, on the other hand, also "decenter" from the perceptual state and mentally reenact the transformation involved. Thus he reasons that nothing has been added or taken away, or that the water can be returned to the original container and thus returned to its original height and width. Piaget calls this reversibility. Thus, the preoperational child, centering on a particular aspect or state, uses neither compensation nor reversibility in reaching a solution. The operational child, however, sees these as directly related to the solutions and utilizes one and/or the other in expressing a decision.

One of Piaget's more important discoveries was that these interstage differences follow similar patterns across various tasks and concepts (number, quantity, classification, time, and space).

In terms of the present study, it is being argued that efficient spelling requires a more specific but parallel coordination of structures or patterns. Efficient spelling, like operational thinking, requires a decentration away from strictly perceptual correspondences, in this case away from simply sound-letter relationships. Thus, testing procedures were used which examined each child's ability to decenter along seven Piagetian dimensions: perception (as measured by Elkind's *Picture Integration Test*); class inclusion; and conservation of number, mass, continuous quantity, weight, and volume. (See Appendix for a fuller description of the decentration battery.)

Procedures

Given the hypotheses and working definitions of complexity, quality of response, and stage of development formulated thus far, the following procedures were planned and carried out:

1. Two 18 word spelling lists were constructed including a total of six low frequency examples of each of the five word pattern categories: Short Vowel, Long Vowel, Past Tense, Consonant Doubling, and Derivational Pairs.
2. Spelling lists were administered to 60 elementary school children, 15 each in grades one through four.
3. Two raters independently rated each spelling using the six point scale discussed above (percentage of agreement between raters was between 93 and 100 percent across the sixty spellings of each word). Each child's spelling rating for each of the six examples for each category were then totalled, giving each child an overall rating for each of the five spelling categories.
4. A battery of Piagetian tasks was constructed along the seven dimensions dis-

cussed above: Perception, Class Inclusion, Conservation of Number, Mass, Discontinuous Quantity, Weight and Volume. This battery was then administered and scored for each child.
5. The spelling data were analyzed using a two way analysis of variance for repeated measures design (*16*).
6. Factor analyses for oblique rotations were performed using the five spelling category scores and seven decentration scores for each child.

Results

The results of the analysis of variance indicated that there were significant effects for grade level and spelling pattern categories as well as a significant interaction effect between grade and category (p<.01 for all three). There was a general increase in scores as grade level increased, and a general decrease in ratings for each grade as word complexity increased. Furthermore, the factor analysis revealed that there were two distinct factors, one for spelling categories and one for decentration tasks, but that these factors were significantly correlated (r=.56, p<.01) even when the effects of grade level were controlled (r=.36, p<.01).

Discussion: Spelling Strategies

The results of the analysis of variance supported the three hypotheses generated about how children at different grade levels would attempt to spell different kinds of words. First, as the grade level increased the children seemed to use more sophisticated spelling strategies. This tendency held across all categories. However, second grade was an exception. Not only were the spelling responses similar to first grade attempts, but the performance of the second graders on the decentration tasks was also comparable to that of the first graders. Further communication with the teacher supported the suspicion that this class was, in fact, an academically below average second grade. But these children's consistent performances on both spelling and cognitive tasks tend to confirm the hypothesis that level of spelling strategy and cognitive development are significantly related.

The results of the analysis also supported the hypothesis that, across all four grades, differences in categories would lead to differences in performance. The Short and Long Vowel categories seemed of comparable difficulty, while the Past Tense and Consonant Doubling categories were also equally difficult, though noticeably more difficult than the first two categories. Finally, the Derivational Pairs category was clearly more difficult than the other four.

The children in this study seemed to rely on three different strategies in spelling short vowels. First grade attempts were about equally divided between a closest long vowel strategy and a correct short vowel strategy, with a lower but fair number of transitional attempts. This supported the findings of recent investigations *(2, 3, 21, 22)*. Furthermore, second, third, and fourth grade spellings indicated a progressive decrease in nearest vowel strategies (minimal by third grade). Transitional attempts, on the other hand, were much slower to disappear, showing even slight increases in grades two and three. Through all the grades, the most prevalent strategies involved using the correct vowel, with almost perfect use of the proper short vowel by grade four. These findings were not unexpected. Since the children were tested toward the very end of the school year, even the first graders had the benefit of a year's instruction and a year's experience with written words. Furthermore, short vowels are traditionally dealt with during the first year of school. What is essential to the theoretical basis of this study, is that the children did employ systematic ways of spelling the short vowels, and that more of the spellings conformed to the standard orthographic representation as familiarity and maturity increased.

Long vowel spellings showed a movement from a letter-name strategy to a mastery of the marking system which structures the spelling of the English Long vowels (SKRAP—*scrape*). The first graders seemed unaware of this system, with 60 percent of their attempts being categorized as letter-name. Of the classifiable attempts of the second grade pupils, a much higher proportion showed evidence of a working knowledge of marking principles. Third and fourth graders, as expected, performed extremely well on these words, with over 90 percent of the fourth grade spellings using at least possible vowel marking patterns.

But a use of letter-name strategy did persist into the third grade (17 occurrences, SKED—*skid*). Furthermore, there was no strong evidence for any transitional stages. It seemed that when the marking system was used in the spelling responses, it was handled correctly in all grades. It may be that this finding was due to the immaturity of the second grade sample, and that an average second grade would have provided responses in which transitional strategies were used. But it is also possible that the ability to integrate both the marking system and phonetic principles was more cognitively demanding than mastering either system separately. Thus knowledge of marking principles might have been masked by an inability to use both systems simultaneously. There is not enough evidence at this time to warrant a final statement on this point.

The next two categories, Past Tense and Consonant Doubling, were characterized by a high proportion of 0 responses in both grades one and two. However, most of these unclassifiable attempts did follow a discernible pattern—spelling of the base word with the inflectional ending completely omitted (STAB—*stabbed*). But there may be a reasonable phonological explanation for this phenomenon.

As many linguists *(26, 27)* have noted, a certain amount of consonant cluster reduction is typical in the pronunciation of standard English. (This feature has also received considerable attention in recent studies of social dialects.) Consonant reduction refers to the deletion of a stop consonant *(t, d, p,* or *k)* when it follows another consonant at the end of a word. It is important to realize that in many words when the base form ends in a consonant the addition of *-ed* usually results in a consonant cluster. Thus *raked* and *trimmed* are pronounced (reykt) and (trimd). Given this fact, it may be that many of the unclassifiable responses were in reality letter-name strategies.

For the Past Tense category, the data indicated that correct use of the marking system emerged rather abruptly at the third grade level. It seemed that once the need for the marking system was realized, its implementation developed quite rapidly. Again, the noted general immaturity of the second grade sample limits the conclusions that can be drawn on this point.

The Consonant Doubling category, on the other hand, showed a somewhat different developmental pattern in the third and fourth grades. Though the children went beyond letter-name strategies, a considerable number of third grade responses revealed an unawareness of the doubling principle (HUMING—*humming*), while at the same time a smaller but still significant number of attempts showed an overextension of the principle. For the fourth grade, awareness of the doubling principle had increased, while overgeneralization remained at about the same level. The difference in the two classes also was reflected in the increased number of correct attempts by the fourth graders. Once more the developmental pattern can be reasonably explained in terms of two factors: an increased familiarity with the kinds of words under consideration and the creation and testing of a set of underlying rules. The number of overgeneralization responses for Consonant Doubling supports this contention.

The Derivational Pairs scores indicated that this category was definitely the most difficult. Once again, a high proportion of first and second grade scores were unclassifiable. An examination of the responses revealed younger children often left out whole syllables and blocks of letters, usually at the point of most interest, around the unaccented syllable of the second word in the pair. Unfamiliarity with polysyllabic words was most likely a cause of such responses. However, it is also possible that letter-name strategies were affected by constraints on short term memory. If the children attempted to move across the word in a letter-name fashion, the increased time needed to process the longer words may have led to a short term memory overload for the younger children. As a result, the phonetically least prominent parts of these words, the unaccented syllables, were omitted from the spelling attempts.

The letter-name strategies of first and second grade children were characterized by the omission of the schwa vowel from the unaccented syllable (for example, *combnashon* for *combination*). Very few of the responses for these children went beyond a simple letter-name approach.

Third and fourth grade responses, on the other hand, showed a much more consistent use of a vowel in the unaccented syllable. However, a substantial number of third and fourth grade attempts were also based on a letter-name strategy. Furthermore, only 12 percent of the third grade responses and only 40 percent of the fourth grade attempts showed the use of the same vowel in both accented and unaccented positions. For the fourth graders, the great majority of these were correct spellings. It would seem once again that familiarity and experience were factors in the way the children approached the spellings of these words. But the attempts also seemed to involve growing concepts of how words work. The principles of root word relationships, demanding generalizations and the creation of structures over classes of related words, seem to require a highly sophisticated understanding of the way words are related. Apparently these principles are mastered sometime beyond the fourth grade level.

In summary, the spelling data from this investigation generally support the argument that children progressively develop more sophisticated strategies for dealing with English orthography. However, the transitional stages for Long Vowel and Past Tense categories discovered in earlier research were not noted in the present study. Several possible explanations for this fact were suggested, but the immaturity of the second grade sample limited the applicability of the present data, especially in regard to transitional stages.

Discussion: Spelling and Decentration

The results of the two-factor analyses confirmed the investigator's original general hypothesis that performance on the decentration battery and levels of spelling strategies for each category would be significantly correlated. The fit of the two-factor solution indicated that these two sets of variables did, indeed, measure different things, but the correlation between the two factors confirmed that decentration and levels of spelling strategies were significantly related.

The purpose of the second factor analysis, using the partial correlations generated when grade was controlled, was to minimize that part of the variance predictable by between-grade differences, both maturational and experiential. The findings were that the factor pattern remained essentially the same, and that the two factors were still significantly correlated. This provides empirical data supporting the argument that the structures needed to deal effectively with English orthography are somewhat similar to the structures that must be invented in order for a child to move from preoperational to operational thinking.

Two specific sets of intercorrelations seem especially interesting. The particularly high correlations between the first and easiest spelling category, the Short Vowel category, and the decentration variables suggest that the qualitative difference between preoperational and operational thinking is most important for spelling at that time when the child first moves from a letter-name strategy to more abstractly based relational structures. Because of the effects of the Great Vowel Shift on the English sound-spelling system, a true understanding of the short vowel spellings necessarily involves a transformational system that goes beyond the merely perceptual relationships evident in letter-name spellings. More difficult spelling category strategies, though probably facilitated by more stable concrete operational thinking, did not seem quite as directly related to cognitive development.

The second interesting correlation was the significant relationship in both factor analyses between the Picture Integration Test and Derivational Pairs. Both variables specifically dealt with perceptual relationships between parts and wholes. It may very well be that the ability to internalize the relationship between *combine* and *combination* requires the same kind of active, systematic perceptual exploration necessary for success on Elkind's part-whole test.

Conclusions and Implications

Considering the developing quality of children's spelling mistakes through the grade levels tested and the significant correlations between spelling and cognitive factors in both factor analyses, it seems reasonable to conclude that learning to spell is not simply a matter of enough drill work and/or rote memorization. The development of spelling proficiency seems to involve both cognitive and linguistic processes and, as such, it requires the active, exploring participation of the learner.

Since children's spellings do exhibit stage-like characteristics, it follows that teachers could acquire useful instructional information regarding stage of development, sources of difficulty, and signs of progress by examining the quality of children's spelling attempts as well as by simply determining their correctness.

Furthermore, classroom practices like extensive phonics drills and typical weekly spelling list-test cycle hardly encourage essential active participation and concept formation. It would seem more profitable to construct learning environments in which children have the opportunity to formulate, test, and evaluate their own hypotheses about the orthography. Such environments might logically include activities which encourage and stimulate natural language use through extensive speaking, reading, and writing as means of communication and expression.

Children also need opportunities to compare and contrast words on a variety of levels (sound, structure, syntax, semantics) so that they might systematically discover and utilize both intraword and interword patterns of organization. Activities that foster such comparisons need not be especially complicated or time consuming. Henderson *(14)* briefly suggests a word sorting procedure in which the child sorts or piles word-bank words under examples of useful classifications. It may be helpful for children to see the relationship between the spelling of past tense (typically *ed*) and its various but systematic pronunciations. Children may be asked to classify their *-ed* words as more like *raked, cheated,* or *played.* (Of course there will be some exceptions, and other examples may be thought of as the child proceeds with the activity.)

Dale *(8)* and O'Rourke *(17)* describe the technique of "word webbing" as another activity through which older children may discover word patterns and relationships. In a root web, for instance, words like *sympathy, pathetic,* and *pathology* are linked through their common root *path-,* from *pathos* (suffer). By constructing such webs and checking their accuracy, students can simultaneously extend both their spelling and vocabulary growth through the discovery of underlying, systematic patterns of meaning and spelling.

In effect, children need the opportunity and encouragement to *discover* for themselves the structures governing English spelling, just as they *invent* (in Piaget's terms) the structures which enable them to assimilate reality, and tacitly *construct* the transformational rules which govern the structure of spoken and written language.

Appendix

List of Examples

Short Vowels
a:	craft	(21)*	e:	hem	(14)	i:	drift	(36)
	damp	(27)		speck	(13)		skid	(3)

Long Vowels
a:	tame	(25)	e:	creep	(36)	i:	spike	(5)
	scrape	(18)		thief	(28)		slime	(4)

Past Tense
/t/:	cramped	(8)	/d/:	bragged	(5)	/Id/:	dented	(3)
	raked	(13)		stabbed	(9)		cheated	(18)

Consonant Doubling
Short vowels:	humming	(20)	Long vowels:	wading	(15)
	trimmed	(42)		striped	(7)
	flopped	(5)		dining	(A)

Derivational Pairs
a:	inflame	(7)	e:	compete	(11)
	inflammation	(2)		competition	(28)
	explain	(AA)		repeat	(A)
	explanation	(31)		repetition	(10)
i:	combine	(A)			
	combination	(40)			
	inspire	(32)			
	inspiration	(18)			

*Numbers in parentheses are the occurrences of the word or its uninflected per million words in the Thorndike and Lorge (*21*) overall count. A indicates a word occurs between 50 and 99 times per million words. AA indicates a word occurs 100 or more times per million words.

Decentration Tasks: Procedures

1. *Conservation of Mass*
   Equipment—Playdoh, screen
   Procedure. Use the Playdoh to make two balls of equal size. Show these to the children and make sure they agree that both balls have the same amount of Playdoh. If the children do not agree, adjust the sizes of the balls until they consider them equal. Put one ball behind the screen and leave the other in front of the children. Roll the ball into a sausage in front of the children. Now ask the children if the same ball you rolled into the sausage still has the same amount, or it has more or less than it did before. (It is important that you give children the three choices so that they do not base their decisions on what they think you want them to say.) Then ask them to explain their reasoning. Next, bring the other ball out from behind the screen, reminding the children that the two balls originally had the same amount of dough, and that you have neither added any

dough to them nor taken any away. With both the ball and the sausage in front of them, ask the children whether the balls have the same or different amounts. Next, ask them to explain their reasons.

2. *Conservation of Number*
   Equipment—Eight plastic poker chips of one color and eight of another color, screen
   Procedure. Assemble the chips into two differently colored lines of the same length. Show these to the children and have them agree that both lines contain the same amount by counting the number of chips in each line. Now place the screen between the two rows so that only one row can be seen. Change the length of the row seen by moving the chips farther apart. Now ask the children if that row has less, more, or the same as it did before. Then ask the children to explain their reasoning. Next remove the screen, reminding the children that the rows were originally the same, and that you have neither added nor taken away any chips. Now ask the children whether one row has more or less than the other or whether they both have the same amount. Ask the children to explain their reasoning.

3. *Conservation of Continuous Quantity*
   Equipment—Two identical clear plastic cups, one differently shaped cup, water, screen
   Procedure. The procedure is almost identical to that used for the conservation of mass. Now the shape of the material is determined by the shape of the container rather than by the tester's manipulation of solid material.

4. *Conservation of Weight*
   Equipment—Playdoh, screen
   Procedure. Same as for conservation of mass, except that decisions are made in regard to the weight of the Playdoh rather than in regard to its mass. Thus, a child may hold a ball in each hand in order to agree that they weigh the same. However, once the shape of the ball is changed, the child should not be allowed to weigh the objects again. Judgment should be based on what the child thinks should be true rather than on the actual physical sensation of the Playdoh.

5. *Class Inclusion I*
   Equipment—Paper triangles and squares (there should be more of one than the other), box
   Procedure. Show the children the squares and triangles. They must understand that they are *all* paper and must also agree that there are more of one than the other. Now ask the children whether there are more square (or triangle) things or more paper things. Ask the children to explain their reasoning.

6. *Conservation of Volume*
   Equipment—Two beakers equally filled with water (about halfway), two equal balls of Playdoh, screen
   Procedure. Again, basically the same as conservation of mass. Now the judgments are made on the change in the level of water in the cups if the Playdoh were put in the water. Again, however, the Playdoh should *not* be put in the water. The decisions should be made on what the children think should happen rather than on the physical perception.

7. *Class Inclusion II*
   Equipment—Plastic poker chips, two different colors (there should be more of one than the other)
   Procedure. Same as class inclusion I. Now ask the children if there are more of the greater number colored chips or more plastic chips. Ask them to explain their reasoning.

Scoring Criteria

On the conservation problems, there are two questions—one based on the change in an object itself (identity) and one based on the change in relation to a similar object (equivalence). These two should be marked *yes* if the child makes the correct judgment. Under each, however, is a category for the child's reasoning. As much as possible of the child's explanation should be recorded, and the reasoning category should be marked *yes* only if the child's reasoning is directly related to the question, and only if it makes sense. It should be based on logic rather than on the specific perceptual situation. Thus, a response like "they look like they're about the same" is not acceptable, though the tester may wish to ask for a further explanation. Correct responses are usually based on one of two principles: compensation or reversibility. An example of compensation would be, "Now it's longer but thinner" while reversibility is dependent on the child's ability to see that one could return it to the former state: "If you squished it back together, it would be the same as before." In any case, testers should be careful that their decisions are based on what the child understands, rather than simply on the correct verbal response.

Table 1
Spelling Strategy Rating Scale

Category	Strategy	Score	Examples of Children's Spellings
Short Vowel	unclassifiable	0	krof (craft), scod (skid)
	vowel omitted	1	krft, scd
	closest tense vowel	2	crift, sced
	transitional	3	creft, scad
	vowel correct, incorrect form	4	kraf, scid
	correct form	5	craft, skid
Long Vowel	unclassifiable	0	crop (creep), slom (slime)
	letter-name	1	crep, slim
	transitional	2	crip, slam
	vowel correct, marking incorrect	3	creyp, sliym
	vowel correctly marked, incorrect form	4	creap, sime
	correct form	5	creep, slime
Past Tense	unclassifiable	0	rake (raked), cet (cheated)
	letter-name	1	rakt, chetd
	d-marker	2	rakd, cheatd
	vowel (not e, not o) +d	3	racid, cheatud
	marker correct, incorrect form	4	raced, cheeted
	correct form	5	raked, cheated
Consonant Doubling	unclassifiable	0	flop (flopped), wad (wading)
	letter-name	1	flpt, wadn
	lax, undoubled	2	floped
	tense, doubled	3	wadding
	doubling correct, incorrect form	4	floppid, weding
	correct form	5	flopped, wading
Derivational Pairs	unclassifiable	0	xpln-xplntn (explain-explanation)
	letter-name	1	xplan-xplnashon
	vowel present, unextended	2	explain-explinashon
	vowel incorrectly extended	3	explain-explaination
	vowel correctly extended, incorrect form	4	explain-xplanashon
	correct form	5	explain-explanation

Table 2
Partial Correlations of Decentration and Spelling Variables (Grade Controlled)

	1	2	3	4	5	6	7	8	9	10	11
1. Number											
2. Mass	.19										
3. Cont. Quant.	.57**	.55**									
4. Weight	.46**	.56**	.72**								
5. Volume	.27*	.44**	.37**	.46**							
6. Class Incl.	.30**	.42**	.42**	.29*	.26*						
7. P.I.T.	.20	.41**	.45**	.25*	.23*	.45**					
8. Short Vowel	.27*	.40**	.47**	.42**	.13	.11	.27*				
9. Long Vowel	.28*	.07	.32**	.13	.19	.09	.04	.60**			
10. Past Tense	.15	.15	.38**	.29*	.22*	.21*	.20	.60**	.58**		
11. Doubling	.11	.24*	.34**	.29*	.18	.17	.23*	.72**	.56**	.70**	
12. Derivational Pairs	.03	.22*	.31**	.19	.20	.18	.32**	.54**	.39**	.54**	.65**

*p<.05
**p<.01

Table 3
Intercorrelations of Decentration and Spelling Variables

	1	2	3	4	5	6	7	8	9	10	11
1. Number											
2. Mass	.30**										
3. Cont. Quant.	.61**	.61**									
4. Weight	.53**	.62**	.75**								
5. Volume	.33**	.50**	.43**	.51**							
6. Class Incl.	.37**	.50**	.48**	.37**	.32**						
7. P.I.T.	.28*	.48**	.50**	.33**	.29*	.51**					
8. Short Vowel	.41**	.54**	.54**	.54**	.27*	.29*	.39**				
9. Long Vowel	.42**	.33**	.44**	.34**	.33**	.29*	.23*	.78**			
10. Past Tense	.35**	.40**	.47**	.45**	.35**	.38**	.35**	.78**	.80**		
11. Doubling	.31**	.44**	.45**	.45**	.32**	.35**	.37**	.85**	.78**	.86**	
12. Derivational Pairs	.25*	.42*	.43**	.38**	.33**	.35**	.43**	.73**	.67**	.77**	.82**

*p<.05
**p<.01

Table 4
Frequency Counts of Strategies by Grade and Category

	Rating	Short Vowel	Long Vowel	Past Tense	Doubling	Derivational Pairs
Grade 1	0	5	5	49	45	33
	1	3	54	20	18	43
	2	30	2	8	8	13
	3	13	4	6	0	1
	4	34	13	5	8	0
	5	5	12	2	11	0

Table 4—Continued
Frequency Counts of Strategies by Grade and Category

	Rating	Short Vowel	Long Vowel	Past Tense	Doubling	Derivational Pairs
Grade 2	0	28	23	49	53	55
	1	7	18	14	8	27
	2	13	11	5	8	4
	3	15	4	5	2	2
	4	10	13	10	13	2
	5	17	21	7	6	0
Grade 3	0	1	0	11	7	10
	1	0	17	2	2	29
	2	5	2	0	28	40
	3	20	1	0	10	7
	4	16	28	39	11	3
	5	48	42	38	32	1
Grade 4	0	0	0	6	11	7
	1	0	5	3	1	15
	2	3	2	0	11	31
	3	4	0	0	12	4
	4	18	19	24	5	8
	5	65	64	57	50	25

REFERENCES

1. Almy, M., F. Chittenden, and P. Miller. *Young Children's Thinking: Studies of Some Aspects of Piaget's Theory.* New York: Teachers College Press, Columbia University, 1966.
2. Beers, J. "First and Second Grade Children's Developing Orthographic Concepts of Tense and Lax Vowels," unpublished doctoral dissertation, University of Virginia, 1974.
3. Beers, J., and E. Henderson. "A Study of Developing Orthographic Concepts among First Graders," *Research in the Teaching of English,* 11 (1977), 133–148.
4. Briggs, C., and D. Elkind. "Cognitive Development in Early Readers," *Developmental Psychology,* 9 (1973), 279–280.
5. Cahen, L., M. Craun, and S. Johnson. "Spelling Difficulty: A Survey of the Research," *Review of Educational Research,* 41 (1970), 281–301.
6. Chomsky, N. "Phonology and Reading," in H. Levin and J. Williams (Eds.), *Basic Studies in Reading.* New York: Harper and Row, 1970.
7. Chomsky, N., and M. Halle. *The Sound Pattern of English.* New York: Harper and Row, 1968.
8. Dale, E. *The Word Game: Improving Communications.* Bloomington, Indiana: Phi Delta Kappa Educational Foundation, Fastback #60, 1975.
9. Elkind, D. *Picture Integration Test* (in press).
10. Gates, A. *A List of Spelling Difficulties in 3876 Words.* New York: Teachers College Press, Columbia University, 1937.
11. Hanna, P., and others. *Phoneme Grapheme Correspondences as Cues to Spelling Improvement.* Washington, D.C.: U.S. Government Printing Office, 1966.
12. Harman, H. H. *Modern Factor Analysis.* Chicago: University of Chicago Press, 1967.
13. Heatherly, A. "Attainment of Piagetian Conservation Tasks in Relation to the Ability to Form Hypotheses as to the Probable Content of Story Material among First and Second Grade Children," unpub-

lished doctoral dissertation, University of Virginia, 1971.
14. Henderson, E. "On Learning to Spell," presented to the Psycholinguistics and Sociolinguistics Special Interest Group, International Reading Association Annual Convention, Houston, May 1978.
15. Mazurkiewicz, A. "Toward a Spelling Reform," *Reading World,* 16, 2 (December 1976), 81–87.
16. Myers, J. L. *Fundamentals of Experimental Design.* Boston: Allyn and Bacon, 1966.
17. O'Rourke, J. *Toward a Science of Vocabulary Development.* The Hague: Mouton Press, 1974.
18. Piaget, J. *The Child and Reality: Problems of Genetic Psychology.* New York: Viking Press, 1973.
19. Piaget, J. *Psychology of Intelligence.* Totowa, New Jersey: Littlefield Adams, 1966.
20. Piaget, J., and B. Inhelder. *Psychology of the Child.* New York: Basic Books, 1969.
21. Read, C. "Preschool Children's Knowledge of English Phonology," *Harvard Educational Review,* 41 (1971), 1–34.
22. Read, C. "Children's Judgments of Phonetic Similarities in Relation to English Spelling," *Language Learning: A Journal of Applied Linguistics,* 23 (1973), 17–38.
23. Thorndike, R. L., and I. Lorge. *The Teacher's Word Book of 30,000 Words.* New York: Teachers College, Columbia University, 1944.
24. Venezky, R. L. "English Orthography: Its Graphical Structure and Its Relation to Sound," *Reading Research Quarterly,* 2 (1967), 75–105.
25. Weir, R. H., and R. L. Venezky. "Spelling-to-Sound Patterns," in K. S. Goodman (Ed.), *The Psycholinguistic Nature of the Reading Process.* Detroit: Wayne State University Press, 1968.
26. Wise, C. *Introduction to Phonetics.* Englewood Cliffs, New Jersey: Prentice-Hall, 1957.
27. Wolfram, W., and D. Christian. *Appalachian Speech.* Arlington, Virginia: Center for Applied Linguistics, 1976.
28. Wolfram, W. "Generative Phonology: A Basic Model for Reading," in R. Shuy (Ed.), *Linguistic Theory: What Can it Say about Reading?* Newark, Delaware: International Reading Association, 1977, 32–57.

Spelling Texts and Structural Analysis Methods

DONALD H. GRAVES

Sonya opened her sixth grade spelling book to page fifty-five. It was a Tuesday, and on Tuesdays she completed word exercises from her text to prepare her for a spelling test on the same words on Friday.

She glanced down the page. The first direction stated, "Choose and write the correct homonym: Jack had a paper _____ (root, route)." The second directed her to, "Write *mistaken.* Cross out the prefix." The next asked her to "Write in syllables: *memory, towel, thirsty, upper.*"

Some persons believe these exercises contribute to spelling power or to related language arts skills. A few believe they are detrimental to fostering spelling abil-

---

From *Language Arts,* Vol. 54, No. 1, (January, 1977). © 1977 by the National Council of Teachers of English.

ities. Still another group believes they are harmless, yet important "fill-ins" for teachers while they are busy working with other students.

As in Sonya's case, commercial texts are the foundation of spelling activity for most pupils. That is, most of the spelling exercises, word lists, and approaches used to develop spellers are determined by published spelling materials. The actual materials have seldom been reviewed for content, approach, and effectiveness.

Cohen (1969) evaluated the structural analysis methods of spelling books in use at the time of his study. The findings of the study are timely in the light of renewed interest in spelling by many school systems. This report reviews the Cohen study and provides an update on the exercises contained in nine spelling texts in current use.

Cohen's study concerned the basic issue of the value of word study exercises in spelling textbooks:

It is the value of the word study exercises in spelling textbooks to which this study directs its attention. While there is much indirect evidence concerning the effect of word study exercises that emphasize phonics, syllabication, and affixes on the student's ability to learn to spell, there is little research data on the specific contribution that the spelling book word study exercises make to the learning of assigned words.

To reach his objective Cohen had to complete several study phases. First, he examined nine different spelling books in order to classify exercises and determine the nature of current approaches to the teaching of spelling. Second, he tested the effectiveness of these exercises in a study with children. This was done through a comparison of two approaches to the teaching of spelling: word analysis, and response to meaning and word usage techniques. The goal of this phase of the study was to measure the effects of each type of word study exercise on the student's ability to learn to spell assigned words.

The phase which tested the effectiveness of spelling approaches involved 553 pupils in grades five and six from a suburban community. The classes in the experiment were given a list of twenty words each week for six weeks. One week, the words were studied by exercises typical in spelling textbooks and similar to those used by Sonya. A second week, the words were studied by simple word usage study and a test correction method. Examples of response meaning and word usage study exercises are contained in the following tasks for children.

1. On a separate piece of paper use each of the words from your spelling list in a phrase or sentence under one of the following headings: (One has been done for you to give you the idea.)
WHEN MOTHER AND I HAVE A LITTLE DISAGREEMENT . . .
   I get very *uncomfortable*.
THINGS I WOULD LIKE TO DO WITHOUT . . .
   An *opinion* on how much I've grown from an elderly friend of the family.

2. On a separate piece of paper, put each group of three words in one colorful and interesting sentence. The challenge in this exercise is to link the three words together in the sentence . . . not to just put the three words in a sentence in a disjointed way.

discussion	equipment	disappointment
colonel	shepherd	benefit
disagreeable	appreciate	condemn

In each case the structural elements of the words are not attended to; rather, the child is simply asked to use the word.

By using the alternating plans, three of each student's six weeks involved spelling book exercises and three involved studying the words in usage exercises. Thus, the effectiveness of each approach was measured with the same pupils.

Findings: Spelling Texts

Textbooks employ varying emphases for preparing children as spellers. Cohen identified five categories of exercises common to all of the sixth grade spellers examined. The five categories, their contents, and the aggregate percentage of emphasis by the texts follows:

I. Affixes and Inflectional Endings: prefixes, suffixes, root or base words, plurals, possessive cases	23.7%
II. Syllabication	7.9%
III. Phonics: homophones, silent letters, double letters, phonetic respelling, digraphs, vowel sounds, ending blends, demon phonograms	33.6%
IV. Exercises calling for a response to the meaning of the assigned word	14.6%
V. Word Study Exercises Involving Basic Language Skills: synonyms, antonyms, homonyms, homographs, alphabetizing, contractions, compound words, dictionary skills, parts of speech, pronunciation accents, handwriting, abbreviations, capitalization, punctuation, sentence type identifications, miscellaneous activities	20.2%

A review of the spellers showed no discernible pattern of organization or distribution for the word study exercises.

Findings: Word Study Exercises

Children spell better when they are using language with a purpose; when they are using the response meaning and word study exercises. Students spelled less well when preparatory exercises stressed homophones, attention to affixes and inflectional endings, silent letters, initial consonants and blends, phonetic respellings, and vowels.

Some exercises actually served as deterrents to learning. The study of homophones in which a child is directed to "write two new words in which *ph* sounds like *f*," or "write the word in which *ci* sounds like *sh*" are examples of detrimental exercises. Other exercises which produced poorer spelling than word usage were activities involving silent letters, phonetic respellings, and vowels. A common characteristic of all of these exercises was a directive to deal with changed word forms. Of the analytical exercises that had some degree of success (though not better than word usage) the *form of the word was not changed,* as in calling attention to double letters, initial consonants, affixes, and syllabication.

All of the spelling words used in the study were observed for levels of significance in correct spelling. For eighty-one words spelled correctly (at the .05 significance level) seventy-two were spelled best by the word usage pattern, while only nine were favored by the word study.

Cohen found other tendencies worth noting through small sample data analysis. The study showed that the word usage study method better aided the spelling of high and low mental ability students, high and low academic achievers, both good and poor spellers, male pupils, and sixth grade pupils.

Cohen's findings are not surprising. As long ago as 1929 Ernest Horn questioned exercises that attended to the details and hard spots of words:

Direct experiments in marking hard spots have failed to show results as good as are obtained without use of such devices. Single hard spots are exceptions and what is hard for one person may not be hard for another. Teaching hard spots is no guarantee that these abilities will be transferred to other words.

In 1947 Thomas Horn examined the overall effectiveness of spelling books when he compared a corrected test method with the spelling textbooks' test-study procedure. In Horn's study, one group of children prepared for tests through the use of the spelling text, while another used a test-corrected test procedure with no study of the words. Horn found that the test-corrected test procedure could account for ninety to ninety-five percent of the children's achievement. Horn believed that the small margin of possible improvement did not warrant the large amount of time children spent in spelling books. Through this approach children merely study the words they do not

PERSPECTIVES

know, rather than becoming involved in exercises with words they already know.

Research Update

Have spelling books changed since the Cohen study was completed in 1969? To answer this question a survey was made of nine spelling books published since 1971. Three of the publishers were the same. The data in Tables I and II show the similarities and differences in spelling book emphases over the last twenty-five years, first in the Cohen study (Table I), then in the 1976 update (Table II).

Table III shows the trend in the use of word study exercises for all nine spelling books between the time of the Cohen study and the 1976 update.

Table I
Percentages of Word Study Exercises in the Cohen Study

Word Study Exercises by Major Category	(Merrill) 1957	(Webster) 1960	(Houghton Mifflin) 1955	(Silver Burdett) 1957	(Lyons & Carnahan) 1959	(World Book) 1960	(Ginn) 1956	(McCormick-Mathers) 1958	(Row Peterson) 1961
1. Affixes and inflectional endings	24.4	20.5	46.0	25.9	13.5	16.3	29.0	27.7	15.1
2. Syllabication	10.1	5.0	1.5	5.5	4.4	6.3	10.7	7.7	18.3
3. Phonics	18.5	47.7	24.4	30.5	42.4	58.0	25.4	38.0	22.2
4. Responding to the Meaning of the Word	19.7	13.7	10.5	18.1	24.4	6.5	16.6	16.6	9.1
5. Language Arts Skills	27.3	13.1	17.6	20.0	15.3	12.9	18.3	10.0	35.3

Table II
Percentages of Word Study Exercises in Current Texts

Word Study Exercises by Major Category	(Rand McNally) 1976	(American Book) 1976	(Harper Row) 1975	(McGraw Hill) 1976	(Harcourt Brace) 1974	(Lippincott) 1973	(Noble) 1971	(SRA) 1970	(Houghton Mifflin) 1971
1. Affixes and inflectional endings	18.4	22.8	15.3	7.4	25.0	24.8	24.5	31.4	12.8
2. Syllabication	1.3	5.0	4.7	3.3	5.4	3.6	3.8	7.8	5.1
3. Phonics	32.8	32.6	22.7	27.6	23.0	9.2	21.1	15.8	30.7
4. Responding to the Meaning of the Word	27.1	11.1	24.8	9.7	14.2	11.6	16.6	23.0	19.6
5. Language Arts Skills	19.9	28.5	32.5	52.0	32.4	50.8	34.0	22.0	31.8

Table III
Percentages of the Total Number of Word Study Exercises for Nine Texts

	Cohen Study (1955–1961)	Current Texts (1971–1976)	Degree of Change
1. Affixes and Inflectional Endings	23.7	19.3	−4.4
2. Syllabication	7.9	4.5	−3.4
3. Phonics	33.6	24.6	−9.0
4. Responding to the Meaning of the Word	14.6	17.5	+ 2.9
5. Language Arts Skills	20.2	34.0	+13.8

Reaction and Assessment

Spelling books in 1976 continue to include large numbers of word study exercises. There is still a large proportion of exercises in areas the Cohen study questioned: affixes and inflectional endings, phonics, and syllabication. On the positive side, three areas are less emphasized: affixes and inflectional endings, syllabication, and most of all, phonics. Phonics contributes the least to spelling power.

The greatest change can be seen in the attention given to language arts skills. Since spellers have moved away from the traditional teaching of spelling, they have turned to a heavier involvement in language arts skills. In short, today's spellers are largely language arts skills texts. Rather than remove spelling books from the market place, publishers have filled the vacuum with exercises related to handwriting, synonyms, word origins, and other language arts skill areas. Such exercises may be useful, but why must it be implied that they contribute to spelling power?

On the encouraging side, is the slight increase in word usage and response to meaning activities for children. In the light of the history of research in spelling and the Cohen study, more usage activities are needed.

Spelling is for writing. It is not to develop skills in alphabetizing, recognizing double consonants, or identifying affixes and inflectional endings. These activities may contribute to greater word sense or a wider vocabulary, but the odds are that they do not contribute to greater power in spelling. Fortunately, the Cohen data show that when words are applied in writing, children are more likely to spell them correctly.

The medium of spelling exercises and the spelling of words in isolation on a Friday test may carry the clear message, "spelling is for exercises, not for writing." They exist as so many pushups for the real game that is never played.

The Cohen data, as well as the update on current spelling book practices, point to the need for a reevaluation of spelling books and their contents. If books are to be used, more usage and application of spelling words is needed. The direct linkage between spelling and writing needs further exploration in both practice and in research.

REFERENCES

Cohen, Leo A. "Evaluating Structural Analysis Methods Used in Spelling Books." Ph.D. dissertation, Boston University, 1969.

Horn, Ernest. "The Influence of Past Experience Upon Spelling," *Journal of Educational Research* 19 (1929): 283–288.

Horn, Thomas D. The Effect of the Correct Test on Learning To Spell. *Elementary School Journal* 47 (1947): 277–285.

Correct Spelling—an Inquiry

EDMUND H. HENDERSON

For the past five years I have been studying the question of how it is that children learn to spell (Henderson and others, 1972). My interest has not been altogether unselfish because I happened to have been one student who did not learn to spell very well. Nonetheless, that long-lasting unhappy event did give me some leads in my work. For example, I can list from firsthand experience as well as from empirical evidence, a few ways in which children do not and cannot learn to spell. This has been helpful in narrowing the field of inquiry. Let me begin then by dispelling some of those myths about the world of spelling and how one learns to do it.

The first and most common prescription to the would-be student is "to study the word carefully, break it into syllables, sound it out and then memorize its letters in serial order." This, of course, is a good trick if you can do it, but to do so one must know *in advance* how English words are ordered—syllabled and sounded—and that is precisely what, in my youth, no one knew. In fact, it was generally conceded that English was a most irregular language which simply had to be learned the hard way. Unfortunately, the human mind is so constituted that it has a shockingly small capacity for the storage of meaningless rote associations (Miller, 1956).

At an early age I did succeed in remembering serially and permanently that *b u r e a u* spelled *bureau* and could astound my peers with this feat of exotic wisdom. Yet, I was then, and am to this day, tense in the company of such common words as *lay* and *lie* and *lose* and *loose, soap* and *rope, occurs* and *occurred* and so on. Well, then, how did those other children learn to spell? Brute memory couldn't do it. There was no logic to it; yet many did, and I did not.

Some learned men like George Bernard Shaw pled for reform—"change it so it's spelled as it sounds," they argued. There is a small problem here, of course, as I daresay Shaw and I would say things a bit differently. Phonetic precision could only yield chaos to reader and writer alike. Other wise men (W. B. Yeats, for example) simply disregarded the problem, or so it would appear from a study of their manuscripts. They spelled it as they pleased and left orthography to editors. The latter has always seemed to me an excellent way, but it is hard indeed for the school boy and the college student.

Spelling cannot be taught?

In early college days, when I was promptly condemned to what we then called "Dummy English" (a non-credit section for semi-literates), I was soon called in for a conference by the instructor.

"I perceive, Mr. Henderson," he said, (the salutation "Mr." always rather tickled me at the age of just seventeen), "that your presence in this section derives from your inability to spell." This was high praise indeed, for it implied the possibility that I could both read and write, two things toward which I had, for all the callowness of youth, both a fondness and ambition.

"Well then, sir," I asked, "do you think that you can teach me?"

"Unfortunately," he said, "I cannot. We simply do not know how to teach people to spell." I have often ranked

---

From *The Reading Teacher*, Vol. 28, No. 2 (November, 1974). Reprinted with permission of the International Reading Association and Edmund H. Henderson.

this honest statement with the Neoclassic beauties of the University of Virginia, an equal *in kind* to the vast Jeffersonian gift.

"I am, however," he added, "able to teach you one troublesome word which you will thereafter never forget." The word was "sepArate" which he spelled thus and with exactly the predicted effect. The mnemonic device *will* teach the weakest speller a few words. *Bureau* and *separate* were mastered by me for life, but what about the other 75,000 words a writer must deal with?

"If you read a lot," I was told, "it will help." But I did and it didn't. Indeed, as a contemporary psycholinguist, Frank Smith (1973), has shown, reading at a certain point is the worst of all possible things for spelling. The whole act of reading requires more and more minimal scrutiny of words in order that one may move with greater and greater efficiency to meaning. The better you read the less you will learn about spelling.

Well, then, how about the spelling books? Memorizing words (that is, *all* the words) letter by letter can't be done; we're agreed to that, I hope. But aren't there some rules? Indeed there are, and the most characteristic thing you find about them is that good spellers do not know them, and bad spellers remember them incorrectly. "Words that end in *o* form the plural or inflected form with *es*—Examples: *do = does, potato = potatoes*. That's a good one. But how about the rule that includes some parenthetical assertion about "when the accent is on the penult . . ."? The writer simply hasn't time for such nonsense. Spelling rules have been tried by many well-intentioned educators, but they simply don't work. Mr. Johnson knew *that* and had the honesty to declare it.

How about studying phonics? Children who study phonics learn to spell better than the poor victims of the whole word method. Edmund Burke Huey (1970), who wrote at the turn of the century (1917), tended to agree with this analysis. But phonics alone, he knew absolutely, would not solve the problems of learning to spell. The perception of words, he concluded, is not a simple mechanical event but involves a psychological projection outward from the mind.

Producing Good Spellers

For the next seventy-five years behavioral scientists (or worse, their misunderstanding educational interpreters) labored to produce machine-like methods of varied sorts to teach children words after the manner of Henry Ford in the production of cars. The effects in each case were similar. There has been an awful increase in volume, but overall quality is noticeably not improved. Hopefully we are not lost! A new day *has* dawned and there are *real* grounds to support the belief that the bad speller, like the polluted air and sea, may both be cured. During the past decade a group of substantive scientists have addressed themselves to the kinds of questions raised by Huey so many years ago.

What was this "projection from the mind" that constituted word recognition and orthographic knowledge? For years we were told that good spellers all have excellent "auditory senses". Perhaps so, but so do bad spellers. In fact, their most striking characteristic is that they spell things as they sound! Moreover, if we didn't *all* have excellent auditory senses, we could neither speak nor understand.

We have also been told that good spellers have excellent visual memory. No doubt this was true. By looking carefully at a word they can tell you whether a word is spelled correctly or not. But what is excellent visual memory made of, pray tell? Are people equipped with little "Brownie" cameras in their heads? Obviously not! Though I must confess that there was many a day that I wished it were true, for then, at least, I would have known where to send to get it fixed. (I should avoid a discussion of dyslexia in this paper, but I cannot resist pointing out that it is of the same order as this camera business. Roughly translated, *dyslexia* means that something in "there" doesn't work and we don't know what it is or how to fix it.)

But, to return to the basic question, what were Huey's "projections outward from the mind" underlying the secrets of visual memory for English words? We think now that we begin to know. They were ideas, concepts, "rules," systematic hierarchical orderings of knowledge about English words and how they work.

The work of Venezky (1967) and Chomsky (1970) has succeeded in dispelling one of the greatest myths of all times. The English language is *not* irregular at all. Rather it is fantastically regular and ideally suited to the conceptual capacities of the human mind, and to the different but companion tasks of reading and writing. The bad speller is nothing more than one who, because of physical damage (rare) or shock and ill teaching (more common, I think), fixates at a primitive stage of word knowledge. He goes no further in his cognitive learning and, like all persons under stress, tries less and less effective strategies to cope with his problem. He tries mnemonic devices, spelling rules, spelling-by-sound, and the hopeless task of serial letter by letter memorization.

Logic of Orthography

We still have much to learn about how the child goes about this wonderful process of mastering the logic of orthography. But we are learning bit by bit (Read, 1971; Henderson and Beers, 1974). We know, for example, that some children begin by using their knowledge of letter names. They spell *cat* KT and *cake* KAK. Later, they form the concept of the vowel-requiring syllable. At this point, they seek systematically among their own phonological repertoire for the nearest logical fit on the basis of the sound involved in the letter's name. Thus, the word *that* becomes THET. At the same time they make a negative transfer of this new knowledge so that *cake* is now spelled KEK. Gradually the vowel concept is internalized and the system of markers or signals learned (*oa* for *soap, ee* for *feet,* and the silent *e* for *cake*). Of course, there is overlap and errors will and *must* be made and *tested* so that the true order can be conceptualized. Rote learning exercises, stress, pressure and harassment can play havoc with the timid learner at this point, and it frequently does.

On the basis of our beginning work, we see that average first graders move through the major phases of letter-sound spelling and into basic vowel concepts. Some of the ablest pupils begin to toy with what Venezky calls morphographemic patterns. (For example, the *th* in *anthill* is not pronounced as in *thing* since meaning analysis requires that *t* and *h* be treated separately.) Inflectional endings, of course, are morphemic or meaning elements and must receive this prior scrutiny before they may be affixed to a root. *When* this system is learned, however, great order emerges in English that once appeared not to be there. Are there also underlying historical and semantic rules by which meaning emerges in the orderly surface of written language? Undoubtedly so, and here lies the present cutting edge of psycholinguistic research.

But it *is* this order (in a non-verbal, non-theoretical sense) that young children learn as they learn to spell. They are perfectly equipped to do it. They need only our confidence, encouragement and time. They need lots of activities and things of importance to do and feel and write about. They need the right to be wrong and an uninterrupted opportunity to try and test what will work for them at a pace that is right for them. They need schools that are interesting places to be and teachers of sense and sensitivity. Probably one of the most intriguing questions on earth is whether or not we can supply what is needed.

REFERENCES

Chomsky, N. "Phonology and Reading." *Basic Studies in Reading*. Levin and others, Eds. New York: Harper and Row, 1970.

Henderson, E. H. and J. Beers. A Study of Developing Orthographic Concepts among First-Graders. Unpublished manuscript, 1974.

Henderson, E. H., T. H. Estes, and S. Stonecash. "An Exploratory Study of Word Acquisition among First-Graders at Mid-Year in a Language Experience Approach." *Journal of Reading Behavior*, vol. 4, no. 3 (1972).

Huey, E. B. *The Psychology and Pedagogy of Reading*. (reprinted). Cambridge, Massachusetts: M.I.T. Press, 1970.

Miller, G. A. "The Magical Number Seven Plus or Minus Two: Some Limits on Our Capacity for Processing Information." *Psychological Review*, vol. 63 (1956), pp. 81–97.

Read, C. "Preschool Children's Knowledge of English Phonology." *Harvard Educational Review*, vol. 41, no. 1 (February 1971).

Smith, Frank. *Psycholinguists and Reading*. New York: Holt, Rinehart and Winston, 1973.

Venezky, R. "English Orthography: Its Graphical Structure and Its Relation to Sound." *Reading Research Quarterly*, vol. 2, no. 3 (Spring 1967), pp. 75–105.

Some Spelling Facts

HOWARD E. BLAKE
ROBERT EMANS

Grapheme, morpheme, phonics, phonetics, homograph, homophone, affix, suffix, vowel, consonant, open syllable, closed syllable . . . teachers of spelling today are confronted with terms and concepts which are baffling and confusing.

As teachers of teachers of spelling we too have had difficulty in communication with our students. What is needed is a compact source to which teachers can go for clear cut definitions and examples of the terminology and concepts used in spelling instruction. Successful teachers of spelling know that some children learn spelling best simply by reading, some by studying meanings of words, some by writing words in and out of context, some by oral spelling, some by using phonic and linguistic aids, and some by using a combination of some and even all of these.

Teachers of spelling should know thoroughly the intricacies of each approach to spelling instruction. However, no matter which approach is used they must know the terminology of each and their related concepts. They should understand them backwards and forwards, up one side and down the other, vertically and horizontally. Only when teachers have acquired this knowledge, and an understanding of the potential contribution of the various approaches, are they adequately qualified to teach spelling.

With this point of view in mind, the terminology and concepts for teaching

---

From *Elementary English*, Vol. 47, No. 2, (February, 1970). © 1970 by the National Council of Teachers of English. Reprinted by permission.

spelling which teachers should understand and teach to children when needed are outlined. This is not a thorough paper; rather it points out basic essentials and understandings of word structure. It gives some guidance to teachers as to what they must know. It should be clear by now, we are not advocating the teaching of spelling through any one approach. What we are advocating is that as teachers we must understand the terminology and concepts regarding the teaching of spelling uncommonly well and then use them where and when they are required. We have brought together from many sources some of the information that teachers should have, although they may not present it as such to pupils. We have endeavored to make the definitions, descriptions, and examples as simple as possible. At times, we have had to strike a balance between a complex presentation of a particular discipline and that aspect of it which is really necessary for teachers to know.

Terminology

Phonetics: the science of speech sounds.
Phonics: the application of phonetics to spelling and reading.
Linguistics: the study of human speech. It includes the study of phonetics as well as the study of meanings of words and grammar.
Phonetic analysis: the use of phonics in the spelling of words. Also, used to pronounce a written word in reading.
Structural analysis: the use of meaning units (or morphemes) in the spelling or recognition of words.
Phoneme: a bundle of phonetically similar sounds in language which are distinguishable in that the substitution of one for another changes the meaning of a word. For example: sounds represented by b, m, or the e in bet.
Morpheme: the smallest meaningful unit in the structure of words. Examples: root word, prefix, suffix, inflectional ending.

There are two forms:
(a) *free* which can be used as an independent word. Examples: rain, pin.
(b) *bound* which must be combined with one or more other morphemes. Examples: "-ing", "-s", "-ed", and "pre-".

Grapheme: an alphabetical symbol (letter) representing a phoneme (sound). Examples: *a, A.*

Grapheme-phoneme correspondence: the relationship between a phoneme (sound) and a grapheme (letter) in writing. In English there is not as close a one-to-one relationship between printed symbols and speech sounds as there is in some other languages such as Spanish. Some letters (graphemes) represent more than one sound (phoneme), e.g. the two s'es in "saves." Some sounds (phonemes) are represented by more than one letter or group of letters (graphemes). Examples: the vowel sound in "too," "do," "you," "flue," and "chew."

Consonant: one of the two main categories of speech sounds (phonemes). It is usually produced through the aid of the lips, teeth, tongue or palate. The letters (graphemes) representing the consonant sounds (phonemes) are also sometimes called consonants. There are approximately twenty-four consonant sounds in English. There is generally a higher grapheme-phoneme correspondence between consonants than vowels.

Consonant blend: two or more consonants which occur together without losing their separate identity. Examples: *st*ool, *bl*ack, subje*ct,* persi*st.*

Consonant digraph: two letters representing one consonant sound (phoneme). Examples: *th*is, *th*ick, *sh*arp, *ch*ange, si*ng,* w*h*ere, *ph*one, enou*gh,* ha*nd*. There are eight common consonant digraphs: th, sh, ch, ng, wh, ph, gh, and nd.

Vowel: one of the two main categories of speech sounds (phonemes) which is produced with the oral passage comparatively unobstructed, i.e. the lips, teeth, tongue, or palate are not generally used in modifying the sound as with the consonants. There are basically two sounds which every vowel letter represents: the long and the short sound. There are other vowel sounds, practically all of which occur whenever a vowel is followed by l (fall, tall, wall), r (for, fear, care, corn, horse, board, sure, farm) and w (down, draw, paw). The sounds in these words are actually diphthongs. Long and short sounds comprise the bulk of sounds given to English vowels. The letters (graphemes) representing the vowel sounds (phonemes) are also sometimes called vowels.

Long vowel: occurs whenever the sound of the vowel is the same sound given it when we say the letter as it appears in the alphabet. Examples: *a* in tape, *e* in be, *i* in bite, *o* in go, *u* in use. Most words that have the long vowel sound end in a vowel, or a "silent" e.

Short vowel: heard in these words: *a* in hat, *e* in bet, *i* in hit, *o* in hot, *u* in up. Most words that have the short vowel sound end with a consonant.

The multiplicity of ways in which vowel sounds can be represented accounts for one of the greatest difficulties in English language spelling. Consider the various spellings for each of the long and short vowel sounds:

long a—tape, weigh, tray, great, gauge, fiancee, aye, wait, prey, persuade, bouquet, risque, eh, suede, beta, reign.
short a—hat, laugh, plaid.
long e—be, lead, need, key, machine, people, quay, subpoena, Hawaii, Caesar, suite, Portuguese, deceive, believe, coeliac.
short e—bet, many, said, bread, friend, leopard, heifer, guess, says, bury, aesthetic.
long i—bite, lie, try, sigh, rye, rhyme, aye, sleight, eye, tried, buy, aisle, guide.
short i—hit, sieve, myth, been, busy, women, senate, pretty.
long o—go, toe, boat, yeoman, though, beau, oh, roast, quota, sew, brooch.
short o—hot, trauma, wash.
long u—use, ewe, feud, queue, lieu, you, view, beauty, cue, few, yule, Hugh.
short u—up, flood, rough, does, twopence, money.

There are perhaps other spellings besides these, but this list is indicative of the difficulty of spelling—and in teaching it.

Vowel digraphs: two vowels (letters) together in one syllable representing only one or a new vowel sound.

There are four kinds of vowel digraphs:

(1) First vowel long and second vowel "silent." Examples: deceive, team, pail. These words are spelled by the phonetic reading rule that "when two vowels come together, the first vowel usually does the talking and the second does the walking." (Plenty of exceptions exist for this rule, as represented in the other types of digraphs.)

(2) First vowel "silent" and second vowel long. Examples: great, guide, believe.

(3) First vowel short and second vowel "silent." Examples: breath, dead, feather, heavy, spread.

(4) Neither the short nor the long vowel sound of one or the other of the two letters is heard; rather, they combine to represent a new sound. Examples: does, again.

Diphthong: two vowel letters together in the same syllable representing one sound in which both vowels are heard. Examples: boil, sound, boy. As mentioned before, when l, r, or w follows a vowel, a diphthong is also usually being represented.

Schwa: the sound of a vowel in an unaccented syllable. A vowel in an unaccented syllable is usually not long or short or any other discrete vowel sound; it often is a schwa sound (written ə). Examples: parade, repair, decrease, sofa. A way to remember schwas is to remember the sounds in these key words: *a* in about, *e* in taken, *i* in pencil, *o* in lemon, *u* in circus. (Not all phonetic systems and dictionaries agree with the definition of schwa used here.)

Silent letters: any letter which is not a

part of a blend or digraph that is not heard when the word is pronounced. Example: fi*l*e, *k*nife, sc*h*ool, *p*neumonia, grow. The *e* in great, the *i* in believe, the *a* in weather, and the *o* in jeopardy are parts of digraphs and thus are often not thought of as silent letters. In the latter words the letters mentioned join with another letter to form a sound (phoneme) within the word. A letter to be considered "silent" cannot be a part of a phoneme; it is a whole. Some authorities reason that there are no "silent letters" in spelling. They believe that the so-called "silent letters" are better explained as part of the total grapheme. For example, the "silent" e is a diacritical symbol representing a part of a grapheme which signals the long vowel sound in ate or the *z* sound for the final *s*, as in cheese. Whether or not young children can readily grasp this concept is still in question.

Diacritic mark: a symbol may be added to a letter (grapheme) in order to indicate the pronunciation of the sound (phoneme). Example: the symbol for a long *e* is usually ē; for a short *e*, ĕ. However, this symbol varies from dictionary to dictionary.

Syllable: a unit of sound composed of a vowel and, often, a consonant. May be a whole word or part of a word. A written syllable may or may not correspond to a spoken syllable. Open syllable: a syllable ending with a vowel. Examples: me, so.

Closed syllable: a syllable ending with a consonant. Examples: men, son.

Accent: the degree of loudness (stress) by which a syllable is spoken.

Primary accent: the loudest accent.

Secondary accent: the second loudest accent.

Root word: the base of a word to which affixes are added. Examples: play in playing, playful, and replay.

Affix: a morpheme (the smallest meaning-bearing unit of a word) which is dependent upon another morpheme (a root word or another affix) and modifies the morphemes upon which it is dependent.

There are three types of affixes: prefixes, suffixes, and inflectional endings.

Prefix: an affix coming at the beginning of the word modifying the meaning of the basic word. Examples: pre- in prefix, re- in redone, un- in undo.

Suffix: an affix coming at the end of the word modifying the meaning of the basic word. Examples: -er in teacher, -ty in safety, -ful in forceful.

Inflectional ending: an affix coming at the end of the word to form plurals, possessive cases, comparisons, tenses of verbs, and so forth. Examples: -s in boys, -'s in boy's, -est in biggest, -ed in talked, -s in walks.

Synonym: words having the same, or nearly the same, meaning. Examples: danger, peril, hazard, risk.

Antonym: words having opposite meanings. Examples: big, small; hot, cold.

Homographs: words spelled alike, but with different meanings or pronunciations. Examples: the wind blew, to wind the clock; to convict, the convict in jail.

Homonym: words which sound alike, but with differing meanings and, sometimes, spellings. Examples: one, won; air, heir; bare, bear; dear, deer.

Spelling Rules

One view for teaching spelling is that each word must be memorized separately. Another view is that children should be taught methods which help them learn a system in spelling words without having to commit each of the many thousands of words to memory individually. As part of the process there are various rules which aid the speller. These rules state various generalizations which give clues as to how a word is conventionally spelled. By knowing a given rule a child may have a good clue as to how a word is spelled. However, English spelling is extremely complex. Many exceptions are encountered for almost any rule. These exceptions are seldom haphazard, but usually follow other rules. However, a child would have to learn an extremely large number of rules if he were to rely on them. Consequently, a compromise must be made between learning enough rules to give a system for spelling, but not so many that the learning of such rules becomes a burdensome task. Thus, the selection of which rules are most useful, (i.e., those which do not require too many subrules to explain the exceptions and which are applicable to a large number of words) puzzles both teachers and researchers.

Here are some of the rules that have been validated by research as having wide application. Probably other rules exist which may be more helpful. The teacher should be on the alert for them.

1. Words ending in "silent" e:
   a. A one-syllable word in which the vowel has the long vowel sound followed by a consonant sound often ends with a "silent" e. Examples: make, write, hole, use. This is generally true for the final syllable of a polysyllabic word. Examples: mistake, invite, before, perfume. Words with some other vowel sound usually do not end in a "silent" e. Examples: hit, hat, help.
   b. In some one-syllable words or in some final syllables the long vowel sound is sometimes spelled by a combination of two vowels without a final "silent" e. Examples: feed, coat, unload, repeat.
2. Spelling the i sound as i or y.
   a. When the i sound, either long or short, comes at the beginning or in the middle of a word or final syllable, the letter i is usually the correct letter to use. Examples: ice, advice, bring, admit. Exceptions: system, mystery.
   b. When the i sound, long or short comes at the end of the word it is usually spelled with a y. Examples: fry, why, defy, rely, ready, many, very.
3. Spelling the ai sound as ai or ay.
   a. When the long a sound occurs in the medial part of a word, it usually is spelled *ai*. Examples: train, bait, tail, retain, explain, entertainment.
   b. When this sound occurs at the end of a word it is usually spelled *ay*. Examples: day, bay, anyway, holiday.
4. Words ending in *ful*.
   If the *ful* is a suffix, it is spelled with one l. Examples: beautiful, powerful, wonderful, faithful, graceful, careful.
5. Spelling the k sound as c or k.
   a. The k sound is generally spelled with a c before the vowels a, o, and u. Examples: camel, company, custom, scale, scare, scuffle, delicate, acorn, difficult.
   b. It is usually spelled with a *k* before the vowels e and i. Examples: kettle, kid, sketch, skill, blanket, unkind.
   c. When it follows a long vowel sound, the k sound is usually spelled with a k. Examples: awake, duke, hike, joke, creek, leak, soak, crook.
6. Q followed by u. In English words q is always followed by u.
7. Adding suffixes to words ending in y.
   a. When final y is preceded by a consonant, the y is usually changed to i before adding any suffix that does not begin with i; e.g., relied, reliable. When the suffix begins with i, the y does not change; e.g., relying.
   b. When y is preceded by a vowel, the y does not change when adding a suffix. Examples: played, staying.
   c. Another way of saying the above two points is that when adding a suffix change y to i *except* when: (1) y is preceded by a vowel, (2) the suffix begins with i.
   d. Exceptions: adjectives of one syllable sometimes retain the y before ly and ness; e.g., spryly, dryness.
   e. In one study (3) this generaliza-

tion applied to about 80 words of the 1600 studied and only 3 exceptions were noted.
8. Adding suffixes to words ending in "silent" e.
   a. If the suffix begins with a consonant, generally retain the "silent" e. Examples: lonely, settlement.
   b. If it begins with a vowel, generally drop the "silent" e. Examples: lovable, moving, movable, caring, arguing, guidance.
   c. Exception: Words that end in ce and ge generally reverse these two rules when the suffix begins with a or o. Examples: noticeable, changeable, courageous. Also in a few other words such as dyeing, argument, duly, truly, wholly, judgment.
   d. One study (3) showed that these rules applied to 300 of 1600 words studied. There were only three exceptions on the list.
9. Doubling the final consonant when adding suffixes.
   a. Words ending in a single consonant preceded by a single vowel usually double the final consonant before adding the suffix. Examples: chopped, setting. This rule also applies to longer words when the last syllable is accented. Example: forgotten.
   b. (3) Applied to 74 of 1600 words studied. There were four exceptions, three of which ended with the letter x, which is not doubled.
10. Forming plurals. There are seven ways:
    a. By adding s (most words follow this rule).
    b. By adding es when the pronunciation requires it, such as after s, ss, ch, sh, x.
    c. By changing y to i and adding es when final y is preceded by a consonant: (This is the same aforementioned rule for adding a suffix to words ending in y.)
    d. By changing final f or fe to v and adding es. Examples: scarves, calves.
    e. By changing the internal vowels, as in foot, tooth, mouse, man.
    f. A few words are spelled the same in both singular and plural. Examples: deer, sheep.
    g. A few words change the letters ending the word to form the plural. Examples: datum–data, radius–radii, gymnasium–gymnasia, phenomenon–phenomena, criterion–criteria. (These words are of foreign derivation and are not encountered greatly by elementary school children.)
    h. One study (3) showed that of the 1600 words in fourth, fifth, and sixth grades there were 767 applications of these generalizations and only 31 exceptions. These exceptions included such words as *scarf* and *tooth*.
11. Rule for i before e.
    a. *i* comes before *e* except after *c* and in such words that have a long *a* sound as neighbor and weigh. Exceptions: either, neither, foreign, their, height, leisure, weird, seize. (Some teachers use sentences to display these exceptions as: "Neither is it weird for foreigners to seize leisure, either," or "Neither has leisure to seize the weird thing.")
    b. In Fitzgerald's basic list of 2650 words, 83 contain the *ie* and *ei* combination; only eight are exceptions to the rule.
12. Abbreviations are followed by a period.
13. Proper nouns and adjectives formed from proper nouns begin with a capital letter.
14. Adding the suffix *ly*.
    a. Most words add the suffix *ly* without change in the base word.
    b. The exception occurs when a word ends in y or *le*.
       (1) If the word ends in *y,* change

y to *i* and add *ly*.
Examples: busily, luckily. (This is actually the aforementioned rule for adding suffixes to words ending in y.)
(2) If the word ends in *le,* drop the *le* and add *ly*. Examples: capably, respectably.

Not all children need to learn these rules, but teachers do. A clear understanding of the rules will make it possible to diagnose more professionally a child's spelling needs and to select and recognize those rules which will be helpful.

When children learn spelling rules, they should probably learn them inductively, with the help of the teacher. A rule taught by rote usually is of little value to a child as he will seldom apply it. Rules cannot be considered a central approach to the spelling problem, but if they are approached reasonably and are derived inductively, they are of advantage to many learners.

The purpose of this paper has not been to suggest procedures for the teaching of spelling. Instead, the purpose has been to consolidate much of the spelling terminology and concepts currently used. The teaching of spelling is extremely complex. Consider these well-known poems which point out the complexity of our language and how difficult it must be to learn how to spell.

Our Querr Lingo

When the English Tongue we speak
Why is "break" not rimed with "freak"?
Will you tell me why it's true
We say, "sew", but likewise "few"?
And the maker of a verse
Cannot rime his "horse" with "worse"?
"Beard" sounds not the same as "heard";
"Cord" is different from "word";
"Cow" is cow but "low" is low;
"Shoe" is never rimed with "foe".
Think of "hose" and "dose" and "lose";
And think of "goose" and yet of "choose".
Think of "comb" and "tomb" and "bomb,"
"Doll" and "roll" and "home" and "some".
And since "pay" is rimed with "say"
Why not "paid" with "said," I pray?
Think of "blood" and "food" and "good";
"Mould" is not pronounced like "could".
Wherefore "done", but "gone" and "lone"—
Is there any reason known?
To sum up all, it seems to me
Sounds and letters don't agree.
—Anonymous

"Hiegh-Ho—Spelling by Rule"

When I was in school and I learned how to spell,
They taught me a rule, I remember quite well;
Put "i" before "e"—so I learned when a brat
Except after "c", it's as simple as that.
When memory gets muddy, I think in this vien,
For spelling's a study where science should riegn.
And when deficeint have siezures of doubt.
This rule is sufficeint to straighten them out.
So why need one labor to reach the hieght
Or inviegle a neighbor to set him aright,
When this anceint rhyme will his critics inviegh
And never a crime on his consceince need wiegh.
But while I'm proficeint
At spelling, I've feared
Though the rule is efficeint
The words do look wierd.
—Anonymous

PERSPECTIVES

Take My Word For It

I must confess it puzzles me
A little word like rough
Must always be pronounced to rhyme
With cuff and muff and fluff.

And yet there is another sound;
When one speaks of a cough,
Why must, forsooth, it ever rhyme
With off and doff and toff.

Another funny thing to me,
If I beg in a slough,
I tell the tale to listening ears,
And rhyme the word with goo.

But if by chance in dread disease
Some tissue I should slough,
We're right back where we started
With cuff and muff and fluff.

To make things worse, when we get paid,
We call it filthy dough,
Although I cannot reason why
It must be said just so,

And as a climax, might I add,
In climbing on a bough,
Perhaps to tumble from my perch,
I'm sure I'd screech an "OW"!
—By James Stevens

Pluresy

We'll begin with a box and the plural is boxes
But the plural of ox should be oxen, not oxes.
Then one fowl is a goose but two are called geese,
Yet the plural of moose should never be meese.
You may find a lone mouse or a whole set of mice,
Yet the plural of house is houses not hice.
If the plural of man is always called men,
Why shouldn't the plural of pan be called pen?
If I speak of a foot and you show me your feet,
And I give you a boot, would a pair be called beet?
If one is a tooth and a whole set are teeth,
Why should not the plural of booth be called beeth?
Then one may be that, and three would be those,
Yet hat in the plural wouldn't be hose.
And the plural of cat is cats and not cose.
We speak of a brother and also of brethren,
But though we say Mother, we never say Methren.
Then the masculine pronouns are he, his and him,
But imagine the feminine she, shis, and shim.
So English, I fancy you all will agree,
Is the funniest language you ever did see.
—Anonymous

This year—I firmly made a vow—
I'm going to learn to spell.
I've studied phonics very hard.
Results will surely tell . . .

"I thought I heard a distant cough
But when I listened, it shut ough."
Oh, dear, I think my spelling's awf.
I guess I mean't I heard a coff.

"To bake a pizza—take some dough
And let it rise, but very slough."
That doesn't look just right, I noe.
I guess on that I stubbed my tow.

"My father says down in the slough
The very largest soybeans grough."
Perhaps he means "The obvious cloo
To better crops, is soil that's nue."

"Cheap meat is often very tough.

We seldom like to eat the stough."
I'm all confused—this spelling's ruff.
I guess I've studied long enuph.
—Isabelle Smythe

BIBLIOGRAPHY

1. Betts, Emmett A. "Phonics: Vowel Principles." The ABC Language Arts Bulletin, Vol. III, No. 2, American Book Co., N.Y., 1950. 4 pp.
2. Carlson, Thorsten. "Developing Insights in Spelling." Language Arts Notes, No. 8, World Book Co., 1957. 4 pp.
3. Miller, Martha. "A Study of the Applicability of a Selected Set of Generalizations to a Word List in Spelling." Unpublished Master's Thesis, San Diego State College, 1955.
4. Gray, William S. On Their Own in Reading. Glenview, Illinois: Scott, Foresman and Co., 1960.
5. Horn, Ernest. "Phonetics and Spelling." Elementary School Journal, May, 1957, pp. 424–32.
6. Fitzgerald, James A. The Teaching of Spelling. Milwaukee, Bruce Publishing Co., 1951.

Speaking and Spelling

PATRICK GROFF

What effect do various aspects of children's speaking have on their ability to learn to spell? This is a critical issue that brings to mind other related questions. By improving children's articulation or production of speech sounds can we help develop their spelling skills? Does the use of a nonstandard dialect interfere with normal growth in spelling competence? Does systematic and intensive teaching of phoneme-grapheme correspondences, that which we call phonics, help children to learn to spell? Only if answers to such questions are available is it possible for teachers to determine if certain presently used practices in the teaching of spelling are legitimate.

From *Language Arts*, Vol. 56, No. 1 (January, 1979). ©1979 by the National Council of Teachers of English. Reprinted by permission.

Speech Errors and Spelling

While accurate responses to these three questions are somewhat difficult to come by, there is research information that does offer some rather definitive answers to at least two of them. In the first instance, we can say with some certitude that there is little relationship between errors in children's articulation and their faults in spelling. Despite the lopsided weight of opinion to the contrary in the past, as represented by the comments of Boyd and Talbert (1971), there is "disappointingly little evidence from experimental studies that suggests the relationship between speech and spelling seen by Boyd and Talbert and other writers of like persuasion" (Groff 1973, p. 89). This research on children's speech errors and their spelling leads to the inevitable conclusion that speech therapy to correct the problems children have in articulating speech sounds is not likely to have much effect on their power to spell. While there are various studies that have come to this conclusion, perhaps the one by Ham sums it up best. During his study of the relationships between the misspellings and the misarticulations of children, Ham recalls, "At no time was any spelling error related to the type of mispronunciation, e.g., the child who said *wabbit/rabbit* was more likely to misspell the word than the child who said the word correctly, but the misspelling would not involve the w/r substitution" (1958, p. 296). Read concluded that "Idiosyncracies of a child's pronunciation do not always affect his spelling" (1971, p. 5). Ham's data prompt us to challenge Read to demonstrate that there is, in fact, any such influence at any time. Thus, the massive task of reforming children's faulty articulation is not necessary before the successful teaching of spelling can be commenced.

Nonstandard Speech and Spelling

This conclusion about children's faulty articulation and their spelling leads to a second consideration, that of the role nonstandard speech or dialect has in children's learning to spell. Those who in the past have wrongly identified children's misarticulation of speech sounds as a major cause of spelling problems also have said that nonstandard speech falls into this classification. While present-day linguists remind us of the error in supposing that children who speak nonstandard English inevitably have articulation problems, this notion does continue to be held in some educational quarters. Even some experts in spelling who are not otherwise susceptible to this error in judgment do advise teachers that a stilted or pedantic standard pronunciation of a word by nonstandard English speaking children is likely to be useful for the purpose of mastering spelling. Teaching nonstandard speaking children in this way (to produce what for them are artificial pronunciations of words) to help prevent the spelling problems that stem from their dialect, is the counsel given teachers by Hanna, Hodges and Hanna (1971). Unfortunately, there is no evidence that this is a worthwhile recommendation.

This judgment is not intended to imply that there is no connection between nonstandard speech and spelling errors. While little research, indeed, has been devoted to this issue, we can conclude nonetheless that some relationship does seem to exist between these two linguistic phenomena. The reliable investigations of this issue have come since 1972. In that year Kligman, Cronnell and Verna (1972) studied second-grade low-income black children and spoke Black English (BE), a nonstandard English dialect. They found that the children made at least ten percent BE-related spelling errors on each of thirty-eight of forty-three groups of words that exemplified these forty-three speech features of BE. For example, they found that forty-seven percent of the spelling errors in words like *hatched* were dialect-related errors. That is, *hatch* was chosen as the correct spelling of *hatched* (and likewise, *cook* for *cooked, pass* for *passed* and *kiss* for *kissed*) forty-seven percent of the time by these children. In this study it was also found that BE-speaking pupils made significantly more BE-related spelling errors than did a group of standard English-speaking children. This latter finding was duplicated in a follow-up study of the dialect-related spelling errors of second-grade pupils who spoke BE (Kligman and Cronnell 1974). With the second-grade subjects of the Kligman and Cronnell (1974) study it had previously been found (Cronnell 1973) that sixty-one percent of their spelling errors in words ending in the consonant sound /s/ and in the consonant cluster /st/ were BE-related spelling errors, e.g., *bites* was spelled as *bite,* and *chased* was spelled as *chase.*

But do these BE-related spelling errors persist into the middle grades? To answer this question Groff (1978) had low-income pupils in the middle grades who spoke BE spell the test words used in the Kligman, Cronnell and Verna (1972) study. It was found that the BE spelling errors previously found to be made by second grade BE-speaking children did not continue in large part into grades four, five, and six. This investigation indicated, to the contrary, that only a few features of BE dialect continue by the middle grades to have any significant effect on the spelling of BE-speaking children. The middle-graders of this study exhibited BE-related spelling errors, of ten percent or more, on words that exemplified only six speech features (out of forty-three) of this dialect that were tested. Following are: a) examples of words in which these six features are found, b) the BE-related spelling errors made on them, and c) the percent of BE-related spelling errors made on them.

1. spill: *speel* (ten percent)
2. hatched: *hatch* (twenty percent)
3. moved: *move* (seventeen percent)
4. lips: *lip, lis* (thirty-three percent)
5. fires: *fire, fize* (ten percent)
6. tests: *test, tesses* (forty-five percent)

The evidence from DeStefano (1972) suggests, in addition, that there may be some lessening of the effect of BE on children's spelling in their written compositions versus words they spell from lists. She found that the absence of the -*s* inflection (e.g., the pronunciation of *bite* for *bites*) in the talk of BE-speaking fifth graders accounted for forty-five percent of their entire nonstandard speech forms, and for sixty percent of their nonstandard speech verb forms. DeStefano reports that not once did she find words with the -*s* inflection spelled without the *s* (*bites* written as *bite,* for example) in the written compositions of these children. Groff (1978) found that 9.1 percent of his subjects who spelled from lists left off the *s* in such words.

Regardless of the extent to which these different studies have discovered BE to be related to spelling errors, the investigators have concurred on one implication of their findings. This is that *under no circumstances should the spelling teacher try to change children's BE dialects with the hope that a reform to standard English would improve their spelling abilities*. This idea is wrong, researchers insist, since the proposed change in dialect is far too comprehensive and complex a matter for classroom teachers to attempt to manipulate.

Phonics and Spelling

Third, we need to inquire as to the importance of the teaching of phonics as a means of developing children's spelling abilities. While the modern teaching of phonics does not aim at reforming or otherwise changing children's articulation or dialect, as such, it does require children to pay close attention to the speech sounds they utter and to match these with letters or graphemes that are used to represent these phonemes. For this purpose modern phonics programs dismiss the traditional notion that children must first speak a certain set of phonemes in words "correctly" before they can use phonics as an aid to their spelling progress. It is now widely accepted in recent books on phonics teaching that this instruction must be adapted to the dialect the pupil speaks. It is "mandatory," one such text argues, that "teachers in any locality must compare the speech sounds of their pupils with the ones used here [in this text on phonics] and not hesitate to add, subtract, or exchange the sounds that they hear in their pupils' dialect which differ from 'Western' dialect given in this book" (Groff 1977, p. 91).

Also available are several reviews of research on the positive effects of the teaching of phonics on children's learning to spell. These various summations have come essentially to the same conclusion as did Cramer in 1969 that "the weight of evidence tends to support the view that instruction in phonics of various types does provide some help in spelling achievement" (p. 502). These critiques reflect a later summary of the research that "Overall, the evidence now indicates that phoneme → grapheme correspondences of some consistency do exist in English and that the spelling difficulty of an individual word should be related to the magnitude of the correspondences with the word" (Cahen, Craun and Johnson 1971). From this it would follow, of course, that a learning of these correspondences (phonics) should be mandatory.

The Argument Against Phonics in Spelling

In the past few years, nonetheless, there have been several notable challenges to the intensive use of phonics by children as a means for their learning to spell correctly. One group of objectors to phonics instruction believes that in the primary grades children should learn to spell on their own, simply by writing. No attempts should be made to correct these spellings because nonstandard spellings at this grade level are "natural," as Gentry and Henderson (1978, p. 636) put it. "In the primary grades," they insist, "a child must be encouraged to spell as best he or she can and not be held accountable for adult spelling standards" (1978, p. 633). If the teacher will simply "nurture the child with language activities that are interesting, enjoyable and satisfying" then "children will learn the conventions of English orthography and become capable spellers" it is claimed (Cramer 1976, p. 467). This tenet reflects Smith's contention that "written language is related directly to meaning, and not to sound" (1972, p. 1084).

Another reason that the intensive use of phonics for spelling "is not reasonable nor reliable" with young children is offered by Tovey (1978, p. 220). He noted that for 619 misspelled words he found in first-graders' compositions fifty-three percent had been spelled phonemically correct, that is, in accordance with their speech sounds. Tovey concluded from this that "It is highly improbable that 'sounding-out' alone will produce lexical [correct] spellings" (1978, p. 232).

Yet other detractors of the use of intensive phonics for spelling claim phonics is inappropriate because "children do not understand word-attack principles" (Beers, Beers, and Grant 1977, p. 242). These writers believe children use instead a "letter-name strategy" in their attempts to spell words (1977, p. 239). This point of view is derived from Read's findings (1971) that pre-school children systematically use the letters, *a, e,* and *i* to spell /a/, /e/, and /i/ speech sounds, and that they otherwise understand the fact that certain pairs of vowels alternate regularly in derivationally related word forms in English (e.g., *line-linear, please-pleasant*). Read (1971) infers that pre-school children have a knowledge of these phonological categories and relations, and that they seek to relate letters to them in some generally systematic manner, even when they spell the speech sounds in bizarre ways (e.g., /ĭ/, /ĕ/ and /ŏ/ as *e, a,* and *i*).

It has also been said that the intensive application of phonics is faulty since the most complete examination so far of phoneme-grapheme correspondences as potential cues to spelling improvement (Hanna, et al. 1966) does not support it. This study found that eighty-seven percent of words could be written, with a maximum of one error, using phoneme-grapheme correspondence rules. Since an application of these phonics rules will not result in total error-free spelling Petty argues that its intensive use "may just muddle the learning technique for most pupils" (1969, p. 88). Accordingly, he advises that only five phonics rules be taught. These involve the spellings of *make-making; busy-busily;* and *run-running; qu* for /kw/; and the non-use of *v* alone to spell the last sound in any word. Hillerich agrees that "it does no good to teach rules about vowels" for spelling purposes (1977, p. 305). Such teaching will interfere with children's development of proofreading abilities, he goes on, since it will cause children to "get in the habit of approximating spellings phonetically," which he deems undesirable (1977, p. 305).

The conclusion that phonemic spelling purportedly produces low spelling accuracy, leads Simon and Simon to suggest that the best learning method in spelling is the "generate and test" procedure (1973, p. 117). This is a trial and error process in which children generate as many alternative spellings of a word as seem probable to them and then test which of these is the correct spelling through their word recognition abilities. By drawing on word-recognition information, in combination with usual enthusiasm to use phonemic cues for spelling, "a child can use his growing reading vocabulary to bootstrap his spelling competence," they contend (Simon and Simon 1973, p. 130). This deduction appears to concur, to a degree at least, with both Smith's contention (1972) that one learns best to spell by simply memorizing words and/or by remembering their spellings through analogy (e.g., telegra*ph-ph*onograph or *lie-ly*ing), and Chomsky's observation that good spellers among children "rely on an underlying picture of the word that is independent of its varying pronunciations" (1970, p. 303). The finding that "deaf children spell remarkably well" (Hoemann, et al. 1976) would also seem to support these views.

The detractors of phonics for spelling point finally to recent research on this issue as evidence of its lack of superiority over nonphonics methods. Since the latest review of this research quoted in this discussion (Cahen, Craun and Johnson 1971) there have been at least two studies that have found that intensive phonics brings on no significantly greater gains in spelling than do non-phonics approaches (Grottenthaler 1970; Warren 1970). Because the similar non-phonics methods described here were not found inferior to the more complicated phonics approach it was deemed that they are preferable. It has been found that children's knowledge of the graphemic options available for spelling is slightly less correlated with spelling achievement in sixth and eighth grade ($r = .80$ and .75) than is oral reading in these grades ($r = .86$ and .82) (Cheek 1972).

The Argument for Phonics in Spelling

One must rush to say that the arguments against the intensive use of phonics in spelling programs themselves do not stand unchallenged. Those who favor phonics for spelling can point to an even larger number of recent research studies which have shown that the intensive use of phonics not only equals the effectiveness of non-phonics approaches but brings on significantly greater gains in spelling than do the latter (Baker 1977; Block 1972; Dunwell 1972; Gold 1976; Schwartz 1976).

Thus, the thesis that spelling is best developed by simply nurturing children with general language activities, expecting them to learn to spell as a result of their growing recognition of words, has come under fire. From his review of the research on reading and spelling Blair notes that "good readers may or may not be good spellers" (1975, p. 604). To assume that spelling ability will inevitably accompany word recognition is too risky a postulation, the research reveals. The majority of the research that has examined the comparative relationship to spelling of phonics versus word-recognition ability also questions the proposition that correct spelling in large can be developed as a consequence of growth in word recognition. MacGregor (1976) found that children's phonetic analysis is more closely related to their spelling achievement than is their reading vocabulary. Smith (1977) found that the correlation between children's understanding of spelling rules and their spelling ability was higher ($r = .92$) than the correlation between their spelling and their reading comprehension scores (r = .72). A review by Valmont (1972) of the research on children's abilities to observe whether a word one has written is spelled either correctly or incorrectly also does little to support the notion that word recognition is the predominant influence in spelling achievement. He found that "persons at all age levels show a lack of ability to correctly identify misspelled words" (1972, p. 1221). Those who can make such successful identifications, Valmont discovered, have among their other attributes a superior ability in phonics. Wallace (1968) directly investigated the supposition that children have the ability to choose words as being correctly or incorrectly spelled on the basis of their similarity to true English words. He found there was no significant difference between their ability to choose between words highly similar to actual English spellings, and those somewhat less similar to correct spellings. Small differences in the spellings of words thus are likely to escape the notice of children. In short, their word recognition abilities appear of little help in this respect. Nor do such abilities seem to particularly help deaf children who can spell much better than they can read.

Advocates of phonics for spelling also warn teachers about some of the evidence or comments offered by their opponents. For example, Yee (1969) concluded that his teaching of ten phonics "spelling" rules did not bring on significantly greater results than did a non-teaching of them. An inspection of his "spelling" rules, however, makes it immediately apparent that four of these were rules of reading, and not about spelling at all. Nor is there evidence that phonics ability for spelling interferes with proofreading.

They would object, as well, to the findings of Petty, Murphy and Mohan as to the effects on spelling of the use of the initial teaching alphabet (i.t.a.), with third, fourth, and fifth grade children, as proof "that little would be gained from teaching patterns of sound-to-symbol generalizations" (1974, p. 313). To use i.t.a. in this way, in a manner for which it was never intended, with children who have had years of traditional spelling experience, appears a highly curious and inappropriate manner by which to evaluate phonics in spelling. The results of this obviously strange use of i.t.a. must be contrasted with numerous studies that have shown when it is used as an *initial* teaching tool it has repeatedly been demonstrated to be an effective aid to spelling development (Block 1972).

The advocates of phonics also contend that because phonics instruction does not lead to letter-perfect spelling accuracy that this is no reason for mistrusting the functions it can and does serve. If by following the rules of phonics, they reason, children can spell ninety percent of words with a maximum of one spelling error per word, surely this should be a highly cherished academic goal to be eagerly worked for. The evidence that preschool children, untutored in phonics, spell in bizarre ways, said to be "natural" for them, does not gainsay the need to accelerate an abandonment of such unacceptable spellings, phonics proponents argue. To assume that one should not intervene with phonics teaching to speed up the forsaking by children of their preschool eccentric spellings seems a queer question, indeed, for teachers to take. The repeated observations that children have strong urges to spell words phonemically, that is, as they sound (Manolakes 1975), signals to the phonics advocate that this impulse should be directly exploited for spelling purposes rather than be systematically ignored, as phonics opponents would have it.

Conclusions

It has been demonstrated in this discussion that conclusions about two of the major aspects of children's speaking and spelling are relatively easy to come to. The research demands that we now put little faith in the supposition that specific speech errors and spelling errors have some kind of cause and effect relationship. Equally convincing are the findings from research which indicate that some relationship does exist between "Black English" (BE) and certain kinds of spelling errors made by children who speak this nonstandard dialect. No researcher of this problem suggests that the BE-speaking child must reform his or her dialect so that it approximates standard English. The only special teaching in spelling they recommend be given to words that reflect BE-related spelling errors is to carry out somewhat more intensive spelling exercises in which BE-speaking children listen carefully to the way they pronounce the words whose spelling is affected by their dialect, and then to note carefully how they are spelled.

It is also clear, however, that a third important aspect of children's speaking and spelling, the use of phonics for spelling, is far more difficult to appraise. The fact that research and opinion can be found to either support or disparage this practice is representative of the present highly controversial nature of this issue. Since fairly reasonable arguments can be made both for and against the use of intensive phonics in spelling programs it remains for individual teachers to judge which of these conflicting contentions is the more logical, which is supported by the more impressive research, in short, which is the more convincing.

REFERENCES

Baker, Gertrude. "A Comparison of Traditional Spelling with Phonemic Spelling of Fifth and Sixth Grade Students." *Dissertation Abstracts International* 38 (November 1977):2514-A.

Beers, James Wheelock; Beers, Carol Strickland; and Grant, Karen. "The Logic behind Children's Spelling." *Elementary School Journal* 77 (January 1977):238–242.

Blair, Timothy R. "ERIC/RCS." *Reading Teacher* 28 (March 1975):604–607.

Block, J. R. "But Will They Ever Lern to Spel Korectly?" *Educational Research* 14 (June 1972):171–178.

Boyd, Gertrude A. and Talbert, E. Gene. *Spelling in the Elementary School.* Columbus, OH: Charles E. Merrill, 1971.

Cahen, Leonard S.; Craun, Marlys J.; and Johnson, Susan K. "Spelling Difficulty—A Survey of the Research." *Review of Educational Research* 41 (October 1971):281–301.

Cheek, Martha D. "Relationships of Oral Reading, Spelling and Knowledge of Graphemic Options." *Dissertation Abstracts International* 33 (December 1972):2608:A.

Chomsky, Carol. "Reading, Writing and Phonology." *Harvard Educational Review* 40 (May 1970):287–309.

Cramer, Ronald L. "The Influence of Phonic Instruction on Spelling Achievement." *Reading Teacher* 22 (March 1969):499–503.

———. "The Write Way to Teach Spelling." *Elementary School Journal* 76 (May 1976):464–467.

Cronnell, Bruce A. "Black English and the Spelling of Final Consonant Clusters." *Dissertation Abstracts International* 34 (December 1973):3015A–3016A.

DeStefano, Johanna S. "Productive Language Differences in Fifth Grade Black Students' Syntactic Forms." *Elementary English* 49 (April 1972):552–558.

Dunwell, Stephen. *Report on WRITE: Computer Assisted Instruction Course in Written English Usage.* Poughkeepsie, NY: Shared Education Computer Systems, Inc., 1972.

Gentry, J. Richard and Henderson, Edmund H. "Three Steps to Teaching Beginning Readers to Spell." *Reading Teacher* 31 (March 1978):632–637.

Gold, Virginia Y. "The Effect of an Experimental Program Involving Acquisition of Phoneme-Grapheme Relationships Incorporating Criterion

Referenced Tests with Evaluative Feedback upon Spelling Performance of Third Grade Pupils." *Dissertation Abstracts International* 37 (October 1976):1959A–1960A.

Groff, Patrick. "Children's Speech Errors and Their Spelling." *Elementary School Journal* 74 (November 1973):88–96.

———. *Phonics: Why and How*. Morristown, NJ: General Learning, 1977.

———. "Children's Spelling of Features of Black English." *Research in the Teaching of English* 12 (February 1978):21–28.

Grottenthaler, John. "A Comparison of the Effectiveness of Three Programs of Elementary School Spelling." *Dissertation Abstracts International* 31 (November 1970):2004-A.

Ham, R. E. "Relationship between Misspelling and Misarticulation." *Journal of Speech and Hearing Disorders* 23 (August 1958):294–297.

Hanna, Paul R., et al. *Phoneme-Grapheme Correspondences as Cues to Spelling Improvement*. Washington: U.S. Office of Education, 1966.

Hanna, Paul R.; Hodges, Richard E.; and Hanna, Jean S. *Spelling: Structure and Strategies*. Boston: Houghton Mifflin, 1971.

Hillerich, Robert L. "Let's Teach Spelling—Not Phonetic Misspelling." *Language Arts* 54 (March 1977):301–307.

Hoemann, Harry W., et al. "The Spelling Proficiency of Deaf Children." *American Annals of the Deaf* 121 (October 1976):489–493.

Kligman, Donna Schwab; Cronnell, Bruce A.; and Verna, Gary B. "Black English Pronunciation and Spelling Performance." *Elementary English* 49 (December 1972):1247–1253.

Kligman, Donna and Cronnell, Bruce. *Black English and Spelling*. Los Alamitos, CA: SWRL Educational Research and Development, 1974.

MacGregor, Sister Marilyn. "Multiple Regression Analysis of Essential Variables Contributing to Spelling Achievement." *Dissertation Abstracts International* 37 (September 1976): 1308A–1309A.

Manolakes, George. "The Teaching of Spelling: A Pilot Study." *Language Arts* 52 (February 1975):243–247.

Petty, Walter. "The Teaching of Spelling." *Bulletin of the School of Education,* Indiana University 45 (November 1969):79–98.

Petty, Walter T.; Murphy, J. Brien; and Mohan, Madan. "Spelling Achievement and the Initial Teaching Alphabet: Analysis of Errors." *Elementary School Journal* 74 (February 1974): 309–313.

Read, Charles. "Pre-School Children's Knowledge of English Phonology." *Harvard Educational Review* 41 (February 1971):1–34.

Schwartz, Sybil. "A Developmental Study of Children's Ability to Acquire Knowledge of Spelling Patterns." *Dissertation Abstracts International* 36 (January 1976):8028-A.

Simon, Dorothea P. and Simon, Herbert A. "Alternative Uses of Phonemic Information in Spelling." *Review of Educational Research* 43 (Winter 1973):115–137.

Smith, Frank. "Phonology and Orthography: Reading and Writing." *Elementary English* 49 (November 1972):1075–1088.

Smith, Howard W. "Intelligence, Reading and Spelling Abilities." *Dissertation Abstracts International* 38 (November 1977):2676-A.

Tovey, Duane R. " 'Sound-It-Out': A Reasonable Approach to Spelling?" *Reading World* 17 (March 1978):220–233.

Valmont, William J. "Spelling Consciousness: A Long Neglected Area." *Elementary English* 49 (December 1972):1219–1221.

Wallace, John. "Spelling Ability and the Probability Texture of English." *Journal of Educational Research* 61 (March 1968):315–319.

Warren, John H. "Phonetic Generalizations to Aid Spelling Instruction at the

Fifth-Grade Level." *Dissertation Abstracts International* 31 (October 1970):1699-A.

Yee, Albert H. "Is the Phonetic Generalization Hypothesis in Spelling Valid?" *Journal of Experimental Education* 37 (Summer 1969):82–91.

Handwriting and Spelling: Their Current Status in the Language Arts Curriculum

WALTER T. PETTY

Spelling and handwriting have traditionally been important elements of the elementary school curriculum. As measured by the amount of time devoted to their teaching and by teacher effort, the importance of their roles has ranged from very considerable to only moderate. Since the impact of Sputnik, a greater emphasis has been placed on the three R's. Thus, both spelling and handwriting are again receiving greater teaching attention than was the case only a few years ago.

While it may be generally agreed that these subjects are currently receiving more curricular emphasis, this does not necessarily mean that they are being better taught than formerly. Disturbing as it may be, there appears to be evidence that teaching practice has tended to remain influenced far more by habit than by research evidence. For example, Groff (20) reported that a survey of opinions of directors of elementary education in seventy-two metropolitan areas showed that the teaching of handwriting is based on public opinion rather than on research evidence. A similar conclusion regarding spelling was reached by Richmond (45) as a result of a detailed study of forty-one sixth-grade children.

This report is a summary of the status of handwriting and spelling teaching today with particular reference to established findings of research and to research recently concluded. Brief consideration is also given to the relationships between handwriting and spelling as facets of the total language arts. This report is not intended as a comprehensive one of the research in these areas, nor are the references cited the only ones which could be cited. Reference is made in many instances only to well-documented research summaries. The report is simply one which sets the stage for somewhat more detailed summaries which will follow.

Spelling Programs Today

Actual procedures followed in the teaching of spelling throughout the country are considerably influenced by the commercial materials used. Since teacher practices may have considerable bearing upon what appears in a textbook, tradi-

---

From *Elementary English*, Vol. 41, No. 8 (December, 1964). ©1964 by the National Council of Teachers of English. Reprinted by permission.

tional procedures may receive reinforcement with the result that a cycle of practices with little research validity is operating. That this supposition has considerable observational validity is testified to by Horn's (29) statement that "... the chief problem today [in teaching spelling] appears to be a more critical and universal application of the [research] evidence now available."

Spelling programs generally give at least some consideration to vocabulary studies which show the words written most frequently (4). Spelling lists published in recent years have tended to include fewer than 4,000 words, thus reflecting this consideration. However, the actual words in such lists and the grade levels suggested for teaching particular words vary considerably from list to list (29). This variance is often the result of improper attention to the existing evidence on which words should be included and when the teaching of a particular word should occur, as well as the treatment given phonic or linguistic rules and generalizations (24). Treatment which gives undue stress to rules having limited application results in the selection of words for which the rules apply and fails to choose words of greater social utility (46, 50).

Teaching Spelling

The superiority of the test-study approach over the study-test approach in teaching words has long been established (17, 31). The test-study procedure calls for beginning the unit of instruction with a test which identifies for each pupil the words he does not know how to spell. This procedure is efficient and helps to build favorable attitudes toward spelling (13, 30). Another help for building favorable attitudes is a procedure known as the corrected test, which focuses upon specific spelling problems through having each pupil check his own test. This has been shown to be the most efficient single procedure for learning to spell (30, 31).

The test-study approach and the corrected-test are basic elements of method identified by research to be essential which are ignored by many teachers. Another inferior procedure in widespread use is the contextual presentation of the spelling words. This presentation presumably develops the meaning of the word; however, since most such presentations simply use the words rather than develop their meaning, and since carefully selected spelling words have ordinarily been in the pupils' speaking, understanding, and reading vocabularies, any so-called development of meaning is largely a waste of pupil time. The list presentation of words is more efficient and fosters a more favorable learning attitude (8, 30, 31).

Early studies pointed out the faulty reasoning in expecting improved spelling ability to result from increasing the time devoted to spelling instruction (14), yet time allotments have recently been increased. In most instances not more than seventy-five minutes per week should be devoted to spelling instruction, and there is evidence that even less time accomplishes equal achievement (29). In most schools, spelling is taught five periods per week, principally because of the ease in the administration of such a program. However, there is considerable evidence which suggests that fewer periods may be satisfactory (29), particularly if the corrected-test technique is used (32).

One of the most common causes of low spelling achievement is poor study habits (18, 48). Many children do not follow the study "steps" suggested in most commercial spelling materials and generally known to teachers. Although these steps focus upon sensory impression and attempted recall, use of the corrected test enhances the steps' effectiveness as study procedures (29, 30).

How well a pupil learns to spell depends largely upon his interest. The pupil's interest in and his attitude toward spelling determine what he will do toward attempting to learn, how hard he will work, and how persistent he will be in his learning effort. The development of the desired interest and attitude may be accomplished by: (1) selecting genuinely useful words; (2) limiting study to those words which tests have shown the pupil unable to spell; (3) fostering definite and efficient study habits; (4) showing pupils that they are achieving and progressing; and (5) using materials which have inherent appeal (29, 30).

Recent Research in Spelling

As has been stated previously, an apparent need in spelling instruction is the application of the evidence regarding its teaching that has been produced by research. By and large this application has not been made. Further, there has been a disappointing amount of significant and new research in recent years (37), with the paucity probably due both to the difficulty of attacking some problems and to the financial encouragement given to investigating other curricular areas.

The value of the corrected test was borne out in Schoephoerster's study (52), though application of this procedure probably has still gained little teacher acceptance. The instructional possibilities of individualized spelling plans were shown in Eisman's study and the suggestion made that variation in study plans may be needed for pupils with different perceptive abilities (9). The question of identifying image types still remains moot, though training in visual imagery showed an effectiveness in learning spelling (36, 44). The precise kind of imagery training and the value for all pupils remains unsettled.

Programmed instruction received research attention (2, 6, 19). While spelling would appear to lend itself to such instruction, results of the research did not clearly bear out this view. Undoubtedly this is an area which will and should receive more research attention.

Identifying and classifying spelling errors has continued to interest researchers (33, 43), with some clarification of the attention which needs to be given to letter positions and to meanings of homonyms. The controversy over the value of phonics in teaching spelling has also continued, with extensive claims being reported concerning the "regular" representation of phonemes (24). Several recent studies (22, 42, 49) indicate that phonetic rules do not apply to a substantial percentage of words pupils are called upon to spell. The position is still prevalent that teaching of sound-to-letter and letter-to-sound relationships may prove of value (29).

Handwriting Programs Today

Recent surveys of the status of handwriting instruction indicate that handwriting programs are also largely tied to commercial handwriting systems (34, 40). As many as sixteen commercial programs are in use, with another ten commercial systems being used which emphasize other facets of the language arts. These latter ten, therefore, are classified as only partial handwriting programs (26, 40). The various handwriting programs show considerable divergence in letter forms, sequence in the introduction of letters, and recommended teaching practices (26).

Evidence has also been presented that as high as 30 percent of all school systems have no handwriting program and as many as 50 percent of all schools have no separate handwriting period (34). Teachers in these school systems undoubtedly make at least some incidental effort to improve handwriting, though the surveys generally fail to establish the extent of this.

The absence of handwriting programs in many school systems may result from the lack of attention often given handwriting in teacher education programs (7). Also, of course, the social valuing of other curricular areas over that of handwriting has had its effect. In a crowded school curriculum something has to go; for a teacher with little ability himself to write well, with handwriting ranking low in popularity with him and his fellow teachers (25), and with little social pressure, an easy area to eliminate or denigrate is the handwriting program.

Handwriting Instruction

The most recent survey of handwriting instruction of an extensive nature was that made in Wisconsin in 1951 (23). Studies in Texas (41) and in Monmouth County, New Jersey (25), though more recent, were less extensive. However, they both substantiated the findings of the Wisconsin study. These studies showed a number of factors as basic to handwriting instruction: (1) legibility is considered the most important objective in programs, with slant, letter formation, and spacing of next importance. Speed of writing should receive the least stress; (2) practice periods of about ten minutes' duration each, either daily or on alternate days, are generally favored; (3) the introduction to manuscript writing is made in the first grade, with transition to cursive usually occurring in the early third grade; and (4) teachers, in general, are aware of the importance of the proper handwriting position, adjustments necessary for the left-handed child, and of the paper and writing instruments to use.

The handwriting position in general acceptance in practice and supported by research (15, 38) is to use the pen or pencil as essentially an extension of the forearm, with the movement combining vertical and side strokes to produce a moderately slanted letter formation. The body, of course, must be in a position for the forearm to move freely and without strain. The principal adjustment to be made for the left-handed pupil is one of reversing the slant of the paper, though a slightly more pronounced slant is preferred by the left-handed pupil writing cursive form than by the right-handed pupil (10).

Copying to learn the formation of letters is favored over other methods; most commercial handwriting programs recognize this (40). Handwriting paper generally used recognizes the need to reduce the space between the lines as pupils advance in age and in writing skill. Pupils also prefer to use conventional writing instruments, since these seem to work as well as specialized ones for different grade levels. Research on such instruments is continuing and instruments designed from research evidence may ultimately result (28).

Handwriting Issues and Recent Research

Analyses of adult handwriting reported in 1960 have shown the need for handwriting instruction with much of the instructional emphasis being upon the maintenance of earlier learned skills (55). The fact that adults' handwriting departs from many of the forms as originally learned led to the suggestion that some letter forms in current use should be modified (51).

Issues in the teaching of handwriting which have been of concern for some years continue to be unsettled. These include: (1) whether or not both manuscript and cursive forms should be taught; (2) whether or not practice on letter forms and handwriting movements should occur isolated from meaningful writing; (3) how handwriting should be evaluated; and (4) how instruction may be individualized to care for differences in pupil abilities.

Most schools teach both manuscript and cursive forms so this issue is largely one of appraising the consideration which should be given to custom in the continuance of teaching cursive writing. The extent to which manuscript writing may be done with comparable speed remains controversial (12, 21). There is a trend toward the maintenance of skill in manuscript form throughout the grades, even after cursive has been introduced. Tradition and society's feelings concerning the esthetic qualities of cursive writing will probably mean continued teaching of both forms.

Using a functional approach exclusively versus giving some attention to training in motor skills may be an issue only to the extent that some schools have no handwriting periods and may, thus, do little formal handwriting teaching. The role of motor learning will be discussed in a later chapter in this bulletin, but evidence to date appears to recognize the need for practice of a motor-drill nature (16, 38, 54). There is evidence that some letters are more difficult to form than others, which led to the opinion that there should be direct teaching of letter forms and continued practice on them (39). However, the nature and condition of the practice which would achieve the handwriting objectives has only recently begun to receive the experimental attention needed to settle the issue.

Evaluation of children's handwriting is simply nonexistent or is quite informal. Few schools evaluate in the formal sense through the use of commercial scales. One reason for this may be that such evaluation possibly would show relatively low scale scores (3), though a more important social reason may be that regular use of a standard scale may destroy the individuality of handwriting (25). Handwriting scales are increasingly being mentioned in reports of research, but in order for scales to be used properly teachers need training in their use (11). The evaluation needed may not occur until new scales are developed which reflect current handwriting standards and which provide self-diagnosis (1, 27). Also, further clarification is needed as to just what constitutes handwriting quality and handwriting legibility before more usable scales can be developed (47).

Some commercial handwriting materials may not foster the individualized instruction generally needed. This is particularly true with respect to the emphasis given rhythmic count in forming letters (27). A teacher may allow variance, however, in such count for different pupils and, if he has a program of diagnosis and evaluation, may possibly approach an individualized handwriting program. Taking into consideration (1) the objective of legibility, (2) the recognition of pupil differences in abilities, and (3) the awareness that pupils actually develop personalized forms of writing (51, 53), programs which provide for instruction which recognize handwriting individuality would seem to be imperative. Since an increasing number of commercial systems make such provision, more individualized handwriting instruction should appear (40).

Handwriting and Spelling in the Language Arts Program

Spelling and handwriting competencies are influenced by reading, listening, and written and oral composition, just as skills in these latter areas are influenced by spelling and handwriting abilities. Studies have shown positive correlations between abilities in the various language arts (5, 35), but not as high as might be expected (57). The extent to which these correlations increase or decrease as pupils mature is a matter not clearly established (35, 56).

Many of the interrelationships that are present are very likely due to the presence of common elements in each facet and to the fact that an experience affecting one cannot be isolated from the others. For instance, pupils certainly do learn to spell many words as a result of reading and other activities. Spelling pretests regularly show that pupils know how to spell many of the words on such tests (32). Too, a number of researchers have reported that mispronunciations and speech articulatory defects are often related to spelling disabilities (29) and, of course, illegible handwriting at least leads one to question the spelling accuracy of the words written. Copying words as a part of handwriting instruction may account for learning the spelling of some words since the motor-mental effort made is a type of sensory impression basic to learning spelling.

Certainly, as handwriting improves, all written work is facilitated with the result of increased benefits to spelling (29). Likewise, pronunciation and articulation which give due recognition to letters representing sounds mean that these letters and perhaps their order in words are seen and may be recalled when spelling is attempted. It would seem, though, that learning in one language arts area that has carryover to another takes place in a larger context than just relating one aspect to another. That is, genuine interrelated learning would seem to result best from an instructional program which teaches all of the language arts in a communication framework (5).

Recognition of the interrelationships of the language arts, however, should not be interpreted as support for an incidental approach to the teaching of the various facets as opposed to systematic programs. Neither should systematic attention preclude correlating the language arts with other curricular areas not integrating related skills. A genuine communication program acknowledges the interrelatedness of all of the language arts as well as the need for specific teaching attention to specific skills.

REFERENCES

1. Bezzi, Rocky, "A Standardized Manuscript Scale for Grades 1, 2, and 3," *The Journal of Educational Research,* 55 (April, 1962), 339–340.
2. Buzby, John J., and Lester Mann, "The TMI Self-Tutoring Program Compared with Teacher and Flash Card Taught Programs," *The Journal of Educational Research,* 55 (August, 1962), 585–586.
3. Covert, Sidney, *An Evaluation of Handwriting in Certain Iowa Schools.* Doctor's thesis. State University of Iowa, 1953.
4. Davis, Bennie Joe, *A Study of the Vocabulary Overlap Between Words Written by Children and Words Written by Adults.* Master's thesis. The University of Texas, 1954.
5. Early, Margaret J., "Communication Arts," *Encyclopedia of Educational Research.* Chester W. Harris, (ed.). New York: Macmillan, 1960.
6. Edgerton, Alice K., and Ruth W. Twombly, "A Programmed Course in Spelling," *The Elementary School Journal,* 62 (April, 1962), 380–386.
7. "Educators Enthused over Handwriting Instruction Programs," *Handwriting Foundation Newsletter,* 143 (February 6, 1962).
8. Edwards, Mary Ann Rigsby, *An Evaluation of the Casis School Instructional Program in Spelling.* Master's thesis. The University of Texas, 1953.
9. Eisman, Edward, "Individualized Spelling," *Elementary English,* 39 (May, 1962), 478–480.
10. Enstrom, E. A. "The Relative Efficiency of the Various Approaches to Writing with the Left Hand," *The Journal of Educational Research,* 55 (August, 1962), 573–577.
11. Feldt, Leonard S., "The Reliability of Measures of Handwriting Ability," *Journal of Educational Psychology,* 53 (December, 1962), 288–292.
12. Fitzgerald, James A., "Research in Spelling and Handwriting," *Review of Educational Research,* 22 (April, 1952), 89–95.
13. ———, *The Teaching of Spelling.* Milwaukee: Bruce Publishing Company, 1951.
14. Foran, Thomas G., *The Psychology and Teaching of Spelling.* Washington, D.C.: Catholic Education Press, 1934.
15. Freeman, Frank, *The Handwriting Movement.* Chicago: The University of Chicago, 1918.
16. Gates, A. I., and G. A. Taylor, "Acquisition of Motor Control in Writing by Pre-School Children," *Teachers College Record,* 24 (1924), 459–468.
17. Gates, A. I., "An Experimental Comparison of the Study-Test

Methods in Spelling," *Journal of Educational Psychology,* 22 (January, 1931), 1–19.
18. ———, *The Psychology of Reading and Spelling with Special Reference to Disability.* Contributions to Education, Number 129. New York: Teachers College, Columbia University, 1922.
19. Gibson, Mrs. R. E. "Final Report on the Westside High School Teaching-by-Tape Project," *Bulletin of the National Association of Secondary School Principals,* 44 (January, 1960), 56–62.
20. Groff, Patrick J., "From Manuscript to Cursive—Why?" *Elementary School Journal,* 61 (November, 1960), 55–62.
21. ———, "New Speeds of Handwriting," *Elementary English,* 38 (December, 1961), 564–565.
22. ———, "The New Iowa Spelling Scale: How Phonic Is It?" *The Elementary School Journal,* 62 (October, 1961), 46–49.
23. *Handwriting in Wisconsin.* University of Wisconsin, Department of Education Committee for Research in Handwriting. Madison: University of Wisconsin, 1951.
24. Hanna, Paul R., and James T. Moore, Jr., "Spelling—From Spoken Word to Written Symbol," *Elementary School Journal,* 53 (February, 1953), 329–337.
25. Harris, Theodore L., "Handwriting," *Encyclopedia of Educational Research.* Chester W. Harris (ed). New York: Macmillan, 1960.
26. Herrick, Virgil E., *Comparison of Practices in Handwriting Advocated by Nineteen Commercial Systems of Handwriting Instruction.* Madison: Committee on Research in Basic Skills, University of Wisconsin, 1960.
27. ———, (ed.), *New Horizons for Research in Handwriting.* Report of the Invitational Conference on Research in Handwriting. Madison: University of Wisconsin Press, 1963.
28. ———, "What Research Says about Writing Tools for Children," *NEA Journal,* 50 (February, 1961), 49–50.
29. Horn, Ernest, "Spelling," *Encyclopedia of Educational Research.* Chester W. Harris, (ed.), New York: Macmillan, 1960.
30. ———, *Teaching Spelling: What Research Says to the Teacher.* Washington, D.C.: Department of Classroom Teachers and American Educational Research Association, 1954.
31. Horn, Thomas D., "Research in Spelling," *Elementary English,* 37 (March, 1960), 174–177.
32. ———, and Henry J. Otto, *Spelling Instruction: A Curriculum-Wide Approach.* Bureau of Laboratory School Publications Number 2. Austin: The University of Texas, 1954.
33. Jensen, Arthur R., "Spelling Errors and the Serial-Position Effect," *The Journal of Educational Psychology,* 53 (June, 1962), 105–109.
34. King, Fred M., "Handwriting Practices in Our Schools Today," *Elementary English,* 38 (November, 1961), 483–486.
35. Loban, Walter D., *The Language of Elementary School Children.* NCTE Research Report No. 1. Champaign, Illinois: National Council of Teachers of English, 1963.
36. Mason, Geoffrey P., "Word Discrimination Drills," *Journal of Educational Research,* 55 (September, 1961), 39–40.
37. Michael, William B., "A Short Evaluation of the Research Reviewed in Language Arts and Fine Arts." *Review of Educational Research,* 34 (April, 1964) 249–256.
38. Myers, Emma, *A General Review of Handwriting Instruction.* Master's thesis. State University of Iowa, 1954.
39. Newland, T. Ernest, "An Analytical Study of the Development of Illegibilities in Handwriting from Lower Grades to Adulthood," *Jour-

nal of Educational Research, 26 (December, 1932), 249–258.
40. Noble, J. Kendrick, Jr., "Handwriting Programs in Today's Schools," Elementary English, 40 (May, 1963), 506–512.
41. Owen, Mary E. (ed.), "Just Where Do We Stand in Handwriting?" Instructor, 63 (1954), 57.
42. Petty, Walter T., "Phonetic Elements as Factors in Spelling Difficulty," Journal of Educational Research, 51 (November, 1958), 209–214.
43. Plessas, Gus P., "Children's Errors in Spelling Homonyms," The Elementary School Journal, 64 (December, 1963), 163–168.
44. Radaker, Leon D., "The Effect of Visual Imagery upon Spelling Performance," Journal of Educational Research, 56 (March, 1963), 370–372.
45. Richmond, Arnie E., "Children's Spelling Needs and Implications of Research," Journal of Experimental Education, 29 (September, 1960), 3–21.
46. Rogness, Alton S., Grouping Spelling Words According to the Rule. Doctor's thesis. Colorado State College of Education, 1953.
47. Rondinella, Oreste R., "An Evaluation of Subjectivity of Elementary School Teachers in Grading Handwriting," Elementary English, 40 (May, 1963), 531–532.
48. Russell, David H. Characteristics of Good and Poor Spellers. Contributions to Education, Number 727. New York: Teachers College, Columbia University, 1937.
49. Sah, Loretta J., A Study of Spelling Performances. Master's thesis. Sacramento State College, 1964.
50. Sartorius, Ina C., Generalizations in Spelling. Contributions to Education, Number 472. New York: Teachers College, Columbia University, 1931.
51. Schell, Leo M. and Paul C. Burns, "Retention and Changes by College Students of Certain Upper-Case Cursive Letter Forms," Elementary English, 40 (May, 1963), 513–517.
52. Schoephoerster, Hugh, "Research into Variations of the Test-Study Plan of Teaching Spelling," Elementary English, 39 (May, 1962), 460–462.
53. Seifert, Eloise P., Personal Styles of Handwriting in Grades Six, Seven, Eight, and Nine. Doctor's thesis. Boston University, 1959.
54. Shane, Harold G., Research Helps in Teaching the Language Arts. Washington, D.C.: Association for Supervision and Curriculum Development, 1955.
55. Templin, Elaine M., "How Important Is Handwriting Today?" The Elementary School Journal, 61 (December, 1960), 158–164.
56. Templin, Mildred C., "Phonic Knowledge and Its Relation to the Spelling and Reading Achievement of Fourth Grade Pupils," Journal of Educational Research, 47 (February, 1954), 441–454.
57. Winter, Clotilda, "Interrelationships among Language Variables in Children of the First and Second Grades," Elementary English, 34 (February, 1957), 108–113.

Excerpts From Spelling: Learning and Instruction—Research and Practice

ROBERT J. FITZSIMMONS
BRADLEY M. LOOMER

Historically, spelling has been one of the most frequently investigated areas of the curriculum. However, improvement in spelling programs in the elementary schools does not seem commensurate with research efforts. Petty (1969) has stated "that much has been learned but the knowledge has not been used. The problem in spelling really is the application of what is known" (p. 79). For example, the results of the findings of E. Horn (1926), Fitzgerald (1951), T. Horn & Otto (1954) indicate that a basic writing vocabulary of approximately 2,800 to 3,000 well-selected words, highly useful both in child and adult writing, is a desirable spelling goal for the elementary school child. To require a child to master a much larger basic writing vocabulary in the elementary school is out of harmony with research. E. Horn (1924) stated "that the thousand most used words comprise, with their repetitions, about 90 per cent of the total of child and adult writing" (p. 87).

A second area in which a great deal of research has been done is methods of learning to spell a word. In the investigations done by Fitzgerald (1951), the following techniques for learning to spell a word have been found valuable: (1) Look at the word carefully; (2) Say the word; (3) With eyes closed, see the word; (4) Cover the word and then write it; (5) Check the spelling. If the word is misspelled, start again with Step Number 1.

There is also a wealth of research

Copyright © 1978 by Curriculum Associates, Inc. Reprinted by permission.

findings indicating that the test-study method of teaching spelling is more effective than the study-test method. Gates' (1931) study has shown that the test-study method of teaching spelling, when properly used, is superior to the study-test method. T. Horn's (1947) study as well as subsequent studies done by Hibler (1957) and Montgomery (1957) clearly show that use of the test-study method is superior to the study-test method.

A fourth area which has been researched extensively is the concept of time allotment. Fox & Eaton (1946) and T. Horn (1947) in their studies showed that schools with large time allotments in spelling secured the same or no better results than schools with more moderate allotments. The data from more recent investigations support these conclusions. T. Horn (1969) states that "it appears likely that the time allotted for direct study of spelling in excess of 60 minutes a week may be spent more advantageously in other areas" (p. 1286).

Fitzgerald (1951) states:

> ... although many spelling investigations have been carried out during the past half century, improvement in the working of spelling has been slow. One of the chief difficulties seems to have been that the results of research and experimentation were not readily available to the teacher. Although additional investigations are necessary to solve some of the more complex problems of spelling, many of the immediate spelling problems can be solved by the use of available research findings ... (pp. 2–3).

Christine & Hollingsworth (1966) also make note of the large number of studies done in the area of spelling. They concluded that, "Many studies concerning spelling instruction have been made in the twentieth century, yet many pupils have learned to spell incorrectly" (p. 565).

Leading authorities such as T. Horn, Fitzgerald, and Hanna are of the opinion that there is available professional knowledge based on research that would go far toward preventing and solving spelling problems. This opinion is reflected by E. Horn in his statement on spelling in the 1960 edition of *The Encyclopedia of Educational Research* which concludes with ". . . the chief problem today appears to be a more critical and universal application of the evidence now available" (p. 1350). Campanale (1962) also concurs with E. Horn when he states that, "If instruction in spelling were planned in a more definite fashion, utilizing pertinent research findings, it could be made more meaningful" (p. 446).

Ernest Horn (1944) declared that the problem in spelling was to implement what research had been done, not to do more research. Much has been learned, but the knowledge has not been used effectively. More specifically he stated that,

The evidence is sufficiently complete and convincing to enable schools to teach spelling with substantial professional efficiency. Shortcomings in the teaching of spelling are therefore due not so much to the absence of satisfactory evidence as to the lack of knowledge of existing evidence, to the failure to apply it intelligently, or to erroneous interpretations (p. 6).

As regards the teaching of spelling, one is concerned with what the elementary teacher actually knows about the specific procedures and useful techniques available in the teaching of spelling. In general terms, is the elementary teacher knowledgeable about research-supported procedures in the teaching of spelling? Does the teacher, in fact, utilize research-supported techniques in conducting the spelling program in his classroom?

Information known ten, fifteen, twenty years ago is still known today. But is the knowledge applied any more universally today than previously? It was the purpose of this study to find the degree to which a representative sample of Iowa elementary teachers were aware of research and non-research supported procedures in spelling and to what degree those procedures were utilized in classrooms.

Research-Supported Procedures in Spelling

Presenting spelling words in list form, initially, is a more successful method than presenting spelling words in sentence or paragraph form.

Winch (1916)
Hawley and Gallup (1922)
McKee (1924)
E. Horn (1944, 1954, 1963)
Strickland (1951)

The spelling words of highest frequency in child and adult writing should be studied by elementary school children.

Thorndike (1921)
E. Horn (1924, 1926, 1939, 1960)
Hollingsworth (1965)
T. Horn (1969b)

The major contribution of spelling games is the stimulation of pupil interest.

Fitzgerald (1951)
E. Horn (1960)
T. Horn (1969b)

The child correcting his own spelling test, under the direction of the teacher, is the single most important factor in learning to spell.

T. Horn (1946)
Louis (1950)
Beseler (1953)
Tyson (1953)
Thomas (1954)
Schoephoerster (1962)
E. Horn (1963)
Christine and Hollingsworth (1966)

In order to learn to spell, it is not necessary for children to learn the meaning of the majority of their spelling words.

    E. Horn (1960)
    Petty (1968)
    T. Horn (1969b)

Spelling lists derived from the various curricular areas are of little value in increasing spelling ability.

    E. Horn (1919, 1926, 1960)
    Fitzgerald (1951, 1953)
    T. Horn (1969b)

Learning words by the whole method is a better technique than learning words by syllables.

    T. Horn (1947, 1969b)
    Humphry (1954)

Due to the nature of the English language, most attempts to teach spelling by phonic rules are questionable.

    E. Horn (1919, 1954, 1957, 1960, 1963)
    Archer (1930b)
    Sartorius (1931)
    King (1932)
    Foran (1934)
    Fitzgerald (1951)
    Jackson (1953)
    T. Horn (1969a, 1969b)

Time allotted for the study of spelling should be between an hour and seventy-five minutes per week.

    Larson (1945)
    T. Horn (1947)
    E. Horn (1960)

The test-study method is superior to the study-test method when working with most spellers.

    Kingsley (1923)
    Gates (1931)
    Blanchard (1944)
    T. Horn (1946)
    Edwards (1951)
    Shubik (1951)
    Fitzgerald (1953)

    Hibler (1957)
    Montgomery (1957)
    Witty (1969)

Procedures in Spelling Not Supported by Research

The presentation of words in syllabified form has proven to have an advantage over the method of whole word presentation.

    T. Horn (1947, 1969b)
    Humphry (1954)

A child's interest in learning to spell is secondary to rewards he might receive for achievement in spelling.

    Columba (1926)
    Diserens and Vaughn (1931)
    Thorndike (1935)
    Forlano (1936)
    D. Russell (1937)
    Sand (1938)
    E. Horn (1960, 1967)

Writing words several times each helps insure spelling retention.

    Abbott (1909)
    E. Horn (1967)
    Green (1968)
    Petty (1968)

Using phonic rules, for most words, is a worthwhile instructional procedure.

    E. Horn (1919, 1954, 1957, 1960, 1963)
    Archer (1930b)
    Sartorius (1931)
    King (1932)
    Foran (1934)
    Fitzgerald (1951)
    Jackson (1953)
    T. Horn (1969a, 1969b)

It is helpful to have children look at "hard spots" in a word to improve spelling ability.

    Tireman (1927)
    Masters (1927)

Mendenhall (1930)
Rosemeier (1965)

For the majority of children, studying spelling words before a pre-test is a highly valuable procedure.

Kingsley (1923)
Gates (1931)
Blanchard (1944)
T. Horn (1946, 1969b)
Fitzgerald (1951)
Hibler (1957)
Witty (1969)

Time allotment for spelling should vary according to the child's need.

Larson (1945)
T. Horn (1947)

Children should devise their own individual method by which they study each word.

E. Horn (1944, 1954, 1960)
Fitzgerald (1951, 1954)
T. Horn (1969b)

Writing words in the air is a valuable means of helping the child practice the spelling of a word.

Green (1968)
Petty (1968)

Presenting spelling words in sentence or paragraph form, for the first time, is more successful than the spelling list presentation.

Winch (1916)
Hawley and Gallup (1922)
McKee (1924)
E. Horn (1944, 1954, 1963)
Strickland (1951)

SUMMARY OF THE FINDINGS

(Item 6, Part II) Research Supported: Presenting spelling words in list form, initially, is a more successful method than presenting spelling words in sentence or paragraph form

Summary of What the Field Research Indicates

In the study conducted by Hawley and Gallup (1922), they stated that, "If teachers wish to test pupils on the new words of the week, as is advocated by the best authorities, and if they desire to have the spelling work reviewed within the allotted spelling time, they will use the list methods" (p. 267).

E. Horn (1944), McKee (1924) and Winch (1916) all concurred that the presentation of words in context is less efficient than their presentation in list form, except in so far as context is necessary to identify the words in giving a test.

E. Horn (1936) stated that,

Research has consistently shown that it is more efficient to study words in list than in context. Words studied in lists are learned more quickly, remembered longer, and transferred more readily to new context. Occasional lessons may be justified in which words are presented in context for the purpose of encouraging children to do certain types of writing . . . (p. 16).

(Item 8, Part II) Research Supported: The spelling words of highest-frequency in child and adult writing should be studied by elementary school children

Summary of What the Field Research Indicates

Hollingsworth's (1965) research was conducted in order to determine if E. Horn's (1926) list of *10,000 Words Most Commonly Used in Writing* was still useful as a basis for present spelling lists. Hollingsworth's results agreed with the known research. E. Horn's study showed a very small amount of loss or gain in word usage.

In attempting to determine the age of his 5,000 words of greatest-frequency in the *10,000 Words Most Commonly Used in Writing,* E. Horn (1939) stated:

Less than 4 per cent of these words have come into the language since 1849, and less than 10 per cent have come in since 1749. More of these words were in the language before 1099 than have come into the language since 1799 (p. 134).

T. Horn (1969b) stated:

There is as yet no field-tested substitute for direct instruction on the basic core of high-frequency words needed in child and adult writing (p. 1285).

(Item 10, Part II) Research Supported: The major contribution of spelling games is the stimulation of pupil interest.

Summary of What the Field Research Indicates

Games and special devices are often suggested as an aid to spelling. The evidence of Fitzgerald (1951), E. Horn (1960) and T. Horn (1969b) suggested that some of these games may be of some benefit. They should supplement rather than supplant systematic instruction.

(Item 11, Part II) Research Supported: The child correcting his own spelling test, under the direction of the teacher, is the single most important factor in learning to spell

Summary of What the Field Research Indicates

As a result of T. Horn's (1946) investigation into the value of the corrected test as a teaching technique, he concluded that:

(1) As measured by a final weekly test or by recall tests after an interval of seven days, the corrected test alone will contribute from 90–95 per cent of the achievement resulting from the combined effect of the pronunciation exercise, corrected test and study; (2) In some classes the corrected test alone is sufficient for mastery or near-mastery of a typical spelling lesson by the upper third of the class; (3) The corrected test appears to be the most important single factor contributing to achievement in spelling (p. 29).

The value of the corrected test was also borne out in Schoephoerster's (1962) experiment designed to ascertain the comparative value of three variations of the test-study plan of teaching spelling.

The study completed by Christine & Hollingsworth (1966) concurs with T. Horn's earlier experiment that the corrected test appears to be the best single factor contributing to success of achievement in spelling.

(Item 14, Part II) Research Supported: In order to learn to spell, it is not necessary for children to learn the meaning of the majority of their spelling words

Summary of What the Field Research Indicates

E. Horn (1960) stated that, "Since the words taught in the first six grades are those most often used by children in writing, most of these words are familiar to the children. The arbitrary practice of teaching the meaning of each word is therefore a wasteful practice" (p. 1346).

T. Horn (1969b) concurred with the aforementioned.

(Item 15, Part II) Research Supported: Spelling lists derived from the various curricular areas are of little value in increasing spelling ability

Summary of What the Field Research Indicates

E. Horn in his studies of 1919, 1926 and 1960 pointed out the fact that little was to be gained by teaching a large number of words.

PERSPECTIVES

T. Horn (1969b) said:

> ... those who contend that a locally devised list of words (if based on counts approaching those of Fitzgerald, E. Horn, and Rinsland) will deviate significantly from the high-frequency words already identified are in for disillusionment, as evidence has already shown that the high frequency vocabulary in children's and in adult writing is very similar. Over and above the security segment of the spelling curriculum, pupils should be free to pursue their own special interests and needs and should be encouraged to do so. Nevertheless, local school districts can better employ staff time in other ways than in attempting to develop a local list of spelling words to be learned (p. 1288).

(Item 17, Part II) Research Supported: Learning words by the whole method is a better technique than learning words by syllables

Summary of What the Field Research Indicates

T. Horn's (1947) investigation was undertaken to determine the effect of the visual presentation of words by syllables on learning to spell, and to discover which types of words, if any, benefit from syllabic presentation, and to what degree.

Four conclusions were thought to be warranted from Horn's study. First, there was no advantage in presenting words in syllabified form. Second, no generalized group gives any indication of an advantage to syllabified presentation. Third, no advantage in syllabic presentations was found at either the superior or inferior levels of ability. Fourth, for words which, if syllabified, may cause errors in spelling, there was evidence of a disadvantage if presented in syllabified form.

In T. Horn's (1969b) review of spelling studies he stated that, "The visual presentation of words in syllabified form has not demonstrated any advantage over the undivided method of word presentation, and for some words (e.g., *purpose, therefore*) there is a negative effect" (p. 1289).

(Item 18, Part II) Research Supported: Due to the nature of the English language, most attempts to teach spelling by phonic rules are questionable

Summary of What the Field Research Indicates

In E. Horn's (1954) study he found it possible to conclude that "the limited success in attempts to teach pupils to learn and apply even a few spelling rules suggests that we should not be too optimistic about the practicability of teaching the more numerous and complicated rules or principles in phonetics" (p. 234).

With greater finality, E. Horn (1957) wrote that, "There seems no escape from the direct teaching of the large number of common words which do not conform in their spelling to any phonetic or orthographic rule" (p. 432).

T. Horn's (1969b) review of spelling research also concurs with earlier studies done by E. Horn et al.

(Item 19, Part II) Research Supported: Time allotted for the study of spelling should be between an hour and seventy-five minutes per week

Summary of What the Field Research Indicates

Larson's (1945) study was done to determine the relationship that exists between the efficiency of spelling instruction and the time allotted to spelling. The conclusions from this study are summed up with the statement that the reduction from 100 minutes to 60 minutes has little adverse effect on achievement.

T. Horn (1946) stated, "... time allotted for the study of spelling in excess of 60 minutes a week may be spent more advantageously in other areas" (p. 30).

E. Horn (1960) said, "What is needed is not more time but spirited, efficient use of instructional procedures" (p. 1346). Finally, he warned against the notion that a large time allotment will automatically raise spelling achievement.

(Item 20, Part II) Research Supported: The test-study method is superior to the study-test method when working with most spellers

Summary of What the Field Research Indicates

Studies done by Hibler (1957) and Montgomery (1957) clearly showed that the test-study method with an immediate correction of the list, was superior to the study-test method.

Walter Petty (1969) stated, ". . . there is an accumulation of research evidence going back about 40 years which shows the value of the pre-test in building positive attitudes in children toward spelling instruction and in resulting high spelling achievement."

(Item 1, Part II) Not Supported by Research: The presentation of words in syllabified form has proven to have an advantage over the method of whole word presentation

Summary of What the Field Research Indicates

T. Horn's (1947) investigation was undertaken to determine the effect of the visual presentation of words by syllables on learning to spell, and to discover which types of words, if any, benefit from syllabic presentation, and to what degree.

Four conclusions were thought to be warranted from his study. First, there was no advantage in presenting words in syllabified form. Second, no generalized group gives any indication of an advantage to syllabified presentation. Third, no advantage in syllabic presentation was found at either the superior or inferior levels of ability. Fourth, for words which, if syllabified, may cause errors in spelling, there was evidence of a disadvantage if presented in syllabified form.

In T. Horn's (1969b) review of spelling studies he stated that, "The visual presentation of words in syllabified form has not demonstrated any advantage over the undivided method of word presentation, and for some words (e.g., *purpose, therefore*) there is a negative effect" (p. 1289).

(Item 2, Part II) Not Supported by Research: A child's interest in learning to spell is secondary to rewards he might receive for achievement in spelling

Summary of What the Field Research Indicates

Studies conducted by Columba (1926), Diserens and Vaughn (1931), Forlano (1936), D. Russell (1937), Sand (1938) and E. Horn (1960, 1967) indicated that intrinsic incentives for learning to spell, such as positive attitudes and interest, are preferred to the extrinsic incentives of school grades and competition.

(Item 3, Part II) Not Supported by Research: Writing words several times each helps insure spelling retention

Summary of What the Field Research Indicates

The practice of intervening recall has been shown to be beneficial in all fields of learning and the studies done by Abbott (1909) and E. Horn (1967) showed the usefulness of recall for both initial learning and review lessons.

Green and Petty (1968) studies have shown that children should not be required to make repeated writings of words without intervening attempts at recall. The practice of having a child copy a word five times, or ten times, encourages poor habits and attitudes.

(Item 5, Part II) Not Supported by Research: It is helpful to have children look at "hard spots" in a word to improve spelling ability

Summary of What the Field Research Indicates

Tireman (1927) in concluding his study stated, "After a study of over 4,000 pupils in grades four, five, and eight involving a half-million spellings, one is impressed with the consistency with which the data show that marking hard spots is of little or no value" (p. 116–177).

He continued,

> The essential fact in spelling is to write all of the letters and have them in right order. Anything that diverts from this does harm. The fact stands out that the pupils who studied words with the hard spots marked made poorer scores than those who studied lists with the words unmarked. In other words, the people who advocate marking the hard spots are not only suggesting a useless device but possibly a harmful one (p. 117).

The studies of Masters (1927), Mendenhall (1930) and Rosemeier (1965) also concurred with Tireman's (1927) study that calling attention to "hard spots" was of little or no value to the pupil.

(Item 4, Part II) Not Supported by Research: Using phonic rules, for most words, is a worthwhile instructional procedure

Summary of What the Field Research Indicates

In E. Horn's (1954) study he found it possible to conclude that "the limited success in attempts to teach pupils to learn and apply even a few spelling rules suggests that we should not be too optimistic about the practicability of teaching the more numerous and complicated rules of principles in phonetics" (p. 234).

With greater finality, E. Horn (1951) wrote that, "There seems no escape from the direct teaching of the large number of common words which do not conform in their spelling to any phonetic or orthographic rule" (p. 432).

T. Horn's (1969b) review of spelling research also concurs with earlier studies done by E. Horn et al.

(Item 7, Part II) Not Supported by Research: For the majority of children, studying spelling words before a pre-test is a highly valuable procedure

Summary of What the Field Research Indicates

The field research has shown that for the majority of children, studying spelling words before a pre-test is not a highly valuable procedure.

Studies done by Hibler (1957) and Montgomery (1957) clearly showed that the test-study method was superior to the study-test method.

Walter Petty (1969) stated, ". . . there is an accumulation of research evidence going back about 40 years which shows the value of the pre-test in building positive attitudes in children toward spelling instruction and in resulting high achievement."

(Item 9, Part II) Not Supported by Research: Time allotment for spelling should vary according to the child's need

Summary of What the Field Research Indicates

Larson's (1945) study was done to determine the relationship that exists between the efficiency of spelling instruction and the time allotted to spelling. The conclusions from this study are summed up with the statement that the reduction of time from 100 minutes to 60 minutes has little adverse effect on achievement.

T. Horn (1946) stated ". . . time allotted for the study of spelling in excess of 60 minutes a week may be spent more advantageously in other areas" (p. 30).

E. Horn (1960) said, "What is needed is not more time but spirited, efficient use of instruction procedures" (p. 1346). Finally, he warned against the notion that a large time allotment will automatically raise spelling achievement.

(Item 12, Part II) Not Supported by Research: Children should devise their own individual method by which they study each word

Summary of What the Field Research Indicates

The field research done by E. Horn (1944, 1954, 1960), Fitzgerald (1951, 1954), and T. Horn (1969b) has shown that there should be a systematic approach whereby children learn to study each word.

(Item 13, Part II) Not Supported by Research: Writing words in the air is a valuable means of helping the child practice the spelling of a word

Summary of What the Field Research Indicates

Concerning the writing of words in the air, Green and Petty (1968) stated that:

The practice of writing words in the air is of doubtful value. This practice takes time and does not give the child a realistic image of the word. Supposedly this practice is to give a kinesthetic impression of the word, but the result is questionable, since arm and hand movements are generally not the same as in writing a word. A kinesthetic impression may be useful to a few very poor spellers, but such impression could better be gained through fingertip impression in sand or on the blackboard (p. 332).

(Item 16, Part II) Not Supported by Research: Presenting spelling words in sentence or paragraph form, for the first time, is more successful than the spelling list presentation

Summary of What the Field Research Indicates

In the study conducted by Hawley and Gallup (1922), they stated that, "If teachers wish to test pupils on the new words of the week, as is advocated by the best authorities, and if they desire to have the spelling word reviewed within the allotted spelling time, they will use the list method" (p. 310).

According to the results of McKee's (1924) study, it appeared that the list format was the most effective way to present spelling words for study.

T. Horn (1952) has stated the crucial question, "When the spelling needs are identified, what is the most efficient method of study? Once again going to the research, our best available evidence, not opinion, favors the list method" (p. 267).

E. Horn (1944), McKee (1924) and Winch (1916) all concurred that the presentation of words in context is less efficient than their presentation in list form, except in so far as context is necessary to identify the words in giving a test.

E. Horn (1963) stated that,

Research has consistently shown that it is more efficient to study words in list than in context. Words studied in lists are learned more quickly, remembered longer, and transferred more readily to new context. Occasional lessons may be justified in which words are presented in context for the purpose of encouraging children to do certain types of writing . . . (p. 16).

EDUCATIONAL IMPLICATIONS

On the basis of the findings of this study, the following educational implications seem warranted:
1. An important conclusion from this study, and one having significant implication, is that a serious gap appears to exist between the existing research in spelling and its application in the classroom. Ample evidence of this was revealed in the analysis of the data. For example, spelling research has indicated (Item 14, Part II) that in order to learn to spell, it is not necessary for children to learn the meaning of the majority of their spelling words. For the large majority of students the meaning of the word is already known and to spend additional time on word meaning detracts from spelling ability. In spite of this evidence, this study has shown that a total of 1,007 (79.3%) teachers out of 1,270 indicated that they either disagreed or strongly disagreed with the procedural item. A second example can be seen in procedural Item 18, Part II. The field research on this time has shown that due to the nature of the English language, most attempts to teach spelling by phonic rules are questionable. In spite of this evidence, a majority of teachers in this study, 692 (55.0%), indicated they either disagreed or strongly disagreed with the procedural statement. The majority of these respondents also indicated they almost never or infrequently employed this procedure in their classes. It would appear that these responses can be construed as additional evidence of the need for better communication between available field research in spelling and its application by elementary teachers.
2. A majority of the procedural items in Part II of this study were based on field-test research which has been known for over a quarter of a century. But this study has indicated the lack of a universal application of the evidence now available.

Perhaps a major factor for a teacher's failing to know this research and to apply it in the classroom is the fact that many publishers of spelling materials have not made results of the field-tested research available to teachers through their spelling series.

I. RECOMMENDATIONS APPLICABLE TO TOTAL PROGRAM:

A. It appears that educators can profit by periodically assessing their procedures, practices, and methods. The following suggestions are based upon a careful review of research. They should systematically be included in every good spelling program.
1. The words in the spelling program should reflect the known information as to which words are most frequently and likely to be used by students. These words have immediate and permanent value. In most schools this amounts to 3,000–4,000 words. In high ability schools this list might be cut in half with more attention given to the high frequency words with demonstrated persistent difficulties. The easier words will most likely be learned incidentally. Word lists to be consulted are Horn, Rinsland, Fitzgerald, *The New Iowa Speller*.
2. Where to place a word in the spelling program is dependent upon a number of factors. First, the child's need of the word; second, the difficulty level of the word with the more difficult words reserved for later in the program; and, third, the phonetic difficulty encountered within the word. There are excellent sources available for analyzing word difficulty by age or grade level (*The*

New Iowa Speller, and the Iowa Test of Basic Skills).

The developed program of spelling must relate to two major concerns: maintenance of spelling ability, and growth of spelling ability. Of the two factors the second is most likely to be overlooked. It would seem worthwhile to select words for study that not only maintain a level of spelling proficiency, but at the same time enlarge the students' ability to spell more words, which implies growth. This may be achieved by carefully insuring that each grade or age level has words that are both maintenance in nature and growth in nature. Too much emphasis on purely a maintenance program would tend to evidence itself in little group or grade growth on standardized achievement or skill tests. A careful balance between maintenance and growth should show spelling improvement on standardized tests. A good discussion of grade placement is found in Horn's NEA publication cited in the bibliography.

3. The self-corrected test procedure has been found to be the single most worthwhile learning activity (per unit of time) yet to be devised. It is clearly appropriate for all ages and abilities.
4. A systematic approach to the study of each word is paramount for good learning. This involves, as stated earlier, pronunciation, visual imagery, reinforcement both orally and written, and systematic recall of words. Frequent opportunity to use spelling words in written words contributes greatly to the maintenance of spelling ability.
5. A good crisp spelling program of between 60–75 minutes per week should be sufficient to both maintain and improve spelling ability.
6. Utilization of a pre-test is a must. The child then studies those words that are shown difficult for him as evidenced by the pre-test. The pre-test coupled with the child's correcting of his own spelling is the single most important factor leading to spelling growth. A proper maintenance program will retain this growth.
7. The child's attention should be directed to each word as a total word. Little gain occurs by breaking it into syllables.
8. There are very few rules that will provide the student with concrete spelling direction. Emphasis must be on teaching the child to learn the ways that words are spelled and not depend upon any one approach or way to spell a speech sound.
9. Schools should systematically and periodically establish inventory lists to measure both group and individual improvement. Each grade or level ought to establish beginning of year, middle of year, and end of year inventories. Student progress should be thoroughly charted. The emphasis on testing should be directed toward proper testing. The chosen standardized test may or may not be closely related to the spelling instruction program of the school. If the words of your program are totally different from the standardized test, you have no accurate measure of your program's effectiveness. Generally, it is recommended that inventory tests, with class norms, individual norms, and school norms be established within the district or school over the specifically stated spelling program. Standardized tests then give additional information.

The developed testing program ought to answer two questions: a) how well is our spelling program maintaining spelling ability? and b) how well is our spelling program providing for additional spelling growth?

10. The latest developments relating to

linguistically based spelling (Hanna) programs bear watching. From this approach may come fruitful insights into the relationship of sound to letter (phoneme-grapheme) correspondence. At the time of this writing the relationship of linguistic principles to improved spelling is rather tenuous.

B. Pupil interest is crucial to spelling improvement. The development of a positive attitude toward spelling improvement is the key to improvement. The replacing of positive attitude by letter grades or competition with others detracts from genuine spelling growth. At the same time recognize that mere pride in spelling alone is no substitute for efficient and meaningful practice periods. But the two aspects, coupled with pupil interest, are bound to result in student gain.

C. Recognize that contemporary spelling programs generally follow one or two approaches. The first approach highlights the use of a pre-determined list of frequently written words and stresses the formation of perceptual images (visually and aurally), along with positive reinforcement, and proper habits of study.

The second approach, generally labeled linguistic, places much more priority on sound and letter associations. In this approach a greater emphasis is placed on phonics and phonetics. The utilization of sound letter rules is generally recommended. There is a much greater emphasis on grouping words in phonemic families. This approach stresses those words that can be said to exhibit accurate phoneme-grapheme relationships. (See Hanna in bibliography).

While the above two approaches are said to be different, they still embody some common elements such as pre-testing, systematic word study, corrected test, and both visual and auditory discrimination exercises.

D. The role of learning has not been totally established in most spelling programs. In view of this a look at the research shows enough evidence to support the following recommendations:
1. Utilize words that are frequently needed by pupils, thus providing a needed stimulus.
2. Provide proper visual and oral opportunities to see and hear the word.
3. Immediate reinforcement of the word through self-correcting is essential.
4. Provide systematic reinforcement of the word; preferably in many different situations.
5. In addition provide meaningful opportunities for systematic recall of the word. Mainly through periodic assessment and functional writing.
6. Accurate spelling ability is most likely the result of "overlearning" which fixes the word image in the pupil's mind.

E. Use of inventory tests is definitely recommended. Preferably during the first or second week of school an inventory test of about fifty words should be given. Its purpose is to discover how well the pupils can spell, before study, the words which make up the lessons for the semester. The words should be systematically sampled from lessons which make up the semester's work. This will give the teacher a good idea of growth occurring during the term. In addition, special programs can thus be inaugurated for both high and low spelling ability students. Also, accurate record keeping allows pupils to see what growth has occurred; a motivational factor in learning to spell. Above all, make sure the child is thorough in his spelling approach. Repeat process for second semester.

F. Constant attention to reviewing those words with known difficulty, obtained through inventory tests, standardized tests, or in consultation with *The New Iowa Speller,* will enhance spelling ability. A definite weakness of many spelling programs lies in that they do not systematically reacquaint the students with those words with known difficulties.

G. Oral spelling lessons should not occur very frequently. Spelling ability is defined as the ability to write the word rather than spell it aloud. The neurophysiological bonds established by writing and seeing the written word are much more valid than the oral approach.

H. A school's testing program ought to be comprehensive. The program should include teacher made, inventory, and standardized tests. Included should be the development of class, school, and system norms in spelling. These norms should be utilized in helping teachers establish realistic goals for students.

I. It appears that the incorporation of a student kept record of words most likely to be misspelled is helpful. The pupil keeps a continuous log of words with which he has had difficulty. This serves as a constant reinforcer for directing attention to his own peculiar spelling needs. This practice highlights the development of the student's self responsibility toward spelling growth.

J. Recognize that tremendous variability exists between the popular spelling series available to schools. These differences are due chiefly to the failure of the publishers to insist that available evidence be followed. Some of the more common differences center around the following:
1. Method of presenting words.
2. Procedures suggested for word study.
3. Emphasis upon phonics.
4. Relationship of spelling to reading and handwriting.
5. Use of rules for spelling.
6. Selection of words to be learned.
7. Grading of words (level or grade).
8. Indication of word difficulty.
9. Placement or grouping of words for instruction.
10. Method of showing spelling growth.
11. Procedures for diagnosing spelling deficiencies.
12. Standardized norms for evaluation.
13. Sensory modes employed (visual, oral, aural, haptic, or kinesthetic).
14. Quality of teacher manual which accompanies the series.

K. It is worthy to emphasize the relationship between time alloted to spelling and the development of pupil spelling ability. The wise educator will quickly realize that increasing time allotment will not automatically raise spelling achievement. What is needed is to recognize that spirited spelling lessons with efficient recall techniques are the keys to improved spelling programs. If students are studying words that testing has shown are specific problems for them, improvement is likely. In most situations a weekly spelling program allotment of 60–75 minutes is sufficient.

II. RECOMMENDATIONS FOR SPECIFIC PROCEDURES

Column or List Form

It would appear from the data available within this study that more direct effort should be exerted to present words for study in a column or list form. It is recommended that spelling be taught as spelling and words to be learned presented in list or column fashion.

Teachers appear to be confusing some of the spelling goals with reading goals. The responses to the statement pertaining to teaching the meaning of each spelling word affirm this. It is strongly recommended that teachers be aware of the fact that the meanings of most, if not all, spelling words in the typical spelling program have already been assured through both the child's reading and composition program. Hence, more attention to meaning detracts from the pupil's effort to concentrate on spelling the word.

Clear understanding must be made between the presentation of spelling words and the practice of language in written form. It appears that many educators are under the impression that if the word appears in either sentence or paragraph form that this will lead to better spelling. Research has demonstrated that it is more efficient to present words for study in list or column form. The presenting in list form has the advantage in that it focuses specific attention upon each and every word as a separate problem. On occasion you may wish to get a measure of a child's spelling ability by analyzing how the child spells selected key words which are embedded within a sentence. In this procedure a complete sentence is dictated and the child writes the total sentence. Only the key selected words within the sentences are analyzed for spelling ability. This, however, is entirely different than the objective of how best to present words to children for spelling instruction.

Social Utility

School systems are urged to give serious thought to what, and how many, spelling words should be included in the spelling program. It appears that teachers are of the opinion that the inclusion of more words, especially words from various curricular areas, will make the pupil a better speller. No doubt the recent attention to individualized instruction has supported this belief. The fault lies in that many of these additionally selected words are of little value in developing spelling ability because they may not be the words the student is most often called upon to write. This is not to imply that the individual child should not be free to pursue his individualized interest and needs for spelling. It does call attention to the fact that schools would be further ahead if they developed a spelling program around a core of words the pupils were most likely to use or need in the future.

"Hard Spots" & Syllabification

1. Schools would do well to re-emphasize the fact that learning to spell a word should involve the child forming a correct visual image of the whole word. The attempt to divide words into parts or syllables has not proven to be a superior technique. Concentrated attack on each whole word as a specific learning problem is recommended. It is extremely important that the pupil learn the ways to spell each sound and not search only for the way to spell a sound. There is no escaping the fact that a large number of common words do not conform to any generalized phonetic or orthographic rule.

2. There may still continue some indecision as to whether the spelling of a word follows the synthetic or analytic approach. The advocates of the synthetic approach believe better spelling occurs by concentrating on the total word as a specific and individual problem. Research seems to favor the synthetic approach.

The analytical technique attempts to emphasize the characters (letters) that make up the words. They seek to improve spelling ability by increasing the pupil's awareness of the likenesses and differences of individual letters within the word.

3. Some spelling series have attempted to improve spelling ability by drawing attention to so called "hard spots" within a word. Research has consistently shown this technique to be of little value. Some series color "hard spots" to draw attention of students to it. Again, it is important to realize that children learn words as whole units and not individual parts.

Test-Study-Test Format

1. For the majority of grades in the elementary school the teachers are advised to utilize the test-study-test approach to spelling instruction. Proper testing is aimed at identifying which words are difficult for each child. The pupil's learning should therefore be directed toward those words with which he has demonstrated trouble. The subsequent study period, which concentrates on each child's difficult words, places the focus on learning rather than merely

maintaining the correct spelling of words already known to the pupil. This correctly places emphasis on gain in spelling ability by being able to spell words in the future that were spelled incorrectly in the past.

Individualization of Spelling

1. There seem to be contradictory forces operating when the topic of individualized spelling arises. On the whole it appears that teachers are highly in favor of having each child develop his own particular approach to spelling each word. In reality the best procedure is the spelling program which provides the child with a systematic approach (steps) to spelling improvement. Schools would be well advised to incorporate the research efforts into a deliberate and systematic instructional program. As such, the following is recommended:

a. First, having the pupil get a correct visual-aural impression of the word by seeing the word while it is pronounced correctly.
b. With eyes closed have each child try to see the specific word. Have the child pronounce it and then try to recall how the word looked in the book.
c. Open your eyes and look at the word to see if you spelled it correctly.
d. Focus attention upon the word with attention again given to pronouncing it correctly.
e. Again close your eyes to see the word as you attempt to spell it aloud.
f. Look again in the book to see if you had the word spelled correctly.
g. You may wish to write the word a couple of times, each time covering the previous spelling, so you don't copy from the first spelling. If you don't make any mistakes, go on to the next word following the same procedure. Be careful that you follow the procedure step by step.

It is recommended that a procedure such as described above be utilized for each child regardless of ability in every classroom.

2. Helping students who appear to be low in spelling ability deserves special recognition. Immediate and careful remediation of the problem is imperative. It is best to first isolate the cause for low spelling ability. In general, this seems most likely to be lack of interest, poor proofreading skills, little writing ability, no direction concerning what words are in need of additional study, dawdling, no method of attacking a word, or improper use of the self-correction technique. In some cases the cause may be due to organic deficiencies (sight, hearing, motor ability). It is recommended that the low spelling ability student stress the steps outlined earlier in the above recommendation. In some cases splitting the week's spelling list into two or three sub-lists might aid by making the week's work more manageable for the student.

Self-Correction

1. There is a great deal of uncertainty by teachers as to the value of the self-corrected test procedure. It is strongly recommended that schools develop a clear perception of what the corrected test procedure is, and furthermore actively seek to implement the technique within the spelling program. It is clearly evident that teachers, in general, are unaware of the value of the corrected test procedure in spelling improvement. A good source for reference is Thomas Horn's MA Thesis at the University of Iowa (cited in bibliography).

The self-correction technique does several things for the student. It provides him with an immediate opportunity to see what words cause him difficulty. It also allows him to see the part of the word that caused him difficulty. In addition, he can immediately set about to correct any errors he may have made. In last analysis, the procedure calls the student's attention to how critical his own perceptions concerning self-improvement are to the learning process.

Rote and Air Writing

1. Educators should place less reliance on the old method of having the child write each word several times in hopes that this will cement the word in his mind. In effect what this does is encourage poor habits and attitudes. The teacher should place much more emphasis on systematic recall of the words. The emphasis within the study period should be directed toward recalling the visual image of the word rather than merely impressing this image through repeated writing of the word.

2. The practice of having children practice by writing words in the air is highly suspect. Its greatest danger lies in the fact that it does not allow the child to form a realistic image of the word as does writing it on paper. At the same time be careful to insure that the writing of the word on paper is meaningful to the pupil and not merely perfunctory. This same criticism is also applied to the practice of having the child spell orally.

BIBLIOGRAPHY

Abbott, E. E., "On the Analysis of the Memory Consciousness in Orthography." University of Illinois Psychological Monograph 11, 1909.

Archer, C. P., "Shall We Teach Spelling By Rule." *Elementary English Review,* Vol. 6–7, March, 1930. (a)

Archer, C. P., "Transfer of Training in Spelling." University of Iowa, Iowa City, No. 5, 1930. (b)

Bauer, N., *The New Orleans Public School Spelling List*. New Orleans: Honsell and Brothers, Ltd., 1916.

Beseler, D. W., "An Experiment in Spelling Using the Corrected Test Method." Unpublished master's thesis, Central Washington State College, Ellensburg, 1953.

Blanchard, Sr. M. Gervase, "An Experimental Comparison of the Test-Study and the Study-Test Methods of Teaching Spelling in the Eighth Grade." Unpublished master's thesis, Fordham University, New York, 1944.

Blommers, P., & Lindquist, E. F., *Elementary Statistical Methods in Psychology and Education*. Boston: Houghton Mifflin, 1960.

Burr, E. J., "The Distribution of Kendall's Score S for a Pair of Tied Rankings." Biometrika, Vol. 47, 1960.

Campanole, E. A., "Survey of Methods in the Teaching of Spelling." *Elementary English,* Vol. 39, May, 1962.

Carroll, H. A., "Generalization of Bright and Dull Children." Contributions to Education, No. 439. New York: Bureau of Publications, Teachers College, Columbia University, 1930.

Christine, R. O. & Hollingsworth, P. M., "An Experiment in Spelling." *Education,* Vol. 86, May, 1966.

Columba, Sr. Mary, "A Study of Interests and Their Relations to Other Factors of Achievement in Elementary School Subjects." Catholic University, Washington, D.C., 1926.

Cook, W. A., "Shall We Teach Spelling by Rules?" *Journal of Educational Psychology,* Vol. 3, June, 1912.

Diserens, C. M., & Vaughn, J., "The Experimental Psychology of Motivation." *Psychological Bulletin,* Vol. 28, January, 1931.

Edwards, C. W., "A Comparative Study of Two Techniques of Spelling Instruction." Unpublished master's thesis, University of Iowa, Iowa City, 1931.

Fitzgerald, J. A., "The Vocabulary, Spelling Errors, and Situations of Fourth, Fifth, and Sixth Grade Children's Letters Written in Life Outside the School." Unpublished doctoral dissertation, University of Iowa, Iowa City, 1931.

Fitzgerald, J. A., *The Teaching of Spelling*. Milwaukee: Bruce Publishing Company, 1951.

Fitzgerald, J. A., "The Teaching of

Spelling." *Elementary English*, Vol. 30, January, 1953.

Foran, T. G., "The Psychology and Teaching of Spelling." *Catholic Education Press*, 1934.

Forlano, G., "School Learning With Various Methods of Practice and Rewards." Teachers College, Columbia University, New York, 1936.

Fox, W. H., & Eaton, M. T., "Analysis of the Spelling Proficiency of 82,833 Pupils in Grades 2 to 8 in 3,547 Teaching Units of the City Schools in Indiana." *Bulletin of the School of Education,* Indiana University, Bloomington, Vol. 22 (2), 1946.

Gates, A. I., "An Experimental Comparison of the Study-Test and Test-Study Methods in Spelling." *Journal of Educational Psychology,* Vol. 22, No. 1, June, 1931.

Goodman, L. A., & Kruskal, W. H., "Measures of Association for Cross-Classifications." *Journal of American Statistical Association*, Vol. 49, 1954.

Green, H. A. *The New Iowa Spelling Scale.* Bureau of Educational Research and Service, University of Iowa, Iowa City, 1955.

Greif, I. P., "Abstracts of Research in Spelling Instruction." Unpublished master's thesis, University of Iowa, Iowa City, 1956.

Hanna, P. R., & Moore, J. T., "Spelling From Spoken Word to Written Symbol." *Elementary School Journal,* Vol. 53, February, 1953.

Hanna, P. R., et al., "Linguistic Clues for Spelling Improvement." Report to U.S. Office of Education on Project Number 1991 for the period January 1, 1963 to December 31, 1964.

Hanna, P. R., "The Teaching of Spelling." *National Elementary Principal,* Vol. 45, November, 1965.

Hawley, W. E., & Gallup, J., "The List Versus the Sentence Method of Teaching Spelling." *Journal of Educational Research*, Vol. 5, 1922.

Hays, W. L., *Statistics for Psychologists*. New York: Holt, Rinehart and Winston, 1963.

Hibler, G. H., "The Test-Study Versus the Study-Test Method of Teaching Spelling in Grade Two: Study I." Unpublished master's thesis, The University of Texas, Austin, January, 1957.

Hodges, R. E., & Rudorf, E. H., "Searching Linguistics for Cues for the Teaching of Spelling." *Elementary English,* Vol. 42, May, 1965.

Hollingsworth, P. M., "Spelling Lists—Outdated?" *Elementary English,* Vol. 42, February, 1965.

Horn, E., "Principles of Methods in Teaching Spelling as Derived from Scientific Investigation." *Eighteenth Yearbook of National Society for the Study of Education,* Part II, Bloomington, Illinois, February, 1919.

Horn, E., "The Curriculum for the Gifted: Some Principles and an Illustration." *Twenty-Third Yearbook of National Society for the Study of Education,* Part I, 1924.

Horn, E., *A Basic Vocabulary of 10,000 Words Most Commonly Used in Writing*. College of Education, University of Iowa, Iowa City, 1926.

Horn, E., "The Validity and Reliability of Adult Vocabulary Lists." *The Elementary English Review,* Vol. 16, 1939.

Horn, E., "Research in Spelling." *The Elementary English Review,* Vol. 21, January, 1944.

Horn, E., "Phonics and Spelling." *Journal of Education,* Vol. 136, May, 1954.

Horn, E., "Phonetics and Spelling." *Elementary School Journal,* Vol. 57, May, 1957.

Horn, E., "Spelling." *Encyclopedia of Educational Research,* (3rd ed.) New York: Macmillan, 1960.

Horn, E., *Teaching Spelling: What Research Says to the Teacher*. Department of Classroom Teachers, American Educational Research Association of the National Education Association, November, 1967.

Horn, T., "The Effect of the Corrected Test on Learning to Spell." Unpublished master's thesis, University of

Iowa, Iowa City, 1946.

Horn, T., "The Effect of a Syllabic Presentation of Words Upon Learning to Spell." Unpublished doctoral dissertation, University of Iowa, Iowa City, 1947.

Horn, T., "That Straw Man: The Spelling List." *Elementary English*, Vol. 29, May, 1952.

Horn, T., & Otto, H. J., *Spelling Instruction: A Curriculum-Wide Approach*. Bureau of Laboratory School, University of Texas, Austin, 1954.

Horn, T., "Research Critique." *Elementary English*, Vol. 46, February, 1969. (a)

Horn, T., "Spelling." *Encyclopedia of Educational Research*. (4th ed.) New York: Macmillan, 1969. (b)

Humphry, M. O., "The Effect of a Syllabic Presentation of Words Upon Learning to Spell." Unpublished master's thesis, University of Texas, Austin, 1954.

Jackson, J., "The Influence of Word Analysis Upon Spelling Attainment." *Journal of Educational Research*, Vol. 45, October, 1953.

Jones, F. W., "Concrete Investigation of the Materials of English Speaking." University of South Dakota, Vermillion, 1913.

King, L. M., "Learning and Applying Spelling Rules in Grades Three to Eight." Teachers College, Columbia University, New York, 1932.

Kingsley, J. H., "The Test-Study Method Versus Study-Test Method in Spelling." *Elementary School Journal*, Vol. 24, 1923.

Larson, I. M., "Time Allotment in the Teaching of Spelling." Unpublished master's thesis, University of Iowa, Iowa City, 1945.

Lester, J. A., "Delimitation of the Spelling Problem." *English Journal*, Vol. 6, June, 1917.

Likert, R., "The Methods of Constructing an Attitude Scale." In Fishbein, M., *Readings in Attitude Theory and Measurement*, Wiley and Sons, New York, 1967.

Louis, R., "A Study of Spelling Growth in Two Different Teaching Procedures." Unpublished master's thesis, Central Washington State College, Ellenburg, 1950.

Masters, H., "A Study of Spelling Errors." Unpublished master's thesis, University of Iowa, Iowa City, 1927.

McKee, P., "Teaching and Testing Spelling by Column and Context Forms." Unpublished doctoral dissertation, University of Iowa, Iowa City, 1924.

McKee, P., *Language in the Elementary School*. Chicago: Houghton Mifflin, 1939.

Mendenhall, J. E., "An Analysis of Spelling Errors: A Study of Factors Associated With Word Difficulty." Teachers College, Columbia University, New York, 1930.

Montgomery, M. A., "The Test-Study Method Versus the Study-Test Method of Teaching Spelling in Grade Two: Study II." Unpublished master's thesis, University of Texas, Austin, January, 1957.

Parten, M., *Surveys, Polls and Samples*. Cooper Square Publishers, New York, 1966.

Wood, M., *NUCROS*, University of Iowa Computer Center.

Petty W., & Green, H., *Developing Language Skills in the Elementary Schools*. (3rd ed.) Boston: Allyn and Bacon, 1968.

Petty, W., "The Teaching of Spelling." *Bulletin of the School of Education*, Indiana University, Bloomington, Vol. 45, No. 6, November, 1969.

Rinsland, H. D., *A Basic Vocabulary of Elementary School Children*. New York: Macmillan Company, 1945.

Rosemeier, R. A., "Effectiveness of Forewarning About Errors in Response—Selective Learning." *Journal of Educational Psychology*, Vol. 56, 1965.

Russell, D. H., "Characteristics of Good and Poor Spellers." Teachers College, Columbia University, New York, 1937.

Sartorius, I. C., "Generalizations in

Spelling." New York Bureau of Publications: Teachers College, Columbia University, New York, 1931.

Schoephoerster, H., "Research Into Variations of the Test-Study Plan of Teaching Spelling." *Elementary English,* Vol. 39, 1962.

Shukik, H. M., "An Experimental Comparison of the Test-Study and the Study-Test Methods of Teaching Spelling in Third Grade." Unpublished master's thesis, Fordham University, New York, 1951.

Sand, H. J., "An Evaluation of the Effects of Marks as Incentives to Pupil Growth in Spelling Ability and of the Comparative Values of Equated Scales and Informal Tests as Measurements of the Progress." *Journal of Educational Research,* Vol. 31, 1938.

Strickland, R., *The Language Arts in Elementary School.* Boston: D. C. Heath, 1951.

Thomas, R. L., "The Effect of the Corrected Test on Learning to Spell, Grades Four, Five, and Six." Unpublished master's thesis, University of Texas, Austin, 1954.

Thorndike, E. L., "The Teacher's Word Book." Teachers College, Columbia University, New York, 1921.

Thorndike, E. L., *The Psychology of Wants, Interests, and Attitudes.* New York: Appleton-Century, 1935.

Thorndike, E. L., "The Teaching of English Suffixes." Teachers College, Columbia University, 1941.

Tidyman, W. F., "Survey of the Writing Vocabularies of Public School Children in Connecticut." Washington, D.C. United States Bureau of Education: Teachers Leaflet No. 15, 1921.

Tireman, L. S., "The Value of Marking Hard Spots in Spelling." Unpublished master's thesis, University of Iowa, Iowa City, 1927.

Turner, E. A., "Rules Versus Drill in Teaching Spelling." *Journal of Educational Psychology,* Vol. 3, October, 1912.

Tyson, I. M., "Factors Contributing to the Effectiveness of the Corrected Test in Spelling." Unpublished doctoral dissertation, University of Iowa, Iowa City, 1953.

Watson, A. E., "Experimental Studies in the Psychology and Pedagogy of Spelling." Unpublished doctoral dissertation, Teachers College, Columbia University, New York, 1926.

Winch, W. H., "Additional Researches on Learning to Spell." *Journal of Educational Psychology,* Vol. 7, 1916.

SECTION TWO

Issues

- Correct spelling is a mechanical skill and, like math or any other mechanical skill, it gets rusty from disuse.
    Robert Hillerich

- ... the purpose of spelling instruction should be to prepare students to spell words independently. However, the practice provided by spelling books most commonly involves writing the words that are printed on the page.
    Bruce Cronnell
    Ann Humes

- Already we are a nation tongue-tied and pen-frozen by linguistic anxiety.
    Russell Tabbert

INTRODUCTION

The issues that surround spelling instruction are closely related to those that have arisen in reading. Quite naturally, then, phonics instruction is a central concern of educators who are interested in spelling. Hillerich takes the position that ". . . schools have done an excellent job of creating phonetic misspellers," while Cronnell and Humes suggest that even though spelling texts are phonics-based, they are more concerned with teaching words rather than spellings. Irvine also criticizes contemporary spelling texts, suggesting that many of the activities they contain are interesting, but do not provide students with the consistent practice they need to become good spellers.

McFeely makes an interesting point about syllabication generalizations and spelling, a point that can easily be extended to other types of spelling rules. He argues that ". . . the child must already know how to pronounce the word in order to syllabicate it." Those of us whose knowledge of spelling extends no further than the "*i* before *e* rule" would surely agree with him.

Mazurkiewicz and Kasdon have opposing views regarding teachers' knowledge of phonics. Mazurkiewicz, as a result of survey research he conducted, contends that neither teachers nor their professors know enough about phonics to use their knowledge profitably to teach spelling. Kasdon replies that Mazurkiewicz's results are in error—that his questions are incapable of being answered because of the way they are worded.

The issue of dialect and spelling is raised by Tabbert and by Kligman and her colleagues. Although it appears as if there is some relationship between dialect and spelling, none of the authors suggest that corrective measures be taken to modify children's speech to make it conform to "standard" English.

The chapter closes with a comment by Mazurkiewicz on spelling reform. Although it is unlikely that such reform will take place in the foreseeable future, the arguments he musters in support of change in orthography are compelling.

Let's Teach Spelling—Not Phonetic Misspelling

ROBERT L. HILLERICH

Many criticisms of education are ill-founded, but critics of instruction in spelling and written expression are right on target. For the past thirty-five to forty years the schools have done an excellent job of creating phonetic misspellers. Why should this be, when research in the area of spelling is more clear and in more agreement than that in any other area of education? The obvious reason is that, if all one wants to do is teach spelling, there is no way to justify a spelling *book*. Publishers of spelling programs would be out of business.

To justify their existence, most spelling programs devote their efforts to teaching various kinds of generalizations with the intent of enabling children to

From *Language Arts*, Vol. 45, No. 3 (March, 1977). © 1977 by the National Council of Teachers of English. Reprinted by permission.

spell words they have never studied specifically for spelling. On the other hand, we've known since the research of Ernest Horn in 1957 that no one can be assured of the correct spelling of a word that has not been examined specifically for spelling. It is simple to come up with phonetic possibilities, but impossible to be certain of the "correct" spelling.

Let's examine the nonsense word /nē' dər lē/ as an example. The sounds to be represented are easy enough to identify: the /n/ in initial position, then /ē/, /d/, /ər/, /l/, and /ē/ in final position. To arrive at the spelling, one could consider *n* as the most likely beginning letter, although the other reasonable possibilities are *kn (know), gn (gnaw), pn (pneumonia),* and *mn (mnemonic).* The /ē/ in medial position could be spelled *ae (aegis), e (between), ea (meat), ee (meet), ei (neither), ie (chief), eo (people), ey (keynote),* or *oe (amoeba);* /d/ is easy—it is *d* or *dd;* /ər/ could be *ar (liar), er (term), ir (first), or (worm), ur (turn), ear (learn), our (journey), eur (chauffeur),* or *yr (myrtle);* /l/ again is easy as either *l* or *ll,* but final /ē/ could be *ay (quay), i (ski), ee (see), ey (key), y (baby), e (be),* or *ois (chamois).* In fact, we have demonstrated that the nonsense word could be spelled in $5 \times 9 \times 2 \times 9 \times 2 \times 7$ or 11,340 different ways. Of course, if one were unfamiliar with the influence of position, seventeen different spellings of /ē/ would have to be considered for both occurrences, increasing the possibilities to 52,020!

Whether one looks at the research on language itself or the research on the effects of teaching generalizations to children, the obvious conclusion is that no one can develop generalizations that will assure correct spelling of a word that has not been examined specifically for spelling. The evidence from analysis of the language (Hanna *et al.* 1966) indicates that a computer with 203 rules was able to spell 17,000 English words with only 49 percent accuracy; in fact, the same 203 rules led to poorer spelling than that done by live fifth grade children (Simon and Simon 1973). In other studies (Bredin 1972; Hillerich 1966; Hillerich 1971*b*), children who used some of the major spelling programs were compared with those who followed the researched approach to spelling. The latter spelled better after spending only three-fifths the time in spelling as compared with those who used traditional spelling workbooks.

How Does Research Indicate that Spelling Should be Taught?

First, if all the teacher is interested in is teaching spelling, there is no need for any spelling book. All that teacher needs is a good word list, developed through a pretest with immediate correction by the child, followed by instruction on the study method, and including a record of student progress. Such an approach can be conducted in one hour a week instead of the usual twenty to thirty minutes a day wasted in most commercial programs.

Secondly, however, such an approach will assure only a basic security list. To do the job completely, several other elements must be incorporated—namely, the development of a "spelling conscience," the ability to use a dictionary for spelling, and lots of writing.

The Word List

A well-selected word list of 2500-3000 words will account for 96 percent of all words anyone will ever write in a lifetime (Horn 1960; Hillerich 1976). It must be obvious that we quickly reach a point of diminishing returns in attempting to study words. As Ernest Horn (1926) pointed out, the three most frequently used words *(I, and, the)* account for at least ten percent of all words in print. The ten most frequently used words account for twenty-five percent: the child who knows only those ten words can spell correctly one-fourth of all the words that individual will write in a lifetime. The hundred most frequently used words account for well over fifty percent of all words used by children or adults.

The unabridged dictionary lists over 450,000 entry words. This means that the security list of some 3,000 words still leaves a gap of over 447,000 words to make up the other four percent of words to be written. It is impossible for anyone to guess which of those words will be needed in the future. Efficient use of a dictionary must account for these.

Words for spelling instruction ought to be arranged so that children at the beginning level will learn to spell those words that young children use most frequently in writing. As youngsters mature, word lists will gradually incorporate words most frequently used by adults as well.

Within a grade level, word lists ought to be arranged so they are equal in difficulty. In reading instruction, we expect the first story in a grade level to be easier than the last because children increase in reading skill. In spelling, however, an unknown word is an unknown word. Therefore every word list for a given level ought to be equal in difficulty. Children should not begin the year with lists where they know how to spell all the words and conclude the year with lists where they know none of the words.

Any good commercial program will develop the word lists from studies of both children's and adults' writing. Traditionally we have relied on Rinsland's (1945) count of words used by children in writing and on the Thorndike and Lorge (1944) count of adult writing. Any modern spelling program must also take into consideration the more recent word counts of Kucera and Francis (1967) (adult printed material) and Carroll and others (1971) (elementary books, grades three–nine). Ideally the Rinsland list will also be augmented by a modern count of words used by children in their writing.

Since no generalizations should be taught through the lists, words do not need to be grouped according to spelling. However, children should be placed in the word lists at levels where they already know how to spell fifty to seventy-five percent of the words in each list. Any child who consistently misses more than fifty percent of the words on a pretest is in a list which is entirely too difficult. Not only is the child overloaded for spelling study, but this would also indicate that the child does not know how to spell many of the words on a lower level list—words that are more important because they are more frequently used. One certainly looks much more ridiculous misspelling *the* and *was* than misspelling *secretary* or *established*.

Pretest with Immediate Correction by the Child

Research evidence indicates that the use of a pretest with immediate correction by the child accounts for about ninety-five percent of all learning that takes place in spelling (Horn 1947). This is one of the most important factors in a good spelling program and the one neglected in most commercial programs.

The pretest is administered in typical spelling-test fashion *before* the child looks at the word list. This pretest is not a test of the child; it represents the child's testing of the word list to discover which words need to be studied. The child should write each word in column form as the words are dictated. When the entire list has been dictated, the teacher will give the correction while also showing the correct spelling on the board or on a transparency, so children both hear and see the correct form as they correct their papers. Students will merely check those words spelled correctly. When a word is misspelled, the child will write the correct spelling beside this misspelled word.

This pretest approach has several values. First of all, it identifies for the child those words that need to be studied, thereby justifying the study method. There is no justification of the study method in most programs where a child is given a list of twenty words, fifteen of which the child already knows how to spell (Hughes 1966). Why should anyone go through the laborious study method with fifteen words that are already known? On the other hand, when five or six of the twenty words are identified as unknown, there is reason to apply the study method.

Secondly, we've known from the turn of the century that it does no good to point out "hard spots" in words because different people have different hard spots in the same word (Hillerich 1976). However, through use of the pretest youngsters discover their own personal hard spots in the words misspelled—they discover what mistakes they made and where they made them.

Study Method

Strangely enough for spelling programs that espouse a generalization approach to spelling, most still agree upon the study method established by Ernest Horn (1919) for learning to spell words from a list approach. It is an effective way to study a word specifically for spelling and involves visual, auditory, and kinesthetic modalities. Briefly, the study method involves these steps:

1. Look at the word and say it to yourself.
2. Close your eyes. Try to see the word as you spell it to yourself.
3. Check to see if you were right. (If not, begin again at step 1.)
4. Cover the word and write it.
5. Check to see if you were right. (If not, begin at step 1.)
6. Repeat steps 4 and 5 two more times.

The study method is an essential part of a good spelling program and one that must constantly be taught, retaught, and reviewed with children if they are to be successful spellers.

Record of Progress

The record of progress is nothing more than a graph. This is also an element agreed upon in most spelling programs. Actually children need to see that they are making progress in any area, so the record of progress should not be unique to spelling.

In the pretest approach, the record of progress takes on another facet. First of all, children should record the number of words spelled correctly on the pretest. No great point should be made of this score, or children will be encouraged to look at the words before the pretest. If they do, short-term memory could get them through the pretest without their actually knowing how to spell some of the words. Secondly, the number of words learned on the posttest should be added to the record of progress to show "how many words I learned by studying." This latter point is where the emphasis should be placed.

Other Essentials for Good Spellers

The foregoing elements will take care of the security list in spelling, and mastery of that list will enable correct spelling of ninety-six percent of all words anyone will write in a lifetime. On the other hand, this is not enough—to be ninety-six percent accurate in spelling. Now we depart from the study of spelling per se to get into the related elements neglected in spelling programs for the past forty years—elements probably more important than the spelling itself.

After all, spelling should not even be considered an academic area. It doesn't

ISSUES

belong with science, math, social studies, or reading; it belongs with the publications of Emily Post and Amy Vanderbilt. *Correct* spelling is nothing more than a courtesy to the reader. The whole point in learning to spell is to be an effective writer. Individuals can listen, speak, and read effectively without ever knowing how to spell a single word; the only time one needs to spell is in writing. Hence, spelling ought to be recognized and taught as one element of mechanics in written expression.

Using a Dictionary for Spelling

While practically every spelling program and every reading program teach children how to use a dictionary, there is practically no program that teaches children how to use a dictionary specifically for spelling. Any teacher from fourth grade up has had the experience of telling a youngster to check a spelling in the dictionary and having the youngster reply, "How'm I going to find it if I don't know how to spell it?" We must teach children how to find a word when they don't know how to spell it!

Using a dictionary for spelling is an entirely different activity from using a dictionary for pronunciation or for meaning, the two elements usually taught in commercial programs. Readiness for this skill should begin in first grade where a teacher will present a word orally that children certainly don't know how to spell, such as *mischief,* and ask children "With what letter do you think *mischief* would begin?"

As soon as youngsters are familiar with alphabetical order in a dictionary, they should be asked, "In what section of a dictionary would you begin in order to find that word?"

Children from second grade on need experience in exploring the possible spellings of vowel sounds. While it does no good to teach rules about the vowels, children can be given experience in discovering possible spellings of vowel sounds. For example, take the vowel sound /ē/ as in *eel*. Once children have learned to identify that sound—usually in second grade—they can use their readers, library books, or other printed material to collect as many words as they can find that have the vowel sound /ē/ in them. They may then, initially with the help of the teacher, make a composite list and sort the words according to the spelling of that sound. The group's list on the board may look something like this:

Spellings of /ē/

e	ee	ea	y	ey	eo
me	see	eat	candy	money	people
she	week	read	baby		
he	green		very		
be	feet		any		
	three				

To apply this activity to the use of a dictionary, the third grade teacher, for example, will give children a word they don't know how to spell, such as *bane,* and ask children what letter *bane* would begin with, where they would begin to look in a dictionary, how they think the vowel sound is spelled, and have them check suggested spellings until the correct spelling is found. In other words, use of a dictionary for spelling is nothing more than educated guessing. However, we must provide the education in order to enable effective guessing.

Spelling Conscience

Unfortunately the evidence is not so clear on how we can develop a spelling conscience—a desire and concern for spelling correctly. However, we know that children *can* spell better than they *do* spell.

There are two important aspects that can be brought in to help youngsters use the knowledge they already have. First, let's let them in on the secret that mature writers know: spelling is a courtesy to the reader. For example, no adult, in writing a grocery list, grabs the dictionary to be sure that *cantaloupe* is spelled correctly; that person puts down something resembling *cantaloupe* and goes to the grocery store to buy it. On the other hand, that same individual, writing a letter of application for a job, will double-check every word about which there is a doubt. Let's let children know that correct spelling is a courtesy to be taken care of when a piece of writing is going somewhere important, and let's get off their backs about correcting their spelling every time they put pencil to paper.

Secondly, because youngsters get in the habit of approximating spellings phonetically, they don't do a good job of recognizing when they don't know how to spell a word, and they often don't spot the misspellings in proofreading. This problem can be corrected if, from the very first writing experiences in first grade, children get in the habit—when they don't know how to spell a word—of putting down the initial letter or several letters they know, drawing a line, and continuing with their writing. Then, when the writing has been completed, it is time for the cleanup; they will ask how to spell the unknown words if they are primary children, or they will use a dictionary for those words if they have been taught how to use a dictionary for spelling.

This technique has another advantage in terms of written expression: children don't get into the habit of interrupting their thoughts in the middle of a sentence just because they don't know how to spell a word, or—worse—of using a simpler or less appropriate word merely because they know how to spell that word.

Lots of Writing

Correct spelling is a mechanical skill and, like math or any other mechanical skill, it gets rusty from disuse. If children are to maintain and further their spelling skills, they must do lots of writing. More importantly, they should do lots of writing because that's the only reason they are learning to spell to begin with. If they aren't going to write there is no point in wasting precious instructional time in learning to spell.

In the teaching of writing the emphasis should be on teaching children to communicate ideas. Teachers' comments on the papers should be reactions to those ideas and encouragement of the positive aspects of the writing. There should be *no corrections* on children's papers. This does not mean that the teacher ignores mechanical errors; it means that the teacher will make personal note of the mechanical errors as indications of the need for further teaching of those skills.

Results of the usual "teaching" of writing have been clearly demonstrated in the national assessment of written expression (Educ. Comm. 1972). By high school age, students have gotten the message; they have learned how to avoid red marks by writing short, simple sentences (because they can punctuate these correctly) and by using simple, common words (because they can spell these correctly). Is this the goal of instruction in written expression, to develop writers of correct inanities?

Evidence is also clear on this point: Children who write frequently and receive no correction on their papers will write more, have more creative ideas, enjoy writing more, and—at worst—will make no more mechanical errors than do those who receive correction on their papers (Gee 1972; Taylor and Hoedt 1966). According to most studies, those who do not receive corrections make even fewer errors in capitalization, punctuation, and spelling (Hillerich 1971*a*; Hillerich 1971*c*; Nikoloff 1965).

Research evidence suggests that formal spelling with word lists should not begin until second grade (Battenberg and Hillerich 1968), but the first grade teacher should also provide lots of writing experience with a focus on the high frequency words. In fact, children can write rebus stories where they draw pictures for some of the nouns they want to use in their writing.

In first grade, the teacher may focus on just a few high frequency words in order to assure automatic spelling of those. For example, just eight words (*the, a, is, was, in, on, and, it*) account for eighteen percent of all the words anyone uses in writing. Of course, the first grade teacher also ought to develop the habit in children of putting down only the first letter or so and drawing a line when a word is unknown. Then, after the writing is completed, the teacher can supply the spelling of the unknown words.

If teachers follow the research in spelling, the basic security list, accounting for ninety-six percent of all words used in writing, can be accomplished in about three-fifths the time normally devoted to spelling. This will allow the additional time for the development of writing skill, without which spelling skill is useless. It will also allow time for teaching the use of a dictionary for spelling, which will encourage the spelling conscience and the use of more appropriate, though more difficult, words in writing.

It's time that we let children in on the secret that writing is the important thing and that correct spelling is a courtesy that we will take care of before a piece of writing goes anywhere important. Let's get that mechanic of correct spelling done more quickly and more effectively so that we have more time to develop children who can write, who do write, and who enjoy writing.

REFERENCES

Battenberg, Donald, and Robert Hillerich. "Effectiveness of Teaching Spelling in Grade One." Unpublished study. Glenview, IL, 1968.

Bredin, Dorothy M. "Evaluation of Third Grade Spelling." *School District #69 Bulletin*. Skokie, IL, June 1972.

Carroll, John; Davies, Peter; and Richmond, Barry. *The American Heritage Word Frequency Book*. Boston: Houghton Mifflin, 1971.

Educational Commission of the States. *Report 8, Writing: National Results—Writing Mechanics*. Denver: Educational Commission of the States, February 1972.

Gee, Thomas C. "Students' Responses to Teacher Comments." *Research in the Teaching of English* 6 (1972): 212–221.

Hanna, Paul and others. *Phoneme-Grapheme Correspondences as Cues to Spelling Improvement*. Washington: U.S. Office of Health, Education, and Welfare, 1966.

Hillerich, Robert L. *Analysis of Words Used in Creative Writing, Grades 1–6*. Unpublished study. Glenview, IL, 1966.

———. "Comparison of Two Approaches to Spelling Instruction." Unpublished study. Glenview, IL, 1966.

———. "Evaluation of Written Language." *Elementary English* 48 (1971*a*): 109–112.

———. "A Second Comparison of Two Approaches to Spelling Instruction." Unpublished study. Evanston, IL, 1971*b*.

———. "A Second Evaluation of Written Language." *Illinois School Research* 7 (1971*c*): 28–31.

———. *Spelling: An Element in Written Expression*. Columbus: Charles E. Merrill, 1976.

Horn, Ernest. *A Basic Writing Vocabulary*. University of Iowa Monographs in Education, First Series, Number 4, April 1926.

———. "Phonetics and Spelling." *Elementary School Journal* 57 (1957): 424–432.

———. "Principles of Method in Teaching Spelling as Derived from Scientific Investigation." In Eighteenth Yearbook, Part II, Chapter II,

National Society for the Study of Education. Bloomington: Public School Publishing Company, 1919. (page 72)

Horn, Thomas D. "The Effect of the Corrected Test on Learning to Spell." *Elementary School Journal* 47 (1947): 277–285.

———. "Research in Spelling." *Elementary English* 37 (1960): 174–177.

Hughes, James. "The Myth of the Spelling List." *National Elementary Principal* 46 (1966): 53–54.

Kucera, Henry, and Francis, W. Nelson. *Computational Analysis of Present-Day American English*. Providence: Brown University Press, 1967.

Nikoloff, Syra. "The Relationship of Teacher Standards to the Written Expression of Fifth and Sixth Grade Children." Ph.D. dissertation, State University of New York at Buffalo, 1965.

Rinsland, Henry. *A Basic Vocabulary of Elementary School Children*. New York: Macmillan, 1945.

Simon, Dorothea, and Simon, Herbert. "Alternative Uses of Phonemic Information in Spelling." *Review of Educational Research* 43 (1973): 115–137.

Taylor, Winnifred, and Hoedt, Kenneth. "The Effect of Praise Upon the Quality and Quantity of Creative Writing." *Journal of Educational Research* 60 (1966): 80–83.

Thorndike, Edward, and Lorge, Irving. *The Teacher's Word Book of 30,000 Words*. New York: Bureau of Publications, Teachers College, 1944.

Elementary Spelling: What's Really Taught

BRUCE CRONNELL
ANN HUMES

The content of elementary-school instruction is frequently based on the content of textbooks (1). Teachers usually do not have the time or the resources to devise all their own instruction, and they must depend on what is available. According to a study conducted by the Educational Products Information Exchange Institute (2), investigators in on-site observations noted that 90 percent of what is done in classrooms is based on commercially prepared materials. Consequently, what students learn is often what their textbooks present. In the study reported here, elementary-school spelling textbooks were examined to determine the nature of current spelling instruction. The results of the study add to our understanding of instruction in schools and provide data for developing assessment instruments based on both the content that students have been taught and

---

Reprinted from *The Elementary School Journal*, Vol. 81, No. 1 (September, 1980). By permission of the University of Chicago Press. © 1980. Copyright is held by the University of Chicago.

ISSUES

the manner in which that content is presented and practiced.

This paper describes the three aspects of the study: the coding indexes used to describe spelling textbooks, the coding process, and some results of the analysis. The present study of spelling instruction is derived from similar earlier studies of reading and mathematics (3).

Coding indexes

To describe spelling textbooks, two indexes were prepared: the Content Index and the Performance Mode Index. The Content Index describes the spellings being taught; the Performance Mode Index describes the ways in which this content is presented and practiced.

The Content Index was derived from previous studies of spelling (4, 5) and from a preliminary analysis of a number of spelling textbooks. The Index includes twenty-nine major categories of spelling content:

> Consonants
> > Invariable single consonants
> > Variable consonants
> > Consonant digraphs
> > Miscellaneous doubled consonants
> > Miscellaneous silent consonants
>
> Vowels
> > Short vowels
> > Long vowels
> > Vowel-r
>
> Affixation
> > Inflectional suffixes
> > Derivational suffixes and endings
> > Endings
> > Prefixes and beginnings
> > Affixation processes
>
> Structures
> > Dictionary skills
> > Homophones
> > Compounds
> > Irregular words
> > Contractions
> > Abbreviations
>
> Syllabication
> Special sets of words
> Segments
> Whole words
> Nonspelling
> Miscellaneous

Several features of this list should be noted. Nonspelling categories were included because many textbook series include these categories. Handwriting and Grammar are two examples. Some of the other categories listed here—Syllabication and Miscellaneous Silent Consonants—are of questionable value to spelling, but were included because they, too, are found in many series. The organization of the major categories was determined in part by the computer program that had been established for the previous research in reading and mathematics. However, the decision to use available programming rather than set up new programming did not have a serious effect on either coding or analysis.

Each major category includes up to 50 subcategories that define specific spelling content. Most of these subcategories are mutually exclusive, for example, short /e/ spelled *e*, short /e/ spelled *ea*. However, when appropriate, another subcategory can be used in conjunction with the preceding subcategories to delineate specific uses; for example, the position of a spelling—initial, medial, or final—can be indicated. In most major categories, an "Other" code was established to permit coverage of unspecified content of low frequency.

The Performance Mode Index was derived from a description of the instructional specifications for a research-based spelling program (6). The performance modes were numbered 51 through 99 so that they could be used in conjunction with all 50 content subcategories previously described. Performance modes numbered 51 through 60 are verbs describing the motor skills that the student must use to complete the textbook exercises; two examples are "underline" and "write." Performance modes numbered 61 through 99 are noun phrases, that is, direct objects of the verbs. These noun phrases describe the stimulus-and-response characteristics of the textbook exercise. Two examples of these categories are "word that rhymes" and "word for picture." Together, the verbs and the noun phrases form directions for completing the exercises: "underline word that rhymes," "write word for picture." A variety of performance modes in textbook exercises can be described by the many possible combinations of the verbs and the noun phrases.

Procedures

Seven commonly used commercial spelling textbook series were selected for initial coding (7–13). Each instructional exercise was coded for a major category of content. At least one subcategory code was also used when—as was usually the case—specific content was being practiced. For example, one subcategory for the major category Contractions could be *n't*. Next, two Performance Modes codes were used—one verb and one noun phrase—to describe the task to be performed by the student. Any content or task not covered by the available codes was described in prose.

The coded data were keypunched for computer processing. The codes were sorted first by spelling series, then by grade level, and finally by major content area. Within each major category of content, subcategories were listed in (page) order of appearance in the textbook. The computer printout converted the numerical codes into their prose descriptions, thus providing an easily read listing of spelling content and practice. A sample computer listing is presented in Figure 1.

Results

Current popular spelling programs are much alike in the early stages. In almost all the programs studied, instruction begins with simple consonants and short vowels. However, in one program, consonants are not taught in the first year; that program is designed as a half-year program. The teacher's manual gives the reason why consonants are not taught in spelling in the first year: "...the basal reading program is the appropriate place to establish such foundation skills [consonants]" (13, p. T4).

After the introduction of simple consonants and short vowels, textbook series are less alike, varying in content and in sequencing. All series include, in varying sequences, a certain number of high-frequency spellings. Lower-frequency spellings vary from program to program, differing in their presence and absence, as well as in their grade level of introduction.

A few examples suggest this variability. In four programs, the letter *x* is taught in first grade; in two other programs, it is taught as late as third and fifth grades; in one program, the letter *x* is never explicitly taught. Two programs introduce ten or more long-vowel spellings in first grade; three programs introduce five to seven long-vowel spellings in first grade; the other two programs do not teach any long-vowel spellings until second grade. The *oy* spelling is taught in first grade in one program, in third grade in two programs, in fourth grade in two other programs, and not at all in the remaining two programs. The *be-* prefix is taught in third grade in two programs and in sixth grade in another; it is not taught at all in the other four programs. (Affixes are subject to much variation.) Thus, although the content of the spelling programs is much alike, there is great diversity as to when and whether certain content is taught.

Once spelling programs introduce content, they frequently return to it year after year. Most textbooks have a considerable amount of review and reteaching, particularly of vowels. After a vowel spelling is taught, it is usually repeated at each later grade. A few consonants and many suffixes also get this repetitious treatment. Repetition may sometimes be justified if the spelling is difficult, but in many cases the repeated

ISSUES

```
PROFICIENCY VERIFICATION SYSTEM
SORT PROCEDURE FOR SPELLING
PAGE 33

PROGRAM:   5,  GRADE:   3

SKILL:   22    LONG VOWELS

PAGE:     PAGE CONTENTS:
  47      LONG /O/ - OA* WRITE* WORD THAT COMPLETES SENTENCE
  47      LONG /O/ - O* WRITE* WORD THAT COMPLETES SENTENCE
  47      LONG /O/ - O . . . E* WRITE* WORD THAT COMPLETES SENTENCE
  48      LONG /O/* WRITE* WORD THAT COMPLETES SENTENCE
  48      LONG /I/* WRITE* WORD THAT COMPLETES SENTENCE
  50      LONG /I/ - I . . . E* CHOOSE AND WRITE* WORD(S) WITH SEGMENT
  50      LONG /A/ - A . . . E* CHOOSE AND WRITE* WORD(S) WITH SEGMENT
  50      LONG /(Y)U/* OTHER SPELLING* CHOOSE AND WRITE* WORD(S) WITH SPECIFIED SOUND*
          O . . . E* TREATED AS IRREGULAR * LOSE, PROVE
  60      LONG /A/* CHOOSE AND WRITE* WORD(S) WITH SPECIFIED SOUND
  60      CHOOSE AND WRITE* WORD(S) WITH SPECIFIED SOUND
  60      UNDERLINE* LETTER(S) FOR SPECIFIED SOUND
  60      LONG /I/ - I* CHOOSE AND WRITE* WORD(S) WITH SPECIFIED SOUND
  65      LONG /E/* CHOOSE AND WRITE* WORD(S) WITH SPECIFIED SOUND* (FINAL E MARKER)
  65      LONG /A/* CHOOSE AND WRITE* WORD(S) WITH SPECIFIED SOUND* (FINAL E MARKER)
  65      UNDERLINE * WORDS WITH 2 VOWELS TOGETHER
  66      LONG /A/ - A . . . E* WRITE* WORD FROM PRONUNCIATION SYMBOLS* ASTE * TREATED AS IRREGULAR
  70      LONG /(Y)U/ - OO* CHOOSE AND WRITE* WORD(S) WITH SPECIFIED SOUND
  70      LONG /(Y)U/ - OO* WRITE* WORD FOR PICTURE
  71      LONG /(Y)U/ - OO* WRITE* WORD THAT COMPLETES SENTENCE
  71      LONG /(Y)U/ - OO* CHOOSE AND WRITE* PRONUNCIATION SYMBOL FOR SOUND
  71      LONG /(Y)U/ - OO* WRITE* WORD FOR PICTURE
  72      LONG /(Y)U/ - OO* WRITE* WORD THAT COMPLETES SENTENCE
  73      LONG /(Y)U/
  73      LONG /(Y)U/ - OO* WRITE* WORD THAT COMPLETES SENTENCE
  78      LONG /(Y)U/ - OO* WRITE* WORD THAT COMPLETES SENTENCE
```

Fig. 1.—Sample computer listing

spellings are simple; short /a/ spelled *a* and /sh/ spelled *sh* are frequently covered in each of Grades 1 through 6; the *-s* and *-es* suffixes (primarily for plurals) are commonly covered in each of Grades 2 through 6.

Spelling textbooks seem to have two conflicting bases that may account for the repetition of content. One basis is phonics generalizations and spelling rules; the other basis is grade-level word lists. Words from these lists are presented at higher grade levels than are the spellings they contain; for example, the word *bay* is commonly taught in Grades 4 and 5 although the spellings in the word are taught in Grades 1 and 2. Thus, textbooks must review spellings to have a reason for teaching new words. Therefore, despite the purported use of phonics, rule-based approaches, spelling textbooks commonly are concerned with teaching words rather than spellings.

The seven spelling series analyzed differ not only in content but also in the amount and the kind of instruction and practice they offer. Five programs provide instruction and practice on consonant clusters (blends); the other two programs provide no explicit instruction on clusters. However, words that have consonant clusters are included in all series; thus students' ability to spell such words may vary considerably, depending on the amount and the nature of instruction and practice in their particular textbooks.

Analysis of the performance modes provides a description of the spelling practice that students receive. Frequently textbooks offer little practice. Spelling books are usually similar in length; but, at the same grade level, the number of responses per page varies considerably from program to program. Because time on task may be important in school success (14), programs that offer little practice may produce poorer spellers than programs that offer more practice.

Additionally, the relevance of the spelling practice is often questionable. Every program has exercises that seem suspect; one example suggests the irrelevance that may be found. (The program will not be named; examples could be cited from all programs.) In a second grade lesson on *wh* (which occurs only initially in words), students write *wh* only eight times; for the remaining 18 items, they write the endings of words beginning with *wh*. Although relevance is hard to measure, it clearly influences students' learning; students cannot be expected to learn from practice that does not focus on the content to be learned.

A disturbing feature of most spelling programs is that they rarely require students to perform realistic spelling tasks. In "real-world" spelling, students must generate a spelling on their own, in response to a need, internal or external. Thus the purpose of spelling instruction should be to prepare students to spell words independently. However, the practice provided by spelling books most commonly involves writing the words that are printed on the page. Sometimes the spelling task explicitly directs students to copy words. More often the task requires students to choose a listed word and write it—another kind of copying task. Some tasks can be completed without looking at the words printed on the page; however, some, if not many, students probably complete all their spelling practice by merely copying the words printed on the page. This kind of practice is not in keeping with the goal of self-generated spelling, a goal that textbooks frequently ignore, although a wide range of appropriate formats for practice could be used (6). (Students might be asked to spell a word for a picture, or a word that completes a given sentence, or a word that fits a particular story content, or a word that has a specified sound.)

Conclusion

This study of spelling textbooks adds to our understanding of what students are exposed to when commercially prepared materials are used to teach spelling in elementary schools. This knowledge is particularly valuable in designing assessment instruments, for it helps in the construction of tests that parallel instruction. To test students on what they have not been taught is unfair; analysis of the content and the nature of instruction is a necessary preliminary step to designing tests that accurately assess learning.

REFERENCES

1. The work upon which this article is based was performed pursuant to Grant No. OB-NIE-G-78-0209 with the National Institute of Education, Department of Health, Education, and Welfare. Larry Gentry, Teanna Boscon, and Roxanne Denson contributed to the coding and the data analysis described here.
2. Educational Products Information Exchange Institute. *Report on a National Study of the Nature and the Quality of Instructional Materials Most Used by Teachers and Learn-*

ers. Report No. 76. New York, New York: Educational Products Information Exchange Institute, 1976.
3. A. Buchanan and P. Milazzo. "Designing an Instruction-Referenced System for Large-Scale Evaluation of School Achievement." Paper presented at the Third Annual Conference of the California Society of Educational Program Auditors and Evaluators, Los Angeles, California, May, 1977.
4. B. Cronnell. *Beginning Spelling: A Linguistic Review of Six Spelling Series*. Technical Report No. 35. Los Alamitos, California: SWRL Educational Research and Development, 1971.
5. P. Russell. *An Outline of English Spelling*. Technical Report No. 55. Los Alamitos, California: SWRL Educational Research and Development, 1975.
6. A. Humes. *Instructional Specifications for the SWRL Spelling Program*. Technical Note No. 3-76-07. Los Alamitos, California: SWRL Educational Research and Development, 1976.
7. H. F. Benthul, E. A. Anderson, A. M. Utech, and M. V. Biggy. *Spell Correctly*. Morristown, New Jersey: Silver Burdett, 1971.
8. T. E. Glim and F. S. Manchester. *Basic Spelling*. Philadelphia, Pennsylvania: Lippincott, 1977 (revised edition).
9. W. Kottmeyer and A. Claus. *Basic Goals in Spelling*. New York, New York: McGraw-Hill, 1976 (fifth edition).
10. R. Madden and T. Carlson. *Harbrace Spelling Program*. New York, New York: Harcourt Brace Jovanovich, 1974.
11. W. N. Novicky, S. Dorocak, M. C. Faulhaber, M. Himes, K. McNerney, R. Petruziello, and R. Wolfert. *Growth in Spelling*. River Forest, Illinois: Laidlaw, 1975.
12. L. L. Ort and E. E. Wallace. *Word Book*. Chicago, Illinois: Rand McNally, 1976.
13. O. Thomas, I. D. Thomas, and A. Lutkus. *The World of Spelling*. Lexington, Massachusetts: D. C. Heath, 1978.
14. J. B. Carroll. "A Model of School Learning," *Teachers College Record,* 64, (May, 1963), 723-33.

If You're Not a Spelling Genius, Beware of Friday

PATRICIA McCUNE IRVINE

While we've been fighting the chronic war of school bussing in this country, our newspapers sneaked in a not surprising informational morsel the other day: our high school students can neither read nor write up to par. Which means they can't spell, either. (Actually, some of us suspect there is a whole bunch of other things they can't do).

Nevertheless, high echelon educators are attempting to rectify the situation—with curriculum changes—special teachers, more frequent testing.

But as an interested taxpayer, I should

From *Spelling Progress Bulletin*, Vol. 21, No. 3 (Fall, 1981). Reprinted with permission.

like to suggest that shutting the barn door in high school is too late. By then, we've already lost the horses. Doesn't everyone know kids should be taught to read and write and spell correctly in elementary school?

Now writing is the true key to reading. They go together—read and write. But better the other way—write and read. Because if the kids write well, they can read well. No question about that. And writing is a lot easier for good spellers. Webster often stands on the desk untried because non-spellers can't get the hang of him. Did you ever wonder what happened to those flat little spelling books with nothing but lists and lists of words that we drilled into our heads? Write the word and cover it and write it again—and again. Until perfection?

I'm not sure of the fate of composition classes in the lower grades, but I know what happened to spelling. It became Language Study—where words are discussed—and related. They are meaningful—and they are understood. This is sometimes pleasant. But the actual spelling: that is, the juxtaposition of the letters in a word—is not properly studied, not necessarily learned.

"Spelling" books suggest studying. They refer to a study plan, to study steps, and often simply give the order to study per se. However, the week goes something like this:

Monday—*Meeting New Words.* This is logical and a step in the right direction. Most "spelling" periods are 20 minutes long and rarely exceed 30 minutes, so with from 10 to 20 new words involved, the introductions have to be fast. One a minute, more or less. Although this places your genius speller in the catbird seat, his slothful friends are in a peck of trouble. Monday is not entirely fair to them.

So on Monday, we look at the pictures and read the story. We say each new word after the teacher. We find each new word in the story. We underline it. We write the new word in the space provided—and it is provided in a way which makes it easy to copy if we are unable to write it from memory.

And that's for Monday. The lesson is over and we are happily acquainted with our new words. But only the natural talents know how to spell them. Nothing solid in the way of accomplishment for the run-of-the-mills.

Tuesday—*Using My Words.* The pleasant thing about Tuesday is that we don't always have to use the words in the same old way. We do look at the picture again, read the story once more, draw a line under each spelling word one more time, but in the remaining few minutes we surge forward.

We use the words. We fill in blanks. We write words that rhyme. We write the name for each picture. We play a crossword puzzle game. (Time falls away here in great chunks.) We write words that are spelled the same but mean different things. You know, like *pen* and *pen*. We write words that sound the same but are spelled differently: you know, like *by* and *buy*. We fill in the missing word. I tried this one recently and although I'm preciously close to being a spelling genius myself, I found I looked back to the list for the desired word so I wouldn't inadvertently write *cottage* for *house*. Once you look you might as well copy the word. And if I were writing the opposite of *soft,* without checking I might not know for certain the proper word was *hard.* After all, it could be *loud.*

But Tuesday is a wonderfully fun day. Even if you do get a neck-ache by constantly looking back.

Wednesday—*My Trial Test.* This shoots the whole spelling period. Anyone who isn't a spelling genius had better look to Thursday.

Thursday—*Learning About Words.* About? Nevertheless, if we thought Tuesday was fun, on Thursday we are ecstatic. There are so many things to learn about words (spelling notwithstanding), and such fascinating ways to learn them. For instance, we can put a ring around each vowel. Or draw lines under same. We write the word that begins with *gr*. Write the word that has a double *t*. Write the word that ends in *ce*. Write *play* and add *s*. Add *ing*. Add *ed*. Put a ring around the silent letters (or draw lines under same). We write names for the nearby pictures. We underline (or draw rings around) letters that are the same in different words. We write words that rhyme. (We've also done this on Tuesday.) We put words in alphabetical order. We write longer words made from shorter words. We write the vice versa. We learn about singulars and plurals and abbreviations. Marvelous day!

But if you can't play the piano by ear, you'd better practice. If your thumb is other than green, you'd better fertilize the garden patch. If the chef's hat doesn't fit your head, you'd better watch the ingredients you put into the casserole.

If you aren't a spelling genius, beware of Friday.

Friday—*What Have I Learned?* Notice the question? Notice the lack of finality? Not What *I Have* Learned, with definite clarity, but What *Have I* Learned, hopefully, inquiringly, as if the whole matter might be subject to dispute.

Everyone will agree botanical scrutiny, however fascinating, does not get the ivy planted, and nutritional consideration, no matter how important, does not put the cheese souffle on the table. The electric toaster has to be plugged into the socket, and daily practice is the only way to master the piano. Or the game of football.

By the same authority, language investigation, both important and fascinating, will never teach anyone to spell.

Actually, I don't really advocate returning to that flat, little meaningless spelling book, with its lists and lists of words to drill into heads.

But unfortunately, inconsistencies exist between our oral and our written language. One cannot tell how to spell an English word by its pronunciation and vice versa. Our words were created by different peoples and are rampant with borrowings, distortions, diminutions and embroideries. Our spelling has become deceptive, frustrating and often clumsy. It is highly traditional and needlessly complex and has become a *basic source of academic failure*. Some say spelling cannot be taught effectively and those with less literate life styles are doomed. So what do we do now?

The logical answer, of course, is to simplify and reorganize, tidy up the situation. Create simplified spelling.

But no real agreement as to how to do this exists among the experts. We have pedagogical objections and practical objections and emotional objections.

Theoretically, the best spelling system would combine consistency with simplicity. In the ideal, a character would always represent the same sound and the same sound would always be represented by the same character. And then—presto—we would have correlation between spelling and pronunciation.

Or would we?

Once, when I emerged from a California drug store with a young friend visiting from New Zealand, he referred to 'tykes.' I glanced around and saw none and asked him to repeat, which he did. Three or four times. "What about the *tykes?*" The tykes. Tykes. Tykes. He was very exasperated with me. I asked him to spell the word. And he did. T-a-x, *tykes.*

Everyone has had a little difficulty understanding other English-speaking people, whether from another country or simply another part of our own country. To add pronunciation symbols to simplified spelling—even if it would do any good—is asking for the moon. No one uses the ones we've borrowed with words from other languages—such as café. And we all know the difficulties of syllabic stress, depending on use as a noun or a verb, such as *con*duct or con*duct, reb*el or reb*el*—and the change in phrasal stress from isolated pronunciation to connected speech. Homophones would create difficulty—remember *by* and *buy*? Well, what do you do about *pear* and *pair* and *pare,* to everyone's satisfaction? And *ant* and *aunt?*

Some prejudices and natural resistance to spelling reform can best be overcome by gradual steps, altho the illogic in our word structure will no doubt persist. We can flow from *although* to *altho,* from *though* to *tho,* and from *through* to *thru,* and perhaps even from *photograph* to *foto.* But it is unlikely that any system of simplified spelling will be satisfactory to everyone, and for that reason, it's best not to wait too long for it. I have a postal card sent in 1911 to the Spelling Board of New York, from someone pledging to use simplified spelling in business letters—but that was 70 years ago. What happened? Perhaps we're still not ready. But we needn't wait—simplified spelling isn't the only answer. We mustn't give up too easily. Mountains can be moved. In the here and now.

So I do advocate having a Spelling Class in connection with Language Study, in elementary school. And a Writing or Composition Class, also. Every day. Communication is a basic skill which eventually determines success or failure in most areas of our very competitive life and the ability to spell correctly frees the writer to concentrate on the content of his communication.

Anyway, it's the school's task to develop proficiency in spelling—no matter about the inconsistencies and degree of difficulty. If a third-grader can know and thoroughly understand every electronic game on the market today and very young computer specialists can learn that machine's capabilities and limitations, the ability to spell correctly cannot be totally out of reach, if you're willing to put enough time to it. I believe pupils should be made to understand that no one becomes an expert at anything without consistent and insistent practice—the electronic game player or the baseball pitcher or the pianist or the spelling champ. A lot tougher courses than spelling will come up in their career. They should understand that.

Spelling should be taught as a practical tool for writing, and not as an academic discipline. Spelling correctly is useful knowledge and, if as some say, it is contrary to human nature to learn anything unless it offers a definite advantage, it might behoove us to sell the advantage, and to instill in the kids such emotions as desire, interest, pride and the necessity for it all. Reveal the advantages. The learning process would become easier with a few positive emotions going for it. I thought it was fun to spell M-i-s-s-i-s-s-i-p-p-i out loud when I was a child because of the rhythm and lilt it created. And because it was a long word and made me feel brainy. And I thought it was fun to spell E-g-y-p-t because of the three letters with tails in a row. And because the 'y' was a special surprise. Nobody has any fun any more.

Because no general rules are dependable and rote learning must be used, spelling becomes an interminable process. So spelling words must become meaningful. Therefore, a class could devise its own special spelling book with the words that are needed for class projects. Words that are in the pupils' speaking and reading vocabularies, with meanings being explained if not known. If the Westward Movement is being studied in the classroom, create usable lists from words needed or requested for the daily compositions—*pioneer, mountain, Indian, Kentucky, westward, movement,* etc.

If the Space Age is being studied in the classroom, let the spelling words be useful for daily composition—*missile, orbit, atmosphere,* etc.

Spelling lists also should be learned in related groups with endings that rhyme, to facilitate the learning of many words almost simultaneously—*care, dare, rare,* etc. And the same rhyme endings with alternate spellings—*bear* and *pear,* or *fair* and *hair.*

Another group of words that relate to each other are actual family members known in daily life—*father, mother, brother, aunt, niece,* etc. And perhaps some Christmas thank-you notes could be written in daily composition class after that holiday.

Our Language Study can give us many groups of words that relate to each other. I, personally, was always a stickler for requiring the class to spell our states correctly—all of them. A matter of pride. But perhaps that was a personal thing and taught more as a discipline.

A writing vocabulary is developed, then, by first concerning ourselves with the practical needs of the pupils. But they must write something every day.

Kinesthetic treatment can be particularly helpful to slow learners, when audio-visual imagery is impaired. This method of tracing words requires more individualized attention, but blackboard use in a schoolroom is possible, as well as help from more advanced classmates.

If more practice is necessary to retain what is learned in school, home study should not be shunned. Parents can be a critical factor in the learning process. Some of them have dropped the ball. Or don't care.

Excellence should be rewarded. What's wrong with a prize for the best composition on the Westward Movement or the Space Age, or even a short fiction piece? Why not offer an award for distinction in sixth grade spelling? Why not give our spellers something to strive for? Good old-fashioned competition is an effective incentive. Every child is not like every other and let us not be afraid of excellence—knowing that some may attain it while others fail. Is that not the condition of life itself? Quality spelling should be our goal, not a uniformity of nothingness—because of fear—that provides real quality to no one at all.

Remember, writing is a lot easier for good spellers. And reading is a lot easier for good writers.

Draw rings around the vowels if you wish. Underline, rhyme, play, get acquainted, look at pictures, and read the stories. But if you can't write or read or spell, what difference does it make which high school the bus takes you to?

Syllabication Generalizations: Help or Hindrance to Communication?

DONALD C. McFEELY

As a professor of reading, I am asked many questions from my students and in-service teachers about reading. One topic of concern is the importance of teaching children about syllables through syllabication generalizations.

In order to answer the many questions I receive, I must turn to my own research (McFeely, 1974) or to the literature that is replete with articles and books related to syllabication. When I or my students go to the literature, that is when a state of confusion becomes apparent. I should like to touch briefly the surface of this literature.

Research on the Syllable

Lenneberg (1967) notes that: "Since the time of ancient grammarians and inventors of scripts there has been an aware-

From *Spelling Progress Bulletin*, Vol. 21, No. 2 (Summer, 1981). Reprinted with permission.

ness of some rhythmically occurring events in speech, namely the syllable (p. 115)."

Kenyon (1928) explains syllables on the principle of sonority or degree of audibility. He explains that vowels are the most sonorous of all speech sounds. Therefore, the phonetic center of a syllable is its point of greatest sonority. Boundary lines are the point between them of least sonority, which may or may not be silent. This, he states, may fall between a vowel and a consonant, or on the consonant itself if it is one of the least sonorous.

Research on Syllable Boundaries

In order to apply syllabication generalizations to words, it has been assumed that syllables have boundaries of where it (the syllable) begins and ends as the child pronounces each syllable. A number of authorities (Groff, 1971; Hall, 1964; Jones, 1950; Malone, 1957) feel that it is difficult and sometimes impossible to determine precisely where a syllable begins and where it ends.

Based on the findings of the linguists and the problem of determining boundaries of the syllable, Groff (1971) concludes that it is impossible to accept some of the evidence of *dictionary syllabication* because "there is no theory in linguistic literature to our knowledge that supports dictionary syllabication as a system by which boundaries of the syllable should be defined (p. 27)."

Evolution of Syllabication Generalizations

For years educators have advocated the use of dictionary syllabication. Dolch (1938) maintains that "what the schools definitely need is a teaching of phonics of polysyllables (p. 124)." Dolch (1945) further believes pupils "must have a method of attack, that is, conscious rules to follow (p. 278)."

Betts (1959) supports Dolch's idea by proposing a sequential program wherein the child, in this sequential order: (a) identified vowel letters, (b) counted the number of syllables in a word, (c) noted which were accented, and (d) decided on which vowel rule would help know this (pp. 261-262).

William S. Gray (1960) has been very influential in advocating dictionary syllabication. He states that "if pupils are to progress in reading they should learn how to apply visual clues to vowel sounds in two-syllable words. To do so, they must learn how to divide printed words into syllables (p. 44)."

Anderson (1968) offers rules for dividing words into syllables and states, "...through teaching syllabication children will be able to pronounce new words through applying the rules that might be relevant, arrive at correct spelling, and break words at the end of a line of writing in accordance with syllabic principles (p. 175)."

Bush and Huebner (1970) conclude that breaking words into syllables may help the reader in many ways and that, "children have to learn to use a number of generalizations in breaking words into syllables (p. 319)."

Syllabication as a form of structural analysis has been advocated by various authorities.

Dechant (1970) discusses syllabication as a skill of structural analysis and states that, "Syllabication must receive attention at all levels of reading instruction. For most pupils, learning in this area is greatest during the intermediate grades (p. 319)."

DeBoer and Dallman (1970) state that, "Syllabication can aid in the identification and recognition of words (p. 131)." However, they feel it is "not essential to the recognition or pronunciation of a word to know exactly where some of the breaks between syllables occur (p. 131)."

Durkin (1970) contends that when a child has to deal with syllabication of an unknown word, he needs to consider a number of generalizations, all concerned with syllabication. She concludes that:

ISSUES

When a child encounters a word which is unknown to him in written form, a phonic analysis generally should be attempted. With such an analysis, the first job is to consider the likely syllabication of the word because the syllable is the basic unit of pronunciation (p. 236).

Jones (1971) doesn't advocate memorizing the rules but feels that "principles of syllabication and accent are helpful in arriving at the pronunciation of a word (p. 169)." Strang, McCullough, and Traxler (1967) discuss the problem of secondary students in word recognition and state that "those who do poorly [in syllabication] should be given additional practice (p. 228)."

Cordts (1960) also believes rules of syllabication are useful although as she states, "Unfortunately these rules too, like most rules, have their exceptions (p. 173)." Cordts lists five rules that she feels are useful:

1. When there is one consonant between two vowel sounds, the consonant usually goes with the next syllable, if the preceding vowel is "long," and with the preceding syllable if the vowel is "short" or has a sound other than "long."
2. When there are two or more consonants between the vowels in a word, all the consonants go with the next vowel, if the vowel is not "long," the first consonant stays with the preceding syllable and the others go with the following syllable.
3. When there are two identical consonants between the vowel sounds, the word is divided between the consonants.
4. When each of two vowels in a word forms a separate syllable, the word is divided between the vowels.
5. When a word is composed of two complete words, the word is divided between the words in the compound word (pp. 173-175).

An analysis of the rules advocated by Cordts implies the child must already know how to pronounce the word in order to syllabicate it. For example, in Rule 1, the child needs to know that the first vowel in *hero* is long to divide the word *he/ro* and the child needs to know that the first vowel in *radical* is short to divide the word *rad/i/cal*. The same holds true for Rules 2 and 4. In Rule 2, the child needs to know that the vowel in *program* is long to divide the word *pro/gram*, and that the vowel in *capsule* is short to divide the word *cap/sule*. In Rule 4, the child needs to already know that the *u* and *i* in the word *ruin* are in separate syllables.

If the purpose of syllabication is to aid the child to pronounce unfamiliar words by breaking them into smaller parts to apply phonetic skills, then Rules 1, 2 and 4 as advocated by Cordts seem to be too complex and erroneous. In addition, as written, Rule 2 is not understandable.

Criticisms of Syllabication Generalizations

The critics of dictionary syllabication base their conclusions on the lack of research and the findings of linguists. Russell (1961) concludes that "research studies have not given clear evidence of the values of structural analysis when taught by itself as a technique of word recognition (p. 312)."

Spache (1963) concludes that there is little relationship between retention of syllabication rules and success in analyzing words into syllables (p. 236). He further states that, "it is doubtful that they [syllabication rules] are long remembered or have any great functional value for maturing readers (p. 236)."

Stauffer (1969) maintains that "syllable rules are of some value in spelling, and it is in spelling class that they are frequently taught (p. 359)." Stauffer challenges the advice of many reading experts and especially Gray (1960) by concluding, "No pupil has learned to be on his own in reading by memorizing the hundreds of rules supplied in *On Their Own in Reading* by Gray (p. 358)." Stauffer does concede that syllables "are of some value in the early learning-to-read stages when on occasion, if a child syllabizes a word and then speaks it, he may identify it as a spoken word he knows (p. 359)."

In addressing himself to the question of teaching generalizations, Stauffer (1969) states:

This examination of the rule circumstance points up quite clearly the futility of either rules or generalizations. . . . it suggests loudly and firmly that from the beginning of reading instruction attention should be focused 100% on comprehension rather than on word-recognition rules, because 100% comprehension will always have 100% utility (p. 368).

Schell (1967) considers dictionary syllabication as being inaccurate instruction. He contends that not only do such "instructional techniques frequently fail to distinguish between reading and spelling...[but] it appears that sometimes it is not clear whether pronunciation or syllabication comes first (p. 134)."

The present emphasis on linguistics has influenced the critics of dictionary syllabication. Wardhaugh (1969) in discussing rules for syllabication found in phonics programs, states that:

Reading teachers are asked to teach children to divide words . . . such rules are often quite circular, have almost nothing to do with the actual sound patterns of English and almost everything to do with line-breaking conventions, and hardly any possible application beyond the typesetter's domain (p. 9).

Wardhaugh further concludes that the rules of syllabication are much too complicated as presently stated. In fact Wardhaugh claims that if a child can use the rules of syllabication, he (the child) really doesn't need them because the use of these rules requires the child to have the very knowledge that the rules are supposed to be teaching (p. 9).

Lefevre (1964) supports Wardhaugh's conclusions that syllabication rules have almost nothing to do with the actual sound patterns of English. Division of words into syllables, according to Lefevre, "is primarily a printer's device rather than a problem of reading or writing; words should seldom be artificially uttered as if the syllables were actually separated in speech (p. 177)."

Research on the Utility of Syllabication Generalizations

Sartorious (1930) reports one of the first studies concerned with the utility of phonic generalizations. Her study is related to spelling rather than a specified vocabulary. Oaks (1952) analyzed 1,966 words to determine which were conformations and which were exceptions to eight generalizations. Oaks recommends not to include the generalization, "When in a word of more than one syllable, the final syllable ends in the letters 'en,' the 'n' becomes syllabic and is pronounced, but 'e' is silent because of its infrequent occurrence (p. 617)."

A number of studies have evolved that have investigated the varying degrees of utility of phonic generalizations, which have included syllabication generalizations (Bailey, 1967; Clymer, 1963; Emans, 1963; McFeely, 1974; Parker, 1968).

For the purpose of this paper, two syllabication generalizations have been analyzed. These are as follows:

1. If the first vowel sound in a word is followed by two consonants, the first syllable usually ends with the first of the two consonants. VC/CV

2. If the first vowel sound in a word is followed by a single consonant, that consonant usually begins the second syllable. V/CV

Table 1 presents the findings of these studies as a means of comparison. Table 1 indicates the investigator, the number of applicable incidents and conformations, and the percentage of utility.

An attempt has been made here to analyze only two generalizations from various studies. A more in-depth discussion can be found in a previous study done by this writer (McFeely, 1974).

For the purpose of this paper, I analyzed the VCV generalization and tried to determine could teachers offer students an alternative if the generalization is an exception. For example, if students apply the VCV generalization to a word such as *vivid,* they would find the dictionary pronunciation would divide the word *viv-id,* not *vi-vid* as the generalization would indicate. What would happen if the teacher would tell students to try the V/CV generalization and try to pronounce the word to determine if it "sounds" right? If not, divide the word after the consonant VC/V.

Table 1
Utility level of various syllabication generalizations

Generalization	Bailey	Clymer	Emans	McFeely	Parker
1. If the first vowel sound in a word is followed by two consonants, the first syllable usually ends with the first of the two consonants. VC/CV.	$\frac{1311}{1689} =$ 78%	$\frac{404}{563} =$ 72%	$\frac{648}{811} =$ 80%	$\frac{1305}{1546} =$ 84%	$\frac{628}{741} =$ 85%
2. If the first vowel sound in a word is followed by a single consonant, that consonant usually begins the second syllable. V/CV.	$\frac{638}{1283} =$ 50%	$\frac{190}{427} =$ 44%	$\frac{313}{659} =$ 47%	$\frac{1109}{2014} =$ 55%	$\frac{385}{730} =$ 53%

The number of exceptions from a previous study (McFeely, 1974) was analyzed. I found 2,014 incidences of the VCV pattern with 1,109 conformations for a 55% utility. This meant that there were 905 exceptions. When I applied a VC/V generalization to these words, I found 863 conformations or a degree of utility of 95%. It would seem teachers could increase the usefulness of the VCV generalization by telling students to try to divide the word after the consonant if it doesn't sound right after they divided after the vowel.

Conclusions

At this point I need to answer the question, "Is teaching syllabication generalizations a help or a hindrance to communication or more specifically to reading?" Now the reader must make his/her own decision as to the usefulness of syllabication. It is apparent from the review of literature that there is no agreement from the various so-called authorities in reading as to the value of syllabication generalizations. Teachers can choose any side they want.

I for one, however, have taken a position that it is not so much *if* we teach syllabication generalizations but *how* we teach. I would agree with Rosati (1973) that we should teach the student to experiment with syllabication rather than consider syllabication to be based on rules for dictionary accuracy.

Burmeister (1968) recommends teaching those generalizations that indicate the highest utility. She recommends that "teachers place more confidence in some generalizations than in others and that they be particularly cautious when instructing children in the use of phonic generalizations which appear to have limited value. Teachers should advise children to examine words in which these generalizations might apply in two or more different specific ways until oral recognition is achieved (p. 95)."

My suggestion to teachers is that knowledge of syllabication can be helpful to students when they need to divide a "big" word into "smaller parts" in order to pronounce the word. I inform them, however, that syllabication cannot guarantee "correct" pronunciation since I feel that there is not always such a thing as correct pronunciation. I usually give the following steps in using syllabication generalizations:

Tell the students to do the following:
1. Look for compound words.
2. Look for a prefix or suffix. Try to pronounce the word.
3. Look for a VCCV. If the word has a VCCV, divide it VC/CV and try to pronounce the word.
4. Look for a consonant-le. Try to pro-

nounce the word before the consonant and after the consonant.
5. Look for a VCV. Divide after the V/CV. If it doesn't sound right, divide after the VC/V.

These five steps are based on a priority of high to low degree of utility based on the various studies mentioned in this paper.

Syllabication generalizations can be useful in the hands of creative, knowledgeable teachers who understand that syllabication generalizations are only one of the tools that students can use to pronounce unfamiliar words. Students need to be taught to use their knowledge of syllabication generalizations when they meet an unfamiliar word in their reading. Students need to understand that the generalizations do not always work and that they (the students) should utilize a systematic approach when attempting to apply the generalizations.

The question that teachers need to ask themselves is a question that was asked of me as I tried to defend my rationale for not teaching the VCV generalizations, "Isn't a 40% help better than 0% help?"

REFERENCES

Anderson, Verna Dieckman. *Reading and Young Children*. New York: The Macmillan Co., 1968.
Bailey, Mildred. "The utility of phonic generalizations in grades one through six." *The Reading Teacher*, v. 20, 1967, pp. 413-418.
Betts, Emmett A. "Phonic: syllables," *Education*, v. 79, 1959, pp. 557-564.
Burmeister, Lou E. "Selected word analysis generalizations for a group approach to corrective reading in the secondary school." *Reading Research Quarterly*, v. 1, 1968, pp. 71-95.
Bush, Clifford L. and Huebner, Mildred H. *Strategies for reading in the elementary school*. New York: The Macmillan Co., 1970.

Clymer, Theodore. "The utility of phonic generalizations in the primary grades," *The Reading Teacher*, v. 16, 1963. pp. 252-258.
Cordts, Anna. *Phonics for the reading teacher*. New York: Holt, Rinehart & Winston, 1960.
DeBoer, John J., and Dallman, Martha. *The teaching of reading*. Holt, Rinehart & Winston, 1970.
Dechant, Emerald V. *Improving the teaching of reading*. Englewood Cliffs: Prentice-Hall, 1970.
Dolch, Edward. "Phonics and polysyllables," *Elementary English Review*, v. 15, 1938, pp. 120–124.
Dolch, Edward. "How a child sounds out a word," *Elementary English Review*, v. 22, 1945, pp. 275-280.
Durkin, Dolores. *Teaching them to read*. Boston: Allyn & Bacon, 1970.
Emans, Robert. "The usefulness of phonic generalizations above the primary grades," *The Reading Teacher*, v. 20, 1967, pp. 419-425.
Gray, William S. *On their own in reading*. Chicago: Scott, Foresman, 1960.
Groff, Patrick. *The syllable: its nature and pedagogical usefulness*. Portland: Northwest Regional Educ. Laboratory, 1971.
Hall, Robert. *Introductory linguistics*. Philadelphia: Chilton, 1964.
Jones, Daisy Marvel. *Teaching children to read*. New York: Harper & Row, 1971.
Jones, Daniel. *The pronunciation of English*. Cambridge: The University Press, 1950.
Kenyon, John Samuel. *American pronunciation*. Ann Arbor: George Wohr, 1928.
Lefevre, Carl A. *Linguistics and the teaching of reading*. New York: McGraw-Hill, 1964.
Lenneberg, Eric H. *Biological foundations of language*. New York: John Wiley & Sons, 1967.
Malone, Kemps. "Syllabication," *College English*, v. 18, 1957, pp. 202-205.
McFeely, Donald C. "Syllabication usefulness in a basal and social studies

vocabulary," *The Reading Teacher*, v. 27, 1974, pp. 809-814.

Oaks, Ruth E. "A study of vowel situations in a primary reading vocabulary," *Education*, v. 72, 1952, pp. 604-617.

Parker, Jessie Joe. "The utility of phonic generalizations and their application to the history and geography vocabularies in certain specified textbooks adopted for grades four, five, six," Unpublished doctoral dissertation, Louisiana State Univ. and Agriculture and Mechanical College, 1968, No. 68 16323.

What Do Teachers Know About Phonics

ALBERT J. MAZURKIEWICZ

In a replication and extension of Reid's study, Downing[1] reported that two words teachers often use in reading instructions, *word* and *sound*, were poorly understood by Scottish five year olds while Clay[2] found that New Zealand children had difficulty differentiating between letters and words. Based on classroom experiences with children and teachers, the author hypothesized that these findings might also be demonstrated among the U.S. children and that, if so, its cause might be traced to the teacher's lack of knowledge of the meanings of words she uses in instructing children. It would appear that if a teacher is unable to define and then use such terms as vowel, consonant, vowel sound, diphthong, digraph, glided, long, cluster or blend, syllable, etc., in identifying such elements in words and syllables, then the child to which that teacher is exposed has little other opportunity to learn such meanings. Spache[3] in his replication of Aaron's study[4] of teachers' knowledge of phonics indicated that "the extent to which teachers can and do teach their pupils various phonics and syllabication skills is, of course, dependent upon their own knowledge of the underlying principles and conventions." Aaron stated this slightly differently: "How much teachers know about these skills has a bearing upon the extent they teach them." Both studies confirmed the hypothesis that teachers had an inadequate knowledge of phonics and syllabication generalizations as they were then being taught while Ramsey's, Gagan's, and Schubert's studies[5,6,7] produced similar findings on tests they devised. It can be inferred that the teacher's lack of knowledge of phonic generalizations also indicates a lack of knowledge about accepted definitions of terms, but the inference is questionable.

To study the hypothesis that teachers do not know the meaning of words they use in instruction, the author devised a questionnaire which included each of the above terms and administered it during the first session of class to 118 experienced teachers (grades one thru six) in his three graduate classes in the Spring

From *Reading World*, Vol. 15 (March, 1975). © 1975 by the College Reading Association. Reprinted by permission.

TABLE I
Correct Responses to Definition of Terms
N = 118

Terms Defined	No. Correct	Percent Correct
Vowel	4	3.4
Consonant	7	5.9
Diphthong	9	7.6
Long vowel	6	5.1
Consonant blend	64	54.2
Digraph	47	39.8
Glided sound	1	.8
Syllable	17	14.4
Consonant cluster	5	4.2

of 1971. The responses were judged for adequacy using both dictionary definitions[8,9] and definitions found in reading texts.[10] A response was termed correct if it approximated the meaning found in any of the sources. Table I illustrates the results of this preliminary study. That this group of teachers did not know the meanings of terms used in teaching reading is self-evident from the data.

That this sample of teachers did not know the meanings of the most common terms, vowel and consonant, is indicated by the above results and the number (83 percent) who responded to the request to define the terms by listing the vowel or consonant letters, responding "I don't know" or giving no response. Some 53 percent (52.5) of this preliminary study group indicated they possessed low-level operational definitions of the term vowel by listing the vowel letters while 84.7 percent indicated essentially that "consonants were sounds which were not vowels."

The responses to "glided" and "consonant clusters," terms which have only recently come into vogue as replacement for the terms "long vowel" or "diphthongs" and "consonant blends," suggest that this sample of teachers either has developed only a slight understanding of these terms from the materials used in their classrooms or that materials which use this terminology are relatively scarce in the school districts in which these teachers work. Since little use of the terms is found in current texts or professional literature, little significance is attached to these low responses.

In any case, the low level of understanding by this sample of teachers, representative of 26 teacher training institutions in eleven states, of terms frequently used in teaching reading, suggests that elementary teachers as a whole might similarly lack such knowledge. If, in fact, we can generalize beyond this study, it would appear that elementary pupils cannot reasonably be expected to know the meaning of terms teachers use when teachers themselves indicate a state of ignorance. Certainly a working knowledge of such terminology is required of teachers who teach reading so that explanations to children can be unambiguous. Certainly if the child is required to recognize a syllable, know certain vowel or consonant letter-correspondences, or discriminate between digraphs and diphthongs, he should possess accurate definitions or adequate information to work from.

A follow-up study with this group of

teachers was done to refine a questionnaire for use in a larger study. This questionnaire was designed to obtain information on teachers' knowledge of the number of vowels and consonants in the alphabet and language, and 3 frequently used generalizations. Based on the above tabular information, three variations of each question on vowels and consonants, were established as shown below. The terms consonant, vowel sounds and consonant sounds were substituted for vowel and vowel letters in the general format of the questions noted below:

    Form A 1. How many vowels are there in the alphabet?
    Form B 1. How many vowels are there in the language?
    Form C 1. How many vowel letters are there in the alphabet?

to make up the second, sixth and seventh questions. This procedure was followed to determine the extent to which teachers (grade one thru six) discriminate between the words *vowels* and *consonants* as sounds, and *vowels* and *consonants* as letters. A random distribution of 39, 40, and 39 copies of each form of the questionnaire produced responses which indicated that the form of the question did not appreciably affect the quality or nature of the response. For example, in response to question one, the teachers in each group responded with 5, 5 plus, 5 plus *w* and *y*, 6, 7, 5 and sometimes *w* and *y*, in almost equal proportions (97.4, 95, 100) to each of the three versions. Interviews with respondents confirmed the hypothesis that these samples of teachers use the words vowel and vowels as synonymous with vowel letters and, at this level of questioning, seem unaffected by the use of the word *alphabet* as opposed to *language* in the question. Only when the question included the term *sounds* after either vowels or consonants did the teacher respond differently. This use of the terms *vowel* and *consonant* to denote letters is in contrast with dictionary and other definitions. It suggests that pupils' response to teacher questions could be affected by a lack of understanding of what responses the teacher desires since she seems to mean sounds when she uses the word letters and letters when sounds are called for. Certainly a gross lack of precision in the use of such terminology is indicated.

Since possession of a definition does not necessarily mean ability to apply it correctly, the researcher was interested in extending the scope of his study to include assessment of teacher's knowledge of certain generalizations, as well as her knowledge of certain phoneme-grapheme relationships. The questionnaire referred to above, which asked for the number of vowel and consonant sounds, vowel and consonant letters and the generalization teachers would use to teach the sound of the first vowel in *cake, road,* and *lady* was devised to assess the current state of teachers' knowledge. It was hypothesized that a sample of experienced teachers would know the number of vowel and consonant letters in the alphabet, but to lesser extent know the number of vowel and consonant sounds in the language and that some confusion between the two would be evident. It was further hypothesized that, despite the number of studies reported in the literature on the inadequacy of the generalizations taught to children, a sample of experienced teachers would have knowledge of the three most frequently used long vowel generalizations and little or no knowledge about their effectiveness or utility.

A "phonics competency examination" was also devised which assessed teacher's knowledge of a variety of consonant grapheme-phoneme correspondences as well as her ability to use prior knowledge of diphthongs, consonant blends, long and short vowels, etc. and to recognize the correct response among choices provided.

The Sample

A sample of 300 teachers from 26 school districts surrounding Kean College of N.J. in a 35 mile radius was selected by inviting teachers at grades Kindergarten through 6 to volunteer to participate in the study. It was noted at the outset that teachers at all seven grade levels exhibited insecurity about their knowledge of phonics and thus a record of the number of teachers indicating reservations about participation was made. Two hundred and nine of the 300 who were approached indicated reservations about participating in the study while 15% of those approached refused to participate.

Such comments as "I want to study phonics one of these days," "I'm not at all good at phonics," or "I need to go back to school to study phonics" were frequently offered as reasons for their refusal to participate even though the purpose of the study "to find out what teachers know about phonics" was explained as being helpful to the author and others in planning appropriate teacher-education courses or in-service education workshops and that anonymity of their responses was guaranteed. Although anonymity of the respondent would be normally followed, a high degree of concern that responses might be used against teachers in some way was voiced.

Of the original sample of 300, 252 teachers completed both the questionnaire and the phonic examination. Analysis of the responses indicated that this sample of teachers received reading instruction from faculty at 57 different teacher-training institutions but that 71 percent (178) received reading instruction by full-time and adjunct faculty at three local institutions: Jersey City State College, Paterson State College, Newark State College. Amounts of training varied from "reading was included in a language arts course" to a required six credits. Teacher experience in the grades K through 6 ranged from as little as one year to as much as 28 years.

Procedures & Results

The two instruments were administered sequentially, sometimes individually, sometimes in small groups. No coding of either instrument was done to eliminate the concern of teachers that somehow matching of the information on the questionnaire with the Examination results might in fact be traced to an individual and that the responses would reflect on that teacher's competency. Since accountability and reduction in force are current conditions of the profession, it is understandable that teachers would feel threatened but only if competency in this area was questionable or poor. While the data to be gathered might support such a conclusion, the inference that a large number of teachers feel inadequately prepared, or perceive themselves as having weaknesses of some considerable dimension, is inescapable.

1. Questionnaire data

Analysis of the results appears to confirm teachers' perception.

Table II, indicating the correct responses to the seven content items on the questionnaire indicates that teachers generally know the number of consonant and vowel letters in the alphabet but that a few are unsure of the number of vowel letters and a larger number do not know the number of consonant letters. Analysis of each teacher's responses indicated that no one recognized the letter *u* as being used to represent consonant and vowel sounds and that subtraction of 5, 6, or 7 from 26 to arrive at the number of consonant letters was generally practiced. While responses from 4 thru 7 for the number of vowel letters in the alphabet were deemed acceptable, fully 25 percent responded 5 to 6, or 6 to the question. Since logically if either *w* or *y* is considered a vowel, the other must be, some teachers either exclude one or the other. Interview information confirmed this and showed that teachers generally included *y* but excluded *w*. The protocol "Y represents /ie/ or /εε/" accurately describes teachers' reasoning for its inclusion and stands in marked contrast to professional text information on the

TABLE II
Correct responses to questions on letters, sounds, & generalizations
N = 252

Question	No. correct	Percent correct	"correct" responses
No. of vowel letters	248	98.4	4 thru 7
No. of consonant letters	237	94.0	19 thru 22
What procedure would you follow or how would you teach the sound of the 1st vowel in			
cake	198	78.6	e at end indicates 1st vowel is long
road	148	58.7	Two vowels together, 1st long
lady	56	22.2	Vowels in open syllables are long
No. of vowel sounds	127	50.4	11 to 24
No. of consonant sounds	94	37.3	23 or 24

function of *w* as a vowel letter. That no one indicated *u* as also a consonant is understandable since the literature generally ignores its duality in representing the consonant sound of *w*.

It would appear that teachers are aware of the three long vowel generalizations currently carried in professional texts[11] but to differing extents in each case. It should be noted that Aaron (and Spache) included these in his study as reflecting what was taught or carried in reading series to be taught and that Durkin's tests of phonics[12] had, until moving to out-of-print status, tested these. While only 22 percent of the sample use or would teach the discredited and wrong generalization "vowels in open syllables are long," an additional seven percent used a generalization ("the *y* at the end makes the preceding vowel long") which is questionable at best and the remainder of the sample would simply "tell the child the sound of the letter" or "didn't know."

While current research supports the use of the first generalization based on 83 percent utility,[13] some 21 percent of the sample seem to be unaware of its existence or have been led not to use it by earlier research. While less than 59 percent know and would use the generalization "two vowels together in a word, the first vowel is long" or some variation thereof, 41 percent would "tell the child the sound," "teach the spelling pattern as representing the sound /o/," or didn't know.

Interview information supports the inference that almost all of the teachers in this sample who did not use the generalization also did not know of the existence of the generalization and that no one of the teachers were aware of any of the research on the utility of the phonic generalizations.

The question on vowel sounds produced responses ranging from "5 through hundreds" with 25 percent of the sample responding "I don't know." Since disagreement among linguists exists on the answer to this question, sympathy for the teachers who responded "hundreds" can be expressed but since, in general, agreement exists within the span 11 to 24, it can be seen that almost 50 percent of the sample have either not been instructed, are unable to count the typical usage of five long, five short, /ou/, /oi/ and broad *a,* or are influenced to guess by the numbers of spelling patterns or graphemic options available to represent the sounds. This low knowledge or awareness of vowel sounds status is, however, somewhat better than that reflected in data on the awareness of the number of consonant sounds. Almost 63 percent indicated either no knowledge or gave responses which suggested that a subtraction of 5 (vowel letters) from 26, alphabet letters was being made.

Interview protocols only rarely indicated that "since dictionaries or reading experts couldn't agree, how am I supposed to know," but often indicated that "no instruction had been given," "We were never expected to learn them," or that "there are so many vowels that I can't begin to count them." Further inquiry, as a follow-up to the last statement when given, confirmed the earlier view that teachers confuse letters or graphemic options with sounds. Three percent of the sample were aware, however, of dialect or variations in pronunciation and reported this as the reason for not being able to indicate the number of vowels in the language.

2. Phonics Competency Examination
   a. Consonants

Using multiple choice technique, test items were constructed, tried and revised with successive small groups of teachers until satisfactory items were developed. A total of 45 items were included in the instrument, 11 items of which asked for a statement justifying the choice made. The item format for consonants was identical; a typical question was as follows:

Which word, (or words), has the "Hard C" sound?
a. cent
b. cycle
c. certain
d. city
e. none of these

Instructions included circling the letter of the answer considered correct and recording that letter in the space to the left of the question. Table three indicates the range of consonant information tested and the results from this sample.

Two consonant situations are deserving of specific discussion: Voiced (Hard) *C* and the sounds of *S*. While 90.5 percent of the sample of teachers identified the "hard *c*" in the initial position before *a, o,* and *u,* only 39.7 percent identified the "hard *c*" in cycle. This disparity in results suggests that the sample has relatively little difficulty in identifying the "hard *c*" in initial positions but may be inattentive to the use of a second *c* in a word, are inattentive to sounds inherent in words, use "rules" as though they apply to initial positions only, or have a limited knowledge of "hard *c*" as found in words.

The items $s = z$, zh, sh, and $s = s$, sh, zh, z show disparity in results which suggest that this sample of teachers, when confronted with the full range of sound choices that *s* represents are less able to recognize the four phonemes *s* represents or at any rate increase their error in choosing the correct response. Even so, less than half of the sample know the four sounds of *s*.

In terms of the consonant information tested, it cannot be stated otherwise than that this sample of teachers do not exhibit much in the way of knowledge of

TABLE III
Correct Responses: Consonant Phonic Knowledge
N = 252

Content of Question	Percentage Correct
Hard c (Initial and medial position)	65.1
Hard g	82.5
voiceless th (none present)	68.3
Voiced th	49.2
Silent Consonant (Bell)	52.4
S = /z/, /zh/ and /sh/	49.2
ch and c = /sh/ and /k/	61.9
x = /k/	33.3
qu = /kw/	87.3
ch = /tsh/, /sh/, /k/	49.2
s = /s/, /sh/, /zh/, /z/	41.3
bl = 2 sounds among ch, sh, and z spellings	38.1
Identification of consonant clusters	50.8
4 spellings of the /sh/ sound	95.7
4 spellings of the /zh/ sound	76.2
x represents two sounds	66.7

consonant sound information or, at least on this instrument, are unable to apply whatever knowledge they have to identifying words or spelling patterns which represent the range of information available about consonant grapheme-phoneme relationships.

b. Vowels

Knowledge of vowels and their grapheme options were tested by several different forms of items. In addition to the use of multiple choices, 14 items followed the pattern: "on each of the following, all of the words or letters belong together, or one word doesn't belong." Ten of these items also asked for "the reason for the choice" to sample teachers' thinking and/or knowledge. Another six items used the pattern: "one word in each group doesn't belong. Write the word and indicate the reason for your choice." Three items among those testing vowel knowledge were designed to test the respondent's knowledge of the diphthongal nature of "long" vowels.

Table IV indicates the results obtained from those items which tested vowel knowledge as reflected by instruction which classifies vowels as long, short or diphthongal and excludes *i* and *u* spellings as representing diphthongs. At this level of instruction the use of a question which includes the word *child* as representative of a diphthong would be incorrect; however, an attempt to determine whether teachers can apply a definition of diphthong to such a word was of value in that it allowed contrast with a following item where the typical *oi* as in *spoil* was used. The difference in "cor-

TABLE IV
Correct responses: Vowel Phonic Knowledge
N = 252

Question	Percentage correct
1. a before r	76.2
2. long o in nonsense syllables	44.4
3. long o in real syllables	71.4
4. long o in real words	90.5
5. short e	79.7
6. Definition of diphthong	27.0
7. Identification of child as diphthong /i/	17.5
8. Identification of spoil as diphthong	55.6
9. short e among long e spellings	73.0 and 97.9% correctly stated the reason for choice.
10. four diphthongs or long vowels	39.7 and 91.3% correctly stated the reason for choice.
11. four spellings of ō	76.2 and 97.9% correctly stated the reason for choice.
12. four spellings of ē	95.2 and 88.3% correctly stated the reason for choice.
13. four spellings for schwa sound	33.3 and 50.0% correctly stated the reason for choice.
14. broad a among short vowels	76.2 and 79.2% correctly stated the reason for choice.
15. oi diphthong among long vowels	55.6 and 91.4% correctly stated the reason for choice.

rect'' responses on these two items (17.5 and 55.6) while indicating the low level of teachers' knowledge of diphthongs also suggests that some teachers comprehend and apply a diphthong definition which reading textbooks rarely cite or discuss.

As can be seen in items 2, 3, 4, this sample is most capable of identifying the "long o" in real words, but less capable in real syllables and least capable in nonsense syllables. The 44.4 percent correct response to "long o" when nonsense syllables are used to test phonic knowledge suggests that almost 56 percent of this sample have little real knowledge of the graphemic environment effects on the nature of the vowel sound.

Item 13, testing the schwa sound, which used the words *above, the, kingdom,* and *April* suggest this sample's understanding as reflected in typical instruction yet, at the same time, the item must be questioned for use since 42.9

ISSUES

percent chose *April* as indicating no schwa sound. Since the variant pronunciation of *April* with the "short i" exists, it's reasonable to conclude that a large number of teachers used this pronunciation. Yet, analysis of the reasons for the choice indicated that only 50 percent of this sample knew why they had chosen the word. On this basis it seems more reasonable to conclude that knowledge of the schwa sound is not very high.

While the percentage correct responses on items one thru fifteen are generally higher than those indicated for consonants, teachers in this sample do not demonstrate more than a moderate level of competence. Protocols for choices, but particularly among incorrect responses, indicate a high level of ambiguity and little to allow confidence that the child receiving instruction would obtain explanations which would be of much help in forming "rules" for further decoding use.

Protocols Analyzed

Items 40 and 41, not included in the above information on consonants were reserved for examination here to illustrate both teacher knowledge and their explanations. Items 40 and 41 were included in the group of items where the directions were: "One of the words in each question doesn't belong. Circle the correct choice and justify your choice below the question." Item 40 included the choices *ph*one, *s*ure, *e*xit, thou*gh* and, as noted, the teacher's attention was focused by underlining on the given graphemes representing sounds. While 66.7 percent correctly chose the word *exit*, only 23.8 percent knew why. Incorrect protocols from those choosing *exit* included:

x is not a digraph (5.4 percent responded thusly)

x is not a diphthong (2.9 percent responded thusly)

x is not a glide

x is not two sounds

x is one letter–one sound (10.8 percent responded thusly)

x is not a blend sound

x because all other spellings indicate sounds of blends. (10.8 percent)

Based on the above, it would appear that teachers have memorized certain spelling patterns as representing digraphs, blends and diphthongs, and do not really understand what these terms mean. This appears to confirm the data reported in study one (Table I) but also suggests that a significant number are unaware of sounds x represents.

Item 41 included the choices *th*ink, *p*hoto, *s*hould, and *ch*ild. The correct choice *child* should have been based on a knowledge that this pattern represented two sounds. While 14.3 percent chose *child* correctly, only 1.6 percent knew why. Protocols, however, included, "*ch* harsher than others," "*ch* not a digraph." While it can be argued that the item is unfair since few professional texts carry the information that *ch* represents two sounds in words like *child* (*chill, chew,* etc.) and that therefore this information would most probably not be communicated to teachers in training, of more interest is the fact that 60.3 percent chose *photo* wrongly, that 18 percent indicated it was not a blend, and 8 percent indicated it was not a digraph. The inference in the first case is that *th, sh,* and *ch* are blends and, in the second, are digraphs. The inference that teachers have an inadequate understanding of terms used in teaching reading is inescapable.

Among the choices is item 44, *time, tame, note* and *mete,* no one who chose *child* as representing a diphthong chose time correctly as the only diphthong (Level one of understanding) while 4.8 percent chose *note* correctly (Level 2 understanding where long o is considered the purest of vowels) but no one knew why. Of more interest, however, was the fact that 65.1 percent chose *mete* with 12.2 percent indicating that "there is no such word," 4.7 percent indicating that "the final vowel was heard," and 8.4 indicating that "it didn't follow the silent e rule."

Conclusions and Implications

Based on the results of this study and within its limitations, but particularly of teacher sample, the conclusions that teachers have an inadequate knowledge of terms used in reading and a low level of ability to apply them to words typically found in reading materials seem evident. Moreover, the conclusion that teachers exhibit a low level of phonic knowledge as this was measured by the phonic competency examination is warrantable and, more than 10 years later, confirms findings of other studies which used more restricted measures. Since teachers used such terms as glides, diphthongs and long vowels to describe the same sounds, it would appear that instruction they received has varied but also that some learning can be attributed to the teacher's guides and/or materials they use in instruction. Weaknesses not only include a lack of knowledge of the consonant and vowel letters, but also the vowel and consonant sounds, phonic knowledge as reflected in generalizations, phoneme-grapheme correspondences and graphemic options for phonemes.

Implications for teacher or in-service training include not only a need for specific instruction but also for insuring competency, and a clarity in definition of terms. Of major concern should be an attempt to orient teachers to the sounds symbols represent so as to reduce their strong tendency to think and respond about symbols in visual terms.

REFERENCES

1. Downing, John. "Children's Concepts of language in learning to read," *Educational Research,* 1970, 12, 106-112.
2. Clay, M. "Emergent Reading Behavior," unpublished doctoral dissertation, University of Auckland, Auckland, New Zealand, 1966, (Reviewed by Samuel Weintrank in *The Reading Teacher,* 1968, 22, 63-67.)
3. Spache, George D. and Bagget, May E. "What do teachers know about Phonics and Syllabication?" *The Reading Teacher,* 1965, 99.
4. Aaron, Ira. "What Teachers and Prospective Teachers know about Phonic Generalizations." *Journal of Educational Research,* 1960, 530, 323-330.
5. Ramsey, Z. Wallace. "Will Tomorrow's Teachers know and Teach Phonics?" *The Reading Teacher,* 1962, 15, 241-245.
6. Gagan, Glen Scott. "A Diagnostic Study of the Phonics Ability of Elementary Teachers in the State of Utah." Doctoral Dissertation, Colorado State College, 1960.
7. Schubert, Delwyn G. "Teachers and Word Analysis Skills," *Journal of Developmental Reading,* 1959, 2, 62-64.
8. Stein, Jesse. *The Random House Dictionary.* New York: Random House, Inc. 1967.
9. Schubert, Delwyn G. *A Dictionary of Terms and Concepts in Reading,* Springfield, Illinois: Charles C. Thomas, 1964.
10. Betts, Emmett A. *Foundations of Reading Instruction,* New York: American Book Co., 1950.
11. Fry, Edward. *Reading Instruction for Classroom and Clinic.* New York: McGraw Hill Book Co., 1972.
12. Durkin, Dolores. *Phonics Test for Teachers and Phonics Knowledge Survey.* New York: Teacher College Press, 1964.
13. Mazurkiewicz, Albert J. "The Diacritic e" *The Reading World,* 1974, 14.

What the Professor Doesn't Know About Phonics Can Hurt!

ALBERT J. MAZURKIEWICZ

In a recent study, Mazurkiewicz (1975) demonstrated that classroom teachers K-6 had an inadequate understanding of terms used in reading instruction as well as a low level of ability to apply them to words typically found in reading materials. Moreover, he demonstrated that as a group they lacked a knowledge not only of the consonant and vowel letters in the alphabet but also the vowel and consonant sounds in the language, phonic knowledge as reflected in generalizations, phoneme-grapheme correspondences and graphemic options used to represent phonemes. The conclusion that some of this weakness was attributable to the nature of their pre-service education experiences was supported by verbal statements volunteered by a number of teachers. This latter conclusion suggests that the Austin-Coleman (1963) finding that teachers felt (because of the brevity of the course) that they were "provided with only a superficial knowledge of phonic principles and their application" may still be somewhat valid.

It is also true that an examination of instructional materials for in-service instruction and textbooks for pre-service instruction allows the recognition that research findings since 1963 have had relatively little impact on the field, are given scant attention, are contradicted in terms of illustration or exercises, or that rules and generalizations are provided for instructional purposes which are contraindicated by research. Further, a lack of clarity of definitions and meagreness of information on phonics characterize most textbook materials. While it might be inferred that some teacher inadequacy is also related to pre-service and in-service instructional materials, it might also be conjectured that teacher inadequacy cannot be wholly blamed on these since college instructors would responsibly add to, edit, and instruct to provide teachers-to-be with correct information, and in turn, newer teachers would edit instructional materials so as to eliminate inadequacies they meet rather than be influenced by repetitive use to accept and internalize inadequate if not incorrect information.

As suggested above, a number of lines of investigation are possible in any attempt to account for classroom teacher inadequacy in the decoding area of reading instruction: the elements of pre-service training, the degree of competency, if any, achieved, the influences of textbook material on that which is known, the influence of professorial instruction, the nature of the material provided by the professor, the influence of teacher's reading of research, etc.

Hypotheses

Of first priority, it appeared to me, would be an investigation of what the college-university instructor knows about phonics, the priority he/she places on learning various elements, his/her definitions of terms and their adequacy, the degree to which he/she insures competency, his/her view of the adequacy of

From *Reading World*, Vol. 14 (December, 1975). © 1975 by the College Reading Association. Reprinted by permission.

the materials used, his/her editing of them, etc. It was hypothesized that college-university professors would generally agree
   1. on the definitions of terms most frequently used in reading instruction
   2. on the number of consonant and vowel letters in the alphabet
   3. on the number of consonant and vowel sounds in the language, and
   4. on the identification of graphemes used to represent such elements on blends, digraphs, diphthongs, long and short vowels.

It was further hypothesized that professors would exhibit a high degree of sophistication about the English language and exhibit knowledge based on wide reading across the field.

Instruments

To meet the purposes of the study, a questionnaire was devised which was based wholly on information supplied in reading texts since 1968. The questionnaire, made up of several sections, was designed to develop data not only on definitions of terms, but whether an instructor used or expected teachers-to-be to know certain terms, his/her knowledge of the graphemes which illustrated his/her use of the terms, the priority placed on certain types of information, his/her view of the adequacy of texts used, etc. In this report only the data relating to his/her phonic knowledge are utilized, with the remainder deferred for later treatment. A phonics competency examination was also developed for use with this population. It was designed to serve as a check on the consistency with which instructors responded from one type of instrument to the next.

Since the purposes of the study were to be hidden as much as possible, a letter inviting colleagues to participate in the study was couched in general terms and the invitation indicated that on completion of the first questionnaire a validation study of a phonics competency examination would be sent for completion as a second part of the study.

Sample

To meet the purposes of the study, and to allow for generalization, a random sample of the identifiable professors teaching reading in the colleges and universities of the nation was established as most viable. To develop the population, two mailing lists used by publishers for mailings of text information were purchased with duplicate names culled to create one composite list. Additionally the teacher education membership list of the College Reading Association was obtained to add to the list, again with duplications eliminated. A composite list of 2482 identifiable professors of reading in the 50 states was thus created. To insure that the list was largely complete, invitational letters which went to a twelve percent (298) random sample of the population asked also that colleagues be invited to participate in the study and to list their names. The additional names provided were then checked against the composite list to determine the adequacy of the list. Since only seven percent of the additional names provided were not found on the composite list, it was concluded that the list was to a great extent representative of the whole population, that as little as 6 percent of the original 12 percent random sample would adequately reflect the total and the responses of those instructors who additionally volunteered to participate at each institution could be used as a subsample to check on the findings from the sample. A provision to extend the invitation to 20 percent of the sample was found needless since 74.5% (222) of the random sample agreed to participate and completed the questionnaire to varying degrees within the time limits provided. It has been feared that, as with most questionnaire studies, only a small percentage of the sample would respond favorably and that a lesser number would complete the questionnaire since in this case the questionnaire would prove to be an onerous task. Although 87.6% (261) of the invitees agreed to participate, 13.1% did not return the questionnaire. An 8.9% sample, however, of the total population was available for study and, within the constraints of questionnaire studies, seemed more than adequate.

Since the initial questionnaire was a long one, it's surprising that a larger percentage of non-returnees did not materialize. The large number of responses almost seems suspect until one recognized that many felt that responding to the questionnaire was a unique learning experience, that some professors discussed the study with others not invited (a possible source of contamination) and generated interest to the point that non-invitees felt left out and asked to be included in the study and that still others, while questioning the purpose of the study and guessing (wrongly to a large extent) about its purpose, felt professionally committed to participate having accepted the invitation.

The study was undertaken in October and November, 1974, and completed questionnaires accepted thru March, 1975. As each response to the invitation was received, a coded questionnaire was mailed to insure confidentiality of the responses and to allow for mailings of the validation instrument on receipt of a coded response since no names were to be attached to the questionnaire itself. Some individuals chose to abrogate this confidentiality procedure by signing their name, others attempted to completely hide their identification by cutting off the code number. Comments accompanying returned questionnaires, partially or wholly completed, indicated that a large percentage of the sample felt threatened by the questions posed, were unsure of answers, sought refuge in quoting texts or indicated some answers were checked in texts or dictionaries. Some comments were caustic while others sought information about the sources for correct responses to the questions.

Of the 222 responding educators, 61.7 percent held a Ph.D. or Ed.D., 26.1 percent held an M.A. and 3.2 percent the B.A., while the status of 9 percent is unknown since the information was not supplied. Teaching experience ranged from as little as one year to as much as 45 years and at the college or university level from one year to thirty years.

Determining Adequacy of Responses

Since dialect differences in the nation could cause responses to differ, Kenyon and Knott's (1953) *A Pronouncing Dictionary of American English* was used as a basic source book while information on the etymology of words was sought in the *Oxford English Dictionary* (1971). Reported research of Clymer, Bailey, Emans, Burmeister, Mazurkiewicz, Venezky, Groff, Berdianky, *et al.,* and usages of terms such as glided and unglided related to the work of Shuy, were utilized as the basis for testing the adequacy of responses. Definitions of terms were judged adequate when no contradiction existed between the definition and any illustrations given as well as when the definition agreed with an accepted form as found in dictionaries. Illustration of a vowel by listing vowel letters rather than giving a definition was rejected as inadequate, for example, as was a definition of a digraph which referred to a unique sound, a special sound, etc. since there is nothing unique about the sounds of English. To avoid undue repetitions additional information by which adequacy is judged is found in the discussion following each question or item sampled.

Results and Findings

1. What do you teach about the number of vowel letters in the alphabet?
   a. nothing – 24.6%

b. that there are 5 to 9 vowel letters – 73.0%
   a, e, i, o, u – 23.72%
   a, e, i, o, u/y – 18.64%
   a, e, i, o, u/y, w – 54.25%
   a, e, i, o, u/y, w, l – 1.7%
   a, e, i, o, u/y, w, h, r – 1.7%

While at first glance it would appear that number of vowel letters is so obvious based on past experience that teachers would not need to be taught this, fully 73% of the sample find this of some importance.

In examining the responses to the question "What do you teach about the number of vowel letters in the alphabet in comparison to the number of vowel sounds in the language (q. 4), it can be readily seen that a significantly larger number of professors (73.0%) believe the letters representing vowel sounds are more important to teach than they (37.8%) do the number of vowel phonemes.

While it can be conjectured that professors find more certainty about the number of the vowel letters in the alphabet and therefore teach this characteristic of the orthography, it can readily be seen from the data that professors do not agree on that number. Over three percent add "sometimes" "l" or "h and r" besides "y and w" to a, e, i, o, and u. A degree of linguistic sophistication is suggested in these responses since the semi-vowels as identified by phoneticians are included for instruction by this group. It can also be seen that over fifty-four percent of the sample teach *a, e, i, o, u* and sometimes *y* and *w*, that almost 19 percent would reject *w* but include *y* and that almost 24 percent reject both *y* and *w*.

Since data exists to indicate that *u* is used as a vowel only about 92% of the time, that *y* is used as a vowel some 97 percent of the time, and *i* is used as a vowel 85-86% of the time, it can be demonstrated that all of the population is teaching partially erroneous information while about 77 percent are clearly in error. The conclusions that "traditional wisdom" to some extent is utilized in instruction, that relatively few professors have modified their instructional informational bank as a result of research evidence accumulated in the last twenty years, and, perhaps, that the largest majority of professors are not even aware of such information seem possible.

2. Based on the above, what do you teach about the numbers of consonant letters?
   a. nothing – 36.4%
   b. that there are _____ consonant letters in the alphabet. – 56.8%
      19 – 16.7%
      20 – 11.9%
      21 – 71.4%
   c. no response – 6.8%

Based on the above, it can be seen that fewer professors teach the number of consonant letters than teach vowel letters. A high degree of consistency in teaching that certain letters are sometimes consonants if they are also identified as sometimes vowels was shown by making an item analysis of the responses.

It might be conjectured that fewer professors feel the need to specify a number in regard to consonants on the basis that simple subtraction would provide the information, but it can be concluded that more than half of the sample find some value in providing the data.

3. What do you teach about the number of sounds or phonemes in American English?
   a. nothing – 20.3%
   b. that there are _____ sounds in the language. – 74.3%
      32-44   1.82%
      35   1.82%
      35 to 44   7.27%
      38   1.82%
      39   1.82%
      40   3.64%
      40 +   1.82%

ISSUES

40-41	1.82%
41	0
43	1.82%
44	52.72%
44 +	3.64%
46	3.64%
48	1.82%
50 +	1.82%
more sounds than letters	3.64%
at least 44 but as many as 47	1.82%
numerous, many, indefinite, etc.	7.27%

c. no response – 5.4%

The data shows that almost three fourths (74.3%) of the sample teach that there are at least 32 and as many as an indefinite number of sounds in American English. While more than half (52.7%) of this subsample teach that there are 44 sounds or phonemes, a wide variety of information is supplied to teachers at the graduate and undergraduate levels. Although a few indicate that this or that linguist indicates 46, each of these teach only 44, apparently in agreement with the sound base used by typical collegiate dictionaries. Over 11 percent use terminology which allows for no specific number and is, at best, misleading if the function of phonics relates primarily to the grade levels K thru 3 or 4. Although alphabeteers such as Pitman, Malone, Dewey, Goldman-Lynch, etc. have utilized a 39 or 40 sound base for their instructional purposes, little better than 5 percent (5.5) of the subsample indicate an agreement with these usages, though more choose 40 than 39. It would appear that the largest number are in agreement with the 44 sound base found in typical collegiate dictionaries but no information is available to indicate the degree of consistency between the two.

4. What do you teach about the number of vowel sounds or phonemes in American English?
a. nothing – 52.7%
b. 10 – 20 – 37.8%

10	– 3.57%
11	– 3.57%
13	– 14.29%
15	– 3.57%
16	– 10.71%
17	– 10.71%
19	– 7.14%
20	– 3.57%
20 +	– 42.86%

Although Kenyon and Knott indicate that there are 22 vowel sounds in speech and it can be shown that most dictionaries identify 20, less than five percent of the sample indicated that they teach the number 20 while almost 43 percent indicate that there are more than 20. Since Kenyon and Knott identify 3 variations of u before r in the first syllable of *further* and distinguish between short u and schwa, all of which could be discarded since other linguists do not identify these differences, or discriminate only by way of accent for the short u as opposed to the schwa, a reduction to 18 vowel sounds is possible. Surprisingly, no one chose this number as something they teach. When one notes that Kenyon and Knott identify another phoneme between the *a* of *ah* and the *aw* of *jaw* as being found in w*a*tch which most others identify as either the *a* in *ah* or the *o* in *pot* and further note that Kenyon and Knott also identify one additional *a* sound as being between the *a* in *sang* and the *a* in *ah* and presumably spoken by some easterners in the word *bath*, we recognize the phonetician at work but can also recognize that few of us untutored to this degree discriminate these two intermediate sounds. While we can thus reduce to a 16 vowel sound base what needs to be taught, less than 11 percent of this sample teach that number.

Since the range of responses varies from 10 to 20+ with a concentration at more than 20, one wonders about these extremes. At the lower end, 10, it can be inferred that the response related to the addition of 5 "short" and 5 "long" while at the other extreme, 20+, that this response is related more to a recognition of dialect differences than to real knowledge about the number of vowel phonemes in the language since only a small percentage of the population showed a high degree of sophistication about the sound-symbol correspondence, etc. in the language. While these might be correct inferences, there is no external evidence to support them and must be discarded in favor of the generalization that a wide range of information, some of it questionable, is supplied teachers-to-be as to the number of vowel phonemes in the language by about forty percent of the total sample.

5. As opposed to vowel sounds, what do you teach about the number of consonant sounds in English?
   a. nothing – 55.4%
   b. 21-27+ – 33.8%
      21-   – 8.0%
      22-   – 4.0%
      23-   – 0%
      24-   – 28.0%
      25-   – 2.7%
      26-   – 5.3%
      27-   – 13.3%
      27+   – 30.7%
   c. N.R.   – 13.5%

Although Kenyon and Knott, for example, identify 28 consonants, three of which are identified as two sounds, /hw/, /tʃh/, and /dʒ/, they also add syllabic l, m, and n which most often are identified as containing the reduced schwa and thus also represent two sounds. Technically, therefore, only 22 consonant sounds are reflected in speech. It is also true that some linguists do not discriminate the voiced and voiceless th, indicating that one is the allophone of the other. On this basis, we could identify 21 consonant sounds. However, most do discriminate these two sounds and most will add /tʃh/, and /dʒ/ to the sound system for a total of 24. Despite the confirmation of this as found in most dictionaries, of the 23.8 percent who indicated that they teach the number of consonant sounds, 72 percent indicated that they teach that there are more or less than 24 consonant sounds with more opting for 27+ (30.7 percent) than any other number provided. While four percent indicated that there were 21 consonant sounds, 28 percent chose the number 24 in agreement not only with typical dictionary phonetics but also with the number typically taught in decoding programs.

If that which the teachers will deal with is the raison d'etre for any element in instruction about decoding, only this 28 percent can be deemed correct.

But of interest also is the fact that 9.5 percent indicated that there were 44 sounds in English and then proceeded to supply numbers of vowels and consonant sounds which either added up to more or to less than 44. It appeared also that a few simply subtracted 5 (vowel letters) from 26 to arrive at the number 21 for an answer to the question about the number of consonant sounds in the language since, again, their total did not agree with the supplied total.

Certainly there is a wide margin of difference in what professors teach about the number of consonant sounds. It seems evident, too, that most who do provide this information, teach or use numbers which are misleading in relation to the reality of decoding materials or dictionary usage.

6. Do you teach or discuss the term digraph?
   yes – 89.2%
   no – 6.8%
   N.R. – 4.1%

Although a slightly smaller percentage of the sample teach or use the term digraph (as opposed to 91.9 percent teaching or using the term diphthongs, 90.5 percent long vowels and 91.2 percent

ISSUES

short vowels), no implication of a trend to avoid the term is suggested. It seems as important in teaching reading as do the others.

7. Which of the following do you identify as digraphs?
   th   –   100%
   oa   –   68.6%
   ph   –   82.9%
   ch   –   100%
   N.R. –   6.2%
   ee   –   64.3%
   sh   –   91.4%
   ai   –   65.7%
   gh   –   77.1%

While 10.9 percent indicated either no response or that they did not teach or use the term, almost half of this same group chose to identify what they understood the term to mean by identifying digraphs in item seven. When two separate analyses, with and without this group's information, were made, so little difference in the results was obtained that both sets of responses were combined as one.

It can be seen, that a large part of the sample identify both consonant and vowel digraphs but that only two (*th* & *ch*) are universally identified as digraphs. Of the four consonant digraphs most often identified in the literature (*ph, sh, th, ch*) and in reading programs, *ph* is least often identified by the sample and *sh* next least often. It would appear that the term digraph is somewhat confusing to professors since neither *sh* or *gh* can be excluded if *ch* and *th* are so identified since *th* represents two phonemes, *ch* represents three and is also silent while *sh* and *ph* consistently represent only one phoneme.

No attempt to justify the varying percentages indicated for vowel digraphs can be made since there is no basis in the literature to justify one more than another. Rather, we can conclude by examining individual responses that personal knowledge or lack of it is operational.

The addition of *nk* and *ng* by a number of respondents to the list of digraphs (among several others) is interesting in that none also added *nc, nx* or *nq* as of a similar value to *nk* and that over 11 percent (11.4) of the sample apparently extend the meaning of "digraph as representing one sound" to include *nk* which represents two. This is in direct contrast to many of the respondent's definitions which do not allow for a two-sound contingency. The results suggest inattention to correspondences of symbol-sound, inadequate knowledge or even a lack of understanding of the definition used.

While a number of texts and/or materials do identify *ng* as a digraph as identified by 17.1 percent of the sample, only 5.5 percent appeared to be aware that this was true only in short words ending in *ng* and, by convention, their derivations. It might be noted (as an aside) that *n* before *c, k, x, q,* and *g* usually represents the /ŋ/ sound, that *g* is morpho-phonemic, acts as a diacritic before and after *n,* and that both Random House and Webster's Unabridged identify n = ŋ in *finger, anxious, anklet, Lincoln, single, conquer,* etc.

8. Do you discuss or teach the term diphthong?
   yes – 91.9%
   no – 5.4%
   N.R. – 2.7%

9. Which of the following do you identify as containing diphthongs?
   day   – 17.6%
   see   – 7.4%
   out   – 94.1%
   go   – 8.8%
   shout – 17.6%
   ice   – 11.8%
   oil   – 98.5%
   use   – 10.3%
   arm   – 10.3%
   put   – 0.0%
   chill – 1.5%
   mother – 4.4%

120

Although about 92 percent of the sample indicate that they teach or use the term diphthong, 10.3 percent of this portion of the sample appear also to use the term interchangeably with the term glided as seen later. However, the data shows that neither *out* or *oil* are identified consistently as representative of diphthongs and that all words but *put* are identified as containing elements which are representative of diphthongs. Since 1.5 percent of the sample indicate a knowledge of the existence of vowel *and* consonant diphthongs earlier, it's not surprising that *ch*ill is identified by 1.5 percent as containing a diphthong. While it can be conjectured that some portion of the sample of 4.4 percent are identifying the *er* in *mother* as the "murmuring diphthong" as used by some writers, no confidence can be placed in the conjecture since there is no evidence in the questionnaire to support it. It can be seen, however, that from 10 to 17 percent of the group are correctly identifying diphthongs in *day, shoot,* and *ice* while 10.3 percent are erroneously indicating a diphthong is found in *arm*. This last is considered an error since none of the linguistic, phonic, or other such material examined supports such an identification. It can be seen that only a small percentage of the sample identify the vowels in *ice* and *use* as diphthongs and that this contrasts with what is more typically held.

We can conclude that this sample most nearly follows the older notion that only *oi* and *ou* are diphthongs but that not all are able to identify correctly even these two, that end of syllable vowels are inconsistently identified as diphthongs and that a large number (17.6%) hold that *oo* in *shoot* is a diphthong. Since some authors do state that *oo* as in *shoot* is a glided vowel, there is some justification for this choice.

The overall findings here support the conclusion that the sample identify diphthongs inconsistent with either the glided, long vowel or diphthongal schools of usage. In fact, error predominates.

10. Do you use the term long vowels?
 yes – 90.5%
 no – 5.4%
 N.R. – 4.1%

11. What do you identify as long vowels?
 cake – 98.5%
 red – 0
 seal – 89.6%
 now – 1.5%
 road – 88.1%
 good – 0
 use – 95.5%
 arm – 0
 ice – 97.0%
 short – 3.0%

Although over 90 percent of the sample teach or use the term long vowel, no one of the vowels usually designated as long was identified in this fashion by 100% of the sample while /εε/ and /œ/ were identified less frequently than /ue/ or /ie/—the two vowels most often identified as diphthongs in teacher texts. Had /ue/ and /ie/ been identified less than the others, it could be inferred that their diphthongal usage accounted for their being identified to a lesser extent. Instead it must be concluded that over 11 percent of the sample have difficulty in identifying all of the long vowel sounds and that 1.5 percent are unable to identify that the word *cake* contains the long *a*.

The minor identification of *now* and *short* as containing long vowels might suggest additional difficulty but since the word *short* is pronounced with the long *o* in some dialects, the conclusion is not wholly tenable. However, the word *now* is not shown to have a pronunciation of /œ/ by Kenyon and Knott and this does suggest some incomplete knowledge of the meaning of the term *long vowel*.

12. Do you discuss short vowel sounds?
 yes – 91.9%
 no – 3.15%

13. What do you identify as the short vowel sounds?
    - man – 100%
    - ride – 0.0%
    - get – 100%
    - but – 100%
    - shoe – 4.4%
    - should – 8.8%
    - farm – 5.9%
    - know – 2.9%
    - fell – 0.0%
    - use – 55.0%
    - no – 45.0%
    - day – 55.0%
    - seed – 45.0%
    - stop – 5.0%
    - wood – 5.0%
    - shoe – 20.0%
    - art – 5.0%
    - out – 40.0%
    - cap – 0.0%
    - cup – 0.0%
    - boil – 50.0%
    - her – 0.0%

While 91.9 percent indicate that they discuss short vowels, less than 9 percent (8.8) identify *ou* in *should* as short, while 4.4 identify *oe* in *shoe* and 2.9 percent identify *ow* in *know* as short. Since /ω/ in *should, wolf, wood* and *put* is always classified as short, in contrast to /ω/ in *food* as long, in the classification system of long, short, broad, and diphthongal, it appears that some 82 percent of the sample are unaware of this or at least are in error in identifying the short vowels. Some confusion also exists in a small portion of the sample in the classification of /ω/ and /œ/. In the classification system of short, long, broad, and diphthongal, broad is not considered short and thus the 2.9 percent who identified the *a* in *farm* as short are also in error.

It can be concluded that while a small portion of the sample exhibit serious error in identifying long or broad vowels as short, most of the sample exhibit difficulty in application of the term short to one fourth of the short vowels exhibited.

14. Do you teach the terms glided or unglided?
    - yes – 27.02%
    - no – 71.62%
    - N.R. – 1.35%

15. What do you identify as the glided sounds?
    - side – 55.0%
    - born – 10.0%

The term glided, used or taught by only 27 percent of the sample, appears to be used interchangeably with the term diphthong by 35% of the sample since each of these identify *oi* and *ou* as both diphthongs and glided vowels. 20 percent appear to be using the term similarly to that of Ruddell, Clymer, and Shuy (Ginn 360) but do not appear to have grasped its meaning well since they do not identify all of the words containing vowels which ordinarily are considered glided and others identify unglided sounds as glided. It can be concluded that the term glided to identify the so called long vowels and diphthongs has not found acceptance in the field as yet and that those who use the term are largely confused about its usage, referring mostly to the vowels /ie/, /ue/, /ae/, /oi/ as glided, to a lesser extent to /œ/, /εε/ and /au/, and to /ω/ least often. Error in identification also exists.

16. Do you discuss or teach phonic generalizations?
    - yes – 90.5%
    - no – 6.8%
    - N.R. – 2.7%

The data speak for themselves as to the relative importance professors of reading place on discussing or teaching phonic generalizations but, as can be seen in the responses to question 17, a high degree of erroneous information is apparently supplied.

Although as seen in item 16, 9.5% of the sample did not respond or indicated they did not discuss or teach phonic generalizations, a larger number of the sample as seen in the data for question 17 did not respond to certain items and some of the 9.5 percent chose to respond to question seventeen ignoring the instruction to skip the item. It appeared that the wording of the question which related to *teach or expect students to know* attracted respondents despite the direction and thus it seemed desirable that all of the data be utilized for analysis. A subsequent analysis of the responses only from those who indicate they teach phonic generalizations merely

17. Which of the following generalizations do you teach or expect students to know?

	Yes	No	No Response
a. Vowels in open syllables are usually long.	N 78.38	14.86	6.76
b. The final e in short words is usually silent and indicates that the first vowel is long.	Y 83.8	8.1	8.1
c. When there are two vowels together in a word, the first is usually long and the second silent.	N 63.51	28.4	8.1
d. Vowels in closed syllables are usually short.	Y 77.0	14.9	8.1
e. Vowels in open syllables are usually short.	Y 8.1	79.7	12.2
f. Vowels in open syllables are long and short, try the short sound first.	Y 10.8	77.0	12.2
g. Vowels in closed syllables may be short or long, try the short sound first.	Y 47.4	39.2	13.5
h. The *e* at the end of a word is a diacritic (signal or marker) which is usually silent and indicates a change from the expected in the preceding consonant or vowel.	Y 37.84	48.65	13.50
i. C before e, i and y is usually soft.	Y 82.4	8.1	9.5
j. C before a, o, and u is usually hard.	Y 72.97	17.56	9.46
k. G before e, i and y is usually soft.	Y 81.08	9.46	9.46
l. G before a, o and u is usually hard.	Y 75.68	14.86	9.46

N and *Y*, representing No and Yes, indicate the direction responses should have taken according to research.

intensified the results on the yes-no responses by at best 1.2% while diminishing the no response category data by 2.7%.

When an item covering essential information had previously been marked, respondents tended not to respond to an item which stated a negative or reverse view or about which they had doubts. This last is suggested by the number of respondents who placed question marks next to an item.

When compared to research on utility or validity of the generalizations, it can be concluded that the majority of this sample of professors are teaching erroneous information in 2 of the first 3 cases: *a* and *c* as opposed to *b*, but it should be noted that 4 percent of the sample responding yes to generalization *a*, added the modification so that the item read "vowels in open *accented* syllables are usually long." Since research does not support this modification to any great extent, the data suggest a lack of awareness of the research on the utility of this generalization in either form.

Although 77 percent indicate that they do teach that vowels in closed syllables are short (d), more than half of this group also teaches that vowels in closed syllables may be short or long (g) while 45 percent find this expanded generalization apparently has no value. It would also appear that a needless redundancy in instruction is provided by teaching both generalizations.

While only 8.1 percent teach the correct generalization that vowels in open syllables are usually short (e), three fourths of this group also teach that vowels in open syllables may be short or long (f), but not all of those who rejected item a (vowels in open syllables are usually long), (14.86%) teach either of these variations, generally opting for the no response category. While again, some redundancy in instruction is suggested, some lack of knowledge or hesitation to use alternatives is implied by those who reject item a, and most teach the incorrect generalization that vowels in open syllables are usually long.

Item h (diacritic e) shows a moderately high acceptance though research on this item is of relatively recent vintage. Almost 49 percent (or up to 62%) either are unaware of the utility of this generalization, have fixed on *b*, a secondary generalization of less value, or see little reason to utilize *h*.

It would appear that although generalizations *i* thru *l* find high favor, the lesser number teaching *j* and *l* suggest that some reject the need to teach them as being obvious and partially redundant.

We can conclude that while some seeming redundancy exists in instruction, a large percentage of the sample persist in teaching or requiring teachers to know poor if not incorrect (for decoding) generalizations, indicating either a lack of awareness of research or a rejection of it in favor of tradition, personal bias, etc. While it might suggest a reluctance to change, it might also suggest that many professors do not read across the field post master's or doctoral studies and are unaware of research in this area.

18. Do you discuss or teach the term blends?
    yes – 91.89%
    no – 6.76%
    N.R. – 1.35%

Although the term blend is shown to have high popularity in usage or instruction, the data from question 19 suggests that it is used in a restricted sense by the largest number of professors and that even here disagreement on what the term means or how it should be used exists.

19. What do you identify as blends?
    bl – 98.5%
    at – 2.9%
    tl – 22.1%
    cr – 94.1%

na – 0
fl – 98.5%
thr – 67.6%
st-e – 11.8% when e is omitted
str – 91.2%
nd – 44.1%

Although 98.5% agree that bl and fl are blends, lesser numbers identify *cr, str,* or *thr* similarly. While almost 3 percent hold that at is a blend a similar reverse (na) is not so identified. While 44.1 percent identify nd as a blend, some 5 percent needed to add a dash before *n* (-nd) to indicate that this would be a final blend, and, obviously, the largest number reject it entirely.

As one type of check on the linguistic sophistication of the sample, items 20 and 22 were inserted in the questionnaire and will be discussed together. Item 21 will follow.

20. What do you teach about the u in tongue?
   a. nothing – 71.6%
   b. complete in
      a few words – 25.7%
   c. N.R. – 2.7%

The following represent the variety of protocols found among the completion responses made. Only where a large number gave a similar response are the percentages indicated.

a. derivation–gue is silent	5.26%
b. rare occurrence, language artifact, no rule	
c. silent–a remnant of morman language	
d. it is there to retain hard g	10.5%
e. dumb German word with a syllabic glottal	
f. silent	26.3%
g. schwa sound	3.51%
h. derivation from lingua	
i. irregular spelling–as a signal to help identify pronunciation which differs from long, strong.	
j. ue is silent–g takes hard sound	8.77%
k. foreign word–ue is silent– French origin	
l. ue is silent	26.3%

Since the Oxford English Dictionary indicates that the spelling *tung* was modified to *tong* by ME convention and later was added to indicate the *ng* was not pronounced /ndʒ/, etc., and that *ng* represents /ŋ/, a velar sound, it can be inferred that a large percentage of this subsample exhibits erroneous information and misapplies the marker notion of *u* between *g* and *e*, but that at least 5 percent suggest a knowledge that *n* before *g* represents /ŋ/, and that at least 58 percent of the subsample teach that *ue* is silent.

22. What do you teach about the *n* in angle?
   a. nothing – 48.6%
   b. it's a consonant – 2.7%
   c. *n* and *g* equal one sound similar to the final sound in si*ng*. – 18.9%
   d. completions as below – 27.0%
   e. N.R. – 2.7%

Protocols representative of the completions include:
* Perhaps the teacher should know *n* and *g* = /ŋ/ as in *sing*—teaching this to children seems senseless—1.7%
   an is the first syllable, *gle* second. *An* pronounced /an/–15.0%
? The *n* before *g* or *k* usually represents /ŋ/ phoneme–5.0%
   At times letter *n* stands for /ŋ/ sound

---

*Indicates errored responses

ISSUES

but there are numerous exceptions 6.7%
n represents /ŋ/ 6.7%
* context can carry the day 5.0%
* *n* and *g* represent digraph and together they produce a sound unlike that of either single consonant 8.3%
In pronunciation, the *g* gets double effect in that it is joined to *n* to make the /ŋ/ sound and is repeated as /g/ in the last syllable. 5.0%
Last letter of accented first syllable. 3.3%
* Vowel in initial position is usually short. 6.7%
? For syllabication, treat as consonant: an/gle, for pronunciation treat as digraph representing /ŋ/ as in *sing* 6.7%
* One of the vanishing sounds in American English—we don't like to make glottals 1.7%
VC/CV 8.3%
? It's a consonant; encourage blending 5.0%
? Nothing to avoid confusion in syllabication 3.3%
n = /ŋ/–divide an/gle 5.0%
? n in environment of g and k = /ŋ/ 5.0%

1. It ends syllable, 2. It is a good example in phoneme-grapheme correspondence of the *n* by itself representing the /ŋ/ sound, 3. In writing the word divide after *n*. 3.3%

The data indicate slightly less than half of the sample deal with *n* in *angle* in some fashion, that 33.3 percent of the total sample identify *b, c,* or other errored responses as indicative of their procedure, and that at least 65.5% (to a possible 77.8%) of this subsample teach material which is errored on one or more bases.

The protocols reveal some gross misinformation about the phoneme-grapheme correspondence of the language but also reveal that 11.7 percent of the total sample possess a high degree of sophistication about the phoneme-grapheme correspondence of the language and are imparting this to teachers.

21. What do you teach about the *e* in the last syllable of such words as *table, circle, turtle?*
    a. nothing – 34.2%
    b. completion – 60.4%
    c. no response – 5.4%
Representative Protocols:
  part of a syllabic consonant and is silent
  schwa 11.2%
  consonant plus schwa plus 1
  schwa vowel in unaccented syllable 6.7%
  schwa sound tur/təl 7.5%
  *silent—indicates *a* is long table 4.5%
  indicate syllabic *l* or reduced schwa preceding *l*
  e takes schwa sound in *le* endings (dictionary says so)
  ble is blend
  e sound is controlled by the *l*
  *1. *e* at the end of a word is silent, 2. a blend at the end of a word usually has an *e* which is silent
  *it is silent and these types of syllables are the only ones in the English language which have no vowel sounds 4.5%
  **le* is a dominant cluster, likes to take the consonant before it with it.
  *c + le - consonant generalization 11.9%
  *silent and blends last 2 consonants 3.0%
  see what a named book says
  *silent 14.2%
  *unvoiced
  it is silent. The vowel sound in the syllable is schwa inserted between the *c* and *l*.
  *in control of vowel sounds
  the sound of *ul* is represented by *le*

---

*Indicates errored responses

ISSUES

silent: there is a vowel sound in *le* endings: b'l
1. anticipate endings (ing, er) which very frequently cause the preceding two consonants to *blend*. (cf, table, circling, etc.) 2. indicates stress in conjunction with *l* (cf, mattel mattle)

While over 34 percent of the sample indicates that they teach nothing about the final *e* in consonant plus *le* words, some 60 percent do and of these over 50 percent teach questionable if not incorrect information. The asterisk preceding the protocols indicates those which are considered incorrect or of questionable value.

Of the variety of additional items, one which asked for the professor's definition of the term digraph is of particular importance since the protocols offer an opportunity to note the variety of definitions used and their application as viewed by their definers. While 89.2 percent of the sample indicated that they teach or use the term digraph (q.6) and placed high value on teachers' knowing the definitions of the term (a ranking of 82.19 as found in part 1, question 22), only eleven percent (11.2) of the sample appeared to supply a definition that was adequate, that is, was not in application shown to be contradictory of the spelling patterns used to illustrate it. The patterns listed below following a protocol were those of the respondent who often listed these following his definitions or are those patterns he chose in response to question 7 which asked him to identify digraphs among the patterns listed.

*symbols for 2 letters representing a single sound: (nk, ch, ng in angle); 2 consonants one of which is h; they make one sound; teach as a group: (th, ph, ch)
*2 successive speech sounds: (nk, ng, th, oa, ch)
*2 letters that make one sound – different from originals: (not ph, but ch, wh)
*Combination of 2 letters resulting in one unique speech sound: (th, ph, ch, ee, gh)
*Combinations of certain vowels or certain consonants which represent one sound: (for consonants digraphs – a single sound) ng, ch, gh, sh, oi
*2 or 3 letters together, treated as only one sound
*2 letters representing a special speech sound: (th, oa, ph, ch, ee, but not gh); a combination of 2 letters, either vowels or consonants as a nonemonic we write two but we hear only one sound: (ch, oa)
*2 letters (or more) that when put together make new sound and not just representing the two original letters (or more): (ch, oa, ee); a combination of two vowels or two consonants representing one sound: (ch, oa, ph)
*2 letters – only one sound: oa, ee, oi (not ph, ch, th, gh, sh)
*2 letters making one sound: th, oa, ch, ee, etc. (but not gh)
*2 letters representing one phoneme not represented by either letter alone: th, wh, sh, ch (sometimes a phoneme often represented by another letter: sh, ph)
2 consecutive consonants or two consecutive vowels which represent one distinct sound: (ch, ng, th, oa, ph, etc.)
*Combination of 2 consonants as having a unique sound unlike either consonant or combination of 2 vowels or a vowel and consonant which represent one speech sound: (sh, oa, et, ot)
1. A group of 2 successive letters; 2. a group of 2 successive letters whose sound value is not what

---

*Indicates errored responses

might be expected for each letter such as the consonant digraphs ch, sh, etc.; 3. a group of certain successive vowel letters which represent a single sound such as the v. dig. ea in bread.
*2 consonants when sounded do not hear the sound of either consonant: (ch, sh)
2 consonants or 2 vowel graphemes representing one consonant or vowel phoneme: (ch, gh, th, oa, ph)
*2 successive speech sounds: (th, oa, ch, ee, sh, oi, nk, ng)

Only four of the definitions are considered to be satisfactory since some form of contradiction is apparent in each of the others. *nk* is a digraph when the term simply means two letters, but nk in *ink* represents both /ŋ/ and /k/, not one phoneme; *c* and *s* and *h* in *ch, sh,* and *wh* represent the phoneme /ch/ in *cello,* /ʃh/ in *sure* and /h/ in *who* respectively; none of the phonemes represented by the graphemes *ch, sh,* etc. are *unique* or *special* to American speech; three letters is by definition a trigraph; etc. While technically we recognize *ch* as representing /tʃh/, this is typically accepted as one phoneme for instructional purpose and is not considered incorrectly used here.

Conclusions and Implications

Based on the results of this study and within its limitations, the conclusions that college professors who teach teachers to teach reading do not agree on what reading terms should be taught, their definitions, or on the generalizations to be used in phonic analysis is inescapable. Such a conclusion is not surprising; however the evidence also indicates that only a small percentage of the sample had a satisfactory knowledge of those decoding elements he deems it important for teachers to know, that gross misinformation characterizes his instruction to teachers, that contradictory information is supplied teachers, and that college professors, as reflected in this sample, are generally poorly instructed about or meagerly conversant as a result of self-study with those elements which are basic to reading instruction.

The implication is clear that teachers of reading are inadequately prepared and, as a consequence, teach children with far less than a good understanding of principles involved in phonics and word analysis.

It might also be concluded that reading is not a science, since any science requires definitions in exact, precise terms, and as an art, the teaching of reading leaves much to be desired.

BIBLIOGRAPHY

Austin, Mary C. Coleman Marrison, *et al, The First R,* New York: The Macmillan Co., 1963, p. 166.

Kenyon, John S. and Knott, Thomas A. *A Pronouncing Dictionary of American English,* Springfield, Mass.: G. & C. Merriam Co., 1953.

Mazurkiewicz, Albert J., "What Do Teachers Know About Phonics" *Reading World,* March, 1975, p. 165-177.

Oxford English Dictionary, New York: Oxford University Press, 1971.

Phonics? Phonetics? Phonemics? A Reply to Mazurkiewicz

LAWRENCE M. KASDON

When I read Mazurkiewicz' article, "What the Professor Doesn't Know About Phonics Can Hurt" (1975b), the same uneasiness came over me as when I read his previous article, "What Do Teachers Know About Phonics" (1975a). I agree with Mazurkiewicz' thesis that instructors have a clear responsibility to impart accurate knowledge about phonics to all students if they are to be well taught.

My basic criticism of his study as reported in the December 1975 issue of the Reading World is that many of his questions are incapable of being answered because of the way they are worded. One of the principle components of validity of a questionnaire is that the questions be clearly and unambiguously stated. His questions, at times, can have as their referents the disciplines of phonetics, phonemics, or phonics. In his comments, Mazurkiewicz shifts among these three disciplines (particularly phonics and phonetics) while addressing himself to a single question and the responses to it. Certainly he should allow his respondents this same advantage. Unless he specifies in terms of which of these three disciplines a question is to be answered, the responses to many of his questions are incapable of being answered. Furthermore, although he does mention dialect, he does not appear to have been aware as to how it may have colored some of the responses. It seems to me that not including the element of dialect in his analyses, if it could have been done, further weakens some of his analyses.

Because Mazurkiewicz appears to equate "sounds" with "phonemes," let me offer some working definitions of *phonetics* and *phonemics* in order to clarify the discussion that follows. May I add, before proceeding, that in my lexicon *phonetics* or its written symbols are not the same as *phonics*. Phonics, as used in reading, deals with the relationship between graphemes and phonemes. I shall briefly define *phonetics* as the science devoted to the study, analysis, and classification of human speech sounds. One of the major branches of phonetics which has a bearing on our discussion is articulatory phonetics, which is concerned with usable speech sounds in terms of the mechanism of their production by the human vocal apparatus. In transcribing these sounds in written form, phoneticists make use of various alphabets, including many symbols from our Latin alphabet.

Later in my discussion it will become clearer why I am including the quotation from Gleason on phoneticians' attempts to catalogue all human speech sounds. Gleason (1961) stated:

> Phoneticians at one time set as their goal the exact and detailed description of every sound. As work proceeded, it soon became evident that this objective could never be reached. The human vocal apparatus can produce an infinity of sounds. The only limit of the number which can be identified is the instruments used...

Many of the differences in the sound system of human speech that a phonetician may be able to observe may not be important phonemically, for they do not influence the message. *Phonemes* have

---

From *Reading World*, Vol. 15 (October, 1976). © 1976 by the College Reading Association. Reprinted by permission.

been variously described as the "significant" or "functional" units of speech sounds of a given dialect of a language. One of the difficulties is that there is frequently disagreement among linguists as to the number of phonemes in a given language, particularly when the situation is complicated by considering the dialects of that language. A phonemic inventory is usually arrived at by comparing statements such as *Give me a bit* and *Give me a beet*. Through such contrastive analysis a linguist arrives at a catalogue of segmental phonemes.[1] A phoneme is not really a single sound but a class of sounds which is perceived by a native speaker as the same sound. For example, the sounds represented by *p* in *pit, spit* and *sip* are articulated slightly differently; they are allophones of the same phoneme. In other words, a phoneme usually consists of a bundle of allophones or sounds. (I am using allophones and sounds synonymously.)

Before dealing further with some of my points of disagreement with Mazurkiewicz, I must make one additional point which I feel is essential in any attempt to discuss phonics—the number of segmental phonemes varies with the dialect of American English under discussion (e.g., Francis, 1958, p. 447, f.n. 2). Ives and Ives make the point most cogently:

> ...The phonemic principle was developed for analyzing an internally consistent corpus, and attempts to extend it to a variety of dialects of the same language have resulted in the suppression or oversimplification of some phonological facts. Yet, a teacher cannot evade these facts, for they appear in her classroom.

A friend of mine told me that when he was studying reading at a university in Boston, the professor, a native of Boston, remarked, "I can only teach phonics in Boston."

Question 3 reads: "What do you teach about the number of sounds or phonemes in American English?" Is the respondent to answer in terms of sounds or phonemes? In 3b "that there are ____ sounds in the language." To the initiated it would indicate that Mazurkiewicz is talking about phonetics. Questions 4 and 5 raise the same problems as 3. Could this ambiguity possibly account in part for the range of numbers in the answers and for some of the apparent inconsistencies on the part of the respondents?

Before leaving question 4 ("What do you teach about the number of vowel sounds or phonemes in American English?"), I should like to comment on his reactions to the answers to this question. He discusses pronunciation symbols in dictionaries as if they represent phonemes. These symbols are used to reduce the redundancy by which the various sounds of the language, including its dialects, can be most economically represented in written form. Thus, the schwa sound /ə/ heard in the second syllable of the words *heaven* and *lemon* can be represented by the same pronunciation symbol. In the introduction to many dictionaries, e.g., Kenyon and Knott (1953); Webster's Third (1961), etc., there are detailed discussions of the various sounds that each pronunciation symbol may represent. It does not matter whether or not dictionary editors use a greater or lesser number of pronunciation symbols for a given language. Unless the dictionary user is a phonetician, he will pronounce the respelled words for pronunciation in terms of his dialect. The map should not be confused with the territory.

Mazurkiewicz' confusion about phonetics and phonemics is apparent when he writes on page 118: "...When one notes that Kenyon and Knott identify another phoneme between the *a* of *ah* and

---

[1] In addition to the *segmental* phonemes, linguists refer to a second classification of phonemes, the suprasegmental phonemes—pitch, stress, and juncture. Some linguists classify pitch, for example, according to three levels while others use four levels. Hence, there is no agreement as to the number of suprasegmentals. Technically, when discussing the number phonemes in a language, one should include both segmental as well as suprasegmental phonemes.

the *aw* of *jaw* as being found in *watch*.... We recognize the phonetician at work...." He goes on further to reduce the number of vowel sounds by eliminating fine distinctions that Kenyon and Knott make so that he arrives at a figure of 16 vowel sounds "which need to be taught." First of all, the sounds do not need to be taught since most users of the dictionary already speak the language, albeit in their own dialect. Secondly, adding or subtracting the number of pronunciation symbols does not yield the number of phonemes in a dialect. Such a figure is arrived at, as stated earlier, by contrasting minimal pairs.

For the sake of brevity I shall desist from entering into a detailed explication of my disagreement with his discussion of question 5, regarding the number of consonant sounds in English. Much of my opposition to his statements in this section is contained in my remarks about question 4.

In question 7 (a task in identifying digraphs in a list of words) I should like to make one or two observations. Since Mazurkiewicz did not specify whether or not he was using a phonemic, phonetic or phonic referent, it is possible that the respondents used their own. Also, within each of these disciplines various writers use somewhat different definitions as to what constitutes a digraph and, therefore, categorize them somewhat differently. I had difficulty in following his logic, particularly his conclusions in the last sentence of the second paragraph on page 120. Perhaps the fault is mine; therefore, I shall not attempt to comment on this point.

Mazurkiewicz' discussion of glides and diphthongs leaves me somewhat puzzled that he can reach a definite conclusion that error in identification exists. Van Riper and Smith (1972) point out that linguistic scholars have identified 36 diphthongs in American English, "even though most of them have only regional popularity." I would submit that it would take a more sophisticated analysis of the responses than the published data permits, particularly in terms of regional or dialectical variation. I base my conclusion on this topic on such references as Francis (1958) and Gleason (1968) where rather detailed descriptions of the possible glides and diphthongs for the various dialects of English are discussed. Since Mazurkiewicz did not possess knowledge of the various respondents' dialects, the respondents may not have been "confused" about glided sounds.

In any case the significant question(s) for teaching phonics in reading is not to arrive at a given number of vowel or consonant phonemes but rather to be familiar with what are the options in terms of grapheme-phoneme relationships. This determination of options is in turn influenced by the conditions which can determine the selections of one phoneme over another when decoding a word. One cannot survey phonics without considering the influence of such elements as environment, accent, morphemes, semantics (meaning), context, syllabication, syntax, dialect, etc. Such a task is not simple as there is no agreement among linguists about grammar as witness the various schools of linguistics. (A current description of several of these schools is given in Southworth and Daswani [1974].) To complicate matters much of the research in phonics has been done on word lists that have since been updated, e.g., Carroll, et. al., *The American Heritage Word Frequency Book* (1971). Dictionaries change because they reflect the change in language. To make matters worse, the editors of Webster's Third have changed some of the rules of syllabication of written words and have practically given up on syllabicating spoken words.

Linguists continue to study dialects and there is much controversy about their place in the reading program. All of these eddies, crosscurrents and flows will have to be considered in any study of phonics and reading. The development of a paradigm for phonics must be

ISSUES

considered in terms of the total reading-language context.

BIBLIOGRAPHY

Carroll, John B., Davies, Peter and Richman, Barry. *The American Heritage Word Frequency Book.* Boston: Houghton Mifflin, 1971.
Francis, W. N. *The Structure of American English.* New York: Ronald, 1958.
Gleason, J. A., Jr. *An Introduction to Descriptive Linguistics,* rev. ed. New York: Holt, Rinehart and Winston, 1961.
Gove, P. B., ed. *Webster's Third New International Dictionary of the English Language Unabridged.* Springfield, Mass.: G. & C. Merriam, 1961.
Ives, S. & Ives, J. P. Part I. "Linguistics and Reading." In *Linguistics in School Programs,* A. H. Marchwardt, ed. The Sixty-ninth Yearbook of the National Society for the Study of Education, Part II. Chicago: National Society for the Study of Education, 1970.
Kenyon, J. S. and Knott, T. A. *A Pronouncing Dictionary of American English,* Springfield, Mass.: G. & C. Merriam, 1953.
Southworth, F. C. and Daswani, C. J. *Foundations of Linguistics.* New York: The Free Press, 1974.
Van Riper, C. G. and Smith, D. E. *An Introduction to General American Phonetics,* 2nd ed. New York: Harper & Row, 1962.

Dialect Difference and the Teaching of Reading and Spelling

RUSSELL TABBERT

> The collapsing of /ɑ, ɔ/ is a characteristic of many pronunciation dialects, especially of those dialects that do not accompany the language of achievement.[1]
> John W. Black

There is a yacht in the harbor in Valdez, Alaska named *The Knotty Girl.* In Alaska's special Congressional election campaign some supporters of the Democratic candidate Emil Notti wore buttons proclaiming "I'm a Notti Body." In both of these punnings is an important moral, that is, a pedagogical moral for teachers of reading and spelling and, as the quote above reveals, for some teachers of teachers.

Check any dictionary, reading system, or spelling book and you will almost always be informed that *knotty* and *naughty* are pronounced differently. The first syllable of *knotty* has an "ah" vowel (phonemically /ɑ/) while the first syllable of *naughty* has an "aw" vowel (phonemically /ɔ/). But now check your pupils' pronunciation of *knotty* and *naughty* or

[1] "On Improving the Speech of Children," in *On Teaching Speech in Elementary and Junior High Schools.* J. Jeffery Auer and Edward B. Jenkinson, eds. Bloomington: Indiana University Press, 1971, p. 67.

From *Elementary English,* Vol. 51, No. 8 (November, 1974). © 1974 by the National Council of Teachers of English. Reprinted by permission.

132

of a number of other similar pairs such as *Don-dawn, tot-taught, cot-caught.* The chances are good that some or all of the students will not make the "ah"-"aw" distinction; they will pronounce *knotty* and *naughty* exactly alike. In fact, check your own speech; you may not have the contrast either.

This state of affairs is no cause for alarm. We are not dealing with nonstandard dialect or sloppy articulation or speech handicaps or non-achieving language, whatever that might be. The situation is simply this. There is a sound change taking place in North American English which is resulting in the merger of two previously contrasting sounds (phonemes). The resulting single phoneme is usually articulated somewhere between the "ah" and "aw" positions, further back in the mouth than "ah" and with less lip rounding than "aw." Like most linguistic change, this merger is a slow, virtually imperceptible process, probably happening more between generations than within the speech of individuals.

Furthermore, like other instances of change, this one is not taking place uniformly over a whole area. Thus we have a situation where in certain parts of the country the merger is well established for all speakers: for example, Eastern New England and an area of Eastern Ohio and Western Pennsylvania. The merger is also apparently well advanced in Canada. In other areas the speakers still generally maintain the "ah"-"aw" contrast: for example, large areas of the Midwest. And in still other areas the situation is mixed, but moving towards the merger: for example, the West. Although complete information for a more precise statement of the situation is not available, there is little doubt that millions of speakers have merged the two vowels and that the merger is spreading.

This situation has several implications for the teaching of reading and spelling. First of all, the correspondence between pronunciation and spelling goes further awry. That is, dialects with the "ah"-"aw" merger have moved another step away from the presumed ideal of a single and consistent spelling for each distinctive sound. Though not perfect, the unmerged dialects are closer to the ideal. The letter *o* alone between consonants and without a following "silent e" quite regularly stands for the "ah" sound (*lot, hop, copper,* etc.). The representation of the "aw" sound is less consistent, but there are some regularities: *aw (saw, flaw,* etc.); *au (maul, faucet,* etc.); *al(l)* (*ball, salt,* etc.); and *ough (cough, bought,* etc.). But now in the dialects with "ah"-"aw" merger, one sound is spelled in all of these various ways.

Of course this kind of discrepancy between pronunciation and spelling is hardly new to English. Ever since the Renaissance, when English spelling became more or less permanently fixed by the introduction of printing, there have been irregularities, and new ones have been added as further sound changes took place. Just for example, consider the *k* of *knotty* and the *gh* of *naughty,* both of which at one time represented pronounced sounds. Or closer to our "ah"-"aw" merger was the coalescence of words with an "ē" sound, spelled *ee* (*sheep, deed, knee,* etc.), with a portion of a set of words formerly pronounced with an "ā" vowel and spelled *ea* (*leap, read, meat,* etc.). Many more examples could be cited, for one of the chief reasons that English spelling is irregular is that we do not allow spelling to adapt to changing pronunciation. And since sound change is a constant feature of a living language, we can expect, over the long run, further sound-spelling divergence.

For the short run, though, we need not be unduly pessimistic. This most recent divergence does not necessarily mean new and serious reading and spelling problems. Because there is already inconsistency in our spelling, including single sounds spelled in several ways, the awareness and acceptance of irregularity must come early in the learning to

ISSUES

read and spell processes. Therefore students with "ah"-"aw" merger will learn to treat the diverse spellings of their single merged sound as just another instance of a familiar phenomenon.

In fact the most serious potential for problems may be in the reading and spelling instruction itself, from the materials because almost all present only the dialect in which "ah" and "aw" are still distinct, and from the teachers because, in using such materials, they may attempt to impose a distinction on pupils who do not have it.

Unless the teacher realizes what the situation is and makes adjustments to the materials, the pupils with merged "ah"-"aw" will be confused and misled by the discussions and exercises. This would be particularly true in approaches which emphasize sound-symbol correspondences, such as the initial teaching alphabet or the various "phonics" and "linguistic" approaches. Typical is *The Palo Alto Reading Program* by Theodore E. Glim (Harcourt, 1968) in which "ah" and "aw" are presented only as distinct phonemes with no hint to the teacher or student that this is not the situation for everybody. In books 3, 4, and 5 of *The Roberts English Series: A Linguistics Program* (Harcourt, 1966, 1970) there is a careful and detailed presentation of the sound-spelling correspondences in English, but always for a dialect in which "ah" and "aw" are distinct. Though the teacher is cautioned that some Americans have merged the vowels, there is no suggestion that this should make any difference in the use of the materials. And the pupils get no hint of it. Phonics manuals and texts present only the "ah"-"aw" contrast. For example, Arthur W. Heilman in *Phonics in Proper Perspective: Second Edition* (Charles E. Merrill, 1968) simply states that "the letter *a* has the sound *ô (aw)* when it is followed by *l, ll, w, u*." No qualification is made for other dialects. And the initial teaching alphabet, devised in England to fit British pronunciation, uses the following respelling symbols, *a* as in *father; au* as in *ball;* and *o* as in *box*.

The most unfortunate result of failing to understand this "ah"-"aw" merger would be for the teacher to diagnose it as a speech deficiency and to attempt to "correct" it by drilling the distinction. There is nothing to be gained and much to be lost in such a procedure. It is not necessary because (1) the merger is not a speech defect, but rather part of the child's normal speech pattern; (2) the speech pattern is a standard dialect spoken by millions of Americans; (3) except perhaps for some minor additional difficulty in learning correct spelling, the merger will cause no problems in language use. Listeners will not be uncertain whether the speaker means *naughty* or *knotty* (and so forth) because the linguistic and extra-linguistic context will make clear which is intended.

Such an attempt to impose the "ah"-"aw" contrast is dangerous because it focuses negative attention on the child's speech. The student is made consciously aware that the teacher finds something wrong with his pronunciation. But when the teacher tries to explain what is "wrong" and show how to do it "right," the child is confused and frustrated. Because he doesn't make the contrast, he will have difficulty hearing it in somebody else's speech, except in minimal pairs such as *cot-caught*. And even when he does hear it, he won't be able to make it because he won't know what to do. The classroom teacher is not a speech therapist and will not know the techniques for getting the necessary tongue and lip positions. A speech therapist will, but that would be the worst possible thing that could happen—to send a child to speech correction because he has a dialect difference.

Already we are a nation tongue-tied and pen-frozen by linguistic anxiety. Our language use is guided more by fear of being "wrong" or different than by confidence that we have something important to say and adequate means of saying it. Unfortunately language arts instruction has contributed to this anxiety by a persistent emphasis on the negative—by showing or implying to the child that his language is "wrong." But, and here's the moral, this approach has relied on two false notions about English: (1) that it is single, uniform, and unchanging and (2) that it should be pronounced, as nearly as possible, according to the spelling.

Language arts teachers and materials specialists must accept the variety in English, for it is not necessary that everyone speak the same in order to learn to read and spell and use the language fluently. And these, after all, are the goals. In addition, they must understand the nature of this variety. They must be able to recognize the important dialect differences and be able to create and adapt their materials and techniques accordingly. Not a terribly knotty problem.

Black English Pronunciation and Spelling Performance

DONNA SCHWAB KLIGMAN
BRUCE A. CRONNELL
GARY B. VERNA

The question of nonstandard dialect pronunciation interference in school performance has often been raised in relation to reading. This is understandable considering the crucial nature of the reading task for school success. It is curious, however, that the question of dialect interference in spelling has been largely ignored until quite recently (e.g., Brengelman, 1970). Because spelling is based on oral stimuli, it is quite possible that there is a greater potential for dialect interference in spelling than in reading. Dialect pronunciation may interfere with the spelling of unfamiliar words for Black English (BE) speakers in the same way that standard pronunciation may interfere with the spellings of unfamiliar, irregularly spelled words for Standard English (SE) speakers. (For example, a BE speaker who does not pronounce the /l/ in "wild" might spell it as *wide* just as an SE speaker might spell "half" as *haff*.)

An examination of the spelling errors made by dialect speakers should be an indication of the extent to which dialect pronunciation is related to incorrect spelling output. A few such studies have been done (e.g. Graham and Rudorf, 1970; Boiarsky, 1969). They found that significant differences in the patterning of spelling errors did exist and that the errors of the dialect speakers reflected pronunciation differences. While these studies were of regional, rather than social dialects, informal evidence indicated that similar results would be found in the study of the relationship between BE and

---

From *Elementary English*, Vol. 49, No. 8 (December, 1972). © 1972 by the National Council of Teachers of English. Reprinted by permission.

spelling output. Wolfram and Whiteman (1971) found selected interference in an examination of compositions by 10th grade BE speakers in Washington, D.C. An analysis made by Briggs (1968) of the compositions of 9th–11th grade Black students in Alabama, listed a total of 312 spelling errors of which nearly 50% appeared to be dialect-related. However, Briggs' report was rather casual and incidental to her discussion of grammatical and lexical differences. The observations were not specifically intended to be related to the speech of the students. Thus, the research relating social dialects to spelling performance is scanty indeed, which suggested the need for further study.

SOME FEATURES OF BLACK ENGLISH PHONOLOGY

The social dialect which has come to be known as Black English has been well described by linguists [e.g., Labov, Cohen, Robins, & Lewis (1968); Shuy, Wolfram, & Riley (1967); and Legum, Pfaff, Tinnie, & Nicholas (1971)]. Their studies were used in compiling a list of phonological (and, in some cases, grammatical) features of the dialect. It should be emphasized that the features of BE described by these studies do *not* occur without variation even for a single speaker of the dialect. Within the competence of each BE speaker is the ability to change styles to conform to varying cultural and social contexts. In formal situations, for example, the BE speaker may use more features of SE. Thus, the occurrence of any BE feature is subject to many incompletely defined linguistic and sociolinguistic environments. It is also important to recognize that BE is a fully independent, rule-governed dialect and that the following description of BE phonology is merely a statement of its relationship to SE. A contrastive analysis of the two dialects was made in order to predict which features of BE pronunciation might be expected to interfere in spelling output.

Single Final Consonants

Many of the pronunciation features of BE which differ from SE occur at the ends of words. In many words where single final consonants occur in SE, the consonant is often devoiced or absent in BE, especially if the following word begins with another consonant. Final stop consonants (/d/, /b/, /t/, /g/, /k/, /p/) are most likely to be devoiced or absent in BE, but others (e.g., /z/, /r/, /l/, /n/) may also be reduced.

Final Consonant Clusters

The absence or partial absence of final consonant clusters is frequent in BE pronunciation. Such words as "post" and "card" may be pronounced /pos/ or /kar/. The first member of a final cluster may be similarly reduced in BE if it is /l/ or /r/. Such words as "bulb" and "warm" may be pronounced /bəb/ or /wɔm/.

Initial Consonants

The initial consonants /ð/ as in "these" and /θ/ as in "threw" may be realized as their stop equivalents, /d/ and /t/, in BE.

Vowels

There are several common differences in vowel pronunciations in BE and SE. /ɛ/ before nasal consonants in SE (as in "pen") is often pronounced /ɪ/ in BE (though it may also be pronounced /ɪ/ in regional dialects of SE). Other vowel differences are absence of glides and heightened vowels before liquid or nasal consonants in BE. For example, /ay/ as in "ride" may be pronounced /a/, and /ɪ/ before /l/ may be pronounced /i/. Thus the pronunciations of *lot* and *light* or of *fill* and *feel* may closely resemble each other.

BE Pronunciation Features Which Affect Grammatical Markers

The absence or reduced form of final consonants and clusters often neutralizes grammatical information which is present at the ends of words in SE pronunciation. Whether or not phonological differences indicate underlying structural differences is still being investigated by Labov and others. For the purposes of a spelling study, however, it seemed appropriate to ignore that distinction.

In English there are three pronunciations of the past tense marker; /d/ after voiced sounds as in "moved," /t/ after unvoiced sounds as in "cooked," and /ɪd/ after /t/ or /d/ as in "waited." All are spelled *ed*. These markers are often absent in BE pronunciation.

In English there are also three pronunciations of the plural, possessive, or third person singular marker; /z/ after voiced sounds, as in "drives," /s/ after unvoiced sounds as in "Pat's," and /ɪz/ after /s/, /z/, /š/, /ž/, /č/, and /ǰ/ as in "watches." All are spelled *s* or *es*. These markers are also often absent in BE pronunciation. Because of reduced final consonant pronunciations, contractions such as "we'll," "we're," or "he's" may become simply "we" or "he" in BE.

A STUDY OF SPELLING AND *BE*

By undertaking a study of the relationship of BE pronunciation as described to spelling performance, it was hoped that the following questions would be answered.

1. Do BE-speaking children make more spelling errors than non-BE speakers of a comparable socioeconomic group?
2. Do BE-speaking children make more dialect-related errors (i.e., misspellings which are phonetic representations of the child's speech) in spelling than non-BE speakers? How comparable is the spelling performance of the two groups if dialect-related errors are discounted?
3. Which features of BE pronunciation are related to the greatest number of dialect-related errors?
4. Do BE-speaking children make more or less dialect errors on words in which phonological features affect grammatical markers?

Participants

To answer the above questions, children from four second-grade classrooms in each of two schools in Los Angeles were asked to participate in a spelling study. One school was predominately Black and the other was predominately White. All non-Black children in the predominately Black school were excluded from the study as were all Black children from the predominately White school. An informal survey indicated that the Black children were, for the most part, BE speakers and that the White children spoke SE. All children with any other language influences (e.g., foreign born parents) were excluded. Each dialect group was composed of 61 children (BE, 24 boys and 37 girls; SE, 34 boys and 27 girls). The mean ages (BE, 7.10; SE, 7.11) and mean reading scores (BE, 20.2; SE, 21.3 on Form 12A of the Cooperative Primary Reading Test) of the children in both schools were approximately the same.

Test Content

Spelling tests were devised to be administered to the children. Test items were written including three examples of each of 43 pronunciation features derived from the description of BE phonology.

ISSUES

In order to minimize the children's spelling by memory rather than by rules of correspondence, test words were chosen which were not found in the spelling books the children had been using.

Test Format

In order to control spelling responses and to minimize the testing of auditory and writing skills, a multiple-choice format was chosen for the testing procedure. It has often been noted that the multiple-choice spelling test is easier for children than the dictated word test but this was not of concern as some words chosen were particularly difficult to spell for the age group tested. For each word, one or two errors were constructed which would reflect a likely BE pronunciation. For example, since it was expected that a BE-speaking child might pronounce the word "mouth" as /mawf/ or /mawt/, the errors constructed for "mouth" were *mouf* and *mout*. For each test word, an equal number of nonpronunciation related errors were offered (e.g., letter reversals, consonant or vowel misspellings, or intrusive letters). These errors were constructed so as to be neither related to possible dialect differences nor phonologically possible misspellings (e.g., *bred* was not used as a nondialect-related error for "bread").

A sentence which was not definitional but which gave a clear context was constructed for each test word. All sentences were devised so that test words were followed by words beginning with consonants, as this is the most favorable environment for the occurrence of many BE features. In order to minimize the testing of reading skills instead of spelling skills, each sentence (including the test word) was read to the children by the examiner. This test format and method of administration may have reduced effects of dialect in that children's spellings were not self-stimulated, but comparisons of results showed dialect-related error rates similar to those found in studies made of spelling errors in free composition (e.g., Briggs, 1968).

Procedures

Testing was conducted on three consecutive days. An SE-speaking White female administered all tests to assure uniform pronunciation of test words and standard testing procedures in all classrooms. Each day's testing session was 20-30 minutes long. Students circled their answers and their responses were coded and processed by computer in order to group responses by item and by rule across various sets of children.

RESULTS AND DISCUSSION

Analysis of the responses showed that BE speakers made more incorrect responses (44%) than did SE speakers (36%) and boys made more incorrect responses (46%) than girls (35%). Analysis of variance showed that these differences were significant (F $[1,118]$ = 8.52, p $<.01$ for dialect and F $[1,118]$ = 11.43, p$<.01$ for sex). Furthermore there was a significant difference between error types (dialect-related and nondialect-related, F $[1,118]$ = 44.22, p$<.01$), with nondialect errors (23%) outnumbering dialect errors (16%). The interaction between speaker group and error type was significant (F $[1,118]$ = 6.83, p$<.01$). For nondialect-related errors, error rates were approximately the same for both groups (24% for BE speakers, 22% for SE speakers). However, for dialect-related errors, the groups differed considerably (19% for BE speakers, 12% for SE speakers). In addition, there were significant differences in performance on individual features tested for both dialect and nondialect-related errors (F $[42,2520]$ = 58.40, p$<.01$ and F $[42,2520]$ = 96.33, p$<.01$, respectively for BE speakers and F $[42,2520]$ = 32.89, p$<.01$ and F

[42,2520] = 78.61, p<.01 respectively for SE speakers).

The results of the study, then, support the hypothesis that dialect pronunciation has a significant relationship to the number and type of spelling errors made. Because of the test construction and response bias (e.g., Black children had interference from both dialect and the nature and difficulty of English spelling whereas White children had no comparable pronunciation-related errors to choose from), no direct comparison can be made of the general spelling abilities of the two groups. It does appear, however, that spelling performance, if based only on the number of nondialect errors made, does not differ significantly for the two groups. While the BE speakers clearly made more dialect-related errors, it is interesting to note that White children had some of the same dialect-related spelling difficulties that Black children had. The features on which the most dialect errors were made, as well as the features on which the least were made, were similar for both speaker groups. No comparable results were found for nondialect errors. This similarity between groups is not surprising since many children in second grade may still have spelling interference from incomplete phonological or structural development of language and since casual speech of some White children may well contain some of the features of BE (Garvey & McFarlane, 1970).

DISCUSSION OF THE DIFFICULTY OF SELECTED FEATURES

Regardless of dialect group, there was a significant difference in performance depending on which pronunciation feature was being tested. In other words, interference appeared to be selective. The features are discussed below in terms of numbers of children who chose dialect-related errors at least once. Only those which caused considerable difficulty for one or both groups are discussed in detail.

1. /ɛ/ before a nasal may be pronounced /ɪ/ (e.g., "pen" may be pronounced /pɪn/ and spelled *pin*). Over half the children in both groups chose such an error. There is good evidence (e.g., Labov *et al*, 1968) that this pronunciation is a strong feature of BE, which could explain the marked tendency for BE-speaking children to spell words correspondingly. Evidence is also appearing (Metcalf, 1971) that SE speakers in Southern California lose the vowel distinction in the same environment. If this is true, it is understandable that SE speakers would also often spell /ɛ/ with *i* before nasals if they have learned to spell by correspondence rules.

2. /sks/ or /sts/ at the end of a plural noun or third person singular verb may be reduced to /sk/ or /st/ (e.g., "desks" may be pronounced /desk/ and spelled *desk*). About two-thirds of the BE speakers chose such an error at least once; however, about half of the SE speakers chose it at least once, which may indicate that it is merely a problem of child language development. Templin (1957) noted that even the simple final clusters /sk/ and /st/ were not mastered until age seven. Presumably, these clusters plus a plural or third person morpheme would not be mastered until even later.

3. /t/ or /d/ in past tense verbs may be deleted (e.g., "moved" may be pronounced /mʊv/ and spelled *move*). About two-thirds of the BE-speaking children chose such a pronunciation-related error, while about half the SE speakers were attracted by it at least once. Both the /t/ and /d/ forms of the past tense were clearly more difficult for both groups than the /ɪd/ form. This was expected for the BE speakers at least, since /ɪd/ as in "waited"

ISSUES

does not form the difficult final consonant cluster. Berko (1958) found that none of the three past tense forms were correctly produced even 90% of the time by first graders; thus the high error rate is not surprising.

4. The plural marker /ɪz/ may be deleted (e.g., "dresses" may be pronounced /drɛs/ and spelled *dress*). The dropping of the plural marker was a common misspelling for both groups. It was expected that /ɪz/ would be the easiest form to hear and spell, for BE speakers, at least, since it does not form a final cluster when added to a noun; the reverse was true, however. About half the children in each speaker group chose a spelling which reflected the deletion of the /ɪz/ plural. It is suspected that the general process of child morphology acquisition was, in this case, more influential than dialect or pronunciation. Graves and Koziol (1971) report that "The /s/ and /z/ allomorphs (of the plural) seemed mastered by most children by the first grade while the /ɪz/ allomorph was not completely mastered by most children until the third grade."

5. /ɛ/ before a consonant other than a nasal may be pronounced /ɪ/ (e.g., "wet" may be pronounced /wɪt/ and spelled *wit*). This was the only pronunciation "rule" which was related to more dialect errors for SE speakers than for BE speakers. Over half the SE sample chose such a dialect error whereas only somewhat over one fourth of the BE sample chose one. "Get" pronounced /gɪt/ is certainly commonly heard in casual speech in Southern California as elsewhere (Metcalf, 1971) and, for the SE sample studied at least, it may be spreading to other words as well. The vowels are close phonetically and the merger would not be unreasonable.

6. Medial /l/ may be deleted (e.g., "bulb" may be pronounced /bəb/ and spelled *bub*). Such a dialect error was made at least once by over half the BE speakers studied. Apparently, it is an insignificant problem for SE speakers as only about one-fourth of the SE-speaking children were attracted to such an error.

Questionable results were obtained for the relationships of the following pronunciation tendencies to spelling; it is possible that further testing would reveal the effects to be significant. Initial consonants, devoicing or deletion of final stop consonants such as /b/ and /d/ and the changing of final /θ/ as in "mouth" to /f/ appeared to have some effect on spelling for BE speakers but not overwhelmingly so. The same can be said of changes in vowels before /l/, /n/, or /r/, deletions in contractions, deletions of /z/ and /s/ plural markers and /z/ markers on possessives, passive pronouns and third person singular verbs, and of the past tense marker /ɪd/.

Some BE pronunciation features appeared to have very little relationship to spelling. Changes in medial vowels (e.g., /ay/ as in "ride" pronounced /a/) did not affect spelling for many students nor did deletions of /r/ in the initial cluster /θr/ as in "threw." None of the rules affecting single final consonants had much relationship to spelling errors except, in most cases, the voiced stops and /θ/. Less than one-fourth of the children in either dialect group chose errors related to devoicing or deletion of other final consonants. The same was true, surprisingly, of final consonant clusters. Neither first nor second members of the clusters were often omitted in spelling. The reduced form or absence of final clusters in BE pronunciation is well documented, but they are apparently well enough perceived to cause little spelling difficulty. Wolfram and Whiteman (1971) support the finding in their study of compositions written by BE speakers. They found that monomorphemic (nongrammatical) final clusters are not reduced or omitted as frequently as those including grammatical markers. Thus, "mist" would more often be spelled correctly than "missed." This may indicate that the grammar of BE is, in these cases, interfering with spelling to a greater extent than is the BE pronunciation.

Although deletions of spellings of the voiced form of the third person singular /z/ (as in "drives"), were a bit more frequent; deletions of final *s* pronounced /s/ (as in "cooks") on third person singular verbs and possessive nouns occurred for less than one-fourth of the speakers in each group. This, too, was surprising, considering the extent to which they are reported to be absent in BE pronunciation. Spelling deletions of plural *s* markers were made by nearly twice as many children. The Wolfram and Whiteman study (1971) showed a comparable situation. It reported 19% absence of *s* on third person singular verbs while 44% of the plural *s*'s were missing for those students who made such deletions. Briggs' study of compositions (1968) also suggests a higher absence of plural markers than of third person singular markers.

CONCLUSIONS AND IMPLICATIONS

Pronunciation differences in BE are significantly related to the spelling output of those children who speak the dialect. However, it appears that only selected features cause enough difficulty to justify pedagogical concern. Although the present study cannot lead to specific conclusions about spelling instruction that would help BE-speaking children (and, in some cases, SE-speaking children) to become better spellers, it does suggest that special concern with spelling instruction for BE speakers may be justified. Some educators (e.g., Baratz, 1969) have made suggestions which focus on strengthening the BE speaker's command of SE in order to alleviate dialect interference in reading. This solution is beyond the scope of a spelling program and may be, furthermore, a questionable procedure in terms of both community support and pupil motivation. It is possible, rather, that modified instructional materials or procedures could be developed that would help the BE speakers (and in some cases SE speakers) to better understand the relationship of their own pronunciation to English spelling.

BIBLIOGRAPHY

1. Baratz, Joan, "Who Should Do What to Whom and Why?" *Florida FL Reporter,* (Spring/Summer, 1969) 75-77.
2. Berko, Jean, "The Child's Learning of English Morphology," *Word,* 14 (1958) 150-177.
3. Boiarsky, Carolyn, "Consistency of Spelling and Pronunciation Deviations of Appalachian Students." *Modern Language Journal,* 53 (1969) 347-350.
4. Brengelman, Frederick, H., "Dialect and the Teaching of Spelling," *Research in Teaching English,* 4 (1970) 129-138.
5. Briggs, Delores, *Deviations From Standard English in Papers of Selected Alabama Negro High School Students.* Unpublished doctoral dissertation, University of Alabama, 1968.
6. Garvey, Catherine and Paul McFarlane, "A Measure of Standard English Proficiency of Inner-city Children," *American Educational Research Journal,* 7 (1970) 29-40.
7. Graham, Richard and E. Hugh Rudorf, "Dialect and Spelling," *Elementary English,* 67 (1970) 363-376.
8. Graves, Michael and Stephen Koziol, *Noun Plural Development in Primary Grade Children.* Child Development, 42(4) (1971) 1165-1173.
9. Labov, William, Paul Cohen, Clarence Robins and John Lewis, *A Study of the Non-standard English of Negro and Puerto Rican Speakers*

in New York City. Columbia University Cooperative Research Project No. 3288, 1968.
10. Legum, Stanley, Carol Pfaff, Gene Tinnie and Michael Nicholas, *On the Speech of Young Black Children in Los Angeles.* Technical Report No. 33, 1971, Southwest Regional Laboratory, Los Alamitos, California.
11. Metcalf, Allen, A., *Riverside English.* University of California at Riverside, 1971.
12. Shuy, Roger, Walt Wolfram and William Riley, *Linguistic Correlates of Social Structure in Detroit Speech.* USOE Project No. 6-1347, 1967.
13. Templin, Mildred, C., *Certain Language Skills in Children.* Minneapolis: University of Minnesota Press, 1957.
14. Wolfram, Walt and Marcia Whiteman, "The Role of Dialect Interference in Composition," *Florida FL Reporter,* 9 (1971) 34-38, 59.

Toward A Spelling Reform

ALBERT J. MAZURKIEWICZ

If children have difficulty in telling time based on the circular 12 hour-60 minute clock we now recognize that the substitution of the digital clock eliminates the complex learnings involved in this type of telling of time and telling time is learned as the child learns to recognize and use numbers. Later teaching of the 12 hour-60 minute clock, building on knowledge of digital time clocks, proceeds easily and well.

If the reader or writer-to-be of English, whether he/she is a child, illiterate adult, or foreign language speaker, is of concern at all, the problems inherent in the task need a similar analysis and a similar substitution.

Though reformed orthography procedures exist and are an immediate and parallel solution to the telling time problem, the same process of analysis and substitution of a simpler procedure is not always the case in learning to read.

While transition to reading the complex spellings of English is accomplished with ease, some children taught using a reformed orthography in the first grade have some of the same problems of developing efficiency in commanding the printed page at later levels as the child taught using conventional print since teachers often fail to carry on the instruction necessary for the child to internalize to the point of automaticity some aspects of the complex spellings of English. Developing efficiency in conventional print needs continuing attention since we cannot expect the reader to be self-motivated to puzzle out the complex grapheme-phoneme correspondences of increasingly more difficult matter. In fact, research has shown[1] that few young adults will even use dictionaries to determine the pronunciation of a word since the procedure is an interference in the reading act. Research also shows that if a child needs to refer constantly to other sources for aid in decoding print, he turns away from the task just because it is a task and also because it is a task which is often unrewarding.

From *Reading World,* Vol. 15 (December, 1976). © 1976 by the College Reading Association. Reprinted by permission.

The analysis of the learning to read activity (and reading well) indicates that the orthography as conventionally printed is a major handicap. The work of Downing and colleagues[2] on the use of i.t.a. has demonstrated conclusively that traditional orthography is a significant handicap to the child's task of learning to read. Soffietti[3], in his linguistic analysis of the language, demonstrated that traditional spelling was the primary cause of failure in learning to read. Makita[4], in a study of the extent of reading disability among Japanese children as compared with United States populations demonstrated that the incidence of disability was about one-half of one percent as opposed to the average twenty-five percent found in the U.S., and convincingly demonstrated that this difference could be attributed to the spellings of English, that Pitman's i.t.a. compared favorably to the Japanese phonetic form and could provide the basis for an attack on the problem.

Since the initial teaching alphabet in reading and writing instruction has been shown to be one viable alternative and other reformed orthographies exist for the same purpose, why then a spelling reform? Like all alphabetic innovations of the past, gross misinformation, the pressure of the market place where large corporations with their huge staffs of representatives and investments of countless millions in conventional reading materials overwhelm the "opposition," insecure educational administrative staffs who are preservers, or believe they are to be preservers, of the status quo and make administrative or public relation rather than educational decisions, parental concern that spelling might be negatively affected, etc. have combined to limit the employment of such educationally sound alternatives as i.t.a. and only a limited usage can be expected in the future.

Certainly spelling reform is not needed for those of us who are literate. But research has demonstrated that countless millions are barely literate, that millions of others read badly or, if able, read little, and that countless thousands of young children continue to suffer failure, ego-damage and frustration. Others continue to spell badly even after 12 or more years of education.

Additional research[1] examining another aspect of the development of literacy—learning to write (spell) the language—has demonstrated that children and young adults often choose to write a word they know how to spell rather than the word that first came to mind, rarely use a dictionary to check the spelling of a word ("since I can't find it because I don't know how it's spelled"), and suffer embarrassment because their spellings don't conform to the "accepted" ones.

Even the words "accepted spellings" indicate a problem since most children and adults are unaware that ofttimes their spellings are equally correct alternative spellings. Instruction on these is rarely, if ever, given, since teachers are as unaware of these alternatives as the children they teach and, if a choice is given, the more difficult of two alternatives is often taught on the assumption that it is the "preferred" and therefore *the correct spelling*[8,9,10].

But conventional spelling is also racist and the *arbiter elegantiae* of social class or status. There is a marked tendency to use the spellings a person writes as a measure of his literacy or social status: good spellers are associated with the well-educated upper class, poor spellers with the poorly-educated lower class. Rewards, in terms of employment, promotion, etc. are often related similarly for as Perrin and Smith[5] point out in their *Handbook on Current English:*

The man who writes with no misspelled words has prevented a first suspicion of the limits of his scholarship, or in the social world, of his general education and culture.

Recent Reform

Arguments against spelling reform abound in the literature, yet, as anyone familiar with the subject knows, each of these are errored on one or more bases and nearly all may be traced to sentiment. It is also true that enough attention to peculiarities inherent in English spelling has been demonstrated or experienced so that one sample of 230 educators, businessmen, and secretaries[6] showed that 88 percent favor some type of spelling reform while another sample of almost 800 educators confirmed this finding[7] indicating a wide spread current interest.

Responses such as that of a manager indicated that "In my high school graduating class, half of the class could hardly spell the easiest words," or of a teacher who stated that "Many times when I'm writing reports, I have to consistently refer to the dictionary to check spellings," or that of another teacher, "the more phonetic the spelling, the easier it would be for children to succeed in spelling and related tasks," or still another "Modern spelling reform would prove an invaluable aid to better reading success by many who now find reading and related skills an impossible barrier," are illustrations of the felt need for reform.

While the reformer has not been able to have much direct effect in recent years in producing change, it is notable that no research other than that cited above exists to support a change. Many reformers and alphabeteers exist, but little evidence exists that these reformers have proceeded logically to marshall support. In spite of this lack, reform, slowly and inexorably, has taken place with little or no outcry. Changes in spelling have occurred primarily in the realm of business and industry and these have been adopted by the public at large. *Yogurt*, popularized as a food by television commercials in the U.S., and spelled five different ways (all of which are equally correct) has been accepted as the standard spelling. In one study[8], a sample of 910 teachers and parents only vaguely recalled that *yogourt* and *yoghourt* were alternative spellings a few short years ago and none would replace the phonemic *yogurt* with any of the five previously used spellings. A group of psychologists when tested on the spelling of *donut* questioned whether there was another way of spelling it. When shown the spelling *doughnut*, individuals remarked "Oh yes, but we haven't used that for years; that's obsolete."

Oddly enough, the spelling of *draught*, mispronounced by many to rhyme with *caught* for the game of checkers (draughts) is hardly recognized as the spelling for *draft* beer with the switch by beer manufacturers from the antique spelling to the phonemic *draft* only a few years ago. The wholesale abandonment of *ue* after *g* in *epilog, analog, catalog* and *monolog* by millions and by publishers of catalogs, producers of analog computers, makers of television dramas, etc. is resisted by relatively few. The American brand of catsup, pronounced /ketchup/, and alternatively and equally correctly spelled *catchup, catsup,* or *ketchup* has been formalized on labels as *ketchup* by industry. In fact one study[9] of product names currently under way shows that over 450 different items have been respelled to represent their pronunciations (e.g., Snack-*Pak*), are spelled to provide instant identification with the hoped for or planned purpose of the product (*Fab* suggesting fabulous, *Duz*—does everything, etc.), or show the most phonetic alternative of several available (ketchup). The use of the macron in Nodōz and Nestlē to indicate the pronunciation of the glided vowel is paralleled in corporate names: Apēco.

Resistance to spelling reform, identified by Lounsbury[11] as primarily based on sentiment, is often encouraged by managing editors of publishers whose style sheet or house manual indicates what spellings are acceptable in its publications. Equally correct alternative spellings as identified by Deighton[12] for 2,000 words in four collegiate dictionaries are given short shift. *Catalogue* may still be foisted on children in spelling materials and workbooks, in readers and phonic programs, because editors believe that they are the final arbiters to keep the language "pure" and, if a choice is available, will apparently choose the more complex, the more unphonetic, the more irregular spelling.

The following is a sample of alternative spellings, both of which are correct:

antennas–antennae
aunty–auntie
buses–busses (for transportation)
practise–practice
busing–bussing (for transportation, not kissing)
blond–blonde
bluish–blueish
brocoli–broccoli
brunet–brunette
calory–calorie
cigaret–cigarette
curst–cursed
drafty–draughty
gasolene–gasoline
gelatin–gelatine
glamor–glamour
defense–defence
license–licence
liquify–liquefy
beefs–beeves
bran-new–brand-new
cagy–cagey
develop–develope
drout–drought
pinocle–pinochle

While it is commonly reported that there is only one correct spelling for every word in the language, the above list *is* representative of some 2400[13] words having alternatively correct spellings as found in various collegiate dictionaries. Although the belief that there is only one correct spelling has been supported by many teachers in the spellings they accept, by the uniform usage to be observed in newspapers and magazines, resistance to such arbitrary behavior has also been noted. One publisher in its books has dropped the apostrophe in such words as *dont, wont, cant*; another allows its authors the freedom to spell *aids* as *aides* when instructional materials are referred to; another avoids teaching the so called "*es* rule after words ending in *o*" to indicate the plural spelling of *tomatos, zeros, potatos, tobaccos, nos, mottos*; newspapers generally use *buses* rather than *busses*, etc.

Oddly enough, teachers when informed that each spelling in a list similar to that above was correct[10] and asked what they would do as a result of this knowledge were first surprised, indicated little knowledge of the availability of alternatives, and that they would modify their teaching behavior to include teaching "bright" children that there are equivalent spellings but would hold lesser able children to one spelling. When asked which spelling that would be, the almost uniform response was that which was shown in workbooks or spelling texts. The assumption that when the more phonetic, the more regularly spelled words found their way onto lists or into spelling materials, then teachers would teach these spellings, suggests one way to move spelling reform forward.

A first examination of this problem using parents, teachers and seventh and eighth grade children in one suburban community[8] indicated that only 4 percent of the population were aware of some of these alternatives, that responding to the questionnaire was a learning experience since most examined their dictionaries after completing the questionnaire, and that parents often excused their spelling knowledge by pointing out that "I went to school some 20 or 30 years ago and spelling has changed."

The expectancy of change suggests a predisposition to accept change and reinforces the findings of Stern's study[6] that spelling reform would be supported.

Direction for Change

It would certainly be incorrect for me to state "this is the way it should be" since no one individual's prejudices should dictate the direction for change. Rather we can rely on research and the documented views of many reformers in history to establish a commonality for direction. Rather than a reform *of* the orthography—if such it can be called since "unphonetic, irregular and illogical as it is, modern English spelling does not merit the name *orthography* which is made up of two Greek words meaning 'correct writing' "[14]—it is my belief that a reform *in* orthography should be aimed for.

If those words which do not consistently follow the consonant and vowel rules as established for reading instruction[13] were made to conform, learning to read and write would be vastly easier since no exceptions to generalizations would exist and only 25 to 30 rules would need to be learned and readily mastered. We might move in the direction of an elimination of unnecessary silent letters and might start with those which were inserted based on false etymology (the *b* in *dumb* and *doubt* for example), but not those which are morphophonemic (the *b* in *bomb, bombard,* the *g* in *sign, signal*); the elimination of the diacritic silent e following *v, z,* etc. where the signal today is meaningless or redundant, the reduction of the number of alternative graphemes to represent the sounds of English, the addition of the diacritic *e* following vowels to provide digraphic representations, etc. are but some of the possibilities.

Since research has demonstrated that a moderate reform would be most acceptable at this time[7] by the largest number of people, if we care that children should not be subject to the risk of failure and unnecessary frustration in learning to read, should not risk ego damage and being turned off from the adventure of education, we can start moderately by shifting to the use of alternative and equally correct spelt words which use the past tense morpheme *t* in such words as *curst, spelt,* etc., to those which are more phonemic, less complex, *thru* rather than *through, tho-though,* etc. We could adopt (SR1), spelling reform one[16], which establishes the principle of spelling the unglided *e* in such words as *sed, hed, thred.*

We could encourage more business and industries to utilize additional phonetic spellings and expect that television and other advertizing media will establish these as the accepted spellings since nearly all of a sample of 500 adults[16] indicated that many of the words they now write have been learned from these sources.

Whatever the rationale we choose to adopt, there is little doubt that support for a reform exists, that we can effectively use modern means of exploitation and that a reform is possible if we take the initiative to move one to the fore.

REFERENCES

1. Mazurkiewicz, Albert J. "A Comparative 10th Grade Study of i.t.a.-T.O. Beginnings", *Reading World*, Vol. 14, No. 4 (May, 1975).
2. Downing, John. *The i.t.a. Symposium*, National Foundation for Research in England and Wales, Slough, 1967.
3. Sofietti, James P. "Why Children Fail to Read: A Linguistic Analysis," in Mazurkiewicz, Albert J., *New Perspectives in Reading Instruction*, Pitman Publishing Company, 1968.
4. Makita, Kiyoshi. "The Rarity of Reading Disability in Japanese Children," *American Journal of Orthopsychiatry*, Vol. 38, No. 4., July, 1968, 599-614.
5. Perrin, Porter G. and Smith, George H. *The Perrin-Smith Handbook of Current English*, Scott, Foresman and Co., Fairlawn, N.J., 1962.
6. Stern, Ruth. "Interest in Spelling Reform," Unpublished Research Report, Kean College of N.J., 1973.
7. ———. *Educators Acceptance of Spelling Reform*, Unpublished Master's Thesis, Kean College of N.J., 1975.

8. Mazurkiewicz, Albert J. and Berk, Barbara. "Spelling Equivalency Awareness," *Reading World*, Vol. 15, No. 3 (March, 1976).
9. Mazurkiewicz, Albert J. "Spelling Reform in Industry and Business," *Reading World*, Vol. 15, No. 4 (December, 1976).
10. _____ , and Gould, Jane. "Spelling Preferences and Instructional Considerations," *Reading World*, Vol. 15, No. 2 (May, 1976).
11. Lounsbury, Thomas R. *English Spelling and Spelling Reform*. Harper and Brothers, New York, 1909.
12. Deighton, Lee C. *A Comparative Study of Spellings,* Hardscrabble Press, Inc., Pleasant Meltler, N.Y., 1972.
13. Emery, Donald W. *Variant Spellings in Modern American Dictionaries,* (Rev. Ed.) Sponsored by the Washington State Council of Teachers of English. Washington, D.C. National Council of Teachers of English, 1973.
14. McKnight, George. *Modern English in the Making,* Appleton-Century Crofts, Inc., N.Y., 1928.
15. Mazurkiewicz, Albert J. *Teaching About Phonics,* St. Martin's Press of New York, 1976.
16. _____ , and Roth, Charlotte. "Affects on Adult Spelling Choices," *Reading World,* Vol. 15, No. 3 (October, 1976).

SECTION THREE

Foundations of Instruction

- ... in teaching spelling as a part of word study, the teacher supplies a *context* that is missing in many spelling programs.
  Edgar Dale
  Joseph O'Rourke

- ... a child's knowledge about written words is acquired systematically, developmentally, and gradually.
  James Beers

- Contradictions in spelling exist between those used by this sample of instructional materials, teacher choices of "correct" spellings, and between teachers who are charged with teaching spelling.
  Albert Mazurkiewicz
  Jane Gould

INTRODUCTION

Spelling instruction would be more enjoyable for both teachers and students if they were more aware of the principles on which this instruction is based. One is the alphabetic basis of our language. The millions of adult Americans who are poor spellers might find it hard to believe, but our language has a highly consistent orthography. It is far from perfect, but as Hanna, et al. show, the relationship between sounds and letter representations in English is more predictable than has traditionally been thought.

A second principle is that spelling instruction enhances vocabulary development. This conclusion comes from Dale and O'Rourke, whose work on vocabulary is unsurpassed among contemporary educators.

Children grow into spelling. As they mature, they use different strategies to form their words. Several of our contributors describe the various stages of spelling through which children progress and discuss how knowledge of these stages can be used by teachers.

There is no single "right" way to spell. Nicholson and Schachter found that proficient spellers use their knowledge of language, internalized rules, and visual associations when they write words. They make the recommendation that teaching activities need to be based on all three kinds of knowledge, a recommendation that can hardly be disputed.

Despite the regularity of our language, it contains a great number of variations. Some words have perfectly acceptable alternative spellings. Mazurkiewicz and Gould found that teachers are relatively unaware of acceptable alternative spellings, but would be willing to teach them. Betts adds that many of the most frequently used words do not conform to regular patterns, and that teachers should mix a liberal dose of common sense with their spelling instruction if they hope to alleviate the frustration experienced by many schoolchildren.

The Alphabetic Base of Spelling

PAUL R. HANNA
RICHARD E. HODGES
JEAN S. HANNA

Features of American-English Orthography

Before describing this study—which was known as Project 1991 and was conducted at Stanford University—we should first review some of the features of American-English spelling that were considered in carrying out the research. As has been repeatedly pointed out, few

---

Paul R. Hanna, Richard E. Hodges, Jean S. Hanna: *Spelling: Structure and Strategies,* Pages 80–98. Copyright ©1971 by Houghton Mifflin Company. Used by permission of the publishers.

of our speech sounds have single spellings representing them in all words of the language. This is, of course, precisely the problem that complicates the mastery of our orthography.

An American-English writer—as opposed to a writer whose language has a highly consistent alphabetic orthography—is required to play odds, to assess the *probability* that a given phoneme is spelled a particular way in the word he proposes to write. Helped by such additional cues as his visual or neuromuscular memory of the word, or of other words of similar pattern, he usually does achieve a functional mastery of the orthography, although some parts of words present special problems. In short, an ability to spell correctly in our language is largely dependent on the person's knowledge of how closely a given phoneme *approximates* the alphabetic principle of a unique graphic symbol for each phoneme.

Further discussion of sound-letter relationships also must take into account the factors of position and stress. Phonemes are not randomly strung together to form syllables and words. Most have favored positions; and a few, such as /ng/, are not used in certain positions at all. Moreover, the stress patterns of American-English speech sometimes affect the pronunciation of phonemes while the graphemic symbol remains unchanged— and sometimes the reverse occurs. Therefore, in order to determine the productive patterns of American-English spelling, at least three factors must be considered:

1. How phonemes are spelled when position and stress have no effect on them, i.e. when they strictly adhere to the alphabetic principle. For example, the consonant /p/ is almost always spelled *p* (cf. *pit, spot, top*)— regardless of where it occurs in a word and how it is stressed.
2. How the position of a phoneme in a syllable or word affects its spelling. For example, the /f/ sound is normally spelled *f* at the beginning of a syllable or word (*farm*), spelled *ph* when it is the second element in a consonant cluster (*sphere*), and spelled *ff* when it terminates a word (*off*). Moreover, *gh,* another spelling of /f/, represents this phoneme only at the end of syllables and words, as in *cough, rough,* and *laugh' ter.*
3. How syllable or word stress affects phoneme-grapheme correspondences. As noted above, stress may affect the pronunciation but not the spelling. For example, the second vowel sound of *civ'il* occurs in an unaccented syllable and has a pronunciation much like the vowel sound in *rug,* a vowel sound called *schwa* (/ə/). When *civ'il* is changed to *ci vil' ian,* the previously unaccented syllable becomes stressed and the /ə/ changes to /i/, but the *spelling* of the two vowel sounds remains the same. In addition, stress may change the spelling but not the sound, as is seen in the spelling of final /k/ in *at' tic* and *at tack'.*

PHASE I: AN ANALYSIS OF PHONEME-GRAPHEME RELATIONSHIPS

With these three factors in mind, the Stanford researchers employed computer technology to analyze the sound-letter relationships in 17,000-plus words, with the intention of clarifying the alphabetic nature of American-English spelling. What, then, were some of their major findings?

Simple Phoneme-grapheme Correspondences

In terms of the first factor, simple phoneme-grapheme correspondences, it was found that the great majority of consonants had single spellings which were used 80 percent or more of the time in the 17,000-plus words investigated. On the other hand, only a handful of vowel sounds had single spellings which occurred with such high frequency. Table 7-1 presents a sample of the phonemes which were represented most consistently by one specific grapheme, and examples of words in which they occur.

It can be seen from this table that a person is likely to be able to spell many consonant phonemes and a small number of vowel phonemes (the so-called "short" vowels) correctly if he is aware of the most commonly used graphemic representation of these phonemes. Obviously,

Table 7-1
Samples of Highly Productive Simple Phoneme–Grapheme Correspondences

Phoneme	No. of Occurrences in 17,000+ Words	Most Common Spelling	No. of Occurrences in 17,000+ Words	% of Use of This Spelling	Examples	
*Consonants**						
/b/	2303	*b*	2239	97.2	*b*ig	ta*b*
/d/	3691	*d*	3611	97.8	*d*ig	ma*d*
/l/	5389	*l*	4894	90.8	*l*ake	he*l*p
/m/	3501	*m*	3302	94.3	*m*an	ha*m*
/n/	7656	*n*	7452	97.3	*n*ow	ca*n*
/p/	3449	*p*	3296	95.6	*p*ill	sto*p*
/r/	9390	*r*	9119	97.1	*r*un	ca*r*
/t/	7793	*t*	7528	96.6	*t*in	po*t*
Vowels						
/a/	4340	*a*	4192	96.6	*a*t	c*a*n
/e/	3646	*e*	3316	90.9	*e*bb	p*e*n
/o/	1662	*o*	1558	93.7	*o*n	t*o*p
/u/	1410	*u*	1212	85.9	*u*s	c*u*p

* Other productive phoneme-grapheme correspondences noticed at this level of analysis included /g/ spelled *g* as in *go*, /h/ spelled *h* as in *him*, /th/ spelled *th* as in *thin*, /th̶/ spelled *th* as in *then*, /v/ spelled *v* as in *vat*, and /w/ spelled *w* as in *win*.

however, words are made up of many other phonemes. Are all of the remaining phoneme-grapheme correspondences completely inconsistent with the alphabetic nature of the orthography, or can useful sound-letter patterns be detected?

Positional Effects on Spelling

In order to resolve this issue, the researchers analyzed the 17,000-plus words in terms of the second factor listed on page 151: the effect of the position of a phoneme in a syllable or word on the spelling of the phoneme. Table 7-2 presents some phonemes, their most common spelling in a specific position, the percentage of times that they were represented by that spelling in that position, and some examples.

The table clearly shows that many phonemes—particularly vowels—have quite predictable spellings in certain positions. For example, although /ā/ is spelled *a* only 45 percent of the time in the 17,000-plus words, it is spelled *a* 81 percent of the time when it ends a syllable that does not end a word. In summary, we can say that the position of phonemes in syllables and words distinctly influences the spelling of many of the phonemes.

The Effects of Stress on Spelling

The results of Project 1991 were not as clear-cut regarding the effect of stress on the spelling of phonemes as the effect of position. However, the factor of stress should not be dismissed as irrelevant, since the form of a word is integrally related to its *total* phonetic characteristics—including its stress pattern. Linguists re-

Table 7-2

Samples of the Effect of Position on Phoneme–Grapheme Correspondences

Phoneme	No. of Occurrences in 17,000+ Words	Position in Syllable and Most Common Spelling	No. of Occurrences of Spelling in That Position	No. of Occurrences of Phoneme in That Position	% of Use of This Spelling	Examples
/ā/	2248	In final position, *a*	860	1062	81.00	f*a* vor
/ē/	2538	In final position, *e*	1740	1921	90.6	l*e* gal
/i/	7815	In medial position, *i*	2772	3346	82.6	b*i*g
/ō/	2587	In final position, *o*	1629	1771	92.00	n*o* tice
/yü/	1188	In final position, *u*	770	870	88.5	c*u* bic
/f/	2019	In initial position, *f*	1381	1630	84.7	*f*an
/k/	4712	In initial position, *c*	2287	2607	87.7	*c*oin
/ng/	615	In medial position, *n*	129	134	96.27	si*n*k
/s/	6326	In medial position, *s*	373	385	96.9	be*s*t

153

fer to the study of this relationship as *morphophonemics*. Table 7-3 presents some useful insights about certain phoneme-grapheme correspondences that emerge when stress is taken into account.

The Stanford study we have been summarizing pointed up the basically alphabetic nature of American-English spelling. It showed that, contrary to traditional viewpoints, the orthography is far from erratic. It is based upon relationships between phonemes and graphemes—relationships that are sometimes complex in nature but which, when clarified, demonstrate that American-English orthography, like that of other languages, is largely systematic.

PHASE II: A COMPUTER PROGRAMMED TO SPELL

To find out whether these observed phoneme-grapheme relationships could be useful in spelling words, the Stanford group undertook a second investigation in which a computer was programmed to spell the 17,000-plus words by using the orthographic insights gained from the first phase of the study. Much like a person who can distinguish American-English phonemes, who knows the various ways in which these phonemes can be spelled, and who knows the productive principles that determine how these phonemes are usually spelled in particular situations, the computer was to attempt to spell the 17,000-plus words on the basis of the previously demonstrated sound-letter relationships, including the factors of position and stress. Table 7-4 lists some of the relationships that were highly productive in terms of helping the computer spell correctly. Table 7-5 provides examples of phoneme-grapheme correspondence factors that did not work as well as might have been expected.

It should be kept in mind, of course, that the spelling principles used in Phase II of the Stanford project were humanly derived: the *researchers* selected those sound-letter relationships that appeared to predict most reliably the spellings of the respective phonemes. Therefore, it is possible that some errors of judgment

Table 7–3

Samples of the Effect of Stress on
Phoneme–Grapheme Correspondences

Phoneme	Most Common Spelling and % in 17,000+ Words	Conditions for Predicting That Spelling	Example
/ch/	*ch* (97%)	In initial position of primary-stressed syllables	*ch*ar′ coal
/j/	*g* (82%)	In initial position of unstressed syllables	co′ *g*ent
/sh/	*ti* (84%)	In initial position of unstressed syllables	frac′ *ti*on
/y/	*y* (98%)	In initial position of primary-stressed syllables	*y*es′ ter day
/y/	*i* (86%)	In initial position of unstressed syllables	on′ *i*on

Table 7-4

Selected Sample Cases in Which the Algorithm Was Found Highly Productive

Phoneme	Spelled	Condition in Which Phoneme Occurred	Example	No. of Times Phoneme Occurred Under Stated Condition	No. of Times Spelled Correctly	% of Predictability
Consonants					
/b/	*b*	All other cases[a]	*b*oy	2283	2237	98.00
/ch/	*t*	In initial position of unaccented syllable and followed by /ə/	na'*t*ure	124	124	100.00
	ch	All other cases	*ch*art	284	278	97.9
/d/	*d*	All other cases	*d*og	3681	3620	93.3
/f/	*f*	All other cases	*f*ish	1959	1576	80.4
/g/	*g*	All other cases	*g*o	1283	1180	92.0
/h/	*h*	All cases[b]	*h*ere	778	762	97.9
/hw/	*wh*	All cases	*wh*at	89	89	100.00

155

Table 7-4—Continued

Selected Sample Cases in Which the Algorithm Was Found Highly Productive

Phoneme	Spelled	Condition in Which Phoneme Occurred	Example	No. of Times Phoneme Occurred Under Stated Condition	No. of Times Spelled Correctly	% of Predictability
		Consonants—continued				
/k/	c	All other cases	cow	3881	3342	86.1
/ks/	x	All other cases	mix	233	233	100.00
/kw/	qu	All cases	queen	196	191	97.4
/l/	l	All other cases	lamp	5242	4858	92.7
/′l/	le	All cases	ta′b*le*	662	631	95.3
/m/	m	All cases	man	3503	3304	94.3
/′m/	m	All cases	chasm	97	97	100.00
/n/	n	All cases	new	7662	7458	97.3
	n	In medial position	sink	131	129	98.5
/ng/	ng	In word-final position	sing	319	317	99.4
/p/	p	All other cases	push	3443	3299	95.8
/r/	r	All cases	run	9394	9123	97.1
/s/	s	All other cases	say	5354	4337	81.00
/sh/	ti	Initial position of unaccented syllables	fic′*ti*on	851	729	85.7
	sh	All other cases	ship	448	365	81.5

[a] "All other cases" indicates that other "rules" were included for spelling the phoneme in question, in addition to the rule shown.
[b] "All cases" indicates that the "rule" was the only one included in the algorithm for spelling the phoneme in question.

Table 7-4—Continued

Selected Sample Cases in Which the Algorithm Was Found Highly Productive

Phoneme	Spelled	Condition in Which Phoneme Occurred	Example	No. of Times Phoneme Occurred Under Stated Condition	No. of Times Spelled Correctly	% of Predictability
		Consonants—continued				
/t/	t	All other cases	toe	7764	5528	97.0
/th/	th	All cases	*th*ing	411	411	100.00
/th/	th	All cases	*th*is	149	149	100.00
/v/	ve	In word-final position	ha*ve*	238	238	100.00
/v/	v	All other cases	*v*et	1126	1126	100.00
/w/	w	All other cases	*w*et	573	563	98.3
/y/	i	In unaccented syllables	jun'*i*or	73	63	86.3
/zh/	si	In all cases when followed by /ə/	fu'*si*on	50	49	98.00

Table 7-4—Continued

Selected Sample Cases in Which the Algorithm Was Found Highly Productive

Phoneme	Spelled	Condition in Which Phoneme Occurred	Example	No. of Times Phoneme Occurred Under Stated Condition	No. of Times Spelled Correctly	% of Predictability
		Vowels				
/ā/	*a*	In syllable-final, but not word-final, position	pla′ cate	930	860	92.5
/a/	*a*	All cases	cat	4340	4328	99.7
/ä/	*a*	All cases	arm	580	536	92.4
/ē/	*e*	In syllable-final, but not word-final, position	le′ gal	1832	1715	96.6
/e/	*e*	In initial position	etch	760	752	98.9
/e/	*e*	In medial position	bet	2789	2565	92.0
/ə (r)/	*e*	All other cases	but′ ter	2132	1667	78.2
/ī/	*i—e*	In medial position when next phoneme is word-final	dime	439	398	90.7
/i/	*i*	All other cases	tip	5845	5506	94.2
/ō/	*o*	All other cases	told	1710	1615	94.4
/oi/	*oy*	In word-final position	toy	22	22	100.00
/ou/	*ou*	In initial position	out	72	70	97.2
/ou/	*ow*	All other cases	now	80	72	90.0

Table 7-4—Continued

Selected Sample Cases in Which the Algorithm Was Found Highly Productive

Phoneme	Spelled	Condition in Which Phoneme Occurred	Example	No. of Times Phoneme Occurred Under Stated Condition	No. of Times Spelled Correctly	% of Predictability
		Vowels—continued				
/ȯ/	*o*	In all cases	b*o*ss	127	123	96.8
/ȯ (r)/	*o*	In medial position and followed by /r/	c*o*rn	287	280	97.6
/o/	*o*	All other cases	t*o*p	1588	1573	99.1
/u̇/	*u*	All other cases	p*u*ll	182	149	81.9
/yü/	*u*	In syllable-final, but not word-final, position	c*u*' pid	828	777	93.8
	u—e	In medial position	c*u*be	277	225	81.2
/u/	*u*	All other cases	c*u*p	1267	1161	91.6

Table 7-5

Selected Sample Cases in Which the Algorithm Did Not Work as Well as Expected

Phoneme	Spelled	Condition in Which Phoneme Occurred	Example	No. of Times Phoneme Occurred Under Stated Condition	No. of Times Spelled Correctly	% of Predictability
Consonants						
/j/	g	In initial position	gem	456	336	73.7
/k/	k	When preceded by /ng/	drink	152	97	63.8
/s/	c	In final position of a stressed word-final syllable	lace	129	58	45.0
/z/	z	In final position, preceded by /ī/	or' gan ize	148	97	65.5
	s	In all other cases[a]	clos' et	752	571	75.9
/zh/	s	In all other cases	cas' u al	52	34	65.4

[a] "In all other cases" indicates that other "rules" were included for spelling the phoneme in question, in addition to the rule shown.

Table 7-5—Continued
Selected Sample Cases in Which the Algorithm Did Not Work as Well as Expected

Phoneme	Spelled	Condition in Which Phoneme Occurred	Example	No. of Times Phoneme Occurred Under Stated Condition	No. of Times Spelled Correctly	% of Predictability
		Vowels				
/ā (r)/	*a*	In medial position	ca n*ar*' y	104	65	62.5
/ē/	*ea*	In medial position	r*ea*d	380	167	43.9
	e	In final position of a stressed, non-word-final syllable	h*e*' ro	77	55	71.4
/ē (r)/	*ea*	In medial position in a word-final syllable	f*ea*r	49	14	28.6
/ī/	*igh*	In medial position, followed by /t/	f*igh*t	146	78	53.4
/ō/	*o—e*	In medial position of a word-final syllable	d*o*m*e*	226	150	66.4
	o	In medial position of a non-word-final syllable	g*o*l' den	271	176	64.9
/ȯ/	*au*	In final position of a non-word-final syllable	f*au*' cet	124	79	63.7
/ü/	*oo*	In medial position, all other cases	f*oo*d	218	158	72.5

161

were made in the selection of principles, while some principles were inadvertently overlooked—e.g. the fact that /ou/ is normally spelled *ou* in the medial position of syllables. It should also be understood that the total set of "rules," which is called the *algorithm,* included only phonological information. It did not encompass, as will be seen, important morphological and contextual information needed for a comprehensive mastery of American-English orthography.

But despite these drawbacks, the computer spelled almost 50 percent (49.8%) of the 17,000-plus words correctly—a total of 8,483 words. To be sure, 50 percent accuracy in spelling words is not sufficient for written communication. But what this finding does point to is the generalization that nearly half the words in ordinary usage can be correctly spelled solely on the basis of a functional understanding of the relationships between spoken sound and written symbol. Undoubtedly, with refinement of the algorithm, a second run through the computer would have resulted in an even greater percentage of correctly spelled words. (It should be pointed out, however, that the power of the algorithm lies in its *cumulative ability* to relate phonemes to orthography; the sum of the individual sound-letter principles is considerably more important than are the individual principles viewed unrelated to each other.)

The analysis of computer errors

Equally revealing was the finding that the computer misspelled an additional 37 percent of the words (6,195 words) with but one error, 11.4 percent (1,941 words) with two errors, and only 2.3 percent (390 words) with three errors or more. And when the *kinds* of errors made were examined, some most interesting facts about our writing system emerged. Let us see what the most common causes of misspelling were for the "one-error" words.

The first type of computer error was in spelling compound words; for example, *playground* was misspelled as *pla-ground*. In this instance, the computer, not yet equipped with a knowledge of compounding, was unable to tell that the two independent words *play* and *ground* were combined to form a single word with a single unit of meaning, and treated *playground* as two *syllables*. In doing so, it followed the sound-to-letter principle that /ā/ at the end of syllables not ending words (as in *va' cate, na' tion, ba' by*) is usually spelled *a*. Had the computer applied the principle that /ā/ at the end of *words* (as in *day, say, play*) is generally spelled *ay*, this particular misspelling and similar errors in other compound words would not have occurred. In effect, the computer—unprogrammed for such refinements—was unable to detect that compound words are comprised of shorter words, and therefore treated the shorter words as syllables.

A second type of error was made because the researchers did not program the computer to double the spellings of certain phonemes. The word *address,* misspelled by the computer as *adress,* is a good illustration. *Address* is ultimately of Latin origin and is composed of a prefix representing Latin *ad-* and a root representing Latin *directum.* Although when *address* occurs in speech, the final /d/ of *ad-* and the first /d/ of *-dress* are combined so that only one /d/ is pronounced, the spelling of each /d/ remains in the written word. The combining of sounds is quite common in English words that are constructed by combining roots and affixes; but since the programmers did not supply the computer with the "word building" rules of our language, the computer identified only one /d/ in *address* and spelled it accordingly.

Numerous other instances of how a knowledge of *morphology* (how words are formed in a language) would have enabled the computer to spell many of the one-error words correctly were observed in this early phase of the Stanford study. These observations underscored the fact that an orthography represents *language,* and therefore reflects many principles other than phonological that are inherent in the structure of the spoken code.

Another important finding was that many of the computer's misspellings occurred in borrowed words whose original spellings had been kept more or less intact. Although the major "lender" languages—French, Spanish, Italian, Greek, and Latin—possess alphabetically based orthographies, they sometimes use graphemes that differ from ours for their phonemes. For example, the computer misspelled *mosquito* as *mousketo,* failing to take into account the fact that in Spanish, /k/ is often spelled *qu* and /ē/ is often spelled *i.*[1]

Although the bulk of the misspelled words could be accounted for on the basis of the word-building and word-borrowing proclivities of our language, there remained a residue of misspelled words that fell into two categories: 1) a comparatively small number of words in which certain graphemic representations of phonemes are so unpredictable that a knowledge of phonology and morphology is of little help, e.g. *one, acre, iron, forecastle, colonel, victuals, boatswain,* and *of;* and 2) certain words—called *homophones* or *homonyms*—whose similar pronunciation but different spelling creates special problems, e.g. *bare* and *bear, peer* and *pier,* and *aisle, isle,* and *I'll.* Sound-to-letter principles can be used to spell these words, of course, but the choice of principles depends upon the meaning of the word being used—which the computer was not programmed to know.

The Phase II investigation indicated, then, that about half of the words in ordinary speech can be spelled correctly by the application of principles based on the alphabetic nature of the American-English orthography. And most of the remaining words can be spelled correctly if one couples a knowledge of sound-letter correspondences with a knowledge of the characteristic word-building and word-borrowing patterns of our language. Later research which builds morphological and contextual clues into the computer program will no doubt improve the computer's score.

IMPLICATIONS FOR SPELLING PROGRAMS

The two-phased study we have just described represents the increasing interest of curriculum makers in taking into consideration the *nature* of the subject matter to be taught. In this particular case, linguistic insights into the nature of our orthography provided a fresh point of view regarding how spelling might be taught and, most important, identified *what* should be taught. In Part Two of this book, one modern approach to the teaching of spelling will be explained in detail—an approach that makes use of linguistic information about our written code and of our increasing understanding of the learner and the processes of teaching and learning. But for now, let us recapitulate the major points about American-English orthography which early phases of the Stanford study demonstrated.

The first important fact is that the American-English orthography is an alphabetically based orthography, i.e. it employs graphic symbols to represent the speech sounds, the phonemes, of language. And although our orthography does not perfectly conform to the alphabetic principle that one and only one graphic symbol shall represent each phoneme, there is a more consistent relationship between sounds and letter representations than has traditionally been thought. This consistency is demonstrated by the fact that about half of all the words we would normally use in writing were spelled correctly by a computer that was

---

[1]The unusual spelling *ou* for the /ə/ of *mosquito* resulted because the computer had been programmed to spell /ə/ with *ou* when it was followed by /s/.

programmed (somewhat imperfectly) with certain sound-letter principles of our writing system. Such principles, along with further refinements, could become a part of the pupil's spelling repertoire and be applied in spelling words he could pronounce but whose spellings may be unfamiliar. Reinforced by good habits of proofreading, his functional awareness of the alphabetic nature of our writing system could free him from rote memorization of each word.

A second important fact that emerged from the Stanford study is that just as there is pattern and system in the relationships between phonemes and their graphemic representations, there is also pattern and system in the ways words have been created, and continue to be created, in our language. This morphological factor helps to account for many of the seemingly demonic spellings that occur in written American English. A knowledge of morphology contributes importantly to the pupil's development of a power to spell, as well as being inherently interesting.

A third important fact demonstrated by the study is that the number of so-called "spelling demons" scattered throughout our writing system is relatively small (about 3 percent of the core vocabulary fell into this category). Furthermore, such mavericks cause spelling difficulties only because certain *parts* of them depart radically from the basic alphabetic principle. Thus, although the word *women*—for example—may be called a spelling demon, the truly demonic part lies only in the unique spelling of /i/ in the first syllable. The other four phonemes are spelled just as one would expect, so that only one-fifth of this word presents a problem for the speller. In sum, certain words do contain rare, even unique, spellings of phonemes, and such words need to be mastered by whatever means available to the pupil. But these few words hardly constitute a basis for assuming that the entire language is orthographically chaotic, and that most words are spelling problems.

A rational and comprehensive spelling program should begin with the three facts just listed and lead the pupil toward discovering and applying useful generalizations regarding our writing system.

Pronunciation and Spelling

EDGAR DALE
JOSEPH O'ROURKE
HENRY A. BAMMAN

This unit does not try to set up a basic program of spelling. We assume that such a program is always going forward in the schools. Our purpose is to show how pronunciation and spelling are related to vocabulary development. Earlier we noted that word development is concept development and that concept development involves noting similarities and differences. This often means being sensitively aware of the sounds and spellings of words. If a student commonly mispronounces a word, he is likely to misspell it.

The student mistakes *effect* for *affect* partly because he does not distinguish the *e* from the *a*. Perhaps he doesn't hear the difference, or perhaps his parents and teachers do not give enough attention to early oral language development. Often,

---

Pages 163–194 of *Techniques of Teaching Vocabulary*. © 1971 by Field Educational Publications. Reprinted by permission of the Benjamin/Cummings Publishing Company.

spelling errors occur when words sound the same: *principle, principal*. Here the syllables *-pal* and *-ple* have the same sound. Hence, one must often depend on the context to know how a word is to be spelled.

Pronunciation is important in vocabulary development because it involves discrimination between sounds that combine to form words and concepts. Thus, students must make distinctions between the sounds of words such as *wear* and *where, ever* and *every, while* and *wile*. Likewise, students must learn to make discriminations in spelling, distinguishing between *stake* and *steak, pain* and *pane, flew* and *flu*.

We have assumed that in the typical school, accurate spelling is considered important. Actually, nearly all words that children and young people write are correctly spelled, but our standards are high and we object to the misspelling of two or three words on a list of 150. Bad spelling, if nothing else, is annoying to the reader. Moreover, it requires a large amount of a teacher's time to mark misspelled words and then try to reteach them.

We know that spelling ability ranges widely. Possibly there is a sharp difference in the innate ability of persons to visualize the arrangement of word parts and letters. However, most students can sharply improve their spelling skills by (1) developing a spelling conscience, (2) noticing word structures, and (3) being aware that certain words are commonly misspelled and need to be double-checked until they are well known. Since the number of words that are commonly misspelled is relatively small, students who are alerted to their own personal "demons" should show rapid improvement.

Communicating Clearly

The chief reason for discriminating between sounds is to communicate clearly. There are other reasons. For example, the relationship between the pronunciation of words and social acceptance is important. We refer here to accepted standards of schools, professions, business, and industry, where correct pronunciation may be of prime concern; where it is important, for example, not to pronounce *our* like *are*, or *for* like *fur*, especially if mispronunciation not only is unacceptable but leads to misunderstanding as well.

Pronunciation and spelling are means by which we send and receive words and exchange ideas. Students need to be reminded that poor enunciation, mispronunciation, and incorrect spelling distract the listener or the reader and cause static in the communication system.

The teacher can help students become more aware of pronunciation by having the class listen to recordings of speeches by both Americans and Britons. Students might then note the differences between American and British pronunciations. (In England, *laboratory* is pronounced *la_boratory, schedule* becomes *shedule*, *garage* is *garage*.

Practicing Pronunciation

We sometimes mispronounce words because we spell them incorrectly, though more often the reverse is true. Students are nevertheless embarrassed when they mispronounce words that others know well. Obviously, then, it is best to create a situation in which students' pronunciation can be corrected in the spirit of constructive criticism.

Students should be encouraged to take note of mispronunciations they hear and discuss them in class. Common mispronunciations might include *ashfalt* for *asphalt*, *chimley* for *chimney*, *athalete* for *athlete*, *attackted* for *attacked*, *ast* for *asked*, *excape* for *escape*.

Such key words can be spelled aloud or written on the chalkboard. Members of the class can repeat each one to themselves until the correct pronunciation is firmly implanted. The teacher might also prepare tapes that spell out key words, allow intervals for the student to pronounce each one, then present the "accepted" pronunciation in each case.

Students may be at the stage where they are aware of errors in pronunciation or usage on television and radio. One distinguished commentator talked about something as being "the penultimate of success." He meant "the last word." *Penultimate* (from Latin *paene,* almost, and *ultima,* last) means next to the ultimate, almost last—it does not mean the highest achievement. Words heard mispronounced over the air include *fortay* for *forte* (fort), *skism* for *schism* (sizzem).

The teacher might record voices of the class members so they can listen to themselves talk. This can be done during regular class discussion periods. This experience helps students note and correct their own pronunciation errors, as well as enjoy a new experience.

Variety in Pronunciation

Few words are limited to one pronunciation. Words that change the accented syllable when they change from noun to verb or adjective are common. We "*refuse* to be laughed at" but we "empty the wastebasket into the *refuse* container." Other words, while not changing their general meaning, shift from one part of speech to another:

a. He wrote an *abstract* of the article.
b. He *abstracted* the material from the article.

Some words are pronounced more than one way though their meaning or part of speech does not change. You may say "adver*tize*ment" and the television announcer says "ad*ver*tisement"; but the word is the same, and both pronunciations are acceptable. Actually, our pronunciation is influenced by where we live, what we have been taught, or what our friends and family say.

In dealing with pronunciation, differences in regional dialect must be considered. Therefore, we do not suggest a preference for one pronunciation over another. As previously suggested, the main reason for "careful" pronunciation is to communicate clearly and avoid ambiguity or confusion. Therefore, the teacher need not stress one, exclusive pronunciation of a word, since family background, regional traditions, experience, travel, and preference all influence the pronunciation of words and the changing of pronunciations.

Spelling Problems

Teachers might remind students that while the pronunciations of many English words slowly but constantly change, their spelling became static centuries ago. For example, when Chaucer wrote "The Knight's Tale," the word *knight* was pronounced *k-nicht* (the *ch* having the Greek *chi* sound). It is now pronounced *nite* but still retains the original spelling, *knight.* The word *night* has gone through the same process: the pronunciation has changed but the spelling has not. Another example is the variation of pronunciation of *gh* words, in which the *gh* is silent or stands for the same sound as *f*: li*gh*t, bri*gh*t; furlou*gh,* plou*gh;* rou*gh,* enou*gh.*

Other silent letters are found in *knee* and *knife.* The *k* was once pronounced, as was the *g* in *gnash* and *gnarled.* The *e* and *a* in *sea, break, wealth,* etc., were once separate sounds. The *w* in *two,* now silent in English, is pronounced in the Scottish word for *two—twa* (pronounced *twah).* The *w* in *answer* was once pronounced *(answear),* and the *w* is still pronounced in a word related to *answer—swear.*

Unlike students in ancient Rome, our students have a fairly difficult time learning to spell. Roman students learning Latin knew that each consonant had only one sound and that each vowel had only two sounds, long and short. Italian children today learning their highly phonemic language have little difficulty with spelling because of the high degree of one-to-one correspondence of phoneme and grapheme, in which one letter stands for one sound. To gain such ideal correspondence it would be necessary to follow the advice of George Bernard Shaw, who recommended a completely new system of English spelling. To illustrate the inconsistency of present spelling, he pointed out that *ghoti* could be pronounced *fish*:

gh in *laugh* = *f*
o in *women* = *i*
ti in *nation* = *sh*

Aside from phonemically irregular words, one of the chief causes of poor spelling is careless pronunciation. *Government* is often mispronounced and therefore spelled *goverment*, *quantity* becomes *quanity*, *probably* becomes *probly*, *bronchial* becomes *bronichal*, *vanilla* becomes *vanella*, and *arctic* becomes *artic*. (Actually, the latter pronunciation of *arctic* is now acceptable though the spelling is not.)

Spelling and Vocabulary Study

Vocabulary acquisition precedes reading skill, since students must already know words in order to read (*decode* written symbols). However, if the student is to go beyond decoding to *encoding* (writing), he must gain skill in letter discrimination. He must *spell* (place the graphemes of a word in conventional order) before he can write, or encode with skill. While the decoder (the reader) recognizes the word *descend*, the encoder (the writer) has to reproduce the grapheme relationships that make up the word *descend*. Therefore, the skillful encoder (the student who spells words correctly) is in a better position to recognize *descend* in reading and in addition is likely to learn more easily the related words *descending*, *descendant*, *descendants*, *ascend*, and *ascendant*. Students who can spell (encode) can easily read (decode) and are likely to have less difficulty with writing skills.

The most effective spelling program works simultaneously with vocabulary study. Since over 80 percent of English words are phonemically regular, we may be neglecting a ready-made method of learning words and how to spell them: encoding language patterns and word patterns.

The language code, which we must decode to read and encode to write, has order; otherwise we could make no generalizations about the language. This order is quite clear. For example, the *ou* sound is peculiar to different words such as *house*, *louse*, *couch*, *grouch*, *slouch*. From them the student can generalize about the *ou* pattern and the sound it represents. Exceptions to this generalization are easily learned later.

From recognizing meaningful syllables, the student can proceed to a study of the parts of words (roots and affixes). The spelling of words should include encoding sounds, symbols, syllables, and meaningful syllables or elements such as *ab* (from), *ad* (to), *ante* (before).

In addition to making generalizations about regular patterns of graphemes that make up sounds, symbols, and syllables, the student needs practice in making discriminations. He should note that variations in word meanings are often distinguishable by the arrangement of similar letters or even by the addition or omission of a letter: *rat*, *rate*; *hat*, *hate*; *bat*, *bait*, *bate*; *singing*, *singeing*; *dying*, *dyeing*.

The lack of a solid relationship between spelling and vocabulary skills is apparent when students spell *bare* as *bear*, *there* as *their*, *fete* as *fate*. The significance of choosing the correct letter in spelling is easily seen in words such as *homily* and *homely*, *blackhead* and *blockhead*, *mallet* and *mullet*, *winch* and *wench, cook* and *kook*. Anagrammatic words result from the transposition of letters. The position of a letter makes a big difference in words such as *lair* and *liar, dairy* and *diary, lie* and *lei, complaint* and *compliant, trial* and *trail, causal* and *casual*.

It is clear, therefore, that the study of spelling is important for these reasons, to name a few:

1. Incorrect spelling can cause the reader to misunderstand the meaning of a word: *set* for *sit, red* for *rid, loath* for *loathe, ingenious* for *ingenuous*.
2. Correct spelling is needed to make discriminations in meaning: *import* or *export, antiwar* or *antewar, dissect* or *bisect, immigrate* or *emigrate, hypertension* or *hypotension*.
3. The student who knows how to spell a word can obviously find it faster in a dictionary.
4. Knowing how to spell is a social matter. Ability, education, and literacy are attributes often associated with spelling skill.
5. Poor spelling wastes the time of both teacher and pupils.
6. Spelling and pronunciation are related. Linguists recognize the relationship between pronunciation and spelling skills. Students who spell a word correctly usually pronounce it correctly.
7. Poor spellers may avoid using words they know in their written work. They thus deprive themselves of the means to express their thoughts as fully as they might.

We have pointed out the relationship between spelling and vocabulary, noting that spelling enables the decoder (the reader) to encode (to write). Encoding gives the student practice in discriminating regular letter patterns that form meaningful syllables—roots and affixes that are generative of many words.

Knowing how to spell correctly is a combination of remembering letter patterns that represent sounds *(sleek, slick; angel, angle)* and recognizing letter discriminations that distinguish between the meaning of one word and that of another *(heir, air)*.

Organizing Words for Spelling Study

As we have previously pointed out, in teaching spelling as a part of word study, the teacher supplies a *context* that is missing in many spelling programs. Combining spelling and word study makes the learning of spelling a more relevant activity; it integrates it with a study of the written language. Effective word study helps the student make associations, form patterns, relate one concept to another. An effective spelling program organizes materials in terms of word-attack skills, learning whole words and their meanings, learning word parts and their meanings, analyzing elements, and rebuilding whole words by synthesizing elements.

Just as the teacher helps the student generalize about word formation, so he can help the student make generalizations about spelling. The teacher can arrange words to be learned and spelled in groups that help the student make visual and aural associations. For example, the student can readily see patterns in the following sets of words:

multiply	omit	multitude
multiplicand	permit	altitude
multiplier	admit	aptitude
multiple	commit	attitude
multiplication	submit	fortitude
multitude	remit	beatitude

Such arrangements visually and aurally reinforce the learning of letter patterns that the student must know to be a good speller.

Spelling and Word Analysis

English is in some respects phonemically irregular. The *f* sound in *photo* is not spelled like the *f* sound in *first*. The *f* sound and the *u* sound in *muff* are found in words like *enough* and *rough*. Note the *shun* sound in *carnation,* the *a* sound in *they*. These few examples indicate that irregularities exist in the grapheme-phoneme relationships in English; and because of this irregularity many words are difficult to spell.

But, linguists have pointed out that there is a great deal of regularity in English sounds and corresponding symbols. This means that many prefixes, roots, and suffixes (actually syllables and compounds of syllables) appear in predictable positions in respect to phoneme-grapheme correspondence. This becomes increasingly important as the pupil develops greater sophistication in his approach to his spelling problems.

We know that speech comes before writing and that syllabication helps the student pronounce a word. For example, dictionaries give the pronunciation-syllabication of words such as *fanatic* (*fa·nat'ic*) and *fanciful* (*fan'ci·ful*). This type of entry is an aid to the student in pronouncing the words, but it should be pointed out that syllabication does not always help the student see the meaningful parts of words; it does not help him decide whether *fa, fan,* or *fanat* are meaningful word parts. In short, the student gets no hint about how to classify meaningful parts as a way of remembering the spelling of a word. The teacher must supply this help.

Let's consider the word *telegram.* Dictionaries give the syllabication of *telegram* as *tel'e·gram.* An approach to spelling emphasizing meaningful part combinations would stress not *tel* but *tele,* meaning distant. Such an approach would tie in directly with a systematic study of key prefixes in the early grades. Thus the teaching of *tele,* for example, as a meaningful entity, offers an effective way of attacking the spelling of this word. Students learning *tele* as a unit meaning distant would be unlikely to spell *telegram* as *telagram, telegraph* as *telagraph,* and *telephone* as *telaphone*—all common spelling errors.

Likewise, students who know that the prefix *im-* means "not" are less likely to forget to use two *m*'s (one for the prefix and one for the root) in the word *immortal*.

Therefore, in addition to learning phonetic syllabication in spelling activities, the student needs to be aware that word elements with meaning also exist, that the phonetic syllabication of *atom* (found in the dictionary as *(at'om)* tends to prevent his learning that the word *atom* is made up of two meaningful parts, *a* and *tom,* from *a* (not) + *tom* (cut), referring to the early notion that an atom was the smallest particle of matter and could not be cut.

This does not mean that students are to disregard the syllabic sounds of words found in phonetic keys. Rather, we suggest that, in addition to phonetic aids, greater emphasis be placed on the meaningful word elements as an aid to spelling and reading, and as a word-building device. For example, the dictionary listing of *biology* as *bi·ol'o·gy* helps with pronunciation, but the student should also know that this syllabic arrangement does not have meaning. A meaningful formation is *bio* (life) + *logy* (study of).

Classifying Words as an Aid to Spelling

Through the systematic teaching of prefixes, roots, and suffixes (meaningful word parts), and by analyzing words, the teacher can give the student spelling help, as illustrated in the few words listed below.

Prefixes

ab sent	*re* fund
ab duct	*re* play
ad verb	*cent* ennial
ad here	*cent* imeter

169

FOUNDATIONS OF INSTRUCTION

Prefixes

mono plane	*tri* cycle	de *script* ion	pre *dict* ion
mono rail	*tri* vial	pre *script* ion	*dict* ionary
bi cycle	*contra* dict	in *spect* or	dis *aster*
bi sect	*contra* ry	*spect* ator	*aster* isk
anti social	*uni* lateral	*bell* igerent	pro *ject*
anti septic	*uni* form	re *bell* ion	re *ject*
mis spell	*sym* phony	*vis* ible	*tract* or
mis state	*sym* pathy	super *vis* e	sub *tract* ion
trans plant	*peri* scope	bi *cycl* e	un *equ* al
trans fer	*peri* phery	en *cycl* opedia	*equ* ator
super natural	*syn* thesis	dis *miss* al	in *volv* e
super structure	*syn* tax	*miss* ionary	re *volv* er
fore head	*anti* toxin	*grad* uate	*voc* ation
fore most	*anti* venom	de *grad* e	con *voc* ation
inter national	*di* urnal	con *junct* ion	sur *viv* or
inter val	*di* chotomy	*junct* ure	re *viv* e

Roots

tele *graph*	*aud* ition	*manu* facture	e *duc* ate
steno *graph* er	in *aud* ible	*manu* al	ab *duc* t
un *arm* ed	*tele* vision	*anima* l	*para* sol
arm y	*tele* phone	in *anima* te	*para* chute

		Suffixes	
neur *alg* ia	trans *port* ation	psycho *logy*	tonsill *itis*
nost *alg* ia	*port* able	mytho *logy*	appendic *itis*
micro *phon* e	*uni* form	depend *able*	part *icle*
sym *phon* y	re *form*	avail *able*	cut *icle*

Suffixes

invent *ive*
extens *ive*

book *let*
ring *let*

assist *ance*
resist *ance*

friend *ship*
penman *ship*

ill *ness*
full *ness*

brother *hood*
neighbor *hood*

induc *tion*
dic *tion*

civil *ize*
crystall *ize*

real *ist*
art *ist*

material *ism*
social *ism*

conservat *ory*
observat *ory*

audit *orium*
natat *orium*

din *ette*
kitchen *ette*

mole *cule*
minus *cule*

inspect *or*
act *or*

free *dom*
king *dom*

Spelling and Context

Vocabulary instruction aimed at helping the student understand how language develops can contribute to his spelling skills. Linguists divide the study of language structure into three areas: (1) *phonology*, the system of sounds used in a language (Latin *phon*, sound), (2) *syntax*, the arrangement of words to form sentences (Greek *syn*, together + *taxis*, arrangement), and (3) *morphology*, the forms of words brought about by inflection and derivation (Greek *morphe*, form + *logy*, study of).

Recent studies indicate the following:

FOUNDATIONS OF INSTRUCTION

1. Spelling is a more consistent symbolic representation of speech than was formerly believed. Eighty percent of the time, a phoneme is consistently represented by a grapheme.

2. The arrangement of phonological (sound) elements is consistent in consonant-vowel, vowel-consonant, and consonant-vowel-consonant positions. The speller does not have an unlimited choice of position for placing letters.

3. These consonant-vowel, vowel-consonant patterns are readily learned through the teaching of meaningful syllables and word elements (morphological elements): prefixes, roots, and suffixes.

Too often students are asked to learn the spelling of each word as a discrete act, a separate task unrelated to former learning. For effective learning the student must see the word *jumping* as an inflected form (morphological change) of *jump*. He must note the morphological aspects of language: compounds, prefixes, suffixes, roots, and derivatives that point up the relationships between words. He must get the idea that every word he spells is not a new experience.

The student can learn to generalize about spelling as he generalizes about words and derivatives. He can learn that words such as *mate, fate, rate* (having the long *a* sound) generally have a final silent *e*. The same is true of other vowels in words with a long *i*: *kite, site, rite*. Exceptions such as *bade* (pronounced *bad*) and *forebade* (short *a* with silent *e*) can be discussed after the concept is learned.

Additional generalizations and rules that can help students spell correctly are offered in the lessons that follow. We believe, however, that organizing spelling lessons to coincide with the study of morphology gives the student a contextual structure for the study of spelling.

It is often thought that presenting spelling words in the context of sentences is of great help to the student. It may help him relate one word to another, one idea to another. However, it offers no structure for learning to spell,

FOUNDATIONS OF INSTRUCTION

no principles he can follow, no way to help him organize his formerly learned knowledge to apply to newly learned knowledge about spelling.

Students who relate spelling practice to word study, who are taught to recognize certain syllables as meaningful units, readily recognize these units when they turn up in new words (the *anti* in *antifreeze* is spelled the same as the *anti* in *antidote*). If the student knows how to spell *bicycle*, he can be shown that he already knows how to spell one part of *bisect*. If he can spell *circus*, and is taught to recognize *circu* (around) as a unit, it is a short step to the spelling of harder words—*circuit, circuitous*, etc. If he has been taught *epi* (upon) in *epitaph*, the words *epilogue, epidemic*, and *epithet* will be easier to spell.

Spelling Rules

Spelling rules are possible only because there is predictable structure in words. In prefixes such as *pre-, pro-, eu-, dys-*, and many others, the letter patterns are stable and can therefore be easily learned once they are observed.

Roots have regular letter patterns that help the speller who is aware of the roots. It is easy for students to recognize the spelling of recurring roots such as *vis* in *vision, television, visionary, televise*, and *visor* if they are alerted to these roots.

A student who knows the root *labor* (work) is unlikely to misspell the word *laboratory* as *labratory* (leaving out the *o*). A student who knows the root *rupt* (break) and the prefix *inter-* (between) will be less likely to misspell *interrupt* as *interupt* (with one *r*).

Since letter patterns form meaningful units that make up words, it is possible to form generalizations about them, in the form of spelling rules. For example,

Use *i* before *e*
except after *c*
or when sounded like *a*
as in n*ei*ghbor or w*ei*gh.

The rhyme is good to remember when spelling words such as *relieve* and *deceive*, or *believe* and *receive*, although there are some weaknesses in the rule (discussed later in the lesson). Note that we might make up a related rule about verbs, using *e* after *c*: If the noun form contains *cep*, *c* will be followed by *ei*.

re*cep*tion	rec*ei*ve
per*cep*tion	perc*ei*ve
de*cep*tion	dec*ei*ve
con*cep*tion	conc*ei*ve

Existing spelling rules are often helpful, and at the appropriate time the teacher may wish to discuss and review some of the following rules and spelling hints. We include here only a few examples illustrating each principle. Students might be encouraged to gather additional illustrative examples and discuss them in class.

Spelling Hints

1. We make most singular words plural by adding *s* (*book, books; magazine, magazines; puzzle, puzzles*).

2. We make singular words ending in *s, ss, sh, ch, x*, and *z* plural by adding *es* (*bus, buses; glass, glasses; wish, wishes; church, churches; box, boxes; topaz, topazes*).

3. Some plural spellings do not follow rules; rather, there are internal changes to indicate plural (*man, men; woman, women; child, children; mouse, mice; goose, geese; tooth, teeth*). Some plurals are the same as the singular nouns (*deer, deer; sheep, sheep*).

4. We add only *s* or *es* (not *'s*) to make names plural (*Bill*, two *Bills; Mary*, two *Marys;* Mr. and Mrs. *Brown*, or the *Browns;* the *Joneses*).

5. For nouns ending in *y* preceded by a consonant, change the *y* to *i* and add *es* (*army, armies; baby, babies; city, cities; berry, berries*).

6. For nouns ending in *y* preceded by a vowel, merely add *s* (*monkey, mon-*

keys; play, plays; valley, valleys; turkey, turkeys).

7. In general, we drop the final *e* of a root word before adding a suffix beginning with a vowel *(-ing, -er, -ed, -ent, -ence, -er, -able, -ible)*. Examples: *love, loving; care, caring; circle, circling; range, ranging; love, lovable.*

8. In general, we keep the final *e* of the root word before adding a suffix beginning with a consonant *(-ment, -ness, -less, -ful)*. Examples: *arrange, arrangement; care, careless; spite, spiteful; humane, humaneness.*

9. A word ending with a consonant preceded by a single vowel usually doubles the consonant before adding a vowel suffix. Examples: *skip, skipping; scan, scanning.*

10. A word of more than one syllable ending in a single consonant preceded by a single vowel, and with the accent on the final syllable, doubles the consonant before adding a vowel suffix. Examples:

begin	beginning
compel	compelled
prefer	preferring
refer	referring
control	controlling
commit	committed
forgot	forgotten

But if the accent is not on the final syllable, we do not double the consonant.

cancel	canceled
counsel	counseled
benefit	benefited
bigot	bigoted

Note: The rule works most of the time, but *canceled, traveler,* and *kidnaper* are sometimes spelled (mostly in Britain) *cancelled, traveller,* and *kidnapper.*

11. To retain the soft sound of the *c* (*s* sound) and of the *g* (*j* sound) in words ending in *ce* and *ge*, we keep the final *e* *(peace, peaceable; replace, replaceable; arrange, arrangement; advantage, advantageous; notice, noticeable; change, changeable).*

12. Words ending in two vowels (a vowel + final *e*) retain the final vowel *(e)* before adding a suffix. Examples: *see, seeable; shoe, shoeing; canoe, canoeing.*

13. Check the dictionary for nouns ending in *o* before adding *es* for the plural. Although there are about a dozen common *o* words whose plurals end in *es* (*vetoes, mosquitoes, potatoes, tomatoes, heroes, volcanoes, echoes, embargoes, torpedoes, Negroes, buffaloes*), some of those words may add only *s* to form the plural *(buffalos, volcanos)*. Other words that add only *s* are *silos, cameos, radios,* and *dynamos.*

14. In general, we add *s* to the main word of a compound (*brothers*-in-law, *sisters*-in-law, *attorneys*-at-law). We add *s* to compound words ending in *ful* (*teaspoonfuls, tablespoonfuls, cupfuls, mouthfuls, basketfuls*). (But note *manservant, menservants.*)

15. Loan words from Greek and Latin often cause difficulty. English plurals are often used with these words. Either the Greek and Latin plurals or the English plurals are acceptable.

16. A contraction is two words joined with an apostrophe to show the omission of a letter or letters: *we'll* (we will), *haven't* (have not), *they've* (they have), *who's* (who is, who has). The word *apostrophe* comes from Greek *apostrophos* (from *apo,* away + *strephein,* to turn).

In addition to its use in contractions, the apostrophe is used to show ownership *(boy, boy's; dog, dog's; man's* best friend, *man's* inhumanity to man). To singular nouns we usually add *'s (girl, girl's)*. To plural nouns not ending in *s* we add *'s (men, men's)*. To plural nouns ending in *s*, we add just an apostrophe *(girls'* bikes). If a singular noun ends in *s* or an *s* sound, we add just an apostrophe *(Illinois'* population; his *conscience'* sake.) If a noun of one syllable ends in *s*, we add *'s (Tess's* book).

17. We form the plural of numbers,

FOUNDATIONS OF INSTRUCTION

Greek or Latin Singular	Greek or Latin Plural	English Plural
alumnus	alumni *(masculine)*	
alumna	alumnae *(feminine)*	
medium	media	mediums
datum	data	
radius	radii	radiuses
spectrum	spectra	spectrums
stadium	stadia	stadiums
fungus	fungi	funguses
criterion	criteria	criterions
phenomenon	phenomena	phenomenons
locus	loci	
dictum	dicta	dictums
crisis	crises	
oasis	oases	
thesis	theses	
formula	formulae	formulas
forum	fora	forums
fulcrum	fulcra	fulcrums
gladiolus	gladioli	gladioluses
index	indices	indexes
memorandum	memoranda	memorandums

signs, letters, and words used as words by adding *'s (a's; 9's; &'s; p's* and *q's.* You used too many *said's).*

Predicting Spelling Difficulties

Students need to be reminded that certain words are often misspelled, and thus be alerted to check these words after spelling them. But spelling not only involves the ability to put letters together in the correct form, it also requires the attitude or concern to see that it is done. We need, in other words, a spelling conscience. We must care whether we spell correctly or not.

Sometimes we can use memory devices such as rules, but they do not always work. And even if we improve our spelling by learning certain principles and by using memory devices such as noting roots and affixes, we will still misspell words unless we are able to predict and doublecheck the words which we might misspell, and then learn them thoroughly.

We have included here a list with a number of words often misspelled, although they are not, on the whole, difficult words such as those included in the usual lists of "spelling demons." In developing this list of words we have made use of Arthur I. Gates's *Spelling Difficulties in 3,876 Words*[1] and Harry A. Greene's *The New Iowa Spelling Scale,*[2] listing only those words scored below 50 percent on the Iowa Spelling Scale at the eighth-grade level. The student would first be asked to check the words in the list that he thinks he might misspell. The words he checks are probably the ones he needs to look up when he is writing.

[1] Arthur I. Gates, *Spelling Difficulties in 3,876 Words* (New York: Columbia University, 1937).
[2] Harry A. Greene, *The New Iowa Spelling Scale* (Iowa City: State University of Iowa, 1954).

Word (% Correct)	Most Common Misspelling	Word (% Correct)	Most Common Misspelling
abandon (49%)		boys' (39%)	
absolutely (41%)	absolutly	bulletin (38%)	bullitin
abundant (47%)	abundent	bureau (32%)	
acceptable (48%)		campaign (28%)	campain
acceptance (44%)	acceptence	cancellation (30%)	
accepting (49%)		candidate (41%)	
accommodate (24%)	accomodate	capacity (44%)	
accompanied (42%)		ceased (40%)	
accordance (49%)	accordence	challenge (49%)	
accustomed (30%)		characteristic (28%)	
achievement (36%)		children's (45%)	
acknowledgment (25%)		chocolate (48%)	
acquaint (28%)		chorus (44%)	
acquire (35%)	aquire	Christian (49%)	Christain
adequate (22%)		circuit (27%)	
adjourned (43%)		circumstance (45%)	curcumstance
administration (45%)	addministration	civilization (42%)	civilazation
advertisement (46%)	advertisment	cocoon (45%)	
affidavit (15%)		collateral (12%)	
agricultural (40%)		colonel (31%)	
all right (41%)		columns (40%)	
altar (34%)		commencement (42%)	commencment
amendment (43%)	ammendment	commercial (49%)	
analysis (22%)		commission (45%)	commision
annual (43%)	anual	committed (37%)	
anticipate (27%)	antisipate	committee (34%)	
anxiety (21%)		communicate (48%)	
appetite (36%)	appitite	communication (48%)	comunication
applicant (43%)		compel (43%)	
appreciated (48%)		competition (39%)	
approximately (21%)		compliment (39%)	complement
artificial (38%)	artifical	conceive (39%)	
association (47%)		condemn (33%)	condem
attorney (40%)		congratulations (41%)	
authority (45%)		conscience (24%)	concience
available (41%)		conscious (13%)	
bankruptcy (19%)		consequence (33%)	
bearing (46%)		continuous (25%)	
benefit (39%)	benifit	controversy (27%)	
bicycle (45%)		convenience (23%)	
bough (36%)		correspond (42%)	
boundary (49%)	boundry	correspondence (34%)	
bouquet (45%)		council (40%)	

FOUNDATIONS OF INSTRUCTION

Word (% Correct)	Most Common Misspelling	Word (% Correct)	Most Common Misspelling
counsel (17%)		exhaust (42%)	
courteous (34%)	courtious	exhibition (29%)	exibition
courtesy (41%)	curtesy	existence (23%)	
crisis (31%)		experienced (46%)	
criticism (12%)		extension (49%)	extention
curiosity (35%)	curiousity	extraordinary (33%)	
cylinder (25%)		extremely (43%)	
day's (46%)		facilities (31%)	
debtor (38%)		faculty (48%)	
deceive (49%)		familiar (40%)	
definite (38%)		fascinating (20%)	
definitely (21%)		February (47%)	Febuary
definition (40%)		financial (34%)	
delegate (41%)		flu (41%)	
deny (48%)		foliage (26%)	
descend (29%)	decend	foreign (48%)	
despair (35%)		fortunately (36%)	
discipline (14%)		fraternity (35%)	
discussed (49%)		gratitude (40%)	graditude
distinguish (36%)		grieve (47%)	
distribution (49%)		guarantee (16%)	
doctrine (36%)		guardian (47%)	gaurdian
dormitory (24%)		ignorance (47%)	ignorence
earnestly (48%)		Halloween (49%)	
economy (42%)		handkerchiefs (49%)	
edition (47%)		heir (48%)	
efficiency (13%)		hygiene (31%)	
efficient (25%)		icicles (31%)	
elapsed (46%)		illustration (44%)	
eligible (31%)		imagination (46%)	
eliminate (36%)		immediately (33%)	
embroidery (34%)		immense (28%)	
employees (42%)		immortal (44%)	imortal
enclosure (47%)		incident (46%)	
encouraging (38%)		incidentally (12%)	
enthusiastic (41%)		inconvenience (33%)	
epistle (18%)		indefinitely (10%)	
equipped (24%)	equiped	individual (41%)	
exceptionally (37%)		inevitable (24%)	
excessive (37%)		initial (35%)	
execute (42%)		initiation (23%)	
executive (31%)		innocent (43%)	inocent
exercise (49%)		inquiry (46%)	

FOUNDATIONS OF INSTRUCTION

Word (% Correct)	Most Common Misspelling	Word (% Correct)	Most Common Misspelling
inspiration (45%)		originally (37%)	
installation (33%)		ornaments (47%)	
instinct (44%)		pamphlet (29%)	pamflet
institutions (46%)		pamphlets (32%)	
intellectual (22%)		paradise (46%)	
intelligence (37%)		parliament (16%)	parliment
interrupt (43%)	interupt	partial (29%)	
interval (49%)		particularly (47%)	
intimate (33%)		patience (44%)	
jealous (48%)		patronage (42%)	
laboratory (38%)	labratory	peasant (47%)	
legislation (48%)		peculiar (36%)	pecular
legislature (44%)		perceive (28%)	
leisure (43%)		peril (27%)	
liability (46%)		permanent (46%)	
license (31%)		petition (35%)	
lieutenant (18%)		philosophy (21%)	
liquor (43%)		physical (47%)	
loyalty (48%)		physician (38%)	
luxury (43%)		pigeon (45%)	
magnificent (49%)	magnificient	pilgrims (41%)	
manufacturer (37%)		politician (21%)	
materially (44%)		positively (44%)	positivly
mathematics (35%)		possess (31%)	
maturity (46%)		possibility (45%)	posibility
mechanical (44%)		practically (36%)	
merchandise (45%)	merchandize	precious (48%)	
merely (49%)		precisely (23%)	
minimum (38%)		preference (43%)	
mortgage (16%)	morgage	preferred (42%)	
mountains (44%)		presence (46%)	presense
multiplication (41%)		principle (39%)	principal
murmur (38%)	murmer	prior (38%)	
mutual (41%)		privilege (22%)	
necessarily (22%)		probability (45%)	
niece (47%)	neice	professional (46%)	
occasionally (32%)		psychology (7%)	
occurred (28%)	occured	pursuit (33%)	
offense (39%)		quantities (45%)	
official (46%)	offical	receipt (33%)	
opportunities (34%)		receiving (45%)	recieving
oppose (49%)		recognized (45%)	
ordinarily (29%)		recommend (30%)	

FOUNDATIONS OF INSTRUCTION

Word (% Correct)	Most Common Misspelling	Word (% Correct)	Most Common Misspelling
recommended (31%)		temporarily (20%)	
references (41%)		temporary (41%)	temperary
referred (48%)		tendency (42%)	
refrigerator (44%)		they're (40%)	
regretting (41%)		thorough (24%)	
reign (35%)		thoroughly (22%)	
remembrance (36%)	rememberance	tongue (48%)	
remittance (41%)		tournament (39%)	
representative (36%)	representitive	tradition (47%)	
requisition (14%)		tragedy (30%)	
responsibility (40%)		transferred (37%)	transfered
restaurant (21%)	resturant	unanimous (25%)	
reverence (49%)		undoubtedly (25%)	
scarcely (43%)		unfortunately (40%)	
schedule (37%)		universal (49%)	
scheme (43%)		unnecessary (25%)	unecessary
scholarship (46%)		urgent (43%)	
scissors (40%)		utilize (37%)	
sensible (49%)		vacancies (39%)	
separate (41%)		vague (37%)	
separately (37%)		variety (42%)	
shepherd (39%)		veil (38%)	
similar (43%)	similiar	vein (43%)	
sincerely (49%)	sincerly	vicinity (45%)	
skiing (43%)		whether (49%)	
skis (29%)		wholly (46%)	
solemn (30%)		woman's (46%)	
sorority (18%)		wretched (25%)	
specific (35%)		wrought (33%)	
squirrel (41%)			
statistics (35%)			
statues (28%)			
straightened (45%)			
substitute (49%)	subsitute		
succeeded (42%)	succeded		
successfully (46%)			
succession (42%)			
sufficient (22%)	sufficiant		
sufficiently (29%)			
supplement (34%)			
survey (42%)			
suspicion (22%)			
sympathy (45%)			

The list has implications for other grades also. The word *bicycle,* with a spelling score of 45 percent at the eighth-grade level, will be difficult for students below this level. The word *counsel* (17 percent at the eighth-grade level) will still be difficult for students beyond the eighth-grade level.

After the student has used this master spelling list, which he should keep in his notebook, the teacher might give a series of spelling tests on a number of words taken from it. After each test the student can check himself against the master list

FOUNDATIONS OF INSTRUCTION

to see whether he can spell the words he predicted he knew how to spell, or whether those words are in reality his personal spelling "demons." (The list can be expanded periodically.)

By using this table the teacher will be prewarned about the spelling-difficulty level of certain words. Foreseeing his students' probable spelling problems, he can then plan ways of eliminating them.

Of course, the teacher can tell how hard these words are by consulting Greene's book. One advantage of the table, however, lies in Gates's listing of the most common misspellings of certain words, as it enables the teacher to alert the student to the most probable source of his misspelling. It shows, for example, that the most common misspelling of *absolutely* is *absolutly* (not retaining the final e of *absolute*), or that the most common misspelling of *bulletin* is *bullitin*.

The Role of Accent in Words

The development of oral and written language skills requires extensive practice in auditory discrimination. The teacher may point up the importance of pronunciation in changing the meaning of words by showing the student that the meaning of certain words depends on accent (special stress or force given a syllable), for example, conVICT (verb) and CONvict (noun).

The following lesson emphasizes the role of accent in words and points out that words spelled alike often change their meaning or part of speech according to where the accent falls. A verb may become a noun, or vice versa; a noun may become an adjective. The student needs to know that the way he pronounces a word, the way he accents a syllable, often gives a certain meaning to the word or influences the listener's comprehension of the meaning intended.

The student may use the following list of words to practice pronunciation. The teacher may use the list with the overhead projector to illustrate that words spelled alike are not necessarily pronounced alike, and that accent often changes the meaning of a word.

ABsent	abSENT
ABstract	abSTRACT
ADdress	adDRESS
ALly	alLY
COLlect	colLECT
COMpact	comPACT
COMplex	comPLEX
COMpound	comPOUND
COMpress	comPRESS
CONcave	conCAVE
CONcert	conCERT
CONcrete	conCRETE
CONduct	conDUCT
CONfine	conFINE
CONflict	conFLICT
CONserve	conSERVE
CONsole	conSOLE
CONtent	conTENT
CONtest	conTEST
CONtrast	conTRAST
CONverse	conVERSE
CONvert	conVERT
CONvict	conVICT
DEfense	deFENSE
DIgest	diGEST
EScort	esCORT
ESsay	esSAY
EXport	exPORT
EXtract	exTRACT
FREquent	freQUENT
IMport	imPORT
IMpress	imPRESS
INcense	inCENSE
INcline	inCLINE
INcrease	inCREASE
INsert	inSERT
INside	inSIDE
INsult	inSULT
INtern	inTERN
INvalid	inVALID
INvert	inVERT
OBject	obJECT
OFFset	offSET

FOUNDATIONS OF INSTRUCTION

OUTlay	outLAY
OUTreach	outREACH
PERmit	perMIT
PREsage	preSAGE
PROceeds	proCEEDS
PROGress	proGRESS
PROJect	proJECT
PROtest	proTEST
REcess	reCESS
RECord	reCORD
REdress	reDRESS
REFuse	reFUSE
REgress	reGRESS
REject	reJECT
RElapse	reLAPSE
RElay	reLAY
REprint	rePRINT
RErun	reRUN
REset	reSET
REsole	reSOLE
REsurvey	reSURVEY
REtail	reTAIL
REtake	reTAKE
REtread	reTREAD
REwrite	reWRITE
RUNdown	runDOWN
SUBject	subJECT
SUFfix	sufFIX
SURvey	surVEY
SUSpect	susPECT
TRANSfer	transFER
TRANSplant	transPLANT
TRANSport	transPORT

Note: Certain words do not necessarily change their meaning because of shift of accent. Furthermore, people in certain parts of the country may pronounce some of the above listed words in different ways. For example, as a noun, *address* may be pronounced either "*ad*dress" or "ad*dress*." Debatable points can often be settled by consulting the dictionary.

Pronunciation Demons

Many students hesitate to use words they know simply because they are unsure of how to pronounce them. The words listed below (many of which are hard to spell) are often mispronounced. Careful attention to many of them should help the average upper-grade student. Note that some words may be pronounced two ways:

abdomen: *ab* domen (ab *do* men)
abstemious: ab *stee* mious
affluence: *aff* luence
alias: *ale* ius
altimeter: al *tim* eter
anathema: a *nath* ama
antipodes: an *tip* o *dees*
apropos: appro *poe*
archetype: *ark* etype
bade: bad
bayou: *by* oo
bestial: *best* yal
cerulean: se *rule* ian
chiropodist: ki *ropp* edist
chiropractor: *ky* ra *prak* ter
comparable: *com* parable
condolence: con *do* lence
covert: *co* vert (*cuv* vert)
crevasse: cre *vass*
dais: *day* uss (*dye* uss)
decadent: *dek* a dent (de *kay* dent)
demoniacal: demon *eye* ical
despicable: des *pick* able (*des* pick able)
desultory: *dess* ultory
devotee: devva *tee*
diphtheria: dif *theer* ia
disheveled: di *shev* eled
dour: *dow* er (also as in *doer*)
effete: eh *feet*
efficacy: *eff* icasy
endemic: en *dem* ic
ephemeral: eh *fem* eral
exacerbate: ex *ass* erbate
exquisite: *ex* kwizit (ex *kwiz* it)
facade: feh *sahd*
finis: *fin* is
flaccid: *flak* sid
formidable: *form* idable
forte: fort (what one does well)

180

FOUNDATIONS OF INSTRUCTION

forte: for *tay* (played loudly)
genuine: *jen* you in
gondola: *gon* dola (gon *doe* la)
halcyon: *hal* see on
haphazard: *hap* hazard
harbinger: *har* bin jer
hedonism: *heed* onism
height: *hite*
heinous: *hay* nous
hospitable: *hos* pitable (hos *pit* able)
impious: *imp* ious
impotent: *imp* otent
incognito: in cog *neat* o (in *cog* nito)
incomparable: in *com* parable
incongruous: in *kong* gruous
indefatigable: inde *fat* igable
indict: in *dite*
indigent: *in* dijent
infinite: *in* finite
infrared: *in* fra *red*
ingenuous: in *jen* uous
interdict: *in* ter dict (n.), inter *dict* (v.)
intricacy: *in* tricasy
irremediable: irre *meed* iable
irreparable: ir *rep* erable
irrevocable: ir *rev* ocable
lamentable: *lam* entable (la *ment* able)
lichen: *like* n
machinations: *mack* in *na* tions (*mash* i *na* tions)
maintenance: *main* tenance
maniacal: man *eye* acal
metonymy: me *ton* ome
minuscule: *min* us kyool (min *us* kyool)
mischievous: *mis* che vus
naive: na *eve*
obdurate: *obb* durate
obese: oh *beese*
onerous: *on* erous (*own* erous)
onus: *own* us
ophthalmologist: *off* thal *moll* ogist
plebeian: ple *bee* an
plethora: *pleth* ora
podiatrist: poe *dy* atrist
posthumous: *pos* chumous
preferable: *pref* erable
prelate: *prell* ate
pseudo: *sue* doe

qualm: kwawm (kwom)
quay: *key* (kway)
quietus: kwy *eet* us
redolent: *red* olent
respite: *ress* pit
ribald: *rib* ald (*rye* bald)
scabrous: *sca* brus (*skay* brus)
schism: *sizz* im
scion: *sigh* un
secretive: *seek* retive (se *cree* tive)
solace: *soll* iss
specious: *spee* shuss
splenetic: sple *net* ic
succinct: suck *sinkt*
taciturn: *tass* iturn
telemeter: te *lem* eter
travail: tra *vale* (*trav* el)
typography: ty *pog* raphy
ultimatum: ulti *mate* um
vagary: *vague* ary (va *gary*)
valet: *val* it (va *lay*)

Inflections in Language

Students often have difficulty learning words because they don't relate an unfamiliar word to any known word. Many English words are formed merely by inflectional change, so spelling a "new" word may merely involve adding a syllable or changing a letter of a known word.

Students can benefit from the transfer involved in forming new words from words already known. For example, *exemplify* will not appear so hard if it is associated with *example*.

The following list provides pairs of related words with their grade-level scores as found in the Dale nationwide study, *The Words We Know—A National Inventory*. Note that *example* is known on the fourth-grade level, but *exemplify* (an inflectional form of *example*) is not known before the tenth-grade level. *Exemplify* could be learned earlier and more easily if the student were shown that it is merely another form of the word *example*. (Actual percentage scores above grade 12 are included.)

FOUNDATIONS OF INSTRUCTION

Selected List from Dale's *The Words We Know*

active (4)–activate (12)
adaptable (8)–adaptability (12)
break (4)–breakage (10)
captive (6)–captivate (13–88%)
catechism (8)–catechize (13–58%)
clarification (6)–clarify (10)
college (4)–collegiate (12)
competing (6)–competitive (10)
decision (6)–decisive (12)
decorate (6)–decor (12)
demolish (6)–demolition (10)
deprive (6)–deprivation (10)
elephant (4)–elephantine (12)
emblem (6)–emblematic (12)
erase (4)–erasure (8)
error (6)–erroneous (12)
erupt (6)–eruptive (10)
escape (4)–escapade (10)
evacuate (6)–evacuation (12)
example (4)–exemplify (10)
ferocious (8)–ferocity (12)
flirt (6)–flirtation (10)
globe (4)–globular (8)
habit (4)–habitual (10)
herb (8)–herbivorous (12)
infant (6)–infancy (10)
information (6)–informant (10)
injury (4)–injurious (8)
migrate (6)–migratory (10)
nice (4)–nicety (10)
nominate (4)–nominee (8)
note (4)–notation (10)
opinion (6)–opine (16–42%)
opportunity (6)–opportune (12)
oval (8)–ova (13–83%)
pacify (8)–pacifist (12)
part (6)–partition (12)
penalty (6)–penal (12)
persuade (6)–persuasive (10)
pharmacist (8)–pharmaceutical (12)
pilgrim (4)–pilgrimage (10)
plural (4)–plurality (10)
pollen (6)–pollinate (10)
population (6)–populace (12)
portrait (6)–portray (10)
pretend (4)–pretense (12)
quiet (4)–quietude (10)
real (4)–reality (8)
recommend (6)–recommendation (10)
remedy (6)–remedial (13–53%)
resolution (8)–resolute (12)
response (6)–responsive (12)
result (6)–resultant (12)
revel (6)–revelry (10)
savage (6)–savagery (10)
simple (4)–simplify (8)
slavery (4)–slavish (16–63%)
sober (6)–sobriety (12–63%)
true (8)–truism (13–74%)
type (4)–typical (10)
unanimous (8)–unanimity (13–66%)
vein (6)–venous (12–33%)

Note: It is apparent from glancing at the few words listed above that students, in general, are not making connections between related words. It is true that a student may have no need of certain words before he is a junior or senior in high school (for example, *cognizance*), but if the word *infant* is known by 78 percent of sixth-graders, *infancy* could be taught earlier. It is now known by only 70 percent of the students in the tenth grade.

The teacher will note that many of the word pairs listed above are separated by as much as an eight-year span. If the spelling program emphasized the relationship of words formed from common roots, if the inflections of words were stressed to show that many words are slightly changed forms of words the student already knows, an appreciable gain could be made in spelling ability and in word knowledge.

Confused Pairs

The exercise below indicates one way to alert students to words often confused because of pronunciation or spelling similarities. The difficulty of the word pairs ranges from easy to hard, thus elementary teachers or teachers at the higher levels can select appropriate word pairs for their students.

As noted earlier, through faulty pronunciation or bad spelling habits students often confuse one word for another. This sometimes results in humorous situations or *malapropisms* (misused words).

Instructions: The student draws a line to the word or phrase in column B that makes him think of the word in column A.

Example:

their — here
there — cat

A	B
slick	seal
sleek	ice
popular	girl
poplar	tree
mole	on bread
mold	on body
famine	hunger
feminine	woman
angle	wings
angel	corner
champagne	politics
campaign	drink
palm	leaf
psalm	song
decal	sticker
ducal	duke
allusion	indirect reference
illusion	not real
scow	frown
scowl	boat
squaw	storm
squall	Indian
curtsy	manners
courtesy	to bow
gamble	romp
gambol	dice
narrow	thin
marrow	bone

A	B
which	choice
witch	magic
alleys	partners
allies	narrow streets
surplus	garment
surplice	extra
sink	a metal
zinc	in the kitchen
tired	weary
tried	attempted
inspire	put life into
expire	die
quiet	very
quite	not noisy
ever	always
every	all
saucer	magician
sorcerer	plate
anecdote	remedy
antidote	funny story
umpire	British
empire	referee
trial	test
trail	path
ellipse	sun
eclipse	oval
diagram	a sketch
diaphragm	membrane
respectively	with politeness
respectfully	in this order
canary	preserving food
cannery	yellow feathers
apostle	letter
epistle	disciple
specter	watcher
spectator	ghost
morbid	about to die
moribund	gruesome
gaunt	thin and bony
jaunt	travel

FOUNDATIONS OF INSTRUCTION

FOUNDATIONS OF INSTRUCTION

Note: The teacher may wish to construct additional items from the following list, choosing pairs that are suitable for the level of the students.

loath	formally	pastor	perspicuity
loathe	formerly	pasture	perspicacity
baron	putrefy	emulate	affect
barren	petrify	immolate	effect
illegible	canon	precedents	inimitable
ineligible	cannon	precedence	illimitable
eminent	respiration	loping	batten
imminent	perspiration	lopping	baton
missile	latitude	apprehension	dissect
missive	lassitude	comprehension	bisect
augur	irreverent	revolution	interment
auger	irrelevant	evolution	internment
persuade	weather	confident	flaunt
dissuade	whether	confidant	flout
venal	borne	bland	except
venial	born	blend	accept
immigrate	creditable	presence	ascent
emigrate	credible	prescience	assent
wander	cunning	euphemism	commiserate
wonder	conning	euphuism	commensurate
antewar	immorality	ingenious	bauble
antiwar	immortality	ingenuous	bubble
blazer	bedlam	caribou	indigent
blazon	beldam	carabao	indigenous
presence	below	presentment	interpellate
presents	bellow	presentiment	interpolate
amoral	exceptional	eerie	incredible
immoral	exceptionable	aerie	incredulous
continuous	decry	ibex	noisy
continual	descry	ibis	noisome
introspective	acronym	filet	squid
retrospective	acrostic	fillet	squib
faker	paladin	fictitious	selvage
fakir	palanquin	facetious	salvage
hallow	gallon	refractory	relic
hollow	galleon	refectory	relict
cavernous	squab	oscillate	advantageous
carnivorous	squad	osculate	adventitious

FOUNDATIONS OF INSTRUCTION

Visualizing Word Pairs

Sometimes it helps children in the lower grades to have confusions within word pairs presented visually. From the list above, here are some illustrations that the teacher might use for display:

hare   hair

angel   angle   pear   pair

fir   fur

Malapropisms

Malapropisms (named after Mrs. Malaprop in Sheridan's play *The Rivals*) involve the misuse and mispronunciation of words. For example, *enervating* might be used when *energizing* is intended.

The following malapropisms have been taken from the play and set in contemporary usage. Students are to fill in the blanks with the correct word for the misused italicized word.

Answers

alligators	1. In Florida swamps we saw many *allegories*. The right word should be a _ _ _ _ _ _ _ _ _ _.
phraseology	2. His grammatical *physiognomy* is perfect. Right word: p _ _ _ _ _ _ _ _ _ _.
obliterate	3. An atom bomb would *illiterate* the whole city. Right word: o _ _ _ _ _ _ _ _ _.
injunction	4. The management requested a *conjunction* against the union. Right word: i _ _ _ _ _ _ _ _ _.
influence	5. The Senator has much *affluence* with these men. Right word: i _ _ _ _ _ _ _ _.
intuition	6. For judging people she relies too much on her *tuition*. Right word: i _ _ _ _ _ _ _ _.
desisted	7. She *persisted* from talking any longer. Right word: d _ _ _ _ _ _ _.

FOUNDATIONS OF INSTRUCTION

Answers

allusions	8. His *delusions* to classical antiquity were lost on us. Right word: a _ _ _ _ _ _ _ _.
affection	9. I'm happy to be the recipient of her *infection*. Right word: a _ _ _ _ _ _ _ _.
cogitation	10. The process of deep thought is known as *agitation*. Right word: c _ _ _ _ _ _ _ _.
approached	11. The gallery around the green was hushed as the golfer *reproached* the ball. Right word: a _ _ _ _ _ _ _ _ _.
enveloped	12. Soon the mountain darkness *developed* us. Right word: e _ _ _ _ _ _ _ _.
impression	13. The mayor's speech made a great *oppression* on him. Right word: i _ _ _ _ _ _ _ _ _.
commiseration	14. The prisoner at the bar hoped for some *commensuration* from the judge. Right word: c _ _ _ _ _ _ _ _ _ _ _.
fragrant	15. We were attracted by the sweet, *flagrant* odor of the flowers. Right word: f _ _ _ _ _ _.
sects	16. The group was made up of different religious *sex*. Right word: s _ _ _ _.
refuge	17. She thought of her aunt's house as a *refuse* from her troubles. Right word: r _ _ _ _ _.
reference	18. The student looked through the *reverence* book for more facts. Right word: r _ _ _ _ _ _ _ _.
prescribed	19. She took the medicine that the doctor had *subscribed*. Right word: p _ _ _ _ _ _ _ _ _.
repository	20. The mind is a *suppository* for facts and experiences. Right word: r _ _ _ _ _ _ _ _ _.
persecution	21. *Ben Hur* describes the Roman *prosecution* of the Christians. Right word: p _ _ _ _ _ _ _ _ _.
conception	22. He has a good *inception* of his role in the project. Right word: c _ _ _ _ _ _ _ _ _.
infection	23. Bill was laid up with a leg *inflection*. Right word: i _ _ _ _ _ _ _ _.
angles	24. We were able to study the problem from several *angels*. Right word: a _ _ _ _ _.
pulmonary	25. Mr. Brown's breathing difficulty results from a *preliminary* disease. Right word: p _ _ _ _ _ _ _ _.
prodigy	26. The pianist was a child *progeny*. Right word: p _ _ _ _ _ _.
superficial	27. Despite the bad accident, the boy suffered only *supercilious* cuts. Right word: s _ _ _ _ _ _ _ _ _ _.
geography, contiguous	28. In Sheridan's play *The Rivals* (Act 1, Scene 2), Mrs. Malaprop, speaking of her daughter, says, "I would have her study *geometry* so she'd know about *contagious* countries." She meant: g _ _ _ _ _ _ _ _ and c _ _ _ _ _ _ _ _ _.

Note: The teacher may present this lesson in other forms. One way is suggested in item 29 below, with the choices supplied.

apprehended reprehended	29. The policeman _ _ _ _ _ _ _ _ _ _ the speeder and the judge _ _ _ _ _ _ _ _ _ _ _ him. *(reprehended, apprehended)*

FOUNDATIONS OF INSTRUCTION

Phonemically Irregular Words

Words with phonemically irregular letters (e.g., words in which *e* and *ei* have the sound of *a*, as in th*ey* and sl*eigh*) often present spelling problems. Notice the following:

The *a* in *snake* has the sound of the *e* in *they*.
The *a* in *take* = the *ei* in *eight*.
The *a* in *care* = the *e* in *there*.
The *a* in *stare* = the *ei* in *heir*.

The exercise below presents additional illustrations of words in which some letters have the same sound as others. Example: The e in *she* = the i in *machine*.

Answers

poli*c*eman	1. The e in *he* = the i in pol___ceman.
sa*y*s	2. The e in *set* = the a in s___ys.
s*ai*d	3. The e in *wet* = the ai in s___d.
m*a*ny	4. The e in *penny* = the a in m___ny.
rh*y*me	5. The i in *ice* = the y in rh___me.
h*y*mn	6. The i in *him* = the y in h___mn.
b*u*sy	7. The i in *slim* = the u in b___sy.
w*o*men	8. The i in *skim* = the o in w___men.
s*e*w	9. The o in *show* = the e in s___w.
w*a*nd	10. The o in *pond* = the a in w___nd.
s*o*n	11. The u in *up* = the o in s___n.
d*o*ne	12. The u in *cup* = the o in d___ne.
c*o*me	13. The u in *pup* = the o in c___me.
w*oo*l	14. The o in *wolf* = the oo in w___l.
enou*gh*	15. The f in *fur* = the gh in enou___.
*ph*onics	16. The f in *fun* = the ph in ___onics.
t*ou*ch	17. The u in *sun* = the ou in t___ch.
*c*atastrophe	18. The k in *kill* = the c in ___atastrophe.
anti*q*ue	19. The k in *kick* = the q in anti___ue.
*ch*orus	20. The k in *kiss* = the ch in ___orus.
*c*ent	21. The s in *space* = the c in ___ent.
fix*ed*	22. The t in *sit* = the ed in fix___.
*o*f	23. The v in *violin* = the f in o___.
q*u*een	24. The w in *win* = the u in q___een.
wa*s*	25. The z in *whiz* = the s in wa___.
na*ti*on	26. The sh in *sheen* = the ti in na___on.
so*ci*al	27. The sh in *shield* = the ci in so___al.
tha*n*k	28. The ng in *going* = the n in tha___k.

Note: This exercise can be varied as follows:

The *e* in *she* = the ___ in *machine*.

187

FOUNDATIONS OF INSTRUCTION

A Self-Test on Words Often Misspelled

Instructions: Some of the following words are correct as they are. Some have a letter or letters left out. Some blanks will not be filled, while some will need *one or more* letters. If the word is correct, leave it alone. Cover the answers until you have completed the item.

Answers

hypoc*ri*sy	1. h _ pocr _ sy
g*au*ge	2. g _ _ ge (measuring instrument)
Cinc*inn*ati	3. Cin _ ci _ _ at _ i
lia*i*son	4. lia _ son
It's correct.	5. excel _
It's correct.	6. an _ oint
priv*i*lege	7. priv _ l _ ge
sacr*i*leg*i*ous	8. sacr _ l _ g _ ous
ex*hi*larating	9. ex _ il _ rating
ac*commo*date	10. ac _ om _ _ date
con*sen*sus	11. con _ en _ us (agreement)
embar*ras*sed	12. embar _ as _ ed
misch*ie*vous	13. misch _ _ v _ ous
hemo*rr*hage	14. hemor _ _ age
oc*cu*rrence	15. oc _ ur _ _ nce
paraph*er*nalia	16. paraph _ _ nalia
questio*nn*aire	17. questio _ _ air _
liqu*e*fy	18. liqu _ fy
infe*r*red	19. infe _ red
sil*houet*te	20. sil _ ouet _ _

More about *ie* and *ei* Words

The old rule "*i* before *e* except after *c* or when sounded like *a* as in *neighbor* or *weigh*" is helpful to the student only in a limited sense. While it is true that when a long *a* sound is represented the spelling is always *ei* (*eight, feint*), the rule does not apply to many words having the long *e* sound. Here, for example, are some *ei* words that do not fit the "*i* before *e* except after *c*" rule. In these words the *ei* sounds like long *e*.

   caffeine (*also* caffein)
   either
   neither
   leisure
   protein
   seize
   sheik
   codeine (*or* codein)

Some proper nouns that don't follow the rule are:

   Neil
   Keith
   Leila
   Sheila
   Cassiopeia
   Pleiades

FOUNDATIONS OF INSTRUCTION

Notice, also, that close interpretation of the rule would cause us to spell *conscience* as *consceince*, and that the rule does not apply to words like *science, nescience, omniscient, species,* and *financier*, which have *i* before *e* after *c*.

In the following exercise, the student checks his spelling skill by writing *ei* or *ie* in the blanks to complete the words. The correct spellings are given on the left.

Answers

*ei*ther	1. _ _ ther
fr*ie*ze	2. fr _ _ ze
misch*ie*vous	3. misch _ _ vous
w*ei*gh	4. w _ _ gh
aggr*ie*ve	5. aggr _ _ ve
f*ei*nt	6. f _ _ nt
r*ei*gn	7. r _ _ gn
f*ie*nd	8. f _ _ nd
ach*ie*ve	9. ach _ _ ve
rec*ei*ve	10. rec _ _ ve
rec*ei*pt	11. rec _ _ pt
shr*ie*k	12. shr _ _ k
s*ei*ze	13. s _ _ ze
h*ei*ght	14. h _ _ ght
p*ie*ce	15. p _ _ ce
s*ie*ge	16. s _ _ ge
rel*ie*f	17. rel _ _ f
misch*ie*f	18. misch _ _ f
l*ie*utenant	19. l _ _ utenant
conc*ei*t	20. conc _ _ t
for*ei*gn	21. for _ _ gn
br*ie*f	22. br _ _ f
r*ei*n	23. r _ _ n
fr*ie*nd	24. fr _ _ nd
ch*ie*f	25. ch _ _ f
perc*ei*ve	26. perc _ _ ve
c*ei*ling	27. c _ _ ling
th*ie*f	28. th _ _ f
th*ei*r	29. th _ _ r
n*ei*ghbor	30. n _ _ ghbor
n*ei*ther	31. n _ _ ther
l*ei*sure	32. l _ _ sure
ach*ie*vement	33. ach _ _ vement
al*ie*n	34. al _ _ n

Answers

inv*ei*gle	35. inv _ _ gle
all*ie*s	36. all _ _ s
bel*ie*f	37. bel _ _ f
b*ie*nnial	38. b _ _ nnial
countr*ie*s	39. countr _ _ s
conc*ei*t	40. conc _ _ t
*ei*ther	41. _ _ ther
handkerch*ie*f	42. handkerch _ _ f
*ei*ghth	43. _ _ ghth
n*ie*ce	44. n _ _ ce
f*ei*gn	45. f _ _ gn
s*ei*zure	46. s _ _ zure
s*ei*ne	47. s _ _ ne
rel*ie*ve	48. rel _ _ ve
qu*ie*t	49. qu _ _ t
dec*ei*t	50. dec _ _ t
al*ie*nation	51. al _ _ nation
bes*ie*ge	52. bes _ _ ge
arm*ie*s	53. arm _ _ s
b*ei*ge	54. b _ _ ge
bel*ie*vable	55. bel _ _ vable
d*ei*gn	56. d _ _ gn
w*ei*rd	57. w _ _ rd
chow m*ei*n	58. chow m _ _ n
hyg*ie*ne	59. hyg _ _ ne
fr*ei*ght	60. fr _ _ ght

Spelling Compound Words

Many English words are made by compounding simple words *(suit + case = suitcase)*. The practice of making compounds out of simple words is a good way for elementary students to learn one of the principles of language: many words are formed through combining words which retain their original spellings and original meanings.

Simple Words	Compounds
grand + daughter	_ _ _ _ _ _ _ _ _ _ _
bath + house	_ _ _ _ _ _ _ _
can + not	_ _ _ _ _ _
shirt + tail	_ _ _ _ _ _ _ _
book + keeping	_ _ _ _ _ _ _ _ _ _
rough + house	_ _ _ _ _ _ _ _ _ _
under + rated	_ _ _ _ _ _ _ _ _ _

FOUNDATIONS OF INSTRUCTION

Simple Words	Compounds
over + run	_____
out + trick	_____
beach + head	_____
cut + throat	_____
out + talk	_____
high + handed	_____
head + dress	_____
out + think	_____
red + dogging	_____
house + coat	_____
step + parent	_____
over + reach	_____
wash + house	_____
grand + dad	_____
room + mate	_____
dumb + bell	_____
with + hold	_____
dog + gone	_____
over + rated	_____
fish + hook	_____
night + time	_____
cat + tail	_____
over + rule	_____
metal + like	_____
over + ride	_____
yellow + wood	_____
out + last	_____
mid + day	_____
sand + box	_____

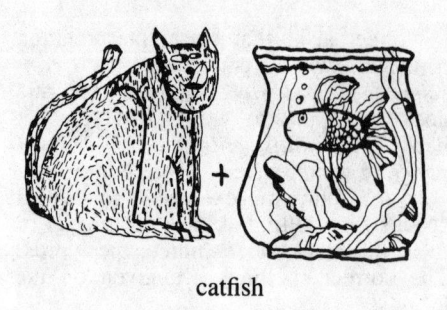

catfish

Krazy Kompounds

The elementary teacher can emphasize the use of compounds in word formation by simple drawings. Students might enjoy making some of these illustrations. Some may be puns.

birddog

Prefixes and Spelling

This lesson emphasizes the importance of recognizing prefixes in spelling words. Using the following forms, the teacher may present key prefixes in words that are often misspelled because of the failure to notice these prefixes.

Part One

Look carefully at these words. They are separated into prefix and root. Write the whole word in the blank:

Prefix and Root   **Whole Word**

mis + spell   _____
mis + spend   _____
mis + state   _____
mis + step   _____
mis + treat   _____
mis + use   _____
mis + understand   _____
mis + take   _____
mis + read   _____
mis + place   _____
mis + shapen   _____

Notice that if the root begins with *s* you must have two *s*'s in the word.

Part Two

Here is a list of words that could add the prefix *dis-* to form new words. In each blank put (2) if you think the new word should have a double *s,* and (1) if you think the word should have only one *s.*

1. _1_ ease
2. _2_ solve
3. _2_ similar
4. _1_ appear
5. _2_ service
6. _2_ satisfied
7. _1_ regard
8. _1_ able
9. _1_ appoint
10. _1_ advantage

Now write out each new word in the spaces below.

1. _____
2. _____
3. _____
4. _____
5. _____
6. _____
7. _____
8. _____
9. _____
10. _____

Sesquipedalian Words

Students sometimes like the challenge of learning to spell a *sesquipedalian* word—a big word (from Latin *sesqui,* one and one half + *ped,* foot)—literally, a word a foot and a half long. Many students have heard the word *antidisestablishmentarianism.* This word describes a doctrine *(ism)* that is against *(anti)* the idea of opposing *(dis)* the establishment—or the doctrine that an established national church (as the Church of England) should be maintained.

But the longest word in the dictionary is not a nonsense word. In one word, what name would you give a *miner's disease of the lungs* caused by the constant inhalation of irritant mineral particles such as superfine silicate or quartz dust?

Here it is: *pneumonoultramicroscopicsilicovolcanoconiosis.*

It has forty-five letters—the longest word in Webster's *Third New International Dictionary.* Long as it is, you can learn to spell it and analyze its meaning if you look at its component parts (a mixture of Greek, Latin, and English).

pneumono / ultra / micro / scopic / silico / volcano / con / iosis

pneumono: related to the lung (as in *pneumonia*)
ultra: beyond, exceedingly, super
micro: very small
scopic: related to sight
(*ultramicroscopic:* exceedingly small to the sight)
silico: related to hard stone or quartz, a mineral
volcano: related to volcanic dust; very fine particles of rock powder
con: dust (from Greek *konis*)
iosis: disease

Now put it back together: a lung disease caused by inhaling superfine silicate dust is
pneumono / ultra / micro / scopic / silico / volcano / con / iosis

A town in Wales has a name with fifty-eight letters:
Llanfairpwllgwyngyllgogerychwyrndrobwllllandysiliogogogoch.

Spelling Pointers

The following information on some of the characteristics of English spelling might be used as discussion points or review items.

1. When the final letter of a prefix and the first letter of a base word or root are the same, both letters must be written. For example:
dis + similar = dis*s*imilar
under + rate = unde*rr*ate

2. When the last letter of a base word and the first letter of a suffix are the same, both letters must be written, for example:
tail + less = tai*ll*ess
soul + less = sou*ll*ess

FOUNDATIONS OF INSTRUCTION

3. Using the overhead projector or the chalkboard the teacher might list the following words and ask the students to make a generalization about their spelling: quintuplet, quick, quilt, quibble, acquire, quit, quite, quotation, eloquent, acquit, tranquility, quantity, quality, quiet.
Spelling hint: The letter *q* is followed by *u*.

4. In some words *k* is added to *c* to make sure we give *c* the hard sound (*k*) rather than the soft sound (*s*). For example:
A politi<u>c</u>ian (*c* has a soft sound) was politi<u>ck</u>ing (*c* has a hard sound). Without the *k, politicking* might be pronounced as *politissing* or *politiseing*.

Here are some other *ck* words:

a. Shella<u>c</u> the chair. *But:* I shella<u>ck</u>ed the chair.
b. The crowd was in a state of pani<u>c</u>. *But:* The crowd became pani<u>ck</u>y—they pani<u>ck</u>ed.
c. Yesterday we went on a picni<u>c</u>. *But:* We were picni<u>ck</u>ing yesterday.
d. Children often froli<u>c</u> on the lawn. *But:* The children froli<u>ck</u>ed on the lawn.
e. A mime is an actor who mimi<u>c</u>s. *But:* The clown mimi<u>ck</u>ed the ringmaster.

Note, however, that this spelling (adding *k* to *c*) applies only to certain words. Mimicry, for example, does not add a *k*. The point of this and other exercises in this unit is to alert students to the characteristics of English spelling, to point up the regularities that exist, and to emphasize the need to consult the dictionary for help with irregular spellings.

Vowel Spelling Strategies among First and Second Graders: A Growing Awareness of Written Words

JAMES WHEELOCK BEERS
CAROL STRICKLAND BEERS

When asked why he had written the word *ride* as RIAD, a six year old replied, "I heard two sounds between the *r* and the *d*." Another first grader had also spelled *ride* the same way, but had a different response to the same question: "Well, *boat* has an *a* after the *o*, so I put an *a* after the *i* in *ride*."

Two youngsters misspell *ride* identically and yet each provides a different reason for that spelling. One child supports a spelling strategy with knowledge of English sounds, while the other reveals awareness of an orthographic principle in English. Both six year olds have developed knowledge of words, although the application of that knowledge is incorrect. It is true that the *i* in *ride* is more a diphthong /aI/ than a single vowel sound. It is also true that many words in English have orthographic markers that influence the pronunciation of a preceding vowel (*a* as in *goat* or *beat*). What is particularly interesting in view of these contrary explanations for the same misspelled word is the fact that

From *Language Arts,* Vol. 57, No. 2 (February, 1980). © 1980 by the National Council of Teachers of English. Reprinted by permission.

both six year olds are actually the same child. The first explanation was elicited at the beginning of his first grade experience and the second came at the end of the school year.

The spelling strategies revealed by this first grader give us a glimpse at the youngster's knowledge about words. Chomsky (1970) has suggested that a child learns to spell by applying knowledge of English phonology to an underlying abstract form of words called lexical units. As the child's knowledge of the English sound system grows, these lexical units emerge as correctly spelled English words. Venezky (1967), while recognizing the importance of a child's awareness of English phonology, believes that a child must learn the graphemic and morphophonemic features of English words if he or she is to become a good speller. These graphemic features are the acceptable letter combinations in English (BFHLW is not acceptable) and the letter markers which affect the pronunciation of other letters (*a* in *boat, e* in *hope*). Morphophonemic features indicate that meaning elements in words are pronounced according to their phonetic or morphemic boundaries. For example, the plural form *s* is pronounced /s/ in *cats, trucks,* and *ships,* but /z/ in *dogs, trains,* and *cars*; *sh* is pronounced /sh/ (not /ʃ/) in *mishap.* While Chomsky's theory of learning to spell relies on phonology and an abstract dictionary of words, Venezky's view of English spelling places more emphasis on the surface features of words. These are somewhat opposing views of English spelling and yet the six year old cited earlier seems to have confirmed both. He used his knowledge of English phonology in his first spelling of *ride,* but relied on his awareness of markers for his second spelling of *ride.*

Read (1971, 1973) and Beers and Henderson (1977) have already demonstrated that preschool children and first graders rely heavily on their understanding of English sounds when they begin to write. Children are aware of the similarities among phonetic features of vowel sounds and use that awareness in their spelling attempts. Tenseness is one phonetic feature. A vowel sound is considered tense or lax based on the degree of tenseness in the tongue and floor of the mouth during the articulation of the sound. By placing the thumb firmly against the skin under the lower jaw one can readily see the *e* in *Pete* is tense and the *e* in *pet* is lax. It is the similarity in tenseness which causes *bed* to be spelled BAD or *hit* to be spelled HET. In both of these misspellings the letter names *A* and *E* correspond very clearly to the short *e* and *i*, respectively, and the phonetic feature of tenseness is used by the children to spell the vowel elements.

The conclusions in both the Read and the Beers and Henderson studies also suggest that changes in spelling strategies used by children occur sequentially and systematically, not haphazardly. Later spellings indicated that the youngsters were cognizant of additional characteristics of written words. This was particularly true in the Beers and Henderson study of first graders' writing attempts. Misplaced markers were noted as well as the use of morphophonemic elements. These same sequential changes in spelling strategies were noted in six to ten year olds in an additional study by Beers, Beers and Grant (1977).

In light of the results of these exploratory studies which saw support for Chomsky's and Venezky's spelling views, the present research was conducted to answer two questions: Does knowledge about written words develop sequentially in beginning readers and writers? Are the youngsters able to apply their knowledge about familiar words to the writing of unfamiliar words?

Procedure

Seventy-five first graders and seventy-one second graders of average or above-average intelligence were asked to spell a list of twenty-four words (see Appendix A). The list was comprised of two high and two low frequency words from six vowel categories (short *a,* short *e,* short *i,* long *a,* long *ee, ea,* and long *i*). The twelve high frequency words were located on the 500 most frequently used words list, and the twelve low frequency words came from below the 1000 most frequent words (Lorge and Thorndike, 1944). The list was randomly ordered for each of five test administrations that occurred monthly during the second half of the school year. Each child's monthly spelling of each word received a score of one to four, which represented the sequential changes in vowel spelling patterns identified in the Beers and Henderson study (1977). (See Appendix B for a more detailed look at the scoring criteria.)

Results

Sign tests were performed on the five scores of each child's twenty-four words to determine if the scores changed sequentially from lower to higher scores. If a child moved from a low score to a higher score four of the five times he or she spelled a word, a plus was received; a child whose scores did not change sequentially received a minus; a child whose scores showed no change at all received a zero. The number of signs (plus, minus, zero) was tabulated for each word and analyzed. The results of these sign tests revealed that a proportionately larger percentage of children followed a sequence of spelling scores than children who did not on twenty-three of twenty-four words. An analysis of variance performed on all spelling scores revealed that first graders' scores differed significantly from second graders' scores in all vowel categories. The first graders, however, moved consistently from lower to higher scores while many second graders scored consistently higher in the first four vowel categories. There was also a significant difference between the high and low frequency words scores, although the greatest differences were seen in first graders' spelling attempts.

Conclusions

The results of this study confirm the hypothesis that children's knowledge about words occurs sequentially and systematically over an extended period of time. The youngster's spelling attempts were a reflection of that growing knowledge. The extensive use of letter names for various vowel sounds can be attributed to an understanding of the phonetic feature of tenseness in English vowel sounds. This understanding can be seen in the first graders' spellings of *bed* (BAD), *step* (SAP), *wreck* (RAK), *lip* (LEP), and *lid* (LED). The widespread use of the letter-name strategy by six year olds may indicate the presence of a cognitive constraint upon the pace at which word knowledge develops.

Within the framework of normal cognitive development, it can be argued that many six year olds are functioning within the preoperational stage. Preoperational thought can be characterized by youngsters' inability to decenter, i.e., to release their perception from the one dominant feature of a problem in order to consider other features. As preoperational children solve the conservation of liquid problems, for example, they are unable to consider both the height and width of the new container when asked to identify which container has more liquid. The preoperational child's response is invariably "the tall one." This inability to consider other characteristics of the object while problem solving may also be seen in the widespread use of the letter-name strategy by most first graders in the early stages of this study. When confronted with the problem "how do you spell _____?", for example, the first graders did not consider that one letter may represent many sounds, or that one sound may be represented by many letters. Instead, most first graders focused on the name of the letter as the dominant feature and ignored other features. The presence of this letter-name strategy in the latter stages of the study strengthens the position that cognitive constraints are operating. With unfamiliar words, the first graders continually relied on the letter name to represent the vowel sound, even when they spelled the corresponding high frequency word correctly. This occurred regardless of the instructional method used to teach reading or spelling.

The second graders, on the other hand, demonstrated their awareness of the multidimensional characteristics of letters. They used higher order strategies involving markers (RIAD for *ride*) which indicates these youngsters recognized that marking is another feature of letters. This recognition may have been the result of more instruction, a greater sight vocabulary, or a growing understanding of written words. The ability to decenter may also have influenced their strategies. The fact that markers were used in second graders' spelling of low frequency words points out their growing ability to apply information about familiar words to unfamiliar words (CREKE for *creek*, DIEK for *dike* and SEIT for *seat*). Such an ability reflects a strategy beyond the letter-name level.

The second graders' ability to apply knowledge of familiar words to unfamiliar words may lend support to Chomsky and Halle's (1968) idea of lexical units. They suggest that children will internalize information about words (and build lexical units) only through repeated experiences with words. Once children begin to internalize this information, they will connect information about similar words to their lexical representations so that they can begin to spell words correctly that have similar lexical representations but different pronunciations. This ability was seen frequently in the second graders, as they applied what they knew about words they had not previously spelled.

The mechanism needed to allow a child to transfer information from one set of words to another set may be evolving as the child progresses through Piaget's stages of cognitive development. By the time children have had extensive experience with written words, they need to be at a cognitive level of understanding that can utilize this information. The seven year old in concrete operations can more easily deal with surface features of words in order to make generalizations about specific types of words than can the six year old preoperational child. Perhaps Venezky's notion of graphemic features and marking qualities of various letters are being examined by seven and eight year olds as they attempt to categorize words. If the seven year old is categorizing these surface features at the concrete operations stage, then Venezky's intermediate step between the surface and the deep structure of written language may very well exist.

A child who consistently spells correctly is one who has had a chance to examine many words over a considerable length of time. It is probable that a higher level of abstract thinking is necessary for a child to be able consistently to transform lexical spellings into correctly spelled words, especially with regard to unfamiliar words. It may be that such a complete understanding of written language does not occur within the Piagetian framework until the age of formal operations. Studies by C. Beers (1978) and Zutell (1978) support the notion that level of cognitive development is related to the development of spelling strategies.

Implications

The results of this study suggest that children move through a series of spelling strategies over an extended period of time, regardless of instructional procedures employed in their classrooms. It should be remembered that no attempt was made to control the type of instruction these children received. The pupils were from eight different first and second grade classrooms whose reading programs ranged from strong phonovisual instruction to the language experience approach. Some teachers had formal spelling lessons while others did not. Regardless of the type of instruction, children from all eight classes exhibited the same kinds of spelling strategies throughout the study.

How the children spelled and the time at which their spelling changed has already been attributed to their varying degrees of cognitive development. If this is true, particularly with these younger school children, more care should be taken to be aware of a child's level of cognitive development. Until a child is functioning at the level of concrete operations, he or she may have difficulty dealing with both spelling and word recognition skills.

Children entering the first grade invariably face the task of acquiring word recognition skills. First graders attempt to learn letter-sound relationships and the inconsistencies of these relationships. If children use letters as one dimensional characters when they try to write words, it follows that the same type of strategy might be employed as they engage in word recognition activities. All children in the first and second grades will not be able to see letters as having various characteristics in different words because children develop cognitively at different rates.

Learning to spell involves learning about words, their components, and the relationships among these components, whether they be sound-letter correspondences, syntactic considerations, or morphemic elements. Teaching spelling, therefore, should not be separated from word recognition skills and should be part of any word exploration that occurs in a classroom. It could easily frustrate a pupil or a teacher when a child is expected to deal with letters and words on a variety of levels when he or she may not conceptually be able to go beyond one level. The results of this research, therefore, question the notion that all first and second graders should receive extensive word recognition training or spelling practice with primary emphasis on memorization rather than exploration. What should in fact be occurring is a closer examination (from a cognitive point of view) of what children do as they deal with letters and words. Some children will require more time, and more opportunities to examine words in order to develop a complete understanding of how they are written. Endless repetition of an activity with the hope that such drill will get the skill into the child's head can thwart the youngster's development, not stimulate it.

One final comment needs to be made about learning to spell and its relation to learning to read. To read, a child must be able to recognize words or at least enough words in a running text. Learning to spell is an avenue that children can take to recognize, not just words, but those components of words that distinguish one word from another. Spelling needs to be examined in light of what it can tell children about words in their writing and their reading.

REFERENCES

Beers, C. "The Relationship between Cognitive Development and Reading Performance in Second Graders." In *Developmental and Cognitive Aspects of Learning to Spell—A Reflection of Word Knowledge,* edited by J. Beers and E. Henderson. Unpublished manuscript, 1978.

Beers, J.; Beers, C.; and Grant, K. "The Logic Behind Children's Spelling." *Elementary School Journal* 19 (January 1977): 238-242.

Beers, J. and Henderson, E. "A Study of Developing Orthographic Concepts Among First Grade Children." *Research in the Teaching of English* 11 (Fall 1977): 133-148.

Chomsky, N. "Phonology and Reading."

In *Basic Studies in Reading,* edited by H. Levin and J. Williams. New York: Harper and Row, 1970.

Chomsky, N. and Halle, M. *The Sound Pattern of English.* New York: Harper and Row, 1968.

Read, C. "Pre-School Children's Knowledge of English Phonology." *Harvard Educational Review* 41 (1971): 1-34.

———. "Children's Judgment of Phonetic Similarities in Relation to Spelling." *Language Learning* 23 (1973): 17-38.

Thorndike, R. and Lorge, L. *The Teacher's Word Book of 30,000 Words.* New York: Columbia University, Teachers College, 1944.

Venezky, R. "English Orthography: Its Graphical Structure and Its Relation to Sound." *Reading Research Quarterly* 10 (1970): 75-105.

Zutell, J. "Spelling Strategies of Primary School Children and Their Relationship to the Piagetian Concept of Decentration." *Research in the Teaching of English* 13 (February 1979): 69-80.

Appendix A
The Twenty-four Spelling Words and Accompanying Sentences

1) *hat* — John put on his hat.
2) *back* — He slid down the hill on his back.
3) *stack* — The books were piled up in a big stack.
4) *sap* — Maple syrup is made from the sap of maple trees.
5) *bed* — We went to bed early.
6) *step* — Susan sat on the bottom step.
7) *wreck* — The car was in a wreck.
8) *speck* — The airplane looked like a small speck in the sky.
9) *lip* — Bill cut his lip.
10) *stick* — The dog ran after the stick.
11) *pit* — The steam shovel dug a deep pit.
12) *lid* — He took the lid off the jar.
13) *gate* — Someone left the gate open.
14) *lake* — We went swimming in the lake.
15) *spade* — You use a spade to dig in the garden.
16) *drape* — Sue's mother put a drape over the window.
17) *week* — Friday is the last day of the school week.
18) *seat* — We rode in the front seat of the car.
19) *creek* — Tom and Bill went fishing in the creek.
20) *streak* — Karen saw a streak of light from the window.
21) *ride* — We went for a ride in the country.
22) *light* — Liz turned on the light.
23) *tribe* — The boys belong to an Indian tribe.
24) *dike* — There were floods when the dike broke.

Appendix B
Scoring Criteria with Examples in Each Vowel Category

Category	Strategy	Score	Example
long *a*	omission of vowel	1	GTE (gate)
	letter-name	2	GAT (gate)
	transitional	3	GAETT (gate)
	correct form	4	GATE

FOUNDATIONS OF INSTRUCTION

Category	Strategy	Score	Example
long *ee* or	omission of vowel	1	WK (week)
ea	letter-name	2	WEK (week)
	transitional	3	SEET (seat)
	correct form	4	STREAK (streak)
long *i*	omission of vowel	1	RDE (ride)
	letter-name	2	RID (ride)
	transitional	3	RIEDE (ride)
	correct form	4	RIDE
short *a*	omission of vowel	1	HT (hat)
	letter-name	2	HIT (hat)
	transitional	3	HAET, HET (hat)
	correct form	4	HAT
short *e*	omission of vowel	1	STP (step)
	letter-name	2	STAP (step)
	transitional	3	STAEP (step)
	correct form	4	STEP
short *i*	omission of vowel	1	LP (lip)
	letter-name	2	LEP (lip)
	transitional	3	LIAP (lip)
	correct form	4	LIP

Phonetic Spelling: A Case Study

MARILOU R. SORENSEN
KRISTEN JEFFERS KERSTETTER

A child entering school is traditionally faced with the task of learning to write. The approaches taken to aid the child in this task have been many and varied. Recent psycholinguistic research has given new insight into the area of beginning writing, showing that it is primarily a thinking process of prediction and confirmation.

Marie Clay (1975) suggested that children begin writing in the same manner they learn oral language: by experimenting and becoming active learners. An integrated language arts program that allows children to actively develop a gradual awareness of the arbitrary customs used in written English aids in the formation of concepts about writing and eases the transition from the spoken to the written word.

Similarly, spelling develops when children, making personal decisions, write from their own perceptions of words and put down what they deem representative of the sound and symbol.

Research on early spellers by Read (1970, 1971, 1975) supports the premise that pre-school, kindergarten and first grade children have phonetic acuity that allows them to analyze their writing into component sounds, arriving at roughly the same linguistic organizational patterns.

The environment that contributes to this early spelling and writing is viewed by Chomsky (1971) as a place where children are ". . . allowed to trust their

---

From *Language Arts*, Vol. 56, No. 7 (October, 1979). © 1979 by the National Council of Teachers of English. Reprinted by permission.

own ears and their own judgments. . . . The whole approach introduces him to the written word by making him aware that it belongs to him and grows out of his own consciousness'' (p. 296).

Invented Spelling: A Case Study

At age five Wes entered an open-space K–1 classroom. Language was valued and praised. Storytelling and reading sessions were held daily—sometimes three or four times a day. A rich use of "book language" and descriptive words came from this time in addition to the sharing that his parents did at home.

Among the many choices that children could make throughout the day were quiet reading and writing. Most of Wes' initial experiences with invented spelling came about because he chose the topic and the time to write.

Early in kindergarten Wes was accustomed to the teacher writing words as captions and labels for his pictures and projects. He seemed to understand that the letter-symbol gave meaning to his work.

In October, after completing a Halloween picture, the teacher told him he needed to do the writing himself. Wes wrote:

HRIS A MNSDYA HND HAS
(here is a monster a haunted house)

Only with *house* did he stop and ask, "What comes after *h*?" The teacher replied, "What do you think?" He wrote *AS*.

Even at this point, when the words were not recognized as separate units, Wes followed a common pattern used by young spellers, excluding lax (short) vowel sounds (Read 1975).

When the teacher read the caption Wes was particularly pleased and later produced another illustrated story:

HE IS DNG RNING
BT HE FRGT TO IG
TO DE QEN
(He is dancing, running
But he forgot to get to the queen.)

In this second writing he correctly left a space between word units. Some of the letters were reversed but there was no reversal in letter sequence.

The pattern of Wes sharing his writing with the teacher, an aide or with more advanced writers was already established. Wes' questions might be: "How does this sound?", "Do you think this is good?" or he might add, "I can't think of anymore." Most of the time he just needed someone with whom to discuss and clarify ideas.

The formation of some letters was difficult for Wes. He made no effort to distinguish between upper and lower case letters even though both were displayed throughout the room on charts, posters and banners. Wes often copied letter formation from a book rather than the model of an experience chart or hand-printed labels.

Late in October Wes' attempt at writing *apple* came from two sources, a book and his own sounding-out process:

I HAVE A AEOUPPL
THE SUN SI SUIEING
(I have a apple, the sun is shining)

Already Wes understood the *-ing* ending and used it in its proper place.

By November Wes was referring to experience charts in the room. When he brought a model dinosaur and a book about dinosaurs the teachers transcribed his sharing onto a chart. Later he wrote his own story and used the words on the charts as references:

THIS IS A PCHR UUV DINOSAURS ARE FING WN
GIGANTIC DINOSAURS (copied from chart)
(This is a picture of dinosaurs fighting with gigantic dinosaurs.)

Wes often used words at the end of one sentence to begin the next as a form of word economy, for example in this sentence *dinosaurs*.

On occasion Wes would ask for help

FOUNDATIONS OF INSTRUCTION

to complete a story such as this one written after a trip to a museum featuring a mastodon:

I HAV MADE A DINOSAURS MUZM IT IS NEET THE BONZ R NEET TO *THE PEOPLE* (provided by the teacher) TAKINGE THE DINOSAURS IN MUZM.
(I have made a dinosaur's museum. It is neat! The barns are neat, too. The people are taking the dinosaurs in museum) [taking pictures with cameras]

In this example of MUZM *(museum)* Wes demonstrated a phonetic relationship which is common to many early spellers, using consonants which make their own sound and the tense (long) vowels that use their letter name. Also, he has used the letter *R* as a word unit.

By December Wes was writing with few reversed letters. Sentences were becoming longer and more complex.

I HAV MADE A BAT MOBILE (provided by teacher)
IT'S NET IF YOU PUHS THAT BTN WN SB'S IT THE RUKS GO
(I have made a bat mobile. It's neat. If you push the button when somebody's in it the rockets go)

Wes used the apostrophe correctly (IT'S) as he had seen it modeled, but in this example over-extended it, saying *SB'S* represented "Somebody is in."

When fairy tales were introduced in the classroom, Wes was helped to write about that genre through the introduction of "Once Upon A Time. . . ."

ONCE UPON A TIME (copied from the teacher)
THR WAS A LITL BABY
NAMES TROZN IN THE JUGL
THE JUGL IS DAYGRIN IN THE JUGL
(Once upon a time, there was a little baby named Tarzan in the jungle. The jungle is dangerous in the jungle)

Wes' writing shows where another linguistic decision was made. Words with *l* and *r* are written into syllabic components by dropping the unstressed vowel.

Wes' valentine to the teacher was stuffed in her bookbag. He was sharing a personal note with her, alone:

YOU BE MY VALENTINE
WE WIL LIV TO TGITHR
(You be my valentine
We will live together)

Some of the words on his valentine had been copied from an experience chart of words compiled by the children.

Wes' first autobiographical sketch was written in February:

I HAVE MADE A CNOO
THE URZ ARE PLLING
ITS PREDE ON THE CNOO
ME AND MY SISBR AND MY MOM AND MY DAD
ME
(I have made a canoe
The oars are pulling
It's pretty on the canoe
Me and my sister and my mom and my dad
Me)

Even though the canoe trip had been taken several months earlier, Wes was still exploring those ideas that were most exciting and relevant to him.

In this selection he added a title for the first time, and also noted the ending.

THE MASTADON
HE WAS
RUNING IN THE
STROM AND
IT'S IN THE MUZM
THE END.
(The Mastodon
He was running in the storm and it's in the museum.
The End.)

Usually Wes' writing was an outgrowth of a class or home experience. For example, during a severe blizzard the children could not attend school and the next day Wes wrote:

WOAS WN I WAS A SLEEP
THN WN MY DAD WT TO WRC WN THE PRCH
FOZ ON THE PRCH
NAD WN I WOK UP I SOL THE PRCH
(Once when I was asleep then when my dad went to work when the porch froze on the porch and when I woke up I saw the porch)

Wes was trying to create colorful language but involved himself with complex grammatical structures which he could not master in writing.

FOUNDATIONS OF INSTRUCTION

The ideas that Wes wanted to express in writing were most often worked out through active participation in storytime, art work, rhythm and music or play in the housekeeping or drama corner.

From a movement and music experience came this story:

THIS IS A JUGL THE KING IS KOING IN THE JUGL
WN TRZAN SWING IN THE JUGL HE GRD THE GRIA
(This is a jungle. The king is going in the jungle. When Tarzan swings in the jungle he guards the gorilla)

In the following selection Wes again practiced word economy by using "the helicopter" at the end of one sentence and as the beginning of the next. He continued to delete vowels, for example, FIRD (*fired*). He now attended to the structure of stories. Here he used a title, beginning and ending.

THE KING KOING HIS RDING
GODZLA GOUP FUM THE ROKS
THEN VRSZIS FUM THE SCHOL HUWOS
THEN KING KOING GODZLA IS FIRING
THE HLLUCOPTR IS FIRD
THIS IS THE EUD
(The King Kong His Writing.
Godzilla got up from the rocks
Then verses from the straw house
Then King Kong Godzilla is firing
The helicopter is fired.
This is the end.)

Throughout the school year, Wes' own illustrations had served as a prewriting activity: a time for him to organize his thoughts. He read compositions as well as a variety of trade books, other children's writings, and sources of print such as charts, magazines, labels, tissue boxes, and personal notes given to him by the teacher.

Early spellers appear to have a sense that they can represent *all* words and sounds with written symbols. On an art piece done in March, Wes wrote across the picture of a rabbit:

WISRS
EIR
WTS UP DUK?
E E E
TH TH TH TH TH TH!
(Whiskers, Er. Eh! Eh! Eh! What's up Doc? th, th, th!) (the rabbit chomping a carrot)

This marked his first use of an exclamation point and question mark.

Later in March Wes read *The Very Hungry Caterpillar* by Eric Carle. After making a tissue paper collage caterpillar, he wrote this story:

THIS IS A CADAPILEER.
IT'S PRITTE. IF YOU TUCHT IT
IT WALL TICKL YOU. AND
IT FIELS LIK MUD.
IT SMALS LIK BOLYLOD EGG.
(This is a caterpillar.
It's pretty. If you touched it, it
will tickle you and it feels like mud.
It smells like boiled egg.)

Wes used a *t* for the past tense /t/ in *touched* (TUCHT). The punctuation demonstrated his growing awareness of the grammar of his language.

Another aspect of phonetic spelling attempted by early writers is called affrication (CH replaced *tr*). A story written in April demonstrated this:

GODZILLA HAS BEN
CHRICT.
THE PEOPL DID IT.
TIEED THE ROK TO HIS FOOT.
(Godzilla has been tricked.
The people did it.
Tied the rock to his foot.)

Wes' long and involved stories also included dialogue:

I HAVE A DREEM A BOWT
A ROBREE. THE PLEEMAN
GOT ME WIV DOT YOU
PLA SOM GAYS! NO!
I WOT! HAY IM NOT
A ROBRT! SO SHE LATI
GO OF ME AND I
SAO THE ROBRT
(I have a dream about a robber. The policeman got me. "Why don't you play some games?" "NO! I won't." "Hey, I'm not a robber!" So she let go of me and I saw the robber.)

Wes' understanding of dialogue was evident when he read this story. His voice changed to the proper register with

201

each character. While the humor in the story might be difficult for adults, Wes' five-, six- and seven-year-old classmates howled with laughter.

At the end of March several books were introduced during storytime which used repetition and refrains. Wes' writing not only reflected this form of language but also the excitement of a trip to the zoo:

WE ARE GOING TOO THE ZOO.
WE ARE GOING TOO SEE LOTS OF THING.
A HO HO LOTS OF THING.
(We are going to the zoo. We are going to see lots of thing. A ho, ho, lots of things.)

Wes had developed a "sense of sentence" and used appropriate punctuation.

In May Wes began an unprompted exploration of print and shapes. This letterplay took the form of decorated words; for example, *Dracula, wolf* and *vampire* were written with red dots falling from them ("dripping blood," Wes explained) and the word *fur* was filled in with lines ("hairy fur").

By the end of kindergarten Wes was spelling most of the service words correctly, using punctuation and capital letters. He had developed excellent small motor coordination.

At the beginning of first grade, Wes was back in the same classroom with the same teacher. He appeared eager to write. Beginning and ending sounds were no problem but the confusion of medial sounds bothered him. He often went to the teacher to ask for the spellings "in the middle." He also began to use his word bank that contained fifty commonly written words. In the past, Wes seemed to prefer his own spellings, but at this time he sensed the need to communicate with others who could read his writing.

Wes began to write a book as one of his projects in the first grade:

PAGE 1: THE CREECHERS ARE NOT.
        CUS THAY ARE MELTIN.
PAGE 2: THE SHIP EXPLODED (word supplied by teacher)
PAGE 3: THE SHIP IS GOING TO EXPLOD
PAGE 4: THE DRAGUNS ARE FITING TO GIT THE PEEPL
PAGE 5: A DRAGUN COT A PRSN TO EAT.
PAGE 6: THE WHAL AND THE SCHWID IS TRYING TO KEEP EECH UTHER AWAY.
(The creatures are not because they are melting.
The ship exploded.
The ship is going to explode.
The dragons are fighting to get the people.
A dragon caught a person to eat.
The whale and the squid is trying to keep each other away.)

By this time Wes had searched out other spellers in the classroom for help. They almost instinctively sought out each other to write and share together.

After hearing *The Biggest House in the World* by Leo Lionni four boys cooperated on a mural about the snail. When it was completed, Wes wrote this account on large paper:

THE BIGIST HOWS IN THE WOLD
BY WESLEY, MATT, C, DJ, CH
THE SNAL IS EATING A CABIG
BUT IT CEN NOT MOOV. THE SHAL IS TOO BIG. THE UTHERS SHALS ON
THE SMALL SNALS ARE LIGHT. AND HE DIYDE.
THE END.
(The snail is eating a cabbage.
But it cannot move. The shell is too big. The other's shells on the small snails are light. And he died.
The end.)

As Wes proceeds in first grade he continues to write voraciously to satisfy his curiosity about written language. The atmosphere and circumstances surrounding him are a natural and fertile environment: self-directed activities, emphasis on the child's interest, stimulating materials and respect for individual creativity. Much of his writing comes about because he chooses the topic and the time to write; he writes about things that have meaning to him. Besides the daily stories and language experiences he has a time to silently explore books and is developing his individual "sense of story" from other authors.

Wes' growth in spelling didn't just happen. It came about because of his need and desire to create his language.

His teacher, as well as others, were constantly listening to his work and complimenting, instructing and challenging him. They understood that this familiarity with written language establishes a solid background for use of standard spelling as he continues to write. Above all Wes has learned to trust his own perceptions of language and understands that he has a viable medium for expressing himself.

REFERENCES

Chomsky, Carol. "Reading, Writing and Phonology." *Harvard Educational Review* 40 (1970): 287-309.

———. "Write First, Read Later." *Childhood Education* 47 (1971): 296–299.

Clay, Marie. *What Did I Write?* Auckland, New Zealand: Heinemann Educational Books, 1975.

Read, Charles. *Children's Categorization of Speech Sounds in English.* Research Report No. 17. Urbana, IL: N.C.T.E., 1975.

———. "Children's Perceptions of the Sounds of English: Phonology from Three to Six." Unpublished doctoral dissertation, Harvard University, 1970.

———. "Pre-School Children's Knowledge of English Phonology." *Harvard Educational Review* 41 (1971):1–34.

Developmental Strategies of Spelling Competence in Primary School Children

JAMES W. BEERS

In the past, learning to spell was viewed as a serial learning task coupled necessarily with the proper pronunciation of spelling words. The work of Furness (6), for instance, appeared to show that mispronunciation of words leads to misspellings. Similarly, Jensen (7) concluded that serial learning effects could predict the occurrence of spelling errors in words of varying lengths. Recently, an alternative hypothesis about how children learn to spell has moved away from this mechanistic view. The thrust of this hypothesis is that learning to spell like learning to speak and read is a language

---

Pages 36-45 of *Developmental and Cognitive Aspects of Learning to Spell.* © 1980 by the International Reading Association. Reprinted by permission.

based activity. Following a model akin to the generative-transformational grammar model, researchers now hypothesize that children internalize information about spoken and written words, organize that information, construct tentative rules based on that information, and apply these rules to the spelling of words.

This hypothesis has been tested in several recent studies in which the spelling strategies of preschoolers and primary grade children have been studied. Read (8) examined the spelling attempts of preschool children in the Boston area and found in their attempts a heavy reliance on the preschoolers' phonological knowledge of spoken English. Read also concluded that orthographic knowledge is acquired systematically and not haphazardly. There was little evidence of random spelling errors. The errors that occurred were consistent with virtually every spelling condition and child that Read examined. Read believes that children know how sounds are articulated and use that knowledge in their early spelling attempts. He concluded that early spelling strategies were replaced by later ones which reflected the application of phonological knowledge and not simple letter-phoneme association. For example, long vowels initially appeared for short vowel sounds (MAT-met), followed later by short vowel for long vowel sounds (MIT-meet) as the children attempted to represent vowel elements in written English. Read reasoned that positions of articulation for letter names and sounds represented by letters were readily used by the children in his sample as they sought the correct spelling of words.

Read (9) later examined six and seven year old children's ability to recognize phonetic similarities among sounds and to represent these sounds orthographically. The children in the study were presented with a nonsense word and a pair of real words. They were instructed to select from each pair the word that "sounded like" the nonsense word. First graders commonly matched a short vowel word with a word containing a similar sounding long vowel. For example (pek) was matched more often with *peck* rather than *peek*. The seven year olds also made matches between certain short vowels. For example, the nonsense word (stIp) was matched with *step* more often than *steep*. Read concluded that this shift away from short-long vowel matching was due to maturational factors or the effects of first and second grade instruction in reading and spelling.

Another finding in this study revealed that adults do not necessarily make the same phonetic judgments about sounds and spelling as primary school children do. If this is an accurate assessment of children's recognition of phonetic relationships, then teachers may assign inappropriate reasons for a primary age child's word recognition or spelling attempts. Most reading and spelling programs utilize phonetic analysis, and yet many children may not categorize English sounds according to this conventional analysis.

Beers and Henderson (2) analyzed the spelling attempts of first grade children in one classroom in Laurel, Maryland, over a six month period. Very specific orthographic conditions were examined which included short and long vowel spellings (*get, gate*), morphological markers (*ing, ed, er*) and various consonant spellings. By noting the spelling changes in weekly creative writing stories for each condition over a six month period, several sequential strategies emerged for most of the children examined. Examples of the spelling sequences can be seen in Table 1.

Initially, position or articulation played a major role in many of the spelling patterns examined which demonstrated that these children also relied on their knowledge of how English sounds are articulated. The letter-name strategy saw the most appropriate letter-name being substituted for a particular sound. These letter-name spellings can be seen in FET for *fit* and PAN for *pen*.

Another example of the children's awareness of English can be seen in their spelling of nasal consonants. In an initial position, medial position or final position *m* or *n* appeared correctly (MENE for *many*). When either was part of a consonant blend, however, the *m* or *n* was omitted (JUP for *jump*). Articulation features appear to be the main reason for this consistent omission since nasals are articulated in the position that is used for a consonant that immediately follows the nasal. This explains why a syllable *m* appears before *p* and *b* consonants, *n* before *d* and *t* and *n* as in *ing* before *g* and *k*. Perhaps it is an internalized awareness that the articulation positions for these final consonants are the major influence

FOUNDATIONS OF INSTRUCTION

Table 1
Spelling Pattern Sequence in Selected Categories

Short *e* as in *met*
 1. *a* for *e* - GAT (*get*)
 2. *i* for *e* - WINT (*went*)
 3. correct form

Short *i* as in *sit*
 1. *e* for *i* - MES (*miss*)
 2. correct form - MIS (*miss*)

Long *a* as in *gate*
 1. correct form - GAT (*gate*)
 2. *e* for *a* - GET (*gate*)
 3. *ay* or *ae* for *a* - GAETT (*gate*)
 4. correct form - GATE

Long *e* as in *feet*
 1. *e* for *ee* - FET (*feet*)
 2. *i* for *ee* - FIT (*feet*)
 3. *ea* for *ee* - FEAT (*feet*)
 4. correct form

Nasal consonants - single letter
 1. correct form when not part of a blend - CAM (*came*), MENE (*many*)
 2. omitted when part of a blend - JOP (*jump*), WAT (*went*)
 3. emergence of *m, n* in consonant blend - WANT (*went*)

Flaps as in *patter* and *later*
 1. *d* for *t* or *tt* - PIDER (*pitter*), SWEDER (*sweater*)
 2. *t* for *tt* or *tt* for *t* - BITTIG (*biting*), LITL (*little*)

Morphological ending
 ed as in *wasted*
 1. *d* substituted for *ed* - PETD (*painted*)
 2. *id, ud, ad* for *ed* - STARETID (*started*)

 ed as in *passed*
 1. *t* for *ed* - NOCT (*knocked*)
 2. *et* for *ed* - DRESET (*dressed*)

upon the nasals that causes less concern for the nasal itself in the children's own knowledge of the English sound system.

A second strategy saw the emergence of an awareness of letters representing sounds rather than being sounds themselves. Short vowels began to appear spelled correctly and pre-consonant nasals now regularly appeared. There was still an awareness of the phonological nature of written language although graphemic constraints were being considered by the children at this level.

Finally, a transitional stage appeared in the spellings where the use of orthographic markers (MAED for *made* or PAETT for *pat*) and morphophonemic elements was common in most spellings. The children at this stage were combining information based on knowledge about English sounds, morphemes in written words, and syntax in order to spell words in their creative writing. For example, in the sentence "My dad is raking the leavz" the *z* in *leavz* represents the plural form phonetically, not as a distinct morpheme. The writer also retained the silent *e* in *raking* but omitted it in *leaves*. Children at this transitional stage have not yet learned how English spelling is affected by meaning and syntax, but they are moving away from the idea that pronunciation is the major control on English spelling.

These data also revealed that the children appeared to proceed through many of these spelling pattern sequences at different rates. Some children would pass through the initial step of a particular sequence more rapidly than others, while other children would appear to skip an initial step as though they were more advanced in spelling a particular orthographic configuration. It was found, however, that the sequence of steps for the spelling patterns examined appeared constant for most of the children. For example, the pupils who began to write in February used the level one strategy for a spelling pattern that the November writer used. This observation indicates that later beginning writers follow the same spelling pattern sequences seen in earlier beginning writers. It would appear, therefore, that the spelling pattern sequences are generally invariant regardless of when a child begins to write.

These spelling pattern sequences suggest that children seem to have developed a highly sophisticated knowledge of English phonology. They are acutely aware of the characteristics of English sounds and have established a hierarchy of these characteristics with which to base their initial spelling of English words. The fact that the sequences are relatively consistent indicates that they may be building a set of internalized rules with which to deal with the system of English orthography. It would appear that the child's growing knowledge of English words is not based on simple letter-sound correspondences but on a combination of phonological and syntactic information as it applies to spoken and written language.

A subsequent study (*1*) attempted to statistically validate the spelling noted in the Read and Beers and Henderson studies. One of the difficulties encountered in these two earlier studies was the inability to control what words were spelled by the children or the frequency with which the words were spelled. By controlling these variables, it was hoped that this later study could answer several important questions. First, when asked to spell selected words over a six month period of time, do first and second graders advance as predicted from no attempt, to letter-name spellings, to transitional errors and, finally, correct spellings? Second, what differences occur as a function of high and low frequency in words of comparable length and phonetic structure?

A spelling word list was given to 75 first graders and 70 second graders in Charlottesville, Virginia, once a month between January and May 1974. These children were representative middle class primary school pupils following a standard basal reader curriculum of instruction. Four single syllable words were selected for each of six spelling categories which were long *a (take), e (seat* or *week), i (wide* or *light)*; short *a (hat), e (met),* and *i (sit)*. Two of the words in each category were from the 500 most frequently used words according to the Lorge-Thorndike Word List (*10*) and two were below the 1,000 most frequently used words.

The spelling attempts by the children received a score of 1 to 4. These scores represented the sequential pattern of errors seen in the vowels' spellings in the Read and Beers and Henderson studies. This sequence can be seen in an explanation of the scores. A *1* was given for the omission of the vowel element, *2* for a letter-name spelling, *3* for a transitional-type spelling, and *4* for the correct rendering of the vowel element and its marker if necessary.

The results of a sign test performed on the monthly scores in each child's spellings indicated that a significantly greater number of children's scores changed sequentially on 23 of the 24 words (see Table 2). There were very few children who showed no change from a low score. The majority of those children who made no changes for specific words spelled them correctly throughout the study.

The analysis of variance in each vowel category indicated that the spelling scores of first graders differed significantly from second graders' scores across all vowel categories. A test of the simple effects of time on the two grades revealed that the first graders moved consistently from lower to high scores while many second graders scored consistently on four vowel categories. The high frequency words received higher scores than low frequency words in all but the short *i* category. The difference between high and low frequency word scores was greatest in the first graders' spelling attempts throughout the study.

Several conclusions were drawn from the results of this study. Children between the ages of six and seven years do follow sequential spelling strategies that progress as the youngster develops. The sequence of strategies was most common in first graders for several reasons. A large number of second graders spelled many words correctly throughout the study, which would preclude any sequence in their spelling. In this study it should also be remembered that the scoring system employed was based on the results of the study by Beers and Henderson which had only examined the spelling attempts of a class of first grade children.

The fact that such spelling pattern sequences were found in this larger sample of children might suggest something about the developmental nature of learning to spell. According to Piaget, many

Table 2
Sign Tests on Sequential Scores of the 24 Spelling Words

Word	Sequence	No Sequence	No Change	Z
gate	60	28	57	3.4*
lake	80	24	41	5.4*
drape	87	34	24	4.4*
spade	84	34	27	4.2*
week	54	27	64	2.7*
seat	94	34	17	5.8*
streak	106	38	1	6.0*
creek	94	31	20	6.3*
light	87	32	26	5.8*
ride	57	13	75	5.0*
tribe	86	35	24	4.2*
dike	80	28	37	4.8*
back	53	16	76	5.2*
hat	30	11	104	5.0*
sap	66	28	51	3.8*
stack	61	23	61	4.4*
bed	45	13	87	3.4*
step	86	18	41	6.6*
speck	91	23	31	6.0*
wreck	81	40	24	3.4*
lip	75	26	44	4.8*
stick	61	36	48	2.4*
pit	75	21	48	5.4*
lid	57	52	36	0.4

*$p < .01$

six year old children are still in the stage of preoperational thought which precedes the stage of concrete operations in his theory of cognitive development. One of the primary characteristics of a child at the preoperational level is his centering on the single most dominant characteristic of an object. This centration causes many real objects to be perceived as one dimensional. The inability to perceive other salient features of objects seems to have been reflected in the extremely common use of the letter-name strategy by many first grade children in the early stages of this study. These children were aware of letters but only by their respective letter names. The name of the letter became the single most dominantly used feature to spell vowel elements in all the vowel categories for these children.

The ability of many second graders to use information about high frequency words when faced with spelling low frequency words may account for the fact that second graders consistently spelled all words better than first graders. Second graders generally have a greater sight vocabulary, basic word knowledge and experience with writing words and could apply this knowledge to unfamiliar words.

The transference of information about known words to unknown words may lend some validity to Chomsky's notion of lexical representations and learning to spell. The Piagetian concept of cognitive development may even provide a structure for what Chomsky believed six and seven year olds do with words. Chomsky (4) hypothesized that six year olds do not know everything about the rules that govern the pronunciation of English words. Through repeated exposure to written words the child will gradually internalize enough information about similarly spelled words that may have different pronunciations. The child will link this information about similar words to the lexical representations that correspond closely to written words so he can begin to spell correctly words that have similar lexical representations but different pronunciations.

By the time a child has been continually exposed to written words and their similar letter combinations with different pronunciations, he needs to have a cognitive framework that can make use of these kinds of information. The seven year old who deals in concrete operations has the beginnings for such a framework. He can deal with the surface characteristics of written words and categorize types of words by their orthographic features. He need not be restricted to pronunciation, as he is at an earlier age.

For a child to have lexical spellings continually emerge as correctly spelled words would require an extensive examination of words over a considerable length of time. It would appear, therefore, that a higher level of abstract thinking may be needed to spell unfamiliar words correctly and consistently. It may be that a child through continued exposure to words and types of words finally achieves a more or less complete understanding of written language at the age that formal operations occur in Piaget's theory of development. It may be that such understanding is not totally grasped until this period of development.

The results of a final study (3) indicate that these spelling strategies occur not only in first and second graders' writings but in third and fourth graders' spelling attempts. A list of five high and five low frequency words representing five vowel categories (short a, e, i; long a and i) was given to children in grades one through four enrolled in various schools in Michigan. They had been exposed to different kinds of reading and spelling instruction. The youngsters' misspellings revealed overwhelming reliance on the letter-name strategy in the early grades. The percentage of youngsters using this strategy steadily dropped from second to fourth grade, although some fourth graders still relied on the strategy. The other two strategies which were also found in the earlier studies saw the attempt to use vowel markers like silent *e* and the substitution of one short vowel for another similar short vowel.

This study once again points to the developmental nature of learning to spell. Probably the most significant evidence for this conclusion lies in the way in which the children differed in their spelling of high and low frequency words. Many of the high frequency words were spelled correctly (*hat, bed, gate*) which can be attributed to reading or spelling instruction. These very same children, however, failed to spell the low frequency words correctly (*sap, speck, drape*) regardless of the classroom instruction they received. This finding suggests that, although children may memorize weekly spelling lists, they may not yet recognize the orthographic principles underlying those words; otherwise, they would certainly apply them to less familiar words. This ability to develop and apply the principles of English orthography brings us back to the original hypothesis stated at the beginning of this paper.

Over an extended period of time children internalize what they know about their language. They construct tentative rules based on this knowledge and apply those rules to the spelling of words. The studies presented here reveal that a child's knowledge about written words is acquired systematically, developmentally, and gradually. The acquisition process is too complex to be limited to serial learning or word memorization. We know children do learn the English spelling system. What needs more investigation, however, is how they learn the complexities of the system.

REFERENCES

1. Beers, J. "High and Low Frequency Words: How First and Second Graders Spell Them and Why," paper presented at the International Reading Association Convention, Anaheim, California, May 13, 1976.
2. Beers, J., and E. Henderson. "First Grade Children's Developing Orthographic Concepts," *Research in the Teaching of English,* Fall 1977.
3. Beers, J., C. Beers, and K. Grant. "The Logic Behind Children's Concepts among First Graders," *Research in the Teaching of English,* Fall 1977.
4. Chomsky, N. "Phonology and Reading," in H. Levin and J. Williams (Eds.), *Basic Studies in Reading.* New York: Harper and Row, 1970.
5. Chomsky, N., and M. Halle. *The Sound Pattern of English.* New York: Harper and Row, 1968.
6. Furness, E. "Mispronunciations, Mistakes, and Method in Spelling," *Elementary English,* 33 (1956), 508-511.
7. Jenson, A. "Spelling Errors and the Serial Position Effect," *Journal of Educational Psychology,* 53 (1962), 105-109.
8. Read, C. "Preschool Children's Knowledge of English Phonology," *Harvard Educational Review,* 41 (1971), 1-34.
9. Read, C. "Children's Judgment of Phonetic Similarities in Relation to English Spelling," *Language Learning,* 23 (1973), 17-38.
10. Thorndike, R., and L. Lorge. *The Teacher's Word Book of 30,000 Words.* New York: Teachers College, Columbia University, 1944.

Spelling, Phonology, and the Older Student

SHANE TEMPLETON

The interplay between the spelling system of English and the phonological knowledge that individuals possess has been an intriguing area of investigation for psychologists and educators alike (17, 20). The question most often addressed in the research involves the degree to which knowledge of orthographic structure influences the psychological reality of words and the phonological processes that apply to them. The question is an important one for it is part of a broader concern involving the way in which individuals organize information about the vocabulary of English. In effect, there probably are limits to the amount of information about words that we can expect most of our pupils to glean from spoken language; the rest of the information may arise from an examination of orthographic structure.

In the middle and secondary school classroom, we are concerned not only with the amount but also with the quality of our pupils' exposure to intraword, orthographic structure. Before embracing specific instructional objectives, however, we must have some idea about the nature of pupils' competence with regard to word structure. The investigation of the orthographic-phonological interplay offers just such a glimpse into this competence. Most of the research in this area has involved younger children; only recently has attention been directed toward the older individual (20).

Before discussing a direct investigation into the way in which orthographic and phonological knowledge interact in the older student, I would like to consider briefly the two areas with which I shall be concerned: the nature of the orthographic "beast" and the sound system to which it corresponds.

Spelling and Phonology

English orthography is often considered a highly inefficient system that fails to represent in consistent fashion the relationship between graphic symbols and phonetic expression (1, 2). In much of the professional literature, however, the tide appears to be turning (11, 12). Recent analyses have suggested that, although English spelling may be somewhat irregular when evaluated according to the criteria of strict one-to-one phoneme-grapheme correspondences, a logical system of impressive regularity emerges on a more abstract level (21, 8, 13). English spelling does manifest its fair share of inconsistencies; research undertaken within the past fifteen years, however, suggests that the spelling system generally reflects a structural consistency only partially evidenced in sound-symbol correspondences.

Apart from phonological correspondences, spelling reflects morphological, syntactical, and derivational aspects (19). This view arises in part from Chomsky and Halle's rather extensive and, from a theoretical standpoint, influential analysis of English phonology (8). Chomsky and Halle asserted that, for the speaker-reader of English, the orthography optimally reflects the semantic relationships among words as well as quite effectively

---

Pages 85-96 of *Developmental and Cognitive Aspects of Learning to Spell.* © 1980 by the International Reading Association. Reprinted by permission.

predicting pronunciation. Although this assertion about "optimality" has been challenged (20), the advantages of a spelling system which does not attempt to represent all the phonetic features of a language are widely acknowledged (13). For example, an efficient orthography probably should not represent all the phonological rules that the speaker-reader automatically applies, such as the distinction between the sounds represented by the letter *s* in the words *cats* and *clubs*. The issue of an efficient orthography usually centers on adequate representation; that is, should the orthography represent distinctions that the beginning reader will make, or those of concern to the more mature reader? Actually, a good case can be made for a kind of compromised efficiency in English; the spelling system seems to reflect competencies possessed by both younger and older individuals (18).

In the case of phonology, most phonological rules are mastered by children by the time they begin formal schooling (14). Furthermore, these rules include the distinction among the pronunciations of the plural marker *s*, as in the examples cited earlier. This type of distinction may be termed "lower order" morphological knowledge (3) and pertains to the pronunciation of inflectional endings (such as /s/) in various contexts. These rules are *automatic*; children apply them with scarcely a second thought about what they are doing. Where older students are concerned, however, the issue may not be quite so simple.

There are some phonological rules about which more mature speakers appear to be uncertain; these higher order rules are seldom automatic (3). Studies have shown that many children and adults do not have a firm grasp of the rules of *vowel alternation* (15, 20). These rules include vowel *laxing*, where the tense (long) vowel in certain base, or root, words changes to a lax (short) vowel in derived words, as in pro*fa*ne-profa*ni*ty. Included also are those instances where the tense vowel in a base word is *reduced*, or changed to the *schwa* sound in a derived form, as in in*cli*ne-incl*i*nation. To a large extent, it is possible that knowledge of these higher order rules is dependent on *orthographic* knowledge. Rather than bringing phonological competence to bear on the examination of orthographic structure, the process may be reversed, and the spelling system may influence the generalization of this higher order phonological knowledge.

Many of the words that exhibit these patterns of vowel alternation occur infrequently in everyday spoken discourse (15). The way in which these phonological rules are applied to this body of vocabulary, then, might be based on a deductive process. For example, when an individual knows the pronunciation and the spelling of a base word and a related derived form, he/she can be cued to the pronunciation of words that follow a similar phonological pattern by the similar orthographic structure of these words. To illustrate, let us assume an individual knows the spoken and written representation of *derive* and *derivative*. He/she can then apply this knowledge in figuring out the placement of stress and the pronunciation of the second vowel in the unknown word *appelative*, which follows a similar spelling pattern (including, in this case, the same number of syllables and the same suffix as in the known *derivative*). A more comprehensive and productive awareness of the rules of vowel alternation, then, may arise from the examination of orthographic structure.

The issue of higher order phonological knowledge (in this case, rules of vowel alternation) may at first glance appear to be a rather arcane concern. As suggested earlier, however, the investigation of this knowledge offers a means by which we can better understand how pupils develop knowledge about words and about the complex interplay between written and spoken language.

The Study

In an attempt to determine the correspondence between knowledge of certain higher order aspects of phonology and knowledge of English spelling, I conducted a study involving good spellers in grades six, eight, and ten. I was primarily interested in this "chicken or the egg" question of whether awareness of sound patterns precedes and is necessary for knowledge of spelling patterns, or vice versa. As the preceding discussion suggests, my hunch was in favor of "spelling first."

I chose to study the pupils' awareness, as reflected in pronunciation and in spelling, of the two rules of vowel alternation that have been mentioned: vowel *laxing* and vowel *reduction*. I believed the following results would occur:

1. Among the eighth and tenth graders, an orthographic representation of base words would more effectively cue correct vowel alternation in derived words than would a spoken representation of base words.
2. Eighth and tenth grade students would evidence a higher positive relationship between knowledge of vowel alternation and orthographic knowledge than would sixth graders.

These first two hypotheses were based on the assumption that the older students, quite simply, had been exposed more often to orthographic structure than had the younger students. In the first case, because older students are more familiar with orthographic structure, this structure should more easily engage the appropriate phonological rules than would the spoken representation. In the second case, as a consequence of increased exposure to orthographic structure, older students have had more opportunities to generalize the phonological rules than have the younger students. Thus, we should see a closer correspondence between phonological and orthographic knowledge among the older students.

3. Phonological and orthographic knowledge should be generalizable to unfamiliar words.

For those students who have a good facility with orthographic and phonological structure, there should be a transfer of this knowledge to English pseudowords, or nonsense words, that follow the same orthographic and phonological rules as do actual English words.

4. Contextual information should facilitate correct vowel alternation.

The pronunciation of many English words in isolation is ambiguous. If an individual knows the grammatical slot into which a word can fit, information is provided as to correct stress placement and vowel pronunciation. For example, *duplicate* is pronounced differently depending on whether it functions as a verb or as an adjective.

To test these hypotheses, twenty students at each grade level were randomly assigned to one of two conditions of presentation. In one condition, each student was shown a base word plus a suffix and asked to pronounce the resulting derived word. The word and suffix were then removed and the student was asked to spell the derived word. In the second presentation condition, a base word was pronounced for the student while a suffix was visually presented. The required response was the same as in the first condition; the student first pronounced and then spelled the resulting derived word. Pronunciations were recorded for later analysis.

Twenty-four words were pronounced and spelled by each student. Half of the words were English words; the other half were pseudowords. In addition, half of the words were presented in isolation, and the other half were presented together with a typed sentence in which the derived word could occur. The following diagram illustrates this design.

		Base Word	**Suffix**
Real Words	(Isolation)	CONTRITE	ION
	(Contextual Clue)	URBANE	ITY
		GEORGE'S _____ IMPRESSED ALL OF US.	
Pseudo-words	(Isolation)	PERCOSE	ITY
	(Contextual Clue)	DEPLONE	IC
		TED IS A _____ PERSON.	

Results

The data were subjected to a multifactor analysis of variance with repeated measurements. In addition, intercorrelations were computed among the dependent variables. The following results were obtained:

1. As hypothesized, the orthographic, or visual, presentation of a base word did significantly increase the probability of correct pronunciation of the derived words.
2. Although the correlation between vowel alternation and spelling increases across grades, this relationship was significant only at grade ten.
3. At each grade, students appeared to generalize orthographic knowledge to the pseudowords. There was no significant difference between the spelling of the real words and the spelling of the pseudowords. Phonological knowledge, however, was not generalized; correct vowel alternation was significantly greater for real words than for pseudowords.
4. At all three grades, it was found that presenting a sentence in which a derived word could occur significantly affected correct vowel alternation. In addition, spelling performance was significantly better for words with which a sentence was presented than for words presented in isolation.

Discussion

These findings suggest some tentative conclusions concerning the relationship between phonological knowledge and orthographic knowledge. *Seeing* a base word, as opposed to hearing it, seems to provide a more direct link with the appropriate phonological rules that apply to derivatives of the base word. That this finding occurred even among tenth graders suggests the tenuous nature of knowledge of vowel alternation. If the appropriate rules were fully internalized, then *both* conditions of presentation—visual and auditory—should have equally facilitated correct pronunciation. Furthermore, the relationship between these phonological rules and print is still inexact, as suggested by the nonsignificant correlations between spelling and vowel alternation at grades six and eight. Although orthographic ability did not differ significantly across grades, the relationship between this ability and knowledge of vowel alternation was significant only at grade ten. In addition, the greater stability of orthographic knowledge over phonological knowledge is suggested by most students' ability to spell correctly most of the pseudowords, whereas the pronunciation of these words, even at grade ten, was significantly lower than for real words.

The fourth hypothesis does not appear to relate directly to the matter of phonological-orthographic correspondence. It was tested in order to provide more information about the possible determinants of phonological rules. Results affirmed an intuitive judgment made by most teachers of the structural analysis of words; that is, the application of appropriate phonological rules appears to be at least partially dependent upon syntactic information. When a more "natural" setting was provided for a derived word, it was more often pronounced correctly. Results were quite interesting concerning spelling performance in this regard. A number of possible explanations might be offered as to why visually presented syntactic information significantly affected correct spelling; it may be that more immediately available orthographic information somehow more effectively engages the orthographic mental "machinery." Whatever the case, some very interesting further research is suggested here.

It appears, then, that orthographic knowledge may be a necessary, though not entirely sufficient, condition for higher order phonological knowledge. Most individuals may master knowledge of allowable letter sequences within words, or *intraword conditional redundancies* (10), and appropriate structural transformations (changing certain letters when affixes are added, for example) earlier than certain phonological rules. It would then remain for an individual to deduce the rules of vowel alternation in unknown words occurring in print from known words to which these phonological rules apply. Thus, a more efficient correspondence between an individual's sound system and the orthography may be, as Chomsky (5:17) expressed it, a "late intellectual product."

Implications

We would be putting the cart before the horse if our primary objective were to facilitate the optimal phonological development of our pupils. Not that this is an undesirable objective, it is just that it is secondary to a main focus on more general word knowledge and vocabulary development. Mature readers can understand words in print that they would otherwise hesitate to pronounce. And, as has been pointed out, more unfamiliar words occur in print than in speech. In the case of lower frequency words, then, we can take advantage of what older students may be more familiar with: a *visual*, as opposed to a *spoken*, representation. Eventually, the spoken forms that correspond to the printed examples will be created. If this were the sum total of the relationship between orthographic and phonological knowledge, we would be left with an interesting conclusion of little substance. This, however, is not the case.

Since the publication of Chomsky's *Syntactic Structures* (7), linguists have pointed out that it is extremely difficult (if not downright impossible) to study language devoid of any reference to an underlying logic. What is true for linguists is also true for our students. We want them to become aware of the general patterns that underlie words and to realize that to learn a word does not mean one learns a single discrete item. Rather, one subdivides and, perhaps, expands an existing *meaning* category which is represented by other words that are already known. We want students to realize that many of these related words may be similar in *form* to the new word. It is in this latter regard where the spelling system can be the great organizer.

Perhaps an example will best illustrate

the preceding point. Students who are privy to the knowledge that spelling can represent underlying relationships may be much more likely to perceive the logical connection between *equation* and *equanimity* if they see these words in print than they would if they hear these two words. The orthography *preserves* the relationship; the spoken representation *obscures* it.

Pedagogically, it is difficult to separate spelling instruction from vocabulary instruction (*16*), for one reinforces the other. In fact, for the older student, they are two faces of the same coin—or at least they ought to be. At issue is not a radically new approach to word study but, rather, an awareness on the teacher's part of existing proposals. Our responsibility as teachers is to direct our students' attention to the structure of printed words. C. Chomsky (*5*); Dale, O'Rourke, and Bamman (*9*); and Brengelman (*4*) have suggested some specific ways of accomplishing this, and current texts in reading methodology are beginning to explore these more intriguing aspects. For starters, we can avoid the type of instruction which honors the presentation of *infant* as a fourth grade word yet postpones the introduction of *infancy* until eighth grade (16).

We need to be alert to every opportunity for stretching our students' existing vocabulary structures with other examples that evidence multilevel relationships. Just as primary grade teachers group words according to "families" (*hat/fat/mat;catch/match/scratch*) so, too, can middle and secondary school teachers group words that exhibit similar higher order structural characteristics. These include the words cited earlier that follow similar alternation patterns. For extra challenge, there are always teasers such as *amnesia, mnemonic,* and *Mnemosyne,* whose structural similarities are more obscure yet still can be identified and whose semantic relationships are intriguing.

Furthermore, from the time students are capable of conceptually dealing with word origins (etymology), they can be instilled with a curiosity about exploring the common lexical roots of words. Rather than appearing as an interesting but largely unproductive comment on the development of English (to which "etymology" as a classroom topic often degenerates), this emphasis can provide a fascinating and powerful tool for word analysis.

Smith (*19*) noted that there are differences between the strategies for efficiently handling an unknown word while reading and the strategies for intentionally expanding one's vocabulary and orthographic knowledge. It would be pedagogically unwise to assume, however, that these strategies reflect largely independent cognitive processes for the student. Writing and examining words apart from actual reading ought to facilitate the latter, and vice versa. The observation that good readers are often poor spellers does not weaken this contention; this phenomenon may simply reflect the lack on the part of such individuals of *consciously* attending to aspects of their "intuitive" knowledge of the symbolic and morphological relationships among words.

As evidenced by the subjects in the study reported here, a closer correspondence between orthography and phonology does seem to develop with age and, one might infer, from a longer exposure to written language. By bringing elements of this correspondence to a level at which they can be examined (for example, by noting morphological, syntactic, and derivational features in word structure), this correspondence can be more fully appreciated. It would follow that a central component of the transition to skilled reading ought to be the development of an awareness of the productivity of more abstract orthographic regularity.

Emphasizing the more superficial aspects of the spelling system—sound to spelling-pattern correspondences—may be a bankrupt policy where many of our students are concerned. They require more of a "handle" on the orthography. We ought to be able to provide that handle by more qualitatively directing our students' conscious attention to the written word. On the other hand, many students are able to internalize English spelling with little conscious awareness of whatever rules or generalizations they are using. It is quite possible that most of the students in the study reported here were of this type. Even for these good spellers, there is more to be learned. For the rest of our students (and perhaps ourselves), this conscious examination should not only generate spelling competency but reinforce what I have continually referred to as a qualitatively better way of examining word structure.

It is difficult to assess empirically the quality of the conceptual frameworks that underlie the written word. As this study has suggested, a productive knowledge of orthographic structure may often precede higher order phonological knowledge. Orthography, being a more stable, visually-accessible system, may thus become the basis for a logical analysis of word-level phonology and semantics. Whenever possible, instruction should capitalize on this feature of orthographic structure.

Increasingly, research in this area is providing support for a more empirically based judgment that many reading theorists and educators have held for quite some time: the more information concerning the logic of word structure to which our students are sensitive, the more sophisticated and adaptive will be their interaction with printed language.

REFERENCES

1. Allred, Ruel A. *Spelling: The Application of Research Findings*. Washington, D.C.: National Education Association, 1977.
2. Baugh, Albert C. *A History of the English Language, Second Edition*. New York: Appleton-Century-Crofts, 1957.
3. Braine, Martin D.S. "The Acquisition of Language in Infant and Child," *The Learning of Language*. New York: Appleton-Century-Crofts, 1971.
4. Brengelman, Fred. "Generative Phonology and the Teaching of Spelling," *English Journal*, 59, 8 (November 1970) 1113-1118.
5. Chomsky, Carol. "Reading, Writing and Phonology," *Harvard Educational Review*, 40, 2 (May 1970), 287-309.
6. Chomsky, Noam. "Phonology and Reading," in Harry Levin and Joanna P. Williams (Eds.), *Basic Studies on Reading*. New York: Basic Books, 1970, 1-18.
7. Chomsky, Noam. *Syntactic Structures*. The Hague: Mouton, 1957.
8. Chomsky, Noam, and Morris Halle. *The Sound Pattern of English*. New York: Harper and Row, 1968.
9. Dale, Edgar, Joseph O'Rourke, and Henry Bamman. *Techniques of Teaching Vocabulary*. Palo Alto, California: Field Educational Publications, 1971.
10. Gibson, Eleanor J., Henry Osser, and Anne Pick. "A Study in the Development of Grapheme-Phoneme Correspondences," *Journal of Verbal Learning and Verbal Behavior*, 2 (July 1963), 142-146.
11. Hodges, Richard E. "Theoretical Frameworks of English Orthography," *Elementary English*, 49, 7 (November 1972), 1089-1097, 1105.
12. Howard, Murray. "The Problem of Spelling," *English Journal*, 65, 8 (November 1976), 16-19.
13. Klima, Edward. "How Alphabets Might Reflect Language," in James F. Kavanagh and Ignatius Mattingly (Eds.), *Language By Ear and By Eye*. Cambridge, Massachusetts: MIT Press, 1972, 57-80).
14. Menyuk, Paula. *The Acquisition and Development of Language*. En-

glewood Cliffs, New Jersey: Prentice-Hall, 1971.
15. Moskowitz, Breyne A. "On the Status of Vowel Shift in English," in Timothy Moore (Ed.), *Cognitive Development and the Acquisition of Language.* New York: Academic Press, 1973, 223-257.
16. O'Rourke, Joseph. *Toward a Science of Vocabulary Development.* The Hague: Mouton, 1974.
17. Read, Charles. *Children's Categorization of Speech Sounds in English.* Research Report No. 17. Urbana, Illinois: National Council of Teachers of English, 1975.
18. Read, Charles. "What Level of Representation Do Children Expect to Find in Print?" in P. David Pearson (Ed.), *Reading: Theory, Research, and Practice,* Twenty-Sixth Yearbook of the National Reading Conference. Clemson, South Carolina: The National Reading Conference, 1977, 193-199.
19. Smith, Frank. "Phonology and Orthography, Reading and Writing." *Elementary English,* 49, 7 (November 1972), 1075-1088.
20. Steinberg, Danny. "Phonology, Reading, and Chomsky and Halle's Optimal Orthography," *Journal of Psycholinguistic Research,* 2, 3 (1973), 239-258.
21. Venezky, Richard. *The Structure of English Orthography.* The Hague: Mouton, 1970.

Spelling Skill and Teaching Practice—Putting Them Back Together Again

TOM NICHOLSON
SUMNER SCHACHTER

Since 1969, The National Assessment of Educational Progress has been testing and evaluating the writing skills of Americans between the ages of 9 and 35. In its first appraisal of writing skills six years ago, it found *that 17-year-olds demonstrated serious deficiencies in spelling.* ("Why Johnny Can't Write"—*Newsweek* 12/8/75)

Spelling skill, like Humpty Dumpty, seems to have "had a great fall." So it seems timely to re-think what we do in spelling and try to find out how we can do a better job.

From *Language Arts,* Vol. 56, No. 7 (October, 1979). © 1979 by the National Council of Teachers of English. Reprinted by permission.

Most teachers develop basic spelling skills by encouraging children to use a dictionary (or thesaurus), by having them keep a list of relevant content words, by teaching them to proofread and by encouraging regular revision of personal lists of difficult words. In other words, pupils are encouraged to develop a spelling "conscience."

At the same time teachers try to supplement this approach by teaching children skills which they can use in learning and recalling new words. Yet this is the area of teaching where there is most uncertainty. Should children be taught spelling rules or is the language too irregular for such an approach? Should children learn words as unique items and forget about rules, or, given the fact that the average adult knows between 50,000 and 100,000 words, does the sight word approach place too much burden on the learner? Or should we teach children to spell by using language analogies, such as remembering that *sign* is spelled like *signal?*

The purpose of this article is to put forward a model of the spelling process which can be used to decide when one teaching method is more appropriate than another. It also provides a framework which can be used for diagnosis and for grouping of words.

THE SPELLING PROCESS

Proficient spellers seem to be able to use three kinds of knowledge when writing words. These different kinds of spelling knowledge are sometimes used separately and sometimes together, especially when some parts of words are regular and others are not.

Language Knowledge

The first component, language knowledge, is something all children bring to the spelling task. They come to school with a well developed language competence that enables them to understand English words, to assign meaning to sounds, and to know whether or not words "sound right." This enables them to distinguish sense from nonsense, assign the correct meanings to homonyms, and use prior knowledge to help determine word structures. Language knowledge also assists children in spelling related words. Carol Chomsky (1969) has argued that children can make use of language knowledge in spelling structurally related words, especially those with Latinate forms. For example, knowledge of the word *signal* can be a useful linguistic tool in recalling the spelling for *sign*.

Other examples are *medicine-medical, history-historical*.

Internalized Rules

The second component, internalized rules, whether acquired inductively (by example) or deductively (by generalization), enable children to predict and write the most probable spelling for words. For example, such rules can tell us that *c* or *k*, not *ck* are used at the beginning of a word. Another example of rule knowledge can be seen when we are asked to spell a word that sounds like *keep* but ends with /g/ instead of /p/. Most of us would probably write *keeg* or *keag*. Very few would write *kege, ceeg, kieg, keg*. Yet why do we do this? The reason seems to be that we have an internalized set of rules to handle the predictable diversity of certain sound-symbol relations. We may not be able to articulate these rules, but we use them all the time.

Visual Associations

The third kind of knowledge used in spelling is what seems to be a visual dictionary in our heads of words and their graphic forms. Many of these words have unpredictable spellings and are usually learned as unique structures of graphemes, or as small "associative sets" of words which have the same irregular spelling. An example of an associative set or word family would be a small set of words such as *light, sight, right,* all with similar graphic structures. Of course, some words are so irregular as to be unique, and would need to be stored as unique items in the visual dictionary. Highly irregular spellings (such as *the, was, laugh, ancient*) fit into this category.

Visual associations can help children to develop automaticity in spelling by storing some words as unique items or as small associative sets of pattern words. Visual associations can be used not only to produce a specific spelling but, when the spelling has been recorded, can be used as a verification channel to check the written form with the visual form in memory. This kind of checking behavior occurs in proofreading and also when we try to confirm a probabilistic spelling to see if it looks correct.

By themselves, however, these three kinds of knowledge are unable to account for proficient spelling behavior. Rule knowledge is useful for generating predictable spellings and for predicting the spelling of new words. Yet, it is unable to account for any more than fifty percent of the words the proficient speller can handle (Hanna & Hanna 1974). Visual associative knowledge, although sufficient to allow us to recall words as single associations or as parts of associative sets, is inefficient and laborious as a total strategy. We shouldn't have to carry around lists of tens of thousands of words in our heads. Finally, language knowledge, although important for clarifying meaning and comparing structurally related words, is not enough to enable us to spell all words accurately. Teaching activities, therefore, need to be based on all three kinds of knowledge.

Teaching Applications

Suppose that the following words have been found difficult by some of the children in the class and the teacher wants to prepare a small group lesson to teach these words:

> history
> attack
> cattle
> ancient
> was
> fight
> medicine

The first step would be to classify the words according to whether the teaching activities should be language based, rule based or depend on visual associations (see Figure 1).

FOUNDATIONS OF INSTRUCTION

Figure 1

A Way of Classifying Words for Instructional Purposes

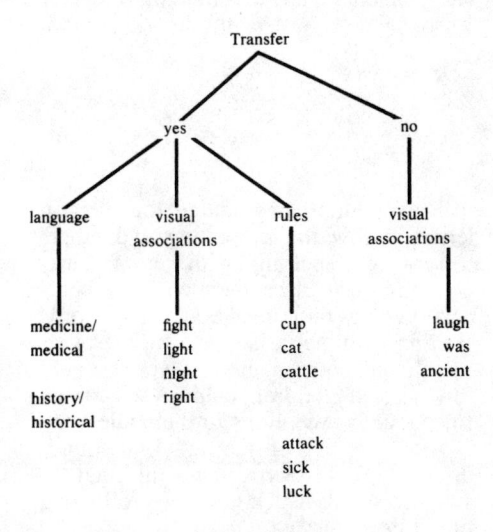

```
                    Transfer
                   /        \
                 yes          no
                /  \            \
         language  visual   rules   visual
                   associations    associations

         medicine/   fight    cup      laugh
         medical     light    cat      was
                     night    cattle   ancient
         history/    right
         historical
                              attack
                              sick
                              luck
```

Teaching Language Relationships

The importance of language structure can be seen with words such as *history* and *medicine*, where knowledge of related forms, such as *historical* and *medical*, will provide sound clues which will enable the child to give the correct spelling rather than common misspellings such as *histery* and *medisine*. Children could be presented with related word pairs, as suggested by Carol Chomsky (1969), to encourage them to take advantage of language cues. Children could work out the missing letters by listening to the related words:

> hist___ry/historical
> si___n/signal
> comp___tent/compete
> medi___ine/medical

Teaching Internalized Rules

The importance of internalized rules can be seen with words such as *attack* (misspelled as *attac*) and *cattle* (misspelled as *kattle*). A practical way to approach

219

FOUNDATIONS OF INSTRUCTION

such words is to have children decide whether or not these words follow some kind of rule. As a class exercise, the children could try to think of a list of words which start with the /k/ sound:

king	cup
kit	cat
kill	cot
kettle	cattle
keg	cap

The children may notice that certain letters follow the *k* spelling and others follow the *c* spelling, with very few exceptions. The class then could hypothesize a possible rule about such words starting with the /k/ sound. But the process should not end there. Over the next few weeks, children could keep watch for possible exceptions to their rules.

After working on the initial /k/ sound, the class could then discuss the final /k/ sound. Words such as the following might be suggested:

back	bike
peck	peek
duck	hike
attack	brake

Children may notice that the final /k/ sound is either *k* or *ck* but not usually *c*, and that there is something about the sound of the vowels that determines whether the spelling is *ck* or *k*.

The teacher could follow up these lessons with spelling-reading exercises such as:

1. The du____ has a sti____ in its bea___.

2. The bi__e is on a pile of ro__ __s.

3. There is a ___at on the truc___.

Teaching Visual Associations

The teacher could group certain words as associative sets or families such as:

fight
light
night
tight
sight

Presenting these as a set of similar patterns may facilitate recall of their spelling.

Other words, however, would need to be learned as unique units because of their unusual spelling. Such words may be highly frequent, such as *was* and *of,* or less frequent, such as *ancient*. These words need to be taught as sight words, using a variety of learning techniques such as saying and writing the words, and then recalling them. They should be practiced in isolation and in context. The learning of some highly irregular sight words can be enhanced by using mnemonics, such as learning about the *lion* in *battalion*. In fact, mnemonics can be especially useful with so-called "demon" words.

DIAGNOSTIC APPLICATIONS

The model we have been using to discuss the teaching of spelling can also be used for diagnosis. If we think of the successful speller as one who can integrate language, associative and rule knowledge, then we need to teach children to use all three skills rather than rely on any one of them.

Language knowledge, for instance, can help us with some words which sound different but are related in meaning (such as *bomb-bombardier* where the *b* at the end of *bomb* is cued by the related word). Yet the child who relies on such a strategy can also be misled (for example, the *s* in *preside* is not cued by the sound of *s* in *president;* nor the *c* in *precede-precedent*).

Some children also get themselves into trouble because they rely on visual associations, that is memorization, of words as unique items and are just not able to remember enough words. They never use language or rule knowledge and so have no way of transferring what is already known to new words, even though the words have predictable spellings. Past instruction may have encouraged these pupils to use only one kind of visual strategy for developing spelling skills:

1) Look at the word.
2) Say the word.
3) Close your eyes. Try to see the word.
4) Look at the word again.
5) Cover the word and try to write it.
6) Check to see if you spelled it right.

Finally, some children rely too much on rules. They either overgeneralize from rules (*hay, pay, day, way*—but *they* then becomes *thay*), or else they adopt a simple rule that all words will be spelled the way they sound (hence *woz* for *was, coff* for *cough*).

Past instruction may have encouraged a rule-governed strategy for developing spelling skills:

1) Say the word correctly. Notice how you make the sounds in the word.
2) Listen to the sounds in the word.
3) Think what letters stand for the sounds in the word.
4) Write those letters clearly and in the right order.

By looking for patterns of errors, the teacher may be able to diagnose a pupil's spelling weaknesses and offer instruction and appropriate groups of words to remediate the problem. We must give pupils the tools for using all three components of spelling behavior. For unless all three kinds of knowledge are learned and used, students are unlikely to become successful spellers. Successful spelling performance involves the integration and interaction of language knowledge, internalized rules and visual associations. Spelling instruction and application should incorporate all three factors in order to enable the student to acquire a variety of spelling skills and strategies.

REFERENCES

Chomsky, C. "Reading, Writing and Phonology." *Harvard Educational Review* 40 (May 1970): 302-309.

Hanna, P. and Hanna, J. "The Teaching of Spelling." In *Language and the Language Arts,* edited by J. de Stefano and S. Fox. Boston: Little, Brown and Co., 1974.

Spelling Preferences and Instructional Considerations

ALBERT J. MAZURKIEWICZ
JANE GOULD

While it appears to be the practice of many dictionary users to assume the first spelling of a word listed in the dictionary to be *the correct* spelling, recent studies by Deighton (1972) and Emery (1973) show that editors of dictionaries have individual ways of indicating *preferred* spellings and that two or more spellings are often listed as correct spellings. The difference between the meanings of *correct* and *preferred*, expressed in literary terms for example, is someone who might *prefer* Steinbeck to Hemingway, that is, "to hold above others." In this sense a prejudice or bias for something is suggested, yet instructional usage of the term *preferred* tends to denigrate an alternative spelling and to foist a spelling on children which may be less phonetic or more irregular because of an assumption that *prefer* means *correct*. The Deighton-Emery studies point out that major dictionaries do not always agree as to which spellings are in fact preferred, and that some dictionaries do not accept frequency as a basis for preference. These dictionaries simply show the variant spellings for a word.

As pointed out by Mazurkiewicz and Berk (1976), the vast majority of their large sample of students, teachers and adults, had a low level of awareness of the existence of equally correct alternative spellings for a random sample of 35 words. They all also showed that a large number of members of the sample often chose a spelling which would not agree with the first spelling as listed in some dictionaries, the so-called preferred spelling, and that there was a detectable trend to use the more regular or simpler spelling of the alternatives available on thirty percent of the words used in their study.

While it might be argued by some purists that the tendency not to use the first spelling listed in a dictionary reflects ignorance, such a puristic position assumes that there is only one correct way to spell words and that even dictionaries which do not conform to an invariant rule are in error. While it can be demonstrated that spelling reform is slowly taking place at this time, in conformance with the history of the language, recent studies on the negative influences of the orthography on reading and writing acquisition and on current interest in spelling reform suggest the need for a quickened pace for change. Change, however, is difficult and a number of byways need exploration before wholesale reform can be rationally undertaken. While certain reforms are apparently being developed in Australia (the principle of SR one), others can be initiated immediately simply by using the more regular of two or three alternative spellings listed in dictionaries. Thus, since *tho* and *thru* are equally as correct as *though* or *through*, *spelt* as correct as *spelled*, etc., consistency in instruction and usage of this kind of known list would immediately provide for meaningful change. Since such correct and more regular alternatives have existed for some time but are less used than might be expected, an investigation into the bases for their limited usage is warranted.

Of specific interest in such an investi-

From *Reading World*, Vol. 15 (May, 1976). © 1976 by the College Reading Association. Reprinted by permission.

gation would surely be a determination of the influence of instructional materials and activities on the pupil in his/her use of alternative spellings. A variety of questions can be raised. Since alternative spellings exist and are equally correct, to what extent do instructional materials contain such information? If excluded, on what basis? What is the direction of choice between alternatives by authors of such materials? Which spellings (more regular or less regular) are taught by teachers? What is the basis for teacher choice of the spelling to be taught? Do teachers teach something about alternative spellings at present? How would they approach this task once equivalency of spellings of words becomes known? What constraints exist to prevent teachers from instructing about equivalent spellings? Or even, what do teachers hold as the meaning of the word *preferred* and why?

Hypotheses

Of the array of questions that can be developed, only a limited number are examined in this study while others are examined in two companion studies in progress. The specific hypotheses of this study were:
1. That at least twenty-five percent of a sample of thirty-two target words would be found among words typically utilized in a sample of materials available for instruction in spelling in grades one thru eight.
2. That altho the sample of thirty-two target words may each be spelled in two equally correct ways, the less regular of the two spellings would be the spelling that was included for instruction in such published materials.
3. That a sample of 50 teachers would have a low level of awareness that the target words are equally correct in each of the two alternative spellings presented.
4. That a sample of teachers who taught spelling would indicate that they rely on the spelling workbooks or "program" for the "correct" spelling of the target words when found among words used in their spelling materials.
5. That the sample of teachers would indicate that they do not teach children about the existence of equally correct spellings for words.

Procedures

To satisfy the purposes of this initial investigation, a selection of materials used most often as the nucleus of a spelling program in local schools was made. The list of 30 target words was initially constructed using the equivalently spelt list of 35 target words developed by Mazurkiewicz and Berk (1976). Since it was recognized that most of the words reported in the Deighton and Emery studies were of a high school and collegiate level of difficulty and that most spelling materials do not continue thru these levels, the final selection of words for study was subjected to the restriction that the words should appear in at least one of two sources, the *Harris-Jacobsen Elementary Vocabulary* (1972) and the *Risland Vocabulary List* (1972). Since the *Risland Vocabulary* continues to serve as a basic source for words in spelling programs as shown by interviews conducted with publishers' representatives who discussed the development of their latest wares at various conferences and conventions, and since spelling programs are most often built to lag one year behind the vocabularies found in graded series of readers, the sources used were deemed appropriate as references for this purpose. Thus only 37.1 percent of the words developed by Mazurkiewicz and Berk were able to be used in this study. Words were added to the list using random selection procedures but subject to the restriction test noted above to complete the list as shown in Table I.

TABLE I
Equivalently Spelled Target Words

dullness	dulness	knowledgeable	knowledgable
drought	drout	blonde	blond
license	licence	judgement	judgment
although	altho	hooves	hoofs
cursed	curst	blueish	bluish
advertise	advertize	lense	lens
brunette	brunet	bussing	busing
gasoline	gasolene	busses	buses
fulfill	fulfil	draughty	drafty
though	tho	totalled	totaled
cigarette	cigaret	theatre	theater
advisor	adviser	grey	gray
likeable	likable	surprise	surprize
socks	sox	ax	axe
leaped	leapt	usable	useable

The target word lists were given individually to a sample of fifty teachers at the late elementary and junior high levels (5th thru 8th grades) who were responsible for teaching spelling as part of the school's curriculum. The directions to each teacher followed those given by Mazurkiewicz and Berk which asked the teacher to determine which of the two spellings were correct or if both were correct to indicate this by writing the letter B before each pair. On completion of this task, each teacher was then interviewed using a series of five questions to determine current procedures in instruction and to obtain reactions to provide data in relation to hypotheses four and five. Recorded responses to the target word lists and to the interview questions were grouped according to frequency. Spelling choices were analyzed for direction of choice (more or less regular) based on the following classification criteria.

Regularity Defined

Each of the two spellings of a word was classified as more phonetic or less phonetic based on its goodness-of-fit to the one symbol-one sound procedure for defining the phonetic nature of languages. Thus *fulfill* containing two *l*'s in the final position was classified as less phonetic than *fulfil* containing one. *Gasolene*, on the other hand, containing an *e* in the last syllable to represent the /ɛɛ/ sound was considered more regular since the letter *e* typically represents the /ɛɛ/ sound and by frequency (Mazurkiewicz, 1976) the letter *i* is used much less often to represent this sound. Similarly *gray* was considered more phonetic than *grey* since by frequency of usage the digraph *ay* vastly outnumbers *ey* to represent the sound /æ/. The spelling *ax* rather than *axe* exemplifies a third criteria for classification when it is noted that the "silent" *e* is dropped. *Theater*, which reverses the order of the letters *er* in *theatre*, reducing the need to think of the final *e* as a signal for the syllabic *r*, illustrates the fourth criterion, while *licence* rather than *license* illustrates the fifth. In this case, the *c* followed by *e*, the diacritic *e*, to represent the sound /s/ was considered more regular based on the research of Mazurkiewicz (1974) which showed that *e* following *s* signals alternative pronunciations of *s*, /s/ and /z/, with the /z/ sound predominating slightly. While it could be argued that

FOUNDATIONS OF INSTRUCTION

the letter *s* in *license* would meet the first criterion of goodness-of-fit to the one sound-one symbol concept more readily, it is also noted that the letters *c* and *s* often represent sounds in common but that in the final position of words *c* followed by *e* is wholly consistent in representing /s/ while the letter *s* in this position is quite variable.

Results and Analysis of Data

Hypothesis one stated that the thirty-two target words would be found among words typically used in instructional materials for spelling in grades one thru eight. To meet the purpose of this initial study three publishers, Houghton Mifflin Co., Follett Publishing Co., and McGraw-Hill, Inc. were contacted to supply a complete list of words contained in the major spelling materials published by them. Houghton Mifflin Company's response indicated that no such list was available, McGraw-Hill did not respond to the request, while Follett Publishing Co. responded by sending a copy of *Individualized Spelling and Writing Patterns* developed by Research for Better Schools, Inc., indicating that the publication had been used as its source.

A detailed examination of each publisher's materials, *Power to Spell* by Hanna, Hanna, Hodges, Rudorf, Berquist and Peterson (1967), *Basic Goals in Spelling*, Kottmeyer and Ware (1964) and *Individualized Spelling & Writing Patterns*, Research for Better Schools, Inc. (1975) produced results as shown below in Table II.

TABLE II
Target Words in Each of Three Sets of Published Spelling Material

Power to Spell Houghton Mifflin Co.	*Basic Goals in Spelling* McGraw-Hill	*Individualized Spelling* Follett Publishing Co.
although	although	although
license	license	license
*theater	*theater	*theater
surprise	—	surprise
*gray	—	*gray
gasoline	gasoline	
advertise	advertise	
*judgment	*judgment	
*ax	*ax	
socks		
cursed		
knowledgeable		
*likable		
*blond		
hooves		
though		
*bluish		
*usable		
*buses		
*drafty		

*more regular according to the criteria

It can be seen that twenty of the thirty target words were found among those used in instruction by Hanna, *et al*, that seven were found in the Kottmeyer material and five were found in the Follett material. Variant word forms of a few of the target words were also found to be contained in each of the three sets of material, but the word as it was used in this study was not presented. *Knowledge*, for example, was found in two of the three sets of material but neither of these presented *knowledgable*. The word *judge* was found in all three sets of material but only two used the word *judgment*, etc.

It can also be seen from the data in Table II that the Hanna, *et al* material contained the largest number (67.70%) of the target words in its instructional sequence while the Kottmeyer contained 21.9 percent and the Follett contained 15.5 percent. While it may seem obvious that little commonality of thought exists between authors on which words are to be taught thru grade eight, the sample of 30 target words is limited and such inference is without foundation. The acceptance of hypothesis one, however, that at least twenty-five percent of the sample of 32 target words would be found among the words typically used in instructional materials for grades one thru eight is possible since an average of 34.7 percent of the words are included for instruction in the three sets of material. But, as has been seen, acceptance of the hypothesis can be made only in relation to the Hanna *et al* materials when each set is considered separately.

Hypothesis two, which states that the less regular of the two alternatives available would be the spelling included for instruction in published material, is similarly supported to a limited extent. Only 10 (50 percent) of the 20 target word pairs used in the Hanna *et al* materials are seen to be the less regular of the alternatives available while 4 of 7 (57.1%) of the Kottmeyer and 3 of 5 (60%) of the Follett are similarly less regular. When viewed collectively, an average of 53.1 percent of the words used are less regular according to the criteria. The inference that some published material for spelling instruction includes spellings for words which are the more regular of two equally correct alternatives and that this varies from publisher to publisher is inescapable.

Analysis and Discussion of Spellings Used

While a preliminary examination showed that two of the three sets of material used the base word *knowledge* but not the derived form *knowledgeable* and it can be inferred that the pupil is expected to construct the derived form by adding the suffix *able* to the root, such a procedure would seem to perpetuate the inclusion of the silent *e* after *g* in such words as seen in the third set, the Hanna, *et al* materials. Since the Hanna, *et al* and Kottmeyer materials include *judge* but spell *judgment* without the silent *e*, an apparent inconsistency in spelling instruction seems to be revealed—particularly when it is noted that *likable*, *bluish*, and *usable* unlike *knowledgeable* drop the final *e* of the root. Since one form of spelling rule exists which indicates that the final *e* in roots is dropped when adding a suffix which begins with a consonant (presumably explaining for formation of *judgment* from *judge*), the retention of the *e* in *knowledgeable* can be said to be in agreement with the converse of this rule, that *e* is retained before suffixes beginning with vowels. But since *likable*, and *usable*, adding the same suffix *able* also exist and since *bluish* similarly drops the final *e* of the root when a suffix beginning with a vowel is added, no consistent usage of "rules of spelling" seems to be predicated as the basis for establishing spellings. Rather, it would appear that some spellings have been chosen from among the correct alternatives available, producing in the case of Hanna *et al* material a goodness-of-fit to regularity as defined above of 50 percent when only the target words used are considered. While further investigation with the authors might reveal some other basis for the choices of word spellings they make, it would appear that each of the several authors, but particularly Hanna *et al*, accept to a moderate degree the more regular of two alternatively correct spellings. A slow evolutionary process in spelling reform can be inferred to be occurring when it is realized that 46.9 percent of the target words used in these three sets of material are the more regular of the alternatives available and that these more regular spellings are not what have usually been considered the preferred spellings.

Study Two

Since a change in the spellings of words seems to be resisted on grounds of sentiment (Lounsbury, 1909), it can be conjectured that some complaints about children's spelling behavior relates to the notion that there is only one way to spell a word. An adult who has been spelling *judgment* as *judgement* all of his lifetime, for example, might view the equally correct alternative form a child uses as a result of instruction as wrong only because of his lack of awareness that equally correct alternative spellings exist and that his spelling is no more correct than that of the child. An indirect way of testing this hypothesis as structured by Mazurkiewicz and Berk (1976) using some 700 students and 350 parents was utilized in the second part of this study. The authors attempted to replicate the findings of Mazurkiewicz and Berk who showed that a sample of teachers at the 7th and 8th grade levels had a low level of awareness that 35 target words were equally correct when spelled two different ways. Since the word lists used by Mazurkiewicz and Berk differed from that used by the authors of this study by over fifty percent as explained above, the attempt at replication is obviously not one of a kind. The procedures used, however, were identical in that teachers were asked to identify whether one or both spellings listed were correct.

Hypothesis three indicated that the sample of teachers would have a low level of awareness that all of the 30 target word-pairs were equally correct. Since no one of the fifty teachers in grades five thru eight indicated that he/she was aware that all of the 30 target word-pairs were equally correct, the hypothesis was accepted and replicates the finding of Mazurkiewicz and Berk tho the word-pair lists used in each study were somewhat different. Further confirmation of the hypothesis is seen in the finding that some degree of awareness concerning alternative spellings of certain pairs of words exists. This teacher sample identified on the average 7.43 word-pairs as correct in either spelling. Using the range (1–11, low; 12–23 moderate; 24–32 high) as suggested by Mazurkiewicz and Berk, a low level of awareness is identified. The mean achievement of 7.43 differs by almost two words from that of the Mazurkiewicz and Berk finding of 5.47 for their sample of teachers. This difference, attributable to the difference in the lists, is more likely accounted for by the high number of teachers who identified both *theatre* and *theater* and *grey* and *gray* as equally correct in this study. These two word-pairs have a high familiarity index and, while used in this study, were not found in the Mazurkiewicz and Berk list. As can be seen in Table III, this sample of teachers more often identified the more unphonetic or less regular spelling as correct for 21 of the 30 target word-pairs. It can also be seen that this teacher sample often made choices which were in agreement with the choices shown in the spelling materials examined. While there appears to be a relationship between the kinds of spellings used in instructional materials and those identified by teachers as correct spellings for the target words, the relationship appears to be a low one since none of the instructional materials used in this study pro-

TABLE III
Percentage of Teacher Choices—More Regular, Less Regular, or Both

More Regular	%	Less Regular	%	Both Correct	No Answer
bluish*	78	blueish	20	2	—
lens	78	lense	4	18	—
busing	76	bussing	20	4	—
buses*	68	busses	16	16	—
draft*	68	draught	8	24	—
totaled	58	totalled	42	—	2
theater*	16	theatre	8	74	1
gray*	12	grey	6	80	1
ax*	26	axe	26	46	2
dulness	—	dullness	100	—	—
drout	2	drought	98	—	—
licence	2	license*	98	—	—
altho	—	although*	96	4	—
curst	2	cursed*	94	4	—
advertize	—	advertise*	94	6	—
brunet	2	brunette	92	6	—
surprize	4	surprise*	88	8	—
gasolene	2	gasoline*	88	6	—
fulfil	8	fulfill	86	4	2
tho	—	though*	86	14	—
cigaret	—	cigarette	84	16	—
adviser	8	advisor	78	12	2
likable*	22	likeable	74	4	—
sox	—	socks*	72	28	—
leapt	6	leaped	70	22	2
knowledgable	32	knowledgeable*	62	2	4
blond*	10	blonde	56	34	—
judgment*	36	judgement	52	10	2
hoofs	28	hooves*	52	14	6
usable*	38	useable	52	10	—

* indicates spelling found in instructional materials

vide instruction on correct alternatives and some of the choices teachers made deviate to a large extent from the spellings included in instructional material. The spelling of *judgement* with the *e* after *g* was chosen as correct by more than half of the sample while two sets of instructional material used the more regular *judgment*. The direction of choice in the case of *blonde* and *useable* was similarly at variance, while a large part of the sample recognized the equivalence of both spellings of *ax, gray,* and *theater*.

Interview Findings

Hypotheses four and five relate to current practices of teachers. These were assessed by an interview conducted individually on completion of the target word lists. While all teachers indicated that they teach spelling, only 84 percent use a workbook or published "program". Sixteen percent indicated that they taught spelling only incidentally, using words from curriculum materials as the basis for a spelling program. Responses to interview questions are noted below.

1. What do you use as the basis for determining the spellings you teach? All teachers indicated that they use the spellings found in the material used, whether it was a curriculum area or published "program". Words are presented as shown in the "program" or curriculum area.
2. a. Do you teach anything about alternative spellings of words? Ninety-eight percent gave a negative reply; 49 negative replies and two positive replies.
   b. Does the material you use provide instruction on alternative spellings?
      1. Two percent responded positively.
      2. Six percent—I don't know.
      3. Ninety-two percent gave a negative reply.
3. What would you use as the basis for determining the spelling to be taught when a question arises about alternative spellings for words found in your "program"?

   All teachers indicated that they would accept the spelling as found in the material as correct but 56 percent further qualified this answer either by indicating the question rarely or never arises (60.7%) or "if it did come up, I would use the dictionary" (39.3%).
4. Since all of the 30 word-pairs on the list you completed are equally correct when spelled either way, what would you do if questions arose about any of these words in your "spelling program"?

   All teachers expressed surprise and 96% indicated a lack of knowledge that words could be spelled correctly two different ways. Most teachers also expressed the desire to check some words immediately in their dictionaries. Responses to the questions when posed again, elicited the responses below.
5. Have you taught any of the words on the list in your spelling program? Twenty-two teachers responded positively. What procedure would you use if a question arose about variant spelling for these words?

   Eighty-two percent of the teachers indicated that they would use the first spelling listed in the dictionary as the basis for instruction; twelve percent indicated that they would not teach the alternatives available but would accept them when written by students. Four percent indicated they would accept an alternative spelling if the dictionary listed it as a correct spelling. Two percent indicated they did not know what they would do since the question has never arisen.
6. Would you be willing to teach var-

Spelling Guide	Respondents
Check with dictionary	42
Reading book and dictionary	1
Spelling programs and dictionary	3
Spelling Dictionary	1
Spelling Programs	2
Teacher across the hall	1

iant spellings of words now that you are aware of some of them? Eighty-four percent responded positively while sixteen percent gave a negative response.

Negative responders elaborated on their responses as follows:
—most frequent spelling should be taught. 8%.
—would refuse to teach them because some would not be acceptable in business letters. 4%.
—would not teach two spellings to most classes but would present alternate spellings to brighter classes. 4%.

Positive responders protocols included:
—I would present variant spellings when I'm aware of them. 2%.
—I would present them only if brought up by students. 12%.
—I would teach both but emphasize the one used more frequently. 2%.
—I would teach "old" spelling when it still has currency. 4%.
—I would teach more than one spelling only to advanced classes. 10%.
—I would stress the most phonetically regular or correct spelling. 12%.

An additional 16 percent of the sample gave supplementary comments reflecting emphatic agreement with the idea of teaching alternatives and allowing the child to make his own choice between alternatives.

Conclusions and Implications

Only one of three sets of instructional materials clearly included at least twenty-five percent of the target words in the scope of words taught. This material, Hanna, *et al*, clearly shows that a large number of regularly spelled alternatives are being utilized in instruction while the remainder includes only a few regular alternatives. An implication that some modest reforms are currently taking place in some instructional material is suggested but the data are limited and further investigation is warranted.

The teacher sample, having initially a low level of awareness of spelling equivalents, largely appears to be open to providing instruction on such alternatives when they are known. Since most teachers emphasize in instruction whatever spelling is used in curriculum or instructional materials, changes that are utilized by authors or publishers would appear to provide a direct basis for change in spelling. If the Hanna, *et al* material is representative of spelling materials, an increasing emphasis on the more regular spelling of two alternatives available would appear to simplify the pupil's task in spelling and aid the process of change.

Contradictions in spelling exist between those used by this sample of instructional materials, teacher choices of "correct" spellings, and between teachers who are charged with teaching spelling. It would appear that some conflict between the spellings a teacher uses and those children may use as a result of instruction is possible. While a plea for conformity to an accepted standard is desirable to avoid such conflicts, it appears more desirable that information be made available about the equality of alternative spellings to prevent denigration of accepted and correct spellings. Perhaps, also, the divergence shown in the way teachers, instructional materials, and adults in general, spell samples of words utilized here in other studies suggests the need to examine realistically the need for a spelling reform.

REFERENCES

Botel, Morton; Holsclaw, Cora; Cammorota, Gloria; and Brothers, Aileen. *Spelling and Writing Patterns*, Follett Publishing Co., 1975

Deighton, Lee C. *A Comparative Study*

of *Four Major Collegiate Dictionaries*. Pleasantville, New York, Hardscrabble Press, 1972

Emery, Donald W. *Variant Spellings in Modern American Dictionaries*. (Rev. Ed.) Sponsored by The Washington State Council of Teachers of English, Washington, D.C. National Council of Teachers of English, 1973

Harris, Albert J. and Jacobson, Milton D. *Basic Elementary Reading Vocabularies*. The Macmillan Co., N.Y. 1972

Kottmeyer, William and Ware, Kay. *Basic Goals in Spelling*. McGraw-Hill, Inc., N.Y. 1964

Lounsbury, Thomas R. *English Spelling and Spelling Reforms*. Harper and Brothers, New York, 1909

Mazurkiewicz, Albert J. and Berk, Barbara. "Spelling Equivalency Awareness", *Reading World*, Vol. 15 No. 3, March, 1976

Rinsland, Henry D. *A Basic Vocabulary of Elementary School Children*. The Macmillan Co., N.Y. 1972

Spelling and Phonics

EMMETT ALBERT BETTS

Everyone knows *about* phonics. And everyone knows about spelling. This is especially true of journalists and parents—and some phonic zealots.

Yes, almost everyone knows ABOUT phonics and spelling, but do they *understand* the relationship between spelling and phonics? 'Tis said that a little knowledge is dangerous. Then some wiseacre asked, "Who knows enough NOT to be dangerous?"

Altho linguists have contributed substantially to one basis of reading instruction, they do not know enough about phonology and grammar to settle "easy" queries about a phonological syllable. Nor do they agree on an inventory of vowel phonemes basic to phonograms. Equally important, their attempts to write basic readers have violated their own premises, resulting in highly debatable materials.

Then, too, psychologists have made significant contributions to the semantic and pragmatic bases of reading instruction and to the psychology of learning, especially motivation, perception, and cognition. As a result a new breed of psychologist, called psycholinguist, has appeared on the educational scene to question methodology and to offer new perspectives. Yet, psychologists, like the linguists, are not prepared to offer educational prescriptions.

Linguistics became a fad during the 1960's—a new shibboleth for some publishers and some authors to exploit, The psychology of learning, another basis of reading instruction, was renamed *psycholinguistics* when applied to verbal learning. This, too, became a vogue, seized upon by some publishers and some authors intent upon exploitation of the "reading" market. The *sociology* of reading, a legitimate concern of serious students of integration, appears to be well on the way to becoming another password in the 1970's. As educationists become increasingly aware of our spelling system and the broad meaning of the alphabetic principle, orthography appears on the horizon as another concept to be exploited—and discarded when one-facet programs are exposed. But

---

From *Spelling Progress Bulletin*, Vol. 16, No. 2, (Summer, 1976). Reprinted with permission.

these and other bases of reading instruction require a depth of understanding and an ability to translate them into the total program for which few are willing or able to pay the cost in terms of scholarship.

Americans—including educationists, psychologists, linguists—love slogans and catch phrases. They invent them to sell ideas and products; they live by them. Phonics and spelling are no exceptions to sloganeering.

More recently orthography, the study of spelling systems, has been reincarnated. Scholars in this discipline have caused educators to take a second, long hard look at the medium with which all educationists deal: the writing system. They raised two issues:
1. How well do spellings predict (i.e., signal) pronunciation?
2. How well do spellings signal morphology—the inflection, derivation, and compounding of words?

Orthographers, therefore, are concerned with the phonemic and/or morphophonemic basis of spelling. How close a fit between phonemes and spellings (phonograms) is necessary and can be justified? How close a fit between morphemes and spellings is necessary and can be justified? More recently this question has become increasingly relevant: For beginners, is it necessary for an initial learning medium (i.l.m; e.g., i.t.a. or WES) to signal more than phonemes? This is, is morphology crucial for the beginner?

Recently, orthographers have pinpointed the spelling system as a major roadblock for both beginners in reading and adults learning English as a second language. While it is a truism to declare that there are many causes of reading disabilities, the spelling system merits consideration, deliberation and investigation, via an interdisciplinary approach, and *subsequent* action by educationists.

Articles on facets of orthography have appeared mostly in five educational magazines: *Elementary English, Harvard Educational Review, Reading Improvement, The Reading Teacher,* and *Reading Research Quarterly.* In addition to these educational magazines, other periodicals on language and orthography are available for teachers and researchers concerned with the medium:

Journal of Verbal Learning and Verbal Behavior, published by Academic Press, Inc., 111 Fifth Avenue, New York, N.Y. 10003.

Language, published by the Linguistic Society of America, Waverly Press, Baltimore, MD 21202.

Spelling Progress Bulletin (a periodical on initial teaching alphabets and spelling reform) published by Newell W. Tune, 5848 Alcove Avenue, North Hollywood, CA 91607.

Visible Language, The Journal for Research on the Visual Media of Language Expansion. (Formerly *The Journal of Typographic Research*), published by MIT Press, Cambridge, MA 02142.

'Tis said that fish will be the last to discover water; that birds will be the last to discover air. Likewise, it can be said that those concerned with reading instruction will be the last to discover the medium, or orthographic code, or writing system, with which they are dealing everyday.

Crucial to note: scholarship in linguistics, psychology (learning, cognition, perception, motivation), sociology, and orthography do not a so-called reading "specialist" make. Likewise, a reading specialist is not made by appointment or by anointment with *lecture* courses on reading instruction; nor is this person to be a specialist in one or all the disciplines contributing to the *bases* of instruction. Instead, the reading "specialist" needs a "working," or pragmatic, indoctrination.

This discussion is organized to spotlight the basic issues in phonics and to direct attention to the many implications of a spelling system that has a loose fit with phonemes and morphemes of language (speech). In brief, these are some, not all, of the CRUCIAL questions:

What special word-perception hazards are inherent in the most commonly used words?

How can awareness of the factors in word perception (e.g., grouping of pronounceable units as *bea, ea, eat* in *beat; closure* to insure linguistic or referential meaning, etc.) contribute to an improved methodology?

To what extent is the alphabetic principle applicable to the English spelling system?

Why do phonic rules tend to be self-defeating?

1. What are the application/exception ratios for vowel and consonant rules?
2. Why do function words (e.g., *to, too, two, of* /əv/, *when* /hwen, wen/) present special word-perception problems?
3. How does stress (accent) complicate vowel rules?

What approaches can be made to legitimate phonics instruction?

What are the implications of the issues regarding phonics versus spelling for the preparation of teachers?

What research is needed to standardize letter shapes?

Is *knowledge* of letter names *one* valid predictor of preparation for beginning reading? If so, does *learning* letter names contribute to word-perception skills for beginners?

Is reading a simple decoding process of relating graphemes to phonemes—of converting writing into the language (speech) code? Stated another way: is there more to word perception than phonics to "unlock," or identify, unknown words during the on-going reading process?

These questions may be more important:

1. What is the chief purpose of phonics in word identification and re-cognition?
2. What are the limitations of phonics for developing independence in word identification?
3. What are the dimensions of language (speech) which enter into word perception during an on-going process of reading?
    a. Is it legitimate to limit word perception, for example, to the relationships between speech sounds and spellings used to represent them?
    b. What is the role of intonation, especially phrase stress, in word perception?
    c. What contributions are made to the study of word perception by structural linguists? By transformationalists?

4. What are the dimensions of orthography (spelling system) which enter into word perception during an on-going process of reading?
    a. Phonemic
    b. Morphemic
    c. Morphophonemic
    d. Semantic

5. Is reading a process of *recoding* via inner speech and of *decoding* the message via grammatical and semantic rules?
    a. Is inner speech (subvocalization) a characteristic of the reading performance of beginners?
    b. Is orthographic representation of speech bound to phonemics alone?
    c. Is traditional, or conventional, orthography via lexical words adequate for signalling semantic relationships, as in *n(a)tion-n(a)tional*?

6. Can reading performance of beginners be escalated via a carefully researched writing system, especially a *spelling* system, which achieves a closer fit to phonology?
    a. Is there a significant advantage in one set of letter shapes for both capital (upper case) and small (lower case)? For example, to eliminate the forms *G* and *g*?
    b. What are the advantages and disadvantages of augmented Roman alphabet, as in i.t.a.? What are the advantages of no-new-letter spellings, as in World

FOUNDATIONS OF INSTRUCTION

English Spelling, especially W.E.S.-i.t.m.? Or, some other proposal?

c. What values accrue for a morphophonemic approach to an initial learning medium (i.l.m.)?

Briefly, this presentation deals in some depth with the issues regarding spelling and phonics:

Beginning Reading Vocabulary—phonology and graphemics of high utility words.

Factors in Word Perception—their recognition in teaching word-perception skills.

Premises and principles of phonics—their relation to curriculum content and to methods.

Phonic rules, or spelling patterns—their validity and hazards (graphotactics).

Letter names—knowledge of letter names as one predictor of readiness for reading, and fact or myth regarding value of learning letter names for learning to read.

VOCABULARY: PHONOLOGY AND GRAPHEMICS

Highly relevant to discussions of phonics, spelling, spelling reform, readability and differentiated instruction are yields of studies of listening, speaking, reading, and writing vocabularies. A rapid survey of evidence on commonly used words reveals significant implications.

What are the commonest words used in communication?

In summary, here are some facts regarding the number of different words (types) that account for a given percent, in round numbers, of running words (tokens):

Percent	Number of Types
10	3
25	9 or 10
50	50
60	100
80	500
90	1000

Ten Percent: Three Little Words

According to Ernest Horn, *A Basic Writing Vocabulary*, three little words—*a, and, the*—comprise 10% of the running words (tokens) used in communication; these three little words are function rather than content words; that is, they have linguistic (syntactic) meaning, not referential meaning. They are commonest not only in the speech of infants and in beginning reading materials, but also in the speech and writing of adults. Furthermore, in propositional speech they usually are unstressed: *a* pronounced /ə/ rather than /'a/, *and* pronounced /ən/, /n/ or /nd/ rather than /'and/, *the* pronounced /th/ or /thə/ rather than /'thē/. Their use in speech involves primarily suprasegmental (intonational) rather than segmental phonemes. How can phonic (graphotactic), especially vowel "principles" be applied to these commonest words?

Ten Words: Twenty-five Percent

In his *Relative Frequency of English Speech Sounds* (1923), Godfrey Dewey concurred, in general, that 10 commonest words form over 25% of the total number used. His nine commonest words: *a, and, the, of, to, in, that, it, is*. His tenth and eleventh words: *I, for*.

Much earlier, Leonard P. Ayres in his *Measuring Scale for Ability in Spelling* reported the ten commonest words: *a, and, the, of, to, in, that, for, you, I*.

All of these ten words are classified as function or syntactic, words. Although only 7% of American English lexicon is used to make clear the structure of sentences, lists of commonest words are freighted with function words. Obviously, these words are needed for communication, but they have syntactic meaning (i.e., exist only in language) and are required to signal parts-of-speech, or content words. That is, meaningful communication is not possible when

FOUNDATIONS OF INSTRUCTION

they are used exclusively, but communication depends upon them.

To test this finding, identify *a, and,* and *the* in the following quotations:

"The true art of memory is the art of attention." (20%)
"By the time a man can afford to lose a golf ball, he can't hit it that far." (17%)
"An attempt has been made to show how the obtained results might be accommodated within a theoretical framework which is psycholinguistically oriented and which conceptualizes the child as a communication channel of limited capacity." (15%)
"The role of speech recording in reading has been a topic of interest to psychologists for many years. The phenomenon has been known by many names, including silent speech, inner speech, subvocalization, phonemic recoding, and acoustic recoding. 'Speech recoding' is used in this paper as a generic term for the transformation of printed words into any type of speech based code, whether it be articulatory, acoustic, auditory imagery, or a more abstract code." (10%)

Here are some relevant comments regarding the ten commonest words used in communication:

1. The words *a, and, the* have been commented on above.
2. The word *of* is respelled /(') əv, ə, 'äv/ in which the letter *f* represents the sound /v/. Of course, the vowel—stressed or unstressed—does not fit the CVC spelling pattern, or short vowel rule.
3. The word *to* is a homonym, also spelled *too* or *two*.
4. The word *in* is a homonym with *inn*.
5. The word *for* is respelled /fər, (') för/ depending on phrase stress.
6. Four words fit the (C)VC spelling pattern, or the short vowel rule. In short, phonic skills may be applied with assurance to 40% of the ten commonest words: *that, in, it, is,* but *s* in *is* is /z/.

Why are the commonest words crucial?

First, they are used necessarily in reading materials for beginners. Therefore, they merit special study in terms of spelling.

Second, a preponderance are function words, tending to be *unstressed* in normal speech. Hence, they create problems in learning word-perception skills because phonic skills usually are developed on isolated word forms which, of course, are stressed.

Third, function words have linguistic rather than referential meaning.

Fourth, the commonest words tend to be irregularly spelled. That is, they are exceptions to phonic, or spelling patterns, introducing special word-perception problems.

Fifty Words: Fifty Percent

In his *The Spelling Vocabulary of Personal and Business Letters* (1913), Leonard Ayres reported that 50 words made up nearly 50% of all running words (tokens) including the ten commonest above:

Word	Respelling
the	/thə, thē, 'thē/
and	/ən(d), (') an(d)/
to	/tə, tu̇, (')tü/
of	/(')əv, ə, 'äv/
a	/'a, ə, (')ā/
in	/(')in, ən, n, 'in/
it	/(')it, ət, 'it/
for	/fər, (')for/
that	/(')*th*at, *th*ət, '*th*at/
is	/(')iz, əz, z, s/
I	/(')ī/
you	/(')yü, yə, yē/
be	/(')bē/
we	/(')wē/
have	/(')hav, (h)əv, v, (')haf/
your	/yər, (')yu̇r, (')yor/
will	/wəl, (ə)l, (')wil/
are	/ər, (')är, (')ȧr/
yours	/'yu̇rz, 'yorz/
not	/(')nät/
as	/əz, (')az/
at	/ət, (')at/
this	/(')*th*is/
with	/(')wi*th*, (')with/
but	/(')bət/
on	/(')ȯn, (')än/
if	/(')if, əf/
do	/(')dü, də/
all	/'ȯl/
so	/(')sō, sə,'sō/

235

FOUNDATIONS OF INSTRUCTION

Word	Respelling
me	/(')mē/
very	/'ver-ē, 'ver-i/
my	/(')mī, mə/
get	/'get/
from	/(')frəm, (')främ/
our	/(')är, (')aůr, (')ȧr/
was	/(')wəz, (')wäz/
time	/'tīm/
put	/'pu̇t/
can	/kən, 'kan/
one	/'wən, (,)wən/
would	/wəd, (ə)d, (')wu̇d/
he	/(')hē, ē/
had	/(')had, (h)əd, d/
go	/'gō/
letter	/'let-r/
been	/(')bin/
when	/(')hwen, wen, (h)wən/
she	/(')shē/
good	/'gu̇d/

The (C)VC spelling pattern, or short vowel rule, fits *as, at, can, had, that; get, letter, when; if, is, this, will, with, in, it; not, but*. These 17 words account for 34% of the 50 commonest words. But what can be said for the spellings of the consonant boundaries in *(wh)en, (th)at, (th)is* versus *wi(th), i(s)—a(s), (c)an?*

One word fits the (C)VC plus final *e*, or split digraph, vowel rule: *time*. But *have*, which is pronounced /(')hav, (h)əv/; before *t*, often /(')haf/ and, therefore, is a double hazard.

One word, *good*, has the *oo* spelling for /u/, but the *oo* spelling also represents /ü/ in *moon*.

Eighty-eight percent, or 44 words, are function words: noun markers (e.g., *the*), phrase markers (e.g., *in*), clause markers (e.g., *if*), verb markers (e.g., *have*), pronouns (e.g., *you*), conjunctions (e.g., *and*), intensifiers (e.g., *not*).

Twelve percent, or 6 words, are content words: class 1, nouns (e.g., *letter*); class 2, verbs (e.g., *go*); class 3, adjectives (e.g., *good*).

The etymology (derivation) of the Ayres list is primarily Old English. Forty-six percent, or 23 words, were different morphologically from the original forms; e.g., *have* was *habban*. 78% were derived from Old English; the remainder from Middle English, Old Norse, Old French, and Indo-European. These data are being reported in a subsequent publication.

Furthermore, here are some crucial questions:

How can phonic skills be applied to the words *to, I, you, of, have, are, from, for, very, was, put, one, on, would, been, is, as, all, our, your, yours, my*—almost half of the 50 commonest?

What phonic rule fits *she, be, he, him?* The words *do, so, go, to?*

Less than a third of the 50 can be said to fit reliably with phonic rules.

If it is assumed that the commonest words have a very high probability of use in beginning reading materials, then it appears that the teacher—and the pupil!—must seek *other* word-perception skills than phonics. What are they? Or, perhaps more important, the teacher needs to give serious consideration to an initial teaching medium which circumvents irregular conventional spellings and makes common words reliable to decode.

Implications

Here are some relevant statements:

1. A preponderance of commonest words are irregularly spelled, therefore, these words have high frequency use in materials for beginners in reading, presenting word-perception hazards.

2. Significant differences in capital and lower case letters add to the word-perception confusion, especially for beginners. (This situation is easily corrected.)

3. Significant differences between manuscript and cursive writing contribute to the learner's difficulties in word perception.

4. Significant differences between handwriting and printing add to the learner's dilemma.

WORD PERCEPTION: FACTORS

Word perception requires far more than (1) applying so-called phonic rules or spelling pattern sequences and (2) memorizing a list of sight words. In fact, a complex of conditions and factors enter into the process of *automatic* word identification and re-cognition.
  1. Readability of material
     a. *Independent* reading level for extensive and study-type activities
     b. *Instructional* reading level for reinforcing motivation, learning new word-perception skills, and developing concepts
  2. Awareness of a personal *need* for identifying an unknown part of a word or a spelling pattern
  3. *Attention* directed to a need
  4. Learning *set,* as a determiner and organizing factor; e.g., hearing syllables in a spoken word before identifying spellings of the syllables
  5. *Grouping* (or chunking) pronounceable parts of a monosyllable or the syllables of a lexical word: e.g., *ca, a,* or *ap* in *cap,* or *lett* in *letter*
  6. *Meaning,* structural (e.g., a function word as *then* or *of*) or referential (e.g., the word *hot*)
  7. *Contrast,* e.g., the sound patterns of /'sit/ and /'sat/ or the spelling patterns of *hat—hate*
  8. *Closure,* perceptual and cognitive. For example, identifying the whole word *park* after being told the sound /är, ȧr/ (except in N.E. United States!) and consummating with cognitive "meaning"
  9. *Feedback* from perception of lexical words to speech and during a directed reading activity, from teachers to learner
  10. *Application* to other words with the same spelling pattern, and finally to pseudo words

The above are samples of conditions and factors in word perception. Other factors enter into the complex processing of lexical words (e.g., dictionary entries) in isolation and within the intonation (rhythm) patterns of speech.

PHONICS: PREMISES AND PRINCIPLES

Here are some statements of premises and principles which appear to merit serious consideration in an assessment of "spelling and phonics":
1. To a degree, writing represents speech; therefore, one approach to word perception is the study of the relationships between the two; i.e., phonics.
   a. Writing (orthography) as a substitute for speech (language) reflects phonemes (via spellings), intonation (via capital letters, italics, and punctuation), and morphology (via roots, affixes, syllabication, etc.)— *all quite imperfectly.*
   b. Monosyllabic words pronounced in isolation always have primary, or strong, stress.
   c. The purpose of phonics is to teach pupils to relate spellings and speech—not to teach them how to pronounce words (i.e., not to teach speech production).
Phonics is the study of the relationship between graphics (letters, punctuation, spaces, etc.) and phonemes, and teaching the child the "sounds" is not the purpose of phonics instruction. That is, phonics instruction deals with relating the two systems—language (speech) and writing.
   d. Corrective speech is not a significant purpose of phonics instruction.
   e. There is scientific evidence to demonstrate that the higher the

spelling-to-sound correlation, the more nearly accurately the words are reproduced. (See Eleanor Gibson, et al, "The Role of Grapheme-Phoneme Correspondence in the Perception of Words.")
f. Graphic signals—e.g., letters, punctuation, etc.—have no meaning *per se*.
g. All letters are silent; some letters are superfluous letters, as *n* in *column*, *t* in *often*.
h. Letters do not have sounds; writing is VISIBLE language.
i. Learning to read requires the development of reading processes far more complex than word perception.
j. Word-perception skills in the ongoing processes of reading function *automatically*, leaving the learner's *one mind* to decode the message.
k. Application of word-perception skills to nonsense, or pseudo, words is a valid test of learning; e.g., to *lat* vs *sat*, *doat* vs *coat*.
l. To escalate reading instruction, there is an immediate need to study word perception at the phoneme-grapheme and higher linguistic and cognitive levels.
m. The concept of "irregular spellings" varies significantly from one researcher to another, ranging from phonemic spellings to morphophonemic spellings.
   (1) Phonemic spellings appear to merit the emphasis in beginning reading, but orthography does signal morphology to a degree.
   (2) Some linguists (e.g., Bloomfield, Fries) tend to emphasize "code breaking" at the phonemic level in beginning reading via spelling patterns.
2. Phonics and look-and-say (word or sight) "methods" are two different approaches to two different situations: (a) regularly spelled words (e.g., *red*) and (b) irregularly spelled words, (e.g., *said*, *you*).
   a. The "visual" method—also called sight, look-and-say, and whole word—in beginning reading instruction appears to have some validity when the high percentage of irregular spellings of common words is given necessary consideration.
   b. The "visual" method is a paired associate learning procedure, but too often it is a tell-the-child-the-word violation of psychological principles of learning.
   c. The "visual-auditory" method—also called phonics—appears to have validity for regularly spelled words, in the phoneme-grapheme sense rather than the morphophonological sense.
   d. The "visual-auditory-kinaesthetic" method—often called the kinaesthetic—is syllable phonics which introduces a *motor* component to reinforce attention (a factor in perception).
   e. The "visual-auditory-kinaesthetic-tactile" method—sometimes called tracing—also is syllable phonics which introduces at least one additional modality to reinforce *attention* (a factor in perception).
   f. Phonic methods are plural; so are "sight" methods.
      (1) Rote memorization; e.g., flash cards
      (2) Paired associate learning; e.g., word and picture
3. Spellings of words are often misleading signals of pronunciation.
   a. The fact that English dictionaries respell all words is admitted by lexicographers to be an indictment of the English spelling system.
   b. Consider these spelling pronunciations on radio and television news programs:

FOUNDATIONS OF INSTRUCTION

Word	Respelling	Mispronunciation
epitome	/e-'pit-ə-me/	ep-i-tome
severed	/'sev-rd/	see-veered
tournament	/'tur-nə-ment, 'tər-/	tour-na-ment
been	/bin/	been
often	/òf-en/	off-ten
temperature	/temp-r-chur, 'temp-ə-, 'temp-ə-, 'temp-r(-)ə, -chər/	-chər or chur as 'tər

c. Both *vowels* and *consonants* are irregularly spelled, but vowel spellings are constrained by a paucity of letters, as in *was, again, been.*
d. Predicting sound from spelling requires consideration of linguistic-orthographic factors.
   (1) Spelling patterns: (C)VC, (C)VC(e), CVVC—35% of "common" words, including function words
   (2) Syllable stress: *surprise, servant, purpose, announced, barometer, e(x)ist* versus *e(x)ercise*
   (3) Phrase stress: function words; e.g., *and, or, of, a, the, to,* etc.
   (4) Highly irregular spellings: *of, one, come-some, their-where-were, what-want, laugh, who, quick,* etc.
   (5) Phonotactical rules: *(kn)ow, (gn)aw, (pn)eumonia, (gh)ost* versus *lau(gh)*
   (6) Morphemic patterns: e.g., *hat-hats, horse-hors(es), mark-marked, land-landed*
   (7) Morphophonemic spellings: e.g., *hymn-hymnal*
   (8) Logograms: +, %, #, $, &

4. Both phonic and spelling rules for traditional orthography tend to be self-defeating.
   a. Rules in phonics tend to be ineffective because exceptions to rules interfere with rather than facilitate independence.
   b. Phonic zealots tend to ignore the influence of the melody of language, called intonation, on word perception. For example, *and* is usually unstressed /an/ or /ən/, not /'and/ in the stream of speech. Or, consider, *has* as:
      /'has/ in *He has to do it*
      versus
      /haz/ in *He has a broken arm.*
   c. Vowel "rules" are high level generalizations. For example, the rule regarding "short" vowels requires a generalization regarding the *different* sounds in *s(a)t, s(e)t, h(i)t, n(o)t,* and *c(u)t.* But what is common to the vowel sounds in these words?
   d. Learning phonic generalizations is a questionable approach to word perception.
   e. Blending in phonics is a misleading and mysterious mixture of orthographics and phonemics.
   f. Teachers do not know phonic generalizations.
   g. The attitude of teachers toward language—with a "monolithic fixation" on correct English—may cause the child with divergent phonology, grammar and usage to be penalized.

5. *Decoding*, a term introduced by some linguists and psychologists, is a misnomer because it is a superficial concept of reading—leading to the same misconceptions entertained by phonic zealots.
   a. Decoding—an often used and mis-

FOUNDATIONS OF INSTRUCTION

used term—embraces (a) decoding writing into speech and (b) decoding the message.
b. Decoding requires both perceptual and cognitive closure to insure comprehension.

6. There have been few innovations in the teaching of phonics since Valentin Ickelsamer introduced the idea during the 16th century.
   a. Awareness of word (lexeme) structure can be developed on regularly spelled words (e.g., *hat* vs *said*) and syllables (e.g., *(sat)isfy*) via a phonics countdown that emphasizes pronounceable units (e.g., *ca, a,* or *ap* of *cap*).
   b. The approach to phonics by Leonard Bloomfield and his disciple, Charles Fries, like the approaches in the Aldine and Beacon systems tends to emphasize consonant boundaries of words and syllables—an often overlooked concept in discussions of vowel spellings.
   c. Systematic dialectal variations are accepted because everyone speaks an idiolect; e.g., some speakers tend to diphthongize the vowel, as in *bed*.
   d. Word-perception skills can be more effectively developed and applied when the readability of the material is at the learner's instructional level.
   e. On-the-spot help is most effective when the learner identifies the part of the word (e.g., *ea* in *each* or *ea* in *neanderthal*) on which help is needed, and receives help on that part followed by the learner's closure.
   (A corollary: need, awareness of success, and other facets of motivation are central to word-perception learning.)
   f. The sequence of phonics instruction depends on the vocabulary of the reading material and, equally important, on the specific needs of the learner.

7. Basic readers based on phonics have fallen into disrepute since the last series was published in the late 1920's; e.g., Moore-Wilson Readers.

8. Word perception is terminated with cognitive closure—arriving at the meaning which includes linguistic and referential.
   a. Content words (e.g., *call, duck*) have referential meaning.
   b. Function words (e.g., *and, of, when*) have linguistic meaning.
   c. An overemphasis on phonics tends to reduce semantic and linguistic input, producing word callers and word-by-word reading.
   d. An underemphasis on phonics contributes to failure in learning the "alphabetic principle."
   e. The relationship between words and their meanings is precarious; e.g., a word may have different denotations and connotations.

9. The reading establishment has been frustrated by the ineffectiveness of phonics but has failed to consider prerequisite, relevant concepts in educational psychology and linguistics (phonemics and grammar) for a laboratory-demonstration course on reading instruction.

10. As a corollary to 9, above, the reading establishment has failed to consider the complex and complicated nature of orthography (spellings and irregular spellings) that represent speech—to take a second look at initial teaching alphabets, not i.t.a. alone, and/or special "self-help" with modified dictionary respellings without diacritical markings.
    a. Use of different capital and "small" (lower case) letters—e.g., G-g, H-h, B-b—introduces unnecessary confusion for beginners in reading, but has a pragmatic, immediate solution.
    b. In T.O. (traditional or conventional) letters are represented by more than one basic shape, as capitals and lower case, manuscript and cursive, as boldface and italics, ligatures (e.g., fi, fl, ff).

c. For many reasons, basic research is needed to assess the relationships between a controlled (revised to achieve regularity) orthography and word perception in the on-going reading processes.
d. An initial teaching alphabet (e.g., i.t.a. or W.E.S.) is a *medium,* not a method, for teaching reading.
e. Research on an initial teaching alphabet probably merits priority over genuine spelling reform.
f. Systematic spellings for beginners in reading permit:
   (1) Prediction of pronunciation: e.g., *one* vs *wun, was* vs *wuz.*
   (2) Learning by analogy: e.g., *have* vs *hav.*

11. Preparation for beginning reading includes visual discrimination of geometric forms called letters, visual-motor skills, auditory discrimination and perception, awareness of speech sounds and spoken words, general alertness to the relationship between speech and writing, etc.

12. Corrective reading and sometimes remedial reading are euphemisms for the failure of first teaching.
    a. A retarded reader with inadequate word-perception skills is likely to be a "poor" speller.
    b. A "poor" speller with a "good ear" for speech sounds is likely to spell words the way they sound; e.g., *wuz* for *was.*

13. Many practices in teaching phonics frustrate the learner, especially the beginner, and produce confusion and retardation; e.g., listening for the sound /b/ in *climb,* attempting to say consonant sounds in isolation, and so on.

14. Preparation for the perceptual-cognitive facet of reading (decoding at phonological, grammatical, and semantic levels) requires a mosaic of competencies and performances.
    a. Competence in producing and understanding sentences, or language facility
    b. Speech production, e.g., sound /y/ in *yellow,* /sh/ in *shoe,* /v/ in *violet.* (Long ago, Leonard Bloomfield commented: "He can be taught to read only after phonemic habits are thoroughly established." p. 501)
    c. A lexicon, reflecting a basic stock of concepts from a *background of information* (Concepts yield vocabulary, not vice versa.)
    d. Skill in visual discrimination of letters and word forms
    e. Ability to name letters of the alphabet, as an awareness of writing
    f. Visual-motor skills for reproducing geometric forms, including letters (e.g., ability to copy an outline of a square and horizontal diamond and to copy letters *A* and *H*)
    g. Ability to perceive relationships in a block design; e.g., copying the correct colors in an alternating black and white, vertically and horizontally, design
    h. Awareness of spoken *words* (This is easily taught quickly and effectively in groups via categories; e.g., colors, furniture, names.)
    i. Awareness of speech sounds, especially vowels (This awareness is quickly learned; e.g., hearing /ē/ in *he,* /ō/ in *home,* /ü/ in *zoo.*)
    j. Visual skills required for singleness and clearness at both reading and blackboard distances
    k. Skill in color discrimination and knowledge of color names (e.g., red, green, blue, yellow)
    l. Hearing, e.g., repeating whispered numbers
    m. Ability to do analogical reasoning; e.g., to perceive relationships between pairs of relevant words, as *sky–blue, grass–green*
    n. Ability to contrast ideas; e.g., to recall opposites, as *big–little*
    o. Ability to classify (categorize) ideas; i.e., to abstract (e.g., how are a kitten and a puppy alike?)
    p. Interests, measured by "What I do"
    q. Memory span, a test of attention

FOUNDATIONS OF INSTRUCTION

    r. Motivation, reflected in ability to write own name, requests for listening to *self-selected* articles in an encyclopedia (e.g., facts on tigers), knowledge of children's literature, requests for "What is this word?" browsing in picture and other books, and so on (This self-actuated behavior reveals facets of motivation: knowledge, skills, values, intent, awareness of success, interest, personal needs, aspirations, attitudes, and so on.)

15. Syllable phonics is deceptive—complex and complicated.
    a. The concept of a syllable is somewhat ephemeral, with syllabic boundaries in question because there is no exact point of syllable division.
    b. The dictionary *respelling,* not the vocabulary entry, is one basis for determining syllable boundaries; e.g., for using kinaesthetic or tactile techniques and other syllabication activities; e.g.,

Entry	Respelling
an.ger	/'ang-ger/
busi.ness	/'biz-nəs/
but.ter	/'bət-ər/
fas.ten	/'fas-n/
freez.er	/'frē-zər/
mo.tor	/'mōt-ər/

      (1) Syllable division in vocabulary entry indicates how syllables are divided in writing.
      (2) Syllable division in respelling indicates a phonological "fact" of pronunciation.
      (Note: The rationale of syllable division is explained in Webster's *New International Dictionary*.)
    c. Polysyllabic words may be analyzed phonologically, morphologically, typographically, or visually, depending upon the principle used.
    d. Syllabication rules "taught" by educationists usually are contradictory and confusing—linguistically and orthographically paradoxical.
    e. Syllabication involves special situations
      (1) Two adjacent vowels; two syllables, e.g., *giant*
      (2) Writing vs. speaking; e.g., *garden:* gar.den vs. /'gard-n/ (See *b* above)
      (3) Words ending in *ed,* as *needed* vs *asked* (*voiceless* consonant) and *dreamed* (voiced consonant)
      (4) Variable syllabication, as *crooked* /'krùk-əd/ and /'krùkt/
      (5) Vowel sound in final syllable
        (a) Primary stress, as in *relate*
        (b) Secondary stress, as in *divide*
        (c) Weak stress, as in *package*
      (6) ng or nk
        (a) /ng-g/ in *anger, longer*
        (b) /ng/ in *sung, strong*
        (c) /ngk/ in *bank, sink*
        (d) /nj/ in *orange, range*
      (7) x
        (a) /ks/ in *box, excuse*
        (b) /k-s/ in *exact, excell*
        (c) /g-z/in *exact, exam*
        (d) /k-sh/ in *luxury*
        (e) /g-zh/ in *anxious*
      (8) Syllabic consonants, as in *cattle* /'kat-l/, *open* /'ō-pən, ōp-n/, eaten /'ēt-n/
    f. The rule that there are as many syllables in a word as there are vowel "places" has hazards, as in *fate–affectionate, moaned, giant, prison*.

VOWEL RULES/SPELLING PATTERNS

Two classic studies on sound-spelling relationships were reported in 1950 by Ruth Oaks on *Vowel Situations* and by Elsie Black on *Consonant Situations*. These investigations, based on the *Betts Basic Vocabulary Studies,* reported the application/exception ratios for time-honored vowel and consonant "rules." Unfortunately, some of the rules don't give the beginners in reading a gambler's chance in their application. Yet those misnomers continue to be quoted in so-called professional literature more than a quarter of a century later.

At this point, findings from the above studies are summarized and reported on selected vowel rules which have been renamed "spelling patterns."

Spelling Pattern I or "Short" Vowel Rule

(Consonant)-Vowel-Consonant, or (C)VC pattern of monosyllables, as in *at–bad–back, it–big–bill, get–bed–bell, cot–fog, but–cup, spin–test–then.*

Exceptions: *was, old, want, find, right, wild, sign, put, star–her–bird–fur, walk, all, saw, haul.* (For each of these exceptions, a rule is available!)

In the Ruth Oaks classic study, based on the *Betts Reading Vocabulary Studies,* this "short" vowel rule had an application/exception ratio of 71/29 for beginning readers.

Two other application/exception studies were made by the author and presented in "Phonics: Methods and Orthography," *Spelling Progress Bulletin,* part I, Vol. XIV, No. 1, (Spring, 1974), pp. 2–6; Part II, Vol. XIV, No. 2, (Summer, 1974), pp. 7–12. Analyses were made of:
1. Edgar Dale, "A comparison of two word lists"
2. A series of basic readers, preprimers to first reader, inclusive. (These data also apply to the other phonic rules listed below.)

The rule for "short" vowels is stated in various ways, loaded with concepts often technical, sometimes awkward, and frequently hedged by qualifiers, as *usually:*
1. *Vowels* are usually "short" in *closed syllables,* e.g., *cat.*
2. *Vowels* are usually "short" when modified by *position;* e.g., *cap, clap.*
3. If there is only one vowel in a word or syllable and it is followed by a consonant, the vowel is usually "short."
4. One vowel in the middle of a word usually has its short sound.
5. When a syllable ends in a consonant, its vowel is usually "short."
6. When there is only one vowel in a stressed syllable and that vowel is followed by a consonant, the vowel has its "short" sound.
7. A single vowel in a closed accented syllable has its "short" sound unless it is influenced by some other sound in the syllable. The consonants that most frequently affect the vowel sounds in the syllable are: *r, l, w.*
8. A *stressed* vowel, followed by one or more consonants in the same syllable is usually "short."
9. When there is only one vowel in a one-syllable word and it isn't at the end, it is usually "short."
10. When a vowel is one of two middle letters in a word of four letters, the vowel is "short"; e.g., *buzz.*
11. When a vowel is *within* a word of more than four letters, the vowel is "short"; e.g., *scratch.*
12. An initial or medial vowel in a word or syllable usually has the short sound when it is the only vowel in a word. (exceptions: *bind, find, mind, night*)

Exceptions to the short vowel rule are made into rules:
1. When *a* follows *w* in a word, it usually has the sound of *a* in *was.* (The author gave *watch* as an example of application! The word *watch* is respelled /'wäch/ but *was* is respelled /'wəz/. Hence, the author's confusion is showing. To finalize the confusion, the author gave *swam* /swam/ as an exception!)
2. When *e* is followed by *w,* the vowel sound is the same as represented by *oo.* (Which *oo?* The *oo* in *look* or the *oo* in *moon?*)
3. The letter *a* has the same sound when followed by *l, w,* and *u.* (We assume *all, saw, caught* are examples of

the /ȯ/ sound, but how about *Albert, algebra, alien, aunt, awry, away, award?* So we have exceptions to the exceptions.)

Notes:
1. In G & C Merriam's *Webster's New Elementary Dictionary* plain *a* /a/, *e* /e/, *i* /i/, two dot *a* /ä/, and *schwa* /ə/ have been substituted for the breve markings, as in /kăt/, /ĕnd/, /hĭt/, /nŏt/, /cŭt/.
2. In English, the "short" vowel sounds predominate. See Godfrey Dewey, *Relative Frequency of English Speech Sounds*.
3. In phonology, the terms *short* and *long* denote duration of a speech sound in its *speech environment;* e.g., the vowel sound in *glad* tends to be longer than the vowel sound in *late*—giving myth to statements of phonic zealots.
4. One author, in fact, stated emphatically that when teaching the short vowel rule for *cat* and *stand,* "Emphasize the sound of *a* (ah), but not detach the sound." This statement, of course, is a double or maybe a triple whammy.

First, the sound /a/ is not respelled *ah,* for the sound /a/ is sometimes called the *ah* sound by phoneticians.

Second, how is the sound /a/ emphasized without distortion?

Third, "do not detach the sound" from what?—one or both consonant boundaries?

Spelling Pattern II, or Final *e* (Split Digraph) Rule

(Consonant)-Vowel-Consonant plus final *e,* or (C)VCe pattern of monosyllables, as in *make–like–joke–duke.*

Exceptions: *come, some, gone, done, one, have, give, move, are, here, were, use, more, shore, horse, prince.*

In the Oaks study, this final *e* rule had an application/exception ratio of 53/47 in beginning readers.

The rule for the split digraph—which the learner has about a 50–50 chance of using effectively—is stated in these fashions, with varying complexities:
1. In a short word ending with a final *e,* the *e* is usually silent and the "preceding" [sic] vowel is "long" or "says its own name."
2. Final *e* lengthens the "preceding" [sic] vowel.
3. The letter *e* at the end of an *accented syllable* usually shows that the preceding *vowel* has its "long" sound.
4. When there are two vowels [sic] in words of one syllable, usually the first is "long" and the second is silent.
5. A *stressed* vowel, followed by a consonant and silent *e* is usually "long."
6. When a stressed syllable ends in *e,* the first [sic] vowel in a syllable has its own long sound and the final *e* is silent.
7. When *e* comes at the end of a word, it doesn't sound (it is silent), and the *a* has the long sound. (This sub-rule is restated for *e, i, o, u.*)
8. Final *e* in a word or syllable signals a "long" vowel and the /s/ sound for *c* in *face, place, piece, palace.*
9. Final *e* in a word or syllable signals a "long" vowel and the /j/ sound of *g,* as in *age, large, hinge, orange.*

Spelling Pattern III, Vowel Digraph

(Consonant)-Vowel-Vowel-Consonant as in *beat–feed, rain–wait, eat–read* /rēd/, *street.* (See below)

Exceptions: *field, great, been, friend, plaid, guest, ready, was–said, build, good–moon, hair–dear, heard, sn(ow), read* (past tense /'red/)

In the Oaks study, the vowel digraph "rule" had an application/exception ratio of 50/50 in beginning readers.

The rule for vowel digraphs, often dutifully hedged, also is stated in various ways:
1. When two vowels [sic, sounds or letters?] of a word are together, the first "vowel" is *usually* "long" and the second vowel is silent.
2. In vowel digraphs, the first vowel

FOUNDATIONS OF INSTRUCTION

[sic] *usually* has its own "long" sound and the second vowel is silent.

3. In *most* vowel digraphs the first vowel has its own "long" sound and the second is silent.

4. When there are two vowels, one of which is final *e,* the first vowel is long and the *e* is silent.

5. When there are two *adjacent* vowels in a syllable, the first vowel has its own "long" sound and the second is silent.

6. A combination of two vowels [letters or sounds?] in a word is called a vowel digraph. Usually the first vowel is long and the second is silent.

Exceptions to the vowel digraph rule are stated as rules:

1. If two *o*'s appear in a word or syllable, they have the short sound of *oo* as in *book* or the long *oo* as in *moon.*

2. Words having the double *e* usually have the long *e* sound. (e.g., *seem;* exception, *been*).

3. In the phonogram *ie,* the *i* is silent and the *e* has a long sound. (e.g., *believe;* exceptions, *friend, sieve*).

Other Spelling Patterns: Vowels

There are more than fifty phonic "rules." Some attempt to justify exceptions to the above three spelling patterns by stating rules for sub-patterns. A few examples follow:

1. Final vowel letters
  a. A final vowel *(a, e, i, o, u)* usually has its long sound when it is the only vowel in a word; e.g., *me, go,* or in a syllable *(o)pen, (ta)ken.*
  b. A final *i* or *y* in a word or syllable may either have the "long" *i* sound; e.g., *(fi)nal, my* or have the "short" *i* sound; e.g., *division, city, baby.*
  c. When a syllable contains only the one vowel *a,* followed by the letters *l* or *w,* the sound for *a* rhymes with the word *saw;* e.g., *ball, paw.* (exceptions, *algebra, Albert*).
  d. A single "vowel" [letters?] followed by *r* in a word or in a syllable has neither its long nor its short sound, but is modified [sic] and controlled [sic] by the consonant [sic] *r;* e.g., *her, bird, fur, word* (the *er, ir, ur, or* represent one phoneme), *arm, farm, corn.*

2. Letter *y*
  a. When *y* is the final letter in a word, it usually has a vowel sound; e.g., *why, dry, pretty.*
  b. When *y* is used within a word, it usually has the long *i* sound; e.g., *scythe, type, dye.* (exceptions, *myth, myrtle, symphony*).

Rules: In Summary

Vowel rules are not necessarily the answer to a beginner's prayer.

1. Rules tend to bog down the young learner with a spate of concepts: *digraphs, vowels, consonants, long* and *short vowels, initial vowel, medial vowel, syllables, closed syllable, open syllable, accent* (stress), etc.

2. *Memorizing* vowel rules is probably as ineffective as *memorizing* long lists of sight words.

3. The application-exception ratios for some rules are so low they become sources of confusion rather than education.

4. Some authors confuse terminology; e.g., mixing *digraphs* (spellings) and *diphthongs* (sounds), using the indefinite term *vowel* for both *sounds* and *spellings.*

5. Some authors use ambiguous terminology; e.g., failing to identify the referent as sound or letters (phonogram) in "when there are two *vowels* in words of one syllable, usually the first is 'long' and the second is silent." What is a *silent* vowel? What are the two vowels in the word *made*?

6. To recognize exceptions to the rule, hedges are used: "usually," "most," "unless it is influenced by some other letter or sound in the syllable."

FOUNDATIONS OF INSTRUCTION

When these precautions are not taken, teachers and pupils are given a sense of *false* security, as in: "... the first vowel **has** its own 'long sound' and the second **is** silent." That is, unfavorable application/exception ratios are obscured.

7. The purpose of an i.l.m. (initial learning medium) is to reduce the complexity of phonic rules via a closer fit between phonemes and spellings.

Learning Letter Names

The following statements appear to be valid:

1. Ability to read letters and numbers appears to be one of the best single *predictors* of achievement in beginning reading, but the causal relationship remains unestablished.

2. To date, there is no real evidence that teaching pupils to read letters and numbers prior to beginning reading facilitates learning to read. In fact, there is evidence to indicate that learning letter names *interferes* with subsequent associative learning of words and pictured objects. Furthermore, there is an increasing fund of evidence that *practice* on letter identification is not significantly related to later achievement in beginning reading.

3. There is evidence that learning the names of geometric forms (e.g., circle, square, triangle) facilitates distinguishing between them. By analogy, it is possible, but not necessarily probable, that learning the names of letter shapes facilitates letter discrimination. (see 4 next)

4. There is no one-to-one correspondence between letter names and the sounds represented by letters; e.g., the letter name *b* /ˈbē/ and the sound represented by *b* in *by* /ˈbī/, or the letter name *y*/ˈwī/ and the sound represented by *y* in *year* /ˈyir/, or the letter name *u* /ˈyü/ and the stressed sound represented in *u* in *but* /ˈbət/ or the unstressed sound represented by *a* in *again* /ə-ˈgen/. In fact, learning the *names* of letters by whatever means tends to interfere with learning *grapheme-phoneme* relationships.

IN CONCLUSION

This session on phonics and spelling can lead educators to grasp the truth of the REALITY of the situation in word perception. True, English writing is an alphabetic system, but this truth does NOT lead to the conclusion that the fit between speech sounds and spellings is a close fit, or even remotely close, for some phonograms and phonic rules. True, that this need to legitimize phonics instruction via direct attention to the spelling system as well as to the psycholinguistic basis of word perception has long been recognized by the world's best scholars—that this need persists and will not go away. True, that the recrudescence of diverse phonic methods and the relentless, unfruitful, nugatory pursuit of phonics is diversionary—away from the central problem, the spelling system.

True, that immediate, common-sense steps can be taken to alleviate the beginning learner's frustration (perceptual conflicts from heterographic spellings) with his attempts to recode writing into speech. But this fact remains: this session will be productive and can have solid, long-lasting impact when everyone here returns to his or her acres of diamonds with the conviction—the involvement and, more important, the commitment—to pursue requisite multidisciplinary scholarship that leads to research on the central problem—the *medium,* or spelling system.

SECTION FOUR

Classroom Practices

- ... the "corrected test technique" which utilizes testing, studying, and retesting ... is the most efficient single method known for learning to spell, often resulting in an error reduction of 50 percent.

  Thomas Horn

- Although a significant number of commonly used words in speaking and writing have consistent spellings for speech sounds, too many crucial words are irregularly spelled.

  Emmett Betts

- The spellings analyzed in this study have demonstrated children's extraordinary abilities to "sound-out" words. Such ingenious abilities to produce phonetic spellings, however, do not alter the lexical nature of English orthography—the spellings generated are still unacceptable.

  Duane Tovey

INTRODUCTION

Here it is, Monday morning, and time to teach a spelling lesson. What should I do first? One suggestion by Horn is to test students before having them study. Another is to follow the advice of Cramer and use samples of children's writing to diagnose their strengths and weaknesses in spelling.

As for the studying part, Betts suggests a procedure he calls the "Phonics Countdown," a method that is based on having children learn the pronounceable parts of words. Tovey recommends teaching spelling in terms of visual patterns rather than sounds; he supports this recommendation by analyzing the misspellings of first-grade children. Not surprisingly, many of the misspellings were of words that had been sounded out successfully.

Cadenhead and his colleagues discuss an approach to spelling instruction that is uncomplicated and apparently successful, while Fisher and others face head-on a central problem in spelling, the distaste most children feel toward this subject. Sofge teaches spelling through the use of audio-tapes that children can use individually, and Campanile-Happ relies on children's interests to compile a word list that is then applied in creative writing. Blair concludes the chapter with a review of the research that classroom teachers will find helpful in planning the spelling curriculum.

Test, Then Study in Spelling

THOMAS D. HORN

Many of the current spelling materials utilize pupil *study before testing*. I'd like to recommend *testing before study*. It has a distinct advantage—to release pupils from studying words they already know. Testing before study tells pupils which words they need to study and lets teachers know which students need additional help and encouragement. This is the theory behind the "corrected test technique" which utilizes testing, studying, and retesting procedures. I feel it is the most efficient single method known for learning to spell, often resulting in an error reduction of 50 percent.

Briefly, the corrected test technique involves pupils taking a spelling test with no previous exposure to the word list, correcting their own tests as the teacher or another pupil spells each word orally, then retesting and correction. Its learning process emphasizes recall and utilizes visual, auditory, and kinesthetic imagery.

When inaugurating the use of the corrected test, it is especially effective to retest and correct immediately following the initial test and correction in order to show the pupils how much they have learned from the first correction. A number of teachers have had a dramatic effect by introducing the corrected test technique saying, "Here is a way you can learn to spell without studying." What a motivational statement that is!

The corrected test is excellent for individualizing spelling instruction since some pupils can pair off, with one assuming the teacher role so you can work with other pupils. Also, the motivational effects of peer teaching, studying only those words that are not already known, immediate reinforcement, and possibilities for flexibility in the selection and number of words to be learned, are extremely positive. In a number of cases, better spellers have elected to learn three to five times the usual number of words in a week. For the less able speller, the

---

From *Instructor*, Vol. 86, No. 4 (December, 1976). Reprinted with permission.

teacher and pupil together may reduce the number of words to be studied at any given time, select high frequency words according to individual needs, and provide for individual assistance such as developing sound-letter relationships through personal practice sessions.

Still another advantage of the corrected test is the focus upon individual and group reduction of errors. When the teacher tabulates on the chalkboard the number of pupils making five errors, four errors, three errors, and so on, and multiplies the number of pupils in each category by its number of errors, the pupils get meaningful practice in multiplication and addition through checking the teacher's operation. Through the focus on error reduction (and if the number of words attempted are adjusted to individual abilities), the less able pupil has a better chance to improve his self-concept and peer status through reducing the group error total rather than rarely or never attaining the hallowed condition of "getting a hundred."

Time for studying the misspelled words may be provided for those needing it immediately following the test, with teacher diagnosis and assistance to those who make excessive errors (a third or more of the test). Students for whom the corrected test technique is particularly powerful may prefer to pair off with another child for peer testing. To maintain a spelling progress report, the results of the final test should be compared with the initial test error totals. Periodic review tests check for the extent of forgetting.

As an example of how able spellers can utilize the corrected test technique to reduce the time spent on spelling to a little less than 30 minutes per week, nine sixth graders in one class elected not only to rely exclusively upon the corrected test but to also cover a new list of 25 words each day. Thus, from October 24 through December 8, words were learned that would otherwise have taken 11 weeks to "learn."

Diagnosing Skills by Analyzing Children's Writing

RONALD L. CRAMER

Diagnosis seeks to examine weaknesses and strengths in order to gain information that will help direct future instruction. If the information gained from diagnosis is pertinent and accurate, as well as properly interpreted and applied, then diagnosis can achieve its purpose.

Children's writing is an excellent source

From *The Reading Teacher*, Vol. 30, No. 3 (December, 1976). Reprinted with permission of the International Reading Association and Ronald L. Cramer.

of pertinent information about spelling and word recognition skills. Let's do an analysis of one child's writing to see how an analysis of misspellings might proceed and how information obtained might be used to direct future instruction. This analysis will be based on a limited sample, of course, although ordinarily such an analysis would cover several writing samples and supplemental information would be collected in any area where uncertainty prevailed.

The story "My Ded Cat" was written by a second grade child. The misspellings are analyzed to show how they can give useful information about spelling and word recognition skills. The content of David's story is far more important than the misspellings. However, that aspect of David's story will not be explored in this article.

> My Ded Cat
> Ones I hade a cat.
> He was white and yellow.
> One night my father
> Come fame my grandfathers house
> Wenn father come home fame
> my grandfathers house he said
> Ruste is ded
> David
> Age 7

David misspelled six different words in his story: *ded* for *dead*, *ones* for *once*, *hade* for *had*, *fame* for *from*, *wenn* for *when*, and *Ruste* for *Rusty*.

On the other hand, David correctly spelled eighteen different words: *my, cat, I, a, he, was, white, and, yellow, one, night, father, come, grandfathers, house, home, said,* and *is*.

Several of the correctly spelled words can be regarded as superior spelling accomplishments for a second grade child. The words *father, grandfathers, white, night, house, said,* and *yellow* are in this category. One can look at David's spelling accomplishments and recognize his growing ability to correctly represent sounds with their appropriate letter and letter combinations. However, it is also instructive to examine David's misspellings for possible evidence of strength or weakness in spelling and word recognition skills. Following is an analysis for each misspelling.

1) *ded* for *dead*. The sound /e/ may be spelled *e* as in *bed* or *ea* as in *dead*. Apparently, at this time, David is unfamiliar with the *ea* option for the /e/ sound. Logically, David spells the sound /e/ with the short *e* spelling he knows. The letter *e* is the most common spelling for the /e/ sound.

2) *hade* for *had*. This misspelling appears to be an over generalization of the final *e* rule (sometimes called the silent *e* rule). David showed that he has considerable awareness of this spelling rule. Notice he has correctly spelled the final *e* pattern in *home, come, white,* and *house*. If David is allowed to continue to test the use of this spelling rule through his creative writings he will soon discover which words take the final *e* marker and which do not.

3) *wenn* for *when*. This misspelling shows knowledge of the second most common spelling for the /n/ sound (the double n). In this case David spelled the /n/ sound as in *tunnel*. Also, David spelled the *wh* digraph in *when* with the letter *w*. Possibly David has not yet mastered the *wh* digraph, although he gets the *wh* digraph right in *white*. A possible explanation for this misspelling is that the word *when* is pronounced /'wen/ in David's dialect rather than /'hwen/. Some misspellings are apparently caused by dialect or pronunciation factors.

4) *Ruste* for *Rusty*. David sensibly spelled the last sound in *Rusty* with an *e* since it has the /ē/ sound. He has not yet learned that the final sound in words like *Mary, hurry,* and *carry* is often spelled with the letter *y*.

5) *fame* for *from*. At first glance this misspelling appears to be David's crudest mistake. However, this misspelling is not as unsophisticated as it might first appear. He has correctly spelled the first and last sounds of *from*. The final *e* in *fame* is probably another instance of over generalization of the final *e* rule. David's problems with *from* are the *r* in the *fr* blend and the vowel *o*. The omission of the *r* in the *fr* blend suggests unfamiliarity with the conventional spelling of this sound. The *o* in *from* is a schwa /ə/, although stressed. This vowel is spelled with the letter *e* in *taken*, the letter *a* in *about*, the letter *i* in *robin*, the letter *u* in *circus*, and the letter *o* in *wagon*. In other words, any vowel letter may spell the schwa sound in an unstressed syllable and sometimes in stressed syllables, as in *from*. Therefore, the letter *a* which David used was not an alto-

gether random guess. Notice that he did use a vowel rather than a consonant to spell the schwa sound. His choice of the letter *a* to represent the vowel sound shows that he was aware of the need for a vowel letter in *from*.

6) *ones* for *once*. *Ones* and *once* may be homophones in David's speech. We know he can spell the word *one* ("One night my father..."). If *ones* and *once* are homophones in David's speech then this spelling logic is impeccable—he simply added the letter *s* to *one* to get *ones*. This misspelling shows good analogical reasoning and good sound discrimination. *Once* ends with the sound /s/ spelled *c*. David spelled the sound /s/ with the letter *s*—the most common spelling for this sound.

An analysis of David's misspellings as well as his correctly spelled words suggests the following tentative conclusions regarding David's word recognition and spelling strengths and weaknesses.

1) David knows many words by sight. We know this because he correctly spelled 75 per cent of the different words used in his story. This information suggests a solid reading vocabulary as well as substantial spelling strength. This conclusion is further strengthened by our knowledge that several of the words he has correctly spelled are words not normally in the spelling vocabulary of a second grade child.

2) David has excellent auditory discrimination acuity and strong letter-sound association skills. He applies his knowledge correctly in most instances, and makes appropriate guesses in all instances where he has misspelled words. His misspellings show an awareness that there is more than one way to spell a given sound.

3) David is aware that certain consonant sounds have variant spellings. This knowledge was revealed when he wrote *wenn* for *when*. Knowledge of consonant variability, and later vowel variability, is an important step toward spelling proficiency.

4) David knows the final *e* rule, which is important for reading as well as for spelling. Naturally, in testing this rule he misapplies it from time to time. Similar instances of over generalization are found in early oral language development. It is recognized in oral language as an important step forward in learning the rules of English syntax. It is a similarly important step in learning the rules of English spelling. Strength is shown in that David does try to apply this rule and frequently he does so correctly—as in *home, come, white,* and *house*.

5) David has excellent control of the letter-sound associations for consonant spellings. He rarely misspells single consonant sounds. When he does misspell consonant sounds the error is associated with blends (*fr* in *from*), digraphs (*wh* in *when*) or variant consonant spellings (*s* for *c* in *once*). In both the blend and the digraph he got the first letter correct but not the second. In *ones* he chose the most common option for the /s/ sound. Finally, his misspelling of the /n/ sound in *when* was caused by knowing too much rather than too little. We suspect that he knows both spellings for the /n/ sound since he uses *nn* in *wenn* and *n* in *grandfathers*.

6) David is beginning to gain control of some difficult vowel spellings. His attempt to spell the schwa vowel (*fame* for *from*), the final *e* spelling (*hade* for *had*), and the /e/ sound spelled *y* (*Ruste* for *Rusty*) may be regarded as steps toward learning these difficult spellings. They are not simply random errors. His guesses represented sophisticated exploration of letter-sound relationships. In all three instances his errors are logical steps in the right direction. Vowel spellings are the most variable and, consequently, take the longest time for children to master.

7) David correctly spelled the blend *gr* in *grandfathers* but misspelled the *fr* blend in *from* and the *wh* digraph in *when*. An educated guess would be that David is ready for some specific instruction on blends and digraphs. However, since there are not enough instances in

this story of the use of blends and digraphs to make a sound judgment, further analysis is appropriate.

8) David uses what he knows to solve what he does not know. This is a significant learning strength and David uses it well. He also reasons well by analogy as was illustrated in several cases. Analogous reasoning is an important thinking ability.

From the analysis we conclude that David is further advanced in spelling proficiency than many second grade children; and that his word recognition abilities are in advance of his spelling ability. In all likelihood he is capable of pronouncing words at a third grade level or higher. This is an educated guess based on the fact that word recognition ability often runs one-half to one grade level higher than the instructional spelling level. Given the opportunity to continue writing, David will likely develop into an excellent speller and capable reader. And, judging from the content of this story, he is on the way to becoming an excellent writer as well.

Perceptual Learning: Phonics Countdown

EMMETT ALBERT BETTS

The phonics countdown, developed in the Reading Research Lab, Univ. of Miami, Fla., is one, but only one method for teaching the pupil how to decode writing. It is used with monosyllables (e.g., *big* or *made*) and with the stressed syllables of words (e.g., the *happ* of *happy* and the *can* of *candy*).

Procedure: Long Countdown

The phonics countdown is a simple procedure for teaching pupils to study (1) *pronounceable* parts of a word, or a stressed syllable, and (2) the relation of the word form to a "life" meaning:
1. "What animal do you see?" (A cat) (A picture of a cat)
2. "What is the first word?" /'kat/ cat
3. "Look at the second word. Say aloud the part that is printed in black letters." /'at/ (c)at*
4. "Look at the third word. Say aloud the part printed in black letters." ca(t)*
5. "Look at the next word. Say the part printed in black." /'a/ (c)a(t)*

*The letters in parentheses appear in color in the pupil's book or on the chalkboard.

6. "What is the sound for the letter *a* in the word *cat*?" /'a/
7. "What is the last word?" /'kat/ cat
8. "Finish this sentence: A cat is _____." (Optional: an animal, pretty, a nice pet, etc.)
"Finish this sentence: A cat likes to _____." (Optional: play with yarn, sleep, etc.)
"How many kinds of cats can you name?"

The emphasis, in this approach to the systematic study of one-syllable words or the stressed syllable of a word, is on

---

From *The Florida Reading Quarterly*, Vol. 10, No. 2 (January, 1974). Reprinted by permission.

CLASSROOM PRACTICES

pronounceable parts. A *pronounceable part* may be:
(1) the *ca* of *cat*, or the *plea* of *please;*
(2) the *a* of *cat* or the *ea* of *please;*
(3) the *at* of *cat* or the *ease* of *please*.

At no time are consonants pronounced in isolation from vowels because they need to be blended with succeeding vowels (e.g., *shar* of *sharp*) or preceding vowels (e.g., *arp* of *sharp*). This use of pronounceable units eliminates a profusion of confusion induced by requiring the learner to say /puh/ and /tuh/ for the *p* and *t* of *pat*, producing the nonsense word /puh-a-tuh/. (Unfortunately, this procedure seems to be somewhat commonplace in too many classrooms).

Phonic countdowns are used on consistently spelled words and stressed syllables (e.g., *tap* /tap/ rather than *was* /wəz/. (Other procedures are used with the host of irregularly spelled words, such as *of* /ov/, *come* /kəm/, and *who* /hü/.)

The same procedure is used with other categories of words:

came	goat	round
(c)ame	(g)oat	(r)ound
ca(me)	goa(t)	rou(nd)
c(a)me	g(oa)t	r(ou)nd
came	goat	round
girl	work	park
(g)irl	(w)ork	(p)ark
gir(l)	wor(k)	par(k)
(g)ir(l)	(w)or(k)	(p)ar(k)
girl	work	park

Note: the phonograms in parentheses in each word are printed in color in textbooks so that the pupil sees the word as a whole but pronounces only the part in black.

Crucial to the use of the phonics countdown are several considerations:
1. Vowel-consonant Blend

When pupils are ready for beginning reading instruction, they can use free association to recall words that rhyme with a word; e.g., *at: cat–hat–sat*. Hence, the pupils are taken from the whole word to its rhyming part because this is an easy initial step in studying the structure of the word.

The first purpose of these activities is to make the pupil *aware* of the patterns of sounds he uses—*not* to teach the pupil the sounds he already uses automatically in his speech activities.

The second purpose is to teach the pupils the relationship between the sound pattern and the letter pattern; e.g., the rhyme /'at/ of /'kat/ and the spelling *at* of *cat*.

2. Consonant-vowel Blend

The next step in studying the structure of the word is the consonant-vowel blend, as *ra* of *rat*. After the pupils are introduced to 3 to 5 situations—e.g., *cat, bat, hat, rat, ran*—they learn that the first parts, *ca, ba, ha, ra,* rhyme.

When the pupils have accumulated a small vocabulary, they will generalize that the *same* consonant-vowel blend in the *same* pattern represents the same sounds, e.g., the *ca* for /'ka/ in *cap–can* of the (C)VC, or (consonant)-vowel-consonant pattern as in *at* and *hat* pattern. At this point, they may be taught the following generalization:

"The words *cat* and *cap* have the same first sounds: /'ka/. What other words begin with the first sounds /'ka/ as *cat* and *cap*?" (e.g., *can, cab, calf, camp, cash, cast, catch*). Or, "Which of these three words have the same first sound /'ka/?: *cat, bat, can*" Or, *fat, cat, cab*. Or, *pat, cat, calf*.

"What is the first part of *cat, cap, can*?" /'ka/
"What is the first part of *cat, cab, calf*?" /'ka/
"What is the first part of *cat, camp, catch*?" /'ka/

3. The Vowel Sound

In beginning reading, the pupil is introduced to the (C)VC spelling patterns, as in *rat, pig, bug, not, get*. In these patterns, the vowel sounds are contrastive and, therefore, can be discriminated easily. Furthermore, the pupils learn one specific spelling pattern (e.g., the sub-

253

pattern *cat–ran*) before being introduced to another spelling sub-pattern (e.g., *big–pig–hit, bug–rug, not–got, get–let*).

Follow-up activities after the introduction of each specific pattern may reinforce the association of vowel sounds with the letters representing them:

"The words *cat, pan, sad* have the same middle sound. What is it?" /a/
"The words *cat, man, nap* have the same middle sound. What is it?" /a/
"The words *cat, sad, rag* have the same middle sound. What is it?" /a/
"The words *cat, ham, lap* have the same middle sound. What is it?" /a/

After two specific spelling patterns have been introduced, the pupils may profit from activities in which they discriminate between contrastive sounds: Say: "Listen to the middle sound of these words to decide whether they are the same or different: *cat–ham, cat–cut, cat–cake, cat–cot, cat–bag, cat–set, cat–lap.*" Say one pair of words at a time and have the pupils say each pair as they listen to the middle sound. Then, have them decide whether the middle sounds are the same or different.

The purpose of the last activity above is to teach the pupil to *hear* sounds he uses automatically, not to teach him to *say* the sounds, which he can do before he *enters* into beginning reading activities.

4. Consonant Boundaries: First Consonants

The total sound pattern of /'kat/ is initiated with the consonant /k/ and terminated with the consonant /t/. For the beginner, the awareness of all three sounds /k/, /a/, and /t/ is a set of new learnings. The vowel is the nucleus of the syllable, but consonants are the margins, or boundaries, of the syllable and, therefore, equally important.

As a follow-up to the first countdown for *cat*, alert the pupils to the first sound /k/:

Say: "The words *cat* and *can* begin with the same first sound. Listen to the first sound of *cat* and *can* as you say them."

"Say some other words that begin with the same first sound." Pupils may respond with *cab, cake, call, camel, keep, key, kick, kind*.

To teach pupils to discriminate between *contrastive* first consonants, say: "Say *cat* and *bat* and listen to their first sounds. Are they the same or different?" Use other pairs: *cat–sat, cat–hat, cat–cab, cat–rat, cat–cap, cat–bat, cat–catch*.

It should be noted that neither the teacher nor the pupils say the name of the letter k /'kā/ or the sound /k/. At this point, attention is directed to *hearing* the sound /k/ in the *whole word cat* /'kat/ and to saying the sound /k/ in the *whole word* (syllable) *cat*.

5. Consonant Boundaries: Last Consonants

The first four patterned words end with consonant *t* /t/: *cat, bat, hat, rat*. The next two patterned words end with consonant *n* /n/: *ran, can*. As the pupil's vocabulary develops, additional consonant letters are introduced. But in each new word, only *one* new consonant letter, as a new learning, is presented—either a first or a last consonant, depending on the sequence of new words in beginning reading materials.

Caveat: It will be noted that neither the pupil nor the teacher says either the names of the consonant letters or the sound of the isolated consonants. The sounds of the whole word *cat* are /'kat/, not the names of the letters /'kā- 'ā- 'tē/. Furthermore, some experienced teachers may be able to say the sound /k/ in isolation, but the sound is often distorted by adding a vowel sound such as schwa: /'kə/. Another plosive, or stop, sound /t/ is distorted into /'tə/ when it is said in isolation. The word is the one-syllable /'kat/, not the two-syllable /'ka 'tə/ or the three-syllable /'kə-'a-'tə/.

Follow-up on a countdown activity may be used to reinforce auditory discrimination and letter-sound associations:

Say: "Say *cat–hot* and listen to the last sounds. Are they the same or different?" Use other pairs: *cat–jam, cat–nut, cat–run, cat–pig, cat–not*.

To further point up the sound /t/, have

the pupils say pairs of words that have vowel sounds other than /a/ and decide if the last sounds are the same or different: *got–pet, rut–pot, lot–pin, sun–sit, him–cut, hit–hot, pig–rot*. Avoid using the cognates /d/ and /t/ as the final sounds in word pairs—because these sounds are too close on the sound spectrum—until the pupils can discriminate between highly contrasted sounds, such as /d/ and /s/.

6. Consonants: Elementary Sounds and Blends

In beginning reading, the pupils first learn the relations between single consonant letters (e.g., *c* and *t* of *cat* and *r* and *n* of *ran*) and elementary sounds (e.g., /k/ and /t/ of /'kat/, /r/ and /n/ of /ran/). Then they are introduced to consonant blends of sounds previously studied; e.g., the *nd* of *and* and *band*.

With the exception of function words (e.g., *a, and*), the first words introduced are within the same spelling pattern: *cat, bat, rat*. For example, the next word may be *bat*, with only one new element added: *b* /b/. Since the pupils have had only one previous experience with this pattern—the word *cat*—they cannot generalize, or discover the alphabetic principle, until they have studied two or more words in that pattern.

New words introduced are within the same specific spelling pattern: *cat, bat*. For example, *bat*, presenting the new element *b* /b/ and *rat*, representing the new element *r* /r/, introduce one new learning at a time. For the first words, care is exercised (1) to select words in which the consonant is represented by one letter (e.g., *hat* rather than *what* or *that*) and (2) to develop the relationship between the sound and the letter representing it. Soon the pupils are able to generalize regarding the *cat–hat–bat* spelling pattern.

This (C)VC generalization is extended for this pattern by using words with *contrasting* final consonants: *cap–can, map–man*. But again, it will be noted that each of the consonant boundaries—first and last—is systematically and painstakingly developed, because each consonant sound and letter is a new learning.

After the pupils have had experience with *sat* and *bad* and similar words, they are in a position to apply their perception skills to *sad*. Or, experience with *ran* and *hat*, for example, makes possible the application of the pattern to *rat*. Or, experience with *cat* and *ran* can be used to identify *can*.

Digraphs—two letters representing a single sound, as in (th)e, du(ck), si(ng), (wh)o—are distributed parsimoniously and developed carefully.

7. Use of Terms: Vowel and Consonant

In beginning reading, one of the major emphases is on decoding writing—relating a sequence of sounds in a spoken word to the sequence of letters in a written word. This major learning is a big order for beginners; hence using the terms *vowel* and *consonant* is not recommended. However, some teachers may be more comfortable if they opt to do so.

8. Function Words

Function words—e.g., *a, and*—tend to be unstressed and shortened in the phases of conversational speech—the norm for oral reading. The word *a* becomes unstressed /ə/, not stressed /'a/, as in *a cat*. The word *and* becomes unstressed /ənd/ or /ən/, not stressed /'and/.

Learning *phrase* stress as well as *syllable* stress is crucial for beginning readers. This learning promotes rhythmical rather than word-by-word reading. For this reason, the function word *a* is usually introduced in the first activity and the function word *and* soon thereafter. Later, function words are distributed as needed in order to take advantage of the pupil's normal intonation patterns, learned before he is ready for beginning reading.

9. Irregularly Spelled Words

Pupil confidence in word-perception skills is developed through an emphasis on *regularly* spelled words; e.g., *cat* and *sat*. This confidence is reinforced by the simple device of respelling irregularly spelled words, *using letter-sound rela-*

tionships previously learned. The word *have,* for example, is presented as *have* (hav), as a self-help aid. Although a significant number of commonly used words in speaking and writing have consistent spellings for speech sounds, too many crucial words are irregularly spelled. Fortunately, however, dictionary respellings for many of these words are with the *at–bet–did–not–but* spelling patterns learned early in beginning reading. Hence, these types of respellings permit rapid perception:

Word	Respelling (Self-help aid)
one	(wun)
what	(hwot)
come	(kum)
from	(frum)
some	(sum)
laugh	(laf)
of	(uv)

This plan has these distinctive advantages:

(1) The pupil always is dealing with known elements. For example, the respellings are all within the *hat–get–but–got–run* spelling sub-patterns which he has learned—or, perhaps, overlearned.

(2) The pupil achieves independence because the special respellings—e.g., *laugh* (laf)—are available as a self-help aid at the moment he needs the help.

(3) The pupil gradually learns that different spellings (letters) may be used for the same sound, as *f* in *if* and *gh* in *laugh.*

(4) The pupil becomes acutely aware of the sounds he uses automatically in speech and relates them to spellings. That is, he learns inductively the alphabetic principle on which traditional orthography is based.

10. Two-syllable Words

One of the crucial factors in word perception is grouping in pronounceable units as the *fa* or *at* in *fat* or the *Bobb* in *Bobby.*

First, the pupils learn through the phonics countdown that the parts of one-syllable words are grouped. For example, the letters of the word *hat* may be grouped as *ha* or *at* to preserve valid consonant-vowel and vowel-consonant relationships. The word *plant* may be grouped as *pla* or *ant*. Furthermore, the *pl* and *nt* of *plant* are subgroups for consonant sounds, which are not said in isolation.

Second, the pupils learn that letters and the sounds they represent may be grouped by syllables. In beginning reading, two-syllable words have relatively simple syllabic division in *better* (better), *penny* (penn-y), *candy* (can-dy), *mother* (moth-er), and *father* (fath-er).

That is, special syllabication situations do not occur until the pupil has mastered the less complex ones. The syllabic division between vowels, as in *giant* /ji-ənt/, is one special situation. The syllabic division represented by the spelling *ng* as in *longer* /ˈlong-gər/, is another.

Pupil confidence derived from success with one-syllable words is *reinforced* through the simple device of showing the syllabic division of the word in terms of *traditional* spelling. Hence, the syllables of the word *pretty* are shown as (prett-y), not as a dictionary respelling /ˈprit-ē/ or as a dictionary entry.

This plan has several distinctive advantages:

a. The pupil learns how to syllabicate the traditional spelling of a word—what he sees when he reads.

b. The pupil achieves an awareness of the double consonant at the end of a syllable which often signals a "short" vowel sound, as in *kitten* (kitt-en) /ˈkit-n/.

c. The pupil learns early to apply one-syllable phonic skills to the stressed syllables of two-syllable words, as in *Randy* (Ran-dy) /ˈran-dē/. That is, he makes a gradual transition to syllable phonics, applying what he already knows.

d. Pupil *motivation* is significantly increased through his understanding of how to group parts of whole words to identify them; e.g., the *thi* or *ink* of *think* or the *Jimm* and *y* of *Jimmy.*

e. Pupil motivation is enhanced through his increasing awareness of what he knows about word perception and about the *application* of his skills to new words.

f. Pupil motivation is given a big boost through the development of positive attitudes toward word perception; e.g., automatically looking for the parts he *knows* as cues to the word.

g. Pupil motivation is further advanced by learning *how* to learn; e.g., by grouping word parts into functional units (as *happ-y* in *happy*) and automatically checking to see if the word makes sense in its sentence—using semantic-syntactic-pragmatic types of context clues.

11. Variant Spelling

A variant spelling of a word is one of two or more appropriate or correct spellings listed in current and reputable dictionaries. The word *rime* is entered in Webster's *New Elementary Dictionary* (1970) as: *rime* var. of RHYME.

Which spelling is used is a matter of personal choice.

To develop pupil confidence and to reinforce his word perception skills for the *like–ride–time* pattern, the variant spelling *rime* is introduced with the word *time*. The optimal, or variant, spelling of *rime* as *rhyme* is introduced later, when the pupil achieves a higher level of competence in both word perception and spelling.

Short Phonics Countdown

A short phonics countdown is used to save time and to teach application of skills:

1. After the pupils (a) have had a long countdown on three to five words within a given specific spelling pattern, and (b) know the consonant boundaries of the new words; e.g., *cat–hat–cap, bet–leg–wet, bake–make–came, out–loud–ground*

hill	make
(h)ill*	(m)ake
(p)ill	(c)ake
pill	cake

*Letters in parentheses appear in color in the pupil's study book or on the chalkboard.

2. After the pupils have learned two contrasting spelling patterns; eg., *hid–big–did* versus *hide–like–ride*. In this instance the spelling pattern of *hid–hide* may be contrasted for cues to the vowel sound.

hid	mad
hide	made

3. After analogous final vowel-consonant blends have been learned; e.g.,

box	park	round
(b)ox	(p)ark	(r)ound
(f)ox	(l)ark	(s)ound
fox	lark	sound

4. After analogous initial consonant-vowel blends have been learned; e.g., *be* of *beg* and *bet*

bad	had	thing
ba(d)	ha(d)	thi(ng)
ba(g)	ha(s)	thi(nk)
bag	has	think

To use this countdown, the final consonants have been learned in relation to other words.

5. After three to five words, a limited category of spelling patterns have been learned; e.g., *he, may, no*

he	may	no
(h)e	(m)ay	(n)o
(m)e	(s)ay	(g)o
me	say	go

To use this countdown, the initial consonants have been learned in relation to other words.

Analogies between words are used in an increasing number of situations in which the pupil contrasts and compares minimal pairs, as for example

hot	he	me	car	feed
got	me	she	tar	feel

CLASSROOM PRACTICES

This is primarily an application procedure.

Vowel plus r

As the pupil progresses in his reading, he meets an increasing number of vowel plus *r* situations, as in *her–bird–work, water–color, air–where*, etc. In some of the situations, the spellings represent an elementary sound (e.g., the /ər/ of *first, her*); in others, the spellings represent diphthongs (e.g., the /är/ *far*). Furthermore, regional differences in speech complicate the situation. To reduce this situation to a manageable one for beginners, all vowel plus *r* situations (1) are presented as phonograms and (2) are taught as cue and probability learnings.

The vowel plus *r* is a stressed elementary sound /ər/ in *bird, her, worm*, etc. Hence, the *ir* or *er* represents the vowel sound and is taught as a consonant-vowel blend *bir* and as a vowel-consonant blend *ird* in the phonics countdown on *bird*.

> bird
> (b)ird
> bir(d)
> (b)ir(d)
> bird

The vowel plus *r* is an unstressed elementary speech sound /ər/ (syllable) in *better* (bett-er), *color* (col-or), *water* (wat-er). Since it is unstressed, a phonics countdown is not used.

In other vowel plus *r* situations, the vowel plus *r* is taught as a phonogram, as in *far–cart–dark, for, there–where*. That is, the phonics countdown is:

> dark
> (d)ark
> dar(k)
> (d)ar(k)
> dark

Stressed Syllables

At first, only two-syllable words in which the first syllable is stressed are taught. Furthermore, the first, or stressed, syllable is a previously taught word, as *can* in *candy* (can-dy), *Bob* in *Bobby* (Bobb-y), and *bet* in *better* (bett-er).

As for the phonics countdowns on monosyllables, the countdown for disyllables is introduced and terminated with a consideration of the *referential* meaning of the word.

A long countdown is made on the first few two-syllable words, as for *little* (litt-le)

> little
> (l)itt(le)*
> (l)i(ttle)
> litt(le)
> little

*Letters in parentheses appear in color in the pupil's study book or on the chalkboard.

As the pupils' understandings of word structure are increased, the countdowns are shortened:

> can   bet   fun
> can(dy)   bett(er)   funn(y)
> candy   better   funny

Later, two-syllable words in which the second syllable is stressed are taught. Moreover, the second, or stressed, syllable has been taught as a word; e.g., *around, away:*

> round   way
> (a)round   (a)way
> around   away

The use of the phonics countdown on stressed syllables teaches the pupils (1) *how* to apply their phonic skills to stressed syllables, and (2) a *set* for seeing and hearing syllables.

The countdown is limited to the stressed syllables for these reasons: first, when a syllable is said in isolation from the word, it is automatically stressed, because stress is a relative phenomenon. For example, the *-er* of *letter* is unstressed /-ər/, not stressed /'ur/, giving rhythm to the word. Second, spelling patterns—e.g., *can* and *candy*—tend to be valid predictors of pronunciations of stressed syllables. Third, cue spellings—e.g., *ar* in *car* and *party*—tend to have the same sound values in stressed syllables, permitting the application of *cue* learning. Hence, the countdown is applied only to stressed syllables in order to preserve their normal pronunciation.

Purposes

The phonics countdown serves these purposes:

1. To teach pupils to hear undistorted sounds which the spellings of a word represent; e.g., the pupil does not attempt (a) to say a (distorted) consonant sound in isolation from the vowel sound of the whole word, or (b) to associate the letter name of the consonant with the consonant sound. For example, the pupil learns to say the monosyllable /'kat/ not /kə/-/a/-/tə/, a three-syllable word. Most people, including children, are not aware of the sounds of speech which they have learned to use automatically.

2. To teach pupils to hear and to say the vowel sound in relation to the undistorted consonant boundaries; that is, the preceding or following consonant sound is always sequenced with the vowel, as /'ka/ for *ca* and /'at/ for *at* of *cat*.

3. To teach pupils to relate a sequence of undistorted *sounds in time* (e.g., /'kat/) to a sequence of *letters in space* (e.g., *cat*)—to understand the alphabetic principle that spellings (writing) represent speech sounds.

4. To teach pupils to identify three types of (stressed) pronounceable units:
   a. Consonant-vowel (e.g., *sou* of *sound*) or vowel-consonant (e.g., *ound* of *sound*)
   b. Vowel, as the *er* of *her*, or glide, as *oi* of *oil*
   c. Stressed syllable, as the *bubb* of *bubble*

5. To teach pupils the organization, or structure, of the word form (e.g., *ca-at* for the /'ka/ /'at/ sound of the whole word)—the structural meaning of the word form.

6. To teach pupils to relate the sequence of the letters to the sequence sounds and the sequence sounds to the "life" meaning of the word (e.g., a *cat* as an animal)—the referential meaning of the word. Meaning—both structural and referential—gives reality to the word form and makes for ease of recall (recognition).

7. To teach pupils to make automatic responses to the informative structural elements of the *whole* word; e.g., to the *bu* or the *ug* of the whole word *bug*.

8. To teach pupils to use two predictors of the letter(s) representing the vowel sound, increasing the probability of identifying the word; e.g., the consonant-vowel blend *dre* of *dress*.

9. To teach pupils *perceptual closure;* e.g., after saying /a/, the child says the whole word *cat*, hearing and saying the sound /a/ in relation to its consonant boundaries, *c* /k/ and *t* /t/. This ability to achieve closure, or completion, of the whole word helps the pupil to achieve independence in word perception and recognition during silent reading. For example, if he asks for help on the word *find* and points to the *i* as the unknown, the teacher tells him the sound /ī/ rather than the whole word. Then the pupil closes, or completes, the whole word by saying /'find/ and by checking to see if

it makes sense in what he is saying. This is a "quickie"—a time saving device that facilitates rather than disrupts the pupils' silent reading.

10. To teach pupils to use *cues* to the sound for the vowel letter(s); e.g., the *ind* of *kind* and *find,* the final consonants *t* and *ll* of *bet* and *fell,* the *ame* of *came* and *game,* the *ou* of *loud* and *sound,* etc.

11. To teach pupils to *group* the letters of the written word into pronounceable units; e.g., not *f-i-r-s-t* but *fir* and *irst* of *first.*
    a. This grouping of letters for sounds focuses *attention* on informative parts of words; e.g., the *up* of *cup.* Attention as a selector of information to be processed is a potent factor in word perception.
    b. Grouping the pronounceable parts of a word reduces the memory burden (attention span) required for word perception; e.g., attending to two groupings as the *ca-atch* of *catch* is not only more productive but also less of a memory burden than trying to decode the *five* letters.

12. To teach pupils to use feed forward—to relate speech sounds to spelling—through hearing and saying the sounds (the *feed*). In this application of skills to unknown words, the pupil has the *feed* (the sounds) to *feed back* from the spellings to the sounds.

13. To teach pupils a *set* to read by structures; e.g., the *pla* or *ane* of *plane,* the *trai* or *ain* of *train,* etc.

Caveats

A phonics countdown is an effective approach to one facet of word perception: the relation between sounds and letters. It is a crucial procedure in the use of V-A-K (kinesthetic) and the V-A-K-T (tactile) developed by Fernald and Keller as well as the V-A (phonic) techniques in word perception. Which of these three techniques is used, of course, depends on diagnosed individual differences in word-learning abilities. Both the V-A-K and V-A-K-T *reinforce* pupil learning via combined modalities: visual-auditory, visual-auditory-kinesthetic, or visual-auditory-kinesthetic-tactile. But the use of these last two techniques emphasizes motor skills as preparation for reading as well as for word learning during beginning reading activities. These techniques require special teacher preparation via carefully supervised laboratory-demonstration courses.

Another caveat: to say that there is a loose "fit" between the sounds of English and the letters used to represent them is a gross and misleading understatement. But in spite of the facts, phonics—the study of the relationships between sounds (phonemes) and spelling (graphemes)—has been touted from the sixteenth century to the present as either *the* way or *one* way to teach reading. A spate of studies has been published on the futility of generalizations, or rules, for spelling, but phonics zealots still reign supreme.

In general, three vowel rules have been served as the hard core of phonics: "short" vowel sounds in closed syllables, as in *at* and *sit;* final *e* to signal the "long" preceding vowel as in *ate* and *made;* two adjacent vowel letters with the first vowel long, as in *eat* and *boat.* The batting averages—the application/exception ratios—in beginning reading for these three rules are: 74%, 53%, and 50%. But only 35% of the commonest words "fit" these three rules. Yes, beliefs in teaching phonic rules—too often, *memorizing* them—are not what they seem to be—they are much, much worse! (Based on studies in our Reading Research Laboratory)

In 1933, Leonard Bloomfield, the innovator and great linguist of his time, suggested the idea of teaching regular spellings first, as in *cat* and *Dan*. However, he issued this caveat: "The real factor of difficulty is the host of irregular spellings which remain, no matter what values are assigned as regular." (p. 501)

Three sets of Bloomfield's regular spellings were made highly visible to the teaching community by Charles Fries as three general spelling patterns: *at–pet–sit–not–cut; ate–like–home; train–eat–coat*. These three "spelling patterns," by this or any other name, are readily recognized by sophisticated teachers as the same old, threadbare, ridiculous "vowel rules."

Why have "vowel rules" and "spelling patterns" continued to be the reading fallacies for centuries? Why do some people persist sometimes, in seeking the impossible: the reconciliation of traditional spellings and speech sounds? Probably for the same reasons that birds will be the last to discover air and fish will be the last to discover water. That is, parents and teachers have not discovered a discipline called orthography which was taught as a required subject in grammar schools, circa 1920. Pseudoconservatives who "get that way by degrees only" might heed this comment by Leonard Bloomfield: "The difficulty of our spelling greatly delays elementary education, and wastes even much time of adults." (p. 501) He continued with this understatement: "There would be no serious difficulty about devising a simple, effective orthography for all types of standard English. . . ." (p. 502)

In brief, an obvious roadblock to reading instruction—an antiquated orthography which has too loose a fit with present-day speech—has been and IS passed by like a stranger on a very dark night.

Hence, a short or long countdown or any other device designed to communicate the "alphabetic principle" is freighted with potential confusion that produces reading disabilities.

BIBLIOGRAPHY

Betts, Emmett A. "Reading: Perceptual Learning." *Education*, LXXXIX, No. 4. (April-May, 1969), 291–297.

Black, Elsie Benson. "A Study of the Consonant Situations in a Primary Reading Vocabulary," *Education*, LXXII, No. 9, (May 1952), 618–623 (Reading Research Laboratory, University of Miami).

Bloomfield, Leonard. *Language*. New York: Henry Holt & Company, 1933.

Bosworth, Mary H. *Pre-Reading: Improvement of Visual-Motor Skills*. Winter Haven, Florida: Winter Haven Lions Research Foundation, Inc., 1967.

DiMeo, Katherine P. *Visual-Motor Skills: Response Characteristics and Pre-Reading Behavior*. Winter Haven, Florida: Winter Haven Lions Research Foundation, Inc., 1967.

Oaks, Ruth E. "A Study of the Vowel Situations in a Primary Vocabulary," *Education*, LXXII, No. 9 (May 1952), 604–617 (Reading Research Laboratory, University of Miami).

"Sound-It-Out": A Reasonable Approach to Spelling?

DUANE R. TOVEY

Linguists have indicated that English spellings are not phonetic but lexical (standard spelling) in nature (Chomsky, 1973). For example—thot, ruf, tri, sik and bred are phonetic spellings for the lexical spellings of *thought, rough, try, sick* and *bread* respectively. Such lexical spellings are not based on perfect one to one sound-letter relationships but are in accord with the patterns/sequences of letters used in English orthography. This seems to suggest that good spellers possess prior knowledge of predetermined letter sequences rather than arbitrarily selecting letters which correspond to sounds they hear. It would appear that the "sound-it-out" strategy—matching sounds to letters—is not reasonable nor reliable unless the spelling of a word is known ahead of time. Spelling should probably be thought of in terms of visual patterns rather than sounds.

Hence, the purpose of this study is to demonstrate the inadvisability of encouraging children to place their confidence in the "sound-it-out" strategy for spelling unfamiliar words. To accomplish this, 590 stories written by first grade children were analyzed. Children wrote these stories on 12″ by 18″ construction paper to describe the pictures they had drawn. Stories varied in length from one to three sentences. Most, however, were only one sentence long. They were written by twenty-seven heterogeneously grouped children who attended a rural school in southeastern Wisconsin.

After copying all the sentences with spelling errors, each misspelled word was subsequently categorized according to particular sound-symbol relationships. The words in each category were then analyzed and discussed highlighting children's extraordinary abilities to "sound-out" words phonetically. The intrinsic problems of such an approach were also noted. Finally, generalizations concerning the limitations of "sounding-out" words were stated.

An Overview

Of the 619 misspelled words analyzed, 326 (53%) were "sounded-out" successfully according to the unique sound-symbol relationships children created. Another 211 (34%) words were not "sound-out" but would be phonetically acceptable if only one change were made. Such changes would involve (1) altering the order of letters *(srping–spring)*, (2) adding, subtracting or substituting consonants *(bowing–blowing; rinding–riding; tine–time)* or (3) adding or substituting vowels *(sumbud–somebody; clomer–climber)* respectively.

The remaining 82 (13%) words failed to evidence any logical spelling strategy *(iwt–to; gonh–going; alaa–apples;* and so on). The identity of these unrecognizable words was determined by using the contextual information found in the accompanying pictures and text. It should be noted, however, that 87% of the 619 words analyzed were either "sounded-out" (53%) or could have been with a single letter alternation (34%). It would appear that children are adept phonetic spellers.

The remainder of this article is an analysis of the 326 words that children "sounded-out" successfully. The analysis was limited to these words as they

---

From *Reading World*, Vol. 17 (March, 1978). ©1978 by the College Reading Association. Reprinted by permission.

An Analysis of the Words that Children "Sounded-Out"

As stated above, 326 (53%) of the 619 misspelled words of this study displayed children's uncanny abilities to "sound-out" words successfully by devising logical and many times ingenious sound-symbol relationships to express their thoughts in print. Read (1971) also found that children who have not learned the conventional spelling patterns of English orthography create their own unique spellings. The categorical lists of words and comments that follow demonstrate (1) the superb cognitive and language competencies children possess for spelling phonetically and (2) some of the limitations and difficulties inherent in such an approach when only lexical spellings are deemed acceptable.

Irregular Consonants and Digraphs— It can be seen in the lists that follow, that children have produced spellings which are logical and in many instances better than standard spellings if phonetic spelling is the desired outcome. In the first column, aren't *sity, dans, rasing, klowne, picknick,* and *sckool* better phonetically than the accepted spellings? Isn't the 'z' in *Jezus* and *timz* (column 2) a better phonetic representation of the given sound than "s"? Doesn't the abbreviated "ch" represent the same sound as "tch"? Aren't *noking* and *piking* (column 3) reasonable phonetic spellings? Does it make a difference phonetically if "ck" is represented by "c" or "kc"? Or if "k" is spelled with a "c" or "ck"? Note the unusual spelling of *ice* (ighs)* and working (whercing)*. In

```
       c                    s                    ck
      (s)                  (z)                   (k)
sity–city            Jezus–Jesus          noking–knocking
dans–dance           timz–times           piking–picking
ighs–ice*            hazs–has
rasing–racing


       c                    s                    ck
      (k)                  (c)                   (c)
klowne–clown         backit–basket        pic–pick
    (ck)             cic–sis              picing–picking
picknick–picnic      cnowman–snowman      sic–sick
      ch                   tch                  (kc)
    (ck)                  (ch)              blakc–black
sckool–school        cech–catch           pikcing–picking
                     haching–hatching
                     waching–watching

                                                  k
                                                 (c)
                                          cilde–killed
                                          bascet–basket
                                          whercing–working*
                                                 (ck)
                                          bicke–bike
                                          licke–like
                                          lick–like
                                          drck–dark
```

* Words referred to in the text which are not in sequential order according to the lists.

these two spellings children seem to be applying spelling patterns generalized from words such as *light* and *where* respectively.

Double Consonants—Most of the following spellings in which children failed to double consonants (columns 1 and 2) are more accurate phonetically than their lexical spellings. Linguists indicate that only one consonant sound is heard in words such as *robber, swimming, staff* and so forth. On the other hand, words where the consonant was doubled inappropriately (column 3) might reflect children's general awareness of the double-consonant phenomenon in English orthography. Is it wise to encourage children to "sound-out" words when the critical factor in spelling is to become aware of the way words pattern?

"Silent" Letters—The two categorical lists that follow again illustrate the ineffectiveness of "sounding-out" unfamiliar words—obviously it is impossible to "sound-out" "silent" letters. The spellings in the first column—*were* (where), *will* (whill), *with* (whith) and *working* (whercing), however, seem to indicate children's consciousness of the presence of "silent" letters in English orthography. It should also be noted that the spellings which delete the "silent" letters (columns 2 and 3) are better phonetic spellings than their standard representation.

Failed to Double Consonants
(should have)

Doubled Consonants
(shouldn't have)

rober–robber	swiming–swimming	dragg–drag
latr–ladder	runing–running	anumall–animal
sumr–summer	wining–winning	fell–feel
somre (of)–summer	dresing–dressing	untill–until
wopr–whopper	geting–getting	firrs–first
beter–better	puting–putting	woss (of)–was
buterflise–butterflies	gramaes–grammas	thiss–this
staf–staff		butt–but
eags–eggs	slipt–slipped	babby–baby
fel–fell	spodid–spotted	purpple–purple
wile–will		watter–water
acrose–across	Tamy–Tammy	lighttining–lightning
	bune–bunny	Dayvvid–David

Silent Letters Used

Silent Letters Not Used

wh	*b*	*h*
where–were	clim–climb	Cristmas–Christmas
whill–will	*u*	waet–what
whith–with	bilding–building	wen–when
whercing–working	*k*	witr–whiter
	now–know	wopr–whopper
	noking–knocking	

Endings of Words—The various spellings of the "ed" ending that follow (column 1) seem to indicate that children are aware that such words end with either the "d" or "t" sound. How many literate adults are aware of that fact? Most writers are probably not aware that the word *chased* ends with the same consonant sound as *cat*. Yet, many of the same persons would probably claim that they "sound-out" every letter of every word as they write.

Note the arbitrariness of "es" spellings (column 2) when words are "sounded-out." Also observe that the "s" in *appls* and *leavs* and the "se" in *buterflise* are more efficient phonetic spellings than "es." The letter "z" as in *timz* (times) is of course the most accurate phonetic representation of the desired sound.

Don't *mountin, appels* and *littel* (column 3) approximate their phonetic spellings in the dictionary more than their lexical entries?

Most children failed to drop the "e" before adding "ing" in words such as those listed below. Few such words were spelled correctly in the stories analyzed.

ed	*es*	*tain* (tin)
(de)	(s)	mountin–mountain
cilde–killed	appls–apples	
likde–liked	leavs–leaves	
rande–rained		*le* (el)
		appels–apples
	(se)	littel–little
(d)	buterflise–butterflies	
liivd–lived		
		Drop "e"—add "ing"
	(z)	comeing–coming
(t)	timz–times	danceing–dancing
chast–chased		diveing–diving
pikt–picked		haveing–having
slipt–slipped		makeing–making
		rideing–riding
		takeing–taking

Long and Short Vowels*—When correct spelling is not determined by the rules of orthography, which of the "long a" spellings that follow (columns 1 and 2) are more logical? That is, gr*a*n or gr*ai*n, th*a*yr or th*e*re, h*a*y or h*ey,* th*ai*r or th*eir,* b*a*r or b*ea*r and so on? Note that the "long a" in most of the remaining words (column 3) is spelled with either "ay" or "aa." This probably indicates children's perception of the two vowel sounds inherent in the so-called "long a." Finally, isn't *annts* (short "a" column) a better phonetic spelling than *aunts*?

It would appear that the following lists of "long e" spellings such as *bech* (beach), *leefs* (leafs) and *babe* (baby) (columns 1 and 2) are better phonetically than their standard spellings. Why are two "e's" needed in *feel, feeding* (column 3) and so forth? Doesn't the "o" in the word *people* and the "i" in *wierd* make such words less phonetic? Note the creative spelling of me–m*y* (puppy), tree–tr*y* (puppy), and eating–e*y*ting (puppy).*

All the spellings of the "short e" seem to be phonetically superior to traditional spellings—except for the unique spelling of eggs–*eags* (bread).*

---

* Because this study deals with phonetics as applied to teaching elementary children, diacritical marks will be limited to those commonly used in phonics.

CLASSROOM PRACTICES

Long a

(ai)
gran–grain
ran–rain
rande–rained
raning–raining
wating–waiting
wateing–waiting

(e, ey, ei and ea)
thayr–there
vary–very
Fairis Wehil–
   Ferris Wheel
hay–hey
thay–they
thair–their
bar–bear
baer–bear

(a–consonant–e)
mayd–made
nayme–name
praad–parade

(ay)
laayeing–laying
plaing–playing

(a–consonant–ing)
taaking–taking
waaking–waking

Short a

(au)
annts–aunts

Long e

(ea)
bech–beach
carem–cream
Ester–Easter
Eyting (puppy)–eating*
leefs–leafs
neet–neat
reeding–reading
screemed–screamed
teecher–teacher
yers–years

(y)
babe–baby
bune–bunny
cande–candy
evre–every
evreabote (read)–everybody
famle–family
prte–party
store–story
heveyie–heavy
redey–ready
verey–very

(ee, e, eo & ie)
fell–feel
feding–feeding
ned–need
tepy–tepee
tepes–tepees
Fairis Wehil–Ferris Wheel

pepl–people
werd–weird

my (puppy)–me
try (puppy)–tree

Short e

(e & ie)
eags (bread)–eggs*
frend–friend

(ea)
fethers–feathers
hed–head
heveyie–heavy
redy–ready

(ai)
agan–again

Observe in the lists which follow that two or more letters were used to represent the "long i" sound in words such as fi*h*er (fire), *igh*s (ice), wr*ie*t (write), fl*iy* (fly) and b*ih*e (buy). Here again children are probably hearing the two vowel sounds present in the "long i."

Notice the inspired spellings of *ice* (ighs),* *invited* (invighted)* and *like* (lighc).* It appears that some children have been impressed by the "igh" representation of the "long i" as in *light, fight* and so on.

---

*Because this study deals with phonetics as applied to teaching elementary children, diacritical marks will be limited to those commonly used in phonics.

CLASSROOM PRACTICES

Long i

(i–consonant–e)
fiher–fire
fiers–fires
fiherman–fireman
ighs–ice*
invighted–invited*
lighc–like*
wriet–write

(y)
fliy (puppy)–fly
fliying–flying
triying–trying
mie–my

(uy)
bihe–buy

Note children's spellings of the "long o" in the lists that follow. Aren't children's spellings of *bot* (boat), *bord* (board), *bloing* (blowing) and *dinusor* (dinosaur) (columns 1 and 2) better phonetic spellings than their lexical representations? Also observe that seven of these "long o" words were spelled with the double "o" (oo) which again seems to indicate children's perception of the two vowel sounds inherent in "long sounds".

Noa (know)* and *throghing* (throwing)* seem to provide more evidence that some of these first grade children are becoming aware of lexical spelling patterns.

Children's "short o" spellings of *are* (or), *want* (wont) and *watch* (woch) are perfect phonetic spellings, identical (ex-

Short i

liivd–lived

Long o

(oa)
bot–boat
bord–board
roored–roared
soop–soap

(ow)
bloing–blowing
noa–know*
throghing–throwing*

(au)
dinusor–dinosaur
dinusore–dinosaur
dinusoer–dinosaur

(o–consonant–e)
brooken–broken
houme (June)–home*
roop–rope
stoor–store

(o–consonant–er)
oover–over
pooster–poster

(oh)
ow–oh

Short o

(a)
or–are
wont–want
woch–watch

(o)
dra*p*ed (p*a*)–dropped*

*Because this study deals with phonetics as applied to teaching elementary children, diacritical marks will be limited to those commonly used in phonics.

267

CLASSROOM PRACTICES

Short u

(o)	(u)	(e)
bruther–brother	b*a*t (*a*bout)–but	th*a* (*a*bout)–the
cuming–coming	*a*ndr (*a*bout)–under	
dus–does	s*o*mre (*o*f)–summer*	
uv–of		

(a)
w*o*ss (*o*f)–was

cept for *are* [or]) to those found in the dictionary.

One wonders whether children's spellings of home–ho*u*me (J*u*ne)* and dropped–dr*a*ped (p*a*)* were intended as marked by the researcher or whether they were simply random spelling errors.

Children's spellings of *brother* (bruther), *coming* (cuming), *does* (dus) and *of* (uv) above (column 1) provide much improved phonetic spellings compared to their lexical representation. Also note the use of "a" (about) in b*a*t (but), *a*nder (under) and th*a* (the) (columns 2 and 3). The "o" in *woss* (was) and s*o*mre (summer)* represents the same vowel sound heard in the word *of*. Again, these relationships might not be the intent of the children but may represent random spelling mistakes.

tive sound-symbol choices, however, must be honored when the standard orthography rules are not considered. All spellings for the items listed are phonetically acceptable except possibly the last item—*shod* (should). Even in this instance, it would appear that the "o" in *shod* represents the given sound phonetically as well as the "ou" in *should*.

Gavir (gave her)* is one of the thirty-six instances in this study where children had difficulty determining whether they were hearing one word or two. This happens as words are a product of written language—oral language has no white spaces to group morphemes (smallest units of meaning) into words.

Final "e"—Most of the children's spellings in columns 1 and 2 which follow coincide exactly with the phonetic

	er, ir, or, ur		*ou*	$\overline{oo}$
(er)		(or)	(ou)	($\overline{oo}$)
gavir–gave her*		whercing–	fownd–found	sp*o*ky (l*o*se)
hir–her		working	owt–out	–spooky
hur–her				

			(ou)	oo
(ir)		(ur)	soop–soup	(ou)
berds–birds		hirt–hurt		cood–could
				shod–should

Other Vowel Sounds—A perusal of the spellings that follow again show the complications that surface when children "sound-out" unknown words. Alternate spellings in the dictionary. Unfortunately, such spellings are not acceptable even though they are "perfect" phonetic spellings.

---

* Because this study deals with phonetics as applied to teaching elementary children, diacritical marks will be limited to those commonly used in phonics.

CLASSROOM PRACTICES

Final "e" Not Used		Final "e" Used Incorrectly
cag–cage	befor–before	agine–again
cam–came	rop–rope	baskete–basket
gam–game	smok–smoke	Baske It–Basket
gav–gave		glade–glad
nam–name		Inedein–Indian
praad–parade	her–here	jame–jam
ras–race	thes–these	lafe–laugh
snak–snake		sike–sick
whal–whale	dans–dance	sisetr–sister
	hors–horse	tage–tag
	hous–house	wile–will
brid–bride		
lik–like		
outsid–outside	ar–are	wateing–waiting
slid–slide	becaus–because	inviteit–invited
tim–time	somthing–something	
valentins–valentines		acrose–across
		applse–apples
		klowne–clown
		Estre–Easter
		flowre–flower
		ovre–over
		overe–over
		sistre–sister
		somre (of)–summer

Spellings in the third column seem to indicate that children are aware of the final "e" phenomenon but have not applied it appropriately.

Schwa Sound—"Short vowel sounds" in unaccented syllables (schwa sound) are so similar that it is usually impossible to distinguish significant differences among them. The need for lexical spelling becomes apparent as one notes the inconsistent spellings of the schwa sound. That is, "e" is represented by "o" and "i" (column 1), "a" by "i," "a," "o" and "y" (column 2), "o" by "e," "i" and "u" (column 3) and so on.

Miscellaneous Categories—Because many teachers have emphasized the sound of "r" (er) and "l" (el), some children logically deleted the vowel preceding the final "r" and "l" in the following phonetic spellings, i.e., *brother* (bruthr) [column 1], *animals* (anamls) and *apples* (appls) [column 3] and so forth.

The effect of diverse pronunciations/dialect on phonetic spelling can be observed in the word lists that follow. Inconsistent spellings, however, are not a problem in a lexical system where dialects and standard pronunciations are represented by the same spelling. A Black child might pronounce *this* as *dis* but will use the standard spelling when writing. The same is true for the Easterner who pronounces *idea* as *idear*.

The remaining categories point out (1) the undesirable effect of pronouncing words very slowly—thus producing additional syllables and therefore distorted spellings, (2) the obvious problems encountered when trying to "sound-out" homophones which represent the same sounds with different symbols and (3) the difficulties faced when the sound of the name of the letter is used rather than the sound the letter represents. This results in the elimination of vowels such as *bhind* (behind), *drck* (dark), *tp* (teepee) and *u* (you).

CLASSROOM PRACTICES

Schwa

appols–apples	anamls–animals	lessen–lesson
backit–basket	anamils–animals	lessin–lesson
Baske It–basket	anumalls–animals	prsin—person
brookin–broken	Cristmis–Christmas	secent–second
opining–opening	dollors–dollars	
presint–present	Indiyn–Indian	decoratens–decorations
rockit–rocket	Inedein–Indian	tulup–tulip
spodid–spotted		
		dinusor–dinosaur
		dinusore–dinosaur
		dinusoer–dinosaur

r = er   l = e

brather (about)–brother	sistr–sister	anamls–animals
campr–camper	sisetr–sister	funerl–funeral
Estre–Easter	sistre–sister	appls–apples
Eastdr–Easter	sumr–summer	applse–apples
flowrs–flowers	somre (of)–summer	bumbl–bumble
flowre–flower	watr–water	mitl–middle
latr–ladder	witr–whiter	pepl–people

Diverse Pronunciations/Dialect

in–and	latr–ladder	cus–cause
brotter–brother	mitl–middle	becus–because
avra–every	secent–second	becuse–because
itsept–except	evreabote (read)–	
gavir–gave her	everybody	invitit–invited
git–get	bedder–better	inviteit–invited
cat-de-cat–kitty-cat	spodid–spotted	meltit–melted
leefs–leafs	decrading–	
are–our	decorating	ken–can
puppy play–	sea–she	cech–catch
puppet play	dis–this	
walken–walking		then–than

Slow—Distorted Pronunciations   Homophones

booys–boys	pepole–people	by–buy	won–one
clowen–clown	suiming–swimming	four–for	two–to
carem–cream	waet (pa)–what	no–know	to–two
Eastdr–Easter	yale–while	merry–Mary	
fiave–five			

Name of Letter Used as Sound

bhind–behind	tp–teepee
drck–dark	tps–tepees
prte–party	u–you

Perfect Phonetic Spellings—Sixty-eight (11%) of the words analyzed in this study were the same as the phonetic spellings in the dictionary—such as *babe–baby, wood–would, staf–staff, puting–putting, brid–bride, bot–boat* and so on. An additional 30 (5%) spellings were not phonetically perfect but much more consistent phonetically than their lexical spellings—such as *beter* (better), *cood* (could), *redy* (ready) and so forth. These were not considered phonetically perfect because of the irregular nature of vowel-*r, c,* final *y* and so forth.

The Wrap Up

The spellings analyzed in this study have demonstrated children's extraordinary abilities to "sound-out" words. Such ingenious abilities to produce phonetic spellings, however, do not alter the lexical nature of English orthography—the spellings generated are still unacceptable.

The spellings analyzed also seem to demonstrate that:
1. There are many ways a given sound can be represented in print. Therefore, one cannot be certain without prior knowledge of lexical spellings, that even a phonetically regular word such as "go" is not spelled goa, gow, goe, gough and so on.
2. Writers are dependent on a knowledge of the visual features of particular words and the way they pattern in the language.
3. It is highly improbable that "sounding-out" alone will produce lexical spellings.

The task seems even more futile when one considers the many dialects and diverse pronunciations of words in a pluralistic society. Is the "sound-it-out" way a reasonable approach for producing lexical spellings? Is it reliable? Is it advisable to encourage children to place their confidence in the "sound-it-out" strategy for producing unknown spellings?

This study does not infer, however, that children should not attempt to write words they don't know how to spell. It merely suggests that children be conditioned to think of spelling in terms of visual patterns and not be convinced that unknown lexical spellings can be produced solely by "sounding-them-out." The illusion that words can literally be "sounded-out" must be recognized and altered in deference to helping children discover the features of words and how they pattern in written language. "Sounding-out", however, will continue to be over-emphasized as long as teachers are convinced that it is not only possible but effective.

REFERENCES

Read, C. "Preschool Children's Knowledge of English Phonology." *Harvard Educational Review,* 1971, 41, 1–34.

Chomsky, C. "Reading, Writing and Phonology." In F. Smith (Ed.). *Psycholinguistics and Reading.* New York: Holt, Rinehart and Winston, Inc., 1973.

Helping Children with Spelling

KENNETH CADENHEAD
BARBARA ASHWANDER
MARVIN USSERY

For two years a personalized program in professional education built around a teacher role framework has been in operation at Auburn University. Students work through a modular program in achieving teacher competences subsumed under the roles of diagnostician, facilitator, interactor, and innovator. The instructional design module calls upon the student to construct educational goals, write instructional objectives, design criterion measures, and plan activities which meet learning requirements of the objectives. As a part of the process used in the module, students diagnose instructional needs of children, and then plan with the children specific activities which will assist them in achieving the instructional objectives.

The program also includes five modules which deal specifically with the teaching-learning strategies of questioning, demonstration, presentation, simulation-gaming, and discussion. As the students progress through these modules they gain a knowledge base for each strategy; they critique a videotape or film where the strategy is used; then they design and implement a lesson where they use the particular strategy with a group of children in a school setting.

The students spend a designated amount of time in a school on a scheduled basis, providing opportunities for them to follow through from initial planning to the implementation stage of the modules. They have many opportunities to work with children, thus assisting the classroom teacher and at the same time gaining valuable experience in their own preservice preparation program.

We worked with a group of special children whose achievement level was very low. The teacher in the school indicated that she would like us to help the children learn how to spell and write the twelve months of the year. With this particular content in mind, we then planned our work, using the basic ideas and processes included in the instructional design and teaching-learning strategies modules.

We began our work by giving the children a brief preview of our activities for the week. We showed them a large chart entitled "Be a Spelling Bee by Bringing the 'Honey Words' from Each Flower to the Beehive." Each time a child learned a new word, he or she would move up one step toward the beehive. This served as a successful motivation for the students. We then administered a pre-test to determine which words the children knew and to establish at what level they would be placed on the chart. This was also done so we would know whether to divide the class into groups according to their previous knowledge of the words. We then handed out a list of the words for study purposes during the week.

Before the presentation, we placed a bee with each child's name on it on the chart next to the number of words he or she spelled correctly on the pre-test. We then divided the class into two groups. One group was composed of children who missed more than five words; the other group was made up of children

---

From *Elementary English*, Vol. 52, No. 5 (May, 1975). © 1975 by the National Council of Teachers of English. Reprinted by permission.

who missed less than five words. This seemed to be the natural division from the results of the pre-test. We presented a chart showing the months of the year. We helped the children learn how to divide the words into syllables. To do this, we used a piece of pegboard and hooked the syllable cards onto it. Any variation of this could be used, but we found the pegboard very durable. The presentation was used mainly to introduce the words and break them down into syllables.

The second day we used demonstration as a strategy to reinforce the concept of syllables. We again reviewed the syllable breakdown of the words with the class as a whole this time. A "Rhythm Chart" was introduced which showed the syllable breakdown with colored paper strips and no letters. Each word was represented by different colors with each syllable being shown by a small strip of paper. We asked the children to clap out the rhythm of the words as they saw it on the rhythm chart. The class really become involved in this activity. We showed them how to use this method with other words that they found difficult to spell.

For the questioning part of the teaching experience, we asked the class fifteen questions concerning many aspects of the months of the year. The questions were designed to provoke thought and not just "yes" or "no" answers. An example: If you clap your hands four times for the word January because it has four syllables, how many times do you clap your hands for the word September? We used different levels of questions to help the children understand how they could remember the words.

On the final day of our program, we played a review game using the syllable cards from the pegboard. The children were seated in a circle and we passed out the syllable cards at random. Then, one by one, they got up and placed their syllable card on the appropriate position on the pegboard, thus building the words from the syllables.

	Pre-test	*Post-test*	*Week Later*
No. correct words			
Ruby	11	12	12
Annice	10	12	12
Chineta	10	12	11
Felicia	10	11	11
Leander	9	12	11
James	9	12	8
David	8	11	9
Cynthia	8	12	10
Monica	7	12	12
Greg	7	12	*
Raymond	7	12	12
Genna	6	11	10
Jill	6	9	10
Beverly	6	12	12
Debra	6	10	6
Freddie	6	*	10
Claude	5	12	8
Chris	5	11	9
Lisa	3	12	12
Mean	7.3	11.5	10

* Absent

After we completed the work with the different strategies, we gave the children a post-test. We were concerned that perhaps they might have just learned the words to "get the bee hive" or to pass the post-test. We decided to let the children write the words again a week later to see if they had retained them. The previous table shows the results of the pre-test, post-test, and the test which was given a week later.

Needless to say, the children were pleased with the results of this work. We

CLASSROOM PRACTICES

felt the experience was not only valuable to the children, but to us as prospective teachers as well. With the help of the children's teacher, we had diagnosed a problem area among the children, and we were able to use various strategies to help the children achieve goals which were identified.

How to Take the YUK Out of Spelling

CAROL J. FISHER
ROBERT RUBINSTEIN
VALERIE SELLERS
SHIRLEY T. SHRATTER
SALLY E. TODD

"KIDS CAN'T SPELL!" claim teachers and parents alike, and the entire country is up in arms wondering what to do about it. But for spelling—more so than for any other subject—teachers need a bag of tricks to get kids involved and motivated.

Here, Carol J. Fisher, INSTRUCTOR's language arts consultant, joins Robert Rubinstein, Valerie Sellers, Shirley Shratter, and Sally Todd, all teachers around the country, to describe their favorite games and those tried-and-true gimmicks that mean superspellers in the classroom!

Robert Rubinstein's word game addicts

I teach word games for a nine-week period. During the first four weeks, students work with crossword puzzles, find-a-word games, weird words, and other challenges. The second half of the course focuses on word-game competition. Each student must complete three crosswords and three find-a-words, with the option of completing as many more as he likes for extra credit. (One student recently completed 267 find-a-words and is still going strong!)

These word games are for the entire class, on one's own, or for the family at home. Some students wind up word-game addicts because the puzzles and games offer unique, personal, and fun ways to build a wide variety of language arts skills. Plus the materials and games are readily available at all skill levels.

Crosswords. Find crossword magazines of varying difficulty at your local newsstand or bookstore. There are crossword puzzles for synonyms, homonyms, and antonyms. Students must spell the answers correctly to solve the puzzles.

Every student then composes his own crossword puzzle of 20 words and 20 clues. The clues must offer clear and logical leads to the answers. The key to creating a crossword is to fill in the answer first and make up the clues to fit. A search in the dictionary may lead to some unusual words.

Find-a-word. These puzzle magazines are also on the newsstands, varying in difficulty and approach. They are especially fun for below-average students who might find crosswords frus-

From *Instructor*, Vol 87, No. 8 (March, 1978). Reprinted by permission.

trating. A student scans a page searching for a group of key letters and learns to recognize a word whether it's printed backward, diagonally, horizontally, or vertically.

Most find-a-word puzzles focus on particular topics, such as holidays, presidents, or famous people. Students find 20 to 40 words concerning that topic. They are given clues and hints. (Some students may need help with the more difficult ones.)

Each student then constructs an original find-a-word of 20 items on a specific topic; the names of old-time baseball teams, for example, or tennis champions. The encyclopedia is a ready source for words on a topic.

Weird words. Do you know what a *fipple* is? *Radix? Helve? Nauplius?* These are "weird words" in the dictionary. A student must find 25 weird words and give for each the part of speech, a definition, and the correct use of the word in a weird sentence. For example, *"Fipple, noun, a plug near the mouthpiece of certain wind instruments. When the musician saw the monkey, he swallowed his fipple!"*

The best source for weird words is a dictionary like *Webster's New World*. Junior high and secondary school dictionaries are not good sources.

Other word challenges. You'll find other word activities in these books: *An Almanac of Words at Play* by Willard R. Espy (Potter) and *Word Play* by Joseph T. Shipley (Hawthorn).

There are also games on additives. For example, add a *d* in front of a kind of liquor (*rum*), and a *b* in front of *eat* to get an African rhythm. Answer: *d* plus *rum* and *b* plus *eat* equals *drumbeat!*

Reverse verses are also intriguing. For example: "In the dark of the night, I may scamper by./Turn me around, I shine in the sky." Answer: *rats* and *star*.

Students can also attempt alpha-sentences. Write a series of sentences with each word in the sentence starting with a consecutive letter of the alphabet. For example: *A bear called Dan entered five gates happy in jumping Kansas. Lately, Molly needs Oregon peas quietly rolling somewhere to understand various ways xeroderma yaps zithers.* The sentences are often strange but the words are used as correct parts of speech.

Word-game competition. In the second half of the nine-week course students are forced to think quickly. Each student must accumulate 450 points in each of four- or five-word game competitions.

Word games include Password, Ad-Lib, Scrabble Crossword game, Probe, and Anagrams. Every time students play games, they add points to those scored in previous games. Even if they lose, they build up credit points. Several students have broken the 1,000-point barrier in "Ad-Lib"!

"Spill" that word, shouts Valerie Sellers

I realized spelling was more than a little problem in my class when several of my third-grade students labeled their papers "spilling." I decided to tackle the subject with new techniques to make the lessons more enjoyable and worthwhile. I added new games and gadgets to the curriculum. But first I didn't throw out my spelling book entirely. I employed these new tricks!

1. Since students have such trouble understanding even the directions for spelling assignments, I assigned one student to explain the various sections before they are tried. Kids loved it!

2. To make sure each child understands the definitions of words used, the class develops its own dictionary of spelling words. Each child is assigned one or two words to define and write on a duplicating master. Everyone receives a copy of the material for his notebook. Each week pupils add to the list and use their dictionaries in other subjects as well.

3. An additional weekly spelling test was added. A child who has difficulty on

Thursday receives an additional chance to try for a perfect paper on Friday. Those successful the first time are rewarded with extra time to enjoy a game or book. Parents comment that their children show a greater interest in spelling with the extra incentive to achieve a perfect score. The tests with perfect scores are displayed each week.

We added games to the learning experience to capture the children's attention. Here are some games my students particularly enjoyed.

Spelling bee. Vary the traditional spelling bee to give extra practice to poor spellers. When a word is missed, the child does not go to his seat but to the end of the line where he will be called upon again. A point is scored against his team. The game ends at a predetermined time with the winning team the one with the fewest points.

Alphabet game. Letters of the alphabet are distributed to children. A leader calls a word and those having the letters for that word form a line in front of the room, holding their letters to spell the word correctly. Redistribute letters frequently so that all class members get a chance to participate in the game.

Spell around. Ask the pupil in the first seat to spell a word you pronounce. Continue around the room and do not stop when a word is misspelled. If the next pupil who follows notices the error, he corrects the mistake. The one who does correct it has "trapped" all the pupils preceding him.

Spelling tic-tac-toe. This is played like the original tic-tac-toe game except with two teams. Make a large tic-tac-toe board on the chalkboard. A leader pronounces a word to the first person on Team One. If the word is spelled correctly, that person goes to the chalkboard and fills in either *X* or *O*. If the word is spelled incorrectly, the same word is pronounced to the first person on Team Two. Continue back and forth until a team wins diagonally, up, down, or across.

Ruler tap. A student comes to the front of the room and chooses a word from a spelling list. He pronounces the word to the entire class and then taps a ruler or pointer until reaching one of the letters in the word. He calls on another who must first tell him the letter he stopped at and then spell the whole word correctly. If he does both correctly, he gets a chance to be the "tapper." If he makes a mistake, another child is chosen to correct the mistake.

For example, the word *clock* might be chosen. The child pronounces the word *clock* and taps the ruler three times. He then chooses a child who must tell him that the ruler stopped on the letter *o* and then spell *clock* correctly.

Spelling relay. The class is divided into two or more teams. Each child is given a slate. The leader pronounces a word and the first person on each team writes the word on his slate. The team member who correctly writes the word first (and so that it is readable) scores a point for his team. The team with the most points wins.

With the use of these activities and games your class will enjoy and improve its "spilling."

Dr. Fisher's favorite bag of tricks

Games make subjects requiring repetition practice livable and more enjoyable. Spelling is certainly that kind of subject. Here are some spelling games to try or they may inspire you to invent others. Be sure all your games, though, actually promote spelling. I have three rules of order:

1. **Write the words!** People do not spell orally except in artificial situations. Words are usually written out or seen in print. Children need to develop a visual image of words, to learn when a word "looks right." A very common game that is sometimes abused is the spelling bee because words are spelled aloud but then are not written, or because poorer spellers generally get the least practice.

2. **Poor spellers should participate**

CLASSROOM PRACTICES

in games, too! If games are to develop skills, leave no one out!

3. **Spell! spell! spell!** A game should promote spelling—not phonics for reading or activities for vocabulary development.

Some of the games below are for individuals, partners, small groups of two to five, large groups, or the whole class and a leader. Adapt all the games to the age level and ability of your students.

The Super Square. Super Square, a version of tic-tac-toe, is for two or four players, each with a partner. The object is to get five squares in a row (horizontally, vertically, or diagonally) before the opponent.

easy, medium, and hard. Each player tells an opponent which level to select.

As in the illustration, colors are placed so that one would have to spell one hard word, two medium, and two easy ones to get five in any direction.

Change the words frequently. Use chips, silver and copper paper clips, pieces of colored paper, and so on, as markers. Write the words on small chalkboards, laminated posterboard, or simply old scraps of paper.

Matches. This board game, for two or four players, is a spelling version of a television game. Children call out two numbers to find a matching pair of words.

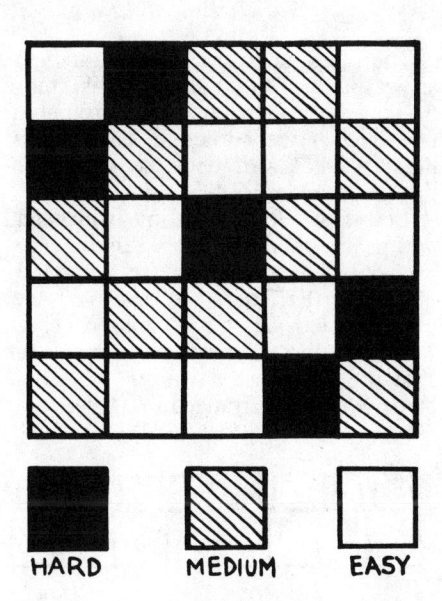

First, words and sentences are printed on cards or slips of paper. A player draws a card, and reads the word and the sentence. His opponent then writes the word. If the spelling is correct, he marks whatever square he chooses. Then the first player spells a word drawn.

Older children may prefer squares in three colors representing easy, medium, or hard words. Use three sets of words—

The top card is plain on one side and has a number on the other side. The card underneath has a word on it. If the correct pair is chosen the player gets five points and the cards are reversed to display a plain side.

When one player or team matches they may call another pair of numbers and continue until they fail to match a pair. Then it is the opposing player or team's turn. The game ends when all pairs are matched. The winner is the person or team with the most points.

Make your board out of heavy poster cardboard. Staple or glue strips of cardboard on it to form 20 pockets that hold two cards each. If you can see through the cards, glue two together or cover with a patterned paper. By having the words to be matched on separate cards, they can be changed by rearranging them between games.

In the illustration, the board is shown with a correct match of the homophones *write* and *right,* numbers 8 and 19. In addition to homophones, the game could match different spellings of the same sound or sets of the same words.

The Big Board. This is a game for small groups. Each player has a personal marker to move along as he spells a word correctly. Each child draws a card with a word on it, reads it for the next player who in turn must spell it correctly.

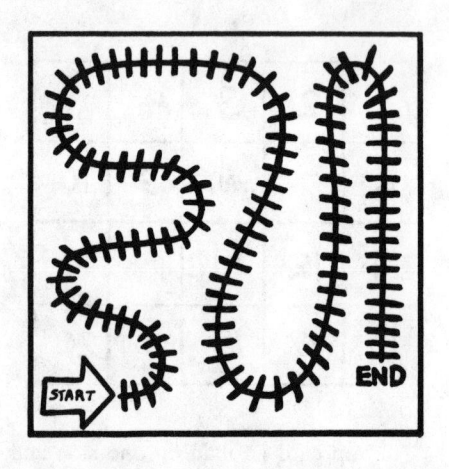

If not spelled correctly, that player loses a turn. Each card has a word, a sentence containing it, and the number of spaces to move if correct. Some cards may say, "LOSE A TURN" or "FREE MOVE: FIVE SPACES." Younger children might have a board with 30 or 40 spaces from start to finish with the words giving moves of two, three, or five spaces. Older children might have 50 or 60 spaces.

Ghoti. This card game is like Fish involving two to five children who try to get pairs of cards to match. Each player is dealt seven cards (five if more than four play). The rest are placed facedown and drawn later.

The dealer starts by asking the next player, "Do you have any _____?" If that person has the word, he must give the card requested. Otherwise, the first player must draw a card from the pile. (You must have one card of the kind you ask for.) The second player asks the next player what he or she wants, and the game continues.

The pairs are various spellings of the same sound. Thus, the cards, like those in the illustration, feature a sound or phoneme at the corner in slash marks, the word below it with the spelling of the sound underlined.

Letter-O. Play this game with small groups of children or the entire class. The object is to spell a word correctly before all the letters are displayed. For example, look at the illustration below. The first three letters of a word are showing. The base has a pocket to hold cards which are arranged in a long row.

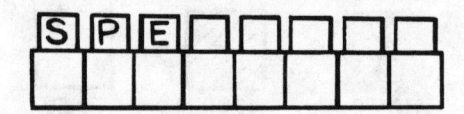

Your librarian may have book pockets you can use. Cut and glue to a heavy strip of posterboard. Put $3'' \times 5''$ cards in them each with a single letter at the top of one side. Arrange cards, one to a pocket, so the plain side is showing and the letters of the correctly spelled word are on the opposite side.

Players take turns guessing what letters might be in the word. If their guess is correct, the letter is revealed and they may guess again. If it is wrong, they lose their turn to the next person or team.

Findit. Here's a game a large group or whole class can play with a skilled leader. Use rows of pockets like the previous game and 3" × 5" cards.

The game begins with all the letters showing. The leader calls out a synonym or definition of a word. Players try to find it in the maze of letters. They answer by giving the row and pocket number of the first letter of the word and then they say the word and spell it. For example, the leader says, "opposite of bottom." Players respond row 1, number 7 *top,* T-O-P; or "a curved entry" is row 2, number 20, *arch,* A-R-C-H; or "birds build a _____," is in row 1, number 4, *nest,* N-E-S-T.

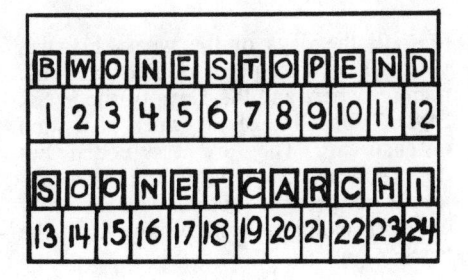

B	W	O	N	E	S	T	O	P	E	N	D
1	2	3	4	5	6	7	8	9	10	11	12
S	O	O	N	E	T	C	A	R	C	H	I
13	14	15	16	17	18	19	20	21	22	23	24

Properly structured and varied, games are both fun and good practice for developing spelling skills.

"Spelling chairs" from Shirley Shratter

This game is similar to Musical Chairs and The Boiler Burst, but you use the week's spelling words. In the fourth grade, we use 20 words. Students first become familiar with all the words. Each child takes a turn saying the word, spelling it, and using it in a sentence. Then we begin our game.

Spelling books are left open on the desks. The child who is "it" secretly chooses one of the spelling words and walks around the room telling a story he has made up. Whenever he mentions one of the spelling words, everyone changes seats. During this game, students constantly scan the spelling list in front of them so they will recognize a word immediately and be able to move faster than the others. This is an efficient and enjoyable way to expedite the process of learning to recognize words and learn the meaning of words when first presented.

Sally Todd and her label fanatics

The phrase heard most in my room is "Who Can Spell It?" As a result my second graders are able to spell common words advanced for their years and they *enjoy* spelling!

We start by labeling every object in our room, including the door, window, closet, and so on. We have mini-lessons throughout the day by my merely saying, "Who can spell . . . *closet,* or *carpet,* or *shades?*" Students try without looking at the word and even the slowest spellers feel success with this practice.

This approach grew out of observing children learning to read and learning a foreign language. In reading, some words are learned merely by memorization. These are usually words that are not phonetic, such as the word *beautiful.* The more meaning the word has for the child, though, the more apt he is to learn it—and remember it. Children learn to read *Halloween* and *Christmas* very quickly.

Do not use words with which children have little experience. What second grader has ever encountered the word *mansuetude?* But sometimes I add words new to kids just for the sheer fun of it. (Millions of children learned to spell the word *antidisestablishmentarianism* this way.)

The technique can be adapted successfully to intermediate as well as primary situations. Follow these guidelines:

1. Label all objects possible in the room clearly.
2. Begin slowly. Label words of objects in the classroom first and then

CLASSROOM PRACTICES

branch out to include other spelling words.
3. Make sure words are familiar to all children.
4. Use the phrase "Who can spell it?" several times a day for reinforcement.
5. Keep the atmosphere casual. I find that spelling a word on a volunteer basis works well.
6. Have the children work with partners for practice.
7. Call on slower children for easier words like *rug*, for example.
8. Ask students themselves to volunteer words and make up a chart of them.

Make spelling a positive subject with your class, and you will see the difference in success!

Teacher-Made Tapes Provide Auditory Aids

ANN SOFGE

Children can be either auditory, visual or kinesthetic learners. But to separate learning into those three divisions will almost surely lead to failure for most students. If one sees a child who is primarily an auditory learner, it is still best to supplement his program with visual and kinesthetic supports. The following methods show how auditory tapes can support visual and haptic approaches. They are not difficult to make, and students work well with them.

The first is the "Days of the Week" tape. Many students on a secondary level feel the need to be able to perform simple "survival-type" tasks. They don't have the equipment to do this on their own. Hence, it is wise to teach them those kinds of daily abilities which will make them more proficient in the eyes of their peers.

The teacher begins the tape by saying, "This is the tape in which you will learn to spell the days of the week. For this you will need magic markers or crayons, tracing paper, and the Days of the Week cards." One day of the week is written on each card. They are color coded, but the colors used are immaterial. The object is to show in contrast the auditory cue. For example, with Wednesday, the teacher says:

The auditory cue for Wednesday is Wed-nes-day. You all know how to spell "day," d-a-y; so all you have to learn is "Wed" and "nes." From now on when I say Wednesday, I want you to think "Wed-nes-day."

The teacher then says:

Put your tracing paper over the card which says "Wednesday"–Wed-nes-day. Trace over each letter while I say it. W-e-d, change color, n-e-s, change color, d-a-y. Wed-nes-day, Wednesday.

Another example of how the auditory cue can work is with the word Saturday. The directions are the same for Saturday. But a secondary auditory cue is given. The teacher says, "You all know how to spell *day* and you know how to spell *sat*, s-a-t. Remember on Saturday you are

---

From *The Pointer*, Vol. 20, No. 2, pp. 41-45. Copyright © 1975. A publication of the Helen Dwight Reid Educational Foundation. Reprinted by permission of Heldref Publications, 4000 Albemarle Street, N.W., Washington, DC 20016.

happy. Saturday is spelled Sat–u–r–happy–day." Most students, once they have used this method, never forget how to spell it.

The children do this tape daily until they are ready to take a test. Having taken the test, and succeeded, they can go to the months of the year. The months are color coded and auditorily cued, the same as the days of the week.

The important thing is that the student sees the large word broken up. He notices "Wed" perhaps in green, "nes" in purple, "day" in red. As the teacher says the letter "W" he is tracing a "W." This gives him a visual and tactile cue to the auditory sound of *Wednesday,* Wed-nes-day.

Dictation

The second auditory tape is for Dictation. The teacher can devise sentences, for example, using the Dolch words. She says on the tape to the student:

This is the Dictation tape. For this tape you will need lined writing paper, tracing paper, a pen or pencil, a chalkboard and chalk, and the cards A1 through 5 with the dictation sentences written on them. Sentence number one is "Today I will clean the house." Look at that sentence on the dictation card, A1. Today—I—will—clean—the—house. See how the sentence starts with a capital letter and ends with a period. Put your tracing paper over the dictation card, and write each word while I say it. Today—I—will—clean—the—house. Be sure you remember the period. Now take the tracing paper away and on your lined paper write the sentence while I say it. Today—I—will—clean—the—house. Remember your period and capital letter.

What is important here is the student may look at the card as many times as he needs to. It is important that the teacher provides a model and does not allow him to fail. He has traced it and then he has written it on his own, but he always has the model he can look at.

Next the teacher says to the student:

Now I want you to make sure you have a clear area on your desk. Write on your desk with your two finger tips each word while I say it. Today—T-o-d-a-y, I—will—w-i-l-l, clean—c-l-e-a-n, the—t-h-e,

house—h-o-u-s-e period. Today I will clean the house.

Next the teacher says to the student, "Now take the card, if you need it, to the board and write the sentence on the board. Ask the teacher to check it to make sure you wrote it exactly right."

The Dictation tape deals with five short sentences at a time. When the student feels he is ready to take the test, the teacher dictates it. If he misses a sentence, or is having trouble with certain words, it is important that the teacher do this: sit down with the child, both with headsets on, listening to the tape. If the student is right-handed, the teacher sits on his right side. She writes the sentence in a bright magic marker color while it is dictated, has him watch, then plays the tape back. He will hear the sentence and will trace over the sentence she had written. The next day, if he feels he is ready, he will take the dictation test again. The same method is followed. If he needs the model, the teacher once again writes the sentence and he traces it.

Flashcard, letter recognition

Another tape for auditory learners is the Flashcard tape. It consists of words taken from the Dolch list. The teacher says on the tape to the students:

This is the Flashcard tape. You will need flashcards one through five, tracing paper, magic marker, a plain piece of writing paper, chalkboard and chalk. The first word on the flashcard is "fight." Look at the word on your flashcard. I want you to think from now on when you hear the word "fight" *fig*(hyphen) *h*(hyphen)*t*. From now on when you hear the word *fight* you will say *fig-h-t*. Take another look at that word. See the little word "fig," the *h,* and then *t*.

On the back of the flashcard is a picture found in an old book or magazine that shows a fight. Say to the student:

See the fight. Now turn the flashcard over. Look at that word again. *Fig-h-t*. Put your tracing paper over the card and write each letter while I say it.

CLASSROOM PRACTICES

Fight. F-i-g, change color, h-t. And again, f-i-g, change color, h-t. Good. Now clear a space off on your desk and shut your eyes. With your two fingers write the letters on the desk while I say them. Close your eyes and try to see that word. *Fight.* F-i-g, h-t. Now go to the board, take the flashcard if you need it, and write the word *fight*.

When the student has finished all the flashcards one through five for the first tape, he asks the teacher to check to make sure he has copied the words correctly.

The next tape is for Letter Recognition. This is best used with the student who has been unable to remember the visualization of a particular letter in the alphabet, for example, a "b." If you know the child cannot remember the direction in which a small letter "b" goes, and he is an auditory learner, this tape may be appropriate. The teacher says to the student:

This is the Letter Recognition tape for the letter "b." You will need the "B" Master Sheet, magic markers, tracing paper, and sandpaper letter "b." I am going to say the letter "b." Every time I say it, you trace one of the b letters on the Master Sheet. (The master sheet has fifteen b's on it with a large capital B on the top.) Ready, begin. b-b, etc.

The teacher leaves enough time in between so she is certain the student can trace that letter at his own pace. At the time he has finished the fifteen b's on the B Master Sheet, the teacher says, "Now take the sandpaper (or felt or carpet) letter and trace over it with your two fingers while I say it." At that point the tape repeats "b" five times and the student traces the sandpaper, felt or carpet letter while she says it.

Other tapes

Another tape is for auditory closure and is called Make the Sentence Right. In it the student does five sentences at a time. There are five flashcards with "A" written on the back. Color code the cards so everyone knows they belong in the same group. On the other side of each card is a different picture. These could each belong in a sentence to make it sound right or to complete it. For example, let's say the pictures were of a kite, a grandmother, a bicycle, the color green, and a smile.

The students have those five pictures on their desks and the tape says:

"Tomorrow I will go fly a   ." Choose the picture which would make the sentence right and put a number one in the corner.

Sentence number two would be:

"I like to ride my   ." Choose the picture which would make the sentence right and put a number two in the corner.

Sentence number three would be:

"My mother wears a   sweater on cold days."

The color green is chosen to make the sentence right. The fourth sentence states:

"I always   at my Dad." Put a four on the card which would make this sentence right.

The last sentence says:

"Tomorrow I will visit my   at her farm." Put a five by the picture which makes the sentence right.

Then the teacher says to the student, "Listen to the sentences one more time and look at the pictures you chose to make sure they fit." The student goes through five pictures at a time. Gradually, they become a little more difficult. Eventually he will have to make a decision in the middle of the tape as to one of two pictures which would be more accurate or make more sense.

The Auditory-Visual Recognition tape follows the concept that before a student can recognize a word he has heard, he can recognize its picture. In this tape a student is told he has a card in front of him that he is to put face down. Then a word will be dictated to him. After a brief delay the teacher will say, "Turn

CLASSROOM PRACTICES

the card over and draw a circle around the picture of the word you say.'' After the student has done this through, perhaps, the Dolch list of nouns, he can try hearing the word and finding it in its written form.

An example would be the dictated word "hand." The student turns over his card and sees four pictures: a hand, a ham, a heart, and a fan. His directions are to circle the picture of the word he heard. In this instance he would circle the hand.

The last tape is the Sound of the Letter. The student has cards with pictures. When he is asked auditorily to discriminate the initial, the final, and the blend consonants, he has the visual cue of the picture to aid him. Eventually the pictures are removed and he must use only his ears. For example, the student has five cards in front of him. He is asked to write the letter of the sound with which the word begins. One of the cards has the color yellow on it, and the tape says:

Look at card A1. Look at the picture on it. Write *A1* on your paper. I will say the word and you will write the letter which makes the sound at the beginning of that word. Yellow. Yellow.

The same directions are given for the final consonant, for an example, the word jump. The tape will say:

Write A8 on your paper. Look at the card A8 and the picture on it. Write the letter of the sound which comes at the end of the word *jump*. Jump.

An example of a blend would be "fly." The student looks at a picture which has a fly on it. He writes A12 on his paper and is asked to write the two letters which make one sound at the beginning of that word. Then, the same auditory discrimination is tested, but without any picture clues or visual clues. The student is asked to listen for initial, final, and blending sounds.

Through tapes students can get the individual help they may be needing. A considerable amount of teacher time is required initially to make them for those who need one-to-one attention. However, as time goes on, and more students appear to need the same kinds of skills, the tapes can be reused. Through this kind of development, it is possible for the teacher to give encouraging notes to the students. For example, "You have done really well." In many cases she may want to tell the students exactly what they have done well, "You have recognized the initial sounds very well." Students achieve better when they understand exactly what they are accomplishing.

We deal with children who are involved in the media of sound. Many of them can remember well all the words to a song, although they might not be able to read them. By combining the auditory strengths of students with visual helps and haptic involvement, we give them the opportunity to learn more thoroughly, and to retain facts and concepts for a longer period of time.

In Spelling We Try Harder

PATRICIA CAMPANILE-HAPP

Last year my two partners in the fifth grade and I switched from a traditional self-contained teaching style to a limited version of specialization. The idea for this move was ours and the rationale behind it was to give our students an opportunity to learn from teachers who had a strong background in a particular field.

This arrangement gave me a chance to implement a dream project of mine: a fifth-grade remedial spelling class that emphasized improvement in written communication skills. My method was to abandon the old spelling lists and use the children's interest in certain areas to compile a reservoir of words. The children were then encouraged to use these special interest words in creative writing.

My class was comprised of those children who, based on last year's teacher's report and on present observations, displayed a retardation of at least a year and a half in spelling and were generally "turned off" to the subject. Based on this knowledge, coupled with findings from informal reading tests, I selected students that I knew had the ability to produce fifth-grade work, but at the time were neither reading nor spelling at that level.

These children also displayed nonwriting behavior. A nonwriter may be a student who feels shy and insecure about writing efforts, and/or a student who makes gross spelling errors.

At the time of selection, I could foresee a problem in having too many students in the class. In order to make the situation more conducive to learning, I had to limit the number. I concentrated on taking only the poorest of the poor spellers/writers, who were not already receiving help from our speech clinician or resource-room teacher. Those children remaining were given routine eye and hearing examinations to rule out any problems that hadn't been caught in previous years. Finally, with this process completed, my class consisted of 18 children. The majority of these students had been placed at spelling levels from one and a half to two years behind grade level; two had been placed three years behind. With the players assembled, we were ready to begin.

A letter explaining the remedial spelling program was sent to the parents. This letter informed them of the plan to have their children participate in a group with other children who were having difficulty in spelling. Emphasis was placed on getting parental help in providing each child with a secure environment, one that advocated patience and understanding. I related my experiences with poor spellers to the parents. I told them that I had found that these students were often very much aware of their spelling problems, and subsequently self-conscious about sharing their written work. I told the parents that if we could build their self-confidence, they would be ready to make real headway.

Besides setting up a secure environment, I had to structure learning conditions so that early in the program my students could see immediate improvement, no matter how small the gain. I used not only their work, but also a positive change in attitude, toward themselves or their work, as an indication of improvement. I also tried to provide the children with lessons that would give them the satisfaction of actually completing an assignment, something that was a much shared concern.

When we first met and discussed our course of action many students expressed feeling "uptight" because they might not be able to complete assign-

---

From *Instructor*, Volume 89, No. 4 (November, 1979). Reprinted with permission.

ments in the proper way or hand them in on time. We discussed in general, the length of assignments and the amount of time it would take to complete them. We decided not to be too rigid on coming up with a standard length and date due; we would do the best we could.

Our group quickly adopted a slogan: "We try harder!" We established a daily working time of 30 minutes for instruction and 15 minutes for review.

During the first group instruction, we chose a topic from which to build our spelling list. Can you guess what was most interesting to my ten-year-olds? Why food, of course! We came up with the following words:

soda	french fries
drink	McDonald's
milk	Hardee's
coffee	Gino's
diner	mayonnaise
potatoes	spinach
lettuce	teriyaki
knife	hamburger
napkin	ketchup (catsup)
beef	gratuity
salad	mustard
entree	menu
dessert	vegetables

Each word list was treated as a spelling unit. The amount of time spent on a list was proportionate to the length and difficulty of the list.

All spelling words were introduced on cassette tape. This allowed the children to hear the correct pronunciation of each word and provided an atmosphere in which the student would not be distracted by outside noises.

Never was a spelling word introduced in isolation. Upon introduction, words were always used in sentences. This showed the students how to use the words in their proper context and also encouraged the use of complete sentences in expression.

After listening to the cassette, the children were given a pretest. Words misspelled by a student were placed on index cards and filed in his own file-card box.

Weekly upkeep of the card files was a must. Any word placed in front of the blue divider card was a word that had yet to be mastered. Any word placed behind the blue card, of course, was mastered. Twice a month, mastered cards were reviewed and rhyming or family words added on the back of the card for the child to spell, thus increasing spelling vocabulary. (During conference time, the child and I would make up sentences that included these additional words.)

These cards were also used in spelling games such as War. In War, each child holds another's card box and asks the owner of the words to either spell a word, spell a family word, put a given word in a sentence, or supply a meaning for a word in the card box. The child who is able to do this for the most cards wins.

I tried to center different kinds of lessons around each spelling list. The lessons worked with rhymes, word structure, and even word origins. The building of word families was often a crucial lesson for a list of words because it reinforced phonetic patterns and enabled students to apply these patterns to yet unfamiliar words.

After completing these lessons, the students wrote stories and poems using the spelling list words. In the case of the food list, we also used the words to design our own menu and to prepare a shopping list. (This last project came in handy later in the year when we had a fifth-grade international luncheon.)

In later weeks, the children's interest led them to household words, words used in the construction trade, television words, and sports words. Some of the children moved on to interests of their own such as weightlifting and photography. I tried to devise special projects for each of the word units. For instance, we learned how to use all the tools mentioned in the construction trade list. We also had a guest speaker teach us how to read simple blueprints, and subsequently, we made our own.

The students also made their own

CLASSROOM PRACTICES

spelling books that had word finds, crossword puzzles, word jumbles, complete-the-sentence, and correct-the-paragraph lessons in them. Basically used as fun homework assignments, the lessons served as a good review and reinforcement of the list words. By the end of the year, every member of the class, including the teacher, was purchasing jumble books or doing jumbles found in the newspapers. It got to be that the last few minutes of every day were devoted to working on jumbles.

Mondays and Wednesdays were conference days. On each day I held nine conferences. While the other students were completing individual work, I would sit down with one student, review his work from the past week, and discuss his outlook on what he had or had not accomplished during that time. Then the two of us would plan an individual course of action for the next week.

Every Friday was our Spill-n-Spell (a popular box game) tournament where three contestants would have five chances to reach a score of 100. At first, the scores were low and errors were made, but students soon caught on. Toward the end of the year they were abandoning the three-letter words and were becoming more adventurous by experimenting with the five-, six-, and seven-letter words, thus increasing their scores considerably.

Even the conventional spelling tests, when given, were unconventional in that the children wrote the entire sentences being dictated. Each sentence contained as many of their spelling words as possible. Such a test provided children with practical experience in spelling as well as in punctuation, and complete sentences.

As you can see from these numerous activities, I tried to make learning enjoyable for my students. If I wanted them to look forward to coming each day, I had to add just enough spice so that those necessary but monotonous activities wouldn't overwhelm them.

By midspring, the group was confident enough in spelling to undertake a big writing challenge—a group newspaper. One of the children brought in his typewriter, and along with the librarian's and my own, we had our equipment. All the children were given a one-week crash course in typing. As for the various news positions, we decided that we would rotate positions for each issue so that each child got a chance at being a reporter, an editor, a typist, and a proofreader. Our paper had straight news columns as well as sports articles, editorials, and critiques of books, movies, and television shows. We even had a column on gourmet cooking!

This article really has no ending because most of the children are still participating in the program, even though they have all moved on to the sixth grade. Last year four children were capable of making the move to the regular spelling group by the end of the second marking period.

In the future, I hope the program will be used to move children in and out of our group, whenever the need arises. I want to make the program a place for the children to touch base when they need that extra help.

Spelling, Word Attack Skills

TIMOTHY R. BLAIR

In the teachers' lounge tomorrow morning give your cohorts a quick spelling test. Ask them to spell the following words: "penicillin," "picnicking," "penitentiary," and "sacrilegious." It's a good bet that there won't be too many perfect scores. We are all aware of the complexities of the English language that render spelling a complicated process at best. However, educators have long considered spelling an important goal in the elementary school (Benthul, 1970). That success in reading and success in spelling are related has been empirically demonstrated and reported in the professional literature. Leo Fay (1971) reported that poor readers are often poor spellers, but good readers may or may not be poor spellers. Fay suggested that part of the reason for the seeming conflict here may be that spelling requires precise knowledge of individual letter combinations whereas meaning in reading can often be obtained from context as well as from the makeup of individual words.

Variance in students' spelling achievement and teachers' awareness of this variance are well documented. With present emphasis on teaching the language arts in relation to each other, spelling and reading are now seen as complementing one another. Evidence of the interrelationship and interdependence between word attack skills and spelling is demonstrated not only in new materials and instructional techniques but also in recent research. The great majority of research completed in the area of spelling instruction and word attack skills has dealt with attempts to account for the observed variance in spelling achievement and attempts to reduce this variance. The bulk of the research in both these areas has centered on methodological variables.

Studies attempting to account for the variance in spelling achievement are greatest in number. Leo Cohen (1969) evaluated various structural analysis methods used in spelling books. The study measured how spelling textbook word-study exercises that call attention to word structure and phonic elements affect learning to spell, retention of learned spelling, and transfer of learned spelling to usage. It was found that structural approaches to spelling which call attention to word-form changes result in more spelling errors than techniques which call only for usage of the words. On the retention test, the structural approach was somewhat favored over usage approaches. In transfer of spelling to usage, usage techniques were favored, but not as statistically significant.

The purpose of a study by Roberta White and Elaine Treadway (1973) was to determine the effects of treatment and prior achievement on spelling proficiency and retention among fifth grade students by comparing three instructional strategies: traditional, word-analysis, and rules generalization. Results indicated that none of the strategies tested was significantly more efficient, and retention over a seven-day time period surpassed the proficiency achieved following the instructional period.

James Frost (1973) investigated the developmental nature of linguistic knowledge revealed in children's spelling. The analysis showed that fewer errors are made as the child progresses through school, and such subtleties as vowel allophones and alternations of letters by position are learned by the twelfth grade. Second graders render more unrecognizable words, make more substitutions, and make more errors than children at any other grade level. The

---

From *The Reading Teacher*, Vol. 28, No. 6 (March, 1975).

study assumed that linguistic resourcefulness changes as a result of formal schooling and that spelling errors represent the child's misjudgments after having searched through his linguistic store of facts regarding the nature of words.

Billie Jo Rieck (1969) studied spelling patterns to 1) find if spelling approaches could be isolated and classified by the use of the JDR Spelling Checklist (an interview-type questionnaire); 2) determine the incidence of approach—visual, auditory, kinesthetic, or combination—used by students in spelling new words; 3) see if a relationship existed between the approach used and such factors as grade, intelligence, and sex; and 4) compare the ability to spell new words with the ability to recognize the written symbol which indicates the pronunciation of a word. Some findings were: students predominately used an auditory approach to spelling; grade level and IQ affected the incidence of the approach used; sex differences did not affect the overall score; in spelling new words, students appeared unable to evaluate correctness; a positive correlation existed between the ability to spell new words and the ability to recognize correct pronunciations and written symbols from pronunciations.

A second set of studies related to spelling and word attack skills attempted to reduce the variance in spelling achievement found among students. The pursuance of reducing variance in achievement scores is the same as the concept of mastery learning discussed by Bloom, Hastings, and Madaus (1971).

Custer Quick (1972) studied the relative effectiveness of three different types of reinforcement strategies on spelling achievement among a sample of disadvantaged and other fourth grade public school pupils. The hypothesis that among disadvantaged groups the concrete reward would have greater effect than either the token or social rewards was not confirmed.

John Grottenthaler (1970) compared the effectiveness of three programs of elementary school spelling instruction to determine which of the programs produced student achievement and favorable attitudes and to determine whether the effects of the several programs differed for pupils in different IQ ranges. The three spelling programs were a word-list mastery approach to spelling, a multilevel sight-sound program, and a spelling-principle mastery approach. Results indicated that no one program was more effective than the others in fostering achievement of children at one of the three ability levels and that no significant differences in either fifth grade student attitudes or achievement resulted from any one of the three programs of spelling instruction.

Stephen Dunwell (1972) investigated a Computer Assisted Instruction (CAI) course, WRITE, used at the Poughkeepsie, New York Middle School to help fifth through eighth graders with spelling and word usage problems. All students received self-paced instructional programs. The teaching was done by examples; the stress was on spelling patterns rather than individual words, and the goal was to have students reach a level of acceptable orthography. Results from the Lincoln Intermediate Spelling Test showed that the experimental group made significantly greater gains. It was concluded that CAI was an efficient means of teaching spelling—that it was sensitive to individual needs, effective for weaker students, and useful for remedial work.

With many studies in spelling instruction reporting no significant differences in a variety of approaches, some researchers have hypothesized that the key variable in the learning situation is the teacher. Richard Hodges (1973) has been an advocate for research on the teacher variable in spelling instruction. While agreeing that a comprehensive understanding of what constitutes effective spelling instruction must take into account the nature of the orthography, the various learner variables, and the instructional method, Hodges believes the area of teacher interaction with students must be taken into account.

REFERENCES

Benthul, Herman F. "Is Spelling Still Important?" *Instructor,* vol. 79 (April, 1970), p. 61.
Bloom, Benjamin S., J. Thomas Hastings, and George F. Madaus. *Handbook on Formative and Summative Evaluation of Student Learning.* New York, New York: McGraw-Hill Book Company, 1971. (ED 049 304)
Cohen, Leo A. Evaluating Structural Analysis Methods Used in Spelling Books. Doctoral dissertation, Boston University School of Education, 1969. (ED 048 269)
Dunwell, Stephen and others. *Report on WRITE: Computer Assisted Instruction Course in Written English Usage.* Poughkeepsie, New York: Shared Education Computer System, Inc., 1972. (ED 083 816)
Fay, Leo. "Reading and Spellings: How Are They Related?" Washington, D.C.: National Reading Center Foundation, 1971. (ED 059 009)
Frost, James Andrew. Development of Competence in Spelling: A Linguistic Analysis. Doctoral dissertation, Case Western Reserve University, 1973. (ED 085 706)
Grottenthaler, John. A Comparison of the Effectiveness of Three Programs of Elementary School Spelling. Doctoral dissertation, University of Pittsburgh, 1970. (ED 049 257)
Hodges, Richard E. Report of the Literature Search in the Area of Teaching Behavior in Spelling Instruction. Paper presented at the meeting of the National Conference on Research in English, New Orleans, February 1973. (ED 078 424)
Quick, Custer R., Jr. The Effect of Three Reinforcement Systems of Spelling Achievement among Disadvantaged and Non-Disadvantaged Pupils. Doctoral dissertation, State University of New York at Albany, 1972. (ED 083 562)
Rieck, Billie Jo Daugherty. An Investigation of Spelling Patterns. Doctoral dissertation, West Virginia University, 1969. (ED 049 226)
White, Roberta, and Elaine Treadway. A Study of the Achievement and Retention Effects of Instructional Strategies in Orthography (Spelling). Doctoral dissertation, New Mexico State University, 1973. (ED 084 502)

SECTION FIVE

Students with Special Needs

- Each student must be taught an efficient, systematic technique to study unknown spelling words.

  Steve Graham
  Lamoine Miller

- The problem was: how do you look up something if you do not know how to spell it?

  Maryann Castelucci

- Misspellings fall roughly into two categories: phonetic misspellings and non-phonetic misspellings.

  Kenneth Howell
  Joseph Kaplan

INTRODUCTION

Students with special educational needs often find spelling a particularly challenging subject. Because of environmental, mental, or physical conditions, these children are deficient in their ability to use standard English, a deficiency that is particularly telling in its effect on spelling achievement.

Golladay compares four methods of teaching spelling to "slow" learners, and Graham and Miller summarize the relevant spelling research and make recommendations concerning instruction for handicapped students. Castelucci asks a question of great importance: can our remedial students use a dictionary? These students are often referred to a dictionary when they cannot spell a word. Is this practice helpful without instruction?

A comprehensive discussion of the nuts and bolts of teaching spelling to students with special needs is provided by Howell and Kaplan. They include in their article a detailed analysis of the spelling errors of a student with an interpretation of why the errors occurred.

The Teaching of Spelling to Low Ability Students

WENDY M. GOLLADAY

One of the most crucial areas of controversy in modern education is the debate over proper teaching methods to be used in the various areas of instruction, although it is now an accepted fact that different methods must be used with students of different abilities. The complete solution to this controversy would, of course, require detailed and complex studies; however, smaller, more specialized studies can be conducted with certain ability groups in specific subject areas to indicate the proper teaching techniques necessary for effective learning. Such is the purpose of this experiment to determine the most effective technique for the teaching of spelling to 7th grade students labeled by the school guidance department as "slow" learners. A group of 40 spelling words (attached as Appendix A), termed "tricky" words or spelling "demons" by grammar experts, was chosen as the subject matter for four classes totaling sixty-three 7th grade remedial reading students. Recommended by their 6th grade teachers for remedial reading, these students had reading levels of 5th grade or below as indicated by a recent reading test (California Reading Test—Junior High Level). A pre-test of the 40 spelling "demons" (scores tallied in Appendix B) showed the students' unfamiliarity with the words, as only 14.3% of the students correctly spelled between 25% and 32% of the words. No one scored over 32%, the mean score being 7.5%.

Four teaching techniques were used in all four classes using 10 of the spelling words at a time. A tachistoscope, which is basically a filmstrip projector made by Educational Development Laboratories, was one method. A word is dictated, used in a sentence, and dictated again. The student writes the word once. The word is then flashed on a screen with the machine automatically set at a speed of ½ of a second, after which the student writes the word a second time. For checking purposes, the word is shown again, and the student writes it a third time with corrections of the first two attempts, circling places needing more concentrated study.

A programmed teaching machine called

From *Elementary English*, Vol. 48, No. 3 (March, 1971). © 1971 by the National Council of Teachers of English. Reprinted by permission.

"cyclo-teacher," made by the World Book Encyclopedia Company, was used as another method. A cycle or wheel of information is put into the machine along with an answer sheet. The student reads the material, writes his answer in the machine, and checks it (receiving immediate reinforcement) before going on to the next frame. Five words are presented on each side of the cycle and repeated two or three times in different contexts.

The third method was a lecture-discussion using the phonic method of learning word sounds. All words were presented on the blackboard, taken apart by syllables, sounded phonetically, and then pronounced and written by the students. With the students participating through questions and answers, the spelling was then discussed.

The final method cannot accurately be called a teaching method as it consisted only of presenting a mimeographed list of the words to be learned by the following day. A schedule of methods used with each class can be found listed as Appendix C.

Word dictation tests were given on the day following each presentation. The results of these tests have been compiled into a chart (Appendix D) which shows the lecture-discussion method as achieving the best test results, as 65% of the students correctly spelled 80% or more of the words using this method. This same 80 percentile level was reached by 36% of the students with the tachistoscope, 33% with the cyclo-teacher, and 28% with the list of words. The mean score out of 10 words was 8 for the lecture-discussion, 6 for the tachistoscope, and 5 for both the cyclo-teacher and list of words.

A result that cannot be seen in the chart but that was made obvious when checking the tests was the number of errors in each word. Fewer letters were missed in each word when the discussion method and tachistoscope were used while the number of letter errors increased appreciably when the list was given or the cyclo-teacher used. Students gave a possible explanation for this disparity when answering a questionnaire (tallied on a sample copy—Appendix E) which was given following the experiment.

According to the results of the questionnaire, most students preferred the lecture-discussion method over the other three and suggested it as the method with which to continue. Least preferred, and the methods that called for more home study, were the list of words and the cyclo-teacher. The reason given by most students was that there was no pronunciation available. This may be the reason for the contrast in scores and letter errors per word. A combination of either a list and the discussion *or* the tachistoscope and a discussion was the suggestion of 26 of 41 students responding to question 5.

The combined results of the study indicate that there is a definite need to familiarize the low ability students with word pronunciation and syllabication if spelling instruction is to be successful. Although the long range results of this instruction have not been tested, the immediate results indicate that low ability students need more than just visual presentation of material and independent study if effective learning is to take place. Applying the results of the examination to a wider context, one can theorize that machines cannot replace teachers, as some have feared, but can aid and supplement the teacher as a reinforcer, the degree of supplementation varying inversely with the ability of the student.

Assuming the opportunity arose for the experiment to be repeated, I would add another teaching method using the tachistoscope followed by a discussion. Duplicating this experiment with higher ability students, and combining the results of the two experiments would be a larger, more important step in the direction of solving the debate stated in the original paragraph.

APPENDIX A
List of Spelling Words Used in Groups of Ten for Experiment

1. certain
2. champion
3. courageous
4. grief
5. artificial
6. tragedy
7. surprise
8. excellence
9. difficult
10. similar
11. undesirable
12. foreign
13. investigation
14. approximately
15. gymnasium
16. hesitate
17. reliable
18. impatience
19. editor
20. resign
21. demolish
22. purposely
23. diagnose
24. inseparable
25. placid
26. observable
27. journalist
28. invincible
29. exaggerate
30. acknowledge
31. fierce
32. negotiate
33. eligible
34. unanimous
35. isolate
36. corduroy
37. convenient
38. camouflage
39. neutralize
40. Tuesday

APPENDIX B
Tally of Pre-test Scores

Number Right Out of 40 Words	Students Achieving the Number
14	1
13	2
12	2
11	2
10	2
9	0
8	3
7	4
6	3
5	7
4	2
Mean– 3	11
2	9
1	7
0	8

APPENDIX C
Schedule of Methods Used With The Four Classes

	Word Group 1	Word Group 2	Word Group 3	Word Group 4
Class 1	tachistoscope	list of words	cyclo-teacher	lecture-discussion
Class 2	cyclo-teacher	lecture-discussion	tachistoscope	list of words
Class 3	list of words	tachistoscope	lecture-discussion	cyclo-teacher
Class 4	lecture-discussion	cyclo-teacher	list of words	tachistoscope

STUDENTS WITH SPECIAL NEEDS

APPENDIX D

Chart Showing Compilation of Test Scores

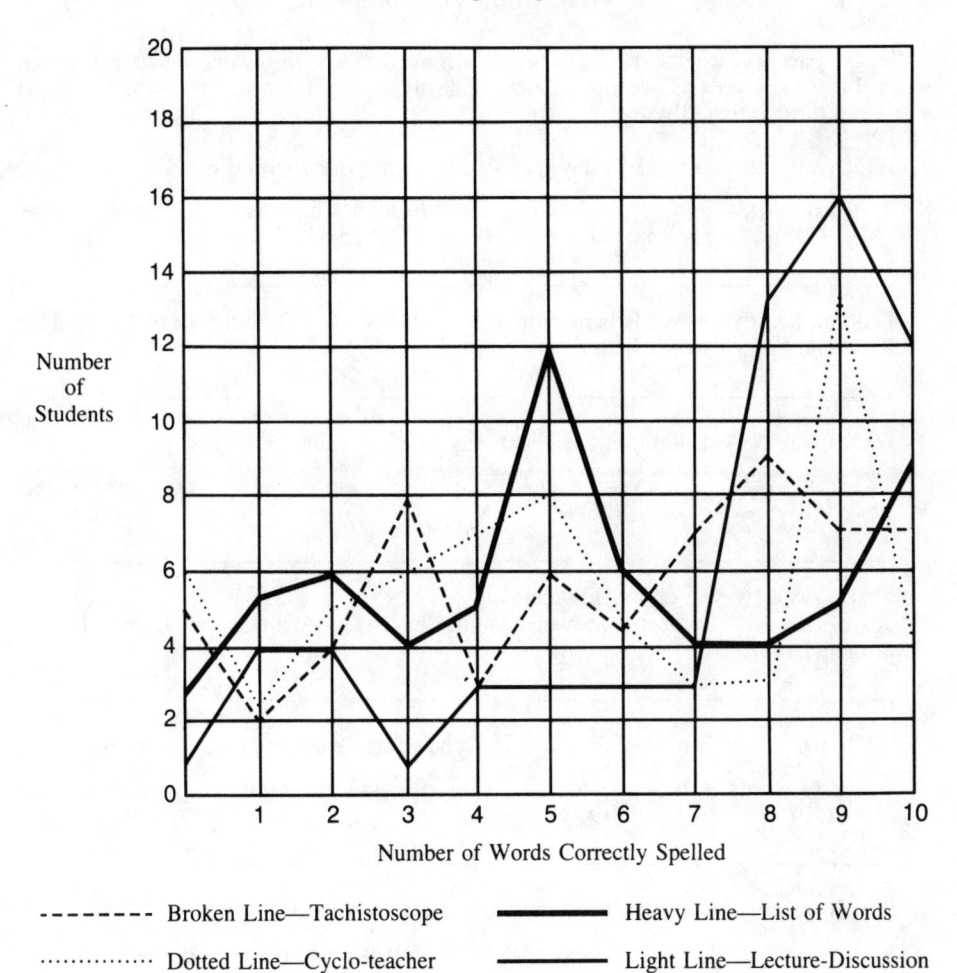

Number of Students

Number of Words Correctly Spelled

- - - - - - - Broken Line—Tachistoscope
·············· Dotted Line—Cyclo-teacher
———— Heavy Line—List of Words
———— Light Line—Lecture-Discussion

APPENDIX E

QUESTIONNAIRE ON SPELLING

For the past few weeks you have been learning your spelling words in four different ways. Please answer the questions below honestly so that I can find out which method you were most satisfied with.

1. Which way do you think is the *best* way to learn your spelling words?

   a. list of words   b. cyclo-teacher   c. discussion in class   d. tachistoscope
       (9)   (11)   (25)   (11)

   Did you learn your words better this way or did you like it better for other reasons? 85% said "learn words better"

2. Which way do you think is the worst way to learn your spelling words?

   a. list of words   b. cyclo-teacher   c. discussion in class   d. tachistoscope
       (18)   (26)   (3)   (7)

   Please say why you chose this method:
   28 of the 41 students answering this answered with some form of "no pronunciation"

3. While using which method did you feel you had to study more on your own?

   a. list of words   b. cyclo-teacher   c. discussion in class   d. tachistoscope
       (29)   (19)   (3)   (11)

4. Which method do you think we should use for the rest of the year?

   a. list of words   b. cyclo-teacher   c. discussion in class   d. tachistoscope
       (10)   (14)   (22)   (9)

5. Would you suggest combining any of the two methods we used? If so, which ones?
   15–c&d   11–a&c   6–c&b   6–d&b   6–a&d

6. Which method do you think we should never use again?

   a. list of words   b. cyclo-teacher   c. discussion in class   d. tachistoscope
       (19)   (30)   (6)   (17)

Spelling Research and Practice: A Unified Approach

STEVE GRAHAM
LAMOINE MILLER

While spelling is neither the most important nor the least important aspect in writing, it is a crucial ingredient. Good spellers are able to express their thoughts on paper without unnecessary interruptions. Poor spellers are hampered in their ability to communicate freely through the written word. For a grocery list or personal reminders, accurate spelling is not essential, but material to be read by others should be free from the distraction of misspelled words.

Spelling is a traditional element of the elementary school curriculum, where considerable amount of time and energy are devoted to its mastery. Moreover, the general public often associates correct spelling with educational attainment, accuracy, neatness and cultivation, while the inability to spell is frequently linked with illiteracy (Personkee and Yee, 1971). Because the public and the educational community emphasize the importance of spelling achievement, the inability to spell may adversely affect an individual's educational and occupational status.

Unfortunately, many school-age children have difficulty learning to spell. The majority of students who are presently labeled handicapped exhibit spelling problems. Learning disabilities, mental retardation, emotional disturbance, and crippling and other health impairments may unfavorably affect spelling performance (Kyte, 1949; Miller & Graham, 1979). These realizations are compounded by an ever present and growing concern that our schools' overall spelling achievement is lower than it was 30 or 40 years ago (E. Horn, 1960).

Unsatisfactory spelling progress may be attributed, in part, to inadequate contemporary classroom instruction, poorly designed commercial materials, and the absence of spelling programs based on research findings. Further, contemporary classroom instruction rarely accounts for individual student differences. On Monday each student usually is introduced to the same list of spelling words. On Tuesday the teacher administers a pretest, and on Wednesday each student uses the spelling words in sentences. Thursday's activities are designed to teach phonic skills and/or words missed on Tuesday's pretest. A final posttest is administered on Friday. This pattern or one that is strikingly similar is common in most American classrooms (Rowell, 1972). Although some students may profit from such large-group oriented instruction, many others do not. Children do not learn at the same rate, nor do they encounter the same difficulties in learning to spell.

The actual spelling procedures used in many classrooms are influenced heavily by commercial materials that form the foundation of most spelling programs. Spelling texts ordinarily offer a set pattern of instruction with little variety (Dieterich, 1973); and a recent survey revealed that direct teacher involvement is limited in most spelling books (Jobes, 1975).

"Teacher proof" materials with little diversity might be acceptable if the content were appropriate. Regrettably, this is not the case. For instance, in a study evaluating current commercial materials, Cohen (1969) identified five major categories of activities or exercises common

---

From *Focus on Exceptional Children*, Vol. 12, No. 2, (October, 1979). Copyright © 1979 by Love Publishing Company. Reprinted by permission.

in sixth grade spellers, and their aggregate percentage of emphasis by text, as follows: phonics (33.6%), affixes and inflectional endings (23.7%), language arts skills (20.2%), word meaning (14.6%), and syllabication (7.9%). Cohen found that some of the exercises actually deterred learning while others were merely ineffectual. As late as 1976, spelling books still contained a large proportion of inappropriate activities (Graves, 1976). Results of the Cohen and Graves studies point to the need for reevaluation of spelling texts and their contents.

As disturbing as it may seem, evidence reveals that instructional practices in spelling are influenced more by habit than by research results. In a study involving 1,289 second through sixth grade elementary teachers, Fitzsimmons and Loomer (1977) found that teachers seldom use research-supported practices in their classroom. The insignificant role of research in spelling *instruction* is paradoxical, since spelling is one of the most thoroughly researched areas in the language arts. Many earlier findings are substantiated by more recent research (Allred, 1977). Even so, improvement in spelling programs is not commensurate with research efforts. While existing evidence will continue to be refined and expanded, it is basically useless if it is not applied.

If handicapped and nonhandicapped students are to receive adequate spelling instruction, teachers need viable alternatives to current spelling texts and instructional practices. The building materials for such options are presently available—a solid research foundation already exists, and the Elementary and Secondary Education Act created a landslide of spelling techniques, approaches, and materials (Fitzsimmons & Loomer, 1977). In designing appropriate alternatives, the present day educator runs the risk of choosing ineffectual activities and/or neglecting the current research foundation. Therefore, spelling instruction should be teacher directed, should contain a variety of relevant instructional options, and should be based on a foundation of research evidence.

THE DEFINITION AND PROCESS OF SPELLING

Unless one first knows the nature of what one is trying to teach, a discussion of methodology and organization seems pointless. Yet, much of the literature evidences this characteristic, mainly because most definitions do not capture the full essence of the spelling process. For example, Hanna, Hodges, and Hanna (1971) define spelling as the "process of encoding, or of rendering spoken words into written symbols" (p. 264). Similarly, Brueckner and Bond (1955) define spelling as the "ability to produce in written or oral form the correct letter arrangement of words" (p. 346). Neither of these definitions is complete. Spelling is not based upon a single act but requires a variety of skills euphemistically called "spelling." *For the purpose of this article, spelling is defined as the ability to recognize, recall, reproduce, or obtain orally or in written form the correct sequence of letters in words.*

Spelling begins with a felt need to spell a word (see Figure 1). This need may be in response to a written assignment, a request for aid, a spelling test, and so forth. Ordinarily, students are able to immediately write or recall spellings of words appropriate to their level of learning with little or no conscious effort. Occasionally, students are able to spell words correctly but first need to use intrinsic or extrinsic strategies to determine if a word is (a) a homonym (semantic information), (b) capitalized (syntactic information), and/or (c) hyphenated (human or written aid). Once they have this information, they immediately recall the word from memory.

If the correct spelling of a word is uncertain or unknown to a student, there are two main resources upon which to

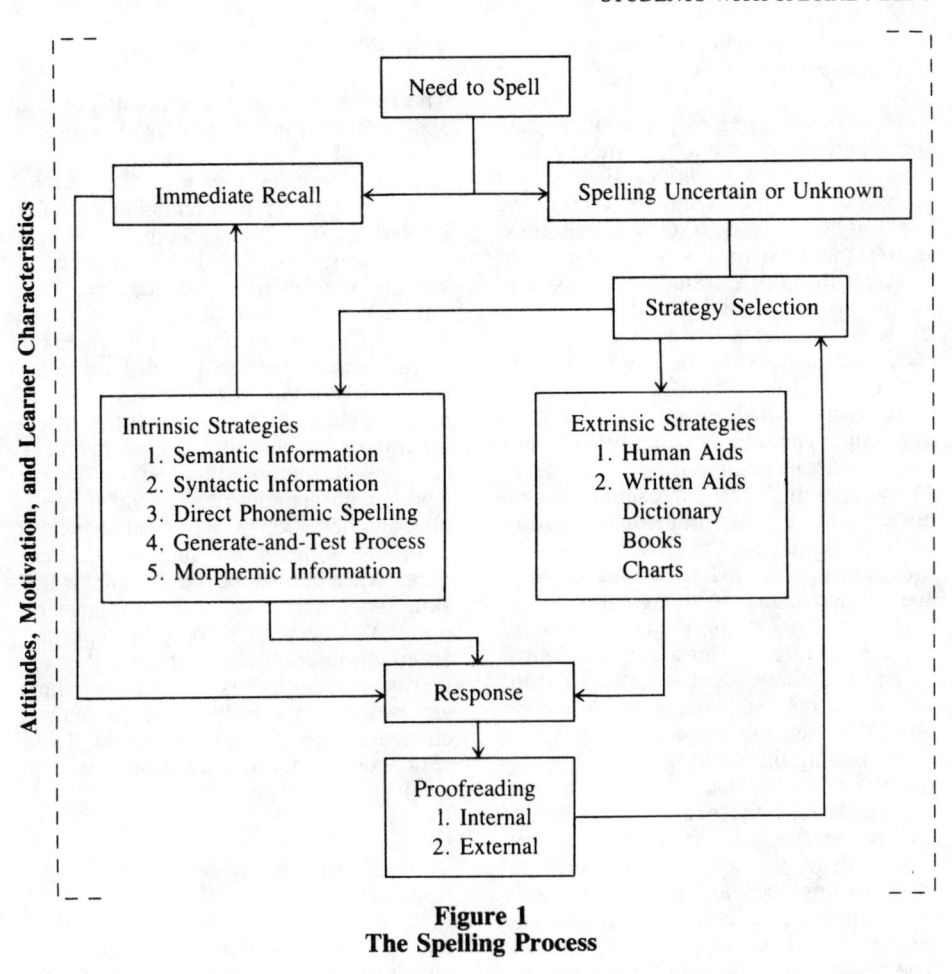

```
                          Need to Spell
                               │
                               ▼
    Immediate Recall ◄──────► Spelling Uncertain or Unknown
                                       │
                                       ▼
                              Strategy Selection

    Intrinsic Strategies                    Extrinsic Strategies
    1. Semantic Information                 1. Human Aids
    2. Syntactic Information                2. Written Aids
    3. Direct Phonemic Spelling                Dictionary
    4. Generate-and-Test Process               Books
    5. Morphemic Information                   Charts

                              Response
                                 │
                                 ▼
                            Proofreading
                            1. Internal
                            2. External
```

(Left margin: Attitudes, Motivation, and Learner Characteristics)

Figure 1
The Spelling Process

draw. One, a person could use *intrinsic strategies* to determine a "possible" correct sequence of sound-symbol associations. These strategies include direct phonemic spelling, the generate-and-test process, and morphemic information (Simon & Simon, 1973). In direct phonemic spelling, students apply their knowledge of phoneme-letter associations and phonemic rules to produce a phonetic spelling of the word. This strategy is successful for only about one of every two words (Hanna, Hanna, Hodges, & Rudorf, 1966). The generate-and-test process is a trial-and-error procedure in which the student produces alternative possible spellings and tries to recognize the correct written response. Although this procedure is superior to direct phonemic spelling (Simon & Simon, 1973), it, too, is prone to error. Each of these two strategies may be supplemented by the use of morphemic information. Auditory recognition of a morphemic element (e.g., *and*) provides spelling information that may be used to derive the correct spelling of words containing that component.

Attitudes, Motivation, and Learner Characteristics

If intrinsic strategies prove inadequate for a particular situation, a student may refer to *extrinsic resources* such as aid from a teacher or friend, the dictionary, spelling books, and so forth. Sometimes, intrinsic and extrinsic strategies are used concurrently; e.g., a student may generate a possible spelling and then use a dictionary to check that response.

A student does not need to be able to recall the full spelling of a word in order to recognize whether or not it is spelled correctly. The process involved in this phenomena is commonly referred to as "proofreading." Once a response is generated either through immediate recall or a spelling strategy, the student may scan the word in an effort to see if it is spelled accurately. Although this procedure is not exact, it often uncovers incorrect spellings. After a suspected error is detected, the student might use extrinsic or intrinsic resources to determine whether or not the response is correct.

In defining the spelling process, a distinction must be made between the mature speller and the beginning speller. A mature speller can immediately spell nearly all of the words encountered on usual writing tasks and can appropriately select intrinsic or extrinsic strategies to correctly spell words that are unknown. The beginning speller, in contrast, has a limited spelling vocabulary and does not have access to a wide variety of spelling skills. Research suggests that students in the primary grades progress through several stages in the development of spelling strategies (Beers, 1974; Beers & Henderson, 1977; Gentry, 1977). First, students tend to omit essential sound features of the word (e.g., vowels). At the next level, spelling is primarily phonetic. During the third stage, attributes of the English orthographic system begin to appear. At the fourth stage, students recognize and recall the correct lexical representation of the word.

THE SPELLING CURRICULUM

The preceding discussion points out that spelling is multifaceted and requires mastery of a variety of skills. Learning to spell is not an easy task. The speller faces many difficulties including, but not limited to, foreign spellings, 26 letters representing 44 sounds, silent letters, variant and invariant sounds, and 300 different letter combinations for 17 vowel sounds (Allred, 1977). To illustrate, the word "circumference" can be spelled over *396,000,000* different ways phonetically (Peters, 1970). In addition to orthographic barriers, the English language contains the largest vocabulary in the world, with approximately 490,000 words plus another 300,000 technical terms.

In planning a spelling curriculum, then, what should be taught and which skills should receive primary consideration? With respect to the latter concern, an enduring controversy regards the regularity of the English language. There are two major theories (and consequent curricular applications) based on divergent views regarding the consistency of English orthography.

Synthetic Alphabet/Whole Word Approach

One theory holds that English orthography is irrational and consequently difficult to master. This view is responsible for the two distinct methodological interpretations that (a) instruction should be based on a special synthetic alphabet (e.g., Initial Teaching Alphabet); and (b) whole words should form the core of the spelling curriculum.

At present, however, special synthetic alphabets are not a viable or pragmatic approach to spelling instruction because they require an additional step in the learning process—transition from the synthetic alphabet to English orthography. Upon cursory examination, the whole word approach also appears to be impractical. The average person uses perhaps 10,000 words freely and can recognize another 30,000 to 40,000 (Monson, 1975). Mentally handicapped students are not likely to be able to memorize this many spelling words.

Fortunately, to be an effective speller, a student does not have to be able to correctly spell all the words in his or her listening, reading, and writing vocabulary. Studies by E. Horn (1926), Fitzgerald (1951a), T. Horn and Otto (1954), and Rinsland (1945) indicate that a basic spelling vocabulary of 2,800 to 3,000 well-selected words should form the core of the spelling program. To illustrate, 8 words account for 18% of all the words children use in their writing, 100 words for 50%, 1,000 words for 89%, 2,000 words for 95%, 3,000 words for 97%, and 4,000 words for 99% (Hillerich, 1977; E. Horn, 1926; Otto & McMenemy, 1966; Rinsland, 1945). After several hundred words have been learned, the law of diminishing returns begins to operate (Allred, 1977). To require a student to master a spelling vocabulary significantly larger than 3,000 words is out of harmony with research.

Phonemic Approach

The second theory views English orthography as a patterned but incomplete system. Supporters of this theory suggest that the systematic properties of orthography should be used in spelling instruction. This view stresses the application of phonics and spelling rules as a means of developing spelling abilities.

There are several notable challenges to the application of phonemic skills. Those objecting to phonics instruction point out that: (a) most sounds are spelled many ways; (b) most letters spell many sounds; (c) more than one-third of the words in the dictionary have more than one accepted pronunciation, more than half contain silent letters, and about a sixth contain double letters; (d) unstressed syllables are difficult to spell; and (e) children do not understand word-attack principles (E. Horn, 1960). In addition, detractors indicate that most misspelled words are phonemically correct (Hahn, 1960; Tovey, 1978) and that intensive phonics instruction is not superior to non-phonics methods (Bedell & Nelson, 1954; Grottenthaler, 1970; Hahn, 1964; Ibeling, 1961; Personkee & Yee, 1971; Warren, 1970).

Those who favor phonics instruction indicate some fairly consistent characteristics of English spelling (Horn, 1960). For example, Hanna et al. (1966) reported that 49 percent of 17,000 words could be spelled correctly using phoneme-grapheme correspondences and another 37 percent could be spelled with only one error. Furthermore, a large body of research supports the contention that intensive phonics instruction creates greater gains in spelling than non-phonics approaches (Baker, 1977; Block, 1972; Dunwell, 1972; Gold, 1976; K. Russell, 1954; Thompson, 1977). Some evidence shows that children learn the more essential phonic principles whether or not formal instruction in phonics is offered (Schwartz & Doehring, 1977; Templin, 1954). In summary, both theory and evidence suggest that phonics instruction may be of some benefit in learning to spell.

Spelling Rules

The issue surrounding use of spelling rules is more clear-cut. Only those rules, with few exceptions, that apply to a large number of words should be taught; and teaching generalizations without regard to utility of the spelling rule is wasteful. For instance, Clymer (1963) found that only 18 of 45 generalizations are useful. Other researchers have suggested that even fewer spelling rules should be taught (Cook, 1912; E. Horn, 1945a, King, 1932). Supporting the statement that spelling rules should be unambiguous, Archer (1930) and Personkee and Yee (1971) indicated that the use of spelling rules may lead to errors because students often misapply generalizations they do not clearly understand. Spelling rules, as a whole, are deemed not very useful in improving overall spelling achievement (Davis, 1969; King, 1932; Turner, 1912; Warren, 1969).

Returning to the question of what should be taught and which skills should receive primary consideration, we suggest that a basic vocabulary of 2,000 to 3,000 words should be supplemented by direct phonics instruction accompanied by limited use of spelling rules. In addition, the student should be able to detect spelling errors (i.e., proofread)[1] and be able to effectively use a dictionary.

Figure 2 presents a spelling scope and sequence divided into eight levels. Each level represents approximately one school year. Depending upon the student's characteristics and the severity of the handicapping condition, the rate of progression through the curriculum may be either decelerated or accelerated. In any case, the fundamental sequence of skills should remain intact.

Within the program, the spelling vocabulary is arranged from the most frequently used words to those used least often. Because of the significant overlap between children's and adult's writing vocabularies (Fitzgerald, 1951b; E. Horn, 1954b), the curriculum is comprised of the words most common to both—attending to the student's future as well as present spelling needs.

Initially, any of a number of lists of "most common words" (e.g., Dolch, Fry, etc.) can be taught. For example, Fitzgerald (1951b) identified a permanently useful core of 449 words for beginners and the retarded, which account for more than 76 percent of the words used in children's and adult's writing. Once the vocabulary in the selected list of "most common words" is learned, additional words are taken from one of the following sources: Fitzgerald (1951b), Hillerich (1976), E. Horn (1926), or Rinsland (1945). Before teaching any word from these sources, the teacher should make sure that the word is already part of the student's listening and reading vocabulary.

Since correct spelling in place of phonetic misspelling is a major goal in spelling instruction, only essential phonic skills and spelling rules are incorporated into the curriculum. The nucleus of the phonics program includes base words, prefixes, suffixes, and consonant, consonant blend, digraph, and vowel sound-symbol associations. Spelling rules are limited to the following:

— Proper nouns and most adjectives formed from proper nouns begin with capital letters.
— Rules for adding suffixes (changing y to i, dropping final silent e, doubling the final consonant).
— The use of periods in writing abbreviations.
— The use of the apostrophe to show possession.
— The letter q is followed by u in common English words.
— English words do not end in v.

Dictionary work includes picture dictionaries, alphabetizing skills, word location skills, independent dictionary skills, and pronunciation skills. Proofreading involves detecting and correcting errors.

THE SPELLING MODEL

The major objectives of the spelling model as presented here are to:

1. Help students become proficient at standard spelling.

---

[1] Research indicates that proofreading skills can be improved and that proofreading programs lead to gains in spelling achievement (Frasch, 1965; McElwee, 1974; Oswalt, 1961; Personkee & Knight, 1967; Valmont, 1972).

	Level 1	Level 2	Level 3	Level 4	Level 5	Levels 6–8
Spelling Vocabulary	25 words	275 words	400 words	460 words	460 words	460 words each
Phonic Skills	consonants →					
		consonant clusters →				
		digraphs →				
	vowels	base words	→			
		suffixes	→			
			prefixes →			
Spelling Rules	capitalization					
			adding suffixes			
			punctuation-abbreviation			
			apostrophes			
			words do not end in v			
			letter q followed by u			
Proofreading		spelling	→			
Dictionary	picture dictionary					
	alphabetical order					
			target word			
			alphabetical guide			
					independent dictionary work →	

Figure 2
Spelling Scope and Sequence

2. Maintain and promote spelling growth.
3. Teach students how to spell words they use in writing.
4. Help students develop effective methods of studying new words.
5. Promote students' use of the dictionary in learning to spell unknown words.
6. Develop in students a spelling conscience—a desire to spell words correctly.

To meet these goals, an effective remedial spelling program must be based on a number of well-defined principles. First, spelling instruction must be direct and not incidental. Studies by Allen and Ager (1965) and Knoell and Harris (1952) found that spelling is an independent skill and that transfer effects from other areas of the curriculum should not be expected. Although students learn many words outside of specific spelling instruction, this incidental learning is applied primarily by the good spellers (Gilbert & Gilbert, 1944; Tyler, 1939). Thus, for poor spellers, basing remedial spelling procedures on reading or other language arts activities may not be justified.

A second assumption inherent in the model presented here is that spelling instruction must be individualized. A wide range of spelling ability and achievement is apparent at every grade level (Ayer, 1951; E. Horn, 1960). The skills and needs of each student are different. Teachers who fail to account for individual differences often rely on hodgepodge procedures that produce hodgepodge results (Schell, 1975). For example, Guiler and Lease (1942) found that pupils at all levels of spelling ability benefited from a program based on individual needs and made substantially greater gains than students receiving instruction formulated on a conventional group basis.

Third, effective remedial spelling instruction depends upon continuous evaluation. Assessment data are used to determine if progress is adequate or if alterations in the instructional plan are necessary. Teachers who do not monitor a student's spelling program carefully cannot adapt instruction to meet individual needs.

Fourth, successful remediation is based upon flexible use of a wide variety of techniques and methods. Regrettably, no one best method or technique has emerged for teaching spelling (Blair, 1975). Likewise, what works with one student may not work with another. Because handicapped students exhibit a diverse range of problems, teachers require access to an extensive assortment of methodological techniques.

Fifth, the effectiveness of spelling instruction is heavily dependent upon the attitudes of both student and teacher. Students must be shown that spelling is personally important to them. Desirable attitudes in students can be encouraged by teachers who (a) provide students with efficient learning techniques, (b) present words of high social utility, (c) emphasize student progress, (d) use a variety of interesting activities and games, (e) structure tasks so that the student can succeed, and (f) limit instruction to relevant and critical skills. Spelling, however, is one of the subjects teachers most dislike to teach (E. Horn, 1960). This is unfortunate, because teachers may be the key variable in students' learning to spell (Blair, 1975).

Assessment

Public Law 94-142 requires that an Individualized Education Program (IEP) must be developed for each student receiving special services. The IEP is a management tool designed to facilitate the process of instructional delivery. While the scope of this article does not allow an in-depth discussion of the IEP, it is necessary to discuss procedures for establishing the present level of performance and evaluating student progress.

Readers interested in a systematic planning model for development of the IEP are referred to Hudson and Graham (1978).

The procedure through which the present level of performance is established has to vary from one student to another. Nonetheless, a suitable analysis should consider the student's (a) readiness for formal instruction, (b) general spelling level, (c) spelling errors, and (d) proofreading, phonic, and dictionary skills. This information is used to plan the student's educational program (i.e., annual goals and short-term objectives).

Before describing specific assessment techniques, a few general principles should be noted:

1. A variety of both standardized and informal procedures should be used.
2. Since writing is the most common response mode in spelling, written tests are preferable to oral tests.
3. Spelling behavior should be assessed in both isolation and written context.
4. Recall tests are more difficult than recognition tests.
5. Results of various assessments should not be considered as discrete, separate entities but should be analyzed for possible relationships.

Readiness

Before direct spelling instruction is planned, the student must be intellectually able and emotionally willing to learn. Students who have not attained sufficient mental maturity and linguistic experiences are scarcely ready to participate in a formal spelling program. How is spelling assessed? Read, Allred, and Baird (1972) recommend that students should be able to: (a) name and write all the letters of the alphabet, (b) copy words correctly, (c) write their names from memory, (d) enunciate words clearly, (e) recognize common letter-sound combinations, (f) write a few words from memory, and (g) demonstrate an interest in spelling. If students do not meet these criteria, they should take part in activities (see Hildreth, 1962) aimed at developing spelling readiness.

Overall Achievement

Various standardized tests are available for measuring a student's general spelling level. Among these instruments are the *Iowa Spelling Scale* (Ashbaugh, 1921), the *Phonovisual Diagnostic Test* (Schoolfield & Timberlake, 1949), the *Ayer Standard Spelling Test* (Ayer, 1950), the *Seven-Plus Assessment* (Lambert, 1964), and the *Kelvin Measurement of Spelling Ability* (Fleming, 1933). Each of these tests examines recall processes and requires that students write words that have been presented orally, used in a sentence, and presented orally again.

Several informal methods are also available for measuring spelling ability at the survey level. Word lists developed by Kottmeyer (1959) and a coefficient of misspelling both yield a general estimate of spelling achievement. Using the latter, the teacher obtains from the student a written specimen containing approximately 200 words. The total number of misspelled words is divided by the number of words written. The resulting coefficient then is compared to suggested grade-level norms (Courtis, 1919; Brueckner & Bond, 1955).

Spelling Errors

Errors that students commit on spelling tests and other written work provide an indication of the nature of the student's spelling difficulties. Error analysis reveals the student's error tendencies and enables the teacher to detect excessive or infrequent types of errors. Most spelling errors are of a phonetic nature (Spache, 1940), occur in the middle of the word (Jensen, 1962; Kooi, Schutz, & Baker, 1965), and involve a single phoneme (Gates, 1937; Hildreth, 1962). A few words do not account for a disproportionate number of errors (Swenson & Caldwell, 1948).

Only a few standardized tests specifically analyze spelling errors. The *Spelling Errors Test* (Spache, 1955) calls for a response to 120 dictated words and permits the examiner to classify the responses according to 13 common error types. The *Larsen-Hammill Test of Written Spelling* (Larsen & Hammill, 1976) is comprised of two subtests—Predictable Words and Unpredictable Words. The test yields a comparative analysis of the student's ability to spell phonetic and nonphonetic words.

Proofreading

Standardized proofreading tests include the *Every Pupil Achievement Test* (Robinson, 1970), the *California Achievement Tests* (Tiegs & Clark, 1970), the *SRA Achievement Series* (Thorpe, Lefever, & Haslund, 1963), the *Northumberland Standardized Test: II English* (Burt 1925), and the *Metropolitan Achievement Tests* (Durost, Evans, Leake, Bowman, Cosgrove, & Reed, 1970). Each of these tests measures recognition processes.

Proofreading skills should be examined in both isolation and context. Some informal proofreading measures are to:

1. Present alternative spellings of a word and have the student select the correct spelling.
2. Introduce different words and have the student decide which words are spelled correctly or incorrectly.
3. Mark words in a sentence and have the student indicate which, if any, of the marked words are misspelled.
4. Have the student mark and correct misspelled words in a sentence, paragraph, etc.

Phonics

In evaluating phonic skills, the analysis should involve sound-symbol associations and not symbol-sound associations. Two standardized tests that meet this requirement are the *Gates-Russell Spelling Diagnostic Test* (Gates & Russell, 1937) and the Spelling subtests of the *Durrell Analysis of Reading Difficulty* (Durrell, 1937). Informal tests corresponding to this principle include the *Diagnostic Test* (Teachers Manual, 1956) and the *St. Louis Spelling Test* (Kottmeyer, 1959).

Dictionary Skills and Spelling Rules

There is a lack of formalized instruments for examining dictionary skills and spelling rules. Therefore, these elements must be examined informally. Dictionary skills can be assessed by directly observing the student locate unknown spelling words in the dictionary. The student's knowledge of spelling rules can be examined by having each student spell nonsense and real words that require the use of a specific rule (see Brueckner & Bond, 1955).

Evaluating Student Progress

Annual goals often are evaluated by administering a standardized test at the beginning of the year and again at the end of the year. This procedure, however, is generally not appropriate for measuring student performance on specific short-term objectives. Daily work products, observation over time, number of trials per lesson, criterion-referenced testing, and applied behavioral analysis are means by which short-term objectives can be measured (see Hersen & Barlow, 1976; Hudson & Graham, 1978; Moran, 1975). For instance, the student's spelling tests and words misspelled on writing assignments may be kept in a spelling folder. Periodically, the teacher should analyze the contents of the folder to determine spelling mastery, error patterns, phonemic skills, etc. This information then may be used to determine if the student is making adequate progress in meeting specific short-term objectives.

Methodological Procedures

The outline in Figure 3 illustrates the basic components of the spelling model. Spelling practices supported by research and those not supported by research are capsulized in Figure 4. Only practices supported by empirical data were incorporated into the model here. Readers interested in a more thorough discussion of research supported practices are referred to Fitzsimmons and Loomer (1977).

Spelling Vocabulary

The beginning step in teaching spelling vocabulary is to determine which words to teach. Many students already know a few words in each lesson (E. Horn, 1960; Swenson & Caldwell, 1948). The student's learning, therefore, should be directed toward words he or she cannot spell correctly. This focuses spelling instruction on acquisition rather than maintenance.

Use of the test-study method indicates which words require study. Through this technique, the student first is given a pretest to determine which words in a particular lesson are unknown to him or her. The test administrator pronounces each word, uses it in an oral sentence, and pronounces it again (Brody, 1944; Cook, 1932; Foran, 1934; Nisbet, 1939). After unknown words are identified, the student studies them. The pretest then is given a second time and the teacher notes which words, if any, are spelled incorrectly. Misspelled words are incorporated into future lessons.

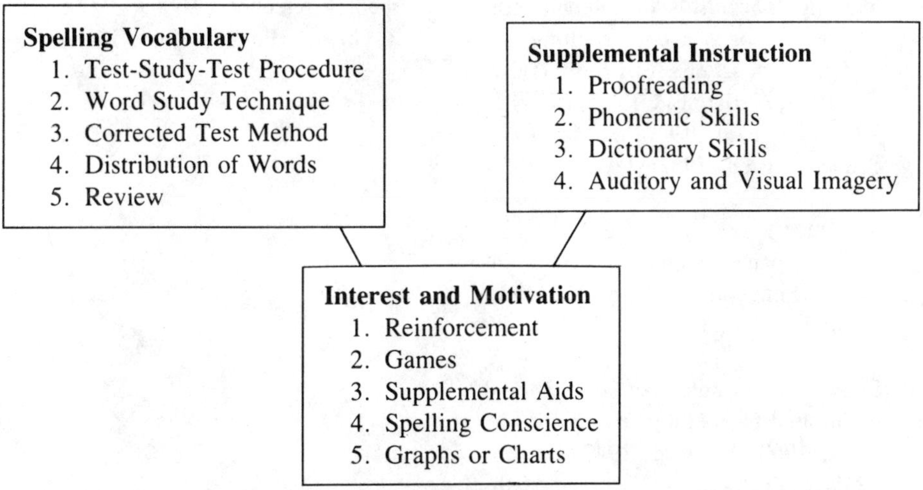

Spelling Vocabulary
1. Test-Study-Test Procedure
2. Word Study Technique
3. Corrected Test Method
4. Distribution of Words
5. Review

Supplemental Instruction
1. Proofreading
2. Phonemic Skills
3. Dictionary Skills
4. Auditory and Visual Imagery

Interest and Motivation
1. Reinforcement
2. Games
3. Supplemental Aids
4. Spelling Conscience
5. Graphs or Charts

Figure 3
Components of the Spelling Model

PROCEDURES SUPPORTED BY RESEARCH	PROCEDURES NOT SUPPORTED BY RESEARCH
1. The test-study-test method is superior to the study-test method (Blanchard, 1944; C. Edwards, 1931; Fitzgerald, 1953; Gates, 1931; Hibler, 1957; T. Horn, 1946; Kingsley, 1923; Montgomery, 1957; Subik, 1951; Yee, 1969).	1. Writing spelling words in the air is a valuable aid in learning new words (Petty & Green, 1968).
2. Learning spelling words by a synthetic approach is a better technique than learning words by syllables (T. Horn, 1947, 1969; Humphrey, 1954).	2. Studying the "hard spots" in words improves spelling ability (Masters, 1927; Mendenhall, 1930; Rosemeier, 1965; Tireman, 1927).
3. It is more efficient to present words for study in a list or column form than in sentence or paragraph form (M. Edwards, 1953; Hawley & Gallup, 1922; E. Horn, 1944, 1954b; McKee, 1924; Strickland, 1951; Winch, 1916).	3. Students should devise their own method for studying spelling words (Fitzgerald, 1951a; E. Horn, 1944, 1954b, 1960; T. Horn, 1969).
4. The single most important factor in learning to spell is the student correcting his or her own spelling test under the teacher's direction (Beseler, 1953; Christine & Hollingsworth, 1966; T. Horn, 1946; Louis, 1950; Schoephoerster, 1962; Thomas, 1954; Tyson, 1953).	4. Student interest in spelling is secondary to rewards received for achievement in spelling (Columba, 1926; Diserens & Vaughn, 1931; Forlano, 1936; E. Horn, 1960, 1967; D. Russell, 1937; Thorndike, 1935).
5. Spelling games stimulate student interest (Fitzgerald, 1951a; E. Horn, 1960; T. Horn, 1969).	5. Writing words several times ensures spelling retention (Abbott, 1909; Petty & Green, 1968; E. Horn, 1967).
6. Sixty to 75 minutes per week should be allotted to spelling instruction (E. Horn, 1960; T. Horn, 1947; Larson, 1945; Rieth, Axelrod, Anderson, Hathaway, Wood, & Fitzgerald, 1972).	

**Figure 4
Research on Spelling Procedures**

Words to be studied should be presented in a list or column form. This is advantageous because it focuses specific attention upon each and every word. If the student does not know the meaning of the word or if the word is a homonym, the teacher may wish to embed the word within a sentence.

Each student must be taught an efficient, systematic technique to study unknown spelling words. Letting students devise their own individual methods is not advisable. An effective word study method can be established by developing a worksheet that specifies the study pattern in a step-by-step manner. Initially, the student uses the worksheet, under teacher supervision, to learn each unknown spelling word. Gradually, the worksheet is faded out as the study method becomes internalized.

An effective word study method concentrates on the whole word and requires careful pronunciation, visual imagery, auditory and/or kinesthetic reinforcement, and systematic recall (i.e., distributed learning and overlearning). Figure 5 presents a variety of word study techniques that, for the most part, meet these stipulations. These authors suggest that the student be taught either the Fitzgerald Method or one of the two methods by E. Horn. If these techniques prove ineffective for a particular student, the Gilstrap Method may be more suitable. Or, a teacher may wish to use one of the other word study techniques (e.g., Fernald Method, Cover-and-Write Method, etc.) with a specific student.

The single most effective technique in learning to spell is followed when the student (under the teacher's direction) corrects his or her own errors immediately after taking a spelling test. The corrected-test method allows the student to (a) see which words are difficult, (b) locate the part of the word that is troublesome, and (c) correct errors. Examples of this technique include the following:

1. Teacher spells word orally. Student corrects word in writing (Hibler, 1957).
2. Teacher spells word, emphasizing each letter as student points to each letter as it is pronounced (Allred, 1977).
3. Teacher spells word and student marks through each incorrect letter and writes correct letter above it (Hall, 1964).
4. Teacher writes word correctly next to misspelled word. Student writes word correctly (Kauffman, Hallahan, Haas, Brame, & Boren, 1978).
5. Teacher writes exact imitation of student's error and then writes word correctly. Student writes word correctly (Kauffman et. al., 1978).

The prevailing practice of presenting all the spelling words at the beginning of the week is not suitable for handicapped students. To present and test a few words daily is preferable. Also, the teacher should intersperse known and unknown words in each spelling test (Neef, Iwata, & Page, 1977). Each newly mastered spelling word should be tested a few days after the initial presentation and then periodically throughout the school year. This helps ensure spelling maintenance and growth.

Many students evidence difficulty in identifying misspelled words, but this skill can be improved through practice (Valmont, 1972). A good way to begin is to provide time to proofread written assignments and stress the importance of spelling consciousness. Proofreading skills may be improved through exercises similar to the following:

1. Have the student locate incorrect spellings in a short list of words (Hardin, Bernstein, & Shands, 1978).
2. Provide practice in detecting words that don't look right in other students' writing assignments (Rudman, 1973).
3. List the number of misspelled words in a composition and have the stu-

Fitzgerald Method (Fitzgerald, 1951a)

1. Look at the word carefully.
2. Say the word.
3. With eyes closed, visualize the word.
4. Cover the word and then write it.
5. Check the spelling.
6. If the word is misspelled, repeat steps 1-5.

Horn Method 1 (E. Horn, 1919)

1. Look at the word and say it to yourself.
2. Close your eyes and visualize the word.
3. Check to see if you were right. (If not, begin at step 1).
4. Cover the word and write it.
5. Check to see if you were right. (If not, begin at step 1).
6. Repeat steps 4 and 5 two more times.

Horn Method 2 (E. Horn, 1954c)

1. Pronounce each word carefully.
2. Look carefully at each part of the word as you pronounce it.
3. Say the letters in sequence.
4. Attempt to recall how the word looks, then spell the word.
5. Check this attempt to recall.
6. Write the word.
7. Check this spelling attempt.
8. Repeat the above steps if necessary.

Visual-Vocal Method (Westerman, 1971)

1. Say word.
2. Spell word orally.
3. Say word again.
4. Spell word from memory four times correctly.

Gilstrap Method (Gilstrap, 1962)

1. Look at the word and say it softly. If it has more than one part, say it again, part by part, looking at each part as you say it.
2. Look at the letters and say each one. If the word has more than one part, say the letters part by part.
3. Write the word without looking at the book.

Fernald Method Modified

1. Make a model of the word with a crayon, grease pencil, or magic marker, saying the word as you write it.
2. Check the accuracy of the model.
3. Trace over the model with your index finger, saying the word at the same time.
4. Repeat step 3 five times.
5. Copy the word three times correctly.
6. Copy the word three times from memory correctly.

Cover-and-Write Method

1. Look at the word. Say it.
2. Write word two times.
3. Cover and write one time.
4. Check work.
5. Write word two times.
6. Cover and write one time.
7. Check work.
8. Write word three times.
9. Cover and write one time.
10. Check work.

References to Other Techniques

Aho, 1967
Bartholome, 1977
Clanton, 1977
Glusker, 1967
Hill & Martinis, 1973
Phillips, 1975
Stowitschek & Jobes, 1977

**Figure 5
Word Study Techniques**

dent search for and correct errors (Valmont, 1972).
4. Underline words that may be misspelled and have the student check their accuracy (Personkee & Yee, 1971).

Phonic skills can be developed through application of a wide variety of activities (see Hanna et. al., 1971; Hillerich, 1976). Specifically, these skills can be taught inductively, in isolation or context, and/or by association. Each of these techniques should be used selectively with handicapped students in teaching sound-symbol associations, prefixes, suffixes, and base words. To illustrate, a student initially might learn to associate a particular sound (e.g., /t/) with its corresponding symbol (t). Later, the student might be asked to write the appropriate beginning letter (t) in response to a dictated word (tap).

E. Horn (1960) indicates that spelling rules should be (a) taught inductively rather than deductively, and (b) developed in connection with words to which the rule applies. Moreover, only one rule should be taught at a time. Both the positive and negative aspects of the rule should be highlighted. The rule also should be systematically reviewed and applied.

An important element in spelling instruction is dictionary training. Students need to know how to use the dictionary for many purposes. Dictionary training activities may include alphabetizing words, approximating the location of a given word in the dictionary, using guide words, dividing words into syllables, and so forth.

Students also may require training in visual and auditory imagery. To be effective spellers, students must be able to easily and correctly perceive the words to be spelled. Hudson and Toler (1949), Mason (1961), and Radaker (1963) indicate that auditory and/or visual training may result in improved spelling achievement.

Interest and Motivation

Positive attitudes are crucial to spelling improvement. As most teachers know, effectiveness of instructional procedures depends greatly upon the student's interest and motivation. Regardless of the quality of the program, progress will be restricted if the student is not motivated to spell words correctly or is not interested in spelling. Since attitudes and methodology are intrinsically bound together, techniques designed to foster positive attitudes should be an integral part of the total spelling program.

How does the teacher promote positive attitudes toward spelling? First, the student must develop a desire to spell words correctly. Spelling consciousness can be stimulated by: (a) showing the student the importance of correct spelling in practical and social situations; (b) providing the student with an efficient method of word study; (c) limiting the spelling vocabulary to words most likely needed in the student's present and near future writing endeavors; (d) encouraging pride in correctly spelled papers; and (e) requiring study of only those words that the student is unable to spell.

Of the sources available to the teacher for promoting positive attitudes, probably none other is as important as the student's awareness of progress or success (E. Horn, 1960). Many handicapped students experience considerable frustration in learning to spell. To minimize the effects of persistent failure, the teacher should dramatize each student success using charts, graphs, verbal praise, and so on. The experience of noting progress may be motivating for both student and teacher.

Whenever possible, the student should maintain the chart or graph himself or herself (Wallace & Kauffman, 1973). For example, the student might first record on a graph the number of words spelled correctly on the pretest, and later add to the graph the number of words spelled correctly on the posttest. This exercise provides a visual representation of the student's progress in learning how to spell new words.

For some handicapped students, the dramatization of success is not, in and of itself, enough to overcome undesirable attitudes. The teacher may have to build into the spelling program rewards for good performance. Studies by Benowitz and Busse (1970, 1976), Benowitz and Rosenfeld (1973), and Thompson and Galloway (1970) reveal that material incentives are successful in improving spelling achievement. If material incentives are used, they should be combined with verbal praise. As the student's attitudes and achievement improve, the material incentives should be slowly phased out. Motivation inspired by intrinsic reinforcement is ultimately preferable to material rewards.

Games and special devices are also often suggested as a means of improving spelling attitudes. Research evidence indicates that certain games may be of some benefit (E. Horn, 1960). Nevertheless, they should supplement rather than supplant direct instruction. Teachers either may develop games of their own or locate games developed by others (see Fitzgerald, 1951a; Hildreth, 1962). Games like hangman, crossword puzzles, scrambled words, spelling bingo, and spelling baseball are enjoyable to most students.

ADDITIONAL CONSIDERATIONS

In designing an appropriate spelling program, the proposed methods, materials, reinforcers, and daily activities should be realistic with respect to the instructional time available. It is recommended that 60 to 75 minutes per week be allotted to spelling instruction. Although a few students may require additional time, most students do not benefit from extended periods of study in spelling (Fitzsimmons & Loomer, 1977).

The time allocated for daily spelling instruction can be supplemented and maximized by the advantageous use of tutors or paraprofessionals. Research indicates that tutors are effective in improving tutees' spelling progress (Bandle, 1949; Lovitt, 1975; Stillberger, 1950).

Additionally, the instructional process may be enhanced by enlisting the cooperation of the student's parents. The involvement of parents as "equal partners" in making decisions related to their handicapped child is implicit in PL 94-142 (Hudson & Graham, 1978).

Of final concern is the effect of dialect upon spelling achievement. Many handicapped students are members of minority groups that converse in a dialect other than "standard" English. Although students from minority groups may spell things the way they hear or say them, under no circumstances should the teacher attempt to change their dialect with the hope that acquisition of standard English will improve their spelling achievement. Instead, it is recommended that students pronounce words affected by their dialect and carefully note how they are spelled.

CONCLUSION

The model presented in this article is intended to provide teachers with a valid, flexible, and systematic guide to spelling instruction. The authors hope that teachers will adapt the model to their own particular students and situations. For instance, in a mainstreaming program, each of the participating teachers might bear responsibility for specific aspects of the spelling curricula. In this way, the efforts of both special and regular educators are coordinated and the likelihood of spelling success maximized.

Finally, spelling instruction in the present program is direct and not incidental. Nonetheless, spelling is an integral part of the writing process and not a discrete, separate skill. The language arts are highly interrelated, and students need a lot of practice using their spelling skills in context (i.e., writing).

REFERENCES

Abbott, E. On the analysis of the memory consciousness in orthography. *University of Illinois Psychological Monograph 11,* 1909.

Aho, M. Teaching spelling to children with specific language disability. *Academic Therapy,* 1967, *3,* 45-50.

Allen D., & Ager, J. A factor analytic study of the ability to spell. *Educational & Psychological Measurement,* 1965, *25,* 153-161.

Allred, R. *Spelling: The application of research findings.* Washington, DC: National Education Association, 1977.

Archer, C. Shall we teach spelling by rule? *Elementary English,* 1930, *7,* 61-63.

Ashbaugh, E. *The Iowa spelling scales.* Iowa City: Bureau of Educational Research and Service, 1921.

Ayer, F. *Ayer standardized spelling test.* Austin, TX: Steck, 1950.

Ayer, F. An evaluation of high school spelling. *School Review,* 1951, *59,* 233-236.

Baker, G. *A comparison of traditional spelling with phonemic spelling of fifth and sixth grade students.* Unpublished doctoral dissertation, Wayne State University, 1977.

Bandle, G. *The influence of group cooperation on spelling achievement.* Unpublished master's thesis, University of Iowa, 1949.

Bartholome, L. Using the typewriter for learning: Spelling. *Balance Sheet,* 1977, *58,* 196-200.

Bedell, R., & Nelson, E. Word attack as a factor in reading achievement in the elementary school. *Educational & Psychological Measurement,* 1954, *14,* 168-175.

Beers, J. *First and second grade children's developing concepts of tense and lax vowels.* Unpublished doctoral dissertation, University of Virginia, 1974.

Beers, J., & Henderson, E. A study of developing orthographic concepts among first grade children. *Research in the Teaching of English,* 1977, *11,* 133-148.

Benowitz, M., & Busse, T. Material incentives and the learning of spelling words in a typical school situation. *Journal of Educational Psychology,* 1970, *61,* 24-26.

Benowitz, M., & Busse, T. Effects of material incentives on classroom learning over a four-week period. *Journal of Educational Psychology,* 1976, *68,* 57-62.

Benowitz, M., & Rosenfeld, J. Three types of incentives and classroom learning of middle and lower-class children. *Psychology in the Schools,* 1973, *10,* 79-83.

Beseler, D. *An experiment in spelling using the corrected test method.* Unpublished master's thesis, Central Washington State College, 1953.

Blair, T. ERIC/RCS. *Reading Teacher,* 1975, *28,* 604-607.

Blanchard, G. *An experimental comparison of the test-study and the study-test methods of teaching spelling in the eighth grade.* Unpublished master's thesis, Fordham University, 1944.

Block, J. But will they ever lern to spel korectly? *Educational Research,* 1972, *14,* 171-178.

Boder, E. Developmental dyslexia: A diagnostic screening procedure based on three characteristic patterns of reading and spelling. *Journal of Learning Disabilities,* 1971, *4,* 297-342.

Brody, D. A comparative study of different forms of spelling tests. *Journal of Educational Psychology,* 1944, *35,* 129-144.

Brueckner, L., & Bond, G. *Diagnosis and treatment of learning difficulties.* New York: Appleton-Century-Crofts, 1955.

Burt, C. *Northumberland standardized*

tests: 11 English. London: University of London Press, 1925.
Camp, B., & Dolcourt, J. Reading and spelling in good and poor readers. *Journal of Learning Disabilities*, 1977, *10*, 46-53.
Christine, R., & Hollingsworth, P. An experiment in spelling. *Education*, 1966, *86*, 565-567.
Clanton, P. *The effectiveness of the letter-close procedure as a method of teaching spelling*. Unpublished doctoral dissertation, University of Arkansas, 1977.
Clymer, T. The utility of phonic generalizations in the primary grades. *Reading Teacher*, 1963, *16*, 252-258.
Cohen, L. *Evaluating structural analysis methods used in spelling books*. Unpublished doctoral dissertation, Boston University, 1969.
Columba, M. *A study of interests and their relations to other factors of achievement in elementary school subjects*. Washington, DC: Catholic University, 1926.
Cook, W. Shall we teach spelling by rules? *Journal of Educational Psychology*, 1912, *3*, 316-325.
Cook, W. The measurement of general spelling ability involving controlled comparisons between techniques. *University of Iowa Studies in Education: 6*, 1932, *6*, 1-112.
Courtis, S. *Measurement of classroom products*. New York: General Education Board, 1919.
Davis, L. *The applicability of phonic generalizations to selected spelling programs*. Unpublished doctoral dissertation, University of Oklahoma, 1969.
Dieterich, D. Diserroneosospellingitis or the fine (language) art of spelling. *Elementary English*, 1973, *49*, 245-253.
Diserens, C., & Vaughn, J. The experimental psychology of motivation. *Psychological Bulletin*, 1931, *28*, 15-65.
Dunwell, S. *Report on WRITE: Computer assisted instruction course in written English usage*. Poughkeepsie, NY: Shared Education Computer Systems, 1972.
Durost, W., Evans, W., Leake, J., Bowman, H., Cosgrove, C., & Reed, J. *Metropolitan achievement tests*. New York: Harcourt Brace Jovanovich, 1970.
Durrell, D. *Durrell analysis of reading difficulty*. Yonkers: World Book, 1937.
Edwards, C. *A comparative study of two techniques of spelling instruction*. Unpublished master's thesis, University of Iowa, 1931.
Edwards, M. *An evaluation of the Casis school instructional program in spelling*. Unpublished master's thesis, University of Texas, 1953.
Fitzgerald, J. *The teaching of spelling*. Milwaukee: Bruce Publishing Co., 1951(a).
Fitzgerald, J. *A basic life spelling vocabulary*. Milwaukee: Bruce Publishing Co., 1951(b).
Fitzgerald, J. The teaching of spelling. *Elementary English*, 1953, *30*, 79-84.
Fitzsimmons, R., & Loomer, B. *Spelling research and practice*. Iowa State Department of Public Instruction and University of Iowa, 1977.
Fleming, C. *Kelvin measurement of spelling ability*. Glasgow: Robert Gibson & Sons, 1933.
Foran, T. *The psychology and teaching of spelling*. New York: Catholic Educational Press, 1934.
Forlano, G. *School learning with various methods of practice and rewards*. New York: Columbia University, 1936.
Frasch, D. How well do sixth graders proofread for spelling errors? *Elementary School Journal*, 1965, *65*, 381-382.
Gates, A. An experimental comparison of the study-test and test-study methods in spelling. *Journal of Educational Psychology*, 1931, *22*, 1-19.
Gates, A. *A list of spelling difficulties in 3,876 words*. Unpublished manuscript, 1937.
Gates, A., & Russell, D. *Diagnostic and remedial spelling manual*. New York: Columbia University, 1937.

Gentry, J. *A study of the orthographic strategies of beginning readers.* Unpublished doctoral dissertation, University of Virginia, 1977.

Gilbert, L., & Gilbert, D. The improvement of spelling through reading. *Journal of Educational Research,* 1944, *37,* 458-463.

Gilstrap, R. Development of independent spelling skills in the intermediate grades. *Elementary English,* 1962, *39,* 481-483.

Glusker, P. An integrational approach to spelling. *Academic Therapy,* 1967, *3,* 51-61.

Gold, V. *The effect of an experimental program involving acquisition of phoneme-grapheme relationships incorporating criterion referenced tests with evaluative feedback upon spelling performance of third grade pupils.* Unpublished doctoral dissertation, University of Southern California, 1976.

Graves, D. Research update: Spelling texts and structural analysis methods. *Language Arts,* 1976, *54,* 86-90.

Grottenthaler, J. *A comparison of the effectiveness of three programs of elementary school spelling.* Unpublished doctoral dissertation, University of Pittsburgh, 1970.

Guiler, W., & Lease, G. An experimental study of methods of instruction in spelling. *Elementary School Journal,* 1942, *42,* 234-238.

Hahn, W. *Comparative efficiency of the teaching of spelling by the column and contextual methods.* Unpublished doctoral dissertation, University of Pittsburgh, 1960.

Hahn, W. Phonics: A boon to spelling. *Elementary School Journal,* 1964, *64,* 383-386.

Hall, N. The letter mark-out corrected test. *Journal of Educational Research,* 1964, *58,* 148-157.

Hanna, P., Hanna, J., Hodges, R., & Rudorf, E. *Phoneme-grapheme correspondences as cues to spelling improvement.* Washington, DC: U.S. Government Printing Office, 1966.

Hanna, P., Hodges, R., & Hanna, J. *Spelling: Structure and strategies.* New York: Houghton-Mifflin, 1971.

Hardin, B., Bernstein, B., & Shands, F. The "Hey what's this?" approach to teaching spelling. *Teacher,* 1978, *94,* 64-67.

Hawley, W., & Gallup, J. The list versus the sentence method of teaching spelling. *Journal of Educational Research,* 1922, *5,* 306-310.

Hersen, M., & Barlow, D. *Single case experimental designs.* New York: Pergamon Press, 1976.

Hibler, G. *The test-study versus the study-test method of teaching spelling in grade two: Study I.* Unpublished master's thesis, University of Texas, 1957.

Hildreth, G. *Teaching spelling: A guide to basic principles and practices.* New York: Holt, Rinehart & Winston, 1962.

Hill, C., & Martinis, A. Individualizing a multisensory spelling program? *Academic Therapy,* 1973, *9,* 77-83.

Hillerich, R. *Spelling: An element in written expression.* Columbus, OH: Charles E. Merrill Publishing Co., 1976.

Hillerich, R. Let's teach spelling—not phonetic misspelling. *Language Arts,* 1977, *54,* 301-307.

Hodges, R. Theoretical framework of English orthography. *Elementary English,* 1977, *49,* 1089-1105.

Horn, E. Principles of methods in teaching spelling as derived from scientific investigation. In *Eighteenth Yearbook, National Society for the Study of Education.* Bloomington: Public School Publishing Co., 1919.

Horn, E. *A basic vocabulary of 10,000 words most commonly used in writing.* Iowa City: University of Iowa, 1926.

Horn, E. Research in spelling. *Elementary English Review,* 1944, *21,* 6-13.

Horn, E. Phonics and spelling. *Journal of Education,* 1954, *136,* 233-235, 246.(a)

Horn, E. What research says to the teacher. *Teaching Spelling,* 1954, *3,* 32.(b)

Horn, E. *Teaching spelling.* Washington, DC: American Educational Research Association, 1954.(c)

Horn, E. Spelling. *Encyclopedia of educational research.* New York: Macmillan, 1960.

Horn, E. *Teaching spelling: What research says to the teacher.* Department of Classroom Teachers, American Educational Research Association of the National Education Association, 1967.

Horn, T. *The effects of the corrected test on learning to spell.* Unpublished master's thesis, University of Iowa, 1946.

Horn, T. *The effect of a syllabic presentation of words upon learning to spell.* Unpublished doctoral dissertation, University of Iowa, 1947.

Horn, T. Research critiques. *Elementary English,* 1969, *46,* 210-212.

Horn, T., & Otto, H. *Spelling instruction: A curriculum-wide approach.* Austin: University of Texas, 1954.

Hudson, F., & Graham, S. An approach to operationalizing the I.E.P. *Learning Disability Quarterly,* 1978, *1,* 13-32.

Hudson, J., & Toler, L. Instruction in auditory and visual discrimination as a means of improving spelling. *Elementary School Journal,* 1949, *49,* 459-466.

Humphry, M. *The effect of a syllabic presentation of words upon learning to spell.* Unpublished master's thesis, University of Texas, 1954.

Ibeling, F. Supplementary phonics instruction and reading and spelling ability. *Elementary School Journal,* 1961, *63,* 152-156.

Jensen, A. Spelling errors and the serial-position effect. *Journal of Educational Psychology,* 1962, *53,* 105-109.

Jobes, N. *The acquisition and retention of spelling through imitation training and observational learning with and without feedback.* Unpublished doctoral dissertation, George Peabody College for Teachers, 1975.

Kauffman, J., Hallahan, D., Haas, K., Brame, T., & Boren, R. Imitating children's errors to improve spelling performance. *Journal of Learning Disabilities,* 1978, *11,* 33-38.

King, L. *Learning and applying spelling rules in grades three to eight.* Contributions to Education, No. 517. New York: Bureau of Publications, Columbia University, 1932.

Kingsley, J. The test-study method versus study-test method in spelling. *Elementary School Journal,* 1923, *24,* 126-129.

Knoell, D., & Harris, C. A factor analysis of spelling ability. *Journal of Educational Research,* 1952, *46,* 95-111.

Kooi, B., Schutz, R., & Baker, R. Spelling errors and the serial-position effect. *Journal of Educational Psychology,* 1965, *56,* 334-336.

Kottmeyer, W. *Teacher's guide for remedial reading.* St. Louis: Webster, 1959.

Kyte, G. Maintaining ability grouping in spelling. *Phi Delta Kappan,* 1949, *30,* 301-306.

Lambert, C. *Seven-plus assessment: Spelling.* London: University of London Press, 1964.

Larsen, S., & Hammill, D. *The Larsen-Hammill test of written spelling.* San Rafael, CA: Academic Therapy Publications, 1976.

Larson, T. *Time allotment in the teaching of spelling.* Unpublished master's thesis, University of Iowa, 1945.

Louis, R. *A study of spelling growth in two different teaching procedures.* Unpublished master's thesis, Central Washington State College, 1950.

Lovitt, T. Applied behavior analysis and learning disabilities. Part II: Specific research recommendations and suggestions for practitioners. *Journal of Learning Disabilities,* 1975, *8,* 504-518.

Mason, G. Word discrimination drills. *Journal of Educational Research,* 1961, *55,* 39-40.

Masters, H. *A study of spelling errors.* Unpublished master's thesis, University of Iowa, 1927.

Mendenhall, J. *An analysis of spelling errors: A study of factors associated with word difficulty.* New York: Columbia University, 1930.

Miller, L., & Graham, S. Reading skills of LD students: A review. *Alabama Reader,* 1979, *6,* 16-25.

Miller, L., & Carpenter, D. Analyzing errors in written spelling (submitted for publication).

Monson, J. Is spelling spelled rut, routine, or revitalized? *Elementary English,* 1975, *52,* 223-224.

Montgomery, M. *The test-study method versus the study-test method of teaching spelling in grade two: Study 11.* Unpublished master's thesis, University of Texas, 1957.

Moran, M. Nine steps to the diagnostic prescriptive process in the classroom. *Focus on Exceptional Children,* 1975, *6,* 1-14.

McElwee, G. *Systematic instruction in proofreading for spelling and its effects on fourth and sixth grade composition.* Unpublished doctoral dissertation, University of Wisconsin-Madison, 1974.

McKee, P. *Teaching and testing spelling by column and context forms.* Unpublished doctoral dissertation, University of Iowa, 1924.

Neef, N., Iwata, B., & Page, T. The effects of known-item interspersal on acquisition and retention of spelling and sight word reading. *Journal of Applied Behavior Analysis,* 1977, *10,* 738.

Nisbet, S. Non-dictated spelling tests. *British Journal of Educational Psychology,* 1939, *9,* 29-44.

Oswalt, W. *The effect of proofreading for spelling errors in spelling achievement of fifth grade pupils.* Unpublished doctoral dissertation, Temple University, 1961.

Otto, W., & McMenemy, R. *Corrective and remedial teaching.* Boston: Houghton-Mifflin, 1966.

Personkee, C. The use of nonsense words to test generalization ability in spelling. *Elementary English,* 1972, *49,* 1233-1239.

Personkee, C., & Knight, L. Proofreading and spelling: A report and a program. *Elementary English,* 1967, *44,* 768-774.

Personkee, C., & Yee, A. *Comprehensive spelling instruction: Theory, research, and application.* Scranton: Intext Educational Publishers, 1971.

Peters, M. *Success in spelling. A study of factors affecting improvement in spelling in the junior-school.* Cambridge: Institute of Education, 1970.

Petty, W., & Green, H. *Developing language skills in the elementary schools.* Boston: Allyn & Bacon, 1968.

Phillips, V. *The effect of a mode of presentation of spelling on reading achievement.* Unpublished doctoral dissertation, University of Illinois, 1975.

Radaker, L. The effect of visual imagery upon spelling performance. *Journal of Educational Research,* 1963, 56, 370-372.

Read, E., Allred, R., & Baird, L. *Continuous progress in spelling: Intermediate teacher's manual.* Oklahoma City: Individualized Instruction, Inc., 1972.

Rieth, H., Axelrod, S., Anderson, R., Hathaway, F., Wood, K., & Fitzgerald, C. Influence of distributed practice and daily testing on weekly spelling tests. *Journal of Educational Research,* 1972, *68,* 73-77.

Rinsland, H. *A basic vocabulary of elementary school children.* New York: Macmillan, 1945.

Robinson, A. *Every pupil achievement test: Spelling.* Emporia, KS: Bureau of Educational Measurement, Kansas State Teacher's College, 1970.

Rosemeier, R. Effectiveness of forewarning about errors in response—Selective learning. *Journal of Educational Psychology,* 1965, *56,* 309-314.

Rowell, G. A prototype for an individualized spelling program. *Elementary English,* 1972, *49,* 335-340.

Rudman, M. Informal spelling in the classroom: A more effective approach. *Reading Teacher,* 1973, *26,* 602-604.

Russell, D. *Characteristics of good and poor spellers*. New York: Columbia University, 1937.

Russell, K. *An evaluation of the effect of word analysis exercises on spelling achievement*. Unpublished doctoral dissertation, Boston University, 1954.

Schell, L. B+ in composition: C- in spelling. *Language Arts*, 1975, *52*, 239-257.

Schoephoerster, H. Research into variations of the test-study plan of teaching spelling. *Elementary English*, 1962, *39*, 460-462.

Schoolfield, L., & Timberlake, J. *Phonovisual method book*. Washington, DC: Phonovisual Products, 1949.

Schwartz, S., & Doehring, D. A developmental study of children's ability to acquire knowledge of spelling patterns. *Developmental Psychology*, 1977, *13*, 419-420.

Shubik, H. *An experimental comparison of the test-study and the study-test methods of teaching spelling in third grade*. Unpublished master's thesis, Fordham University, 1951.

Simon, D., & Simon, H. Alternative uses of phonemic information in spelling. *Review of Educational Research*, 1973, *43*, 115-137.

Spache, G. A critical analysis of various methods of classifying spelling errors. *Journal of Educational Psychology*, 1940, *31*, 111-134.

Spache, G. Validity and reliability of the proposed classification of spelling errors. *Journal of Educational Psychology*, 1941, *31*, 204-214.

Spache, G. *Spelling errors test*. Gainesville, FL: Reading laboratory and Clinic, University of Florida, 1955.

Stillberger, E. *Individual differences of achievement in spelling*. Unpublished master's thesis, University of Iowa, 1950.

Stowitschek, C., & Jobes, N. Getting the bugs out of spelling—Or an alternative to the spelling bee. *Teaching Exceptional Children*, 1977, *9*, 74-76.

Strickland, R. *The language arts in the elementary school*. Boston: D.C. Heath, 1951.

Swenson, E., & Caldwell, C. Spelling in children's letters. *Elementary School Journal*, 1948, *19*, 224-235.

Teacher's Manual. *Portland speller*. Portland, OR: Portland Public Schools, 1956.

Templin, M. Phonic knowledge and its relation to the spelling and reading achievement of fourth grade pupils. *Journal of Educational Research*, 1954, *47*, 441-454.

Thomas, R. *The effect of the corrected test on learning to spell, grades four, five, and six*. Unpublished master's thesis, University of Texas, 1954.

Thompson, E., & Galloway, C. Material reinforcement and success in spelling. *Elementary School Journal*, 1970, *70*, 395-398.

Thompson, M. *The effects of spelling pattern training on the spelling behavior of primary elementary students*. Unpublished doctoral dissertation, University of Pittsburgh, 1977.

Thorndike, E. *The psychology of wants, interests, and attitudes*. New York: Appleton-Century-Crofts, 1935.

Thorpe, L., Lefever, D., & Haslund, R. *SRA achievement series*. Chicago: Science Research Associates, 1963.

Tiegs, E., & Clark, W. *California achievement tests*. Monterey: McGraw-Hill, 1970.

Tireman, L. *The value of marking hard spots in spelling*. Unpublished master's thesis, University of Iowa, 1927.

Tovey, D. Sound-it-out: A reasonable approach to spelling? *Reading World*, 1978, *17*, 220-233.

Turner, E. Rules versus drill in teaching spelling. *Journal of Educational Psychology*, 1912, *3*, 460-461.

Tyler, I. *Spelling as a secondary learning*. New York: Columbia University, 1939.

Tyson, I. *Factors contributing to the effectiveness of the corrected test in spelling*. Unpublished doctoral dissertation, University of Iowa, 1953.

Valmont, W. Spelling-consciousness: A long neglected area. *Elementary English*, 1972, *49*, 1219-1221.

Wallace, G., & Kauffmann, J. *Teaching*

children with learning problems. Columbus, OH: Charles E. Merrill Publishing Company, 1973.

Warren, H. *Phonetic generalizations to aid spelling instruction at the fifth-grade level.* Unpublished doctoral dissertation, Boston University, 1969.

Warren, J. *Phonetic generalizations to aid spelling instruction at the fifth-grade level.* Unpublished doctoral dissertation, Boston University, 1970.

Westerman, G. *Spelling and writing.* San Rafael: Dimensions, 1971.

Winch, W. Additional researches on learning to spell. *Journal of Educational Psychology,* 1916, 7, 93-110.

Yee, A. Is the phonetic generalization hypothesis in spelling valid? *Journal of Experimental Education,* 1969, 37, 82-91.

Can We Assume our Remedial Reading Students Know How to Use the Dictionary?

MARYANN FEOLA CASTELUCCI

Many teachers feel that remedial reading students would have less difficulty reading if they would use the dictionary more often. Certainly this is true. But, can we safely assume that our students know how to use the dictionary correctly? In the past I noticed that students in remedial reading courses were often eager to work with the dictionary but were not sure how to approach it. This semester I gave my class a dictionary exercise which included an exploration of ambiguous spellings that exist for the different sounds of English.

This dictionary exercise was conducted on a class of remedial reading college students aged 19–25. None were students of English as a second language.

Each student had been responsible for bringing a dictionary to class. At the beginning of the 2 hour period I dictated seven words, explaining they probably would not know how to spell most of

---

From *Spelling Progress Bulletin,* Vol. 21, No. 3 (Fall, 1981). Reprinted with permission.

them. They were instructed simply to write down what they heard. I asked the class to work carefully and ask me to repeat any word they did not hear clearly. The words I dictated were: *gnome, gnu, phlebitis, feign, wrest, xenophobia,* and *phenomena.* They were told that 'gnu' (the animal) was not spelled 'new' or 'knew,' 'feign' was not spelled 'fain' or 'fane,' and the 'wrest' that they were looking for had nothing to do with relaxation. In addition to looking up each word, the students had to copy down the syllabication, definition(s), and part(s) of speech.

As I walked around the room and spoke to the students, it seemed clear that what they originally thought was a simple task (i.e. looking up something and copying it down) was turning out to be an arduous task. The problem was: how do you look up something if you do not know how to spell it? Some members of the class commented that this was not unusual for them and when this happened, they usually used another word—a word that was "easier" and "more familiar." This is probably true for many remedial reading students. It seems logical that someone who is having difficulties with language in general is not going to be adept at using the dictionary.

About 20 minutes later, I asked who found any of the words. About one half of the class did not find any. Surprisingly, they were not frustrated. Instead, they were energized with the kind of excitement one has when he is anxious to find something he knows is not within his immediate reach, yet is obtainable. What the other half of the group found gave the others added encouragement to go on. *Phenomena* was the word that some students were able to find. However, most of the students who found it claimed they found it syllabified *phenomenon*.

I told the class that we would get back to the na/non problem, but first we would discuss why some were able to find one of the words. I asked a student how she was able to find 'phenomena.' She recalled that she looked under the letter 'f' for about five minutes and then suddenly thought of the word 'phone.' Remembering that that word begins with the 'f' sound, she recalled that many words with that sound start with 'ph.'

I put the word 'reign' on the blackboard and told the class that if they would employ their classmate's procedure, it would help them find three of the words. At this point, I divided the class into groups of three so that they might share ideas and constructive dialogue.

One of the groups that was working especially hard sounded out the word 'reign' very carefully. One student in the group was saying it sound-by-sound with her eyes closed. All of a sudden she said, "Oh my goodness, that word has a 'g' in it but no 'g' sound!" She hurried to the 'gn' section of the dictionary suspecting correctly 'gnome' started with 'gn.'

Now the class caught on to the reason why they were doing this exercise: the ambiguous spellings can make it difficult when you have to look up a word. But, if we think of words that are familiar to us, we can make our way from the known to the unknown. One student was working on her spelling of 'xenophobia.' She was beginning the word with a 'z,' and was trying to think of words that start with the 'z' sound. I suggested that she think of some common words which start with that sound and repeat the words quickly to herself. In a few minutes her eyes lit up. By thinking of 'xerox,' she was able to get to 'xenophobia.' In this fashion the class was able to look up the rest of the words.

The students also had trouble understanding the syllabification. For instance, many of them wanted to know if the letter 'i' was pronounced the same way each time it appeared in the word 'phlebitis.' They suspected that it was not because each one was represented in a different way (diacritical marks). They knew that there was a pronunciation guide at the beginning of the dictionary, but many of them said that some dictionaries do not give a readable or complete explanation of the sounds of English.

They complained too that sometimes a sound is exemplified in a word they do not know how to say. And, of course, for several reasons, many students do not always use this section of the dictionary. One student said, "Maybe I can use the pronunciation guide, but that won't help me any when I'm trying to sound out a new word and there's no dictionary around." We all agreed this could be a problem.

I referred back to the ability that they had to decode the first sound of the word 'phlebitis.' I asked them to recall how they were able to do it. One student said that she saw an 'f' and instantly pictured the word 'Frank' (her boyfriend's name) and was able to make the necessary sound. I asked if anything similar might be done to sound out the rest of the sounds even though they were not familiar. After some thought the suggestion was made that perhaps they could take the part of the word that was giving them trouble and see if they could remember a word that was made up of or included that spelling (e.g. look up familiar word(s) to see if the symbols in the syllabification were the same as those for either of the 'i's in 'phlebitis'). They tried this out. Much to their pleasure, they found that in most cases it worked. The class felt comfortable and was no longer afraid to deal with the dictionary's symbols once they knew that they represented sounds that had long been part of their speaking vocabulary and were not just part of a crazy code someone recently thought up. It became increasingly evident that my class felt comfortable using techniques they could rely on and, in fact had, to a limited degree, already been using.

When we talked about why so many of them got 'phenomenon' when they were looking up 'phenomena' a similar pattern evolved. I discovered that much of the class did not know the abbreviations for the words: plural, noun, verb, adverb, adjective, etc. No one knew why 'phenomena' did not have a listing of its own. I asked them to look up the word 'parties.' Soon everyone said they found it under the listing for 'party.' We talked about why that was so and several of the class members said the word 'parties' belongs under the listing for 'party' because it is the plural. I insisted that that was not enough proof and instructed them to look under that listing for more concrete proof. After a while, one student said her dictionary had the 'ies' ending but dropped off the rest of the word. When I asked her to illustrate that on the blackboard, she stepped back, considered what she wrote, and then added 'pl.' in front of it. The student said, "This had the letters 'pl.' here, and that must mean 'plural.' It must be the abbreviation for that word." Instantly two things happened. First, the students started to discuss how they were certain that 'phenomena' had to be the plural of 'phenomenon,' just as 'parties' had to be the plural of 'party.' They were so certain because they did not have to take my word for it; they had found it out for themselves.

Secondly, some of the students began to question what the other abbreviations were under the word 'party.' They wanted to know: Could they be the parts of speech? Some students said with confidence that they were, but they were not sure how they knew it. I felt that this was a good entry into the discussion of the parts of speech. I asked what were the main differences between the different definitions of the word 'party' given under the abbreviation 'n.' They broke up into groups to work this one out. I asked them to come to a consensus about the differences in each meaning. Each group basically came up with the same thing: the definitions of 'party' after 'n' was a person or thing and 'party' under 'v' was something someone did. This they said confidently must be what parts of speech are all about. They began to realize that words not only have different meanings, but also have different functions in a sentence.

Thanks to these responses, I feel more comfortable when I ask my class to use the dictionary. The exercises are only a few of many that can be done with a group of college remedial reading students who are just beginning to learn how a dictionary is put together and how they might use it. More importantly, I know they are aware that they have the power to understand many things by using ideas and procedures that have worked successfully for them in the past.

Group work can help to make this type of teaching more successful because the students have the opportunity to work out problems in their own language with others who are at the same or slightly higher level of competency. The students are able to think and speak freely without the fear (which so many of them have) of giving the teacher a wrong answer. If group work is used, however, the students must be shown how to work in a group, i.e., one person does not do all the work, ideas are to be shared, everyone participates, and all tasks are rotated. Like everything else in the encouragement of self-observation in reading, the introduction of collaborative work should include emphasis on procedure rather than on product. And again, we should not assume that our students already know what this means. They all need training in procedures as well as in substance.

Spelling: Diagnosing Basic Skills

KENNETH W. HOWELL
JOSEPH S. KAPLAN
with TERESA SERAPIGLIA

Teachers tend to teach spelling the way it was taught to them. Consequently, most spelling lessons consist of memorizing word lists even though there are years of evidence which show that this isn't the best way to teach students to spell words. Whatever "spelling" is, it certainly is not one independent skill or ability. Nothing correlates particularly highly with spelling. There isn't any syndrome or set of characteristics that typify bad spellers. No one ever says a kid is suffering from "disspellia," because the only characteristic that separates spellers from nonspellers is the number of words they spell correctly.

In order to spell well a student must determine: how the word is pronounced, if it is spelled like it is pronounced, and how it is spelled if it isn't spelled like it's pronounced (Spache, 1940). As an oversimplification, spelling can be viewed as the flip side of reading. When we ask a student to read, we show him letters and ask for sounds. When we ask a student to spell, we give him sounds and ask for letters. Therefore the predictability of the sound/letter correspondence in words is an important concern.

Misspellings fall roughly into two categories: phonetic misspellings and nonphonetic misspellings. Phonetic misspellings can be read as the stimulus word, for example, *order—ordr*. Nonphonetic misspellings can't be read as in *order—audr*. The type of misspelling a student makes is critical. The phonetic speller is actively using phonetic clues (although they are the wrong ones), whereas the nonphonetic speller does not seem to be attending to letter sounds.

A confounding factor in spelling instruction is the observation that many successful spellers simply "see" the word in their mind and copy it onto their paper. Poor spellers seem to lack this skill which is sometimes referred to as "revisualization," or visual memory. When presented with an uncertain word, we will write it out to find out if it looks right. When we do this, we may be comparing the word we wrote to our memory of the word's appearance, or we may simply be checking our spelling by reading what we wrote. In any case, it appears that "revisualization" as a skill cannot be taught. That is, good spellers can do it and bad spellers can't, but teaching it doesn't make bad spellers any better.

There do seem to be some prerequisites to good spelling. One of the most important spelling prerequisites is the ability to discriminate accurately (attend to and perceive) what one hears. If a stu-

---

Pages 174–189 of *Diagnosing Basic Skills: A Handbook for Deciding What to Teach.* © 1980 by Bell & Howell Company. Reprinted by permission.

dent thinks the word *dropped* is pronounced *drop* because he had difficulty perceiving or attending to the endings of spoken words, he will probably write *d-r-o-p* in those instances where *d-r-o-p-p-e-d* would be correct. If he has difficulty discriminating the medial consonant sounds in words, he might perceive *ankle* as *angle* and write it in the wrong context; e.g., "The angle bone is next to the foot." One way to test for this prerequisite is to have the student repeat each spelling word dictated to make sure he heard (perceived) it accurately. Whenever you come across a misspelled word in the student's written work, ask him what word was he trying to write. If he mispronounces the word, you may have a speech and/or regional accent problem to remediate instead of a spelling problem.

Since spelling is only important where written communication is concerned, you must always be aware of the effect that handwriting may have on a student's spelling performance. Students who have not mastered the skill of handwriting are unable to concentrate on the process of spelling. In other words, handwriting should be an automatic skill like operating an automobile. If the average driver had to stop and think about the mechanics of shifting gears every time he turned a corner, it would interfere with his ability to concentrate on the most important facet of driving, navigating safely through traffic. Similarly, thinking about how each letter is written tends to interfere with spelling, whether the student is engaged in revisualizing a word or sounding it out.

Should you suspect that poor performance in writing is interfering with the student's spelling, ask him to spell words verbally before writing them. Make comparisons between his verbal and written spelling. The authors have, on occasion, found students whose spelling errors (on the same words) drop markedly when they are allowed to spell verbally. We have also found that some students cannot spell some words verbally unless they first attempt to write them. In our survey level testing we have often given students the option of spelling the word verbally or in writing. This way we can readily observe the student's preferred response mode. If he begins by writing the letters before he pronounces them, you may assume that he needs visual, kinesthetic, and/or decoding feedback to help him remember the sequence of the letters in the word. On the other hand, if he begins by spelling the word verbally and then attempts to write it, you might hypothesize that the writing act interferes with the spelling. Remember that your assumptions and hypotheses always need to be validated through specific level testing. If you suspect a handwriting problem, administer an informal criterion probe to determine if, in fact, the subject has mastered the prerequisite handwriting skills for spelling.

The most obvious prerequisite to spelling is the ability to recall the letters which make sounds. This phonetic skill is so similar to what is expected while reading that reading and spelling instruction can be used nicely to reinforce each other. Unfortunately, for some mysterious reason educators in this country teach different spelling and reading words at the same grade level. This is not done in other countries where the same word list is often used for both skills. However, in the United States books with different word lists are advertised for each grade level. We assume this is because the procedure allows publishers to sell two different books when one would suffice. At any rate, the decoding table of specifications can be used to test spelling by simply asking "what letter(s) make this sound" and proceeding through the table. In addition, some phonetic generalizations occur reliably enough that students may be able to use them to attack unfamiliar words. These generalizations are outlined in Table 6.1. Of course these generalizations cannot be used at the automatic or even mastery levels, but they may aid a student in reaching accuracy.

Another critical phonetic skill is the

STUDENTS WITH SPECIAL NEEDS

Table 6.1 Phonics generalizations applied to spelling

1. Double the letters *f, l, s,* or *z* in most one syllable words when preceded by a short vowel. Examples are *cliff, sniff, bluff, whiff, cuff, puff, fell, tell, swell, ball, spill, fill, spell, brass, press, cross, miss, fuss, pass, buzz, fizz, jazz.* Exceptions are *bus* and *gas.*

2. The silent *e* at the end of a word makes a short vowel long. Examples are *pin* and *pine, dim* and *dime, hat* and *hate, mat* and *mate, rat* and *rate, cub* and *cube, plan* and *plane, cap* and *cape, at* and *ate, mad* and *made, mop* and *mope, kit* and *kite, rod* and *rode, hid* and *hide, rip* and *ripe, fad* and *fade, cut* and *cute, tub* and *tube, can* and *cane, hop* and *hope, not* and *note,* and *fin* and *fine.*

3. When you hear *k* after a *short* vowel, spell it *ck* and when you hear *k* after a *long* vowel or consonant, spell it *k.* Examples are *neck, dusk, flank, track, hunk, slack, stuck, deck, rink, milk, check, tuck, task, fleck, lack, coke, make, rock, knock,* and *stink.* Use *c* at the end of polysyllabic words when you hear *ik.* Examples are *attic, plastic, metric, cosmic, classic, Atlantic, optic, frantic.*

4. When you hear *j* after a short vowel, you usually spell it *dge.* After a long vowel or consonant you use *ge.* Examples are *age, gadget, lodge, huge, strange, cage, nudge, stage, page, bridge, change, hinge, edge.*

5. When you hear *ch* after a short vowel use *tch.* When you hear *ch* after a long vowel or consonant, use *ch. Ch* is always used at the beginning of a word. Examples are *chop, bench, batch, pinch, church, witch, blotch, pitch, porch, crutch, lunch, sketch, fetch, patch.* Exceptions are *rich, which, much, such, sandwich.*

6. When you have one syllable, a consonant, at the end of a word, preceded by a *short* vowel, and the suffix begins with one vowel, double the consonant. If any one of these conditions is not met, don't double. Examples are *ship* and *shipper, ship* and *shipping, hot* and *hottest, slop* and *sloppy, mad* and *madder, rob* and *robber, star* and *starry, fat* and *fatter, fog* and *foggy, wit* and *witness, grin* and *grinning, mad* and *madly, cold* and *colder, farm* and *farming, dust* and *dusty, rant* and *ranted, boat* and *boating, weed* and *weeding, blot* and *blotter, grim* and *grimmest, rest* and *restless, flat* and *flatly, slim* and *slimmer, feed* and *feeding,* and *win* and *winning.*

7. A word ending in a silent *e* drops the *e* before beginning with a vowel, but does not change before an ending beginning with a consonant. Examples are *hope* and *hoping, dive* and *diving, write* and *writing, tune* and *tuneful, shine* and *shiny, time* and *timer, hope* and *hopeless, take* and *taking, sore* and *soreness, flame* and *flaming, fame* and *famous, care* and *caring, hide* and *hiding, hope* and *hoped, lone* and *lonely, use* and *useful, sure* and *surely, close* and *closely, make* and *making, life* and *lifeless, like* and *likeness, shade* and *shady, noise* and *noiseless,* and *tire* and *tiresome.*

8. Double the consonant when it follows a short vowel. Examples are *capped, caper, capping, moped, mopping, mopped, moping, filling, filed, filing, filled, taping, tapping, taped, tapped, tapper, hopped, hoped, hopping, hoping.*

Table 6.1 Phonics generalizations applied to spelling—continued

9. In words ending in *y*, preceded by a consonant, the *y* changes to *i* before any ending except *ing* or *ist*. In words ending in *y* preceded by a vowel, keep the *y*. Examples are *cry* and *crying*, *rely* and *reliance*, *pray* and *prayer*, *worry* and *worrying*, *joy* and *joyful*, *enjoy* and *enjoyment*, *say* and *saying*, *sleepy* and *sleepiness*, *glory* and *glorious*, *delay* and *delayed*, *merry* and *merriest*, *study* and *studying*, *lonely* and *loneliness*, *pay* and *payable*, *carry* and *carried*, *stray* and *strayed*, *fly* and *flier*, *supply* and *supplied*, *healthy* and *healthier*, *spy* and *spying*, *funny* and *funniest*, *tiny* and *tiniest*, *injury* and *injurious*.

10. When adding *ble, dle, fle* to a word, consider the initial vowel sound. A long vowel or consonant simply needs *ble, dle, fle*. A short vowel continues to need all the help it can get. Examples are *buckle, freckle, puddle, ruffle, stable, rifle, stifle, staple*.

11. While most nouns form the plural by adding *s* to the singular, nouns ending in *s, x, sh,* and *ch* form the plural by adding *es*. A noun ending in *y* preceded by a consonant forms the plural by changing the *y* to *i* and adding *es*. Examples are *cats, dogs, kisses, boxes, fishes, churches,* and *candies*.

12. An apostrophe is used to show the omission of a letter or letters in a contraction. The possessive of a singular noun is formed by adding an apostrophe and *s*. The possessive of a plural noun ending in *s* is formed by adding an apostrophe. Examples are *cannot* and *can't*, *will not* and *won't*, *I had* and *I'd*, *I will* and *I'll*, *had not* and *hadn't*, *Jim's car*, *the dog's bone*, *the groups' scores*.

ability to read and spell clusters. Spelling is a lot like blending in that it requires the student to break the word down, translate it into code, and reassemble it. During the analysis of the word it is best to attend to clusters within the word as opposed to the individual letters. In the word *string*, for example, the student could focus on each letter or on the clusters *str* and *ing*. The Glass Analysis System described in the blending portion of Chapter 4 is an excellent evaluative and instructional technique for spelling.

A sequence for evaluating the student's skill at spelling-related phonetic skills is shown in Figure 6.21. The steps in the inventory are followed on words which the student has previously misspelled. These words are obtained during the survey level testing.

The major controversy in the area of spelling has been whether instruction should focus on the rote learning of each and every word or on the application of a few phonics generalizations (rules) to many words. For years spelling had been taught by rote memorization with the assumption that each word required a separate act of learning. This practice was based on the idea that the English language was nonphonetic and did not readily lend itself to the teaching of phonics generalizations. However, significant research conducted during the 1950s tended to dispute this notion and eventually led to the current philosophy that students need to learn the phonetic patterns in words and how to apply them. Hanna and Moore (1953) analyzed the phoneme-grapheme correspondences in the 3,000 words most commonly taught in spelling programs in the United States and reported these findings: (1) 80% (four-fifths) of all the phonemes (sounds) in the spoken words are predictably represented by graphemes (letters) when the words are written; (2) consonant sounds and blends are regularly spelled more than 90% of the time; and (3) nearly three-fourths of the vowel sounds present no serious spelling problem, since the vowel speech sounds are spelled regularly from 57% to 99% of the time in the vocabulary analyzed (Deverell, 1971). From this data it was concluded that "in spite of its many imperfections, the English system of writing is in origin and in its main features phonetic, or alphabetic" (Hanna & Moore, p. 330).

The findings of Spache (1940) that "good" spellers tended to have greater skill in phonics and better auditory discrimination appear to support the notion that English is phonically regular enough to warrant the teaching of phonics generalizations in the spelling curriculum. The situation seems to parallel the old proverb about giving a man a fish versus a fishing rod. You can teach each word to a student and have him dependent upon you for each word he learns to spell, or you can give him a tool with which he may learn to spell words on his own. Since the phonetic spelling inventory includes words (and word parts) taken from the survey level assessment, it has no standard word list. What is provided in Figure 6.21 is a procedure for designing an inventory using the same words that your student misspelled during the survey level testing. Use each of the performance objectives listed as a basis for a criterion-referenced test. Simply add your content (words and/or word parts) and any directions necessary. You will also need to standardize each CRT in order to determine criteria for accuracy and/or speed. This may be done quickly and easily with a small number of students *who already possess the skills/knowledge being measured.*

Figure 6.21 Informal phonetic spelling inventory

1. *Word Reproduction*: Given words dictated one at a time by the examiner, the student will correctly repeat each word with _____ % accuracy taking no more than _____ seconds per word.

2. *Syllable Isolation*: Given words dictated one at a time by the examiner, the student will correctly say each word with an obvious pause between syllables. This will be done with _____ % accuracy taking no more than _____ seconds per word.

3. *Sound Isolation*: Given syllables dictated one at a time by the examiner, the student will correctly say each sound (phoneme) in a syllable with an obvious pause between sounds. This will be done with _____ % accuracy taking no more than _____ seconds per syllable.

4. *Sound-Symbol Correspondence*: Given sounds (phonemes) dictated one at a time by the examiner, the student will correctly write the letters (graphemes) that make each sound. This will be done with _____ % accuracy taking no more than _____ seconds per sound.

5. *Operational Knowledge*: Given the directions to do so, the student will correctly say and describe all of the steps necessary to phonetically spell unknown words. This will be done with _____ % accuracy taking no more than _____ seconds.

SPELLING ASSESSMENT

Unlike handwriting, where the diagnostician can identify error patterns from a small sample of the student's behavior, spelling requires a relatively large sample of behavior before any reliable estimates can be made. A minimum of 75 spelling errors (up to three per word) is necessary to provide an accurate estimate of a student's error tendencies (Spache, 1940). Few standardized spelling tests afford students the opportunity to make this many errors.

The words used for the spelling assessment may come from the students' speller or from their reading book. A simple procedure for the selection of enough words is to determine the number of words taught at a particular level and then divide this number by whatever amount might yield enough words for a reasonable sample. By "reasonable" we mean *large* enough for the student to make the minimum of 75 errors and *varied* enough to include words representing different kinds of spelling patterns. Considering the format of most spelling texts, you should not simply choose the first 100 words in the book if you want to include a complete and comprehensive variety of spelling words. Let's suppose a book has 500 words in it and you think the student will need to spell at least 50 words in order to make the minimum number of errors. Five hundred divided by 50 equals 10. This means that if you go through the entire spelling book selecting every tenth word, you will wind up with a list of 50 words that is representative of the spelling patterns presented in the text. You are now ready to test.

Use the same stimulus-response modes expected of the student in the spelling lessons (hear to write). Say the word and ask the student to repeat it. If the word has a homonym, then use it in a sentence. Don't worry about time limits. Give the student enough time to write the word down or dictate it to you if she can't write. Encourage her to spell each word. Have her spell it the way it sounds if she can't remember the way it looks. Remember that your goal is to get a sample of her spelling behavior that is large enough to yield a reliable estimate of her error tendencies. If she gives up or doesn't have enough time to spell a word, you won't have enough errors to analyze. Count up to three errors per word. Consider words with more than three different kinds of errors as unrecognizable and don't count them in your total. If an error occurs more than once in a word, count it only once in the total. Keep a running score, if possible, so that you can stop when you have enough errors to analyze. You may wish to take a number of breaks in the testing since it will probably be difficult to motivate the kid to continue to spell words she is having trouble with. It might even become necessary to spread the test over a few days.

Once you have a minimum of 75 errors you may stop the testing and begin error analysis. A useful initial analyzing technique is to categorize the errors. Spache has identified 12 common error types which we have listed with examples in Table 6.2. Categorizing the errors by type may allow you to quickly identify a particular area of phonetic weakness. However, the number of errors in each category cannot always be compared directly to the other categories. The probability of an error occurring is dependent upon the opportunity for it to occur. This means that it isn't possible to omit a double letter in the word *Taylor* or to omit a silent letter in the word *Craft*. The random procedure we described for selecting words from a reader or speller may not provide equal opportunities for all error types; therefore, comparison of the error types to one another can be misleading. However, simply summarizing the errors by type can aid in subsequent analysis.

If an inordinate number of the student's errors are type one, it is not

STUDENTS WITH SPECIAL NEEDS

Table 6.2 Common spelling errors (Spache, 1940)

1. Omission of a silent letter (e.g., *wether* for *weather, reman* for *remain, fin* for *fine*)

2. Omission of a sounded letter (e.g., *requst* for *request, plasure* for *pleasure, personl* for *personal, juge* for *judge*)

3. Omission of a doubled letter (e.g., *suden* for *sudden, adress* for *address, sed* for *seed*)

4. Doubling (e.g., *untill* for *until, frriend* for *friend, deegree* for *degree*)

5. Addition of a single letter (e.g., *darck* for *dark, nineth* for *ninth, refere* for *refer*)

6. Transposition or partial reversal (e.g., *was* for *saw, nickle* for *nickel, bron* for *born*)

7. Phonetic substitution for a vowel (e.g., *prisin* for *prison, injoy* for *enjoy*)

8. Phonetic substitution for a consonant (e.g., *prixon* for *prison, cecond* for *second, vakation* for *vacation*)

9. Phonetic substitution for a syllable (e.g., *purchest* for *purchased, financhel* for *financial, naborhood* for *neighborhood, stopt* for *stopped*)

10. Phonetic substitution for a word (e.g., *weary* for *very, colonial* for *colonel*)

11. Nonphonetic substitution for a vowel (e.g., *rad* for *red, reword* for *reward*)

12. Nonphonetic substitution for a consonant (e.g., *watching* for *washing, inportance* for *importance*)

enough to stop and say that she tends to omit silent letters. You will need to examine each of the misspelled words that include type one errors and determine what kind of type one errors the student tends to make. For example, does she make: omissions of the silent letter *e* at the end of the word, omissions of the silent letter in a vowel digraph such as the *a* in *ea*, omissions of the silent letter in a "sight" word, e.g., *laugh* or *thought*? Similarly, type two errors—omission of sounded letters—require further examination to determine the letter(s) omitted and in what part of the word: beginning, medial, or ending. Does the student omit common suffixes such as *ed, er,* or *ing* or the plurals *es* and *s*? Does she omit the doubled vowels *ee* or *oo* or the doubled consonants after a short vowel? Does she omit the doubled consonants at the end of a word? You will need all of this information in order to specify accurately the student's errors. A sample case should illustrate this procedure.

Example

Ross is a ten-year-old student being mainstreamed in a regular fifth grade classroom. He is currently achieving approximately two years below grade level in spelling, and his teacher has decided to conduct a task analytical diagnosis of his spelling problem. First she completes

STUDENTS WITH SPECIAL NEEDS

a survey level assessment by administering an informal spelling inventory she designed with vocabulary words from the basal spelling program she uses in her class. There are a total of 493 words in the third grade spelling workbook that Ross is using. Based upon his past spelling performance, Ross's teacher predicts that a 60-word spelling test will be necessary to produce the minimum number of 75 errors necessary. By dividing the number of words needed (60) into the number of words in the workbook (493), Ross's teacher is able to determine the ordinal position of each word chosen for the spelling test: 493 divided by 60 equals 8.21 (which is rounded off). Beginning with the first word in the word list, she writes down every eighth word until she has gone through an entire vocabulary list. When she has finished, she has a 60-word spelling test and begins her testing.

Using Spache's most common spelling errors as a guide, she labels each of Ross's errors with a number corresponding to an error type (see Figure 6.22). When this is done, she totals his errors and computes the percentage for each error type. Most of Ross's errors are omissions of silent, sounded, and doubled letters (types 1, 2, and 3). Next the teacher decides to take the process one step further and note the letters and clusters affected by the errors. While this could have been done on the original S/R sheet (Figure 6.22), we have separated it here to make it easier to read. We have also discarded the lower frequency errors and commented on only the most frequently occurring errors. This is shown in Figure 6.23.

Figure 6.22   Ross's survey level spelling test

Stimulus	Response	Error Type (listed as it occurred)
1. keeper	kepr	3,2
2. stories	stry	2,9
3. team	tem	1
4. teach	tesh	1,12
5. cowboy	bboy	8,2
6. why	y	2,1
7. funny	funy	3
8. that's	thats	apostrophe
9. kite	kit	1

329

STUDENTS WITH SPECIAL NEEDS

Figure 6.22 Ross's survey level spelling test—continued

Stimulus	Response	Error Type (listed as it occurred)
10. sorry	*sry*	2,3
11. line	*lin*	1
12. air	*ar*	1
13. became	*becm*	2,1
14. mile	*mil*	1
15. bigger	*bigr*	3,2
16. birds	*lrdz*	2,8
17. animal	*aminl*	6,2
18. I'll	*I l*	apostrophe, 3
19. tribe	*trb*	2,1
20. truck	*truk*	2
21. eight	*at*	7,1
22. won	*on*	2
23. merry	*mry*	2,3
24. helper	*helpr*	2
25. fair	*fr*	2,1
26. send	*sen*	2

330

STUDENTS WITH SPECIAL NEEDS

Figure 6.22 Ross's survey level spelling test—continued

Stimulus	Response	Error Type (listed as it occurred)
27. lunch	lnch	2
28. camp	cap	2
29. set	set	—
30. swing	swim	12,2
31. left	lef	2
32. country	kuntry	12,1
33. street	stret	3
34. visit	vist	2
35. dishes	dish	1,2
36. hadn't	hand	6, apostrophe, 2
37. lock	lok	2
38. almost	allmos	4,2
39. hard	hrd	2
40. pair	pr	2,1
41. most	must	11
42. does	doz	1,8
43. fall	ful	3

331

STUDENTS WITH SPECIAL NEEDS

Figure 6.22 Ross's survey level spelling test—continued

Stimulus	Response	Error Type (listed as it occurred)
44. brothers	bothr	2,2,2 (counted only once)
45. side	sid	1
46. likes	liks	1
47. drink	dnrk	6,2
48. ever	evr	2
49. happiest	hapyst	3,7,2
50. trip	trip	–
51. happier	hapyr	3,7,2
52. tent	ten	2
53. we'll	wel	apostrophe, 3
54. thick	thik	2
55. feeling	feling	3
56. bug	bug	–
57. closed	clozt	8,1,12
58. guess	ges	1,3
59. pretty	prty	2,3
60. color	colr	2

Figure 6.23 Analysis of Ross's spelling errors

1.0 omission of silent letter errors

Stimulus	Response	Comments
team	ten	Doesn't know vowel digraph *ea*?
teach	tesk	Same as above
why	y	Doesn't know "wh" sound?
kite	kit	Doesn't know silent *e* rule?
line	lin	Same as above
air	ar	Doesn't know vowel digraph *ai*?
became	becm	Doesn't know silent *e* rule?
mile	mil	Same as above
tribe	trb	Same as above
eight	at	Not able to revisualize?
fair	fr	Doesn't know vowel digraph?
country	kuntry	Not able to revisualize?
dishes	dish	Doesn't know rule re: adding *e* to *s* after *sh*?
pair	pr	Doesn't know vowel digraph?
does	doz	Not able to revisualize?
side	sid	Doesn't know silent *e* rule?
likes	liks	Same as above
closed	clozt	Doesn't know suffix *ed*?
guess	ges	Not able to revisualize?

2.0 omission of sounded letter errors

Stimulus	Response	Position of Sound	Comments
keeper	kepr	end	Doesn't know suffix *er*?
stories	strz	middle	Doesn't know "or" sound? Doesn't know rule re: conversion of *y* to *ie*? Didn't hear sound (he perceived *stores* for *stories*)?
cowboy	kboy	beginning	Doesn't hear "ow" sound? Or doesn't know diphthong *ow*?
helper	helpr	end	Doesn't know suffix *er*?
fair	fr	middle	Doesn't know vowel digraph?
send	sen	end	Doesn't hear "d" sound?
lunch	lnch	beginning	Doesn't hear short "u"?
camp	cap	end	Doesn't hear "m"?
swing	swim	end	Doesn't hear "g" sound?
left	lef	end	Doesn't hear "t" sound?
visit	vist	end	Doesn't hear short "i" sound?
dishes	dish	end	Doesn't hear plural ending? Or doesn't know how to write plural ending?
hadn't	hand	end	Doesn't hear "t" sound?

STUDENTS WITH SPECIAL NEEDS

Figure 6.23 Analysis of Ross's spelling errors—continued

Stimulus	Response	Position of Sound	Comments
lock	lok	end	Doesn't know rule re: use of *k* and *ck* after vowels?
almost	allmos	end	Doesn't hear "t" sound?
hard	hrd	middle	Doesn't have sound-symbol correspondence?
pair	pr	middle	Doesn't know vowel digraph?
brothers	bothr	beginning	Doesn't hear "r" sound? Doesn't know suffix *er*? Doesn't hear word as plural?
drink	dnrk	middle	Doesn't hear short "i" sound?
ever	evr	end	Doesn't know suffix *er*?
happiest	hapyst	end	Doesn't hear short "e" sound?
happier	hapyr	end	Doesn't know suffix *er*?
tent	ten	end	Doesn't hear "t" sound?
thick	thik	end	Doesn't know rule re: use of *k* and *ck* after vowels?
pretty	prty	middle	Doesn't hear vowel sound?
color	colr	end	Doesn't know suffix *or*?
why	y	beginning	Doesn't know "wh" sound?
sorry	sry	beginning	Doesn't hear "o" sound in word?
became	becm	middle	Doesn't hear "a" sound in word?
bigger	bigr	end	Doesn't know suffix *er*?
birds	brdz	beginning	Doesn't have sound-symbol correspondence?
animal	aminl	end	Not able to revisualize?
tribe	trb	middle	Doesn't hear sound in word?
truck	truk	end	Doesn't know rule re: use of *k* and *ck* after vowels?
won	on	beginning	Doesn't hear sound? Doesn't have sound-symbol correspondence?
merry	mry	beginning	Doesn't hear sound in word?

3.0 Omission of doubled letter errors

Stimulus	Response	Comments
keeper	kepr	Not able to revisualize
funny	funy	Doesn't know rule re: doubling of consonant after a short vowel?
sorry	sry	Same as above
bigger	bigr	Same
I'll	Il	Doesn't know word is contraction for "I will"?
merry	mry	Doesn't know rule re: doubling of consonant?
street	stret	Not able to revisualize

Figure 6.23 Analysis of Ross's spelling errors—continued

Stimulus	Response	Comments
fall	ful	Doesn't know rule re: doubling of letter *l* in one syllable word preceded by short vowel?
happiest	hapyst	Doesn't know rule re: doubling of consonant after a short vowel?
happier	hapyr	Same as above
we'll	wel	Doesn't know word is contraction for "we will"?
feeling	feling	Not able to revisualize
guess	ges	Same as above
pretty	prty	Same

At first it may appear that the teacher is working without a F-AC-T sheet. But while she may not be using the sheet itself, she is still using the format. She has arranged all of the data necessary in the same order as she would if she were using a F-AC-T sheet. As you can see in Figure 6.23, the data under "stimulus" and "response" would comprise the facts while the material under "comments" corresponds with assumed causes. Ross's teacher is simply conserving time and energy (not to mention paper) by consolidating these three stages (fact finding, task analyzing, and hypothesizing) into one operation.

Given the data from the survey level assessment, Ross's teacher has identified the following as assumed causes for his low achievement in spelling:

1. Doesn't know the vowel digraphs *ea* and *ai*.
2. Doesn't know the silent *e* rule and/or how to apply it.
3. Doesn't know the common suffixes *ed* and *er*.
4. Doesn't hear (perceive) consonant and vowel sounds in different parts of words.
5. Doesn't know the phonics generalizations (rules) regarding the use of the letters *k* and *ck* after vowels and/or doesn't know how to apply them.
6. Doesn't know the rule regarding the doubling of consonants and/or doesn't know how to apply it.

Her next step is obvious. She needs to test each of the above hypotheses to determine which are true.

Specific Level Assessment

Specific level assessment in spelling is no different from that in math, reading or language. The objective is to find or write valid criterion measures that will tell you which of the assumed causes are correct. As long as we have gone this far with our illustrative case, we might as well go all the way and take it through the validating stage. Here are Ross's specific level test results:

1. Ross doesn't know vowel digraph *ea*.
   Test: Given the directions to write the letters that make the "ē" sound in words such as *team*, *weak*, *speak*, *teach*, *read*, *reach*, Ross will write the letters *e-a* without hesitation.
   Results: No Pass

STUDENTS WITH SPECIAL NEEDS

2. Ross doesn't know the silent *e* rule.
   Test: Given the directions to verbally state the silent *e* rule, Ross will respond correctly without hesitation.
   Results: No Pass

3. Ross doesn't know how to apply the silent *e* rule.
   Test: Given the words *dim, dime, hide, hid, fin, fine, bit, bite* dictated by the examiner one at a time, Ross will spell each correctly in writing taking no more than ten seconds per word. (Given only if subject passes test #2)
   Results: Not Given

4. Ross doesn't know vowel digraph *ai*.
   Test: Given the directions to write the letters that make the "a" sound in words such as *wait, pain, rain, train, pair, fair, stair*, Ross will write the letters *a-i* without hesitation.
   Results: No Pass

5. Ross doesn't know common suffixes such as *ed* and *er*.
   Test: Given the directions to write the letters that make the "d" and "r" sounds at the end of the words *stopped* and *stopper*, Ross will write the letters *e-d* and *e-r* without hesitation.
   Results: No Pass

6. Ross doesn't hear (perceive) sounds within words.
   Test: Given the directions to say the sounds he hears in a dictated word, Ross will correctly say each sound in the word with an obvious pause between sounds. Words should be used that have consonant-vowel-consonant, CVCV, CCVCCV, and CVCCV relationships.
   Results: No Pass

7. Ross doesn't know the phonics generalizations regarding the use of *k* and *ck* after vowels.
   Test: Given the directions to verbally state the rule regarding the use of *k* and *ck* after vowels, Ross will respond correctly without hesitation.
   Results: No Pass

8. Ross doesn't know how to apply the phonics generalization regarding the use of *k* and *ck* after vowels.
   Test: Given the words *coke, pack, neck, duck, rock, like* dictated by the examiner one at a time, Ross will spell each correctly in writing taking no more than ten seconds per word. (Given only if subject passes test #7)
   Results: Not Given

9. Ross doesn't know the rule regarding doubling of consonants.
   Test: Given the directions to verbally state the rule regarding the doubling of consonants, Ross will respond correctly without hesitation.
   Results: No Pass

10. Ross doesn't know how to apply the rule regarding the doubling of consonants.
    Test: Given the words *filing, filling, hoped, hopped*, dictated by the teacher one at a time, Ross will spell each correctly in writing taking no more than ten seconds per word. (Given only if subject passes test #9)
    Results: Not Given

As you can see from the results above, Ross needs to:

1. Demonstrate a knowledge of vowel digraphs *ea* and *ai*.
2. Demonstrate knowledge of the following generalizations:
2.1 Silent *e*
2.2 *ck* and *k*
2.3 Doubling of consonants
3. Demonstrate knowledge of common suffixes *er* and *ed*
4. Demonstrate ability to perceive sounds within words.

Summary

Handwriting and spelling can be evaluated at the same time by using the spelling test as the survey level handwriting sample. The reading table of specifications in Chapter 4 can be used as a guide for testing the student's knowledge of phonic content. The handwriting check sheets can be used in place of a handwriting table of specifications.

Both handwriting and spelling behaviors are affected by context and time. Therefore, a table for testing both might include the dimensions shown in Figure 6.24. The table shown in Figure 6.24 is not really a table of specifications because it has no content. However, it is sequenced according to difficulty.

One final word. Recognition of misspelling and handwriting errors is a skill which is somewhat independent of production of corrects. However, these proofreading skills put a person in the position to *rewrite*, which is one of the most important things a kid can learn to do. A misspelling or illegibility on an in-class paper is not as dramatic a transgression as the same error on a paper prepared at home. We have only dealt with errors in initial production. Errors in the final product may stem from other problems of equal or greater importance.

	spells/writes by copying	spells/writes from dictation	spells/writes from memory	spells/writes in context
timed				
untimed				

Figure 6.24 A table for evaluating handwriting and spelling

SECTION SIX

Word Lists

- . . . considerable numbers of pupils in the upper grades are misspelling words which come into children's vocabularies at an early age and continue in active use as part of their writing vocabularies for years to come.

    William Guiler

- . . . is it not more important for primary reading materials to reflect what exists in present-day American English, than for sight word lists to reflect what occurs in beginning reading materials?

    Dale Johnson

- Hence, if a beginning reader can read half of the words on any page of any textbook, newspaper, encyclopedia, etc., just by learning a list of 100 words, then those 100 words are a very valuable teaching tool.

    Edward Fry

INTRODUCTION

Any discussion of spelling eventually turns to the topic of word lists. Spelling instruction need not and should not be restricted to words on a list, no matter how well the list is designed, but a word list does give teachers a basis on which they can plan their spelling curriculum.

Guiler's study of primary-grade words frequently misspelled by higher-grade pupils organizes high-utility words according to when they enter children's vocabularies and the frequency with which they were misspelled by eighth-grade students. Times have changed since 1944, but most teachers will agree that today's students are misspelling words in much the same way their peers of 40 years ago did. Leslie Johnson's list of spelling demons complements Guiler's work and is perhaps the best-known compendium of frequently misspelled words.

The issue of the utility of classic word lists is addressed by Dale Johnson, who compares the Dolch list, based on studies done in the 1920's, with the Kucera-Francis list of 1967. Johnson concludes that ". . . the *Dolch Primary Word List* should be replaced by the most frequent words in the Kucera-Francis corpus for whatever teaching, testing, or writing uses that one has for a list of common words." The reader should decide whether this conclusion is warranted, given the data presented by Johnson.

The high-frequency word list that Walker derived from the *American Heritage Word Frequency Book* is only the tip of a monumental iceberg. The body of text from which this list was compiled comprised more than five million words from publications read by American school students. A corpus of this size should give teachers confidence in the validity of the results. Moreover, Walker's description of the process by which the sample was drawn and analyzed will help readers appreciate the effort involved in creating word lists.

The *New Instant Word List* of Fry is a revision of the work he originally did in 1957. Like Dolch's list, Fry's words are better known for their application in reading. The value of Fry's contribution is enhanced by his description of the frequency curve of word usage and his suggestions regarding the use of lists.

Although word frequency counts are usually the basis of spelling instruction, syllable frequency counts should also be used by teachers. The frequency of prefixes and suffixes is disclosed by syllable counts, and, as recent studies have shown, incorrect affixes account for a sizable proportion of spelling errors. Teachers can also use the Sakiey, et al. syllable frequency count to group words for phonics-based or linguistically oriented spelling instruction.

Primary-Grade Words Frequently Misspelled by Higher-Grade Pupils

W. S. GUILER

Alert teachers of spelling are becoming increasingly aware of the fact that considerable numbers of pupils in the upper grades are misspelling words which come into children's vocabularies at an early age and continue in active use as part of their writing vocabularies for years to come. Moreover, there is a growing suspicion that the main reason why these words have not been mastered lies in failure to single out the words so that they will be given adequate study and practice. At the request of a number of teachers interested in this problem, the writer undertook the task of discovering what these particular words are.

Table I presents the words among the four thousand in most common use (1) which come into children's vocabularies in the kindergarten-primary grades and (2) which are misspelled by 5 per cent or more of pupils in Grade VIII. The words are grouped according to their frequency of usage, as determined by Horn's study.[1]

The number in the first column after a word indicates the grade level on which the word appears in children's vocabularies, as determined by the Buckingham-Dolch free-association study.[2] The letter *K* after a word indicates that the word appears in the vocabulary of kindergarten children, as determined by the Kindergarten Union Study.[3] The letter *H* after a word indicates that the word appears in the vocabulary of children up to and including six years of age, as determined by Horn and Packer's investigation.[4] The number in the second column after a word indicates the percentage of eighth-grade pupils who misspelled the word, as determined by Ashbaugh's study[5] and by unpublished study conducted by the writer.

---

[1] Ernest Horn, *A Basic Writing Vocabulary*. University of Iowa Monographs in Education, First Series, No. 4. Iowa City, Owas: College of Education, University of Iowa, 1926.

Reprinted from *The Elementary School Journal*, Vol. 44 (1944). By permission of The University of Chicago Press. © 1944. Copyright is held by The University of Chicago.

[2] B.R. Buckingham and E. W. Dolch, *A Combined Word List*, pp.3-7, 21-185. Boston: Ginn & Co., 1936.
[3] Child Study Committee of the International Kindergarten Union, *A Study of the Vocabulary of Children before Entering the First Grade*. Washington: International Kindergarten Union, 1928.
[4] "The Commonest Words in the Spoken Vocabulary of Children up to and Including Six Years of Age," *Report of the National Committee on Reading*, pp. 186-98. Twenty-fourth Yearbook of the National Society for the Study of Education, Part I. Chicago: National Society for the Study of Education (5835 Kimbark Avenue), 1925.
[5] Ernest, J. Ashbaugh, *The Iowa Spelling Scales*, pp. 125-39. Journal of Educational Research Monographs, No. 3. Bloomington, Illinois: Public School Publishing Co., 1922.

WORD LISTS

TABLE 1
Grade Level of Words Misspelled by Eighth-Grade Pupils and Percentage of Eighth-Grade Pupils Misspelling Word

	Grade Level	Percentage of Pupils Misspelling		Grade Level	Percentage of Pupils Misspelling
The First 500 Most Commonly Used Words					
1. accept	III	5	19. expect	K	7
2. complete	III	5	20. weather	K	7
3. except	K	5	21. whole	K	7
4. feel	K	5	22. course	K	8
5. future	III	5	23. believe	K	9
6. guess	K	5	24. certainly	K	9
7. perhaps	II	5	25. different	K	9
8. possible	II	5	26. position	III	9
9. service	II	5	27. either	K	10
10. sure	K	5	28. forward	II	10
11. their	K	5	29. paid	II	11
12. though	K	5	30. past	K	11
13. through	K	5	31. waste	K	12
14. written	III	5	32. truly	III	15
15. due	II	6	33. whether	K	15
16. no	K	6	34. business	II	17
17. quite	K	6	35. together	K	17
18. write	K	6	36. too	K	17
The Second 500 Most Commonly Used Words					
37. afraid	K	5	66. mention	III	9
38. allow	III	5	67. arrange	III	10
39. doctor	K	5	68. college	K	10
40. fair	K	5	69. insurance	III	10
41. heart	K	5	70. loss	II	10
42. kid	K	5	71. o'clock	K	10
43. manner	II	5	72. suggest	III	10
44. national	II	5	73. university	III	10
45. sometimes	III	5	74. delivery	K	11
46. woman	K	5	75. freight	K	11
47. although	III	6	76. practice	III	11
48. difference	II	6	77. decide	III	12
49. fee	II	6	78. impossible	III	12
50. standard	II	6	79. latter	III	12
51. success	III	6	80. character	II	13
52. vacation	K	6	81. knowledge	III	13
53. wait	K	6	82. ought	K	13
54. beautiful	K	7	83. claim	II	16
55. division	II	7	84. awful	K	17
56. manager	II	7	85. envelope	K	17
57. pa	K	7	86. till	K	17
58. style	II	7	87. writer	III	17
59. touch	K	7	88. maybe	K	21
60. careful	K	8	89. pleasant	II	22
61. dozen	K	8	90. catalogue	III	26
62. met	K	8	91. sense	III	26
63. piece	K	8	92. separate	III	26
64. bit	K	9	93. passed	K	31
65. effort	II	9			

342

WORD LISTS

TABLE 1—*Continued*

	Grade Level	Percentage of Pupils Misspelling		Grade Level	Percentage of Pupils Misspelling
The Third 500 Most Commonly Used Words					
94. breakfast	K	5	124. break	K	8
95. crazy	K	5	125. enter	III	8
96. explain	III	5	126. forgotten	K	8
97. fifteen	K	5	127. invitation	K	8
98. final	III	5	128. minute	K	8
99. fix	K	5	129. firm	III	9
100. gas	K	5	130. loan	III	9
101. honor	II	5	131. neither	K	9
102. husband	II	5	132. sew	K	9
103. nobody	K	5	133. across	K	11
104. truth	III	5	134. fourth	II	11
105. bottom	K	6	135. gentleman	III	12
106. double	K	6	136. proof	II	12
107. fault	III	6	137. happiness	III	13
108. hotel	K	6	138. hospital	K	13
109. intend	III	6	139. prepare	III	13
110. prove	III	6	140. straight	K	14
111. quality	II	6	141. library	K	15
112. satisfaction	III	6	142. surprise	K	15
113. term	II	6	143. terrible	K	15
114. wear	K	6	144. foreign	III	16
115. arrive	III	7	145. meant	II	16
116. main	II	7	146. mamma	K	17
117. quiet	K	7	147. crowd	K	18
118. telephone	K	7	148. lose	II	19
119. uncle	K	7	149. principal	III	21
120. weight	II	7	150. awfully	K	25
121. whose	K	7	151. excellent	II	26
122. worry	III	7	152. convenient	III	38
123. absent	K	8			
The Fourth 500 Most Commonly Used Words					
153. central	III	5	171. worthy	III	6
154. corner	K	5	172. drawn	III	7
155. fancy	K	5	173. group	III	7
156. football	K	5	174. holiday	II	7
157. join	II	5	175. loving	III	7
158. newspaper	K	5	176. modern	III	7
159. piano	K	5	177. nap	K	7
160. skirt	K	5	178. useful	III	7
161. somebody	K	5	179. chief	K	8
162. voice	II	5	180. heaven	II	8
163. avenue	K	6	181. hello	K	8
164. faith	III	6	182. quit	K	8
165. lie	K	6	183. choice	III	9
166. listen	K	6	184. justice	III	9
167. register	II	6	185. motor	K	9
168. rough	II	6	186. worst	III	9
169. spare	III	6	187. admit	III	10
170. strength	III	6	188. cure	K	10

WORD LISTS

TABLE 1—*Continued*

	Grade Level	Percentage of Pupils Misspelling		Grade Level	Percentage of Pupils Misspelling
The Fourth 500 Most Commonly Used Words—*Continued*					
189. fresh	K	10	203. loose	K	15
190. slight	III	10	204. signature	III	15
191. telegraph	III	10	205. operation	II	16
192. choose	K	11	206. pardon	K	16
193. laid	K	11	207. theater	III	17
194. pattern	K	11	208. agency	III	18
195. automobile	K	12	209. soul	III	19
196. commercial	III	12	210. mere	III	25
197. contract	III	12	211. bureau	K	30
198. forty	K	12	212. speech	III	34
199. hug	III	12	213. bulletin	III	49
200. salesman	III	13	214. guarantee	III	57
201. sweetheart	III	13	215. schedule	III	62
202. furniture	K	15			
The Fifth 500 Most Commonly Used Words					
216. deserve	III	5	243. lord	II	8
217. famous	III	5	244. noble	III	8
218. farther	K	5	245. cabinet	K	9
219. habit	II	5	246. million	II	9
220. radio	K	5	247. sleepy	K	9
221. sweater	K	5	248. grown	II	10
222. throat	K	5	249. accident	II	11
223. title	III	5	250. colored	K	11
224. track	K	5	251. queer	II	11
225. waist	K	5	252. exercise	III	12
226. foolish	II	6	253. manufacture	III	12
227. honey	K	6	254. prayer	K	12
228. journey	III	6	255. secret	K	12
229. lazy	K	6	256. silent	III	12
230. row	K	6	257. junior	II	13
231. silence	II	6	258. medicine	K	14
232. sore	K	6	259. tennis	K	15
233. tax	II	6	260. capital	II	16
234. wed	II	6	261. electric	K	16
235. clever	II	7	262. magazine	K	21
236. design	K	7	263. control	III	22
237. fever	III	7	264. variety	II	24
238. struck	K	7	265. apartment	K	25
239. taste	K	7	266. mar	II	31
240. taught	II	7	267. gross	III	35
241. throw	K	7	268. jealous	III	35
242. forth	K	8	269. principle	III	36

WORD LISTS

TABLE 1—Continued

	Grade Level	Percentage of Pupils Misspelling		Grade Level	Percentage of Pupils Misspelling
The Sixth 500 Most Commonly Used Words					
270. dirty	K	5	304. guest	III	10
271. fourteen	K	5	305. post office	K	10
272. garage	K	5	306. scene	III	10
273. golden	K	5	307. collar	K	11
274. lodge	III	5	308. remainder	III	11
275. neighbor	K	5	309. weigh	K	11
276. notion	III	5	310. devil	III	12
277. parents	II	5	311. fed	K	12
278. pupil	III	5	312. laundry	K	12
279. rear	II	5	313. visitor	III	12
280. steady	III	5	314. angry	K	13
281. forever	III	6	315. beach	K	13
282. hen	K	6	316. lonely	III	13
283. rise	II	6	317. fond	II	14
284. wore	K	6	318. grandma	K	14
285. baseball	K	7	319. mood	II	14
286. folk	II	7	320. praise	III	14
287. reliable	III	7	321. editor	II	16
288. rid	II	7	322. patient	III	16
289. captain	K	8	323. hose	K	17
290. headache	III	8	324. concrete	III	18
291. mid	III	8	325. sentence	II	18
292. roll	K	8	326. daddy	K	19
293. engine	K	9	327. succeed	II	20
294. keen	II	9	328. pity	III	21
295. machinery	K	9	329. fate	II	22
296. stiff	III	9	330. demonstration	III	23
297. vain	II	9	331. orchestra	K	24
298. barrel	K	10	332. height	II	28
299. command	III	10	333. attendance	II	29
300. dull	II	10	334. golf	K	29
301. everywhere	K	10	335. led	II	32
302. false	K	10	336. calendar	K	36
303. guard	III	10			
The Seventh 500 Most Commonly Used Words					
337. broad	III	5	352. finger	K	7
338. circle	K	5	353. furnace	K	7
339. gang	II	5	354. gasoline	K	7
340. ocean	K	5	355. introduce	II	7
341. soap	K	5	356. lying	K	7
342. uniform	III	5	357. servant	III	7
343. assembly	III	6	358. tight	K	7
344. cough	K	6	359. bus	K	8
345. curtain	K	6	360. dine	II	8
346. fare	II	6	361. eager	III	8
347. fuel	III	6	362. forest	II	8
348. knee	K	6	363. linen	II	8
349. pole	K	6	364. merry	K	8
350. preacher	III	6	365. parlor	II	8
351. savings	III	6	366. rating	III	9

345

WORD LISTS

TABLE 1—*Continued*

#	Word	Grade Level	Percentage of Pupils Misspelling	#	Word	Grade Level	Percentage of Pupils Misspelling
\multicolumn{8}{c}{The Seventh 500 Most Commonly Used Words—*Continued*}
367.	dying	K	10	382.	shoulder	K	15
368.	faithful	II	10	383.	tremendous	III	15
369.	manual	K	10	384.	stomach	K	16
370.	midnight	III	10	385.	lining	III	19
371.	mix	K	10	386.	rode	K	19
372.	nineteen	K	10	387.	dividend	III	20
373.	slept	K	10	388.	straighten	K	21
374.	breath	II	12	389.	village	II	22
375.	engineer	K	12	390.	enemy	III	23
376.	pledge	III	12	391.	safety	II	27
377.	plow	K	12	392.	carriage	K	31
378.	haste	II	13	393.	hearty	III	33
379.	fountain	K	14	394.	midst	III	37
380.	handkerchief	K	14	395.	role	II	38
381.	gentle	II	15				
\multicolumn{8}{c}{The Eighth 500 Most Commonly Used Words}
396.	cement	K	5	432.	stupid	III	10
397.	flour	K	5	433.	tractor	K	10
398.	sash	II	5	434.	violin	K	10
399.	scout	II	5	435.	dairy	II	11
400.	temple	II	5	436.	fought	K	11
401.	tough	II	5	437.	lest	II	11
402.	ugly	II	5	438.	tale	II	11
403.	garment	III	6	439.	ankle	III	12
404.	mob	III	6	440.	bloom	K	12
405.	moonlight	III	6	441.	hasten	III	12
406.	palace	II	6	442.	wreck	K	12
407.	powder	K	6	443.	bore	III	13
408.	shower	II	6	444.	thirteen	K	13
409.	apart	K	7	445.	strict	III	14
410.	hike	II	7	446.	dentist	K	15
411.	organ	II	7	447.	sane	II	15
412.	penny	K	7	448.	diamond	K	16
413.	pretend	K	7	449.	staff	II	16
414.	progressive	III	7	450.	swear	III	16
415.	rare	III	7	451.	torn	K	16
416.	salad	K	7	452.	underwear	K	16
417.	slide	K	7	453.	haul	K	17
418.	crown	K	8	454.	soldier	K	17
419.	discover	III	8	455.	nonsense	III	18
420.	grammar	III	8	456.	purple	K	18
421.	huge	II	8	457.	grip	II	19
422.	knife	K	8	458.	quarrel	III	19
423.	tone	II	8	459.	divide	II	20
424.	dues	III	9	460.	forenoon	III	20
425.	greet	II	9	461.	tongue	K	21
426.	grocery	K	9	462.	ninety	II	23
427.	merchant	III	9	463.	tear	K	27
428.	eighth	III	10	464.	marvelous	III	30
429.	hungry	K	10	465.	delicious	III	33
430.	rotten	K	10	466.	kindergarten	K	33
431.	strain	III	10				

One Hundred Words Most Often Misspelled by Children in the Elementary Grades

LESLIE W. JOHNSON

What are the spelling difficulties of children in the elementary grades? Have they changed in the past twenty years? These problems prompted a study of spelling difficulties by the National Curriculum Associates.

Cooperating school systems in all forty-eight states were asked to submit creative writings of children. All materials were to be the original effort of each child and free expression. One hundred ninety-nine school systems contributed the creative writings of 14,643 children. The papers of each child were checked for spelling errors by city and grade levels (3 to 8 inclusive). All misspelled words were recorded as well as the number of times they were misspelled. The 14,643 children misspelled 7,260 different words, one of which, was misspelled 967 times.

The following is the first hundred ranking words. The words are arranged according to the number of times they were misspelled: number one, "their"—misspelled 967 times to number one hundred, "money"—misspelled 54 times.

Three factors seemed to enter into causes of misspellings. (1) Imperfection of configurational perception, (2) inability to standardize patterns of words and make them consistently dominant, (3) voids in persistency of effort.

their	you're	because	something	swimming
too	clothes	thought	named	first
there	looked	and	came	were
they	people	beautiful	name	than
then	pretty	it's	tried	two
until	running	went	here	know
our	believe	where	many	decided
asked	little	stopped	knew	friend
off	things	very	with	when
through	him	morning	together	let's
mother	it's	wanted	all right	sometimes
another	started	hear	happened	friends
threw	that's	from	didn't	children
some	would	frightened	always	an
bought	again	for	surprise	school
getting	heard	February	before	jumped
going	received	once	caught	around
course	coming	like	every	dropped
woman	to	they're	different	babies
animals	said	cousin	interesting	money

From *The Journal of Educational Research*, Vol. 44, pp. 154–155. Copyright © 1950. Reprinted by permission of Heldref Publications, 4000 Albemarle St. N.W., Washington, DC 20016.

The Dolch List Reexamined

DALE D. JOHNSON

Most children enter school very fluent in their native language. It is estimated that American pre-school children use nearly 4,000 words in their everyday speech and can comprehend from 6,000 to 48,000 words when they hear them, but most cannot read any words before entering school (Monroe, 1964).

In teaching children to read, the basal reader enthusiasts, many "eclectic" advocates, and most primary teachers have accepted the notion that it is important to teach a sight vocabulary. The sight vocabulary, it has been wisely assumed, should include frequently used words—those already in most children's oral/aural vocabulary. In recent decades most American schools have used one or several basal reading series in which the first books contain tightly controlled vocabularies, presumably composed of the most common English words.

Certainly the most influential sight word list used in the past thirty years has been the *Dolch Basic Sight Word List*, published in 1941. Not only has the Dolch list been the basis for vocabulary selection in many reading series, but it has also been used as a testing device for reading group placement (Zintz, 1966). Perhaps hundreds of thousands of American children have been asked to read and to learn these 220 English words. It is the contention of this author that The Dolch List, as a corpus, has outlived its usefulness and that a more adequate substitute is available.

The *Dolch Basic Sight Word List* was compiled in the mid-1930's from studies done in the 1920's—over forty years ago. One need not ponder long to realize the vast cultural changes since then which have potential impact on learning to read: the publishing revolution, the influence of television, the increasing mobility of the family, to name a few.

In the 1930's Dolch, desiring a short, utilitarian word list useful to classroom teachers, compiled such a list by selecting words common to three then-prominent word lists (Dolch, 1941). The three lists were:

1. *The Child Study Committee of the International Kindergarten Union's Vocabulary List.* This list, published in 1928, contained 2,596 words common to children's vocabularies before entering the first grade. Dolch selected the top 510 words from this list.
2. *The Gates Primary Word List.* Published in 1926, the list contained 1,811 words considered important in children's reading. Dolch used the first 500 words from this list.
3. *The Wheeler-Howell First Grade Vocabulary List.* This list contained 453 words found in ten primers and ten first grade readers published between 1922 and 1929.

Dolch selected 193 words which were common to all three lists. "Dolch then arbitrarily selected twenty-seven words common to two of the lists that he felt 'rounded out' the list. The twenty-seven words that appeared on only two of the three lists were included since they 'seemed to belong' . . ." (Zintz, 1966). Table 1 summarizes the compilation of the Dolch List. Thus the Dolch Basic Sight Word List contains 220 words

---

From *The Reading Teacher*, Vol. 24, No. 5 (February, 1971). Reprinted with permission of the International Reading Association and Dale D. Johnson.

Table 1 The compilation of the Dolch list

List	Date	Number of Words
I.K.U.	1928	510
Gates	1926	500
Wheeler & Howell	1922–29	453
Common to three lists		193
Common to two lists		27
	Total	220

which were considered either common to children (I.K.U.) or important for children (Wheeler & Howell, Gates) over forty years ago. How common are these words today?

In 1967, Henry Kucera and W. Nelson Francis published their *Computational Analysis of Present-Day American English*. Among other things, the book contains a rank ordering of 50,406 distinct graphic words (types) from a corpus of 1,014,232 words (tokens) of natural language text. The corpus is composed of 500 samples of approximately 2,000 words each (1,948 words to 2,240 words) which were selected from fifteen different genre to insure representativeness. Most samples consisted of one continuous passage from a single source, though some samples consisted of collections of shorter pieces, and "...actual samples were selected by a variety of random procedures."

Governing the selection of the samples was the prerequisite that they be accurate, synchronic, and representative of a wide range of styles. To assure synchronicity the data were confined to texts first printed in 1961. The number and type of categories as well as the proportion of the 500 samples assigned to each category were determined by consensus of a conference participated in by W. Nelson Francis, Philip B. Gove, Henry Kucera, John Carroll, Patricia O'Connor, and Randolf Quirk. The categories and numbers of selections assigned to each are as follows (Kucera and Francis, 1967):

Press:	Reportage	44
Press:	Editorial	27
Press:	Review	17
Religious		17
Skills and Hobbies		36
Popular Lore		48
Bibles, Letters, Biographies, etc.		75
Miscellaneous		30
Learned and Scientific Writing		80
Fiction:	General	29
Fiction:	Mystery and Detective	24
Fiction:	Science	6
Fiction:	Adventure and Western	29
Fiction:	Romance and Love Story	29
Humor		9

Notably, the corpus reflects the words of print to which the adult literate reader is exposed. Children's primers and first readers were not sampled. However, considering the thousands of words in the first grader's oral/aural vocabulary, it is reasonable to assume that many of the most frequent words in the Kucera-Francis corpus would be common to the vocabularies of children.

The 1,014,232 "running words" were key punched and the computer processing was done in essentially three stages (Kucera and Francis, 1967): "1] Segmentation of the texts into words, 2] Sorting of segmented words in an ascending (that is alphabetical) order, and 3] The merging of identical words and a count of their frequencies of occurrence."

WORD LISTS

Word frequencies were then listed in rank order.

How does the Dolch list relate to the computational analysis? Of the 220 words on the Dolch Primary Word List, representative of the 1920's, *eighty-two* words or *37 per cent are not* among the most frequently occurring 220 words in the Kucera and Francis corpus compiled in the 1960's. In terms of present day Eng-

Table 2 The eighty-two Dolch words not in the 220 most frequent words of the Kucera-Francis corpus

1. am	22. fast	43. live	64. sleep
2. ask	23. five	44. myself	65. soon
3. ate	24. fly	45. open	66. start
4. best	25. four	46. pick	67. stop
5. big	26. full	47. play	68. tell
6. black	27. funny	48. please	69. ten
7. blue	28. gave	49. pretty	70. thank
8. bring	29. give	50. pull	71. today
9. brown	30. goes	51. ran	72. together
10. buy	31. green	52. read	73. try
11. call	32. grow	53. red	74. walk
12. carry	33. help	54. ride	75. want
13. clean	34. hold	55. round	76. warm
14. cold	35. hot	56. run	77. wash
15. cut	36. hurt	57. saw	78. white
16. done	37. jump	58. seven	79. wish
17. draw	38. keep	59. shall	80. write
18. drink	39. kind	60. show	81. yellow
19. eat	40. laugh	61. sing	82. yes
20. eight	41. let	62. sit	
21. fall	42. light	63. six	

Table 3 The eighty-two words among the top 220 of the Kucera-Francis corpus which are not on the Dolch list

1. more	22. between	43. however	64. hand
2. than	23. life	44. home	65. enough
3. other	24. being	45. Mrs.	66. took
4. time	25. day	46. thought	67. head
5. such	26. same	47. part	68. yet
6. man	27. another	48. general	69. government
7. even	28. while	49. high	70. system
8. most	29. might	50. school	71. set
9. also	30. great	51. untied	72. told
10. though	31. year	52. left	73. nothing
11. back	32. since	53. number	74. night
12. years	33. against	54. course	75. end
13. way	34. used	55. war	76. called
14. should	35. states	56. until	77. didn't
15. each	36. himself	57. something	78. eyes
16. people	37. few	58. fact	79. asked
17. Mr.	38. house	59. though	80. later
18. state	39. during	60. water	81. knew
19. world	40. without	61. less	82. last
20. still	41. place	62. public	
21. men	42. American	63. almost	

WORD LISTS

Table 4 The 220 Dolch words

Rank Order	Word	Number of Occurrences in Kucera-Francis	Rank Order in Kucera-Francis	Rank Order	Word	Number of Occurrences in Kucera-Francis	Rank Order in Kucera-Francis
1.	the	69,971	1	58.	them	1,789	60
2.	of	36,411	2	59.	can	1,772	61
3.	and	28,852	3	60.	only	1,747	62
4.	to	26,149	4	61.	new	1,635	64
5.	a	23,237	5	62.	some	1,617	65
6.	in	34,347	6	63.	could	1,598	66
7.	that	10,595	7	64.	these	1,573	68
8.	is	10,099	8	65.	two	1,412	69
9.	was	9,816	9	66.	may	1,400	70
10.	he	9,543	10	67.	then	1,377	71
11.	for	9,489	11	68.	do	1,363	72
12.	it	8,746	12	69.	first	1,360	73
13.	with	7,289	13	70.	any	1,345	74
14.	as	7,250	14	71.	my	1,319	75
15.	his	7,007	15	72.	now	1,314	76
16.	on	6,742	16	73.	like	1,290	78
17.	be	6,377	17	74.	our	1,252	79
18.	at	5,378	18	75.	over	1,236	80
19.	by	5,305	19	76.	me	1,181	81
20.	I	5,173	20	77.	made	1,125	85
21.	this	5,146	21	78.	after	1,070	86
22.	had	5,133	22	79.	did	1,044	88
23.	not	4,609	23	80.	many	1,030	89
24.	are	4,393	24	81.	before	1,016	90
25.	but	4,301	25	82.	must	1,013	91
26.	from	5,369	26	83.	where	939	96
27.	or	4,207	27	84.	much	937	97
28.	have	3,941	28	85.	your	923	98
29.	an	3,747	29	86.	well	887	100
30.	they	3,719	30	87.	down	895	101
31.	which	3,562	31	88.	because	883	103
32.	one	3,292	32	89.	just	872	105
33.	you	3,286	33	90.	those	850	106
34.	were	3,284	34	91.	how	834	109
35.	her	3,037	35	92.	too	832	110
36.	all	3,001	36	93.	little	831	111
37.	she	2,859	37	94.	good	807	113
38.	there	3,734	38	95.	very	796	114
39.	would	2,714	39	96.	make	794	115
40.	their	3,670	40	97.	own	773	119
41.	we	2,753	41	98.	see	772	119
42.	him	2,619	42	99.	work	760	121
43.	been	2,472	43	100.	long	755	122
44.	has	2,439	44	101.	get	750	124
45.	when	2,331	45	102.	here	750	124
46.	who	2,252	46	103.	both	730	126
47.	will	2,244	47	104.	under	707	130
48.	no	2,201	49	105.	never	698	131
49.	if	2,199	50	106.	know	683	135
50.	out	2,096	51	107.	us	673	139
51.	so	1,984	52	108.	old	660	142
52.	said	1,961	53	109.	off	639	143
53.	what	1,908	54	110.	come	630	144
54.	up	1,895	55	111.	go	626	147
55.	its	1,858	56	112.	came	622	148
56.	about	1,815	57	113.	right	613	149
57.	into	1,791	58	114.	take	611	151

WORD LISTS

Table 4 (continued)

Rank Order	Word	Number of Occurrences in Kucera-Francis	Rank Order in Kucera-Francis	Rank Order	Word	Number of Occurrences in Kucera-Francis	Rank Order in Kucera-Francis
115.	three	610	152	167.	red	197	489
116.	use	589	157	168.	cut	192	504
117.	again	578	160	169.	call	188	513
118.	around	561	163	170.	live	177	545
119.	small	542	166	171.	brown	176	548
120.	found	536	167	172.	read	173	569
121.	went	507	170	173.	cold	171	583
122.	say	504	171	174.	hold	169	590
123.	once	499	173	175.	ten	165	600
124.	upon	495	177	176.	bring	158	631
125.	every	491	179	177.	start	154	648
126.	don't	489	180	178.	fall	147	679
127.	does	485	181	179.	yes	144	696
128.	got	482	183	180.	blue	143	707
129.	always	458	189	181.	try	140	729
130.	away	456	190	182.	ran	134	763
131.	put	437	198	183.	lot	130	792
132.	think	433	199	184.	myself	129	805
133.	far	427	203	185.	ask	128	812
134.	better	414	210	186.	stop	120	872
135.	why	404	215	187.	green	116	903
136.	find	399	220	188.	seven	113	939
137.	going	399	220	189.	wish	110	957
138.	look	399	220	190.	pretty	107	991
				191.	write	106	1003
				192.	eight	104	1025
139.	give	391	230	193.	walk	100	1070
140.	let	384	235	194.	goes	89	1201
141.	white	365	257	195.	carry	88	1223
142.	his	360	263	196.	drink	82	1326
143.	four	359	365	197.	round	81	1348
144.	saw	352	269	198.	fast	78	1389
145.	best	351	270	199.	buy	70	1561
146.	light	333	277	200.	clean	70	1561
147.	want	329	281	201.	sit	67	1647
148.	done	340	288	202.	warm	67	1647
149.	open	319	290	203.	sleep	65	1704
150.	kind	313	295	204.	grow	63	1757
151.	help	311	301	205.	please	62	1791
152.	show	287	320	206.	eat	61	1828
153.	five	286	323	207.	draw	56	2006
154.	gave	285	324	208.	yellow	55	2050
155.	today	284	326	209.	pick	55	2050
156.	tell	268	351	210.	pull	51	2199
157.	shall	267	354	211.	ride	49	2273
158.	together	267	354	212.	funny	41	2719
159.	keep	264	359	213.	hurt	37	3005
160.	full	230	406	214.	wash	37	2005
161.	am	228	410	215.	thank	36	3087
162.	six	220	426	216.	sing	34	3244
163.	run	212	446	217.	fly	33	3331
164.	black	203	465	218.	laugh	28	3793
165.	play	200	474	219.	jump	24	4270
166.	soon	199	476	220.	ate	16	5972

Table 5 The 220 most frequent words in the Kucera-Francis corpus

Rank	Word	Total Occurrences	Rank	Word	Total Occurrences
1.	the	69971	60.	them	1789
2.	of	36411	61.	can	1772
3.	and	28852	62.	only	1747
4.	to	26149	63.	other	1702
5.	a	23237	64.	new	1635
6.	in	21341	65.	some	1607
7.	that	10595	66.	could	1599
8.	is	10099	67.	time	1599
9.	was	9816	68.	these	1573
10.	he	9543	69.	two	1412
11.	for	9489	70.	may	1400
12.	it	8756	71.	then	1377
13.	with	7289	72.	do	1363
14.	as	7250	73.	first	1360
15.	his	6997	74.	any	1345
16.	on	6742	75.	my	1319
17.	be	6377	76.	now	1314
18.	at	5378	77.	such	1303
19.	by	6305	78.	like	1209
20.	I	5173	79.	our	1252
21.	this	5146	80.	over	1236
22.	had	5133	81.	man	1207
23.	not	4609	82.	me	1181
24.	are	4393	83.	even	1171
25.	but	4381	84.	most	1160
26.	from	4369	85.	made	1125
27.	or	5207	86.	after	1070
28.	have	3941	87.	also	1069
29.	an	3747	88.	did	1044
30.	they	3618	89.	many	1030
31.	which	3662	90.	before	1016
32.	one	3292	91.	must	1013
33.	you	3286	92.	through	969
34.	were	3284	93.	back	967
35.	her	3037	94.	years	949
36.	all	3001	95.	where	938
37.	she	2859	96.	much	937
38.	there	2724	97.	your	923
39.	would	2714	98.	way	909
40.	their	2670	99.	well	987
41.	we	2653	100.	down	895
42.	him	2472	101.	should	888
43.	been	2619	102.	because	883
44.	has	2439	103.	each	877
45.	when	2331	104.	just	872
46.	who	2242	105.	those	850
47.	will	2244	106.	people	847
48.	more	2216	107.	Mr.	839
49.	no	3301	108.	how	834
50.	if	3199	109.	too	832
51.	out	2096	110.	little	831
52.	so	1984	111.	state	808
53.	said	1961	112.	good	807
54.	what	1908	113.	very	796
55.	up	1895	114.	make	794
56.	its	1858	115.	would	787
57.	about	1815	116.	still	782
58.	into	1791	117.	own	772
59.	than	1789	118.	see	772

WORD LISTS

Table 5 (continued)

Rank	Word	Total Occurrences	Rank	Word	Total Occurrences
119.	men	763	170.	part	500
120.	work	760	171.	once	499
121.	long	755	172.	general	497
122.	get	750	173.	high	497
123.	here	750	174.	upon	495
124.	between	730	175.	school	492
125.	both	730	176.	every	491
126.	life	715	177.	don't	489
127.	being	712	178.	does	485
128.	under	707	179.	got	482
129.	never	698	180.	united	482
130.	day	797	181.	left	480
131.	same	797	182.	number	472
132.	another	683	183.	course	465
133.	know	683	184.	war	464
134.	while	680	185.	until	461
135.	last	676	186.	always	458
136.	might	672	187.	away	450
137.	us	672	188.	something	450
138.	great	665	189.	fact	447
139.	old	660	190.	though	442
140.	year	660	191.	water	442
141.	off	639	192.	less	438
142.	come	630	193.	public	438
143.	since	628	194.	put	437
144.	against	626	195.	thing	433
145.	go	626	196.	almost	432
146.	came	622	197.	hand	431
147.	right	613	198.	enough	430
148.	used	612	199.	far	427
149.	take	611	200.	took	426
150.	three	610	201.	head	424
151.	states	605	202.	yet	419
152.	himself	603	203.	government	417
153.	few	601	204.	system	416
154.	house	591	205.	better	414
155.	use	589	206.	set	414
156.	during	585	207.	told	413
157.	without	578	208.	nothing	412
158.	again	578	209.	night	411
159.	place	571	210.	end	410
160.	American	569	211.	why	404
161.	around	561	212.	called	401
162.	however	552	213.	didn't	401
163.	home	547	214.	eyes	401
164.	small	542	215.	find	399
165.	found	536	216.	going	399
166.	Mrs.	534	217.	look	399
167.	thought	515	218.	asked	398
168.	went	507	219.	later	397
169.	say	504	220.	knew	395

lish, these eighty-two words rank from 230 to 5,972 in frequency of occurrence. The bottom eighty-two Dolch words, numbering 139 to 220, occur a total of 13,317 times in the computational analysis. The words ranked 139 to 220 on the Kucera-Francis list occur a total of 40,186 times. The bottom eighty-two Dolch words each occur from sixteen to 230 times per million running words, whereas the bottom eighty-two of the top 220 words on the Kucera-Francis corpus each occur from 395 to 665 times.

Four word lists are found on pages 350–354. The first contains the eighty-two Dolch Words which are not among the 220 most frequent words in the Kucera-Francis corpus. The second list contains the eighty-two words which are not on the Dolch list but are among the 220 most frequently occurring words in the Kucera-Francis corpus. (This author sees nothing magical about the number 220. However, since the Dolch list is comprised of 220 words, the top 220 from the Kucera-Francis list are used for comparative purposes.)

The third list is an ordering by rank of the Dolch list words according to their frequency in the Kucera-Francis corpus, together with the number of occurrences in the corpus and their rank order in the corpus. The fourth list is a rank ordering of the 220 most frequent words in the Kucera-Francis corpus, together with their numbers of occurrence. These four lists support the author's contention that if the principal criterion for a basic word list is frequency of occurrence, the *Dolch Primary Word List* should be replaced by the most frequent words in the Kucera-Francis corpus for whatever teaching, testing, or writing uses that one has for a list of common words. This corpus reflects the world of the 1960's— not of pre-Depression America. Critics may state that beginning reading books were not sampled for the study, but in terms of teaching reading this may be in the "cart before the horse" vein. Acknowledging the extent of young children's oral/aural vocabulary, *is it not more important for primary reading materials to reflect what exists in present-day American English, than for sight word lists to reflect what occurs in beginning reading materials?* Certainly such words as *more, through, some* and *few,* from the Kucera-Francis list would be as useful to children in reading as *bring, draw, hold* and *let* from Dolch's.

Since the publication of *Computational Analysis of Present-Day American English,* in 1967, teachers, authors and reading specialists now have access to an invaluable source: a representatively selected list of 50,406 distinct words in rank order, from *the* to *thine.* It seems the Dolch list has outlived its usefulness, and a more adequate substitute is available.

REFERENCES

Dolch, E.W. *Teaching primary reading.* Champaign: The Garrard Press, 1941. Pp. 196-215.

Kucera, H., and Francis, W.N. *Computational analysis of present-day American English.* Providence: Brown University Press, 1967.

Monroe, Marian, and Rogers, Bernice. *Foundations for reading informal prereading procedure.* Glenview, Illinois: Scott, Foresman and Company, 1964. Pp. 4-21.

Zintz, M.V. *Corrective reading.* Dubuque: Wm. C. Brown Company, 1966. Pp. 26-65.

High Frequency Word List for Grades 3 through 9

CHARLES MONROE WALKER

In 1971, Houghton Mifflin Company and the American Heritage Publishing Company cooperatively published the American Heritage Word Frequency Book. This was a detailed report of a computer-assisted study of over five million running words in more than 10,000 500-word samples from more than a thousand publications that American school students are expected to read either by assignment or voluntarily in grades 3 through 9.

The study began with a questionnaire survey of public, parochial, and independent schools in order to determine the range of required and recommended reading to which students are exposed in school grades 3 through 9 in the United States. The survey was conducted in November and December of 1969, using a 10-page questionnaire. The responses represented 71 public school systems, 11 Roman Catholic diocesan systems, and 8 independent (private) schools. (For a complete list of survey respondents, see Carroll, Davies and Richman 1971, pp. 827-30.)

The questionnaire itself was divided into 22 categories that in the main consisted of curriculum or subject-matter areas. These included basic and supplementary reading, English and grammar, composition, literature, mathematics, social studies, spelling, science, music, art, home economics, shop, library (fiction, nonfiction, and general reference), magazines, and religion. Analysis of the responses was done by the Educational Testing Service of Princeton, New Jersey.

In choosing samples of running text to be used in the determination of relative word frequencies of a word corpus that would be as truly representative as possible of the printed language of the American elementary educational system, the attempt was made to 1) choose samples that students would be most likely to encounter in each grade and category, 2) sample each grade and category to an extent that represented its pedagogical importance to every other grade and category, and 3) maximize the diversity of sampling sources within each grade and category.

After a pilot test comparing 500-word and 2000-word samples indicated that 500-word samples would be easier to manage and would yield somewhat greater diversity, it was decided to use at least 10,000 500-word samples from at least 1,000 sampling texts. Text samples were taken at approximately uniform intervals throughout each sampling text. Text materials explicity excluded were headings, captions, footnotes, glossaries, tables, word lists, indexes, teacher's materials, advertisements, phonetic respellings, and paragraph and exercise numbers. Foreign words in normal English context were accepted but long passages in a foreign language were excluded.

Ultimately, 10,043 approximately 500-word samples from 1,657 different volumes (counting each issue of a magazine and each volume of multi-volume reference works as single volumes) were processed. These represented a total of 33,623 pages of text. The texts used constituted only about 16% of the total number listed by questionnaire respon-

---

From *The Reading Teacher*, Vol. 32, No. 7 (April, 1979). Reprinted with permission of the International Reading Association and Charles Monroe Walker.

dents but accounted for 46% of respondent listings because some texts were listed by several respondents. In other words, the texts used were chosen from those in widest use. (For a list of all the texts from which samples were drawn, see Carroll, Davies and Richman 1971, pp. 831-56.)

In this study, because of the limitations of computer keystroking, different forms of the same base word—like *word, Word, words, word's, wordy, worded, wording, wordiness, Words, reword,* and *misworded*—were counted and reported as different words. Since the base word itself is the vital element in word recognition, an analysis was made to determine which of the 86,741 different words in the study involved base words of highest frequency of occurrence in the total study. Such base words obviously would be most important for students to be able to recognize instantly whether in or out of context.

Obviously, as soon as students have learned how the various inflections and derivatives are formed and have been introduced to the formation of possessives, compounds, and contractions, they will be able to handle with ease the variants of a base word that is itself known. Therefore, counts of the regularly formed variants of base words were combined to yield total counts of base words in all forms. Whenever the pronunciation of a base word is changed in a derived form, the two words have been counted as separate words, as *office* and *official*. Similarly, when a derived form was derived so long ago that the relationship of the derivative to the base word has become obscured, as in *every* and *ever,* the two have been counted separately.

A resultant list of the 1,000 words of highest frequency of occurrence was developed in this way. Each of these words appeared at least 534 times in the total of all the sample passages. Together these 1,000 words accounted for 84.6% of all the running words in the study. Consequently, if a student had instant recognition control of each of these thousand words, he or she would seldom meet a reading passage in which more than one word per sentence would need to be decoded by use of context and letter-sound association. Obviously, students unable to recognize these base words in different forms would experience real difficulty in reading because 1) they would be unable to use the known words in a given context to help them identify (or decode) unrecognized words, and 2) they would be unable to put possible word meanings together to make meaning from a flow of language made up of those words.

A similar study reported on at the 1977 Annual Convention of the International Reading Association produced a list of the 800 base words of highest frequency in grades 3 and 4. That list is available free from Houghton Mifflin Company (One Beacon Street, Boston, Mass. 02107, U.S.A.), which used it as a basis for the vocabulary control in its 1976 edition of the Houghton Mifflin Reading Series. Thirty-two words that were on that 800-word list do not appear on the 1000-word list, namely:

alphabet	luck	rhyme
ant	mud	sad
basket	nest	sheep
bowl	nice	sum
butter	park	suppose
button	pig	temper
dish	pole	uncle
feather	prince	wagon
jar	proud	wet
kitchen	rabbit	whale
lion	ranch	

Implications

Perhaps the list of 1,000 words could serve as one factor in a new method of estimating readability. It would certainly seem to offer a better and more up-to-date base for evaluating word difficulty for elementary pupils than other word lists currently in use with readability formulas.

WORD LISTS

Recognizing that students should be able to use contextual clues efficiently in decoding strange words, it is suggested that any text in which the percentage of words not on this list is 30% or higher (meaning that 3 of every 10 words are unknown) is probably too difficult for elementary school students and may be too difficult for most junior high school students.

Following are two lists of those 1,000 base words of highest frequency, one in alphabetical order and one in rank order.

REFERENCE

Carroll, John B., Peter Davies and Barry Richman. *American Heritage Word Frequency Book*. Boston, Mass.: Houghton Mifflin Co. and American Heritage Publishing Co., 1971.

I. Alphabetic list of the 1,000 base words of highest frequency in the 1971 American Heritage computerized study of the vocabulary of published materials used in grades 3 through 9 in the United States

Counts include contractions, inflections, common derivatives formed by the use of taught affixes, and compound words.

Total frequency

a 126,651
able 1,601
about 12,523
above 2,303
act 4,187
add 4,350
afraid 613
after 6,745
again 3,894
against 1,759
age 940
ago 1,388
agree 757
air 4,833
all 17,132
allow 694
also 4,647
always 2,660
am 1,313
among 1,334
an 14,852
and 133,931
anger (y) 625
animal 3,863
answer 3,525
any 7,482
appear 1,712
apple 600
are 35,746
area 2,112
arm 1,281
arrange 660
arrive 577
art (ist) 1,220
as 32,218
ask 4,149
at 23,986
atom 789

baby 1,080
back 6,646
bad 852

ball 1,333
band 595
bank 824
bar 558
base 2,446
basic 586
bat 736
be 25,867
bear 1,104
beat 982
beauty 1,588
bed 1,207
been 7,652
before 5,295
began 2,491
begin 2,702
behind 1,490
believe 1,193
bell 730
best 1,998
better 1,929
between 3,361
big 4,329
bird 2,265
bit 1,005
black 2,197
block 680
blood 850
blow 852
blue 1,441
board 1,152
boat 1,418
body 2,248
bone 764
book 2,526
born 657
both 2,649
bottom 908
bought 598
box 1,630
boy 5,222
branch 618
bread 560

break 859
bright 1,109
bring 1,353
broad 631
broke 967
brother 1,205
brought 1,357
brown 839
build (t) 3,738
burn 1,022
busy 1,421
but 19,206
buy 1,065
by 20,307

call 7,918
came 6,418
camp 660
can 17,811
capital 756
captain 815
car 2,571
card 596
care 2,533
carry 2,525
case 967
cat 1,017
catch 1,163
caught 793
cause (be) 5,402
cell 1,197
cent 846
center (al) 1,743
century 1,014
certain 1,675
chair 755
chance 642
change 4,134
character 795
charge 559
chart 680
check 1,384

chick 552
chief 709
child 959
children 2,704
choose 833
chord 565
circle 1,253
city 3,201
claim 625
 (ac, pro, ex, re)
class 2,146
clean 865
clear 1,480
climb 917
clock (o') 706
close 2,879
clothe 1,089
cloud 932
coast 1,000
coat 597
cold 1,692
collect 820
colony 708
color 2,399
column 636
come 9,265
common 1,417
company 676
compare 732
complete 2,116
condition 589
connect 572
consider 1,012
consonant 955
contain 1,565
continent 625
continue 681
control 818
cook 1,039
cool 913
copy 1,000
corn 733
corner 769

358

WORD LISTS

correct 1,605
cost 842
cotton 658
could 9,469
count 1,229
country 3,553
course 1,452
cover 3,461
  (dis, re, un, under)
cow 1,121
crease (in, de) 899
create 739
crop 775
cross (a, re) 3,185
crowd 734
cry 1,655
current 685
cut 2,424

dad 561
dance 1,293
danger 755
dark 1,651
day 10,056
dead 692
deal 665
dear 552
death 624
decide 1,437
decimal 818
deep 1,432
degree 555
depend 726
describe 1,043
desert 690
design 913
determine 657
develop 1,521
dictionary 952
did 9,213
die 884
differ (ent) 5,492
difficult 811
direct (or, ion) 2,237
discuss 611
distant (ce) 1,348
divide 1,242
division 575
do 13,683
doctor 806
does 5,001
dog 2,241
dollar 719
done 1,589
don't 2,900
door 2,202
double 580
down 7,693
draw 2,946
dream 591
dress 937
drink 551
drive 1,576
drop 1,320
dry 1,404
duck 556
during 1,925

each 14,290
ear 969
early 1,887
earth 3,728

ease (y) 2,677
east 1,347
eat 2,509
edge 1,117
effect 780
egg 1,205
eight 1,077
either 1,033
electric 778
element 774
else 968
end 4,600
enemy 552
energy 1,211
engine (er) 1,288
enough 2,364
enter 703
equal 836
equate (or, ion) 1,369
especial 615
even 4,349
evening 591
event 673
ever 2,299
every 6,243
exact 887
example 2,681
except 879
excite 981
exercise 1,170
expect 777
experience 604
experiment 911
eye 3,274

face 2,388
fact 1,469
fair (y) 829
fall 1,659
family 2,241
famous 721
far 3,040
farm 3,185
fast 1,866
fat 565
father 3,691
favor 573
fear 717
feed 589
feel 2,273
feet 2,545
fell 832
felt 1,236
few 2,860
field 1,619
fig 614
fight 986
figure 1,635
fill 1,348
final 1,536
find 7,512
fine 1,677
finger 988
finish 1,100
fire 2,072
first 7,863
fish 2,488
fit 832
five 1,918
flat 901
floor 1,034
flow 830
flower 1,091

fly (ier, ies) 1,660
follow 4,192
food 3,398
foot 1,424
for 39,333
force 1,444
forest 1,191
form 5,823
forward 609
found 3,532
four 3,394
fraction 1,193
free 1,508
fresh 701
friend 2,500
from 22,811
front 1,544
fruit 752
full 1,447
fun 1,110

game 1,381
garden 837
gas 1,108
gather 641
gave 1,535
general 1,256
gentle 816
get 7,188
girl 2,357
give 6,111
glad 564
glass 1,129
go 9,266
gold 1,414
gone 1,088
good 6,227
got 2,698
govern (or,
  ment, un, able) 1,694
grand 1,334
grass 1,128
gray 633
great 5,718
green 1,534
grew 847
ground 1,880
group 2,667
grow 3,496
guess 745
guide 606
gun 695

had 20,806
hair 1,045
half 2,110
hand 4,486
happen 2,123
happy 1,100
hard 3,156
has 10,471
hat 678
have 23,469
he 47,665
head 3,674
hear 2,440
heard 2,006
heart 1,318
heat 1,357
heavy 1,298
held 1,049
help 5,568

her 11,444
here 4,340
high 4,233
hill 1,021
him 10,703
his 29,387
history 782
hit 774
hold 1,881
hole 896
home 4,574
hope 1,100
horse 2,436
hot 1,369
hour 1,977
house 4,009
how 15,502
huge 612
human 788
hundred 1,919
hunt 1,210
hurry 711

I 30,650
ice 1,255
idea (l) 2,490
if 12,918
imagine 761
in 112,946
inch 1,465
include 1,250
indicate 792
industry 988
insect 794
instant (ce) 556
instrument 1,133
interest 1,869
invent 660
iron 905
is 61,527
island 1,425
it 57,131

job 1,119
join 866
joy (en) 1,151
jump 1,084
just 5,894

keep 3,278
kept 1,131
key 908
kill 965
kind 4,100
king 2,010
knew 2,044
know 8,074

lady 858
lake 964
land 4,347
language 1,337
large 4,423
last 3,231
late (re) 2,908
laugh 1,394
law (yer) 1,007
lay (de, re) 1,779
lead (mis) 1,656
learn 3,489

359

WORD LISTS

least 883
leave 2,220
led 598
left 2,932
leg 1,171
length 1,222
less (un) 1,830
let 3,219
letter 2,615
level 644
lie (lying) 986
life 2,866
lift 685
light (de, ning) 4,114
like (a, ly) 11,742
line 5,515
liquid 540
list 2,278
listen 1,857
little 6,592
live 6,898
locate 796
log 539
lone 1,172
long (a, be) 11,369
look 10,411
lost 842
lot 912
loud (a) 962
love (be, un) 1,738
low (be) 5,553

machine 1,651
made 7,140
magnet 619
main (re) 2,365
major 702
make 11,282
man 6,496
many 12,205
map 1,703
mark (re) 2,628
market 556
mass 597
master 577
match 618
material 1,273
matter 1,255
may 7,750
me 6,209
mean 5,296
meant 539
measure 2,215
meat 725
meet 1,071
melody 894
men 4,149
metal 1,061
method 946
middle 967
might 3,114
mile 2,596
milk 951
million 1,106
mind (re) 1,494
mine 704
minute 1,506
miss 1,359
mix 846
modern 775
molecule 635
moment 964
money 1,728
month 1,107

moon 1,427
more 10,147
morning 1,824
most 8,399
mother 3,806
motion 541
mount (a, dis) 1,161
mountain 2,472
mouth 891
move (re, un) 5,292
much 5,400
multiple (y) 1,461
music 2,653
must 4,338
my 8,132

name 6,010
nation 955
natural 976
nature 546
near 3,766
necessary 745
neck 534
need 4,082
neighbor 739
never 3,257
new 7,427
next 2,738
night 2,877
nine 654
no 8,677
noise 650
noon 801
nor 585
north 2,858
nose 628
not 19,953
note 1,649
nothing 1,453
notice 1,687
noun 1,620
now 7,517
number 8,879
numeral 2,167

object 1,438
observe 960
occur 550
ocean 1,519
of 146,008
off 4,097
offer 558
office 893
often 2,624
oh 1,534
oil 852
old 5,148
on 37,010
once 2,447
one 23,548
only 6,587
open 2,795
operate 746
opposite 663
or 21,292
order 2,076
organ 942
original 564
other 17,256
our 6,047
out 17,257
over 8,130
own 3,646

oxygen 625

page 3,580
paint 1,342
pair 1,253
paper 2,674
paragraph 1,055
parent 576
part 7,319
particular 666
party 767
pass 2,041
past 1,114
path 541
pattern 1,755
pay 941
people 8,291
perhaps 1,236
period 793
person 1,731
phrase 997
pick 1,231
picture 3,933
piece 2,048
pitch 598
place 7,162
plain (com, ex) 2,358
plan 1,645
plane 1,406
planet 712
plant 3,471
play 4,630
please 805
plural 628
poem 732
point 3,849
poor 913
populate 553
port (de, ex, im, re, unim) 4,426
pose (com, dis, sup, im, ex) 2,235
position (ex, dis, com, im) 1,284
possible 1,410
post 568
pound (im, com) 1,590
power 1,679
practice 813
prepare 630
present 1,305
press (ex, im com, de) 2,888
pretty 624
print 693
probable 1,210
problem 2,062
process 748
produce 1,477
product 2,202
proper 559
property 637
protect 802
prove (im, ap dis, re) 1,174
provide 758
pull 1,694
push 1,058
put 4,586

quart 656
question 2,136
quick 1,532

quiet 926
quite 968
quotient 539

race 1,190
radio 791
rail 763
rain 1,701
raise 1,064
ran 1,388
range 546
rather 735
reach 1,868
read 4,509
ready (al) 2,327
real (ist, ize) 2,871
reason 1,224
receive 892
record 1,419
red 2,297
region 1,212
remember 1,893
repeat 633
reply 552
represent 1,221
require 632
rest 1,611
result 1,032
rich 752
ride 1,204
right 5,239
ring 796
rise (a) 854
river 2,578
road (in) 1,706
rock 2,108
roll 991
room 2,509
root 1,071
rope 595
rose (a) 685
round (a, sur) 6,514
row 892
rub 725
rule 1,697
run 2,908

safe 1,019
said 15,309
sail 1,276
salt 630
same 5,030
sand 995
sat 1,138
save 820
saw 3,048
say 5,666
scale 963
school 3,506
science (ist, ific) 2,511
score 601
sea 2,977
search (re) 698
season 621
seat 578
second 2,532
section 940
see 10,789
seed 870
seem 2,779
segment 557
select 634
self 3,738

360

WORD LISTS

sell 678
send 698
sense 974
sent 835
sentence 5,786
separate 812
serve (de, con, re) 1,721
set 4,889
settle 1,263
seven 1,058
several 1,803
shall 1,051
shape 1,370
share 563
sharp 742
she 14, 111
sheet 575
shell 536
shine 638
ship 2,114
shoe 662
shop 641
shore 576
short 2,176
should 3,566
shoulder 661
shout 881
show 6,259
side 7,653
sight 717
sign 1,117
silent (ce) 997
silver 619
similar 609
simple 1,807
since 2,041
sing 1,860
single 904
sister 612
sit 1,191
six 1,849
size 1,273
skill 623
skin 900
sky 1,154
slave 557
sleep 1,177
slip 593
slow 1,754
small 4,613
smell 586
smile 900
snow 1,354
so 11,622
soft 1,111
soil 994
soldier 750
solution 620
solve 1,062
some 18,772
son 965
song 2,216
soon 2,249
sound 8,732
south 2,067
space 2,009
speak 1,262
special 1,496
speech 547
speed 949
spell (mis, re) 4,363
spend 566
spoke 791

spot 692
spread 661
spring 961
square 1,229
stand (out, under) 3,661
star 1,632
start 3,145
state 3,356
station 563
stay 1,452
stead (in) 1,405
steam 546
steel 612
step (in) 1,892
stick 903
still (in) 3,493
stone 926
stood 1,572
stop 2,456
store 1,178
story 3,066
straight 958
strange 1,089
stream 718
street 1,469
stretch 641
string 732
strong 1,501
student 773
study 3,495
subject 1,215
substance 575
subtract 675
success 677
such 4,223
sudden 1,230
suffix 616
sugar 625
suggest 866
suit 690
summer 1,178
sun 3,395
supply 766
support 550
sure (as, en, in, un) 2,422
surface 1,434
surprise 930
swim 665
syllable 1,239
symbol 885
system 1,423

table 1,838
tail (en, de, re) 1,480
take (mis, re) 7,224
talk 2,272
tall 996
teach 1,541
team 846
teeth 538
tell 5,011
temperature 989
ten 1,816
term 665
test (con, at, de, re) 1,421
than 7,984
thank 619
that 48,783
the 374,058

their 13,319
them 11,999
then 12,028
there 16,469
these 11,611
they 28,282
thick 752
thin 716
thing 10,933
think 5,707
third 1,054
this 23,316
those 2,651
though (al) 2,276
thought 3,215
thousand 1,394
three 4,865
through 5,912
throw 639
thus 757
tie 704
time 13,028
tiny 923
tire (at, en, re) 1,354
to 134,781
together 2,746
told (re, un) 2,047
tone 867
too 5,082
took 2,515
tool 588
top 2,034
total 588
touch 848
toward 1,793
town 1,678
track 577
trade 895
train 1,178
travel 1,834
tree 3,200
triangle 713
trip 894
trouble 883
truck 652
true 1,926
try 3,933
tube 722
turn (re) 5,455
twenty 901
two 10,613
type 1,009

under 6,043
unit 1,681
until 2,597
up 15,706
us 3,931
use 15,634
usual 2,336

valley 586
value 987
vary 1,268
verb (ad) 1,864
very 6,001
view (re) 976
village 1,077
visit 1,115
voice 1,683
vowel 1,801

wait (a) 1,647
walk 2,688
wall 1,167
want 4,834
war 1,789
warm 1,512
was 41,685
wash 737
watch 2,419
water 8,068
wave 1,324
way (a) 12,717
we 17,941
wear 839
weather 1,108
week 1,537
weigh (t) 1,260
well 4,712
went 4,133
were 17,207
west 1,881
what 18,828
wheel 1,448
when 16,187
where 6,788
whether 1,060
which 14,036
while 2,892
white 2,720
who 7,765
whole 2,015
whose 799
why 4,164
wide 1,278
wife 663
wild 1,134
will 12,854
win 593
wind 2,146
window 1,181
wing 742
winter 1,149
wire 845
wish 1,160
with 33,953
woman 816
women 622
wonder 1,403
won't 756
wood 2,388
word 19,541
work 7,421
world 3,774
would 11,847
write 11,890
written 1,136
wrong 634
wrote 877

yard 857
year 6,469
yellow 698
yes 1,351
yet 1,326
you 52,939
young 2,336
your 15,572

361

WORD LISTS

II. Rank order of the 1,000 base words

#	Word	#	Word	#	Word	#	Word
1	the 374,058	72	him 10,703	143	before 5,295	213	learn 3,489
2	of 146,008	73	two 10,613	144	move 5,292	214	plant 3,471
3	to 134,781	74	has 10,471	145	right 5,239	215	cover 3,461
4	and 133,931	75	look 10,411	146	boy 5,222	216	food 3,398
5	a 126,651	76	more 10,147	147	old 5,148	217	sun 3,395
6	in 112,946	77	day 10,056	148	too 5,082	218	four 3,394
7	is 61,527	78	could 9,469	149	same 5,030	219	between 3,361
8	it 57,131	79	go 9,266	150	tell 5,011	220	state 3,356
9	you 52,939	80	come 9,265	151	does 5,001	221	keep 3,278
10	that 48,783	81	did 9,213	152	set 4,889	222	eye 3,274
11	he 47,665	82	number 8,879	153	three 4,865	223	never 3,257
12	was 41,685	83	sound 8,732	154	want 4,834	224	last 3,231
13	for 39,333	84	no 8,677	155	air 4,833	225	let 3,219
14	on 37,010	85	most 8,399	156	well 4,712	226	thought 3,215
15	are 35,746	86	people 8,291	157	also 4,647	227	city 3,201
16	with 33,953	87	my 8,132	158	play 4,630	228	tree 3,200
17	as 32,218	88	over 8,130	159	small 4,613	229	cross (a) 3,185
18	I 30,650	89	know 8,074	160	end 4,600	230	farm 3,185
19	his 29,387	90	water 8,068	161	put 4,586	231	hard 3,156
20	they 28,282	91	than 7,984	162	home 4,574	232	start 3,145
21	be 25,867	92	call 7,918	163	read 4,509	233	might 3,114
22	at 23,986	93	first 7,863	164	hand 4,486	234	story 3,066
23	one 23,548	94	who 7,765	165	port (de, ex,	235	saw 3,048
24	have 23,469	95	may 7,750		im, re) 4,426	236	far 3,040
25	this 23,316	96	down 7,693	166	large 4,423	237	sea 2,977
26	from 22,811	97	side 7,653	167	spell 4,363	238	draw 2,946
27	or 21,292	98	been 7,652	168	add 4,350	239	left 2,932
28	had 20,806	99	now 7,517	169	even 4,349	240	late 2,908
29	by 20,307	100	find 7,512	170	land 4,347	241	run 2,908
30	not 19,953	101	any 7,482	171	here 4,340	242	don't 2,900
31	word 19,541	102	new 7,427	172	must 4,338	243	while 2,892
32	but 19,206	103	work 7,421	173	big 4,329	244	press 2,888
33	what 18,828	104	part 7,319	174	high 4,233	245	close 2,879
34	some 18,772	105	take 7,224	175	such 4,223	246	night 2,877
35	we 17,941	106	get 7,188	176	follow 4,192	247	real 2,871
36	can 17,811	107	place 7,162	177	act 4,187	248	life 2,866
37	out 17,257	108	made 7,140	178	why 4,164	249	few 2,860
38	other 17,256	109	live 6,898	179	ask 4,149	250	north 2,858
39	were 17,207	110	where 6,788	180	men 4,149	251	open 2,795
40	all 17,132	111	after 6,745	181	change 4,134	252	seem 2,779
41	there 16,469	112	back 6,646	182	went 4,133	253	together 2,746
42	when 16,187	113	little 6,592	183	light 4,114	254	next 2,738
43	up 15,706	114	only 6,587	184	kind 4,100	255	white 2,720
44	use 15,634	115	round 6,514	185	off 4,097	256	children 2,704
45	your 15,572	116	man 6,496	186	need 4,082	257	begin 2,702
46	how 15,502	117	year 6,469	187	house 4,009	258	got 2,698
47	said 15,309	118	came 6,418	188	picture 3,933	259	walk 2,688
48	an 14,852	119	show 6,259	189	try 3,933	260	example 2,681
49	each 14,290	120	every 6,243	190	us 3,931	261	ease (y) 2,677
50	she 14,111	121	good 6,227	191	again 3,894	262	paper 2,674
51	which 14,036	122	me 6,209	192	animal 3,863	263	group 2,667
52	do 13,683	123	give 6,111	193	point 3,849	264	always 2,660
53	their 13,319	124	our 6,047	194	mother 3,806	265	music 2,653
54	time 13,028	125	under 6,043	195	world 3,774	266	those 2,651
55	if 12,918	126	name 6,010	196	near 3,766	267	both 2,649
56	will 12,854	127	very 6,001	197	build (t) 3,738	268	mark 2,628
57	way 12,717	128	through 5,912	198	self 3,738	269	often 2,624
58	about 12,523	129	just 5,894	199	earth 3,728	270	letter 2,615
59	many 12,205	130	form 5,823	200	father 3,691	271	until 2,597
60	then 12,028	131	sentence 5,786	201	head 3,674	272	mile 2,596
61	them 11,999	132	great 5,718	202	stand 3,661	273	river 2,578
62	write 11,890	133	think 5,707	203	own 3,646	274	car 2,571
63	would 11,847	134	say 5,666	204	page 3,580	275	feet 2,545
64	like 11,742	135	help 5,568	205	should 3,566	276	care 2,533
65	so 11,622	136	low (be) 5,553	206	country 3,553	277	second 2,532
66	these 11,611	137	line 5,515	207	found 3,532	278	book 2,526
67	her 11,444	138	differ (ent) 5,492	208	answer 3,525	279	carry 2,525
68	long 11,369	139	turn 5,455	209	school 3,506	280	took 2,515
69	make 11,282	140	cause 5,402	210	grow 3,496	281	science 2,511
70	thing 10,933	141	much 5,400	211	study 3,495	282	eat 2,509
71	see 10,789	142	mean 5,296	212	still 3,493	283	room 2,509

362

WORD LISTS

284 friend 2,500	358 five 1,918	432 final 1,536	504 wave 1,324
285 began 2,491	359 remember 1,893	433 gave 1,535	505 drop 1,320
286 idea (l) 2,490	360 step 1,892	434 green 1,534	506 heart 1,318
287 fish 2,488	361 early 1,887	435 oh 1,534	507 am 1,313
288 mountain 2,472	362 hold 1,881	436 quick 1,532	508 present 1,305
289 stop 2,456	363 west 1,881	437 develop 1,521	509 heavy 1,298
290 once 2,447	364 ground 1,880	438 ocean 1,519	510 dance 1,293
291 base 2,446	365 interest 1,869	439 warm 1,512	511 engine (er) 1,288
292 hear 2,440	366 reach 1,869	440 free 1,508	512 position 1,284
293 horse 2,436	367 fast 1,866	441 minute 1,506	513 arm 1,281
294 cut 2,424	368 verb (ad) 1,864	442 strong 1,501	514 wide 1,278
295 sure 2,422	369 sing 1,860	443 special 1,496	515 sail 1,276
296 watch 2,419	370 listen 1,857	444 mind (re) 1,494	516 material 1,273
297 color 2,399	371 six 1,849	445 behind 1,490	517 size 1,273
298 face 2,388	372 table 1,838	446 clear 1,480	518 vary 1,268
299 wood 2,388	373 travel 1,834	447 tail (en, de, re) 1,480	519 settle 1,263
300 main (re) 2,365	374 less (un) 1,830		520 speak 1,262
301 enough 2,364	375 morning 1,824	448 produce 1,477	521 weigh (t) 1,260
302 plain (ex) 2,358	376 ten 1,816	449 fact 1,469	522 general 1,256
303 girl 2,357	377 simple 1,807	450 street 1,469	523 ice 1,255
304 usual 2,336	378 several 1,803	451 inch 1,465	524 matter 1,255
305 young 2,336	379 vowel 1,801	452 multiple (y) 1,461	525 circle 1,253
306 ready (al) 2,327	380 toward 1,793	453 nothing 1,453	526 pair 1,253
307 above 2,303	381 war 1,789	454 course 1,452	527 include 1,250
308 ever 2,299	382 lay 1,779	455 stay 1,452	528 divide 1,242
309 red 2,297	383 against 1,759	456 wheel 1,448	529 syllable 1,239
310 list 2,278	384 pattern 1,755	457 full 1,447	530 felt 1,236
311 though (al) 2,276	385 slow 1,754	458 force 1,444	531 perhaps 1,236
312 feel 2,273	386 center (al) 1,743	459 blue 1,441	532 pick 1,231
313 talk 2,272	387 love 1,738	460 object 1,438	533 sudden 1,230
314 bird 2,265	388 person 1,731	461 decide 1,437	534 count 1,229
315 soon 2,249	389 money 1,728	462 surface 1,434	535 square 1,229
316 body 2,248	390 serve 1,721	463 deep 1,432	536 reason 1,224
317 dog 2,241	391 appear (dis) 1,712	464 moon 1,427	537 length 1,222
318 family 2,241	392 road 1,706	465 island 1,425	538 represent 1,221
319 direct 2,237	393 map 1,703	466 foot 1,424	539 art (ist) 1,220
320 pose (com, sup) 2,235	394 rain 1,701	467 system 1,423	540 subject 1,215
321 leave 2,220	395 rule 1,697	468 busy 1,421	541 region 1,212
322 song 2,216	396 govern 1,694	469 test 1,421	542 energy 1,211
323 measure 2,215	397 pull 1,694	470 record 1,419	543 hunt 1,210
324 door 2,202	398 cold 1,692	471 boat 1,418	544 probable 1,210
325 product 2,202	399 notice 1,687	472 common 1,417	545 bed 1,207
326 black 2,197	400 voice 1,683	473 gold 1,414	546 brother 1,205
327 short 2,176	401 unit 1,681	474 possible 1,410	547 egg 1,205
328 numeral 2,167	402 power 1,679	475 plane 1,406	548 ride 1,204
329 class 2,146	403 town 1,678	476 stead (in) 1,405	549 cell 1,197
330 wind 2,146	404 fine 1,677	477 dry 1,404	550 believe 1,193
331 question 2,136	405 certain 1,675	478 wonder 1,403	551 fraction 1,193
332 happen 2,123	406 fly 1,660	479 laugh 1,394	552 forest 1,191
333 complete 2,116	407 fall 1,659	480 thousand 1,394	553 sit 1,191
334 ship 2,114	408 lead (mis) 1,656	481 ago 1,388	554 race 1,190
335 area 2,112	409 cry 1,655	482 ran 1,388	555 window 1,181
336 half 2,110	410 dark 1,651	483 check 1,384	556 store 1,178
337 rock 2,108	411 machine 1,651	484 game 1,381	557 summer 1,178
338 order 2,076	412 note 1,649	485 shape 1,370	558 train 1,178
339 fire 2,072	413 wait 1,647	486 equate 1,369	559 sleep 1,177
340 south 2,067	414 plan 1,645	487 hot 1,369	560 prove (ap) 1,174
341 problem 2,062	415 figure 1,635	488 miss 1,359	561 lone 1,172
342 piece 2,048	416 star 1,632	489 brought 1,357	562 leg 1,171
343 told 2,047	417 box 1,630	490 heat 1,357	563 exercise 1,170
344 knew 2,044	418 noun 1,620	491 snow 1,354	564 wall 1,167
345 pass 2,041	419 field 1,619	492 tire (at, en, re) 1,354	565 catch 1,163
346 since 2,041	420 rest 1,611		566 mount (a) 1,161
347 top 2,034	421 correct 1,605	493 bring 1,353	567 wish 1,160
348 whole 2,015	422 able 1,601	494 yes 1,351	568 sky 1,154
349 king 2,010	423 pound 1,590	495 distant (ce) 1,348	569 board 1,152
350 space 2,009	424 done 1,589	496 fill 1,348	570 joy (en) 1,151
351 heard 2,006	425 beauty 1,588	497 east 1,347	571 winter 1,149
352 best 1,998	426 drive 1,576	498 paint 1,342	572 sat 1,138
353 hour 1,977	427 stood 1,572	499 language 1,337	573 written 1,136
354 better 1,929	428 contain 1,565	500 among 1,334	574 wild 1,134
355 true 1,926	429 front 1,544	501 grand 1,334	575 instrument 1,133
356 during 1,925	430 teach 1,541	502 ball 1,333	576 kept 1,131
357 hundred 1,919	431 week 1,537	503 yet 1,326	577 glass 1,129

363

WORD LISTS

578 grass 1,128	652 else 968	726 oil 852	800 operate 746
579 cow 1,121	653 quite 968	727 blood 850	801 guess 745
580 job 1,119	654 broke 967	728 touch 848	802 necessary 745
581 edge 1,117	655 case 967	729 grew 847	803 sharp 742
582 sign 1,117	656 middle 967	730 cent 846	804 wing 742
583 visit 1,115	657 kill 965	731 mix 846	805 create 739
584 past 1,114	658 son 965	732 team 846	806 neighbor 739
585 soft 1,111	659 lake 964	733 wire 845	807 wash 737
586 fun 1,110	660 moment 964	734 cost 842	808 bat 736
587 bright 1,109	661 scale 963	735 lost 842	809 rather 735
588 gas 1,108	662 loud (a) 962	736 brown 839	810 crowd 734
589 weather 1,108	663 spring 961	737 wear 839	811 corn 733
590 month 1,107	664 observe 960	738 garden 837	812 compare 732
591 million 1,106	665 child 959	739 equal 836	813 poem 732
592 bear 1,104	666 straight 958	740 sent 835	814 string 732
593 finish 1,100	667 consonant 955	741 choose 833	815 bell 730
594 happy 1,100	668 nation 955	742 fell 832	816 depend 726
595 hope 1,100	669 dictionary 952	743 fit 832	817 meat 725
596 flower 1,091	670 milk 951	744 flow 830	818 rub 725
597 clothe 1,089	671 speed 949	745 fair (y) 829	819 tube 722
598 strange 1,089	672 method 946	746 bank 824	820 famous 721
599 gone 1,088	673 organ 942	747 collect 820	821 dollar 719
600 jump 1,084	674 pay 941	748 save 820	822 stream 718
601 baby 1,080	675 age 940	749 control 818	823 fear 717
602 eight 1,077	676 section 940	750 decimal 818	824 sight 717
603 village 1,077	677 dress 937	751 gentle 816	825 thin 716
604 meet 1,071	678 cloud 932	752 woman 816	826 triangle 713
605 root 1,071	679 surprise 930	753 captain 815	827 planet 712
606 buy 1,065	680 quiet 926	754 practice 813	828 hurry 711
607 raise 1,064	681 stone 926	755 separate 812	829 chief 709
608 solve 1,062	682 tiny 923	756 difficult 811	830 colony 708
609 metal 1,061	683 climb 917	757 doctor 806	831 clock (o') 706
610 whether 1,060	684 cool 913	758 please 805	832 mine 704
611 push 1,058	685 design 913	759 protect 802	833 tie 704
612 seven 1,058	686 poor 913	760 noon 801	834 enter 703
613 paragraph 1,055	687 lot 912	761 whose 799	835 major 702
614 third 1,054	688 experiment 911	762 locate 796	836 fresh 701
615 shall 1,051	689 bottom 908	763 ring 796	837 search 698
616 held 1,049	690 key 908	764 character 795	838 send 698
617 hair 1,045	691 iron 905	765 insect 794	839 yellow 698
618 describe 1,043	692 single 904	766 caught 793	840 gun 695
619 cook 1,039	693 stick 903	767 period 793	841 allow 694
620 floor 1,034	694 flat 901	768 indicate 792	842 print 693
621 either 1,033	695 twenty 901	769 radio 791	843 dead 692
622 result 1,032	696 skin 900	770 spoke 791	844 spot 692
623 burn 1,022	697 smile 900	771 atom 789	845 desert 690
624 hill 1,021	698 crease (in) 899	772 human 788	846 suit 690
625 safe 1,019	699 hole 896	773 history 782	847 current 685
626 cat 1,017	700 trade 895	774 effect 780	848 lift 685
627 century 1,014	701 melody 894	775 electric 778	849 rose (a) 685
628 consider 1,012	702 trip 894	776 expect 777	850 continue 681
629 type 1,009	703 office 893	777 crop 775	851 block 680
630 law (yer) 1,007	704 receive 892	778 modern 775	852 chart 680
631 bit 1,005	705 row 892	779 element 774	853 hat 678
632 coast 1,000	706 mouth 891	780 hit 774	854 sell 678
633 copy 1,000	707 exact 887	781 student 773	855 success 677
634 phrase 997	708 symbol 885	782 corner 769	856 company 676
635 silent (ce) 997	709 die 884	783 party 767	857 subtract 675
636 tall 996	710 least 883	784 supply 766	858 event 673
637 sand 995	711 trouble 833	785 bone 764	859 particular 666
638 soil 994	712 shout 881	786 rail (road) 763	860 deal 665
639 roll 991	713 except 879	787 imagine 761	861 swim 665
640 temperature 989	714 wrote 877	788 provide 758	862 term 665
641 finger 988	715 seed 870	789 agree 757	863 opposite 663
642 industry 988	716 tone 867	790 thus 757	864 wife 663
643 value 987	717 join 866	791 capital 756	865 shoe 662
644 fight 986	718 suggest 866	792 won't 756	866 shoulder 661
645 lie (lying) 986	719 clean 865	793 chair 755	867 spread 661
646 beat 982	720 break 859	794 danger 755	868 arrange 660
647 excite 981	721 lady 858	795 fruit 752	869 camp 660
648 natural 976	722 yard 857	796 rich 752	870 invent 660
649 view (re) 976	723 rise (a) 854	797 thick 752	871 cotton 658
650 sense 974	724 bad 852	798 soldier 750	872 born 657
651 ear 969	725 blow 852	799 process 748	873 determine 657

364

WORD LISTS

874	quart 656	905	skill 623	937	win 593	969	bread 560
875	nine 654	906	women 622	938	dream 591	970	charge 559
876	truck 652	907	season 621	939	evening 591	971	proper 559
877	noise 650	908	solution 620	940	condition 589	972	bar 558
878	level 644	909	magnet 619	941	feed 589	973	offer 558
879	chance 642	910	silver 619	942	tool 588	974	segment 557
880	gather 641	911	thank 619	943	total 588	975	slave 557
881	shop 641	912	branch 618	944	basic 586	976	duck 556
882	stretch 641	913	match 618	945	smell 586	977	instant (ce) 556
883	throw 639	914	suffix 616	946	valley 586	978	market 556
884	shine 638	915	especial 615	947	nor 585	979	degree 555
885	property 637	916	fig 614	948	double 580	980	populate 553
886	column 636	917	afraid 613	949	seat 578	981	chick 552
887	molecule 635	918	huge 612	950	arrive 577	982	dear 552
888	select 634	919	sister 612	951	master 577	983	enemy 552
889	wrong 634	920	steel 612	952	track 577	984	reply 552
890	gray 633	921	discuss 611	953	parent 576	985	drink 551
891	repeat 633	922	forward 609	954	shore 576	986	occur 550
892	require 632	923	similar 609	955	division 575	987	support 550
893	broad 631	924	guide 606	956	sheet 575	988	speech 547
894	prepare 630	925	experience 604	957	substance 575	989	nature 546
895	salt 630	926	score 601	958	favor 573	990	range 546
896	nose 628	927	apple 600	959	connect 572	991	steam 546
897	plural 628	928	bought 598	960	post 568	992	motion 541
898	anger (y) 625	929	led 598	961	spend 566	993	path 541
899	claim (ex, pro, ac, re) 625	930	pitch 598	962	chord 565	994	liquid 540
		931	coat 597	963	fat 565	995	log 539
900	continent 625	932	mass 597	964	glad 564	996	meant 539
901	oxygen 625	933	card 596	965	original 564	997	quotient 539
902	sugar 625	934	band 595	966	share 563	998	teeth 538
903	death 624	935	rope 595	967	station 563	999	shell 536
904	pretty 624	936	slip 593	968	dad 561	1000	neck 534

The New Instant Word List

EDWARD FRY

I would like to present a new and totally revised list of Instant Words. The old list of Instant Words has been around for over 20 years (Fry, 1957), and it has aided many classroom teachers and remedial teachers by giving them a research-based list for sight word instruction. The old list has been reprinted in many teacher training textbooks, on filmstrips, and in countless local district curriculum guides and teacher training pamphlets.

The older list contained the most common words in English in rough rank order based on studies by Rinsland (1945), Dolch (1936), Thorndike and Lorge (1944), and others. The new list is based on a newer frequency count of five million running words done by Carroll, Davies and Richman (1971). However, the Carroll, Davies, and Richman list has some flaws that make it less useful for classroom teachers than the edited list presented in this article.

Why are the instant words important?

For readers who are not familiar with the efficiency of high-frequency word lists, let me review the basic principle with

From *The Reading Teacher*, Vol. 34, No. 3 (December, 1980). Reprinted by permission of the International Reading Association and Edward Fry.

statistics from this list. The statistics are absolutely astounding if you have not heard them before.

Half of all written material in English is composed of just the first hundred Instant Words and their common variants. An example of a common variant would be the adding of *s* or *ing* at the end of a base word. Hence, if a beginning reader can read half of the words on any page of any textbook, newspaper, encyclopedia, etc., just by learning a list of 100 words, then those 100 words are a very valuable teaching tool.

The reason for calling these words "Instant Words" is that a student must learn to recognize them instantly in order to achieve fluency in reading, writing, or spelling. A reader who stumbles or has to use phonics on *of* or *which* is going to have a lot of trouble getting the meaning of the sentence or paragraph.

The frequency curve in word usage is long and steep. The first 10 words make up about 24% of all written material; the first 100 words make up about 50% (50.44% if you want to be exact), and the first 300 words presented in this article make up about 65% of all the words written in English. At the opposite end of the scale, Carroll, Davies, and Richman found that some 35,000 words out of 87,000 different words were used only once in 5 million running words, each word accounting for half a ten-thousandth of one percent (.00005%). If percentages don't impress you, try to find a sentence that doesn't use one of the first ten Instant Words; it's possible, but such a sentence is rare.

The Instant Words are in harmony with what might be called the probabilistic model of curriculum. This model asks, "What is the most useful word a student will need to know?" "What is the next most useful word a student needs to know?" etc. In other words, the teacher attempts to teach the most used words first, so that the student can read anything more easily. Of course, the model breaks down a little bit when one looks at the nature of language. The first Instant Words are loaded with structure words like *the* or *and,* so that some less frequent content words like *dog* or *run* need to be taught early to give meaning to the lesson material. However, the Instant Words remain a useful tool for 1) diagnosing reading problems (just ask the student to read them aloud) or 2) in preparing teaching material like flash cards, spelling lists, writing samples, and all sorts of curriculum material from games to worksheets for group or individual instruction of regular or remedial students.

Basis of the New Instant Words

The New Instant Words are based on a mammoth frequency count of 5,088,721 running words. These running words appeared in 500-word samples taken from 1,045 different books in 12 subject matter areas ranging from English to vocational education used in grades 3 through 9. Samples were also taken from library books—both fiction and nonfiction—and from magazines. ["Running words" is the total number of words in a text; for example, a typical novel might be 80,000 running words long.]

It is fairly safe to say that these words, particularly those at the higher-frequency end of the list, are quite typical of all school and adult kinds of reading. However, do not make the mistake of thinking that the 300 Instant Words reported here are for grades 3 through 9. They are for beginning readers of any age: 6, 7, and 8 year olds in first, second, and third grades, remedial students in the middle or secondary grades, and adult functional illiterates.

The Carroll, Davies, and Richman list, as marvelous and as impressive as it may be, is not as useful to classroom teachers as it could be. The frequency count was done by computers, and computers have good memories and good adding abilities, but they are not too bright in making discriminations. The computer was told to count as a word

WORD LISTS

anything with a space on either side of it. Hence, *1943, &* and *F* are all counted as words. But that is not the real problem. The real problem is that alternate graphic forms like *run, RUN,* and *Run* are seen as different words. Common structural variants like *run, runs,* and *running* are also seen as different words. Each different word is given a different frequency count and hence a different rank order.

What the New Instant Word list has done is combine the different graphic forms and the different structural variants to give one frequency for the base word *run* while keeping track of the variant forms or endings (e.g., *ing*). Hence the word *run* now has a single and different position in the rank order rather than six different positions as in the example above. Not all words have variant forms, but more than half of the first 300 Instant Words do, and that is a significant amount. Some 189 or 60% of the first 300 Instant Words had common variants. (A common variant is the root word plus suffix that occurs more than 30 times in 5 million running words.)

The Instant Words
First hundred

First 25 Group 1a	Second 25 Group 1b	Third 25 Group 1c	Fourth 25 Group 1d
the	or	will	number
of	one	up	no
and	had	other	way
a	by	about	could
to	word	out	people
in	but	many	my
is	not	then	than
you	what	them	first
that	all	these	water
it	were	so	been
he	we	some	call
was	when	her	who
for	your	would	oil
on	can	make	now
are	said	like	find
as	there	him	long
with	use	into	down
his	an	time	day
they	each	has	did
I	which	look	get
at	she	two	come
be	do	more	made
this	how	write	may
have	their	go	part
from	if	see	over

Common suffixes: *s, ing, ed*

WORD LISTS

The Instant Words
Second hundred

First 25 Group 2a	Second 25 Group 2b	Third 25 Group 2c	Fourth 25 Group 2d
new	great	put	kind
sound	where	end	hand
take	help	does	picture
only	through	another	again
little	much	well	change
work	before	large	off
know	line	must	play
place	right	big	spell
year	too	even	air
live	mean	such	away
me	old	because	animal
back	any	turn	house
give	same	here	point
most	tell	why	page
very	boy	ask	letter
after	follow	went	mother
thing	came	men	answer
our	want	read	found
just	show	need	study
name	also	land	still
good	around	different	learn
sentence	form	home	should
man	three	us	America
think	small	move	world
say	set	try	high

Common suffixes: *s, ing, ed, er, ly, est*

What all this means is that if you take variations of base word form into account, you will get a different rank list for the most common words in English. The Carroll list is a valuable basic research source, but for classroom teachers it is formidable, expensive, and inappropriate.

The New Instant Words presented here are based on a list of 3000 Instant Words (Sakiey and Fry, 1979), which did the original recombining and ranking. The list presented here differs from the 3000-word list in several aspects which are explained in a technical note at the end of this article for readers who like details. The list of 3000 Instant Words is designed for teachers who want a longer list that is also suitable for more advanced students.

Uses of the new list
The 300 New Instant Words and their common variants make up 65% of all the words in any textbook, any newspaper, or any writing sample in English. It is

impossible to achieve fluency in reading or writing unless these words are known "instantly."

It is intended that this list supersede the old Instant Words (Fry, 1957) because of its newer research base and editorial considerations. The research base is broader and larger than that of lists which use only reading textbooks as a source. The new list is also different from the older list and most lists of high-frequency words because it uses a base word plus common variants (suffixes).

Teachers can use the list in many ways. They can teach just the base word or they can teach the common variants with very little extra effort at the same time that they are teaching the base word.

If teachers teach only the base words, it might be helpful for them to know that the vast majority of the variants are caused by just six suffixes: -s, -ing, -ed, -er, -ly, -est. The variants given in the list are not all that are possible; they are just the most common ones.

The Instant Words
Third hundred

First 25 Group 3a	Second 25 Group 3b	Third 25 Group 3c	Fourth 25 Group 3d
every	left	until	idea
near	don't	children	enough
add	few	side	eat
food	while	feet	face
between	along	car	watch
own	might	mile	far
below	close	night	Indian
country	something	walk	real
plant	seem	white	almost
last	next	sea	let
school	hard	began	above
father	open	grow	girl
keep	example	took	sometimes
tree	begin	river	mountain
never	life	four	cut
start	always	carry	young
city	those	state	talk
earth	both	once	soon
eye	paper	book	list
light	together	hear	song
thought	got	stop	leave
head	group	without	family
under	often	second	body
story	run	late	music
saw	important	miss	color

Common suffixes: s, ing, ed, er, ly, est

Teachers can use the Instant Words as an oral reading diagnostic test of a student's knowledge of the most common words. This test can be either an oral sight reading test or a spelling test. In other words, if reading is the goal, just ask the student to read them aloud; and if spelling is the goal, ask the student to write the word or spell it aloud.

Do not, however, ask the poor student to do too many in one sitting. Use your judgment, and do only as many as the student can do without fatigue or boredom. You might remember that Dolch found that a student needed a third-grade reading ability before mastering his 220 Basic Sight Words.

The same cautions apply to teaching these Instant Words. Do not try to teach too many at one sitting. For some students one or two new words per lesson are plenty while others might master ten or twenty per week. Some repetition and retesting are recommended.

Learning a list of words can be a boring lesson, so liven it up with your entire bag of tricks: oral reading, silent reading, games, flash cards, spelling lessons, writing lessons, easy reading material, and anything you can think of for fun and variation. However, teaching this list of words can also be efficient instruction. It saves time, and it teaches students the words they really need to know most.

You will also need to add some interesting subject matter words like *monster* or *skiing,* so do not feel constrained to teach only this list for reading or writing. In fact, you can let the students tell you what high-interest subject-matter words they want to learn while you are sneaking in the highly efficient words from this list.

The development of another high-frequency word list is not revolutionary, but it is hoped that this one represents a modest step forward and is an example of basic research modified for classroom use.

The list of 300 New Instant Words, while copyrighted for commercial purposes, may be duplicated or used in any manner by classroom teachers in preparing material for their students or by districts for making inservice booklets. A free copy can be obtained by sending a self-addressed, stamped envelope to the author at the Reading Center, Rutgers University, New Brunswick, New Jersey 08903, U.S.A.

REFERENCES

Carroll, John B., Peter Davies, and Barry Richman. *The American Heritage Word Frequency Book.* Boston, Mass.: Houghton Mifflin, 1971.

Dolch, Edward W. "A Basic Sight Vocabulary." *Elementary School Journal,* vol. 36 (1936), pp. 456-60.

Fry, Edward. "Developing a Word List for Remedial Reading." *Elementary English,* vol. 36 (1957), pp. 456-58.

Rinsland, Henry D. *A Basic Vocabulary of Elementary School Children.* New York, N.Y.: Macmillan, 1945.

Sakiey, Elizabeth, and Edward Fry. *3000 Instant Words.* Providence, R.I.: Jamestown Publishers, 1979.

Thorndike, Edward L., and Irving Lorge. *The Teacher's Word Book of 30,000 Words.* New York, N.Y.: Teachers College Press, Columbia University, 1944.

Technical note: The Sakiey and Fry list of *3000 Instant Words* (1979) is slightly different from this new list, because 1) the -*'s* was counted as an -*s* variant, 2) some errors were found—the computer was not quite so accurate as the eyeball, 3) only the base words are given in this list of 300, grouped by frequency and by the suffixes which may appear with them. Thus only three suffixes occur with items in the first hundred words, but six suffixes commonly appear with words from the second and third hundreds. Teachers may extend the usefulness of this list somewhat by supplying their own variants (common suffixes) or by using double suffixes (e.g., *doings* or *laughingly*) which were omitted.

A Syllable Frequency Count

ELIZABETH SAKIEY
EDWARD FRY
ALBERT GOSS
BARRY LOIGMAN

A frequency count of the syllables in an edited list of the 5,000 most common English words generated an unweighted list of the most common 322 syllables in 5,000 words and a list of 290 syllables weighted by the frequency of occurrence of words of which the syllables were constituents. The unweighted list contained 222 nonword-syllables and 100 word-syllables. The weighted list contained 190 word-syllables and 100 nonword-syllables. The latter 290 syllables account for 72 percent of the 5,890,868 syllable tokens in the 5,000 most common English words. These lists are seen as potential base data for the development of curriculum materials in reading, spelling, and other areas. They are also seen as potential base data for investigations and technologies in readability, computer translation, verbal learning, and language acquisition.

Certain aspects of basic knowledge about the syllable are updated and refined in this study. Historically, the syllable was one of the mainstays of the teaching of reading; it played a prominent role in the methodology of the 18th century *New England Primer*. At various times subsequently in the history of instruction the syllable has been featured in reading, spelling, and writing instruction. Syllables continue to merit some importance in those areas. They are more important, however, in dictionary use, speech correction, typography, computer translation, readability, verbal learning, and language research.

The purpose of this study was to develop a syllable rank-order list. The study attempts to answer the questions "What is the commonest syllable? What is the next commonest syllable?" etc.

These questions pose another question, "What does *common* mean?" In terms of this study, it means both an unweighted rank-order list and a weighted rank-order list. The lists are composed of *types* and *tokens*. Types are separate or different syllables; tokens are the occurrences, or frequencies, of the types. Each occurrence of a type is a token. The unweighted list presents the number of occurrences of each different syllable in a list of the 5,000 most common words in an edited list based on the Carroll, Davies, and Richman, or *American Heritage* (1971), count. The weighted list reflects the frequency of occurrence of each syllable in the 5,000 words weighted by the number of times each of those words appeared in 5,088,721 running words. These two lists are then compared.

BACKGROUND

The last major syllable count was done by Osburn (1954). He listed the 15 commonest initial, medial, and final syllables. Unfortunately, the bulk of his syllable count on the 9,000 polysyllabic words of the now dated Rinsland (1945) list did not find its way into the professional literature and, for most practical purposes, is lost.

Three decades earlier Dewey counted phonic syllables (spoken syllables) in

From *Visible Language*, Vol. 14, No. 2, copyright © 1980. Reprinted by permission.

100,000 printed words of adult material. He ranked the 220 most common of the 4,400 different syllables obtained (1923). Later he appended initial, medial, and final positions for these syllables (1950).

Dolch (1938) obtained 8,509 nonword syllables in 3,931 polysyllabic words found in 14,000 running words of elementary texts. There were 1,255 different syllables. His published alphabetical list of the 100 commonest syllables does not answer the question of which is the commonest syllable. The list of 100 syllables is all that is apparently available (Dolch, 1940). Additionally, the Dolch count, like the Dewey and Osburn counts, was an unweighted one.

DATA BASE

The Carroll et al. frequencies that served as the data base were generated by a computerized count of occurrences of different words in 5,088,721 running words. These words were in 10,043 five-hundred-word samples of reading materials used in grades three through nine in 22 different categories. This count yielded 86,741 different words or types. A type might not be a word because numerals such as "1905" and initializations such as "USA" are types. A token is the frequency of a word. For example, the type "the" occurred 373,123 times, or "the" had 373,123 tokens.

Method

The 86,741 different words (types) of the Carroll et al. count, together with their frequencies of occurrence, were on computer data tape deposited at the National Archives for Linguistics in Arlington, Virginia. Punched cards were generated from these tapes for 52,000 words that occurred more than once per five million.

The first phase was to edit the Carroll et al. list. They defined a word as a group of symbols with a space on either side. This facilitated selection, scoring, and counting by the computer. It also had the advantage of nonjudgmental objectivity. However, for the purposes of this study it had the obvious drawback of counting *nonwords* such as "&," "$100," and "1945," and "USA" as words. Also, words which differed only in case of letters such as "Run," "run," and "RUN" were counted as three different words with three different frequencies of occurrence for each word.

Hand editing was necessary to eliminate nonalphabetic symbols and nonwords. Hand editing was also used to combine frequencies for different graphic forms of the same word, such as "Run" and "run," into one word. However, *inflected forms* of the word, such as "runs," "running," and "ran" were not combined; this would have omitted syllables such as "ed" and "ing."

After hand editing, 44,174 word cards remained. Of these words, the count was on the 5,000 most frequent. These words account for 4,513,777 occurrences or 89 percent of the word tokens in the 5,088,721 running words. These 5,000 high-frequency words are all the words that occur more than approximately 15 times per million running words.

The 5,000 most frequent words were then divided into *graphemic syllables*. Graphemic syllables refer to syllables whose boundaries were determined for graphic (written) use. The *American Heritage School Dictionary* (1977) was the authority for this syllabification.

Phonetic syllables are those syllables used in the phonetic or pronunciation part of a dictionary definition; they are said to be more akin to speech patterns. There is a lack of agreement among dictionaries on syllable boundaries, particularly for phonetic syllables.

The computer programs used were based on Fortran Sort-Merge and the Statistical Package for the Social Sciences (Nie, Hull, Jenkins, Steinbrenner, and Brent, 1975).

RESULTS

Unweighted List

There were 9,358 graphemic syllables or syllable tokens in the 5,000 words, an average of about 1.9 syllables per word. These 9,358 syllables were comprised of 3,402 different syllables or syllable types. The different syllables may be divided into word-syllables and nonword-syllables. A word-syllable is one like "the" that is a simple word and may also be part of a larger word like "theater." A nonword-syllable is a syllable like "ing," which never occurs as a single word. Of the 3,402 different syllables, 1,982 or 58 percent are word-syllables and 1,420 or 42 percent are nonword-syllables.

The 322 most frequent graphemic syllables are presented in Table I. These are syllables that occurred in five or more of the 5,000 words. Of these syllables, 222 or 69 percent are nonword-syllables and 100 or 31 percent are word-syllables. The five most frequent syllables, "ing," "er," "a," "ly," and "ed," are all nonword-syllables. The syllables "a" and "ed" were not counted as words because "a" generally functions as a single vowel syllable, and "ed" is a word only when capitalized and used as a nickname. The first word-syllable, "in," has a rank of 10; the second word-syllable, "an," has a rank of 22.

The sum of the frequencies of the 222 nonword-syllables is 3,329 or 36 percent of the 9,358 syllable tokens in the 5,000 words. The sum of the frequencies of the 100 word-syllables is 1,496 or 16 percent of the syllable tokens. Thus, 322 syllables account for 52 percent of the 9,358 syllable tokens.

Weighted List

The rank, weighted frequency, and unweighted frequency of each of the 290 syllables with a weighted frequency of 3,000 or more are in Table II. Of these 290 syllables, 190 or 66 percent are word-syllables and 100 or 34 percent are nonword-syllables. The most frequent syllable of the unweighted list, "ing," drops to rank seven in the weighted list, and "er" drops from rank two to rank eight. Of the first 100 syllables, 72 are word-syllables.

When 3,402 syllable types in the 5,000 words are weighted for frequency of the words in which they appear, there are 5,890,868 syllable tokens. The common 190 word-syllables in Table II account for 3,260,280 or 55 percent of these tokens. The 100 nonword-syllables account for 977,456 or 17 percent of these tokens. All 290 syllables account for 4,237,736 or 72 percent of the 5,890,868 tokens.

DISCUSSION

A relatively small number of syllables account for a large proportion of our written language.

In the *weighted list,* a mere 290 word- and nonword-syllables account for 72 percent of the 5,890,868 syllable tokens in the 5,000 most common words weighted for their frequency. This reflects the J-curve distribution of the weighted frequencies in which a few types occur with high frequency and many types occur with moderate-to-low frequencies.

High-frequency whole words continue to be important. Of the 290 weighted syllables, 190 are word-syllables that account for 55 percent of the 5,890,868 tokens or more than half of all written English. This lends support to the efficacy of teaching a high frequency or basic sight vocabulary such as those developed by Dolch (1936) and Fry (1957), since both the Dolch and Fry list contain a high percentage of the same one-syllable words. For example, the basic word "let" is instantly recognized as a syllable when encountered in such words as "gauntlet," "inlet," and "lettuce." Furthermore, the 190 word-syllables pre-

WORD LISTS

TABLE I The 322 most common unweighted graphemic syllables in the English language ranked in order of frequency in the 5,000 most frequent words.

Rank	Syl.	F.	Rank	Syl.	F.	Rank	Syl.	F.
1	ing	230	40	der	25	80	pre	14
2	er	129		ma	23		tive	14
3	a	124		na	22		car	13
4	ly	119		si	22		ci	13
5	ed	114		un	22		mo	13
6	i	112	45	at	21	85	on	13
7	es	98		dis	21		ous	13
8	re	90		ca	20		pi	13
9	tion	83		cal	20		se	13
10	in	78		man	20		ten	13
	e	67	50	ap	19	90	tor	13
	con	64		po	19		ver	13
	y	63		sion	19		ber	12
	ter	60		vi	19		can	12
15	ex	58		el	18		dy	12
	al	56	55	est	18	95	et	12
	de	55		la	18		it	12
	com	51		lar	18		ma	12
	o	51		pa	18		no	12
20	di	46		ture	18		ple	12
	en	42	60	for	17	100	cu	11
	an	39		is	17		fac	11
	ty	39		mer	17		fer	11
	ry	37		pe	17		gen	11
25	u	36		ra	17		ic	11
	ti	35	65	so	16	105	land	11
	ri	32		ta	16		light	11
	be	30		as	15		ob	11
	per	29		col	15		of	11
30	to	29		fi	15		pos	11
	pro	28	70	ful	15	110	tain	11
	ac	26		ger	15		den	10
	ad	26		low	15		ings	10
	ar	26		ni	15		mag	10
35	ers	26		par	15		ments	10
	ment	26	75	son	15	115	set	10
	or	26		tle	15		some	10
	tions	26		day	14		sub	10
	ble	25		ny	14		sur	10
				pen	14		ters	10

374

Table I—Continued

Rank	Syl.	F.	Rank	Syl.	F.	Rank	Syl.	F.
120	tu	10	160	my	8	200	ton	7
	af	9		nal	8		try	7
	au	9		ness	8		um	7
	ey	9		ning	8		ure	7
	fa	9		n't	8		way	7
125	im	9	165	nu	8	205	ate	6
	li	9		oe	8		bet	6
	lo	9		pres	8		bles	6
	men	9		sup	8		bod	6
	min	9		te	8		cap	6
130	mon	9	170	ted	8	210	cial	6
	op	9		tem	8		cir	6
	out	9		tin	8		cor	6
	rec	9		tri	8		coun	6
	ro	9		tro	8		cus	6
135	sen	9	175	up	8	215	dan	6
	side	9		va	8		dle	6
	tal	9		ven	8		ef	6
	tic	9		vis	8		end	6
	ties	9		am	8		ent	6
140	ward	9	180	bor	8	220	ered	6
	age	8		by	8		fin	6
	ba	8		cat	8		form	6
	but	8		cent	7		go	6
	cit	8		ev	7		har	6
145	cle	8	185	gan	7	225	ish	6
	co	8		gle	7		lands	6
	cov	8		head	7		let	6
	da	8		high	7		long	6
	dif	8		il	7		mat	6
150	ence	8	190	lu	7	230	meas	6
	ern	8		me	7		mem	6
	eve	8		nor	7		mul	6
	hap	8		part	7		ner	6
	ies	8		por	7		play	6
155	ket	8	195	read	7	235	ples	6
	lec	8		rep	7		ply	6
	main	8		su	7		port	6
	mar	8		tend	7		press	6
	mis	8		ther	7		sat	6

WORD LISTS

Table I—Continued

Rank	Syl.	F.	Rank	Syl.	F.	Rank	Syl.	F.
240	sec	6	270	fix	5	300	round	5
	ser	6		gi	5		row	5
	south	6		grand	5		sa	5
	sun	6		great	5		sand	5
	the	6		heav	5		self	5
245	ting	6	275	ho	5	305	sent	5
	tra	6		hunt	5		ship	5
	tures	6		ion	5		sim	5
	val	6		its	5		sions	5
	var	6		jo	5		sis	5
250	vid	6	280	lat	5	310	sons	5
	wil	6		lead	5		stand	5
	win	6		lect	5		sug	5
	won	6		lent	5		tel	5
	work	6		less	5		tom	5
255	act	5	285	lin	5	315	tors	5
	ag	5		mal	5		tract	5
	air	5		mi	5		tray	5
	als	5		mil	5		us	5
	bat	5		moth	5		vel	5
260	bi	5	290	near	5	320	west	5
	cate	5		nel	5		where	5
	cen	5		net	5		writ	5
	char	5		new	5			
	come	5		one	5			
265	cul	5	295	point	5			
	ders	5		prac	5			
	east	5		ral	5			
	fect	5		rect	5			
	fish	5		ried	5			

This table contains all syllables that occurred five or more times in the 5,000 highest frequency English words. These 322 syllables comprise 52 percent of all the syllables (tokens) in the 5,000 words.

TABLE II The 290 most common syllables in the English language ranked in order of frequency in 5,088,721 running words.

Rank	Syl.	Weighted[b]	Unwtd.[a]	Rank	Syl.	Weighted[b]	Unwtd.[a]
1	the	374,747	6	40	tion	20,975	83
2	a	191,870	124		had	20,802	2
3	of	150,386	11		not	20,090	3
4	to	143,284	29		but	19,993	3
5	and	133,921	1		can	19,683	12
6	in	131,121	78	45	so	19,242	16
7	ing	71,958	230		re	18,799	90
8	er	64,846	129		some	18,558	10
9	is	64,816	17		what	18,301	3
10	i	59,077	112		o	18,094	51
	be	57,052	30	50	were	17,207	2
	you	50,999	1		oth	17,172	4
	it	50,254	12		all	17,042	1
	that	47,462	1		out	16,892	9
15	y	46,700	63		we	16,474	3
	on	46,634	13	55	ry	16,278	37
	he	46,532	3		your	16,214	2
	for	44,258	17		when	16,183	2
	was	41,685	2		there	15,692	2
20	ly	40,685	119		how	15,422	3
	an	40,572	39	60	said	15,309	1
	as	35,619	15		up	15,291	8
	are	35,502	1		de	14,977	55
	with	33,817	3		ver	14,953	13
25	ter	32,154	60		ex	14,710	58
	his	30,244	3	65	each	14,290	1
	at	27,710	21		en	14,158	42
	or	27,697	26		which	14,016	1
	they	27,627	1		do	13,744	3
30	al	27,231	56		she	13,657	1
	ed	26,367	114	70	their	13,258	1
	es	24,969	98		them	12,959	2
	this	23,316	1		if	12,912	1
	from	22,810	1		will	12,873	2
35	one	22,644	5		di	12,810	46
	have	22,444	2	75	him	12,542	2
	e	21,956	67		bout	12,507	1
	by	21,746	7		com	12,439	51
	man	21,081	20		ple	12,420	12
					u	12,248	36

Table II—Continued

Rank	Syl.	Weighted[b]	Unwtd.[a]	Rank	Syl.	Weighted[b]	Unwtd.[a]
80	then	12,026	1	120	mer	7,726	17
	her	11,814	2		wa	7,699	3
	no	11,763	12		ten	7,661	13
	words	11,707	1		been	7,651	1
	these	11,611	1		who	7,608	1
85	con	11,598	64	125	ment	7,535	26
	way	11,406	7		use	7,529	3
	per	11,315	29		now	7,465	1
	would	11,191	1		ti	7,451	35
	low	10,801	15		pro	7,447	28
90	un	10,748	22	130	down	7,419	3
	like	10,644	4		find	7,313	2
	long	10,616	6		ar	7,285	26
	has	10,469	2		me	7,256	7
	two	10,144	1		ma	7,231	23
95	my	10,142	8	135	new	7,190	5
	more	10,130	2		lit	7,157	4
	go	10,055	6		made	7,157	2
	write	9,974	2		get	7,029	4
	der	9,844	25		ri	6,956	32
100	tle	9,636	15	140	thing	6,817	4
	could	9,464	2		eve	6,806	8
	ber	9,397	12		us	6,608	5
	did	9,276	3		sen	6,601	9
	ty	9,080	39		read	6,584	7
105	see	8,981	3	145	come	6,467	5
	num	8,955	4		came	6,418	2
	day	8,949	14		where	6,413	5
	time	8,643	3		ture	6,411	18
	most	8,372	3		look	6,286	2
110	make	8,340	1	150	back	6,252	4
	peo	8,281	3		side	6,228	9
	its	8,197	5		fer	6,211	11
	ble	8,159	25		dif	6,201	8
	than	8,057	2		round	6,168	5
115	af	7,934	9	155	pa	6,105	18
	ers	7,911	26		let	5,998	6
	may	7,836	3		tions	5,981	26
	word	7,804	1		just	5,939	2
	first	7,776	1		work	5,932	6

Table II—Continued

Rank	Syl.	Weighted[b]	Unwtd.[a]	Rank	Syl.	Weighted[b]	Unwtd.[a]
160	know	5,926	2	200	ning	4,715	8
	our	5,922	2		cause	4,714	2
	ther	5,913	7		ways	4,685	3
	through	5,909	2		col	4,627	15
	try	5,898	7		am	4,621	7
165	fore	5,870	3	205	par	4,621	15
	called	5,789	1		dis	4,549	21
	great	5,737	5		small	4,509	3
	est	5,728	18		air	4,492	5
	fa	5,705	9		three	4,479	1
170	good	5,629	3	210	put	4,455	4
	used	5,611	1		say	4,442	2
	la	5,608	18		ern	4,409	8
	land	5,597	11		help	4,387	3
	part	5,551	7		self	4,380	5
175	car	5,491	13	215	ny	4,372	14
	el	5,474	18		times	4,361	2
	think	5,445	2		well	4,350	2
	n't	5,433	8		cit	4,331	8
	much	5,388	1		must	4,307	1
180	si	5,218	22	220	want	4,292	2
	set	5,217	10		big	4,254	3
	ent	5,187	6		take	4,252	2
	ven	5,098	8		po	4,247	19
	ev	5,096	7		such	4,223	1
185	too	5,074	1	225	cal	4,197	20
	men	5,064	9		here	4,192	1
	old	5,034	3		why	4,158	1
	same	5,024	1		tell	4,137	2
	ac	5,012	26		went	4,132	1
190	ca	5,008	20	230	line	4,131	4
	does	5,001	2		pen	4,121	14
	sound	4,964	2		mu	4,097	12
	fol	4,932	4		things	4,078	1
	right	4,931	2		moth	4,077	5
195	place	4,883	4	235	gain	4,065	2
	ful	4,867	15		end	4,027	6
	son	4,747	15		pic	4,017	4
	na	4,726	22		im	4,001	9
	tain	4,716	11		to	3,989	16

Table II—Continued

Rank	Syl.	Weighted[b]	Unwtd.[a]	Rank	Syl.	Weighted[b]	Unwtd.[a]
240	years	3,975	1	265	home	3,370	1
	off	3,875	1		give	3,369	1
	name	3,864	2		tween	3,344	1
	high	3,861	7		own	3,313	3
	light	3,809	11		gan	3,285	7
245	head	3,795	7	270	bod	3,276	6
	coun	3,770	6		add	3,254	3
	mon	3,712	9		tence	3,252	2
	pe	3,698	17		ward	3,250	9
	near	3,677	5		hap	3,238	8
250	lar	3,654	18	275	nev	3,238	2
	por	3,595	7		ure	3,208	7
	fi	3,579	15		mem	3,206	6
	bers	3,563	3		mean	3,201	4
	sec	3,557	6		looked	3,197	1
255	ap	3,545	19	280	earth	3,177	2
	stud	3,491	4		ters	3,174	10
	found	3,477	2		cov	3,165	8
	should	3,470	1		ger	3,147	15
	ad	3,431	21		last	3,132	2
260	still	3,424	1	285	nit	3,095	3
	form	3,414	6		show	3,089	2
	need	3,412	2		might	3,077	2
	play	3,392	6		stand	3,058	5
	world	3,383	1		house	3,054	2
				290	got	3,051	3

(a) *Unweighted* Frequency means number of occurrences in the 5,000 different words. This is the same as Table I count.
(b) *Weighted* Frequency means number of occurrences per five million running words using words from the 5,000 word list. For example, the 189th syllable "ac" appeared in 26 different words of the 5,000 word list and these 26 words were used a total of 5,012 times in five million running words.
These 290 syllables account for 72 percent of all the syllables (tokens) in the 5,000 most common words.

sented in Table II make up about half of all written English since the 190 words make up 49 percent of the five million running words in the Carroll count.

Another finding of this study is that only 100 nonword-syllables of the weighted list account for an additional 17 percent of the 5,890,868 syllable tokens. Thus, the 100 syllables account for approximately another sixth of all written English.

These findings cannot be compared with those of earlier counts. Dolch and Osburn counted only polysyllabic words; Dewey used phonemic syllables, all of which were unweighted counts.

The *unweighted count* presented here provides a different orientation than the weighted count. When one looks at the unweighted list, in this analysis of 5,000 common words, the 222 nonword-syllables of Table I make up 36 percent of the total syllables, and 100 word-syllables make up 16 percent of the total. Thus, nonword-syllables assume greater importance on the unweighted list than on the weighted list.

Other researchers provide evidence that the syllable is a viable unit for at least some phases of literacy instruction. The objection to teaching syllables in addition to words and phonemes in reading stems from the belief that graphemic or written syllables have numerous pronunciations. However, Sakiey and Martin (1980) have shown that 92 percent of the syllables found in basal readers in the primary grades have two or less pronunciations. Sixty-six percent had only one pronunciation. Savin and Bever (1970) demonstrated "that even for literate adults the syllable is a far more natural, more easily available perceptual unit than is the phoneme" (p. 322). Using both urban and suburban kindergarten-age children, Allen, Rozin, and Gleitman (1972) found that prereaders were more likely to recognize a meaningful word when segmented syllabically than when segmented phonemically.

Blending of two syllables was found to be easier than blending two phonemes (Brown, 1971) for children of ages 56 to 80 months. Children 4 to 6 years old had more difficulty analyzing words into phonemes than syllables (Liberman, Shankweiler, Carter, and Fischer, 1972). Finally, tachistoscopic studies have shown that the syllable functions as a single perceptual unit (Spoehr and Smith, 1973).

Ruddell (1976) called for "A study of various decoding units . . . and the relationship between these units and early reading success" (p. 35). This is only one of the areas in which high-frequency syllable lists might be employed. They might be used in the development of curriculum materials for developmental and remedial reading as well as in spelling and typing instruction. Syllable frequency lists may also be useful in a wide variety of investigation and technologies of readability, spelling reform, verbal learning, language acquisition, and computer translation.

The unique contribution of this study is in providing a weighted syllable frequency count and in determining that a relatively small number of syllables make up a fairly substantial portion of all written language.

REFERENCES

Allen, M. W., Rozin, P., & Gleitman, L.R. A test of the blending abilities of kindergarten children using syllable and phoneme segments. Unpublished manuscript, University of Pennsylvania, 1972. Cited by L.R. Gleitman & P. Rozin, Teaching reading by use of a syllabary. *Reading Research Quarterly*, Summer 1973, *8*, 447-83.

The American Heritage School Dictionary. Boston: Houghton-Mifflin, 1977.

Brown, D. L. Some linguistic dimensions in auditory blending. In G. Green, ed., Reading: The right to participate. *Yearbook of the National Reading Conference,* 1971, *20,* 227-36. Cited by L. R. Gleitman & P. Rozin, Teaching reading by use of a syllabary, *Reading Research Quarterly,* Summer 1973, *8,* 447-83.

Carroll, J. B., Davies, P., & Richman, B. *American Heritage Word Frequency Book.* Boston: Houghton-Mifflin, 1971.

Dewey, G. *Relative frequency of English speech sounds.* Cambridge: Harvard University Press, 1923. Reprint 1950.

Dolch, E. W. A basic sight vocabulary. *Elementary School Journal,* 1936, *36,* 456-60, *37,* 268-72.

――――. Phonics and polysyllables. *Elementary English Review,* 1938, *15,* 120-24.

――――. Sight syllables versus letter phonics. *Elementary School Journal,* 1940, *41,* 38-42.

Fry, Edward. Developing a word list for remedial reading. *Elementary English,* November 1957.

Liberman, I.Y., Shankweiler, D., Carter, B., & Fischer, W.F. Reading and the awareness of linguistic segments. Unpublished manuscript, University of Connecticut, 1972. Cited by L. R. Gleitman & P. Rozin, Teaching reading by use of a syllabary. *Reading Research Quarterly,* Summer 1973, *8,* 447-83.

Nie, N. H., Hull, C. H., Jenkins, J. G., Steinbrenner, K., & Brent, D. H. *Statistical package for the social sciences.* 2nd ed. New York: McGraw-Hill, 1975.

Osburn, W. J. Teaching spelling by teaching syllables and root words. *Elementary School Journal,* 1954, *55,* 32-41.

Rinsland, H. D. *A basic vocabulary of elementary school children.* New York: Macmillan, 1945.

Ruddell, R. B. Language acquisition and the reading process. In H. Singer & R. B. Ruddell, eds., *Theoretical models and processes of reading.* Newark, Del.: International Reading Association, 1976, pp. 22-38.

Sakiey, E., & Martin, J. *Primary level graphemic syllable lists with pronunciation variations.* Paper presented at the meeting of the College Reading Association, Baltimore, October 1980.

Savin, H. B., & Bever, T. G. The nonperceptual reality of the phoneme. *Journal of Verbal Learning and Verbal Behavior,* 1970, *9,* 295-302.

Spoehr, K. T., & Smith, E. E. The role of syllables in perceptual processing. *Cognitive Psychology,* 1973, *5,* 71-89.

Index

A Pronouncing Dictionary of American English, 116
Abstract thinking, 195
Accent, 40, 179, 180. *See also* Stress
Activities, 2
Affixes, 30, 31, 40
Alphabetic base of spelling, 149, 150–164
Alphabetical order, 86
Alternate spellings, 7, 143, 150, 222–231
 in dictionary, 222
American Heritage Word Frequency Book, 340, 356
Analogies, 257–258
Analysis of misspellings, 249–252
Antonyms, 40
Audio-visual imagery, 98
Auditory discrimination, 165, 251, 322–323
Ayer Standard Spelling Test, 305
Auditory tapes, 248, 280–283, 285

Black English, 46, 51, 136
 features of, 136
 final consonant clusters, 136, 140
 final consonants, 140
 grammatical markers, 137
 initial consonants, 136
 medial vowels, 140
 pronunciation, 135–141
 variation, 136
 vowels, 136
Blending, 239, 326
Borrowed words, 163

California Achievement Tests, 306
California Reading Test, 292
Cassette tapes. *See* Auditory tapes
Classifying
 spelling errors, 55
 words, 219

as an aid to spelling, 169
Closed syllable, 40, 123, 243
Clusters, 325
Cognitive stages, 18
Column form. *See* List form
Commercial materials. *See* Spelling programs
Common spelling errors, 328
Common words used in communication, 234
Composition, 3
Compound words, 162, 171, 189, 357
Comprehension, 101
Computer Assisted Instruction, 288
Computers, 3, 154
 errors, 162
 programmed to spell, 154
Confused pairs, 182
Conservation
 of continuous quantity, 25
 of mass, 24, 25
 of number, 25
 of volume, 25
 of weight, 25
Consonants, 38, 109, 255
 and vowel letters, 114
 blends, 38
 boundaries, 254–255
 cluster reduction, 21
 consonant-vowel blend, 253
 digraph, 38
 double, 20, 264
 elementary sounds and blends, 255
 irregular, 263–264
 nasal, 204
 number of, 117
 sounds, 119
  number of, 131
Contemporary classroom instruction, 297
Contextual presentation, 54
 vs. list presentation, 54. *See also* List form
Contractions, 173, 325, 357

INDEX

Corrected test, 31, 54, 55, 65, 72, 248–249, 309
Cover-and-Write Method, 310
Creative writing, 248
Curriculum, spelling, 248. *See also* Spelling

Decoding, 239–240
Definitions, 298
Derivational patterns, 18
Derivatives, 171
Developmental spelling, 4
Developmental strategies, 203–209
Diacritic marks, 40
Diagnostic Test, 306
Dialect, 131, 166, 250, 269–270, 312
  and spelling, 82
  Black, 269
  difference, 132–135
  dialect-related errors, 137, 138, 139
  effect on phonetic spelling, 269
Dictation, 281
Dictionary skills, 86, 217, 291, 302–303, 306, 319–322
  and spelling rules, 306
Dictionary syllabication, 99
Digraphs, 119, 127, 131, 255, 263–264
Diphthongs, 39, 120, 131
Dolch Basic Sight Word List, 348
Dolch list, 281, 283, 348–355
Double consonants, 264
Double spellings, 162
Durrell Analysis of Difficulty, 306

Early spellers, 198
Effects of stress on spelling, 152
Elementary & Secondary Education Act, 298
English language, 193
  graphemic features, 193
  morphophonemic features, 193
Error analysis, 327
  categorizing, 327
Evaluating student progress, 304–307
Every Pupil Achievement Test, 306
Extrinsic resources, 300

Fernald Method Modified, 310
Field research in spelling, 70
Final *e* rule. *See* Rules, spelling

Fitzgerald Method, 309
Flashcards, 281–282
Function words, 233, 255

Games, 2, 65, 312. *See also* Spelling games, Word games
Gates Primary Word List, 348
Gates-Russell Spelling Diagnostic Test, 306
Generalization of spelling skills, 12
Generalizations, 82, 106
  spelling, 168, 301
Generative-transformational grammar, 203
Gilstrap Method, 309
Glides, 122, 131
Grades, 67
Graphemes, 38
Grapheme-phoneme correspondence, 38, 106. *See also* Letter-sound relationships, Phoneme-grapheme correspondence
Grouping words, 5, 72

Handwriting and spelling, 4, 53–60, 323, 329–337
  evaluating, 337
  in the language arts program, 57
Handwriting errors, 4
Handwriting programs, 55
  handwriting position, 56
  left-handed child, 56
  legibility, 56
  manuscript writing, 56
  speed of writing, 56
Hard spots, 31, 63, 68, 74, 85, 308
High-frequency words, 34, 62, 64, 66, 70, 72, 194, 208, 234, 302, 340, 356, 365–366, 369, 373
  frequency curve, 366
  pronunciation of syllables, 381
Homographs, 40
Homonyms, 13, 40, 163
Homophones, 163
Horn Method 1, 310
Horn Method 2, 310

Individualized Education Program (IEP), 304

384

INDEX

Individualized instruction, 55, 57, 75, 304
Inflection, 171, 181
   endings, 13, 33, 40
   patterns, 17
Initial Teaching Alphabet, 50, 134, 143, 232, 233, 240, 241, 300
Inner speech, 233
Instant words, 365–370
Instructional strategies, 287
   rules generalization, 287
   traditional, 287
   word-analysis, 287
Internalized information, 195
Internalized rules, 150, 218, 219
Intrinsic strategies, 298, 299
Invented spelling, 3, 199
Inventory tests, 72
Iowa Spelling Scale, 305
Iowa Test of Basic Skills, 71
Irregular consonants, 263–264
Irregularly spelled words, 255–256

Kelvin Measure of Spelling Ability, 305
Kinesthetic impression, 69
Kinesthetic method, 98, 238, 260

Language analogies, 218
Language arts interrelationships, 58
Language arts skills, 33
   related to spelling, 33
   for writing, 33
Language knowledge, 218, 219
Larsen-Hammill Tests of Written Spelling, 306
Learning styles, 1, 2, 12, 85, 238, 260, 280
   teachers', 2
Letter recognition, 282
Letter-name strategy, 204, 208
Letter-sound relationships, 72, 196, 251. *See also* Grapheme-phoneme correspondence, Phoneme-grapheme correspondence
   inconsistencies of, 196
Linguistically based spelling, 72
Linguistics, 38, 72, 231
List form, 62, 64, 69, 73, 85, 308, 309
   vs. sentence or paragraph form, 62, 64, 69

Lists, 54, 72. *See also* Word lists
Loan words, 173
Long and short vowels, 265–268
Long vowels, 39, 121, 204, 211, 260
Low-ability students, 292
   teaching methods for, 292
      lecture-discussion, 293
      list of words, 293
      programmed teaching maching, 292–293
      tachistoscope, 292–293

Magazines, educational, 232
Mainstreaming, 312
Malapropisms, 183, 185
Meaning of words, 63, 65, 73
Meaningful parts of words, 169
Memorization, 209
Memory devices, 174
Metropolitan Achievement Tests, 306
Minutes per week. *See* Time allotment
Mispronunciation, 203
Misspellings, 18, 322
   non-phonetic, 322
   phonetic, 322
Mnemonics, 221
Modalities. *See* Learning styles
Morphemes, 38
Morphology, 162, 164, 171, 232
Motivation, 311–312

Nasal consonants, 204
Need to spell, 237, 298–299
New Iowa Speller, 70, 72
Nonstandard speech, 46
Nonwords, 372
Northumberland Standardized Test: II English, 306
Number of consonant letters, 117
   vs. number of consonant sounds, 131
Number of vowel letters, 116
   vs. number of vowel sounds, 117
Number of vowel sounds, 117, 130

Open syllable, 40, 123
Oral spelling lessons, 72
Orthographic markers, 205
Overlearning, 72
Oxford English Dictionary, 125

385

INDEX

Parent cooperation, 312
Perceptual closure, 259–260
Perceptual learning, 252–261
Perceptual strengths, 12. *See also* Learning styles
Phoneme-grapheme correspondence, 17, 48, 126, 149, 151, 163, 210, 215, 301, 325. *See also* Grapheme-phoneme correspondence, Letter-sound relationships
  consistency of, 151
  simple, 151
Phonemes, 38, 129–130
  number of, 117
Phonemic approach, 301
Phonemic families, 72
Phonemically irregular words, 187
Phonemics, 129–131
Phonetic analysis, 38, 100, 204
Phonetic generalizations, 323
Phonetic rules, 55
Phonetic spelling, 198–203, 299
  misspelling, 82
Phonetic spelling inventory, 326
Phonetic syllabication, 169
Phonetics, 38, 129–131
Phonics, 30, 31, 33, 35, 38, 45, 47, 48, 51, 72, 73, 81, 104–128, 129–131, 227–238, 306
  and phonetics, 129–131
  and spelling, 47, 231–246, 301
  generalizations, 92, 101, 122, 239, 324–325
    syllabication, 101
    VC/CV, 101
    V/CV, 101
  in spelling, 49
  vs. word recognition, 49
  objections to, 48
  programs, 47
  rules, 48, 63, 66, 68, 70, 233, 234
  skills, 297, 311
  techniques, 260
  vs. phonemics, 129–131
  vs. phonetics, 129–131
Phonics competency examination, 106, 109, 115
Phonics countdown, 247, 252–261
  long, 252–256
  short, 257–261
Phonograms, 253

Phonological rules, 214
Phonology, 17, 171, 193, 210–217
  and orthography, 17
  generative, 17
Phonovisual Diagnostic Test, 305
Plurals, 173, 325
Possessives, 325, 357
Practice, 12, 93, 309
Pre-consonant nasals, 205
Pre-service instruction, 114
Pre-test, 5, 64, 67, 68, 71. *See* Test-study approach
Preferred spellings, 222. *See also* Variant spellings
Prefixes, 40, 91, 169
  and spelling, 190
  and suffixes, 340
Preoperational stage, 194
Prereaders, 381
Pretest, 57, 84, 85, 285
Primary accent, 40
Procedures not supported by research, 63
Programmed instruction, 55
Pronounceable parts, 233, 237, 247, 253
Pronunciation, 142, 151, 165, 203, 232, 238, 250, 288, 322, 357
  American, 165
  and spelling, 133, 164–192
    discrepancy between, 133
  British, 165
  Black, 135–141
  changed in a derived form, 357
  demons, 180
  differences, 135
  symbols, 130
Proofreading, 49, 87, 164, 217, 300, 306, 309, 337
Pseudowords, 212, 214, 237
Psycholinguistics, 231
Public Law 94-142, 304, 312
Pupil interest, 54, 63, 72, 308

Readability, 357
Reading, 323
  and spelling instruction, 323
  instruction, 1, 114
  terms used in, 114
Record of progress, 85
Reinforcement, 72, 288
  token vs. concrete, 288

INDEX

Related word pairs, 219
Remedial spelling programs, 284, 304
Remedial students, 291
   in reading, 319–322
Remediation, 75, 304
Research-supported procedures, 62
Rewards, 63
Root words, 13, 22, 40, 169
Rote associations, 34
Rote memorization, 209, 325
Rules of syllabication, 100
   unfamiliar words, 100
Rules, spelling, 3, 35, 40, 50, 66, 68, 71, 72, 82, 92, 123, 172, 209, 217, 260, 268–269, 301–302
Running words, 349, 371–372

Schwa sound, 39, 211, 244, 250, 251, 269, 270
Scope and sequence, 6, 8–11
Secondary accent, 40
Self-confidence, 284
Self-corrected test, 62, 65, 71, 75, 84, 308
Sentence or paragraph form, 69, 73
   vs. list form, 62, 64, 69
Serial learning, 203, 209
Sesquipedalian words, 191
Seven-Plus Assessment, 305
Short vowels, 39, 204, 205
   rule, 235–236
      (C)VC spelling pattern, 235–236
   sounds, 121, 260
Sight vocabulary, 348
Silent *e*, 324. *See also* Rules, spelling
Silent letters, 39, 264
Simplified spelling, 7, 96
Sound-it-out approach, 262–271
Sound-letter relationships. *See* Grapheme-phoneme correspondence, Letter-sound relationships, Phoneme-grapheme correspondence
Speaking and spelling, 16, 45
Special children, 272–273
Special educational needs, 291–337
Special interest words, 284
Specialization, 284
Speech errors, 45, 51
   and spelling, 45, 51

Spelling
   and composition, 13
   and context, 171
   and phonics, 231–246
   and phonology, 210–217
   and pronunciation, 168
   and reading, 13, 287
   and vocabulary study, 167
   and word recognition skills, 249
   bee, 276
   books, 95. *See also* Spelling programs
   curriculum, 1, 300
   difficulties, 174
   errors, 305
   games, 274–280, 308. *See also* Word games
   hints, 172
   lists, 64, 97, 285
   logic of, 36
   patterns, 235, 236, 239, 242–244
   phonetic, 263
   purpose of, 2
   readiness, 305
   research, 297–319
   scope and sequence, 6, 8–11, 302–303
   skill, 6, 71, 217–221
   vocabulary, 307
Spelling conscience, 14, 83, 86, 174, 217
Spelling demons, 164, 165, 174, 179, 221, 292, 294, 340
Spelling Errors Test, 306
Spelling programs, 6, 16, 29, 30, 31, 53, 73, 81, 89, 95, 297, 163, 223, 287, 297
   differences among, 73
Spelling reform, 6, 34, 82, 97, 142–146, 227
   alternative spellings, 145
   resistance to, 144
Spelling rules. *See* Rules, spelling
SRA Achievement Series, 306
St. Louis Spelling Test, 306
Stress, 151, 179, 233, 258–259
Structural analysis, 29, 30, 38
Structural approach, 287
Study habits, 54, 64, 69, 85
Study-test method, 248, 308. *See also* Test-study method
Subvocalization, 233

387

INDEX

Suffixes, 40, 91, 169, 302–303, 367, 368, 369
  and prefixes, 340
Syllabication, 30, 31, 33, 74, 98–103, 169, 293, 320–321
  dictionary, 101
  generalizations, 82, 98–103
  rules, 242
Syllabified form, 67
  vs. whole word presentation, 67
Syllable boundaries, 99, 242
Syllable frequency count, 371–381
Syllables, 40, 71, 256, 273
Synonyms, 40
Syntax, 171
Synthetic alphabets, 300
Systematic recall, 72, 76
Systematic word study, 72

Tactile technique, 260. *See also* Kinesthetic method, Teaching approach
Teaching approach, 30, 288
  word analysis, 30
  auditory, 288
  kinesthetic, 288
  meaning and word usage, 30
  visual, 288
Test-study method, 5, 54, 57, 61, 63, 64, 67, 68, 71, 74, 84, 85, 248, 285, 307–308. *See also* Study-test method
  vs. study-test approach, 54, 63, 67, 68
Testing programs, 71, 73
Time allotment, 54, 61, 63, 64, 66, 68, 71, 73, 83, 285, 308, 312
Tracing words, 98, 238

Usage, 7
Useful words, 55

Variant spellings, 251, 257. *See also* Preferred spellings
Visual associations, 150, 168, 218, 220, 221, 311
Visual memory, 35
Visual method, 238. *See also* Whole-word method
Visual-Vocal Method, 310
Vocabulary development, 12, 150, 164
Vocabulary instruction, 54, 215
Vowels
  allophones, 287
  alternation, 211, 213, 214, 287
  digraphs, 39
  laxing, 211
  plus *r*, 258
  reduction, 212
  rules, 239, 242–243, 245, 260–261
Vowel sounds, 38, 110, 193, 253–254, 326
  number of, 117
Vowel spelling strategies, 192–198

Weekly tests, 5, 7, 275–276
Wheeler-Howell First Grade Vocabulary List, 348
Whole-word method, 63, 66, 168, 238, 300, 309
  vs. syllables, 63
Word exercises, 30
Word families, 285
Word games, 274–280. *See also* Spelling games
Word lists, 2, 13, 83, 92, 248, 305, 339. *See also* List form
  from various curricular areas, 63, 65, 74
  locally devised, 65
Word perception, 233, 234, 237, 246
  factors in, 237
Word webbing, 23
Word-attack skills, 168, 287–289
Words
  in context, 171
  in syllabified form, 63
    vs. whole-word method, 63
  often misspelled, 174, 188, 341–347
  self-test on, 188
World English Spelling, 232, 233–234, 241
Writing words in the air, 64, 69, 76, 308
Writing words several times, 63, 67, 76, 308
Writing, 87
  importance of, 87